Discovering Anthropology: Researchers at Work— Anthropology

Carol R. Ember
Human Relations Area Files

Melvin Ember
Human Relations Area Files

Peter N. Peregrine
Lawrence University

PEARSON

Prentice Hall

Upper Saddle River, NJ 07458

© 2007 by Pearson Education, Inc.
Upper Saddle River, New Jersey 07458

ISBN 0-13-227762-X
Printed in the United States of America

Contents

Preface

Most of the articles and books anthropologists write are aimed at scholars, not at college students. This is a problem, for works written by scholars for other scholars are usually too full of jargon for students to digest easily. The chapters here, in contrast, were written with you in mind. They are not reprints of articles published elsewhere, but were composed for you, a student of anthropology. We deliberately commissioned the authors to write about something of interest to them that they thought would be interesting to students.

How do these chapters differ from what you might read in other courses? Usually when we read an article about a piece of research, we find out about the results—what the researchers think they have discovered, what they think they know. Rarely do we get to understand the process. Where do ideas come from? How does an idea get transformed into a research project? What was exciting about the research? What was disappointing? What is the person behind the process like? These questions are rarely addressed in scholarly writing, and they are often absent even in popular accounts of research. Here these questions are central, for the anthropologists who wrote these articles wanted to help you understand the process of discovery. They wanted you to understand not only what they found, but how they went about finding it, and what the experience was like. Most of all, they wanted to excite you about their field—not only about research findings, but about the process of doing research itself.

This reader contains one chapter for each chapter of *Anthropology*, 12th edition. The chapters here were originally parts of a larger set of about 80 that were composed between 1995 and 2000 by a diverse group of anthropologists who set aside their research projects and teaching loads to take the time to write these pieces. The task was easy for some, difficult for others, but enjoyable for all. We want to thank all the authors for their efforts in producing these works for undergraduate students. Before appearing here many of the articles were parts of three different series—*Portraits of Culture: Ethnographic Originals*, *Research Frontiers in Anthropology*, and *Cross-Cultural Research for Social Science*, published by Prentice Hall/Simon and Schuster Custom Publishing, and our thanks go to Pat Naturale, Stephanie Mathiessen, and Kari Mazzola for their help in the initial production of these works. We especially want to thank Nancy Roberts, who has been supportive and helpful throughout the process of developing this collection. The three series now appear in their entirety in a CD-ROM called *New Directions in Anthropology* which is also available from Prentice Hall.

We want to thank you, the reader, for taking the time to explore the product of our collective efforts.

Carol R. Ember, Melvin Ember, and Peter N. Peregrine

From Ethnographer to Comparativist and Back Again

Terence E. Hays

As I sat one night in 1972 during an 'umana ceremony in the men's house of a hamlet in Ndumba, a community in the Eastern Highlands Province of Papua New Guinea, I reflected on how fortunate I was. First, although when most people think of New Guinea they imagine hot, steamy swamps infested with crocodiles, my wife and I had selected a location for our doctoral dissertation fieldwork in the central highlands of the island where we avoided such unpleasant things. The settlement of Ndumba was over six thousand feet above sea level, with a climate that was always springtime, scenery that was gorgeous, and people who were reputedly the friendliest in the region. On that particular night, though, I could hardly breathe, for I was one of about seventy males packed into a windowless structure little larger than an average college classroom; the combination of all those sweaty bodies and hearth-fires generating equal amounts of light and smoke made the air thick and uncomfortably warm.

Still, I was lucky simply to have the chance to take part in the events going on, events which focused on several boys between the ages of ten and twelve. In Ndumba, every year or so, boys in that age range were subjected to a three-day series of rites that inducted them into the community of initiated males, removing them forever from their previous homes with mothers and sisters, who lived in separate houses from adolescent males and adult men. Most of the Tairora-language groups to the north had abandoned such customs in the face of rapidly accelerating acculturation, whereas I was enjoying my second opportunity to witness this important rite of passage.

I had missed a great deal during my first 'umana ceremony, held only a few months after my wife and I arrived in Ndumba when our knowledge of the language was minimal and we were still finding our way around the community. This second chance, a little more than a year after our arrival, promised to yield more informed observations and, perhaps, answers to questions that had arisen in the meantime but could not be resolved from my earlier, sketchy notes.

My purpose in going to Ndumba was not, in fact, to study rituals, or indeed even to do a general ethnography of the community. In 1970, when I was seeking financial support for my intended doctoral field research, funding agencies preferred problem-focused projects, and mine concerned the degree of individual variation one might find in plant knowledge among the adult members of a group of subsistence-based horticulturalists such as Ndumba, who raised sweet potatoes as their staple crop and depended a great deal on the wild plants (and animals) of their heavily forested environment to satisfy their basic needs. I had specific hypotheses I wanted to test: For example, given the division of labor in Ndumba, would men's classifications of forest plants be significantly more detailed than women's, and vice versa for plants growing in and near gardens? My project required enormous time commitments as I worked systematically with a carefully chosen sample of main informants of both sexes and a wide range of ages, and I felt I could give little attention to the seemingly limitless events—dispute settlements, bride wealth distributions, and so on—that would have to be investigated to produce an overall description of Ndumba society and culture.

So why was I devoting at least three days of precious field time to a ceremony, especially when I had "seen it before"? I told myself that I had been trained to appreciate the importance of a holistic perspective, which argues that *all* aspects of societies and cultures are interrelated and that a full understanding of any part (belief, custom, or "institution") depends on placing it in the wider whole from which it takes its form and meaning. Indeed, through an example of the serendipity that makes the research process ever-exciting, yet always unpredictable, I had gained an important insight into the reasons behind the very high frequency of multiple names in the local language for particular plants and animals. Ndumba had an extensive system of name taboos, which forbade anyone from saying aloud the personal names of many people who were related in certain ways. Since many Ndumba people were named after animals and plants, the taboos were extended and one had to come up with an alternative way of referring to the organism.

Still, persuasive as this instance might be of the unanticipated range of information that might be directly relevant to a given research question or topic, if one truly has to study *everything* in order to understand *anything*, surely this is an impossible goal. In any case, it was one I had been forced to reject if my project was to be manageable at all, even with fifteen months of field time available.

The simple fact of the matter was that the 'umana ceremony was too spectacular to ignore, with the entire population mobilized for three days of colorful, exciting events, including taking the initiates in a procession to the forest where their noses were forcefully bled, dramatic attacks on the all-male procession by the women of the community, total seclusion of the boys in the men's house for two days and nights, and a culminating feast. The ceremony encapsulated many of the core themes of Ndumba culture, such as the importance of male growth and strength and a corresponding need to minimize physical contact between the sexes, since that was regarded as weakening for males. One could hardly ask for a more compact, and intrinsically interesting, presentation of symbols and actions that gave access to the very heart of their belief system.

As if the cultural salience of the ceremony were not compelling enough, I had by then been intrigued by a new line of investigation that had opened up, again largely by chance, when I had elicited myths and folktales explaining why certain plants appeared in particular locations in the forest. Stories about men turning into orchids led to others, many of which were of a tragic nature, detailing the deformities and deaths suffered by boys and young men as a consequence of associating "too much" with women. Indeed, the bulk of the narratives told by my male informants had the purported dangers of women as a major theme. Moreover, I was told that many of these stories were first recounted to males in the context of the 'umana ceremony or one that was enacted about ten years later and prior to a man's marriage.

These reports reawakened my interest from undergraduate days in culture and personality, especially regarding the role of socialization practices in the reinforcement and reproduction of world view. People, after all, do not simply *have* customs, such as the residential segregation of the sexes, but presumably they believe that living in a particular way makes sense or works for them, given the nature of things. For example, many investigators have proposed a relationship between "father-absence" in early childhood and later "gender identity conflict" and confusion for males. Thus, it is argued, the absence of a "masculine" role model in the first few years of life somehow leads a boy to identify with his mother (or other women) and adopt a "feminine" self-image. Later, he will either retain this identity or, in the face of social opposition and continuing problems, he might go to the other extreme, adopting an excessively "masculine" way of relating to others, evidenced by emphatic rejection of any hints of "femininity" (including abuse of women themselves) and a tendency toward physical aggression. On the surface, at least, the Ndumba case appeared to fit the second pattern. Given the separation of the sexes in Ndumba households and in nearly every aspect of daily life, most boys (especially those who were sons of prominent fighters or community leaders) spent their early childhood years having very little direct contact with adult, or even teenaged, males, whose quarrels (with women as well as with each other) often resulted in fights employing clubs, axes, or bows and arrows. This propensity toward violence, manifest also in the intervillage warfare that was chronic for Ndumba until the late 1960s, was a common indicator of what some theorists call "hypermasculinity."

Such a proposed link between early childhood experiences and later personality traits must remain, of course, only conjectural and it depends on the notion of unconscious processes, since the child is supposed not to be aware of these conflicts but instead is trying to resolve them at a deeper level. What began to interest me was the idea that experiences after early childhood also could be important, by reinforcing or even redirecting ideas and beliefs fostered by treatment and explanations received earlier. It was in these terms, then, that I began to view the 'umana ceremony in a different light: not only as a dramatic display of Ndumba ideology (especially regarding notions of gender differences and their significance), but also as one of the major ways by which the ideology was perpetuated.

During my first witnessing of the ceremony, I had been struck by the emphasis on "teachings" given by adult males to the initiates, not only in the forest while they were undergoing various ordeals but especially during the days and nights of seclusion in the men's house. While I had understood almost none of the specifics at the time, interpreters had told me that the boys were having various rules and taboos explained to them. It was evident from everyday behavior that many special restrictions—on foods, clothing, and activities—accompanied each stage of the life cycle in Ndumba, but I often had been frustrated by the apparent inability of those questioned to give me detailed rationales for most of them. "My parents say so," or "The elders say we mustn't do this," were as close as I usually came to explanations, at least in the early days of fieldwork. Eventually, though, the hints given by some respondents fell into a pattern: At a given stage of maturity, a person might well not have much of an understanding of the reasons behind particular rules, especially but not exclusively if they applied to a stage the individual had not yet reached. For example, girls and young women in Ndumba (as well as virtually all males) seemed genuinely ignorant of the process of childbirth. As my wife's observations of births confirmed, they would learn about it only when they experienced it for themselves, amidst considerable confusion and shock.

Thus I began to think about the 'umana ceremony, among others, as contexts not only for the expression of core cultural themes but also for their transmission. So, a second opportunity to directly observe this process was especially welcome, and I geared up to pay particular attention to the content of the teachings that would be delivered to the initiates, including the myths and folktales, so many of which, I had been told, were first divulged at this time.

My second 'umana ceremony was, in a word, disappointing. It was as colorful and dramatic as the first had been, but even though by then I had a better-tuned ear for the language (though nothing like fluency) and cooperative interpreters, I recorded only one story told during the many long hours I spent in the crowded, smoky, noisy men's house. There were teachings I was able to follow and transcribe, but they seemed very commonplace (for instance, instructions not to use another man's belongings without his permission, or warnings about taking food from gardens other than those of one's parents). Where were the great revelations I had expected?

I tried to console myself by acknowledging that, on the basis of my notes and photographs from a year before, many of the details were different this time, beginning with only one initiate compared to five on the earlier occasion. But could my proposed "enculturative" aspect of the rites be so dispensable? Perhaps my hunches were simply wrong. With less than three months remaining before we had to leave the field, in the face of this discouragement I returned my full attention to my main project. I completed it as well as I could and went home satisfied with that accomplishment, but still with nagging questions that could not easily be dismissed.

* * *

For the next several years my doctoral dissertation and papers on Ndumba ethnobiology occupied most of the time I could spend on the results of my field research. But then in 1979 I was invited to participate in a scientific conference (and later a published volume) addressing male initiation ceremonies in Papua New Guinea. My wife and I wrote a paper intended to be primarily descriptive, placing the 'umana ceremony and one held for young women at their first menstruation in the broader context of Ndumba society and culture. During the conference, I was struck by both the similarities and differences among the rites reported for a wide range of societies, and also by the myths, varied as well, adduced by the other contributors as relevant to their cases.

With this stimulus, I returned to my Ndumba oral narratives and reread them all carefully. There was no doubt about it: The stories I had recorded, all from male informants but under a wide variety of circumstances, almost without exception contained the common theme of dangers to males posed by contact, especially if it was intimate, with women. For example, one story related how a young man visiting a distant village was tricked into sleeping in the house of a young woman. There was a suggestion, although heavily veiled, that the youth was also seduced by his hostess, but in any case he fell ill when he returned home, and soon died. Despite my frustrating experience with the second 'umana ceremony, my suspicion again seemed plausible that Ndumba oral literature (or at least my sample of it) not only reflected, but provided a kind of rationale—like Aesop's Fables, perhaps—for social arrangements that stressed the physical separation of the sexes, and thus could serve as a key element in an enculturative process that would produce adults for whom such arrangements made perfect sense, with each generation convinced anew, at least in part, through the retelling of the tales.

But if such a link were argued for the Ndumba case, it could remain only plausible unless such patterns could be shown to be generally true for a wide sample of societies. On the basis of the relatively few published narratives then available from other societies in New Guinea it appeared that a "dangers of women" theme was prominent in the stories from some groups, but not others. It also was evident that relations between the sexes also varied considerably, with nuclear family households in some cases contrasting with sex-segregated residence in others, and so on. These impressions were, of course, only that. Might a systematic comparative study yield clear patterns—such as "dangers of women" stories prevailing in societies with rigid sexual segregation—patterns that were not only suggestive but convincing? I resolved to embark on such a project.

Library research soon revealed that others had also thought about these kinds of links. Many studies had been reported, especially in the 1960s and 1970s, claiming to show relationships between portrayals of males and females (often called "gender stereotypes") in various media, and social inequalities between the sexes. Investigators had argued that in our society females were consistently portrayed in such diverse formats as popular songs, television commercials, soap operas, and magazine advertisements as having personality and character traits that contrasted negatively with those of males, thus perpetuating stereotypes that reinforced discriminatory attitudes and practices. Some anthropologists had also explored such possibilities, citing examples, especially from oral literature, that arguably mirrored or reflected the gender ideology and relations between the sexes in the communities they had studied. Almost none of these studies, however, was comparative in nature, and many were no more systematically conducted than had been my own preliminary probes in Ndumba. They were very useful, though, in suggesting ways in which characters in stories might be rated as exhibiting "traits" such as assertiveness, submissiveness, persistence, trustworthiness, and others that are frequently attributed disproportionately to one gender or the other.

In 1980 I received a grant that would support my research for a full year, and I was able to throw myself into it completely. Apart from further work on coding schemes, the other major task was to assemble the relevant ethnographic information and as many narratives as possible for each case to be included in my sample. This entailed not only an exhaustive search of the literature but, given the paucity of published myths and folktales from this area, solicitation from colleagues of stories they had collected. Gratifyingly, many were able to help me, and my corpus of potential narrative materials soon grew (it currently includes over 1,500 texts from about sixty highland New Guinea societies).

My Ndumba materials had been the initial stimulus for this project and I wanted to include them in my comparative study if at all possible. But as my examination of other cases and refinement of my coding systems progressed I became increasingly aware of gaps in my own field data. Not only did I need a larger sample of Ndumba stories than I currently had, but my search for relevant ethnographic information in the work of others continually made me aware of the observations I had not made (or at least recorded) and questions I had not asked. In particular, my working hypothesis concerned the possible impact of hearing stories and participating in ceremonies, not just their content, yet I had no direct evidence of this. With an ethnographer's characteristic emphasis on adult informants, I had somehow not thought to interview the initiates themselves in 1971 and 1972! What, I now wondered, did they think and feel when these experiences were unfolding? I really didn't know.

* * *

As my lucky star continued to shine, the grant I had received for my comparative study included funds to return to the field if I chose to do so. I certainly did, and in 1981 I was back in Ndumba, not only recording additional stories, but seizing the opportunity to conduct extensive interviews with four of the boys (now young men) whom I had seen initiated a decade before and who were still living in Ndumba. The interviews yielded remarkable results, the significance of which has extended far beyond serving their intended purpose; because of them I would ever afterward bring a different perspective to both my ethnographic and comparative work.

The format I adopted was to ask each interviewee, separately, first to describe in as much detail as possible the 'umana ceremony at which he was initiated (and which I had observed), and then to recall as well as he could what thoughts and feelings he experienced at the time. I appreciated fully the fact that such recollections could not necessarily be considered valid reports of mental states from so far in the past, but I was hopeful that, given the absence of any other source of this information, they would be at least suggestive. And "suggestive" they were! My informants seemed to have no difficulty recapturing the emotional turmoil they said they had undergone. Sometimes in choked voices, most of them recounted two particular memories. One concerned their feelings of having been betrayed by previously supportive mothers, who had apparently colluded in their forceful abduction from what they thought of as an "easy life":

"I was angry with my mother because she had sent me away to have these things done to me!" The second memory often cited concerned the fear of women they claimed was induced in them when various teachings were delivered, or stories were told. For example, one interviewee reported remembering a night in the men's house when the initiates were lectured against premarital intercourse: "They said we couldn't associate with girls; if we ever had sex with them, we would die. This is what they said, and it scared us."

Such statements were precisely the kind of evidence I saw as needed to test my hypothesis, but the interviews also yielded two other revelations, each troubling in its own way. The first was that, when asked about the myths and folktales I regarded as parts of the ceremony, my informants explained that they did not remember stories being told at the time, but that they had learned many of them (including the ones I had recorded earlier) over the subsequent years, usually during casual fireside socializing at night in the men's house. That is, they first heard these stories while they were in the 'umana stage of the life cycle, but not as a part of their induction into it. This helped me understand better why my straining ears had not picked up any stories during what I had thought of as my abortive attempts during the second 'umana ceremony. But, as an ethnographer, I gloomily reflected on the virtual impossibility of recording such stories in their natural contexts, given their apparently sporadic and unscheduled recitals. No matter how much time researchers have in the field, they cannot wait around indefinitely for something that might or might not occur.

More problematic, from my comparativist's perspective, was the startling realization that emerged from the interviewees' descriptive accounts of the ceremony at which they were initiated. Not only did each of the four young men's versions differ from the others', but none matched in more than a general way my own records, both written and photographic, of the same events. Some of the differences had to do with minor details, but others were significant indeed, and the same was true when I compared their accounts to those I had elicited earlier from older men—recollections of their own ceremonies and generalized outlines of what such rites entailed. My immediate reaction was simply renewed appreciation of my good fortune in having myself witnessed examples of what I was trying so hard to understand, but the implications soon were to become more disturbing.

My head buzzing with fresh data and a general sense that I was on a productive track, I returned home and resumed my scouring of the ethnographic literature. Like all comparativists, I had been frustrated earlier by information gaps in the published record, sometimes with regard to topics that were so crucial that potential cases, otherwise welldocumented, would probably have to be dropped from my final sample. But now I was faced with additional methodological problems. In a paper I wrote not long after returning from the field, I argued that the demonstrable errors in my interviewees' recall of their own initiation experiences formed patterns of systematic distortion that made a kind of sense given Ndumba notions of appropriate behavior and attitudes with respect to kin of various kinds. (For example, acts of brutality from relatives who were supposed to be supportive were systematically excluded from the remembered accounts.) But wrestling with these materials led me to look more carefully at ethnographers' descriptions of such ceremonies in other societies. In some cases, the researcher provided an account based on personal observations, but in many others—as might have been true of me had I not chosen Ndumba as my field site—they had worked in communities where the ceremonies in question had long been abandoned. Their renditions were necessarily derived from either recollections or generalized statements older informants had given them. While these were not necessarily inaccurate, my experiences as an ethnographer made me now, as a comparativist, question the comparability of the material available. Should "memory accounts" be given the same status as those based on first-hand observations?

With respect to the part of my project that focused on oral narratives, a different set of issues arose, again stimulated by my discoveries as an ethnographer. If I were to reach any conclusions about the possible enculturative role played by the telling of myths and folktales, I obviously needed to know something about their *telling*, and not just the content of the stories themselves. Who told them? To whom? In what context? I had earlier been misled into thinking that the stories I had recorded in Ndumba were told during the 'umana ceremony while, I was now convinced, they were actually told more informally, and probably over a long period of time. I would still argue, for my own case anyway, that the stories could be seen as important transmitters of ideology, since indeed the years spent as an 'umana in Ndumba constituted an extended opportunity for resocialization, as boys—through the everyday contexts of eating, talking, living, and sleeping under the continual guidance and influence of their elders in the men's house—gradually came to view the world in ways they would never have learned when they resided with their mothers, sisters, and younger brothers.

Reexamining the hundreds of stories that I had compiled for this part of my study, I was initially distressed to discover that in very few cases was information provided about the customary contexts in which the narratives were recounted, or about their usual, or even permitted, audiences. One of the advantages of the regional nature of my comparative study, and the region itself, was that most of the New Guinea highlands ethnographers were still alive and known personally to me. Thus I was able to query them for "performance data" regarding the stories they had provided either through publications or personal communications. Perhaps faced with the same logistical problems as I had encountered in Ndumba, almost none of them could answer my questions. Most of their texts had been collected the way mine had, by having an informant sit on an empty kerosene drum and talk into a tape recorder. Should I give up?

My grant period ended, and a return to full-time teaching duties forced my project onto a "back burner" until, in 1984, I received more financial support, this time involving a stay of eighteen months in Australia working as part of a research group focusing on "Gender Relations in the Southwest Pacific." Taking all of my materials with me, I had an extended opportunity to discuss my ideas and problems with colleagues as well as to refine my coding systems, now incorporating information about sources of data (observation, informants' reports, and so on). I obtained hitherto unavailable materials from Australian libraries and archives, and my potential sample size began to increase, as did my optimism. It now appeared that I would have to settle for "weaker" hypotheses, but it began to look as if, even when cases were distinguished in terms of the nature of sources of information, significant variation existed with respect to customs, reported gender ideologies, and portrayals of the sexes in myths and folktales. If meaningful patterns of covariation could be found (such as ceremonies that stressed concerns with male health and growth, fears of female "pollution" through physical contact, and stories including female characters who bring about the downfall of males), there was indeed something that called for explanation, and my general hypothesis—that the narration of myths and folktales was an important means of enculturating the young with regard to gender stereotypes—was one possibility worth pursuing. In any event, the project would yield a database that could be used by other comparativists who were interested in testing different ideas.

My new grant, like the one in 1981, included support for a 1985 trip to Papua New Guinea, where I was able to obtain even more research materials (especially unpublished narratives, from missionary and archival sources) and, ever the ethnographer, to return to Ndumba for a brief visit.

I was astounded by the changes that had occurred, not only since 1971, but even from four years earlier. With the establishment of coffee as a cash crop, and roads linking Ndumba to towns and other outside influences and options, a new prosperity had hit the community, and virtually all members now wore Western clothing and some even sported transistor radios, at the same time that warfare with neighboring settlements had resumed. Perhaps most strikingly, some of the old customs related to male-female relations were disappearing, with many married men now living in the same houses with their wives and children (albeit with separate sleeping quarters). On the other hand, seclusion of women during menstruation and childbirth were still practiced and, I was told, I had just missed an 'umana ceremony held a couple of weeks before I arrived.

My stay this time was necessarily short, but I was able to record a few more stories and obtain some additional "memory accounts" of ceremonies, including the one most recently held, which sounded, of course, as if it had differed in some significant ways from the earlier ones. But more important than a new batch of field notebooks, this time I carried away an appreciation for the dynamic nature of societies and cultures that somehow had not previously been forced upon me quite so vividly.

This brought a new kind of complexity to my comparative project for, on reexamination of the ethnographic materials, it became evident that the long-standing preference in anthropological reporting for using the "ethnographic present" tense disguised what was often a mixing of time references. Thus an author might say in one section "the X maintain separate residences for the sexes," while tucked away in a footnote was the admission that "at the time of fieldwork, men's houses were a thing of the past." Thus I felt I needed to be sensitive in my coding to the disentangling of customs and reported beliefs that were contemporaneous from those that were attributed to a vague "traditional" period. This was required, I believed, because societies are continually changing—more conspicuously at some times than at others, as I had witnessed in Ndumba in 1985, but always, it could be argued, representing a mix of "old" and "new" ideas as people struggle to bring into their lives the harmony and integration our anthropological models too often assume they possess as a matter of course. In our comparative studies, as in our ethnographies, it is necessary to be clear about *what* we are trying to understand and explain, and for that we need to know, for a specified time as well as place, which customs and beliefs in fact *co*-occur.

***

The project I have been discussing has been going on for quite a while, as is evident from the above account. In part this is because the accumulation and selection of materials, development of coding systems, and comparative analysis itself are time consuming, just as is the ethnographic field research on which the whole enterprise depends. Moreover, one typically has other lives to lead simultaneously. In my case, additional delays have arisen because of the continual questioning and rethinking in which I found myself forced to engage. Initially, as I repeatedly encountered gaps in the published record, my primary concern was with the quantity of materials that would be available: Would I have enough stories to allow the drawing of a sufficiently large sample to reach meaningful conclusions; would I have enough information on the more than fifty variables currently included in my ethnographic coding scheme; would I have enough time (in my life) to do it all?

I believe it was my experiences as an ethnographer that made me acutely aware that "quantity" is only part of the story; what matters even more is the *quality* of the data to which one is trying to bring order. The problems I have discussed here are familiar ones to comparativists, if not to most ethnographers, as I discovered when I had the opportunity recently to participate in a summer institute for comparative studies. There the issues surrounding the always-problematic nature of sources of information, clarity about time and space reference, and many others were raised and discussed with a succinctness that made me wonder why it had taken me so long to appreciate them.

Yet it was the hours of sweating (literally as well as figuratively) over notebooks in dripping rainforests and smoky men's houses that drove the lessons home for me. As an ethnographer I was continually faced with the question, as one of my mentors expressed it, of "How do you know it's true?" But even when I could reach a (hard-won) conviction that something

was "true" for Ndumba, the second question awaited: "How do you know it's generally true, which you can't know without comparison?"

So, like anthropology itself, I continue to live with the tension between the particular and the general, taking questions and concerns from my comparative work to the field, and returning to the literature with new sensitivities evoked by my experiences there. And, like the unfolding of an intricate flower, each part of the process opens up fresh paths to explore, for even though societies may not be, "on the ground," the tightly interconnected wholes presented in textbooks, when it comes to research one thing certainly leads to another. A focus on plant classification leads to one on myths about men turning into orchids, and then to stories about the dangers of women, and then to residence patterns, and then to ceremonies, and then. . .

Suggested Readings

Hays, Terence E. "Initiation as Experience: The Management of Emotional Responses by Ndumba Novices." In L. L. Langness and Terence E. Hays, eds., *Anthropology in the High Valleys: Essays on the New Guinea Highlands in Honor of Kenneth E. Read*. Novato: Chandler & Sharp, 1987, pp. 185–235. An analysis of interviews with men ten years after initiation.

———. "Sacred Flutes, Fertility, and Growth in the Papua New Guinea Highlands." *Anthropos* 81 (1986): 435–453. A comparative survey of themes in New Guinea Highlands men's cults.

———. "Tairora," in Terence E. Hays, ed., *Oceania: Encyclopedia of World Cultures*, vol. 2. Boston: G. K. Hall, 1991, pp. 307–310. A general ethnographic overview of Tairora-speakers of the Eastern Highlands Province, Papua New Guinea.

——— "Unlocking the Secrets of the Men's House," *Faces* 9, no. 3 (1992): 34–37. Written for a general audience, this article discusses secrecy in a Ndumba male initiation ceremony.

Hays, Terence E., and Patricia H. Hays. "Opposition and Complementarity of the Sexes in Ndumba Initiation Ceremonies." In Gilbert H. Herdt, ed., *Rituals of Manhood: Male Initiation in New Guinea*. Berkeley: University of California Press, 1982, pp. 201–238. A description and analysis of male and female puberty ceremonies in Ndumba.

Ethics in Archaeology
Mark J. Lynott

My first field experience in archaeology was in the summer of 1971. Like most students at the time, my only opportunity to participate in archaeology was as part of a university field school in archaeological methods. I was a student at Western Michigan University, and the Anthropology Department was involved in a project to conduct salvage excavations at a site in Michigan's Upper Peninsula. The site was a mound and village complex on a point of land along the southern shore of Lake Superior. The opportunity for a summer of adventure in the beautiful north woods was more than enough to attract my attention. I did not realize at the time that, in addition to being introduced to archaeological methods, many aspects of that first summer of fieldwork would also introduce me to ethical issues that I and the archaeological profession would face in the years to come.

My summer of 1971 was spent at the Sand Point site near Baraga, Michigan. The site is comprised of a series of mounds and habitation areas on a point of land along the south shore of Lake Superior. In 1968, a significant part of the site along the lakeshore was privately owned, and the owner planned to greatly modify the landscape and build a resort with cabins and a marina. The presence of archaeological remains at that location became known when human bones were exposed by a bulldozer pushing soil from a sand knoll into swampy areas to level the site. Two years later, Western Michigan began archaeological investigations at the site. Most of the 1970 work focused on excavation of a large mound. My own participation in the project began a year later, and included work on smaller mounds and habitation areas. In addition to learning archaeological field methods, I was also informally exposed to three issues that continue to be relevant to archaeology today.

As a student just getting started in archaeology, I had little knowledge about the laws that govern the management and protection of archaeological sites in the United States. Our project of excavating mounds and village areas of the Sand Point site before they were destroyed by lakeshore developments seemed intuitively the "right" thing to do. It only made sense that someone should study archaeological sites before they were destroyed. Issues of stewardship and conservation of the archaeological record, which we see as a foundation of contemporary archaeology, were less widely discussed and not formally taught at that time. Although salvage archaeology associated with road, pipeline, and reservoir construction was practiced throughout the United States,[1] there was very little literature that addressed the philosophical basis for preserving and protecting archaeological sites. It was not until the appearance of Public Archaeology[2] by Charles R. McGimsey III in 1972 and "A Conservation Model for American Archaeology"[3] by William D. Lipe in 1974 that archaeologists began to refine this paradigm.

During the summer of 1971, my fellow students and I excavated several small mounds at the Sand Point site. The mounds contained human burials and were built from beach sand and soil from the nearby village sites. I recall being thoroughly intrigued by the carefully organized bundles of bones we encountered, and fascinated by our instructor's explanation of different mortuary practices. At the time, I gave no thought to the possibility that our excavations might offend some Native Americans. My own family heritage was unknown to me beyond my great grandparents, so I didn't anticipate that other people would object to the excavation of graves that were a thousand or more years old. I simply viewed the excavation of these mounds before they were to be bulldozed as logical and important to understanding the past. In subsequent years, I would be exposed to the strong and diverse views that exist about archaeological excavation of human remains.

Our instructor in the summer of 1971 was Winston D. Moore, who has studied at Washington State University and worked with Richard Daugherty at the Ozette site near Neah Bay, Washington. The Ozette site is a late prehistoric Makah village that was covered by a mudslide and excavated as a cooperative effort between Washington State University and the Makah tribe. Our instructor's experience at Ozette must have been positive, because in the summer of 1971 he arranged to have two local Ojibwa people join the archaeological field crew. Although he never instructed us on the ethical value of this action, it is plain to me in retrospect that he anticipated and respected their interest and desire to be involved in the archaeological study of their past. Thirty years later, this is still an important issue for archaeologists, and it is being incorporated into formal archaeological training.

Upon completion of my undergraduate training, I entered graduate school in 1973. In retrospect, I see now that my undergraduate years in archaeology were associated with a period when most archeological research was the private domain of university and museum archaeologists. My graduate studies and subsequent career have been associated with the development of cultural resource management. During the past thirty years, I have had the good fortune to participate in the tremendous growth of the archaeological profession. During this time we have seen increasing opportunities for archaeological employment and tremendous public support for archaeological research. Along with these benefits there are also responsibilities and the need for archaeological ethics.

Archaeological Ethics: Origins

As a student in the 1970s, my formal training in archaeological ethics was unfortunately limited. This was typical for most students at that time, and the tradition continues to some extent today. The reluctance to discuss ethics in archaeological courses is probably due in part to the history of archaeology.

Most historians of archaeology point to the nineteenth century as the start of systematic archaeological investigation. At that time, there were no "professional" archaeologists. People who conducted archaeological investigations were either independently wealthy or had other employment to support themselves and their families. The development of museums in cities in the eastern United States in the last half of the nineteenth century generated a demand for artifacts associated with the earthen and stone monuments of North and Central America. This demand

provided a number of self-taught individuals with employment to excavate mounds and earthworks in eastern North America, pueblo ruins in the southwest, and ruins and temples in Meso-America. As reports of these expeditions were published, eastern preservationists became concerned about the loss of important sites to looting and vandalism. This eventually resulted in the passage of federal legislation that protected archaeological sites on federal lands. The Smithsonian Institution and the Archaeological Institute of America were instrumental in passage of the Antiquities Act of 1906, and this likely represents the origins of archaeological ethics in the United States.

Throughout the first half of the twentieth century, archaeology was conducted by a small number of professionals in universities and museums. The number of archaeologists in these early years was small enough that the Annual Meeting of the Society for American Archaeology was often held at a university in cities like Ann Arbor, Michigan; Norman, Oklahoma; and Lincoln, Nebraska. The first Annual Meeting of the Society for American Archaeology was held in 1935 in Andover, Massachusetts, with approximately 75 people in attendance.[4]

Due to the small size of the archaeological profession, the number of research projects and resulting reports were quite few. Even with the growth of the archaeological profession following World War II, the number of archaeologists was still sufficiently small so that all the archaeologists working in a region like the Plains knew each other fairly well. With archaeologists focused mainly on research and teaching, the need for formal statements about ethics was limited.

In a review of the history of archaeological ethics, Charles R. McGimsey III[5] notes that the major federal funding through the River Basin Surveys in the late 1940s and 1950s awakened a desire among the archaeological profession to better define the basic qualifications of an archaeologist. Consequently in 1960, Jesse Jennings, President of the Society for American Archaeology, established a Committee on Ethics and Standards. A year later that Committee published a report titled "Four Statements for Archaeology."[6] The four statements represent the first published ethics policy for the Society for American Archaeology and reflect the concerns of that time. The statements warn of censure or expulsion from the Society for disregard of proper archaeological field methods, buying and selling of artifacts, and willful destruction, distortion or concealment of archaeological data. The fourth statement recommends that archaeologists have formal training consisting of a B.A. or B.S. degree followed by two years of graduate study in archaeology and anthropology, with two years of summer field school experience under the supervision of a trained archaeologist. A Ph.D. in anthropology was highly recommended, but not required.

In 1971 when I participated in my first summer of archaeological fieldwork, this ethics policy was not part of the formal archaeological curriculum. During the 1960s and 1970s, students in archaeology were deeply concerned about changes in the paradigm of archaeology. The writings of Lewis R. Binford and his students promoted an interest in processual theory. Processualist views promoted problem-oriented research and the search for laws and theory through research designs and hypothesis testing. The change from a culture-historical orientation to a processualist orientation dominated archaeological discussion and debate even as the foundations of contemporary cultural resource management programs were being developed.

Cultural Resource Management

When I was an idealistic student, it seemed only logical that archaeologists should conduct research at sites before they are destroyed by construction or other activities. The archaeological heritage that was salvaged by the TVA and River Basin Survey programs, although it did not live up to the standards of processual or "New" archaeology, still served as a reminder of what could be lost without archaeological salvage. Fortunately, through the efforts of archaeologists and other preservationists, the U.S. Congress passed the National Historic Preservation Act of 1966, the National Environmental Policy Act of 1969, and the Archeological and Historic Preservation Act of 1974. These three laws form the core of what has become known as Cultural Resource Management in the United States.

As a graduate student at Southern Methodist University, I had the opportunity to participate in a wide variety of contract archaeology projects throughout northern Texas. At that time, most of the archaeological research associated with Cultural Resource Management was being done by universities. Major projects like New Melones in California, Orme and Santa Rosa Wash in Arizona, and Cache River in Arkansas offered opportunities for enthusiastic young archaeologists to apply processualist approaches on an increasingly large scale. Private sector involvement at this time was just beginning, and public funding for archaeology was on the rise. At the same time, some of the same individuals who had worked to pass the laws that formed the basis for the new Cultural Resource Management movement were able to see the need for an expanded code of ethics for archaeology.

Society of Professional Archeologists

Throughout the first half of the 1970s, members of the Society for American Archaeology discussed the need for certification of archaeologists. After several conferences and meetings, a Society for American Archaeology committee met in Fayetteville, Arkansas in January 1976 and decided to develop certification procedures, a code of ethics, and standards of research performance for a new organization, totally independent of SAA and other existing archaeological societies. In May 1976, the Society of Professional Archeologists (SOPA) was incorporated in Illinois and began the process of establishing a registry of professional archaeologists.

Unlike the earlier ethics code developed by the SAA, the new SOPA code was more comprehensive and more specific. The Code of Ethics addressed the responsibility of archaeologists to the public, colleagues, employees, students, and clients. The Standards of Research Performance addressed the responsibility of archaeologists to be properly prepared and trained for any research they undertake, to implement the research in a systematic and scientific manner, to report the results of the research in a reasonable period of time, and to insure that the artifacts and records resulting from the research are curated in an appropriate institution. The Society of Professional Archeologists also implemented a Grievance Procedure that allowed individuals to charge SOPA-certified archaeologists with violations of the Code of Ethics and Standards of Research Performance. After investigation by the Grievance Coordinator and a hearing in front of the Standards Board, an archaeologist who had violated the Ethics Code and Standards of Research Performance could be admonished, suspended, or expelled from SOPA. The creation of a mechanism to enforce the Code of Ethics and Standards of Research Performance represented a bold precedent for American archaeology.

Between 1976 and 1998, the Society of Professional Archeologists was the only organization in the United States that certified individuals as professional archaeologists. Although there was widespread support for the creation of SOPA, many archaeologists objected to the certification process and never joined the organization. The inability to convince substantial numbers of archaeologists to be certified and accept the Code of Ethics and Standards of Research Performance reduced the effectiveness of the organization. Although expensive, the Grievance Process proved effective and SOPA gradually built a body of case law about ethical behavior.

During this same period, archaeology experienced major growth in employment resulting from the passage of cultural resource management legislation. The number of archaeologists boomed from hundreds to thousands, and raised questions about minimum professional qualifications and standards of performance. During this period, SOPA was the only organization to regularly and explicitly address the ethical issues facing the archaeological profession. However, the relatively small number of dedicated SOPA members were unable to have the full impact they desired on the ethics of the archaeological profession.

1980s and Beyond

While the field of cultural resource management continued to grow, the threat to archaeological resources also grew. Illegal trade in antiquities threatened sites around the world, and archaeologists worked with legislators to pass laws to protect archaeological sites from looting by antiquities hunters. Despite serious efforts by many nations to protect their archaeological heritage, the antiquities trade continued to flourish. Archaeological organizations like the Archaeological Institute of America and the Society for Historical Archaeology developed policies to discourage archaeologists from working with looters and antiquities traders to avoid any appearance of approval of their activities.

At the same time, archaeologists were confronted by an increasing expression of interest among Native Americans in the archaeological record and the treatment of the archaeological record. This interest eventually grew into political activism that resulted in the passage of state and federal legislation relating to the repatriation of human remains and associated artifacts. While some archaeologists opposed these developments as anti-science, others argued that these laws offered an opportunity to build upon a history of cooperation between archaeologists and some Native American groups. However archaeologists felt about the Native American Graves Protection and Repatriation Act (NAGPRA), it fueled further discussion about archaeological ethics.

In 1990, the editors of the *American Journal of Archaeology* (published by the Archaeological Institute of America) and *Latin American Antiquity* and *American Antiquity* (published by the Society for American Archaeology) issued policies that prohibited publication of papers that were based on looted data. In May 1991, Alison Wylie made a presentation to the SAA Executive Board about the ethical issues associated with publishing papers that utilized data from looted sites. The SAA Executive Board recognized that the Society's ethics policy was outdated and the editorial policies of their journals were not fully compatible with Society bylaws. The Executive Board asked Alison Wylie and me to cochair a task force on ethics in archaeology.

With funding from the National Science Foundation and the National Park Service, we were able to organize a three-day workshop (November 5–7, 1993) at the CRM Policy Institute, University of Nevada-Reno. At that workshop, a diverse range of participants drafted six principles of archaeological ethics and agreed upon a process for presenting them to the SAA membership. The six principles developed at the Reno Workshop addressed stewardship, accountability, commercialization, public education and outreach, intellectual property, and records preservation.

The six draft principles were presented to the SAA membership at the fifty-ninth Annual Meeting of the Society in a Special Forum in Anaheim, California. The Special Forum included an introduction, six position papers about the draft principles, and commentaries from five discussants. The proceedings from the Forum were compiled and edited and published by the SAA as a Special Report.[7] The Special Forum and subsequent Special Report were intended to encourage discussion and inform archaeologists about the draft principles. Verbal and written comments were further solicited by the presentation of papers at regional conferences and at discussion sessions at the sixtieth Annual Meeting of the SAA in Minneapolis in 1995.

After reviewing the comments that were received, the Ethics in Archaeology Task Force made editorial and other minor changes and developed an additional principle that addressed the responsibility of archaeologists to publish reports of their research. The principles were then submitted to the SAA Executive Board for review and approval in September 1995. At the next meeting, the Executive Board discussed the draft principles expressing concerns about aspects of two of the draft principles and recommending that an eighth principle addressing training and resources be developed by the Task Force. The Task Force made the recommended changes and resubmitted them to the SAA Executive Board, which adopted them in 1996.

Principles of Archaeological Ethics

The Principles of Archaeological Ethics are statements of ethical goals or ideals. They are intended to guide archaeologists through the increasing complexity of conducting their professional lives in the modern world. The Principles of Archaeological Ethics represent what Alison Wylie[8] has called "ceilings" of ethical behavior, rather than "floors" that might identify minimum acceptable levels of conduct. The Ethics in Archaeology Task Force, in developing the Principles, never intended that they be enforceable. The Principles were intended to stimulate discussion, encourage teaching about ethics, and serve as ethical guidelines.

PRINCIPLE 1: STEWARDSHIP

The archaeological record—that is, in situ archaeological material and sites, archaeological collections, records, and reports—is irreplaceable. It is the responsibility of all archaeologists to work for the long-term conservation and protection of the archaeological record by practicing and promoting good stewardship of the archaeological record. Stewards are both caretakers of and advocates for the archaeological record. In the interests of stewardship, archaeologists should use and advocate use of the archaeological record for the benefit of all people; as they investigate and interpret the record, they should use the specialized knowledge they gain to promote public understanding and support for its long-term preservation.

PRINCIPLE 2: ACCOUNTABILITY

Responsible archaeological research, including all levels of professional activity, requires an acknowledgement of public accountability and a commitment to make every reasonable effort, in good faith, to consult actively with affected group(s), with the goal of establishing a working relationship that can be beneficial to all parties involved.

PRINCIPLE 3: COMMERCIALIZATION

The Society for American Archaeology has long recognized that the buying and selling of objects out of archaeological context is contributing to the destruction of the archaeological record on the American continents and around the world. The commercialization of archaeological objects—their use as commodities to be exploited for personal enjoyment or profit—results in the destruction of archaeological sites and of contextual information that is essential to understanding the archaeological record. Archaeologists should therefore carefully weigh the benefits to scholarship of a project against the costs of potentially enhancing the commercial value of archaeological objects. Wherever possible, they should discourage, and should themselves avoid, activities that enhance the commercial value of archaeological objects, especially objects that are not curated in public institu-

tions, or readily available for scientific study, public interpretation, and display.

PRINCIPLE 4: PUBLIC EDUCATION AND OUTREACH

Archaeologists should reach out to, and participate in, cooperative efforts with others interested in the archaeological record with the aim of improving the preservation, protection, and interpretation of the record. In particular, archaeologists should undertake to (1) enlist public support for the stewardship of the archaeological record; (2) explain and promote the use of archaeological methods and techniques in understanding human behavior and culture, and (3) communicate archaeological interpretations of the past. Many publics exist for archaeology, including students and teachers; Native Americans and other ethnic, religious, and cultural groups who find in the archaeological record important aspects of their cultural heritage; lawmakers and government officials; reporters, journalists, and others involved in the media; and the general public. Archaeologists who are unable to undertake public education and outreach directly should encourage and support the efforts of others in these activities.

PRINCIPLE 5: INTELLECTUAL PROPERTY

Intellectual property, as contained in the knowledge and documents created through the study of archaeological resources, is part of the archaeological record. As such it should be treated in accord with the principles of stewardship rather than as a matter of personal possession. If there is a compelling reason, and no legal restrictions or strong countervailing interests, a researcher may have primary access to original materials and documents for a limited and reasonable time, after which these materials and documents must be made available to others.

PRINCIPLE 6: PUBLIC REPORTING AND PUBLICATION

Within a reasonable time, the knowledge archaeologists gain from investigation of the archaeological record must be presented in accessible form (through publication or other means) to as wide a range of interested publics as possible. The documents and materials on which publication and other forms of public reporting are based should be deposited in a suitable place for permanent safekeeping. An interest in preserving and protecting in situ archaeological sites must be taken into account when publishing and distributing information about their nature and location.

PRINCIPLE 7: RECORDS AND PRESERVATION

Archaeologists should work actively for the preservation of, and long-term access to, archaeological collections, records, and reports. To this end, they should encourage colleagues, students, and others to make responsible use of collections, records, and reports in their research as one means of preserving the in situ archaeological record and of increasing the care and attention given to that portion of the archaeological record that has been removed and incorporated into archaeological collections, records, and reports.

PRINCIPLE 8: TRAINING AND RESOURCES

Given the destructive nature of most archaeological investigations, archaeologists must ensure that they have adequate training, experience, facilities, and other support necessary to conduct any program of research they initiate in a manner consistent with the foregoing principles and contemporary standards of professional practice.

Stewardship

The concept of stewardship is at the center of the Principles of Archaeological Ethics. It has become widespread in archaeology with the development of cultural resource management. The term became a catchword for archaeological site protection following the publication of a booklet titled "These are the Stewards of the Past."[9] Stewardship responsibilities for archaeologists were further defined by William Lipe in one of the most important archaeological papers in the past three decades. In that 1974 paper, "A Conservation Model for American Archaeology," Lipe offered many excellent and logical reasons why archaeologists should work to protect and preserve the archaeological record for future study.[10] A generation of archaeologists embraced this model and worked to weave it into the fabric of current cultural resource management practices.

Recently, Lipe has refined his thinking on stewardship and reminds archaeologists that understanding the past through the study of the archaeological record is the ultimate goal of archaeology. Since the value of many archaeological sites is tied to their information potential, well-designed and implemented archaeological research is important to the advancement of the discipline and benefits the public. "Long-term, frugal consumption of the archaeological record by well-justified research—both problem oriented, and mitigation driven—must be an accepted and integrated part of the preservation program."[11] Although much of my own archaeological training

emphasized that professionally trained archaeologists have the most legitimate interest in the archaeological record, the interest of the general public and specific interest groups in the use and management of archaeological sites and objects is clearly increasing. Coincident with the development of the draft Principles of Archaeological Ethics, Christopher Chippindale[12] published an eloquent dialogue on the importance of holding archaeological resources in "common" for everyone. Since the vast majority of archaeological research and archaeological site management is now funded by the public, this seems to be a practical as well as principled approach. Archaeologists have long recognized that one of the primary factors that distinguish professional archaeologists from looters is that our training, specialized knowledge, and skills permit us to serve a wide range of public interests.

Accountability and Public Education and Outreach

The principles of accountability and public education and outreach reflect the growing awareness among archaeologists that our obligations extend beyond the archaeological community. When I first became involved in archaeology, many archaeologists viewed talking with the media or giving a lecture at a rotary luncheon as something to be avoided. This is clearly changing. Not only do the principles encourage archaeologists to share their specialized knowledge about the past with the diverse public, but archaeologists recognize that most of their work is sponsored by public funding. At a time when there is increasing competition for public funds at all levels, it is clearly in our best interest to share our knowledge and discoveries with the public. The Society for American Archaeology has established a nationwide network of Public Education Coordinators who work with local archaeologists to arrange and schedule public lectures, assist teachers and administrators in adding archaeology to school curricula, and organize and schedule statewide archaeology week activities.

There is also growing awareness among archaeologists that our research and professional activities affect many individuals and groups beyond the archaeological profession. Archaeologists have always been aware of their responsibilities to landowners on whose property they wish to work, but now there is increasing awareness of responsibility to the people whose past we study. Many native people around the world are interested in what archaeology can tell them about their heritage, and some are uncomfortable with the methods of archaeology. In the United States, the

Native American Graves Protection and Repatriation Act recognizes that Native Americans should have a voice in the treatment of human remains and associated funerary objects recovered from archaeological sites. Similar legislation in Canada and other nations is encouraging archaeologists and First Nations to communicate and collaborate on the study of the past.

Commercialization

The loss of archaeological sites and damage to the archaeological record from looters is a major problem throughout the world. A search of almost any American flea market will reveal a dealer selling arrow heads and other artifacts. While many of these may, in fact, be recent replicas, they demonstrate the market for even common and broken objects from the past. The finest archaeological objects usually sell through international auctions. The demand for antiquities is worldwide and is big business. Competition among museums to display the best and finest artifacts also fuels this market. The demand for antiquities is encouraging illegal and unscientific excavation of archaeological sites all over the world.

One of the oldest, and still most important, ethical problems for archaeologists is deciding how to deal with collections owned by amateur archaeologists and art collectors. Archaeology in general, and professional archaeologists in particular, have benefited greatly from information provided by amateur archaeologists. Most professional archaeologists are comfortable working with amateur archaeologists and landowners who collect surface artifacts, record their provenience, and report site locations to professional archaeologists. What becomes more difficult is deciding how to treat individuals who dig for artifacts without proper training.

Ten years ago, *Archaeology* magazine published a special report on the extent of looting in Arkansas.[13] The report emphasized the extent and intensity of the problem. Since it is largely rural and one of the poorest states, many people in Arkansas see digging for artifacts as a way to increase their income. Individuals have been digging prehistoric graves to collect pots and other artifacts for sale for more than a hundred years, and Mississippian and Caddoan pottery from Arkansas is found in private collections and museums around the world. Unfortunately, when an archaeologist examines artifacts from a private collection and provides an opinion about their age, function, or authenticity, that opinion may be used to legitimize the artifacts. A professional archaeologist's opinion might also result in an increase in the sale price of artifacts. This is even more likely when an archaeologist incorporates data from looted contexts into their research and publications. By increasing the commercial value of looted collections, archaeologists unintentionally provide fuel for further looting of archaeological sites. Art and antiquities collectors are very much aware of the literature of archaeology, and opinions, writing, and activities of professional archaeologists have an impact on collecting activities and interests.

Intellectual Property and Public Reporting and Publication

As a student, one of the first informal lessons I received in ethics was a discussion by a professor about the importance of writing reports that describe our excavations. The professor never really said why reporting was important, but it was clear that failure to do so would tarnish our reputations. With most archaeological research today is supported by public funding, the obligation to prepare reports is still widely accepted. The need to publish our research results, particularly books and papers that synthesized work from cultural resource management projects, is particularly important. Most cultural resource management reports are produced in very small numbers, and they are only accessible to specialists and close colleagues. This "gray literature," as it is known, contains a tremendous amount of information that is inaccessible to many professionals and most of the public. For most people working in cultural resource management, it is difficult to find the time needed to synthesize projects and prepare papers and books for publication. However, it is widely understood that this is necessary if we are ever going to fully justify the continuing expenditure of public funds on archaeology.

My student training also included informal lessons about intellectual property. As noted in Principle 5, the knowledge and documents that are created as part of archaeological research are just as much a part of the archaeological record as are artifacts and objects. When I first started in archaeology, many archaeologists viewed their records and notes as personal property. Although they accepted that the artifacts from a project belonged in a museum, they kept the written notes and records in their personal possession. The importance of properly curating records and notes with artifact collections is also addressed in Principle 7. More than one older research collection has been reduced in value through the loss of records and notes that describe the provenience of artifacts or the circumstance of their discovery.

It is logical that project archaeologists should have primary access to the original records and documents for a limited and reasonable period of time. However, when a project report is complete, collections and records should be made available to others. Our stewardship responsibilities require that we share our knowledge, notes, and records with colleagues, to maximize the information potential of the archaeological record.

Records and Preservation

From some of our earliest years in school, we are taught that scientific research includes systematic, objective, and precise experiments or observations that can be replicated under the same circumstances. In archaeology, the process of excavating a site removes artifacts from their original context. This process is destructive in that it leaves little or nothing for future researchers to study, except the artifacts, photographs, notes, and records of the excavation. Once excavated, a site cannot be reconstructed and excavations cannot be replicated. Consequently, we must preserve the artifacts and records from our research so that other archaeologists can decide if they concur with our interpretations of the archaeological record.

The stewardship principle recognizes that the artifacts, records, notes, and photographs from archaeological research are an important part of the archaeological record. Preserving these materials in a museum or curatorial repository is as much a part of a successful archaeological project as developing a research design. We must recognize that the products of our research are valuable resources that permit us to restudy the archaeological record, even after the site(s) from which the data came has been destroyed. The federal government recognizes that artifacts and records from archaeological research are important resources and worthy of preservation, and the Secretary of the Interior has issued detailed guidelines for the preservation of these materials.

The growth of cultural resource management has produced a crisis in the management of archaeological collections. Although some new facilities are being constructed, and some existing facilities are being expanded, there is not enough museum or repository space to properly house all the existing collections. As archaeological research continues, it is essential that we work to help develop new facilities. The preservation of these collections is important to the continued study of the archaeological record, and it is each archaeologist's ethical obligation to insure that artifacts and other products of research are properly curated.

Training and Resources

The growth of cultural resource management has made archaeology a significant business in the United States. Thousands of people are employed in archaeology every year. Increasing competition for contracts and grants have led some archaeologists to undertake projects for which they were not fully qualified. Since archaeology is a destructive process, it is important that practitioners be properly trained for the research they undertake. Principle 8 was developed to remind archaeologists that we must have the appropriate training, experience, preparation, and facilities before undertaking an archaeological project.

Register of Professional Archaeologists

While the Principles of Archaeological Ethics were being developed, the Society for American Archaeology, Society of Professional Archeologists, Archaeological Institute of America, and the Society for Historical Archaeology were discussing the creation of a Register of Professional Archaeologists. The Register was formally established in 1998, from the Society of Professional Archeologists under the joint sponsorship of the other three organizations. The Register of Professional Archaeologists (RPA) adopted most of the procedures developed by SOPA, including the Code of Ethics, the Standards of Research Performance, and the Grievance Procedure.

The grievance procedure and certification process are at the heart of the RPA. Through the certification process, individuals submit their credentials to demonstrate that they have met the minimum education and experience levels necessary to be registered as Professional Archaeologists. Individuals listed on the Register also agree to accept the Code of Ethics and Standards of Research Performance. By doing this, individuals agree to participate in the grievance process if there is a credible challenge to their conduct or research performance. The grievance process establishes a system where any concerned individual can ask that the actions of anyone listed on the Register be reviewed by a panel of professional archaeologists.

The grievance process represents a mechanism, with more than twenty years of success under SOPA, by which archaeologists can investigate the conduct and performance of colleagues. This selfpolicing program provides a venue where legitimate complaints are reviewed, and if necessary, sanctions recommended against individuals who perform substandard work.

Since the establishment of the RPA in 1998, the number of archaeologists who have applied for and received certification as professional archaeologists has more than doubled. While only a small fraction of the individuals currently working at archaeology have been certified by the RPA, the substantial increase in applications for certification is encouraging. This implies that more and more archaeologists recognize and accept that there is a need for a formal ethics code for archaeologists.

Ethics and the Future

After nearly thirty years of participating in archaeology, it is obvious to me that change in our profession, just like society in general, is occurring at an increasing rate. The Principles of Archaeological Ethics that have been adopted by the Society for American Archaeology are intended to serve as guidelines to help archaeologists make informed and wise professional choices in a rapidly changing world. The principles represent ideals, and they are intended to encourage discussion and formal training about archaeological ethics.

Until recently, ethics were not commonly part of formal training in archaeology. This is changing as archaeologists become more informed about their ethical responsibilities and the conflicts that confront us throughout the profession. Continued discussion about the Principles is essential, because we cannot possibly anticipate all the future ethical issues that will face us individually and collectively in the coming years. Consequently, the Principles must be reviewed regularly, and possibly updated or revised as needed. Formal discussion and training about ethics is important to this process, and is the best way to introduce future professional archaeologists to the difficult choices they may face.

As archaeology matures as a profession, there is an increasing need for ethical guidelines. The recent, rapid growth in the archaeological profession has clearly created an environment where the Principles of Archaeological Ethics (developed by the Society for American Archaeology), and the Register of Professional Archaeologists both serve an important function. The combination of ethical ideals, professional certification, and standards of minimally acceptable conduct from these two ethical codes offer guidelines to operate in most of the practical real-world situations being encountered by contemporary archaeologists.

Notes

1. Robert Silverberg, *Men Against Time* (New York: MacMillan, 1967).
2. Charles R. McGimsey III, *Public Archaeology* (New York: Seminar Press, 1972).
3. William D. Lipe, "A Conservation Model for American Archaeology," *Kiva* 39 (1974): 213–245
4. Carl E. Guthe, "Report, Society for American Archaeology," *American Antiquity* 1 (1936): 310.
5. Charles R. McGimsey III, "Standards, Ethics, and Archaeology: A Brief History," in M. J. Lynott and A. Wylie, eds., *Ethics in American Archaeology: Challenges for the 1990s* (Washington: Society for American Archaeology Special Report, 1995).
6. J. L. Champe, D. S. Byers, C. Evans, A. K. Guthe, H. W. Hamilton, E. B. Jelks, C. W. Meighan, S. Olafson, G. I. Quimby, W. Smith, and F. Wendorf, "Four Statements for Archaeology," *American Antiquity* 27 (1961): 137–138.
7. Mark J. Lynott and Alison Wylie, eds., *Ethics in American Archaeology: Challenges for the 1990s* (Washington: Society for American Archaeology Special Report, 1995).
8. Alison Wylie, "Ethical Dilemmas in Archaeological Practice: Looting, Repatriation, Stewardship, and the (Trans)formation of Disciplinary Identity," in M. J. Lynott and A. Wylie, eds., *Ethics in American Archaeology* (Washington: Society for American Archaeology, 2000).
9. Charles R. McGimsey III, Hester A. Davis, and Carl Chapman, "These Are the Stewards of the Past" (Columbia: University of Missouri, Extension Division, 1970).
10. See note #3.
11. Ibid.
12. Christopher Chippindale, "The Concept of the 'Commons,'" *Antiquity* 68 (1994): 191–192.
13. Spencer P. M. Harrington, "The Looting of Arkansas," *Archaeology* 44 (1991): 2231.

Suggested Readings

Green, Ernestene L., ed. *Ethics and Values in Archaeology.* New York: Free Press, 1984.

Lynott, Mark J. "Ethical Principles and Archaeological Practice: Development of an Ethics Policy." *American Antiquity* 62, no. 4 (1987): 589–599.

Lynott, Mark J. and Alison Wylie, eds. *Ethics in American Archaeology.* Washington: Society for American Archaeology, 2000.

Messenger, Phyllis Mauch, ed. *The Ethics of Collecting Cultural Property: Whose Culture? Whose Property?* Albuquerque: University of New Mexico Press, 1989.

Vitelli, Karen D., ed. *Archaeological Ethics.* Walnut Creek, CA: Altamira Press, 1996.

Genes, Bodies, and Species

Jonathan Marks

This chapter is about the biological hierarchy through which changes in DNA ultimately become differences between species. The idea of *hierarchy* is an old and fairly nebulous one in evolutionary biology, generally invoked to differentiate between what geneticists study and what anatomists or natural historians study.[1] What geneticists study—genes and chromosomes—is of course so small that you can't see it with the naked eye, while what anatomists study can be sliced and weighed. Likewise, what geneticists study *causes* what anatomists study—that is, genes "code for" bodies.

And yet, such a biological hierarchy is certainly intended to convey something more than simply gross size of the subject matter—big things versus little things! After all, non-genetic information has a major role in the form of the end products of biological development. And genes only "code for" bodies in a very crude way, for bodies also constitute the manner by which the genes are passed into the next generation—so there is an important sense in which bodies make genes as much as genes make bodies.

The object of this chapter is to link together the small and the large through modern evolutionary theory, and to explore the relationships among genes (or cells), phenotypes (or bodies), and populations (or species). The point will be that cells, organisms, and species are all "individuals"—that is to say, singular entities bounded in space and time and composed of interacting parts; as opposed to "classes," or sets of objects, transcending time and space and composed of members sharing a specific quality or essence.[2] Each of these kinds of individuals can be studied in a particular fashion, and we will explore the manner in which that is so, and the different kinds of evolutionary knowledge that is accessible from each kind of individual.

Genetics: Cells as Individuals and Genes as Machine Code

Cells were recognized in the nineteenth century as the most fundamental form of life. Reproduction and development, whose relationship to one another had previously been very unclear, were now seen to be related through the processes of cell division. While the body at all stages was composed of cells, reproduction and development were the results of two different kinds of cell division. Mitosis was the process by which cells divided into two identical cells, and the body thereby grew; and meiosis was the process by which sperm and egg cells were produced to transmit genetic information into the next generation of organisms. Each sperm or egg has half the amount of genetic information of ordinary cells, and the genetic information they carry differs. Thus, ordinary cells have two copies of each gene and are thus *diploid*, while sperm and egg have one copy of each gene and are thus *haploid*. In addition, ordinary cells all carry a set of identical genetic information, while the genetic information carried within each sperm or egg cell is unique and thus distinct from every other sperm or egg.

Cell generations, then, are similar to those of larger organisms. Cells originate, persevere, and die. They exist in space and have a duration in time. They reproduce. They interact with others like themselves and with the physiological environment in which they exist. They are autonomous biological units.

Another powerful recognition came half a century later, as biologists grappled with the precise nature of the genetic information itself. In a book called *What Is Life?* published in 1944, physicist Erwin Schrödinger suggested that the genetic information could be considered as a kind of code that the cell's mechanism effectively decodes. This idea of the *genetic code*, evoking powerful images of language and machinery, has subsequently become one of the most powerful metaphors in science.[3]

The units of genetic information themselves came to be known early in the twentieth century as "genes."[4] The development of population genetics in the 1930s provided a powerful theoretical model for the processes of evolution, based on a mathematical abstraction, the *gene pool*—a hypothetical summation of all the hereditary elements in a population—a pool in the sense of office pool, not swimming pool.

By focusing on the gene pool, population genetics established a fundamental way of thinking about evolution, a way that completely avoided the recognized biological units: cells and organisms. Population genetics modeled evolution as changes in the gene pool, in which organisms were simply represented by genotypes, transient pairs of genes, each of whose lifespan was far shorter than that of the gene pool itself. The proportions of each genotype were mathematically predictable from the proportions of each gene by a relation that has come to be known as the Hardy-Weinberg Law.[5]

The Hardy-Weinberg Law has two parts. The first part tells us that, given two genetic variants (alleles) in a gene pool, one with a frequency of p and the other with a frequency of q, the ordinary processes of organismal reproduction will sort these alleles into diploid genotypes in fixed proportions. One homozygote (an organism with two identical alleles) will exist with a frequency of p^2, the other with a frequency of q^2, and the heterozygote (an organism with one of each allele) will exist in the population with a predictable frequency of $2pq$. In other words, if 30 percent of the alleles in a gene pool are A1, and 70 percent are A2 (A1 and A2 being two hypothetical variants of the A gene), then we would expect to find 9 percent of the *organisms* to be A1A1 homozygotes, 49 percent to be A2A2 homozygotes, and 42 percent to be A1A2 heterozygotes. The second part of the Hardy-Weinberg Law tells us that these proportions remain constant every generation, as long as no other forces are acting on the population aside from reproduction.

Evolution, then, according to population genetics, is simply a violation of this genetic equilibrium. Studying evolution involves asking a single fundamental question: What causes the proportions of genotypes and genes not to remain constant?

Empirically this question can be studied using genetic markers, bits of genetic material whose transmission can be tracked in populations, even though they may not be functionally significant. After all, this is a corpus of statistical theory that eliminates pheno-types, bodies, and organisms from the picture. The function of a gene—what it does, and its effect on the body—is thus irrelevant here.

So what alters the gene pool? Preferential mating with relatives (*inbreeding*) makes a population more homozygous, but doesn't directly affect allele frequencies. Differential reproduction of particular genotypes (*selection*) will directly affect allele frequencies; as will the introgression of genetic material from another population (*gene flow*). Finally, since real populations are finite in size, the laws of chance dictate random deviations from the predicted mathematical constancy (*genetic drift*). Each of these forces has specific effects: Since the environment is what permits different genotypes to reproduce more or less efficiently than their alternatives, selection permits populations to track their environments genetically; thus selection makes populations different from one another adaptively. Gene flow, on the other hand, makes populations more similar to one another, for it reflects the genetic contact between populations. And finally, genetic drift also makes populations different from one another, but in a nonadaptive way.

Thus, "the spread of genes" is a classic way of visualizing evolution, assuming a direct translation from genetical variant to physical/anatomical variant, and modeling the ways in which a population is altered through time upon the emergence of these new genetic variations. But recently, the precise nature of these genetic variations has come to be examined in greater depth, and has revealed a system of far greater complexity than such simple modeling had considered.

The Genome as Information

The image of genes as blueprints or machine code for the body is immensely powerful. It lies behind the program begun in the 1980s called The Human Genome Project, in which great public and private resources were mustered to generate a comprehensive vision of the blueprints: the DNA sequence of each chromosome. A genome is, formally, the genetic structure of a single reproductive cell: a haploid genetic complement, one of each chromosome.

The chromosomes are visible structures whose purpose seems to be to guide a great mass of DNA through cell division by condensing it into a manageable number of regular structures. Thus, chromosomes are only visible during cell division; at other times the DNA is loose in the cell nucleus, although "anchored" to the nuclear membrane at certain points.

Humans have twenty-three pairs of chromosomes, so the Human Genome Project's goal was to reproduce the detailed linear sequence of each of them. Once we have the gene sequences, and the knowledge that the gene sequence is like machine code for the production of organisms, we will have, as the Human Genome Project's purple prose said, "The Book of Man" or "The Holy Grail of Biology."[6,7]

This misses a crucial part of genetic physiology, however. As we noted earlier, a normal human body cell is diploid; only gametes are haploid. In fact, the human body is constrained to have two, *and only two*, sets of instructions in its cells. While many domestic plants have multiple sets of chromosomes, a condition known as polyploidy, mammalian cells simply can't work that way. A human with three sets of chromosomes (sixty-nine total) is triploid and cannot survive.

Moreover, having one copy (monosomy) or three copies (trisomy) of any specific chromosome is also bad. This is known as the problem of dosage: You need two doses of DNA, not one and not three. Having one copy of a particular chromosome (making forty-five total) is not compatible with life, unless that chromosome is the X chromosome, which still results in a characteristic pathological condition known as Turner's Syndrome. Having three copies of a particular chromosome (forty-seven total) is slightly better, but not much. One can live normally with an extra Y chromosome (because there is very little on that chromosome): One can also survive, but again with distinctive pathological phenotypes, with an extra X chromosome (Klinefelter's Syndrome) or chromosome 21 (Down's Syndrome). The X chromosome can tolerate variation in number more readily than other chromosomes because it has relatively few genes and has its own special mechanism for regulating dosage—since normal males have one X and normal females have two Xs. Chromosome 21 seems to be able to tolerate trisomy because it is so small and has only about 200 genes, rather fewer than chromosome 22, which is about the same size.

The point is that normal development depends not just on the DNA sequence, but specifically on the interactions of *two* DNA sequences. Using the metaphor of DNA as a blueprint or code, it may be easy to miss the importance of the dosage of DNA required; the complex interactions between two *sets* of instructions that seem to add up to more than the sum of their parts.

They say that when the only tool you have is a hammer, everything tends to look like a nail. Unfortunately we don't really have tools for understanding the interaction between two genomes that results in a normal, healthy organism. But we do have the ability to study the structure of an individual genome in its finest detail, and so we do. From the standpoint of evolution, this leads us to the process of mutation. Mutation is a change in the genetic material; alleles differ from one another ultimately because of mutation, and consequently mutation is the source of all genetic differences between organisms and between species. Since the 1980s, our increasing knowledge of the genome has greatly affected our view of mutation.

The genome is composed of DNA, a long series of elementary subunits known as adenine, guanine, cytosine, and thymine, abbreviated A, G, C, and T. These are known as nucleotides or bases. When we speak of a "DNA sequence" we mean simply a long, specific arrangement of those four bases: for example, AAGC-TATATCCAGCA.

The human genome is essentially 3.2 billion of those letters, divided among twenty-three chromosomes. Genes are simply particular regions of the genome that have some kind of function. Here, however, is where a major conceptual revolution in the past quartercentury has occurred. Where it used to be thought that the genes were arrayed like beads on a string—the genome being the string and the genes being the beads—it is now clear that (1) the beads are simply "special cases" of string; and (2) there are very few beads.[8] In other words, the genes are simply functional bits of genome; and genes are rare within the genome. The human genome sequence, published in early 2001, shows that less than 25 percent of the genome consists of genes (30,000 genes, each on average 27,000 bases long), and even within each gene less than 10 percent is actually functional. The Human Genome Project reports that only between 1–2 percent of the DNA actually comprises *coding sequence*.[9]

Moreover, there are complex patterns of redundancy within the genome. These patterns of redundancy are themselves products of the mutational machinery, and contribute to the perpetuation of that redundancy. For example, the most basic kind of mutation is the substitution of one base for another, such as AAGCT to AAGCC. However, a different mutational process called *strand slippage* can insert or delete additional bases, such as altering A*AGAGG*CT to A*AGAGAGAGAGG*CT. That, of course, creates a fundamental pattern of redundancy of bases. It may also increase in intensity over the generations, as an auto-catalytic process. This has now been found to be the cause of a significant class of genetic diseases, which includes Huntington's chorea and fragile-X syndrome.

Another kind of redundancy is created by a widespread "rubber-stamping" process in the genome, whereby one DNA sequence is simply copied next to itself. If this DNA sequence includes a functional gene, it will produce two functional genes next to each other, where formerly there was only one. Three things can happen to this new copy over many generations: (1) It can continue to do the same thing, so the body now has twice as much gene product, which, if beneficial, would then be preserved; (2) if its presence makes no difference to the body, it can degrade by mutation to a state of nonfunction, now called a *pseudogene*; (3) rather than becoming nonfunctional, mutations can alter the properties of the second gene product so that it does something different, which again might be beneficial.

And indeed we find that genes in the genome are found in clusters, some copies of which do identical things, some of which do slightly different things, and some of which do nothing at all. The genes coding for hemoglobin, the best-known genetic system, are located in two clusters, one at the tip of chromosome 11 and the other at the tip of chromosome 16. The one at the tip of chromosome 16 codes for the alpha component of hemoglobin, a protein that is 141 amino acids long, and has two identical genes, side-by-side, churning out the raw material for alpha-globin. There is also, however, a gene just a little ways away, which also makes a 141-amino-acid-long protein, but only does so early in embryonic life, when the needs for gas transport in the tissues are considerably different. And there are also DNA stretches that bear strong similarities to the functional genes but do not themselves do anything: pseudogenes, the result of archaic duplications of DNA that didn't help and didn't hurt, a genetic experiment that neither succeeded nor failed, but whose record remains.

Other portions of the genome appear to be immensely long stretches of simple sequences—just a few letters repeated millions of times, the result of a process (or processes) of massive tandem duplication.

Still other kinds of mutation involve the movement of specific DNA bits from one place to another, known as transposition, or the creation of several copies of a particular DNA bit, and the integration of these DNA copies in many places throughout the genome, known as retrotransposition. The most famous of these DNA segments is known as *Alu*, and consists of a fairly specific stretch of DNA about 300 bases long and intercalated seemingly at random through the genome, over a million times.

Since the genome is far more complex than had been thought by an earlier generation, our ideas about the genome have had to be revised, particularly in relation to evolution. We have tended to conceptualize mutation as a simple process of nucleotide substitution in functional genes in our formal models, but it is now clear that the genome is a dynamic landscape, and can tolerate considerable change without apparent adverse effect. With mutation being the basic source of biological novelty, the implication is that the sources of novelty for evolution are considerably more diverse than considered by earlier generations of geneticists. How do we use this new information to understand the biological history of species?

Representation

From the standpoint of evolution, these different parts of the genome can convey different kinds of information. It is axiomatic, for example, that since most of the genome is nonfunctional, it is not affected by natural selection. Thus, most mutations have no effect on the phenotype and are not weeded out by natural selection, while those that alter the structure of genes generally do so adversely and are consequently eliminated. Thus inter-genic DNA evolves most rapidly, and genic DNA most slowly.

However, in the time since, say, human and chimp have been separate species, very few changes have occurred in the genome. We are over 98 percent genetically identical to chimpanzees and (at least to a first approximation) 100 percent genetically identical to each other; consequently it is hard to use DNA to study the relationships among human beings. However, a particularly rapidly evolving part of the genome is found outside the cell nucleus and is known as mitochondrial DNA or mtDNA. Here, humans and chimpanzees are 9 percent different, and two random humans are 0.2 percent different from each other. Consequently this can be used as a genetic marker for studying the relationships among groups of people.

Genetic markers can be tricky, however. Most of the genome doesn't vary from person to person, and what does vary is often the product of complex mutational processes in the cell and complex population dynamics over the eons. Therefore simple explanations of the patterns are unlikely to be correct. For example, the very first genetic marker was the ABO blood group, now known to be caused by a single gene on chromosome 9, whose product adds a sugar to a molecule coating the surface of a red blood cell. Type A adds one sugar, type B adds a different sugar, and type O adds none. Simple enough.

The distribution of the three alleles, however, is far from simple. All populations of the world have all three of them but in different proportions, with O being universally the most common. Clustering human populations on the basis of the frequencies of these alleles puts very different peoples together who share the same frequencies by accident, such the Poles and Chinese. Moreover, in spite of the fact that most people are type O, chimpanzees are overwhelmingly type A, and gorillas are overwhelmingly type B. It is simply not clear just what is going on, or how can we make easy evolutionary sense of it.

It is also important to bear in mind that these are genetic markers, and not genes *for* physical attributes, such as skin color or facial contour—which even today we have no access to.

By the 1970s it was evident that one could pool several different genetic markers and use high-powered statistics to determine which populations had the most similar clusters of allele frequencies, and might therefore be considered closest relatives. It turned out, however, that the results were always very unstable, and highly sensitive to just which genetic markers were used, just what computer algorithm was used, the demographic history of the population (whether expanding, contracting, or interbreeding), and even the specific people chosen to represent the population, and the specific populations chosen to represent the region.[10]

In one infamous anecdote, a geneticist drew blood from pygmies in central Africa but rejected anyone he thought was too tall; thus the test tubes he brought back from the field didn't reflect the real population, but rather his preconceptions of what the population should have been. Other studies generalized extravagantly about "Africans" from two or three local tribes. Thus, representation is a key issue: An accurate relationship between the samples the geneticist has and what or whom those samples are supposed to reflect cannot be taken for granted.

The problem of representation is crucial when we begin to appreciate that populations are composed of diverse organisms that may, and usually do, have complex histories. Looking, for example, at the relationships among human populations, one is always laboring under the shadow of gene flow. Two human populations may be genetically similar because they diverged recently, or because they have interbred. Human populations are also fluid and symbolically-defined: Marriage, adoption, raiding, alliance, and trade all serve to make the boundaries between them far less distinct genetically than culturally. Thus, if one wished to study the genetic relationships among the Germans, Swiss, and Italians, there may be no real scientific answer to such a scientific-sounding question. The answer you get will depend crucially on who is selected to represent those populations, given that Switzerland lies geographically in between Germany and Italy and has a long and complex social history in relation to them.

The important point is that all comparisons are not equal, nor are all evolutionary conclusions based on

genetic data self-evident. Simply the choice of specimen, from which the DNA is ultimately isolated, may have a major effect on the conclusions of a study, if the hierarchical relationships between person, population, and cell are ignored. On the other hand, this problem might seem to be mitigated if you study the relations among different species. Above the species level, gene pools can only diverge; there can be no interspecies breeding (that is generally what we mean by species, after all). Thus, the relations among humans, chimpanzees, and gorillas might at face value seem an easier question.

Speciation

Population genetics is a classically *transformationist* field, tracking a single gene pool as it changes through time. The diversity of life, however, is a product of divergence, as well as descent. How does one evolutionary lineage become two, so that divergence, presumably by a combination of genetic drift and natural selection, can occur?

The multiplication of lineages is the proliferation or reproduction of species, a series of processes known collectively as speciation. This can be considered analogous to the mitosis of cells or the reproduction of (asexual) organisms—the generation of two individuals or biological units where formerly there was but one.

Speciation requires the division of the gene pool, or more precisely it requires the segregation of organisms into populations that are not in genetic contact with one another. The maintenance of genetic contact (gene flow) acts in opposition to speciation. Once the population is divided into two or more segments, they diverge through time genetically both at random (via genetic drift), and in conjunction with their new environments (natural selection). The key question, however, is how the organisms of those populations ultimately come to regard one another as *different*— that is to say, not as potential mates. Dogs, after all, can be exceedingly promiscuous with other dogs, even with dogs that look quite different, but one never sees them mate with cats.

What is it that permits an organism to recognize another as a potential mate, and thereby worthy of reproductive attention and effort, so that it doesn't squander its time, resources, and energy? How does a rhesus monkey know it's a rhesus monkey and not a pig? And more importantly, how does it recognize another rhesus monkey as a potential mate?

The processes of species formation involve not just genetic divergence, but the development of new specific mate recognition systems.[11] These may be visual, olfactory, or behavioral signals, but they comprise a crucial part of the evolutionary process. Often, one population becomes physiologically incapable of reproducing with another population before they recognize each other as being different species—they may be fertile at different times of the year, or recognize different mating signals, or simply have physically incompatible genitalia. Or it may be that the structure of the chromosomes of one population has changed, so that they may mate and hybridize, but the hybrid is infertile—precisely the situation that exists between horse and donkey.

Three sets of changes, all ultimately genetic, but not easily related to one another, occur together during speciation. The first are the clocklike genetic changes all through the genome, so that regardless of the function (if any) of a particular DNA segment, it can be used as a record of the biological history of the cell, organism, and species it came from. The second are the physical changes to the body, itself a responsive and reactive system. And the third are the physiological, reproductive signals that unite a reproductive community, and distinguish it from others. Species that have been separated for a long period of time are different in all three ways; but recent divergences, or even incomplete divergences, yield important insights into the manner by which molecular, anatomical, and reproductive divergences or incompatibilities are generated in populations separately, but in parallel.

Since these kinds of changes occur together, although at different rates, the relationships of closely related species are no more easy to disentangle with molecular data than they are with classical anatomical data. Returning to the question of chimpanzees, gorillas, and humans, we find that some molecular data appear to link chimps and people, some link chimps and gorillas, and most yield thorough ambiguity. We are consequently obliged to regard the relationships among chimps, gorillas, and humans as a threeway-split or trichotomy.[12]

A question arises when we study the relationships among groups of organisms, whether they are parts of one species, or of several: Is one representative sufficient? Can a single specimen stand as a synecdoche (a metaphor in which the part substitutes for the whole) of a biological group?

Actually we can show quite easily the inadequacy of such an assumption at the level of the species. Imagine a single ancestral species, broadly distributed geographically. Perhaps they are protochimpanzees in equatorial Africa. One group fissions off to the west, and over a few hundred thousand years they become a species of protogorillas. Another group fissions off to the east and over a similar span of time they

become protohominids. To ask which pair of species a few million years later are closest relatives is a nonsensical question: The protochimpanzees would be the ancestors of all three living forms (gorillas, chimps, and humans), the early gene pools of the species would have overlapped extensively, and the relations of their modern descendants would be ambiguous.[13] Indeed, the answer you obtained might depend very specifically on which specimens you chose to represent the species: The chimpanzees from one region might turn out to be slightly more closely related to protogorillas and those from another might be slightly more closely related to protohumans. After all, according to this simple model, they were ancestral to both.

And once again, we find that at places where genetic diversity has been sampled in the apes, it is generally considerably greater than anticipated (especially considering that the apes are all endangered, and living in small ranges in Africa), and also considerably larger than in humans, who have nevertheless expanded to fill up the entire planet.[14]

So, just like the problems of understanding the relationships among human populations if the hierarchical relations of cell, body, and population are ignored, there exists a similar set of problems that accrue if one tries with comparable naivete to understand relationships among species.

Seeing Evolution: The Eye of the Beholder

The processes of evolution to a molecular geneticist involve principally mutation and genetic drift. Random changes to the DNA occur at a calculable rate, and since most of the genome has no function, the changes are generally either unexpressed or neutral (functionally equivalent to their alternatives), and will thus be unaffected by selection. Even in functional regions there is considerable "slop"—insulin derived from the pancreas of a pig, while structurally different, nevertheless still functions well for a human.

The action of selection here is principally to weed out genetic variations that function poorly. Thus, given the structure of a protein and its physiological necessities, randomly altering its structure (by mutation) is far more likely to compromise its function than to improve it. Imagine opening the hood of your car and randomly hitting your engine with a hammer (the equivalent of mutation). While it is theoretically conceivable that you might improve the engine's performance, it is exceedingly unlikely. Most likely you'll screw it up; and if you're lucky you just won't do any serious damage.

A geneticist therefore finds two DNA sequences from different species to differ in very specific ways. Because of the constant pressure of genetic mutation, differences will always be there, but you expect to find the most differences in functionless regions, and proportionately fewer in regions with important genes; and within each gene, you expect to find more differences in specific regions that compromise the structure and function of the protein product the least.

In other words, one expects to find difference when comparing DNA regions across species; when "too much" similarity is found, that is taken as evidence for strong constraints on the particular DNA region, indicative of functional importance. That is precisely how the *homeobox*—a stretch of 180 nucleotides in a small class of genes involved in early embryonic development—was discovered: It was there, almost intact, in the genomes of flies and mice. Since flies and mice have little else in common, this suggested an exceptional physiological importance for the region.

Morphologists see evolution, in the classical sense, quite differently. They anticipate stability of structure, because they work with adapted bodies, not with sloppy genes. Therefore they expect related organisms to be *similar* to one another, and attempt to explain the *differences* by recourse to selection. This is precisely the opposite of what the geneticists do, expecting divergence of DNA sequence and explaining the situation in which sequences are more similar than anticipated!

A geneticist and a morphologist look at the same animals: orangutans (*Pongo pygnaeus*), chimpanzees (*Pan troglodytes*), and humans (*Homo sapiens*). The geneticist finds that most of the genome differs by about 2 percent between humans and chimps, and by about 5 percent between either of them and the orangutan. But certain regions are identical: The geneticist thus frames questions such as, "Why haven't mutation and drift caused this region to diverge more through time? Why is this region so important? What does it do that constrains it from tolerating any change?" The morphologist, by contrast, sees two creatures with hairy bodies, long arms, and small brains, and asks, "Why has the other species lost body hair, changed limb proportions, and expanded its brain?" The morphologist does *not* ask, "Why does the orangutan and chimpanzee retain body hair, long arms, and small brains?" The answer is simple: Those features work. The morphologist expects preservation of functional body systems due to adaptation, and in contrast the geneticist expects decay of DNA sequences due to the constant pressure of mutation.

The geneticist and the morphologist thus see different patterns in their data, see change occurring at different rates, in different modes, and ask different evolutionary questions to explain their findings. While genes, bodies, and species all evolve together (obviously!), it is frequently difficult to unify them into a coherent evolutionary narrative. This is not altogether surprising: The big question in genetics is the complex relationship between genotypes (i.e., genetic constitutions or DNA sequences) and phenotypes (the outward appearances of organisms).

In the simplest case, early geneticists following Mendel found that one phenotype was dominant over another, but a pea heterozygous for a gene (Aa) looked indistinguishable from a pea homozygous for one of the genes (AA). Thus, from what the pea looks like, you cannot tell what alleles it has.

In more complex cases, a phenotype results from the interaction of several genes operating in physiological systems. Not only that, but the developing body is reactive and sensitive to the conditions of growth. Thus, someone may be short-statured because of a particular combination of alleles, or because of nutritional stress during childhood. The body is thus developmentally plastic: A given genetic background may result in different physical forms under different circumstances. The body is sensitive to the conditions of life; it is adaptable.

More than that, the body is also pulled in the opposite direction. Not only does the body change in harmony with the circumstances of growth, but in other ways the body is also very *in*sensitive to genetic variation or environmental shock. The developmental geneticist C. H. Waddington called this property *canalization*—the tendency of the genetic system to be buffered, so that the same phenotype may result from different genetic backgrounds or in different environments.[15]

In other words, the same genotype can produce different phenotypes, and the same phenotype can be the product of different genotypes. With such a level of disconnect between genes and bodies, it's no wonder that molecular and morphological specialists see their subject matter in such different ways.

Conclusion

The ultimate source of all evolutionary difference is mutation, the change in DNA, located in cells. Mutation is a more complex process than earlier generations conceived it to be. The genome is a complex landscape, only being mapped now, and the study of *comparative genomics* is in its infancy.

The fundamental changes that occur initially in a cell ultimately accrue to the body the cell is a part of. Mutations that aid in the survival and reproduction of those bodies—or at least don't hurt them—are perpetuated, and thus become disproportionately represented in the gene pool. New species arise when the gene pool is partitioned, and organisms cease to identify each other as potential mates.

Cells, organisms, and species are the units of contemporary biology—molecular or cellular biology in the first case, physiology and anatomy in the second, and systematic biology in the third. Their connections are real, but sometimes difficult to understand; and it has often been easier to ignore the other levels than to grapple with the complexity they impart to the study of evolution. The marvel is that somehow, the same history of life is inscribed into species in each of their manifold components. It is etched into each body and each cell; the trick is to decode it.

Notes

1. M. C. King and A. C. Wilson, "Evolution at Two Levels in Humans and Chimpanzees," *Science* 188 (1975): 107–116.

2. D. Hull, "Units of Evolution: A Metaphysical Essay," in U. L. Jensen and R. Harré, eds., *The Philosophy of Evolution*. (Brighton: Harvester Press, 1981), pp. 23–44.

3. S. Sarkar, "Decoding "Coding"—Information and DNA," *BioSystems* 46 (1996): 857–864.

4. This was in honor of Darwin, who paradoxically had nothing to do with it. Darwin had proposed a theory of heredity called "pangenesis," which never gained wide acceptance. Darwin himself, of course, became a biological icon for his theory of evolution by natural selection. Decades later, while searching for a name for the elementary particles of heredity first characterized by Mendel, the evolutionary geneticist Hugo De Vries proposed the Darwinian "pangenes." The second syllable stuck. E. F. Keller, *The Century of the Gene* (Cambridge, MA: Harvard University Press, 2000).

5. William B. Provine, *The Origins of Theoretical Population Genetics*, 2d ed. (Chicago: University of Chicago Press, 2001).

6. W. Bodmer and Robin McKie, *The Book of Man* (London: Little, Brown, 1994).

7. Daniel J. Kevles and L. Hood, eds., *The Code of Codes* (Cambridge, MA: Harvard University Press, 1992).

8. J. Marks, "Beads and String: The Genome in Evolutionary Theory," in E. J. Devor, ed., *Molecular Applications in Biological Anthropology* (New York: Cambridge University Press, 1992), pp. 234–255.

9. J. C. Venter, et al., "The Sequence of the Human Genome," *Science* 291 (2001): 1304–1351.

10. J. Marks, *Human Biodiversity: Genes, Race, and History* (Hawthorne, NY: Aldine de Gruyter, 1995).

11. L. R. Godfrey and J. Marks, "The Nature and Origins of Primate Species," *Yearbook of Physical Anthropology* 34 (1991): 39–68.

12. J. Marks, "Blood Will Tell (Won't It?): A Century of Molecular Discourse in Anthropological Systematics," *American Journal of Physical Anthropology* 94 (1994): 59–80.

13. Amos S. Deinard, "The Evolutionary Genetics of the Chimpanzees" (Ph.D. Thesis, Department of Anthropology, Yale University, 1997).

14. G. Ruano, Jeffrey A. Rogers, Anne C. Ferguson-Smith, and Kenneth K. Kidd, "DNA Sequence Polymorphism within Hominoid Species Exceeds the Number of Phylogenetically Informative Characters for a HOX2 Locus," *Molecular Biology and Evolution* 9, no. 4 (1992): 575–586.

15. C. H. Waddington, "Evolutionary Adaptation," in S. Tax, ed., *Evolution after Darwin* (Chicago: University of Chicago Press, 1960), vol. 1: 381–402.

Suggested Readings

Lewontin, R. *The Triple Helix: Gene, Organism, and Environment* (Cambridge, MA: Harvard University Press, 2000).

Marks, J. *Human Biodiversity: Genes, Race, and History* (Hawthorne, NY: Aldine de Gruyter, 1995).

Marks, J. *What It Means to Be 98% Chimpanzee* (Berkeley: University of California Press, 2002).

Monod, J. *Chance and Necessity* (New York: Knopf, 1971).

Simpson, G. G. *The Meaning of Evolution* (New Haven: Yale University Press, 1951).

Chimpanzee Hunting Behavior and Human Evolution

Craig B. Stanford

The Hunt

In a forest in Tanzania in East Africa, a group of a dozen chimpanzees is travelling along the forest floor, stopping occasionally to scan the trees overhead for ripe fruit. The group is composed of five adult males weighing nearly one hundred pounds each, plus several females and their offspring. They come upon a tree holding a group of red colobus monkeys; these are long-tailed leaf-eating monkeys weighing about twenty-five pounds each. This group has twenty-five members, about average for the species in this forest. The male chimpanzees scan the colobus group looking for immature animals or mothers carrying small babies. The colobus, meanwhile, have heard the pant-hoot calls of the chimpanzees approaching for the past several minutes and have gathered up their offspring and positioned themselves in order to defend against a possible attack.

The chimpanzees do indeed attack, the five males—Frodo, Goblin, Freud, Prof, and Wilkie—climbing the larger limbs of the tree. They meet the male colobus, who have descended to counterattack their potential predators. In spite of repeated lunges by the chimpanzees against the colobus group, they are turned back by the colobus' aggressive defense; at one point two male colobus even leap onto Frodo's back, trying to bite him as he runs along a tree limb, hurling them off. In the end, however, the chimpanzees prevail; Frodo scatters the male colobus and manages to pluck a newborn infant off of its mother's belly. Some of the chimpanzees continue hunting, while others gather around Frodo, begging with extended hands for scraps of meat from the baby colobus' tiny carcass. Frodo offers bits of meat to his allies and to females with whom he has a close rela-tionship; rivals, however, are denied meat. Meanwhile, the other hunters capture the mother of the baby, who has strayed too close in her effort to rescue her now-consumed infant and has fallen from the tree to the forest floor. The mother is grabbed by a young chimpanzee, Pax, and flailed against the tree trunk until nearly dead. The alpha (dominant) male, Wilkie, promptly steals the prey from Pax, however, and a number of females and juveniles crowd around him. An hour later, the last strands of colobus meat, bone, and skin are still being consumed amid occasional outbursts of aggression by individuals who have not received the meat they desired.

The Significance of Chimpanzee Hunting Behavior to Human Evolutionary Research

Two of the most important and intriguing questions in human evolution are when and why meat became an important part of the diet of our ancestors. Physical anthropologists and archaeologists try to answer these questions using a number of techniques. The presence of primitive stone tools in the fossil record tells us that 2.5 million years ago, early hominids were using stone implements to cut the flesh off the bones of large animals that they had either hunted or whose carcasses they had scavenged.[1] The pattern of obtaining and processing meat by more recent people has been studied by examining archaeological sites in Europe and elsewhere,[2] and also by studying the hunting and meat-eating behavior of modern foraging people, the so-called hunter-gatherers.[3]

Earlier than 2.5 million years ago, however, we know very little about the foods that the early hominids ate or the role that meat may have played in their diet. We know that the earliest upright-walking (bipedal) hominids, currently classified as *Australopithecines*, evolved in Africa about five million years ago, and that they shared a common ancestor with modern chimpanzees before that time. Modern people and chimpanzees share an estimated 98.5 percent of the DNA sequence, making them more closely related to each other than either is to any other animal species.[4] Therefore, understanding chimpanzee hunting behavior and ecology may tell us a great deal about the behavior and ecology of those earliest hominids. This is the approach I have taken in my field study of the hunting behavior of wild chimpanzees; I especially focus on their relationship with the animal that is their major prey, the red colobus monkey. I am trying to answer the following questions:

1. What are the social and ecological factors that predict when chimpanzees will hunt and whether they will be successful?
2. What is the effect of chimpanzee predation on the populations of their prey animals, such as the red colobus?
3. What are the likely similarities in meat-eating patterns between chimpanzees and the earliest hominids?

In the early 1960s, when Dr. Jane Goodall began her now-famous study of the chimpanzees of Gombe National Park, Tanzania, it was thought that chimpanzees were strictly vegetarian. In fact, when Goodall first reported this behavior, many people were skeptical or claimed that meat was not a natural part of the chimpanzee diet. Today, hunting by chimpanzees at Gombe has been well documented.[5] Hunting has also been observed at other sites in Africa where chimpanzees have been studied, such as Mahale Mountains National Park,[6] also in Tanzania, and Taï National Park in Ivory Coast in West Africa.[7] At Gombe, we now know that each year chimpanzees may kill and eat more than 150 small and medium-sized animals, such as monkeys, wild pigs, and small antelopes. Because of the complex fission-fusion nature of chimpanzee society, in which there are no stable groups, only temporary subgroupings called parties that congregate and separate throughout the day, the size and membership of hunting parties vary greatly, from a single chimpanzee to as many as thirty-five. The hunting abilities of the party members, as well as the number of hunters present, can thus influence when a party hunts as well as whether it will succeed in catching a colobus.

STUDYING CHIMPANZEE HUNTING BEHAVIOR

Studying the relationship between predators and prey of any two species is always difficult, because in order to observe hunts the researcher must accustom both the hunter and the prey to his or her presence. Because the chimpanzees of Gombe are thoroughly used to being followed throughout the day by human researchers, habituating the predators to my presence was not a problem; it has been a slower process, though, to accustom two colobus groups that inhabit the territory of the Gombe chimpanzees to human observers. In addition, chimpanzees do not usually hunt every day and sometimes two weeks will pass without any hunting. During each week in the field, I follow chimpanzee parties in the hope of seeing a hunt and also observe any of several colobus groups that may become the targets of hunts. While this may sound like a chancy way to observe a hunt, in practice it has worked very well. At least one party of chimpanzees at Gombe is followed daily by researchers; at the end of each day, the chimpanzees build leafy nests in trees where they will sleep for the night. The following morning they will often head off together, giving loud pant-hoot calls as they travel. These calls allow me to hike early in the morning to a high point in the valley above the chimpanzees' sleeping trees to listen for the direction in which they are moving. I can then walk to any colobus group that I know to be in the path taken by the chimpanzees in order to reach the colobus before the chimpanzees do. In this way I have been able to observe and record nearly one hundred encounters between chimpanzee foraging parties and colobus (from the perspective of the colobus prey) and watch the colobus' reaction to the approach of potential predators. Early morning, therefore, frequently finds me sitting atop a high point in Kakombe Valley (one of the main valleys used by the chimpanzees) called the peak. It was from this point that Jane Goodall made many of her important early observations of chimpanzee behavior many years ago, and it has served me well in my own research. It is also a beautiful vantage point for seeing the whole valley and the animals that inhabit it: chimpanzee, colobus and other monkeys, eagles soaring past, and sometimes a shy bushbuck antelope. As the chimpanzee parties around the valley awake at dawn and set off on their day of travel and feeding, they usually pant-hoot, and this tells me their direction of travel and the likelihood of their meeting a colobus group.

What Is Chimpanzee Predatory Behavior?

After three decades of research on the hunting behavior of chimpanzees at Gombe and elsewhere, we already know a great deal about their predatory patterns. We know that, although chimpanzees have been recorded to eat more than twenty-five types of vertebrate animals,[8] the most important vertebrate prey species in their diet is the red colobus monkey. At Gombe, red colobus account for more than 80 percent of the prey items eaten. But Gombe chimpanzees do not randomly select the colobus they will kill; infant and juvenile colobus are caught in greater proportion than their availability[9]—75 percent of all colobus killed are immature. Chimpanzees are largely fruit eaters, and meat-eating comprises only about 3 percent of the time they spend eating overall. Adult and adolescent males do most of the hunting, making about 90 percent of the kills recorded at Gombe over the past decade. Females also hunt, though more often they receive a share of meat from the male who either captured the meat or stole it from the captor.

One of the main recent findings about hunting by Gombe chimpanzees is its seasonality.[10] Nearly 40 percent of the kills of colobus monkeys occur in the dry season months of August and September. At Gombe, it appears that this is a time of food shortage, since the chimpanzees' body weights decline.[11] Here, the killing is actually less strongly seasonal than in the Mahale Mountains, where 60 percent of kills occur in a two-month period in the early wet season. Why would chimpanzees hunt more often in some months than in others? This is an important question, because studies of early hominid diets have shown that meat-eating occurred most often in the dry season, at the same time that Gombe chimpanzees are eating most of their meat. And the amount of meat eaten, even though it composed a small percentage of the chimpanzee diet, is substantial. I estimate that in some years the forty-five chimpanzees of the main study community at Gombe kill and consume more than 1,500 pounds of prey animals of all species. This is far more than most previous estimates of the weight of live animals eaten by chimpanzees. A large proportion of this amount is eaten in the dry season months of August and September. In fact, during the peak dry season months, the estimated per capita meat intake is about sixty-five grams of meat per day for each adult chimpanzee. This approaches the meat intake by the members of some human foraging societies in the lean months of the year. Chimpanzee dietary strategies may thus approximate those of human hunter-gatherers to a greater degree than we had imagined.

Several other aspects of hunting by Gombe chimpanzees are noteworthy. First, although most successful hunts result in a kill of a single colobus monkey, in some hunts from two to seven colobus may be killed. The likelihood of such a multiple kill is tied directly to the number of hunters in the hunting party. Interestingly, the percentage of kills that are multiple kills rose markedly in the late 1980s and early 1990s, which in turn meant that many more colobus, overall, were being eaten in the late 1980s compared to five years earlier.[12] This is most likely due to changes in the age and sex composition of the chimpanzee community. The number of adult and adolescent male chimpanzees in the study community rose from five to twelve over the 1980s due to a large number of young males who were maturing and taking their places in hunting parties. One could therefore say that the fate of the Gombe red colobus monkeys is in the hands of the chimpanzee population; this is reflected in the colobus mortality rate in relation to the number of hunters available in a given era.

Although both male and female chimpanzees sometimes hunt by themselves, most hunts are social. In other species of hunting animals, cooperation among hunters may lead to greater success rates, thus promoting the evolution of cooperative behavior. Such cooperation has also been posited as important in our own evolution.[13] Whether or not chimpanzee hunters cooperate is a question that has been debated, and the degree of cooperative hunting may differ from one forest to another.[14] In the Taï forest in the Ivory Coast, Christophe Boesch has documented highly cooperative hunting behavior and meat-sharing behavior after a kill that rewards those chimpanzees who participated in the hunt.[15] The highly integrated action by Taï hunters has never been seen at Gombe. In both Gombe and Taï, however, there is a strong positive relationship between the number of hunters and the odds of a successful hunt.[16] This points out the difficulty of interpreting cooperative behavior; even though Gombe hunters do not seem to cooperate, the greater success rate when more hunters are present suggests that some cooperation is occurring. We are still looking for measures of cooperation that can distinguish true cooperation from hunts in which some chimpanzees hunt and others follow along hoping to capitalize on the efforts of others.

Throughout years of research, Jane Goodall noted that the Gombe chimpanzees displayed a tendency to go on "hunting crazes," during which they would hunt almost daily and kill large numbers of monkeys and other prey.[17] The explanations for such binges have always been unclear. My own research has focused on the causes for such spurts in hunting frequency, with unexpected results. The explanation for sudden changes in frequency seems to be related to whatever factors promote hunting itself; when such factors are present to a high degree or for an extended period of time, frequent hunting occurs. For example, the most intense hunting binge we have seen occurred in the dry season of 1990. From late June through early September, a period of sixty-eight days, the chimpanzees were observed killing seventy-one colobus monkeys in forty-seven hunts. It is important to note that this is the observed total, and the actual total of kills, which includes hunts at which no human observer was present, may be one-third greater. During this time the chimpanzees thus may have killed more than 10 percent of the entire colobus population within their hunting range.[18]

To try to solve the binge question my colleagues and I examined the enormous database of hunts recorded by field assistants over the past decade to see what social or environmental factors coincided with the hunting binges. Knowing that hunting was seasonal helped, in that I expected binges to occur mainly in the dry season, which was indeed the case. But other interesting correlations leapt out as well. Periods of intense hunting tended to be times when the size of chimpanzee foraging parties was very large; this corresponded to the direct relationship between party size and both hunting frequency and success rate. Additionally, hunting binges occurred especially when there were female chimpanzees with sexual swellings (the large pink anogenital swellings that females exhibit during their periods of sexual receptivity, or estrus) travelling with the hunting party. When one or more swollen females was present, the odds of a hunt occurring were substantially greater, independent of other factors. This co-occurrence of party size, presence of swollen females, and hunting frequency led me to ask the basic question, "Why do chimpanzees hunt?"

Why Do Chimpanzees Hunt?

Among the great apes (the gorilla, orangutan, bonobo, and chimpanzee) and ourselves, only humans and chimpanzees hunt and eat meat on a frequent basis. Since neither humans nor chimpanzees are truly carnivorous—most traditional human societies eat a diet made up mostly of plant foods—we are considered omnivores. Therefore, the important decisions about

what to eat and when to eat it should be based on the nutritional costs and benefits of obtaining that food compared to the essential nutrients that the food provides. However, as I discussed previously, there are social influences, such as party size and composition, that also seem to play an important role in mediating hunting behavior. Understanding when and why chimpanzees choose to undertake a hunt of colobus monkeys rather than simply continue to forage for fruits and leaves—even though the hunt involves risk of injury from colobus canine teeth and a substantial risk of failure to catch anything—is a major goal of my research.

In his study of Gombe chimpanzee predatory behavior in the 1960s, Geza Teleki considered hunting to have a strong social basis.[19] Some early researchers proposed that hunting by chimpanzees might be a form of social display, in which a male chimpanzee tries to show his prowess to other members of the community.[20] In the 1970s Richard Wrangham conducted the first systematic study of Gombe chimpanzee behavioral ecology and concluded that predation by chimpanzees was nutritionally based, but that some aspects of the behavior were not well explained by nutritional needs alone.[21] More recently, Toshisada Nishida and his colleagues in the Mahale Mountains chimpanzee research project reported that the alpha there, Ntilogi, used captured meat as a political tool to withhold from rivals and dole out to allies.[22] And William McGrew has shown that those female Gombe chimpanzees who receive generous shares of meat after a kill have more surviving offspring, indicating a reproductive benefit from hunting.[23]

My own preconception was that hunting must be nutritionally based. After all, meat from monkeys and other prey would be a package of protein, fat, and calories hard to equal in any plant food. I therefore examined the relationship between the odds of success and the amount of meat available with different numbers of hunters in relation to each hunter's expected payoff in meat obtained. That is, when is the time, energy, and risk (the costs) involved in hunting worth the potential benefits, and, therefore, when should a chimpanzee decide to join or not to join a hunting party? And how does it compare to the costs and benefits of foraging for plant foods? Because of the difficulty in learning the nutritional components of the many plant foods in the chimpanzees' diverse diet, these analyses are still underway. But the preliminary results are surprising. I expected that as the number of hunters increased, the amount of meat available for each hunter would also increase. This would explain the social nature of hunting by Gombe chimpanzees. If the amount of meat available per hunter declined with increasing hunting party size (because each hunter got smaller portions as party size increased), then it would be a better investment of time and energy to hunt alone rather than join a party. The hunting success rates of lone hunters is only about 30 percent, while that of parties with ten or more hunters is close to 100 percent. As it turned out, there is no relationship, either positive or negative, between the number of hunters and the amount of meat available per capita. This may be because even though the likelihood of success increases with more hunters in the party, the most frequently caught prey animal is a one kilogram baby colobus monkey. Whether shared among four hunters or fourteen, such a small package of meat does not provide anyone with much food.

Chimpanzees and Predator-Prey Systems

The October 7 Massacre

This hunting pattern and its potential effects on the colobus population are best illustrated by my observation of one of the largest colobus hunts observed in the thirty-four-year history of research at Gombe. On October 7, 1992, I located the twenty-five members of my main colobus study group feeding and socializing on a hillside in Kakombe Valley, known as Dung Hill. From 7:00 to 11:00 A.M. they moved slowly across the hill slope and into a ravine known as KK6. It was a quiet morning, and the colobus were relaxed as they munched on foliage and young fruits. But beginning about 9:00 A.M., the distant pant-hoots of one or more chimpanzee foraging parties could be heard coming from further down the valley. The male colobus gave occasional alarm calls, highpitched bird-like calls that warn other group members of nearby danger, but the chimpanzees did not approach. Then, at about 11:00 A.M., the pant-hoots rang out in two directions at close range, coming from both north and south of the location of the colobus group and me. For several minutes these two chimpanzee parties called, then the calls converged and moved toward us. Clearly, two foraging parties had met and become one larger party that was headed in the colobus' direction. For several suspenseful minutes, the colobus and I waited to learn whether the chimpanzees were headed directly toward us.

Minutes later, the vanguard of the chimpanzee party arrived, a male named Beethoven and several of the adult females and their offspring. They were being followed that morning by two Tanzanian researchers, Msafiri Katoto and Bruno Herman. The colobus were wary and alarm calling, but such a small party was not a great risk to them. Then the main party arrived, with all twelve adult and adolescent males and many females and juveniles—thirty-three chimpanzees in all. The hunt began, as usual, with Frodo climbing a tall emergent tree in which some of the colobus group was clustered, and for the next twenty minutes the trees shook and the foliage crashed with the sounds of leaping and calling colobus and equally frenzied chimpanzee hunters. As the hunt progressed, I felt sure that the colobus would succeed in driving the chimpanzees away, but Frodo and the other males managed to scatter the male colobus, whereupon the rest of the group fled and became easy prey. Just in front of me a young colobus whom I had watched all morning as it fed on leaves and played with other juveniles attempted to flee the chimpanzees by leaping onto a branch that unfortunately held a male chimpanzee named Atlas. Atlas quickly grabbed the young colobus and dispatched it with a bite to the skull. Within seconds, an estrous female chimpanzee named Trezia ran up to Atlas and begged for meat. Atlas held the colobus carcass away from her; she then turned and presented her sexual swelling to him, they copulated, and only then did she receive a share of the meat. A few feet away, Beethoven had caught a young infant colobus and was engaging in identical behavior with the female chimpanzee Gremlin. The number of colobus killed, however, was difficult to know because after an hour some chimpanzees were still hunting while others who had captured colobus sat on the ground over a fifty-yard circle eating and sharing meat. My reaction to seeing my colobus being killed and eaten one by one before my eyes was initially one of excitement; I was in the unique position of observing a hunt and knowing both predators and prey as individuals. The excitement paled quickly, however, when Msafiri called out through the forest that there had been at least six colobus killed (the final tally turned out to be seven). Four hours later, the chimpanzees finally finished their feast of colobus meat and the ensuing rest and socializing period and departed the scene of the kill.

A hunt like this one does not occur often at Gombe; indeed, this was only the second kill of seven colobus observed in thirty-four years. But multiple kills of two or more colobus happen more frequently—twenty-one times in 1990 alone—illustrating the powerful influence chimpanzees may have as predators on the populations of prey animals within their hunting range. I estimate that from 1990 through 1993, the colobus kills made by the male chimpanzee Frodo alone have eliminated about 10 percent of the colobus monkeys in the home range of the Gombe chimpanzees.

EFFECTS OF CHIMPANZEE PREDATION ON THE COLOBUS POPULATION

As the above-mentioned hunt describes, one chimpanzee hunting party can decimate a group of red colobus prey in a matter of minutes. What is the likely long-term effect of intensive chimpanzee predation on the colobus population? Using information on the size, age, and sex composition of red colobus groups, combined with knowledge of the hunting patterns of Gombe chimpanzees, it is possible to estimate the impact of predation on the colobus. Based on my monitoring of five colobus groups over the past four years, plus censusing of a number of other groups that occupy the eighteen square kilometers of the chimpanzees' hunting range, I estimate there are about 500 (±10 percent) in the chimpanzees' range. I estimate that from approximately 75 to 175 colobus are killed by chimpanzees annually; I base this estimate on those kills that have been observed, plus the expected number of kills per day in which no human observer was following them in the forest. The annual mortality rate in the colobus population that is due to chimpanzee predation is thus between 15 and 35 percent, depending on the frequency of hunting that year.[24] While 15 percent mortality due to predation has been recorded for other species of mammals, it must be noted that this figure represents predation by chimpanzees only and does not include death at the hands of other predators (leopards and eagles exist at Gombe and eat monkeys) or mortality due to disease, infanticide, or other factors. And 35 percent mortality would mean, if it happened every year, that the red colobus population would almost certainly be in sharp decline. It appears, however, that the average mortality of colobus due to predation by chimpanzees over the past decade has been about 20 percent of the population killed by chimpanzees each year; this figure is comparable to what many other populations of prey animals sustain.[25]

To understand the impact of this mortality on the colobus population, it is important to consider certain aspects of the monkey population. First, female colobus appear to give birth about every two years, and births occur in every month of the year. Since chimpanzees prey mainly upon young colobus (under two years old), female colobus that lose a baby to

chimpanzee hunters are able to begin cycling again soon afterward and to produce a new offspring as soon as seven months later. These two facts, lack of breeding seasonality and mortality of immatures rather than adults, may minimize the impact of predation on the colobus, in that a single infant lost is more quickly replaced than an older offspring or adult would be.

To learn whether chimpanzee predation has the potential to be a limiting factor in the size of the colobus population at Gombe, I compared the intensity of hunting by chimpanzees with the size of red colobus groups in each of the valleys of the chimpanzees' hunting range. The central valley of the chimpanzees' range (their so-called core area) is Kakombe Valley; the chimpanzees made about one-third of all their hunts there over the past decade. As one travels away from the center and toward the northern and southern borders of the chimpanzees' range, their use of the more peripheral valleys is much less frequent, and their frequency of hunting there is also less. Only about 3 percent of all hunts took place at the northern and southern edges of their range. I found that the size of red colobus groups also varied over the area of the chimpanzees' hunting range. In the core area, red colobus groups averaged only nineteen animals, little more than half the average of about thirty-four at the outer boundaries.[26] In other words, colobus groups are small where they are hunted frequently and larger where hunting is infrequent. Moreover, I found that this size difference was due largely to a difference between core area and peripheral groups in the percentage of the groups that was immature colobus. In the core area, only 17 percent of each group were infants and juveniles, while fully 40 percent of peripheral groups were immature. This is a direct demonstration of the power of predation to limit both group size and population size in a wild primate population. From now on, we must consider the possibility that in addition to their other interesting traits, chimpanzees may be among the most important predators on certain prey species in the African ecosystems where they live.

What Does Chimpanzee Hunting Behavior Suggest About Early Hominid Evolution?

Did early hominids hunt and eat small and medium-sized animals in numbers as large as these? It is quite possible that they did. We know that colobus-like monkeys inhabited the woodlands and riverside gallery forest in which early hominids lived three to five million years ago. We also know that these earliest hominids were different from chimpanzees in two prominent anatomical features: they had much smaller canine teeth, and they had a lower body adapted for walking on the ground rather than swinging through trees. They almost certainly continued to use trees for nighttime shelter and for daytime fruit foraging, as do modern ground-living primates such as baboons. In spite of lacking the weaponry such as large canine teeth and tree-climbing adaptations that chimpanzees possess, early hominids probably ate a large number of small and medium-sized animals, including monkeys. Chimpanzees do not use their canine teeth to capture adult colobus; rather, they grab the prey and flail it to death on the ground or a tree limb. And once the prey is cornered in an isolated tree crown, group cooperation at driving the monkeys from one hunter to another would have been a quite efficient killing technique.

In addition to the availability of prey in the trees, there were of course small animals and the young of larger animals to catch opportunistically on the ground. Many researchers now believe that the carcasses of dead animals were an important source of meat for early hominids once they had stone tools to use for removing the flesh from the carcass.[27] Wild chimpanzees show little interest in dead animals as a food source, so scavenging may have evolved as an important mode of getting food when hominids began to make and use tools for getting at meat. Before this time, it seems likely that earlier hominids were hunting small mammals as chimpanzee do today, and that the role that hunting played in the early hominids' social lives was probably as complex and political as it is in the social lives of chimpanzees. When we ask when meat became an important part of the human diet, we therefore must look well before the evolutionary split between apes and humans in our own family tree.

Notes

1. Richard Potts, *Early Hominid Activities in Olduvai Gorge* (New York: Aldine de Gruyter, 1988).
2. Mary C. Stiner and Steven L. Kuhn, "Subsistence, Technology, and Adaptive Variation in Middle Paleolithic Italy," *American Anthropologist* 94 (1992): 306–339.
3. Hillard Kaplan and Kim R. Hill, "The Evolutionary Ecology of Food Acquisition, in Eric Alden Smith and Bruce Winterhalder, eds., *Evolutionary Ecology and Human Behavior* (New York: Aldine de Gruyter, 1992), pp. 167–202.
4. Maryann Ruvolo, Todd R. Disotell, Michael W. Allard, W. M. Brown, and R. L. Honeycutt, "Resolution of the African Hominoid Trichotomy by Use of a Mitochondrial Gene Sequence," *Proceedings of the National Academy of Science* 88 (1991): 1570–1574.
5. Jane Goodall, *The Chimpanzees of Gombe: Patterns of Behavior* (Cambridge, MA: Harvard University Press, 1986); Geza Teleki, *The Predatory Behavior of Wild Chimpanzees* (Lewisburg, PA: Bucknell University Press, 1973); Craig B. Stanford, Janette Wallis, Hilali Matama, and Jane Goodall, "Patterns of Predation by Chimpanzees on Red Colobus Monkeys in Gombe National Park, Tanzania, 1982–1991," *American Journal of Physical Anthropology* 94 (1994):213–229.
6. Shigeo Uehara, Toshisda Nishida, Miya Hamai, Toshikazu Hasegawa, H. Hayaki, Michael Huffman, Kenji Kawanaka, S. Kobayoshi, John Mitani, Y. Takahata, Hiro Takasaki, and T. Tsukahara, "Characteristics of Predation by the Chimpanzees in the Mahale Mountains National Park, Tanzania," in Toshisada Nishida, William C. McGrew, Peter Marler, Martin Pickford, and Frans B. M. de Waal, eds., *Topics in Primatology, Volume 1: Human Origins* (Tokyo: University of Tokyo Press, 1992), pp. 143–158.
7. Christophe Boesch and Hedwige Boesch, "Hunting Behavior of Wild Chimpanzees in the Taï National Park," *American Journal of Physical Anthropology* 78 (1989): 547–573.
8. Richard W. Wrangham and Emily van Zinnicq Bergmann-Riss, "Rates of Predation on Mammals by Gombe Chimpanzees, 1972–1975," *Primates* 31 (1990): 157–170.
9. Goodall, *The Chimpanzees of Gombe: Patterns of Behavior.*
10. Stanford, Wallis, Matama, and Goodall, "Patterns of Predation by Chimpanzees on Red Colobus Monkeys in Gombe National Park, Tanzania, 1982–1991."
11. Richard W. Wrangham, *Behavioural Ecology of Chimpanzees in Gombe National Park, Tanzania* (Ph. D. diss., University of Cambridge, 1975).
12. Stanford, Wallis, Matama, and Goodall, "Patterns of Predation by Chimpanzees on Red Colobus Monkeys in Gombe National Park, Tanzania, 1982–1991."
13. Sherwood L. Washburn and Jane B. Lancaster, "The Evolution of Hunting," in Richard B. Lee and Irven DeVore, eds., *Man the Hunter* (Chicago: Aldine, 1968), pp. 293–303.
14. Curt Busse, "Do Chimpanzees Hunt Cooperatively?" *American Naturalist* 112 (1978): 767–770.
15. Christophe Boesch, "Hunting Strategies of Gombe and Taï Chimpanzees," in William C. McGrew, Frans B. M. de Waal, Richard W. Wrangham, and Paul Heltne, eds., *Chimpanzee Cultures* (Cambridge, MA: Harvard University Press, 1994), pp. 77–92.

16. Craig B. Stanford, Janette Wallis, Eslom Mpongo, and Jane Goodall, "Hunting Decisions in Wild Chimpanzees," *Animal Behaviour* 131 (1994): 1–20.
17. Goodall, *The Chimpanzees of Gombe: Patterns of Behavior.*
18. Stanford, Wallis, Matama, and Goodall, "Patterns of Predation by Chimpanzees on Red Colobus Monkeys in Gombe National Park, Tanzania, 1982–1991."
19. Teleki, *The Predatory Behavior of Wild Chimpanzees.*
20. Adrian Kortlandt, *New Perspectives on Ape and Human Evolution* (Amsterdam: Stichting Voor Psychobiologie, 1972).
21. Wrangham, *Behavioural Ecology of Chimpanzees in Gombe National Park, Tanzania.*
22. Toshisada Nishida, T. Hasegawa, H. Hayaki, Y. Takahata, and Shigeo Uehara, "Meat-Sharing as a Coalition Strategy by an Alpha Male Chimpanzee," in Toshisada Nishida, William C. McGrew, Peter Marler, and Martin Pickford, eds., *Topics in Primatology, vol. I* (Tokyo: University of Tokyo Press, 1992), pp. 159–174.
23. William C. McGrew, *Chimpanzee Material Culture* (Cambridge: Cambridge University Press, 1992).
24. Craig B. Stanford, "The Influence of Chimpanzee Predation on Group Size and Anti-Predator Behaviour in Red Colobus Monkeys," *Animal Behaviour* 49 (1995): 577–587.
25. Stanford, Wallis, Matama, and Goodall, "Patterns of Predation by Chimpanzees on Red Colobus Monkeys in Gombe National Park, Tanzania, 1982–1991."
26. Ibid.
27. Henry T. Bunn and Ellen M. Kroll, "Systematic Butchery by Plio/Pleistocene Hominids at Olduvai Gorge, Tanzania," *Current Anthropology* 27 (1986): 431–452.

Suggested Readings

de Waal, Frans. *Chimpanzee Politics*. Baltimore, MD: Johns Hopkins Press, 1982. A popular account of the political and social intrigue of a chimpanzee colony in the Arnhem Zoo in the Netherlands.

Goodall, Jane. *The Chimpanzees of Gombe: Patterns of Behavior*. Cambridge, MA: Harvard University Press, 1986. A scholarly compilation of Goodall's first twenty-five years of research on the Gombe chimpanzees. The most comprehensive book on chimpanzee behavior ever published.

Goodall, Jane. *Through a Window*. Boston: Houghton Mifflin Co., 1990. A nontechnical book summarizing some of the most exciting discoveries made by Goodall about wild chimpanzees, including warfare, cannibalism, and meat-eating.

Johannson, Donald. Lucy: *The Making of Mankind*. New York: Simon and Schuster, 1981. The story of the discovery of the most important early human fossil yet discovered, where it fits into the human lineage, and what its behavior was probably like.

McGrew, William C. *Chimpanzee Material Culture*. Cambridge: Cambridge University Press, 1992. A scholarly work on the manufacture and use of tools and other aspects of behavior in wild chimpanzees. The book makes valuable comparisons between the different wild chimpanzee populations that have been studied.

Teleki, Geza. *The Predatory Behavior of Wild Chimpanzees*. Lewisburg, PA: Bucknell University Press, 1973. The first study of hunting by wild chimpanzees, Teleki's book describes hunting and the chimpanzees of Gombe in the 1960s, some of whom are also mentioned in this article.

Miocene Apes

David R. Begun

Prelude: A Case History

July in Catalonia can be ideal if you are on the beach, or it can be unbearable if you are in a building with no air conditioning, you have nothing to do, and you are seven. That was my son André's problem one summer day in 1991. He was patiently waiting for me to finish planning for our 1991 field season at the Miocene hominoid locality of Can Llobateres, about twenty kilometers northeast of Barcelona. When I suggested that we take a trip to the site late that afternoon, André was thrilled. We drove to the site to look over the area. I wanted André to run around a bit, and I gave him a pick to poke around with. I was also looking for the type of sediment we knew from previous work to be most likely to contain fossils. The hard green clays of Can Llobateres are the richest in ape fossils, and I wanted to find a new layer of this sediment. André and I had a great time chopping dirt and I did find some green sediment that looked very promising. The next day the field season began officially. My Spanish colleague and I, along with André and a team of excavators, arrived the next morning, and after setting up I showed my colleague the area I considered most promising. Our picks rose together as we prepared to clear away the layer of overburden covering the fossiliferous sediment. As they struck on both sides of the mark I had made the previous day, a tooth popped out. My colleague's pick had hit an upper jaw, or maxilla, dislodging the first premolar tooth. As we watched the tooth roll down the slope, we realized we had something significant. Looking at the spot from which the tooth had come, we saw broken bone. When we finished three days later, we had a nearly complete face, by far the most intact specimen of *Dryopithecus* (discussed later) ever recovered from Spain.

Discoveries in paleoanthropology are often a combination of luck and homework. In the case described above, we were lucky to clean a section right where a beautiful specimen was buried. But we also knew that apes had been found at Can Llobateres, and we knew from the nature of the sediments where our chances of finding good fossils were greatest. Sediments reveal details of the environments in which they were deposited. We knew that fossil apes are associated most often with fine grained sediments indicative of very slow moving water, such as that of a river delta, floodplain, or lake margin. In fact, the goals of our project at Can Llobateres were not only to find fossil apes, but also to collect as much information as possible about the environment in which they lived and died, and their geologic age. This information is combined with data on the anatomy of the fossils to tell us how those organisms lived, what they ate, and how they moved around in their environment.

Our research at Can Llobateres is just one example of many projects on Miocene apes in the last few years. This chapter summarizes research on Miocene apes, its implications for our understanding of ape and human evolution, and the prospects for future work in Miocene ape paleobiology. I will focus on those Miocene apes that are relatively well known and whose general relations to other apes and to humans are reasonably clear.

Background

Before discussing Miocene apes, a few terms must be defined. Hominoids, or the Hominoidea, is a superfamily in the Order Primates that includes all living apes and humans. The Hominoidea is divided into families, the exact number of which is controversial. Most researchers studying Miocene hominoids recognize two families. One is the Hylobatidae (hylobatids), including the gibbons and siamangs (genus *Hylobates*) of Southeast Asia. The other is the Hominidae (hominids), including the great apes and humans. The great apes include the orangutan (*Pongo pygmaeus*) from Indonesia, and the African apes—the chimpanzee (*Pan troglodytes*), the bonobo, sometimes called the pygmy chimpanzee (*Pan paniscus*), and the gorilla (*Gorilla gorilla*). Many researchers, and most text books, continue to separate the great apes and humans taxonomically by recognizing a third family, the Pongidae (pongids) for the great apes. This reflects tradition and a bit of anthropocentrism that often prevents anthropologists from seeing the remarkable similarities between humans and great apes. In fact the overwhelming majority of evidence indicates that African apes and humans are more closely related to one another than either are to orangs. To many paleoanthropologists, this means that African apes should not be placed in a separate family from humans. However, since orangs, African apes, and even the earliest members of the human lineage, *Australopithecus*, all look very similar, at least from the neck up, and since all are so different from hylobatids, two hominoid families separating the lesser apes and the great apes and humans is most practical, and most in agreement with current interpretations of hominoid relations (see later discussion).

Living hominoids share a set of characteristics that distinguish them from other living anthropoids, or higher primates. Their cheek teeth, or molars, have a distinctive arrangement of cusps. Their brains are also somewhat larger than expected for an anthropoid of their size range. But most dramatically, hominoids can be distinguished from other living anthropoids by their postcranial skeleton. All hominoids have skeletons bearing the hallmarks of a suspensory arboreal animal, even those who, like humans, no longer frequent the trees. Hominoids have rather loose but powerful, outwardly facing shoulders, highly specialized elbows to maximize stability in a wide range of positions, mobile wrists capable of adopting a wide range of positions, and long and powerful fingers. All hominoids lack an external tail, and all have specific attributes of the vertebral column, pelvic basin, hip joint, ankle, and foot related to arboreality and more vertical postures.

Apes use these characteristic features to grasp branches and support their body weight from above, unlike most arboreal primates, which move about on top of branches. Humans retain these features because they allow the wide range of arm and hand positions that are crucial to the human way of life, one that is dependent on intensive and elaborate manipulation of the environment.

Hominids (great apes and humans) share many additional characteristics that set them apart from other hominoids (hylobatids). Hominids are all large in body size and relative brain size compared to other hominoids. They have very enlarged front teeth, or incisors, and most have a greatly elongated front part of the palates or upper jaws. They share many other more subtle traits in the dentition and skull, and a large number of features of the postcranium not found in the hylobatids or other primates.

The early history of research on Miocene hominoids has been described in detail elsewhere.[1] Through the 1960s the story of hominoid evolution seemed relatively straightforward. Early Miocene hominoids such as *Proconsul* were thought to be directly related to the great apes (Table 1). Earlier researchers had recognized a closer evolutionary relationship between African apes and humans than between African and Asian great apes.[2] But this view was later abandoned, prematurely as we shall see, and the great apes were lumped together as the descendants of *Proconsul*.[3]

At this time most fossil apes were placed in the genus *Dryopithecus*, a taxon named in 1856 for a lower jaw from France.[4] Many other names had been used for a wide variety of great apelike Miocene specimens from Europe, Africa, and South Asia, including for example *Sivapithecus* from India and Pakistan, and *Proconsul* from Kenya and Uganda.[5] These and many other names were later subsumed under *Dryopithecus*.[6] One group of fossil apes was excluded from *Dryopithecus*. These specimens were most often referred to the genus *Ramapithecus*, and looked more human, mostly by virtue of the thick covering of enamel on their cheek teeth (molars). Figure 1 shows the consensus classification and phylogeny (evolutionary tree) of hominoids as of 1969. It reflects the then accepted division of great apes and humans into "pongids" and "hominids," with the "dryopithecines" as ancestors of the former, and the "ramapithecines" ancestral to the latter.

Three more recent developments in paleoanthropology have completely undermined this view of hominoid evolutionary history. Interpretations or hypotheses in paleoanthropology, as in other sciences, are subject to testing made possible by new discoveries and new techniques for generating data. A field in which ideas are always changing in the face of new discoveries is exciting and dynamic; method is more

Table 1
Fossil Hominoid Taxa and Chronology

Taxa are listed opposite their localities. First occurrences are listed in their entirety; subsequent occurrences are abbreviated. Localities within a row are contemporaneous if separated by a comma or placed in relative stratigraphic position if separated by a period. This table illustrates the incredible diversity of Miocene hominoid taxa. Many remain unnamed (Hominoidea indet.), but when these are combined with named taxa approximately thirty genera of hominoid can be identified. Given that this probably represents a small percentage of the total number of forms that actually existed (known fossils greatly underrepresent taxonomic diversity in the past) and considering the fact that only five genera of hominoid exist today, the Miocene can truly be considered the golden age of apes.

MA	Locality	Taxa
26	Lothidok (Kenya).	Hominoidea (new genus and species)
21	Meswa Bridge (Kenya).	*Proconsul sp.*
20		
19	Tinderet series (Kenya-Kuru, Legetet, Chamtwara, Songhor), Napak (Uganda).	*Proconsul africanus, Xenopithecus koruensis, Limnopithecus legetet, Limnopithecus evansi, Kaleopithecus songhorensis, Micropithecus clarki, Proconsul major, Dendropithecus macinnesi, Rangwapithecus gordoni, Nyanzapithecus vancouveringorum* (N. B. Not all occur at each locality)
17	Rusinga Island, Mwfangano Island (Kenya).	*Proconsul nyanzae, Proconsul hesloni, D. macinnesi, L. legetet, N. vancouveringorum*
	Kalodirr, Buluk (Kenya).	*Afropithecus turkanensis, Turkanapithecus kalakolensis, Simiolus enjiessi*
	Ad Dabtyah (S. Arabia), Sindhi (Pakistan).	*Heliopithecus leakeyi, Dionysopithecus sp.*
16	Sihong (China).	*D. shuangouensis, Platodontopithecus jianghuaiensis,* Hominoid indet.
15	Kipsarimon (Kenya).	2 Hominoidea indet.
	Maboko, Majiwa, Kaloma, Nachola (Kenya).	*Nyanzapithecus pickfordi, Mabokopithecus clarki,* "*Kenyapithecus africanus,*" *Micropithecus leakeyorum*
	Pasalar (Turkey), Devinsk Nová Ves (Slovakia).	*Griphopithecus darwini*
13	Çandir (Turkey).	*Griphopithecus alpani*
	Fort Ternan (Kenya).	*Kenyapithecus wickeri,* 3 Hominoidea indet.
12	St. Gaudens, La Grive (France).	*Dryopithecus fontani*
	St. Stefan (Austria), Can Vila, Can Mata, Castel de Barbera, Sant Quirze (Spain), Chinji (Pakistan).	*Dryopithecus cf., D. fontani, Sivapithecus indicus*
11	Ngorora (Kenya).	Hominoidea indet.
10	Can Ponsic, El Firal (Spain).	*Dryopithecus crusafonti*
	Can Llobateres, Polinya (Spain), Melchingen, Trochtelfingen, Ebingen, Wissberg, Eppelsheim (Germany), Yassioren (Turkey).	*Dryopithecus laietanus, Dryopithecus cf, D. brancoi Ankarapithecus meteai*

(continued)

Table 1
Fossil Hominoid Taxa and Chronology *(continued)*

MA	Locality	Taxa
9	Rudabánya (Hungary), (Austria), Salmendingen (Germany), Udabno (Georgia).	*D. brancoi Mariathal*
	La Tarumba (Spain).	*D. laietanus*
	Ravin de la Pluie, Xirochori, Nikiti (Greece), Nagri (Pakistan, India).	*Ouranopithecus macedoniensis, Sivapithecus sivalensis, Sivapithecus parvada*
8	*Pygros (Greece), Baccinello VI (Italy).*	Graecopithecus freybergi, Oreopithecus bambolii
7	*U-level, Hari Talyangar (Pakistan), Samburu (Kenya), Shihuiba (Lufeng, China).*	S. sivalensis, Gigantopithecus giganteus, *Hominoidea indet.,* Lufengpithecus lufengensis
6	*Lukeino (Kenya), Hari Talyangar (Pakistan).*	*Hominoidea indet.,* Gigantopithecus bilaspurensis
5	*Lothagam (Kenya).*	*cf.* Australopithecus

important than interpretation. A field in which interpretations never change, hypotheses are never falsified, and theories are unaffected by new data, is not much of a science at all.

Of the three recent developments, two fall into the category of new techniques, while the third is categorized as new discoveries. The first development, relatively new to paleoanthropology but with a long history in biology, is molecular systematics. Since the turn of the century, researchers have been attempting to reconstruct evolutionary history using molecules rather than morphology.[7] In the 1960s a number of researchers had concluded on the basis of work on proteins that humans were more closely related to African apes than to orangs,[8] as Huxley had suggested a century earlier on the basis of anatomical comparisons. The antiquity of the split between apes and humans was also dramatically different according to the molecular evidence. Sarich and Wilson estimated that the split could not have occurred more than three to five million years ago,[9] whereas most paleoanthropologists at the time, recognizing *Proconsul* as a great ape ancestor, placed the split sometime before the evolution of this form, at least twenty million years ago. Though Sarich's molecular clock is not widely cited today, his estimate is probably much closer to the truth than the estimate based on *Proconsul.* Modern research in molecular systematics now shows, based mostly on DNA sequencing, how very closely related we are to the African apes and maybe more specifically to the chimpanzee.[10]

The second development, again new to paleoanthropology but with a longer history in paleobiology, is cladistics. Cladistics or phylogenetic systematics is an approach to biological classification that is explicitly evolutionary.[11] All organisms must be classified according to their evolutionary interrelationships. Organisms placed together in a group, or taxon, must be more closely related to the other forms in that taxon than to any organism in another taxon. So, for example, African apes and orangs cannot be grouped to the exclusion of humans, because African apes are more closely related to humans than they are to orangs. This is the main reason the taxon Pongidae is no longer used by many. Taxa like the Pongidae are paraphyletic, meaning they fail to include some lineages, like humans. Including humans with the great apes changes the name of the taxon to Hominidae, because Hominidae was named first. Cladistic methodology provides an explicit protocol for determining ancestor-descendant relationships.[12] The main effect of the application of this method in the analysis of Miocene hominoids has been a thorough re-evaluation of the evolutionary significance of the characteristics used to reconstruct evolutionary relations. Characteristics once thought to indicate a close evolutionary relationship among the great apes, such as large, elongated faces, large canine teeth, very elon-

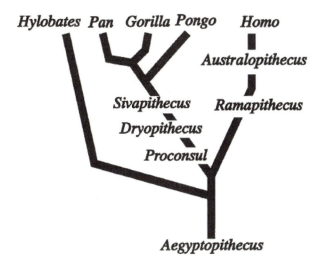

Figure 1
Evolutionary Relations among Fossil and Living Hominoids, as Interpreted circa 1968

Aegyptopithecus, now known to be a primitive anthropoid, was then thought to be an early hominoid, broadly ancestral to all later forms. Most authors placed *Sivapithecus*, *Dryopithecus*, and *Proconsul* in the same genus, *Dryopithecus*, and thought that these were ancestral to living great apes. *Ramapithecus*, now recognized to be a synonym of *Sivapithecus*, was thought by most to be the first "hominid." See text for details.

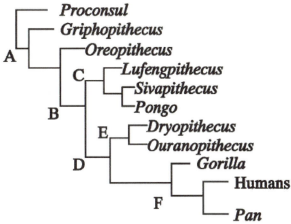

Figure 2
One Interpretation of Relations among Fossil and Living Hominoids

Instead of arranging taxa in an evolutionary tree, most researchers today prefer dendrograms such as this one, which arrange taxa based on relations but avoid speculations about ancestors and descendants. Note, for example, that *Proconsul* is not ancestral to other forms; it simply branched off first. The common ancestor of *Proconsul* and other hominoids is represented by node A, which is not a named taxon but a hypothetical ancestral form sharing characteristics of both *Proconsul* and other hominoids. In this phylogeny, *Sivapithecus*, *Lufengpithecus*, and *Pongo* share a common ancestor at C not shared by any other taxon. They are thus most closely related to one another, and related in the same way to all other taxa, with which they are linked at B. Similarly, *Dryopithecus* shares a common ancestor with *Ouranopithecus* at E, and both share an ancestor with the African apes and humans at D. Humans (including *Australopithecus*) share a common ancestor with chimps (Pan) at F, and are therefore more closely related to chimps than either are to gorillas. See text for discussion.

gated forelimbs, short hindlimbs, and others, are now recognized as primitive characteristics that were also present in the ancestors of humans. Therefore they do not distinguish the human lineage from that of the apes. In contrast, other characteristics, such as well-developed brow ridges, elongated crania, a reduced number of wrist bones, and other details of cranial and postcranial anatomy found only in African apes and humans, suggest that these forms share a period of common ancestry not shared by the orang. Cladistic methods allow researchers to distinguish characteristics indicative of a close evolutionary relationship, or derived characteristics, from those that are more primitive. This type of revision has lead to substantial changes in interpretation of the pattern of relationships among Miocene apes.

The third development of importance to Miocene hominoid research has been new discoveries. The old view of a dichotomy between the "ramapithecines" and the "dryopithecines" has been completely rejected on the basis of new discoveries of both groups. As described later in this chapter, new fossils from Pak-

istan show that *Ramapithecus* and *Sivapithecus* are in fact the same genus. New discoveries of *Proconsul*, *Dryopithecus*, *Sivapithecus*, and completely new forms reveal the pattern of hominoid diversity in the Miocene to be very different from the simple tree that was the consensus in 1969. Figure 2 is a revision of Miocene hominoid classification based on the developments noted earlier. For the rest of this chapter, I will describe these new discoveries and their implications for the evolutionary history of the great apes and humans.

Current Issues and Interpretations in Miocene Hominoid Research

The earliest well-documented Miocene hominoid is *Proconsul*, from sites in Kenya and Uganda up to about twenty Ma (mega-annum, or millions of years ago). One of the most important of these localities is Songhor in southwestern Kenya, near Lake Victoria. Songhor is thought to be about nineteen Ma.[13] Many fossil hominoids are known from Songhor and nearby sites, including species of *Proconsul*, *Rangwapithecus*, and other smaller forms of very unclear evolutionary affinities (see Table 1).[14] Most are probably related to Proconsul, but some, like *Dendropithecus*, may represent a different kind of hominoid, or may not be a hominoid at all.

The specimens from Songhor, apart from a small number of more complete jaws, are fragmentary and include only a few postcranial remains. However, a bit later in time, between about 17.2 and 17.8 Ma, additional similar-looking primates are found at a site on nearby Rusinga Island, in Lake Victoria.[15] Many of these specimens are more complete and provide most of the information we have about the anatomy and evolutionary relations of *Proconsul*.

The Rusinga specimens attributed to *Proconsul* are slightly different from specimens from the older sites, but are currently assigned to the same genus. Based mostly on the evidence from Rusinga, we know that *Proconsul* was a monkey-like arboreal quadruped.[16] Its limbs were roughly equal in length, and its forelimbs lacked most of the characteristics of modern hominoids related to their suspensory locomotor capabilities. *Proconsul* does have a number of features that seem to foreshadow hominoid postcranial anatomy. *Proconsul* elbows, for example, include a specialized ridge similar to but less well developed than a ridge in modern hominoid elbows, designed to maintain maximum stability through the range of motion at the joint. Subtle aspects of the wrists and fingers also suggest mobility and grasping capabilities similar to that seen in living hominoids, but again less well developed than in modern forms.[17] The hip joints and innominate, or pelvic bones, of *Proconsul* also suggest some enhanced ranges of mobility foreshadowing the hominoid condition, as do some details of the anatomy of the feet.[18] Most important, the anatomy of the sacrum, the final section of the vertebral column before the tail, indicates that *Proconsul* was like hominoids in lacking an external tail.[19] Thus, *Proconsul* may

have been a more deliberate climber, venturing out on smaller branches and branch ends, and often adopting more vertical postures than living monkeys.

The anatomy of *Proconsul* jaws and teeth suggest that it was a generalized frugivore, or fruit eater, but probably taking in some leaves as well.[20] The incisors are not as large as in modern great apes, which use these teeth for processing foods with tough coverings, but were similar to those of the frugivorous gibbons and many Old and New World monkeys. These forms generally have diets of 50 to 75 percent fruits, grains, nuts, bark, roots, and other plant parts excluding leaves. The pattern of microwear on the molars of *Proconsul* also indicates a diet similar to that of modern frugivores.[21] The brain of *Proconsul* is known from one specimen, a skull from Rusinga Island. It is very primitive looking in overall morphology and size, and was no more advanced than the brains of living monkeys. In fact in some ways it resembles the brains of living prosimians.[22]

All in all, with its generalized monkey-like morphology but subtle ape-like features, *Proconsul* is a good representative of the ancestor of living apes, and possibly of living hominids. It may be that *Proconsul* was already somewhat specialized in its own direction and is not directly related to modern forms, but the common ancestor of modern hominoids must have been very similar to *Proconsul*.

Contemporary with the latest specimens of *Proconsul* from Rusinga is another set of taxa from northern Kenya. These are the somewhat enigmatic forms *Afropithecus*, *Turkanapithecus*, and *Simiolus*.[23] These forms are known from the sites of Kalodirr and Buluk, in the Lake Turkana region of northern Kenya, the same region that has proven so rich in fossil humans. A fragmentary jaw and some isolated teeth from Saudi Arabia originally attributed to *Heliopithecus* may also be *Afropithecus*.[24] Although contemporary with *Proconsul*, these three species are very different in their cranial and dental anatomy from other early Miocene forms, which makes their correct placement among the hominoids very difficult.

Simiolus is a very small form with unusual cresty teeth and a primitive postcranial skeleton, lacking a number of characteristics that in *Proconsul* foreshadow the hominoid condition.[25] It may not even be a true hominoid but a descendant of a branch that diverged before the hominoids evolved. *Turkanapithecus* is close in size to the smallest species of *Proconsul*. The best specimen of *Turkanapithecus* is a partial skeleton with most of the face and teeth and a number of associated postcranial bones.[26] *Turkanapithecus* has a more projecting mid-face, the region of the nose, than *Proconsul*, and this is reminiscent of more primitive "pre-hominoids" like the thirty-three-million-year-old genus *Aegyptopithecus* from the Fayum deposits of Egypt.[27] Other aspects of the anatomy of *Turkanapithecus* are more similar to *Proconsul*, especially the postcrania, which are very similar in both forms.

Afropithecus is close in size to the largest species of *Proconsul*, but has a distinctive cranial morphology, with a mixture of features resembling *Aegyptopithecus* and *Proconsul*.[28] The upper incisor region or premaxilla of *Afropithecus* is superficially more like that of modern hominoids, being slightly elongated and large, to house the large, thick, upper incisor teeth. Unlike *Proconsul*, *Afropithecus* molars have thick layers of enamel,[29] an extremely hard material that coats the teeth of all primates and of most other vertebrates. This is more like the molars of later more advanced hominoids. The postcrania of *Afropithecus* is nearly indistinguishable from that of *Proconsul*.[30] *Afropithecus* was probably an arboreal quadruped that moved above branches, like modern monkeys, but was a strong climber and spent more time in vertical postures than do living monkeys. The dietary adaptations of *Afropithecus* were probably also similar to those of *Proconsul*, though the thicker enamel of the former suggests a more varied diet that included hard or tough objects, such as nuts and fruits with durable coverings, or foods that tend to wear teeth rapidly, such as those obtained from terrestrial sources that incorporate some grit. *Turkanopithecus*, with its more cresty molars, may have relied more heavily on foods that require extensive cutting and chopping, such as leaves, which must be finely chopped to liberate the few nutrients they contain.

The mixture of primitive and more advanced, or derived, characteristics of *Turkanopithecus*, and especially *Afropithecus*, makes it difficult to place these taxa in a phylogenetic or evolutionary scheme. It may be that both are more primitive hominoids than *Proconsul*, as suggested by the facial similarities with *Aegyptopithecus*, or it may be that *Afropithecus* is derived, given the more modern appearance of its teeth. More fossil material is needed to resolve the enigmatic relations of these relatively newly described Miocene hominoids.

At the end of the early Miocene, about 16.5 Ma, few fossil hominoids are known from East Africa. A small number of fossils similar in morphology to smaller possible relatives of *Proconsul* are known from China and Pakistan.[31] But the record of Miocene apes is relatively barren at that time until about fifteen Ma, at which time a rich record of primates is known from Maboko Island and other nearby localities in western Kenya, close to the early Miocene sites of Rusinga and Songhor. Some of the earliest specimens of true Old World monkeys are known from Maboko, as is a prosimian and several hominoids.[32]

Maboko occurs at the beginning of the middle Miocene, which lasts from about 16.5 Ma to about 11.5 Ma. Along with the early Miocene hominoids that persist at Maboko is a new type of hominoid. This form has thick enamel, like *Afropithecus* and *Sivapithecus*, but more modern looking molars, with less strongly developed cingula than in *Proconsul* and *Afropithecus*. It is most like *Kenyapithecus*, first described from the somewhat younger site of Fort Ternan, also in western Kenya.[33] *Kenyapithecus* is more advanced than early Miocene hominoids in molar morphology but retains many primitive features also found in *Proconsul*, both cranially and, especially, postcranially. However, one important set of differences in the postcranial anatomy of *Kenyapithecus* suggests that it may have been more terrestrial than most other hominoids. Certain characteristics of the shoulder joint in *Kenyapithecus* from Maboko are more like those of terrestrial monkeys such as baboons than are the shoulders of *Proconsul* and other hominoids.[34] The possibility of increased terrestriality in *Kenyapithecus* combined with its thickly enamelled molars suggests a greater dependence on terrestrial sources of food, which tend to contain more grit and therefore tend to wear teeth more rapidly. More will be known about the cranial and postcranial anatomy of *Kenyapithecus* when a large new sample from the Nachola area, west of Baragoi, in northern Kenya is analyzed.[35]

Dentally and postcranially similar hominoids are also known from Europe and Turkey at sites contemporaneous with Fort Ternan. The sites of Çandir and Pasalar, both in Turkey, Devinska Nová Ves (formerly Neudorf) in Slovakia, and Klein Hadersdorf in Austria, have produced cranial and postcranial remains very similar to those of Maboko and Fort Ternan.[36] These forms, called *Griphopithecus*,[37] may, together with *Kenyapithecus*, be the earliest members of the lineage that includes the living great apes and humans. However, the precise placement of this group of hominoids represents a major puzzle in hominoid evolutionary studies. *Griphopithecus* and *Kenyapithecus* have molars and premolars that look more like those of modern great apes than do those of early Miocene forms or those of hylobatids. Yet hylobatids and all late Miocene hominoids (discussed later) have postcranial attributes in common with great apes, all of which reflect the importance of suspensory postures in the trees.[38] So there is a conflict between the evidence for the limbs and the evidence of the teeth.

The earliest substantial evidence of modern hominoid cranial and postcranial anatomy comes at the end of the middle Miocene and the beginning of the late Miocene. In the early Miocene form *Proconsul*, aside from relatively subtle changes in fore and hindlimb anatomy and the less subtle absence of a tail,[39] modern hominoid postcranial anatomy is not present. At Moroto, a site in Uganda from the middle Miocene, about fourteen Ma,[40] a lumbar vertebra is known which looks more modern than any attributed to *Proconsul*, suggesting the presence of a great ape with a short, stiff lower back and a broader torso, like modern forms.[41] By the end of the middle Miocene and into the late Miocene, modern great ape anatomy becomes even more evident. Two forms appear at nearly the same time, one in South Asia (India and Pakistan) and one in Europe. The South Asian hominoid is *Sivapithecus*, and its European contemporary is *Dryopithecus*. *Sivapithecus* is known from many specimens from sites in the Potwar Plateau region of India and Pakistan.

The sample of *Sivapithecus* was formerly divided into several different forms (as discussed earlier) but is now universally accepted as two genera, *Gigantopithecus* for a small number of large to gigantic specimens and *Sivapithecus* for the vast majority of the material. *Sivapithecus* and *Gigantopithecus* are probably closely related to one another, based on considerable similarities in dental morphology.[42] But only *Sivapithecus* is well known from cranial and postcranial morphology, so I will focus on this form here. The face of *Sivapithecus*, known from several palatal specimens and a remarkably complete face, GSP 15, 000, is extremely similar to the faces of modern orangs. This is true in details of the structure of the palate or upper jaw, the zygomatics or cheek bones, the orbits and the region between the orbits, and in the forehead or frontal bone. In fact, it was the discovery of GSP 15, 000, more than any other development (discussed earlier), that convinced most paleoanthropologists that *Sivapithecus* was not a "dryopithecine" but an early member of the lineage of the orang.[43] Other discoveries of smaller jaws and teeth from the Potwar plateau convinced most researchers that Len Greenfield had been correct in recognizing that *Ramapithecus* was simply small individuals of *Sivapithecus*.[44] Greenfield concluded that specimens called *Ramapithecus* differed from *Sivapithecus* only in size and in having smaller canines with a different morphology. Because the canines of *Sivapithecus* all looked very similar to those of male

great apes, and the canines of *Ramapithecus* all looked very much like those of female great apes, Greenfield concluded that all specimens of *Ramapithecus* were in fact females of Sivapithecus, the taxon that had been named first. With the publication of GSP 15,000 it became widely accepted that *Sivapithecus* (now including *Ramapithecus*) was a close relative of the orang, and had nothing directly to do with the origins of the human lineage.

The interpretation of *Dryopithecus* has also changed considerably due to new discoveries. *Dryopithecus* is now known from cranial and postcranial characteristics to be much more modern-looking than *Proconsul*, with which it was once grouped (see earlier discussion). Three partial crania and large numbers of jaws, teeth, and limb bones from various sites in Europe (Table 1) show that *Dryopithecus* has characteristics of the palate, jaw joint, mid face, frontal, and braincase only found in African apes and humans, and one other Miocene hominoid, Ouranopithecus, from the late Miocene of Greece.[45] *Ouranopithecus* is much larger than *Dryopithecus* and has many of the same features found in *Dryopithecus* but in exaggerated form. The Greek form also has many unique features of the face and teeth, and even shares a few traits, such as extremely thick enamel and very small canines, with early humans. Some have suggested that the similarities to humans indicate a close relationship,[46] while others have suggested close affinities to gorillas.[47] However, for a number of reasons, it appears more likely that the similarities to australopithecines occur convergently (that is, they were acquired independently), while the similarities to gorillas are superficial and based on the similar sizes of *Ouranopithecus* and gorillas.

If the characteristics that link *Dryopithecus* and *Ouranopithecus* to African apes and humans indicate a close evolutionary relationship, then these European forms may be more closely related to African apes and humans than are *Sivapithecus* and the orang. This is almost exactly the opposite of the interpretation of these genera twenty-five years ago, based on a smaller number of fossils, that linked a South Asian form to humans and linked *Dryopithecus* to a side branch of the great apes.

Dryopithecus and *Ouranopithecus* both have short faces and poorly developed brow ridges compared to African apes and fossil humans, but both are very similar to African apes and humans in the details of these areas. Given these differences, the view that *Dryopithecus* and *Ouranopithecus* are more closely related to African apes and humans than is *Sivapithecus* is controversial. *Sivapithecus*, after all, has an elongated premaxilla, the front part of the upper jaw, like all great apes, though it is structurally distinct from all but the orang. The issue will probably not really be resolved until African relatives of the African apes and humans are found in the time period between about ten to five Ma. If these relatives more closely resemble *Dryopithecus* and *Ouranopithecus*, which I consider more likely, the Asian forms would have branched off first. If the African relatives share a similar premaxilla with *Sivapithecus* and the orang, that would suggest the European forms diverged first.

Sivapithecus, *Ouranopithecus*, and *Dryopithecus* are all quite distinct from one another in the morphology of their jaws and teeth. *Dryopithecus* has more lightly built jaws and teeth with sharper, more pointy cusps, similar to modern chimps, which are frugivorous in their dietary preferences. *Sivapithecus* and *Ouranopithecus* have more massive jaws, and teeth with lower, more rounded cusps and thick layers of enamel, as in the more primitive forms *Kenyapithecus* and *Afropithecus*. In both forms this suggests the inclusion of harder, tougher, or more gritty objects in the diet, requiring higher bite forces to crack or deform, and/or thicker enamel in response to more rapid wear. These characteristics, which are present in early humans (australopithecines) as well, have also been interpreted as indications of a closer relationship to great apes and humans than to Dryopithecus. However, since similar anatomical characteristics also occur in the clearly more primitive early and middle Miocene forms, it seems more likely that these are simply traits that have changed relatively frequently during hominoid evolution. Even among australopithecines, other fossil humans, and modern great apes, the spectrum of jaw and teeth morphology is tremendous, and it is not obvious which type of morphology gave rise to which. In the final analysis, hominid jaw and tooth morphology are reliable indicators of diet, but not for reconstructing evolutionary relationships. In terms of the jaws and teeth, hominids are mostly what they eat.

The postcranial anatomy of *Dryopithecus* and *Sivapithecus* is not so well documented as in *Proconsul* (and is almost unknown for Ouranopithecus), but the forelimbs and feet are reasonably well known. Both taxa are modern hominoid-like in the morphology of their fingers and elbows, which indicate well developed suspensory capabilities and wide ranges of joint mobility with maximum stability.[48] Wrist and foot bones also indicate mobility of the type typical of modern hominoids, but most tend to retain certain characteristics of more primitive hominoids like *Proconsul*, suggesting that suspensory arboreality may not

have been quite so well developed as in modern forms. The hamate, a bone of the wrist, is more similar to modern hominoids in *Dryopithecus* than in *Sivapithecus*, mostly due to the configuration of the hamate hook, which is more strongly developed in *Dryopithecus* and modern hominoids and is probably associated with more powerful wrist and finger flexion. The shaft of the humerus is also more like modern hominoids in *Dryopithecus*, being slightly curved backwards in side view.[49] This is also thought to be indicative of suspensory arboreality. In *Sivapithecus* the humeral shaft is bent forwards in side view and has very powerful attachment sites for the muscles of the shoulders.[50] This is most similar to large monkeys such as baboons, and may be related to more terrestriality in *Sivapithecus*. Both *Dryopithecus* and *Sivapithecus* were probably basically arboreal. *Dryopithecus* seems to have been more hominoid-like, being highly arboreal and suspensory, but also probably retained the monkey like ability to walk atop the branches. *Sivapithecus* probably ventured to the ground more often, but did not knuckle-walk, as do the African apes when on the ground. Like *Dryopithecus*, *Sivapithecus* was also partly monkey-like, but more similar to terrestrial than arboreal monkeys.

Three other large bodied Miocene hominoids are known, but their relations to other Miocene forms and to living hominoids are even less clearly understood. *Otavipithecus* is only known from a single lower jaw fragment and a few limb bone fragments. It is of middle Miocene age, and shares characteristics with both early and middle Miocene forms. It is interesting that *Otavipithecus* comes from Namibia in southern Africa, and is the first Miocene hominoid from this far south.[51] The other two Miocene hominoids are from the late Miocene and are represented by very large samples of fossils, but remain poorly understood because of their unique combinations of anatomical features. These are *Oreopithecus* from the late Miocene of Italy and *Lufengpithecus* from the late Miocene of China. Both these forms existed between seven and eight Ma, and are the latest surviving Miocene hominoids, along with the last surviving populations of *Sivapithecus*.

Oreopithecus, from Monte Bamboli in Tuscany, is known from more postcrania than any other Miocene hominoid except *Proconsul*. Many jaws and teeth are also known, as are fragments of the cranium. *Oreopithecus* has been called a hominoid by some and a monkey by others.[52] Cranially, *Oreopithecus* is very primitive, with a short face, like gibbons and *Proconsul*, and a very small brain for its body size.[53] Dentally, *Oreopithecus* is highly specialized, with a unique combination of characteristics resembling both hominoids and Old World monkeys. It has small canines, like some hominids, but long teeth with very tall, transversely aligned, pointy cusps, like monkeys. Also like monkeys, their upper and lower molar teeth greatly resemble one another. The dentition of *Oreopithecus* is more functionally than structurally similar to that of Old World monkeys. Both morphologies are probably associated with folivory, or leaf eating, but the differences in the number and position of cusps and cutting ridges, or crests, in each indicate separate origins. Similar kinds of folivore-type teeth are also found in other primates such as New World Monkeys and prosimians.

The postcranial anatomy of *Oreopithecus* is another matter. Much of one skeleton of an *Oreopithecus* individual is known, and a number of isolated pieces from other individuals are known as well. These all indicate a highly advanced suspensory hominoid with forelimb adaptations to hanging and swinging below branches comparable to that of living apes.[54] It is clear that *Oreopithecus* was more advanced in modern hominoid-like postcranial anatomy and behavior than any other Miocene hominoid. More detailed analysis of the entire skeleton of *Oreopithecus* is necessary to reveal whether it is similar in most details to living hominoids, and therefore probably closely related to them, or whether it differs in a large enough number of structural details to suggest an independent evolution of suspensory behaviors in *Oreopithecus*, as seems to be the case with the dentition and diet. *Lufengpithecus* is represented by over one thousand specimens, mostly individual teeth, but also several large cranial specimens and a small number of postcrania, from the site of Lufeng, in Yunnan Province, China.[55] The postcrania include scraps of forelimb material that appear to closely resemble great apes, much like *Dryopithecus* and *Sivapithecus*.[56] Not enough is known to determine what differences, if any, from great apes characterized the postcrania of *Lugfengpithecus*. The teeth of *Lufengpithecus* are very much like many hominids in overall morphology. The postcanine teeth are most like the orang, which, like *Lufengpithecus*, has wrinkled or crenulated enamel on its molars and premolars.[57] The incisors, however, are very similar to those of *Dryopithecus* and *Ouranopithecus* in being quite tall-crowned and narrow. Certain parts of the face, especially around the nose, eyes, and forehead, closely resemble *Sivapithecus* and the orang, while others, particularly the premaxilla and the space between the orbits, are very different from other Asian forms.[58] So *Lufengpithecus*, like *Oreopithecus*, presents an intriguing combination of characteristics from a diversity of hominoids, making the placement of both in the evolutionary framework of the Hominoidea very difficult at present.

Conclusions

The results of the last twenty years of research in Miocene hominoids has produced some dramatic changes in interpretations of hominoid evolution. Hominoid evolution is much more complicated than was once thought, with at least twenty-five different genera known from between about twenty to six Ma. This increase in recognized hominoid diversity may prompt cries of "splitting," but in fact is more in line with the known diversity of primates in other superfamilies, like Old World Monkeys (*Cercopithecoidea*) or New World Monkeys (*Ceboidea*). Living hominoids are but a mere shadow of the former diversity of this group.

Several trends are now apparent in hominoid evolution. Dietary changes are relatively subtle, and involve increased specialization of the front teeth (incisors and canines), probably to increase the ability to process a wider diversity of foods. Modern hominids use their front teeth as tools for removing the various protective coverings of the foods they consume. This ability seems to have developed in the late Miocene. A few hominoids, such as *Oreopithecus* and *Ouranopithecus*, became very specialized in their diets, with unusually enhanced folivore morphology in the former and with huge jaws and teeth suggesting enhanced omnivory in the latter. A more dramatic trend is in the evolution of positional behavior. Monkey-like above branch arboreality imposes limits on the size of animals living in the trees and the ease with which they can move within the canopy. Ape-like below branch arboreality and enhanced limb mobility allows access to smaller branches, where much of the food is. Larger animals have a more difficult time balancing above branches, but can remain in the trees if they can effectively position themselves below branches. The trend to below branch arboreality and increasing body size is apparent from more monkey-like *Proconsul* to more ape-like *Dryopithecus* and *Oreopithecus*. The late Miocene witnesses the appearance of many new and specialized forms of positional behavior. Although no living hominoid moves about in the same way as did any fossil form, all have much in common in their postcranial anatomy. This suggests that the changes in the postcranial skeleton of late Miocene hominoids was extremely successful and flexible, and has led to the development of such diverse patterns of positional behavior as brachiation, knuckle-walking, and bipedalism characteristic of modern hominoids.

The other major conclusion from recent research in Miocene hominoids concerns our understanding of the relations among living hominoids and the place humans occupy among them. There is now widespread agreement among morphologists and molecular systematists that humans are more closely related to African apes than either are to orangs. Furthermore, it is also becoming apparent that humans and African apes are very closely related to one another, such that the precise order in which each diverged from their common ancestor is very unclear. Molecular systematists have been saying with increased frequency that humans and chimps are most closely related among hominids,[59] though many continue to hold that it is just too close to call.[60] Most paleoanthropologists who focus on morphology believe that chimps and gorillas are closest, citing such specialized similarities as knuckle-walking and thinly enamelled teeth.[61] But as we have seen in this review, the significance of these characteristics is not so clear-cut. Enamel thickness is a poor indicator of evolutionary relationships because it changes so often in response to dietary requirements. Knuckle-walking, which is unique to African apes among living forms, is commonly considered to be a recent specialization of the African apes. A more controversial, but in my mind more likely, view is that knuckle-walking characterized our ancestors too. After all, humans do share unusual features of the hand and wrist only with African apes, such as fewer wrist bones, more stability of the joints of the wrist, and shorter hand and finger bones. One real possibility is that humans retain these characteristics because we evolved from a knuckle-walker that needed them to ensure wrist and hand stability while walking on the knuckles. When humans shifted to two feet we lost many features still found in knuckle-walkers, while others were suitable to the tasks important to early bipeds, such as enhanced manipulation.

If humans evolved from knuckle-walkers, a strong possibility given that all three of the closest relatives of humans (chimps, gorillas, and bonobos) are still knuckle-walkers, this tells us something about the history of human descent from the trees. Humans apparently went through a two step process, first becoming sometime terrestrial knuckle-walkers, like living African apes, and then committing themselves more completely to the ground. As knuckle-walkers, the common ancestors of chimps and humans probably exploited resources similar to those exploited by living chimps today. Living chimps and humans still exploit the greatest range of resources of any primate; they are able to range over long distances and in diverse habitats, and they can to use tools to help process foods which would otherwise be unavailable to them. Humans probably diverged from chimps when they became committed to the more completely open ecology of the grassland, requiring a more efficient mode of long distance terrestrial locomotion (bipedalism) and perhaps also an enhanced ability to manipulate the environment with their hands, which bipedalism made possible. These positional changes, which are apparent in the very first humans, *Ardipithecus ramidus*,[62] precede most other changes that today separate humans from other animals. The brain, for example, changed very little, at least in external morphology and relative size, until comparatively late in human evolution, after the appearance of the genus *Homo*. Obligate terrestriality was really the major impetus in human origins, and it appears to have a long history going back to our common ancestors with the African apes. Research on Miocene hominoids has produced many new insights into human evolution in the past twenty years, and we can expect many more in the years to come. Much new fossil material is already known and is being studied. These new data will provide grist for the mill in the continuing endeavor to unravel the mystery of human origins.

Notes

1. Elwyn L. Simons and David R. Pilbeam, "Preliminary Revision of the Dryopithecinae (Pongidae, Anthropoidea)," *Folia Primatologica* 3 (1965): 81–152.
2. Thomas H. Huxley, *Evidence as to Man's Place in Nature* (London: Williams and Norgate, 1863).
3. David R. Pilbeam, "Tertiary Pongidae of East Africa: Evolutionary Relationships and Taxonomy," *Peabody Museum of Natural History* 31 (1969): 1–185.
4. Eduard Lartet, "Note sur un grand singe fossile qui se rattache au groupe des singes superieurs," *Comptes Rendus de l'Academie de Sciences* 43 (1856): 219–223.
5. Guy E. Pilgrim, "New Siwalik Primates and Their Bearing on the Question of the Evolution of Man and the Anthropoidea," *Records of the Geologica Survey of India* 45 (1916): 1–74; A. T. Hopwood, "Miocene Primates from Kenya," *Zoological Journal of the Linnean Society* 38 (1935): 437–464.
6. Simons and Pilbeam, "Preliminary Revision of the Dryopithecinae (Pongidae, Anthropoidea)," pp. 81–152.
7. G. H. F. Nutall, *Blood Immunity and Blood Relationships* (London: Cambridge University Press, 1904).
8. Vincent M. Sarich and Alan C. Wilson, "Immunological TimeScale for Hominoid Evolution," *Science* 158 (1967): 1200–1203; Morris Goodman, "Man's Place

in the Phylogeny of the Primates as Reflected in Serum Proteins," in Sherwood L. Washburn, ed., *Classification and Human Evolution* (Chicago: Aldine Press, 1963), pp. 204–234; Morris Goodman, "The Chronicle of Primate Phylogeny Contained in Proteins," *Symposia of the Zoological Society of London* 33 (1973): 339–375.

9. Sarich and Wilson, "Immunological Time-Scale for Hominoid Evolution."

10. Jonathan Marks, "Genetic Relationships among the Apes and Humans," *Current Opinion in Genetics and Development* 2 (1992): 883–889; Jonathan Marks, C. W. Schmid, and V. M. Sarich, "DNA Hybridization as a Guide to Phylogeny: Relations of the Hominoidea," *Journal of Human Evolution* 17 (1988): 769–786; J. Rogers, "The Phylogenetic Relationships among Homo, Pan, and Gorilla: A Population Genetics Perspective," *Journal of Human Evolution* 25 (1993): 201–216; Goodman, "The Chronicle of Primate Phylogeny Contained in Proteins"; Morris Goodman, B. F. Koop, J. Czelusniak, D. H. A. Fitch, D. A. Tagel, and J. L. Slightom, "Molecular Phylogeny of the Family of Apes and Humans," *Genome* 31 (1989): 316–335; S. Horai, Y. Satta, K. Hayasaka, R. Kondo, T. Inoue, T. Ishida, S. Hayashi, and N. Takahata, "Man's Place in Hominoidea Revealed by Mitochondrial DNA Genealogy," *Journal of Molecular Evolution* 34 (1992): 32–43; B. F. Koop, D. A. Tagel, M. Goodman, and J. L. Slightom, "A Molecular View of Primate Phylogeny and Important Systematic and Evolutionary Questions," *Molecular Biology and Evolution* 6 (1989): 580–612; M. Ruvolo, "Molecular Evolutionary Processes and Conflicting Gene Trees:The Hominoid Case," *American Journal of Physical Anthropology* 94 (1994): 89–113.

11. W. Hennig, *Phylogenetic Systematics* (Chicago: University of Illinois Press, 1966).

12. Daniel R. Brooks and Deborah A. McClennan, *Phylogeny, Ecology, and Behavior* (Chicago: University of Chicago Press, 1991); E. O. Wiley, D. J. Siegel-Causey, D. R. Brooks, and V. A. Funk, *The Compleat Cladist: A Primer of Phylogenetic Procedures* (Lawrence: Museum of Natural History, University of Kansas, 1989).

13. Martin Pickford, "Geochronology of the Hominoidea: A Summary," in J. G. Else and P. C. Lee, eds., *Primate Evolution* (Cambridge: Cambridge University Press, 1986), pp. 123–128.

14. Peter Andrews, "A Revision of the Miocene Hominoidea from East Africa," *Bulletin of the British Museum of Natural History* (Geology) 30, no. 2 (1978): 85–224; Terry Harrison, "The Phylogenetic Relationships of the Early Catarrhine Primates: A Review of the Current Evidence," *Journal of Human Evolution* 16 (1987): 41–80.

15. Alan Walker and Mark F. Teaford, "The Hunt for Proconsul," *Scientific American* 260 (1989): 76–82.

16. Michael D. Rose, "Miocene Hominoid Postcranial Morphology: Monkey-Like, Ape-Like, Neither, or Both?" in Russel L. Ciochon and Robert S. Corruc-

cini, eds., *New Interpretations of Ape and Human Ancestry* (New York: Plenum, 1983), pp. 405–417; Alan C. Walker and Martin Pickford, "New Postcranial Fossils of *Proconsul Africanus* and *Proconsul Nyanzae*," in Russel L. Ciochon and Robert S. Corruccini, eds., *New Interpretations of Ape and Human Ancestry* (New York: Plenum, 1983), pp. 325–351.

17. K. Christopher Beard, Mark F. Teaford, and Alan Walker, "New Wrist Bones of *Proconsul Africanus* and *Proconsul Nyanzae* from Rusinga Island, Kenya," *Folia Primatologica* 47 (1986): 97–118; Michael D. Rose, "Kinematics of the Trapezium-1st Metacarpal Joint in Extant Anthropoids and Miocene Hominoids," *Journal of Human Evolution* 22 (1992): 255–266; David R. Begun, Mark F. Teaford, and Alan Walker, "Comparative and Functional Anatomy of *Proconsul* Phalanges from the Kaswanga Primate Site, Rusinga Island, Kenya," *Journal of Human Evolution* 26 (1994): 89–165.

18. Carol V. Ward, Alan Walker, Mark Teaford, and Isiah Odhiambo, "A Partial Skeleton of *Proconsul Nyanzae* from Mfangano Island, Kenya," *American Journal of Physical Anthropology* 90 (1993): 77–111; Begun, Teaford, and Walker, "Comparative and Functional Anatomy of *Proconsul* Phalanges from the Kaswanga Primate Site, Rusinga Island, Kenya. "

19. Carol V. Ward, Alan Walker, and Mark Teaford, "*Proconsul* Did Not Have a Tail," *Journal of Human Evolution* 21 (1991): 215–220.

20. Peter Andrews and Lawrence Martin, "Hominoid Dietary Evolution," *Philosophical Transactions of the Royal Society of London* B 334 (1991): 199–209.

21. Mark F. Teaford and Alan Walker, "Quantitative Differences in the Dental Microwear between Primates with Different Diets and a Comment on the Presumed Diet of Sivapithecus," *American Journal of Physical Anthropology* 64 (1984): 191–200.

22. W. E. Le Gros Clark and Louis S. B. Leakey, "The Miocene Hominoidea of East Africa," in *Fossil Mammals of Africa* (London: The British Museum of Natural History, 1951); Walker and Pickford, "New Postcranial Fossils of *Proconsul Africanus* and *Proconsul Nyanzae*"; Dean Falk, "A Reconsideration of the Endocast of *Proconsul Africanus*: Implications for Primate Brain Evolution," in Russel L. Ciochon and Robert S. Corruccini, eds., *New Interpretations of Ape and Human Ancestry* (New York: Plenum, 1983), pp. 239–248; Alan Walker, Dean Falk, Richard Smith, and Martin Pickford, "The Skull of *Proconsul Africanus*: Reconstruction and Cranial Capacity," *Nature* (October 6, 1983): 525–527.

23. Richard E. F. Leakey, Meave G. Leakey, and Alan Walker, "Morphology of *Afropithecus Turkanensis* from Kenya," *American Journal of Physical Anthropology* 76 (1988): 289–307; Richard E. F. Leakey, Meave G. Leakey, and Alan Walker, "Morphology of *Turkanopithecus Kalakolensis* from Kenya," *American Journal of Physical Anthropology* 76 (1988): 277–288; Richard E. F. Leakey and Meave G. Leakey, "A New

Miocene Small-Bodied Ape from Kenya," *Journal of Human Evolution* 16 (1989): 369–387.

24. Peter J. Andrews and Lawrence Martin, "The Phyletic Position of the Ad Dabtiyah Hominoid," *Bulletin of the British Museum of Natural History* 41 (1987): 383–393.

25. Leakey and Leakey, "A New Miocene Small-Bodied Ape from Kenya"; Michael D. Rose, Meave G. Leakey, Richard E. F. Leakey, and Alan C. Walker, "Postcranial Specimens of *Simiolus Enjiessi* and Other Primitive Catarrhines from the Early Miocene of Lake Turkana, Kenya," *Journal of Human Evolution* 22 (1992): 171–237.

26. Leakey, Leakey, and Walker, "Morphology of *Turkanopithecus Kalakolensis* from Kenya."

27. Elwyn L. Simons, "New Fossil Apes from Egypt and the Initial Differentiation of Hominoidea," *Nature* 205 (1965): 135–139; John G. Fleagle and Richard F. Kay, "New Interpretations of the Phyletic Position of Oligocene Hominoids," in Russel L. Ciochon and Robert S. Corruccini, eds., *New Interpretations of Ape and Human Ancestry* (New York: Plenum, 1983), pp. 181–210.

28. Leakey, Leakey, and Walker, "Morphology of *Afropithecus Turkanensis* from Kenya"; Meave G. Leakey, Richard E. F. Leakey, Joan T. Richtsmeier, Elwyn L. Simons, and Alan Walker, "Similarities in *Aegyptopithecus* and *Afropithecus* Facial Morphology," *Folia Primatologica* 56 (1991): 65–85.

29. Andrews and Martin, "Hominoid Dietary Evolution."

30. Carol V. Ward, "Torso Morphology and Locomotion in *Proconsul Nyanzae*," *American Journal of Physical Anthropology* 92 (1993): 291–328.

31. Raymond L. Bernor, Lawrence J. Flynn, Terry Harrison, S. Taseer Hussain, and Jay Kelley, "*Dionysopithecus* from Southern Pakistan and the Biochronology and Biogeography of Early Eurasian Catarrhines," *Journal of Human Evolution* 17 (1988): 339–358.

32. Monte L. McCrossin and Brenda R. Benefit, "Recently Recovered *Kenyapithecus* Mandible and Its Implications for Great Ape and Human Origins," *Proc. National Academy of Science* 90 (1993): 1962–1966.

33. Louis S. B. Leakey, "A New Lower Pliocene Fossil Primate from Kenya," *Annual Magazine of Natural History* 13 (1962): 689–696.
34. Brenda R. Benefit and Monte L. McCrossin, "New *Kenyapithecus* Postcrania and other Primate Fossils from Maboko Island, Kenya," *American Journal of Physical Anthropology Supplement* 16 (1993): 55.

35. H. Ishida, M. Pickford, H. Nakaya, and Y. Nakano, "Fossil Anthropoids from Nachola and Samburu Hills, Samburu District, Northern Kenya," *African Study Monographs Supplementary Issue* 2 (1984): 73–85.

36. David R. Begun, "Phyletic Diversity and Locomotion in Primitive European Hominids," *American Journal of Physical Anthropology* 87 (1992): 311–340;

Berna Alpagut, Peter Andrews, and Lawrence Martin, "New Miocene Hominoid Specimens from the Middle Miocene Site at Pa-alar," *Journal of Human Evolution* 19 (1990): 397–422; Peter Andrews and Hans Tobien, "New Miocene Locality in Turkey with Evidence on the Origin of *Ramapithecus* and *Sivapithecus*," *Nature* 268 (1977): 699–701.

37. O. Abel, "Zwei neue menschenaffen aus den leithakalkbildungen des Wiener Bekkens," *Sitzungsberichte der Akademie der Wissenschaften Wien, mathematisch-naturwissenschaftliche Klasse III, Abteilung 1* (1902): 1171–1207; Begun, "Phyletic Diversity and Locomotion in Primitive European Hominids."

38. Rose, "Miocene Hominoid Postcranial Morphology: Monkey-Like, Ape-Like, Neither, or Both?"; Michael D. Rose, "Another Look at the Anthropoid Elbow," *Journal of Human Evolution* 17 (1983): 193–224; Begun, "Phyletic Diversity and Locomotion in Primitive European Hominids."

39. Ward, Walker, and Teaford, "*Proconsul* Did Not Have a Tail."

40. D. Allbrook and William W. Bishop, "New Fossil Hominoid Material from Uganda," *Nature* 197 (1963): 1187–1190; William W. Bishop, J. A. Miller, and F. J. Fitch, "New Potassium-Argon Age Determinations Relevant to the Miocene Fossil Mammal Sequence in East Africa," *American Journal of Science* 267 (1969): 669–699.

41. Ward, "Torso Morphology and Locomotion in *Proconsul Nyanzae*."

42. Jay Kelley and David Pilbeam, "The Dryopithecines: Taxonomy, Comparative Anatomy, and Phylogeny of Miocene Large Hominoids," in Daris R. Swindler and J. Erwin, eds., *Comparative Primate Biology, vol. 1: Systematics, Evolution, and Anatomy* (New York: Alan R. Liss, 1986), pp. 361–411.

43. David R. Pilbeam, "New Hominoid Skull Material from the Miocene of Pakistan," *Nature* 295 (1982): 232–234.

44. Leonard O. Greenfield, "On the Adaptive Pattern of *Ramapithecus*," *American Journal of Physical Anthropology* 50 (1979): 527–548.

45. David R. Begun, "Miocene Fossil Hominids and the Chimp-Human Clade," *Science* 257 (1992): 1929–1933.

46. Louis de Bonis and George Koufos, "The Face and Mandible of Ouranopithecus Macedoniensis: Description of New Specimens and Comparisons," *Journal of Human Evolution* 24 (1993): 469–491.

47. David Dean and Eric Delson, "Second Gorilla or Third Chimp?" *Nature* 359 (1992): 676–677.

48. Rose, "Miocene Hominoid Postcranial Morphology: Monkey-Like, Ape-Like, Neither, or Both?"; Rose, "Another Look at the Anthropoid Elbow"; Mary E. Morbeck, "Miocene Hominoid Discoveries from Rudabánya: Implications from the Postcranial Skeleton," in Russel L. Ciochon and Robert S. Corruccini,

eds., *New Interpretations of Ape and Human Ancestry* (New York: Plenum, 1983), pp. 369–404; Begun, "Phyletic Diversity and Locomotion in Primitive European Hominids."

49. Begun, "Phyletic Diversity and Locomotion in Primitive European Hominids."

50. David R. Pilbeam, Michael D. Rose, John C. Barry, and S. M. I. Shah, "New *Sivapithecus Humeri* from Pakistan and the Relationship of Sivapithecus and Pongo," *Nature* 348 (1990): 237–239.

51. Glenn C. Conroy, Martin Pickford, Brigitte Senut, and John Van Couvering," *Otavipithecus Namibiensis,* First Miocene Hominoid from Southern Africa," *Nature* 356 (1992): 144–148; Glenn C. Conroy, Martin Pickford, Brigitte Senut, and Pierre Mein, "Additional Miocene Primates from the Otavi Mountains, Namibia," *Comptes Rendus de l'Academie de Science Paris Serie II* 317 (1993): 987–990.

52. Terry Harrison, "A Reassessment of the Phylogenetic Relationships of *Oreopithecus Bambolii,*" *Journal of Human Evolution* 15 (1987): 541–583; Fredrick Szalay and Eric Delson, *Evolutionary History of the Primates* (New York: Academic Press, 1979).

53. Terry Harrison, "New Estimates of Cranial Capacity, Body Size, and Encephalization in *Oreopithecus Bambolii,*" *American Journal of Physical Anthropology* 78 (1989): 237.

54. Estaban E. Sarmiento, "The Phylogenetic Position of Oreopithecus and Its Significance in the Origin of the Hominoidea," *American Museum Novitates* 2881 (1987): 1–44.

55. R. Wu, "A Revision of the Classification of the Lufeng Great Apes," *Acta Anthropologica Sinica* 6 (1987): 265–271.

56. Yipu Lin, Shangzun Wang, Zhihui Gao, and Lidai Zhang, "The First Discovery of the Radius of *Sivapithecus Lufengensis* in China," *Geological Review* 33 (1977): 1–4.

57. Kelley and Pilbeam, "The Dryopithecines: Taxonomy, Comparative Anatomy, and Phylogeny of Miocene Large Hominoids."

58. Jeffery H. Schwartz, "*Lufengpithecus* and Its Potential Relationship to an Orang-Utan Clade," *Journal of Human Evolution* 19 (1990): 591–605.

59. Brooks and McClennan, *Phylogeny, Ecology, and Behavior*; Wiley, Siegel-Causey, Brooks, Funk, *The Compleat Cladist: A Primer of Phylogenetic Procedures.*

60. Hennig, *Phylogenetic Systematics.*

61. Peter Andrews, "Evolution and Environment in the Hominoidea," *Nature* 360 (1992): 641–646.

62. Tim White, Gen Sowa, and Berhane Asfaw, "*Australopithecus ramidus,* a New Species of Early Hominid from Aramis, Ethiopia," *Nature* 375 (1995): 88.

Suggested Readings

Andrews, Peter. "A Revision of the Miocene Hominoidea from East Africa." *Bulletin of the British Museum of Natural History* (Geology) 30, no. 2 (1978): 85–224. The most recent and comprehensive revision of the early Miocene Hominoidea. Now substantially out of date in details of taxonomy, it remains a very useful reference for early Miocene hominoid anatomy and diversity.

Andrews, Peter. "Evolution and Environment in the Hominoidea." *Nature* 360 (1992): 641–646. A very recent summary and synthesis by one of the leading authorities in Miocene hominoid studies. One of several recent papers presenting different views of the Miocene.

Begun, David R. "Relations among the Great Apes and Humans: New Interpretations Based on the Fossil Great Ape *Dryopithecus.*" *Yearbook of Physical Anthropology* 37. A recent interpretation of the relations among Miocene and recent hominoids.

Harrison, Terry. "The Phylogenetic Relationships of the Early Catarrhine Primates: A Review of the Current Evidence." *Journal of Human Evolution* 16 (1987): 41–80. A recent and comprehensive summary and synthesis of relations among early Miocene apes.

Kelley, Jay, and David Pilbeam. "The *Dryopithecines*: Taxonomy, Comparative Anatomy, and Phylogeny of Miocene Large Hominoids." In Daris R. Swindler and J. Erwin, eds. *Comparative Primate Biology, vol. 1: Systematics, Evolution, and Anatomy.* New York: Alan R. Liss, 1986, pp. 361–411. A recent survey of large Miocene hominoids, with particular attention focussed on *Sivapithecus.*

Walker, Alan, and Mark F. Teaford, "The Hunt for *Proconsul.*" *Scientific American* 260 (1989): 76–82. A different interpretation of the relations of *Proconsul,* with interesting details of the behavior and biology of this fossil form.

Australopithecus afarensis and Human Evolution

Scott W. Simpson

The two-day drive from Addis Ababa, the capital of Ethiopia, to our field site near the Awash River had left me dusty and tired. The second day began well enough. Just after dawn we reached the western rim of the East African rift. The view from the edge of this massive rip in the earth is extraordinary. At the bottom, two thousand meters below, the barren badlands of the Afar depression stretch away into the haze.

It is difficult to work in the Afar depression. Because the sun always shines in the Ethiopian rift, it can get hot—very hot. Except for the sluggish Awash River, there are no permanent sources of water. We get our water from shallow wells dug in the dry river beds. Despite purification, the drinking water is usually cloudy. Unappealing, but in this treeless desert the tepid dun-colored water is refreshing. Despite these difficulties, we return to this part of the Ethiopian desert year after year because these arid deposits contain fossilized animal bones that provide direct evidence of terrestrial faunal evolution during the Pliocene (5.2 to 1.8 million years ago [mya]) and Pleistocene (1.8 mya to 10,000 ya) epochs. Entombed in the ancient clays, sands, and gravels of the Afar depression are the fossilized bones of innumerable animals. Many hours are spent each day walking across the sediments, examining the thousands of bones and teeth of extinct animals that litter the surface. The dusty landscape and glaring sunlight quickly cause a permanent squint and a bad attitude. After each long day of searching, every new fossil has to be examined and its location carefully recorded. Although most fossils are from long-extinct antelopes, elephants, pigs, monkeys, hippos, and crocodiles, the next one could be an early human ancestor. Finding an ancient hominid fossil produces immediate eupho-

ria. The heat, frustration, bone-jarring rides, and sore feet are all instantly forgotten. Without delay, the sight of a possible human ancestor causes everyone to drop to the searingly hot ground and begin crawling around looking for more. Each little piece of fossilized bone is a rare and important link to the past—a clue that can help answer fundamental questions about our own biological evolution.

Our Family: Apes, Hominids, and Humans

The living African apes, which include humans, chimpanzees, and gorillas, are part of a common evolutionary radiation that began in the Miocene (23.5 to 5.2 mya) epoch. Hominids are upright walking, or bipedal,[1] apes that include humans and our extinct relatives. Anatomically and behaviorally, humans (*Homo sapiens*), chimpanzees (*Pan troglodytes* and *Pan paniscus*), and gorillas (*Gorilla gorilla*) share many common features, such as the absence of an external tail, a conical trunk with shoulder joints that face sideways, absolutely and relatively massive brains allowing greater behavioral complexity and plasticity, prolonged periods of development (including gestation, infancy, adolescence), and single births that are infrequent. If we compare the biochemistry of the different ape species, the similarities among them are even more striking. Modern humans and common chimpanzees, our closest relatives, share approximately 98.5 percent of their nonrepeating DNA (DeoxyriboNucleic Acid).

Even a cursory examination reveals marked morphological differences between humans and the other African apes. Modern humans are large-brained, erect-walking, small-toothed, tool-using apes. Our hair is less pronounced (although no less dense) and we communicate via symbolically based talking and gesturing. African apes have smaller brains and larger canine teeth, are well adapted to tree climbing, and are limited in distribution to the forests and woodlands of equatorial Africa. These differences raise some extremely interesting questions. First, when did the human lineage arise, and second, when and in what sequence did the unique specializations found in modern humans occur?

Researchers use biochemical and anatomical data to answer these questions. Biochemists can study and compare the chemical composition (especially DNA) of living species. Anatomists can examine and compare the shape, function, and development of anatomical structures (bones, teeth, muscles, etc.) in living and extinct animals. Using these two approaches, we can estimate the time when two species separated and reconstruct their evolutionary history.

Despite their morphological and behavioral differences, all modern apes (which include humans) are derived from a common ancestral species, or gene pool. In other words, a now extinct species existed from which the living African apes and humans both descended. Following the separation of these chimpanzee and human lineages, each species continued to evolve and adapt to its environment. Although many of the anatomical differences that distinguish these lineages (including bipedal walking and larger brains in humans) are products of natural selection, other genetic changes have accumulated that have no apparent anatomical counterpart.

Such spontaneous changes are due to silent mutations in the DNA of both lineages. Biochemists can measure the chemical difference between species produced by such mutations. The closer the biochemical similarity between different lineages, the more recent their shared common ancestor. If we measure the degree of biochemical difference produced by mutations in the DNA between species and combine it with an estimate of the mutation rate, the time of the speciation event can be calculated. Current research suggests that hominids became a genetically distinct lineage separated from other African apes approximately five to eight mya.

Explaining why morphological changes occurred in the human lineage seems more interesting to me. Anatomical changes are not random. Bipedalism is not a historical accident. Large brains didn't just happen. These adaptations are the products of natural selection. This means that individuals who displayed brain enlargement or bipedal walking produced more offspring who survived to maturity than individuals who did not. Adaptations can allow individuals to obtain food more successfully, reduce risk from predation, gain and maintain reproductive opportunities, or somehow enhance the survivorship of their offspring. Ultimately, these anatomical changes are always an adaptive response resulting in the production of more babies that survive to adulthood.

Finding Our Ancestors: Hominid Paleontology in Africa
Primitive Hominids from South Africa

To understand changes in functional anatomy, we must learn in which order these anatomical modifications occurred and understand their ecological context. The only way paleoanthropologists can reconstruct the timing and sequence of morphological change in hominids is by analysis of the fossil record. The first primitive hominid fossil was reported by Raymond Dart in 1925.[2] A juvenile skull with associated endocast[3] was recovered from the Taung lime mine in South Africa. The Taung skull, now known to be over two million years old, allowed Dart to define a new primitive hominid genus and species named *Australopithecus africanus*.[4] Although the phylogenetic position of this small-brained, erect-walking hominid as a human relative was vigorously debated, fossil discoveries from the South African cave sites of Sterkfontein and Makapansgat during the next three decades vindicated Dart and proved the validity of the species *A. africanus*. Meanwhile, Robert Broom was discovering fossils of a different hominid species from the South African limestone cave sites of Swartkrans and Kromdraai. Unlike *A. africanus*, this new collection of fossils had larger molar and premolar teeth, smaller canines and incisors,[5] a flatter or less projecting face, and a longitudinal ridge of bone along the top of the skull known as a sagittal crest.[6] Clearly these fossils represented a species different from *A. africanus*. Although they were initially attributed to several different species, they are now included within a single taxon, *Australopithecus robustus* (although some anthropologists contend that these fossils should be named *Paranthropus robustus*). Whatever these extinct species are called, they existed during the late Pliocene and early Pleistocene in South Africa with *A. africanus* (2.8 to 2.2 mya), living earlier than and perhaps giving rise to *A. robustus* (1.8 to 1.0 mya). Anatomically, both species were small-brained (420 cc to 550 cc, which is slightly larger than the brain of a living chimpanzee or gorilla, but only about 40 percent the size of the brain of a modern human), and their molar and premolar teeth were unlike those of both modern humans and apes. For their body size, these species had very large postcanine teeth covered by thick enamel caps. Like the teeth of modern humans, the australopithecine canine teeth were small and very different from the large projecting canines of the other apes. Analysis of their fossilized pelves, lower limbs, and vertebrae demonstrate that both species walked upright on two legs, as do modern humans. Phylogenetically, *A. robustus* is our cousin. They apparently diverged from the lineage that includes modern humans sometime before two mya. Their unique and specialized cranial and dental anatomy makes them an unlikely human ancestor. This evolutionary experiment among hominids became extinct about one million years ago.[7]

THE HOMINIDS OF EAST AFRICA

In 1959 Mary and Louis Leakey discovered a remarkable hominid fossil from early Pleistocene lake margin deposits at Olduvai Gorge in Tanzania.[8] The cranium, known as OH 5 (Olduvai Hominid specimen #5) and dated to approximately 1.8 mya, is now attributed to the species *Australopithecus boisei* (or *Paranthropus boisei*). This specimen and others recovered from Olduvai Gorge, Peninj in Tanzania and around Lake Turkana in Kenya and Ethiopia are best described as extreme versions of the South African *A. robustus*. Similar to the southern species, *A. boisei* had a small brain, a sagittal crest, a flattened face, and large postcanine and small anterior teeth. However, the sagittal crest and molar teeth were larger than, and the canines and incisors were smaller than, those of their South African contemporaries. At approximately the same time (1.8 to 1.0 mya), the two large-toothed, flatfaced species lived thousands of miles apart yet shared many similar adaptations in their skulls and teeth.

In the early 1960s the Leakeys found other early Pleistocene hominid fossils at Olduvai Gorge that were unlike the large-toothed, crested *A. boisei*. Instead, these fossils had smaller molars and premolars and larger brains (greater than six hundred cc). Here was the first good evidence in East Africa of two very different hominid species living at the same place and time. But what was this other, more gracile hominid? Louis Leakey, along with South African anatomist Phillip Tobias and British anatomist John Napier, concluded that these fossils should be attributed to a new species, which they named *Homo habilis*, and which they suggested was ancestral to modern humans.[9] Here was the oldest evidence of the genus *Homo* and it coexisted with the larger-toothed robust australopithecines. Despite these differences, however, both were hominids, meaning they must have shared

a unique common ancestor since their ancestral lineages separated from the African apes.

But what was the common stem hominid from which all subsequent hominids are derived? The only other possible candidate known was *A. africanus*. It had the advantage of being older than both of the East African lineages and it appeared to have a more generalized morphology from which both could arise. However, two problems prevented universal acceptance of *A. africanus* as the last common ancestor (LCA) of all subsequent hominids. First, paleoanthropologists were divided on the phyletic position of *A. africanus*. Some proposed that it was ancestral only to the genus *Homo*, whereas others contended that it was uniquely related to the robust australopithecines. Second, no older (>2.2 mya) fossil material had been recovered from East Africa that could unequivocally be assigned to *A. africanus*. Where was the East African hominid LCA?

HOMINID PALEONTOLOGY IN ETHIOPIA: OMO AND HADAR

One group that worked to resolve this problem was the Omo Research Expedition. This international cooperative effort, led by the American Clark Howell, Camille Arambourg and Yves Coppens of France, and Kenyan Richard Leakey, collected many hominid fossils from the four to one myo (million-year-old) sedimentary deposits along the Omo River in southern Ethiopia.[10] In deposits more recent than 2.5 million years of age, at least two hominid lineages were present, and these were a larger-brained *Homo* and a large-molared robust australopithecine. But in sediments older than 2.5 million years, only one type of hominid was identified. The older sediments (>2.5 mya) from the Usno and Shungura Formations at Omo yielded dozens of isolated hominid teeth but few other skeletal elements. Although these dental remains bore similarities to *Australopithecus africanus*, the unspecialized, primitive nature of these new fossils suggested to Howell and Coppens that the specimens may belong to a new species, perhaps ancestral to all later hominids.[11] Unfortunately, the fragmentary condition of the fossils prevented resolution of the problem.

In the late 1960s Maurice Taieb, a French geologist conducting research for his dissertation on the geologic history of the Awash River in the Ethiopian rift, mapped and surveyed a large basin in the north central portion of the country known as the Afar depression. This area, among the hottest and driest on earth, is a large (~two hundred thousand km^2 or ~seventy-eight thousand mi^2) triangular region where three rifting systems intersect. Three large land masses (East

Africa, Africa, and Saudi Arabia) have been slowly moving away from one another for the last twenty or so million years, and the point from which they are diverging is the Afar triangle. It is a low area extending from 700 m above sea level to about 120 m below sea level. During his geological survey, Taieb noticed that in places the ground was extensively littered with fossils. Subsequently, he was introduced to Donald C. Johanson, who agreed to assist in a reconnaissance survey to evaluate the potential of the area for hominid fossils. In 1972 they explored an area along the Awash River known as Hadar. It was a hominid paleontologist's dream. There were expansive, fossiliferous deposits dated to the crucial period of 2.8 and 3.4 mya. The fossils were entombed in sands and clays deposited by the streams, rivers, and lakes present in the Ethiopian rift during the middle Pliocene.[12] This continuous deposition built a layer-cake of sediments, retaining a record of the plants and animals that lived and died along those wooded lake, swamp, and river margins.

Equally significant to our understanding of the fossils is their geologic context. The East African rift system is volcanically active. Fallout from the many volcanic eruptions becomes incorporated into the sediments. If the eruptions are large, they can form distinct layers in the sediments, known as tuffs. Such tuffs have a characteristic chemical "signature" and also contain unstable (radioactive) isotopes. The unique chemical composition of the tuffs allows geologists to match tuff layers from widely separated localities. Tuffs with the same elemental makeup must have been produced from the same eruption; therefore, the sediments surrounding them must be of similar age. If the crystals in the tuffs have not been too badly weathered, geochemists can estimate their age based on the geochemistry of isotope decay. Isotopes are elemental variants that can decay from an unstable state to a stable state at a known and constant rate. Therefore, the amount of the daughter product (the result of the decay process) depends on the age of the sample. The older the crystals, the greater the accumulation of the stable daughter isotopes. By measuring the ratio of parent to daughter elements, the age of the crystals can be calculated quite accurately.

Hadar, Laetoli, and the Discovery of *Australopithecus afarensis*

Following the initial survey of the area, Johanson and Taieb, now joined by Yves Coppens and Jon Kalb, formed the IARE (International Afar Research Expedition) and initiated a long-term multidisciplinary

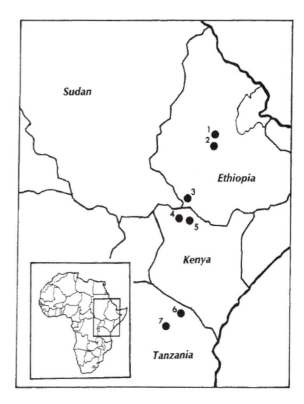

Figure 1
Location of Sites Discussed in Text

1 = Hadar; 2 = Middle Awash; 3 = Omo;
4 = East Rudolf; 5 = West Turkana;
6 = Olduvai Gorge; 7 = Laetoli

research project focusing on the middle Pliocene deposits at Hadar. The group was very lucky. They soon discovered the oldest hominid species, *Australopithecus afarensis*. Hadar is a rich paleontological locality, and their collections of hominid fossils were extraordinary, forcing anthropologists to rethink early hominid evolution. Remarkable hominid fossils were found in each of the first three field seasons (1973–1975). In 1973 they found a hominid knee joint. Despite its great antiquity and extremely small size (smaller than that of a modern human), its bony anatomy clearly showed that it was fully adapted to bipedal walking.

During the 1974 field season at Hadar, Johanson and field assistant Tom Gray discovered what is one of the most extraordinary specimens ever found in hominid paleontology. We know the fossil as "Lucy" (named after the Beatles song "Lucy in the Sky with Diamonds"); more formally, it is known as specimen AL 2881.[13] This number means that Lucy was the first fossil found at the 288th fossiliferous outcrop discovered in the Afar Locality (Hadar). Although other beautifully preserved hominid fossils were also found that year, the quality of Lucy overshadowed the rest. Most fossils are small, battered fragments of teeth and mandibles, with each fragment generally from a separate individual. In contrast, about 40 percent of Lucy's skeleton was found, including her left os coxa (hip bone); sacrum; left femur; portions of her lower leg and foot, including the three bones that comprise the ankle joint; some vertebral fragments; upper limb elements, including portions of the scapula, clavicle, right and left humeri, ulnae, and radii; and some hand bones. Although only a few parts of her cranium were recovered, the associated mandible (jaw bone) was nearly complete. Lucy is an important fossil because her completeness allows anthropologists to study the relationships between the size and shape of structures within a single individual. We can now estimate stature, study the functional anatomy of joints (hip, knee, ankle, shoulder, elbow, wrist), and calculate limb proportions from this 3.2 myo hominid.

In 1975 Hadar revealed its greatest treasure. Site 333, a thin clay deposit, contained over 130 hominid fossils representing at least 13 individuals. The collection includes the remains of very young to very old individuals, and it also spans a broad range of adult size from small (Lucy-sized) to large. Now we could study growth, development, and populational variation in this extinct species.

In all, the five field seasons at Hadar produced more than 250 hominid fossils representing dozens of different individuals sampling a period between 3.0 and 3.4 mya. The upright walking species at Hadar is characterized by a small brain volume (300 to 450cc), canine teeth larger than those of all other hominids but markedly smaller than those of any living ape, and a body mass between 25 and 55 kilograms (55 to 125 pounds). The Pliocene habitat at Hadar showed that these early human ancestors lived in a diverse environment that varied from open to closed woodlands near a permanent source of water.

But Hadar was not the only middle Pliocene site yielding hominid fossils. At the same time, Mary Leakey and colleagues were collecting hominid fossils from the 3.6 myo sediments at Laetoli in northern Tanzania. Laetoli was first surveyed in the mid-1930s by Mary and Louis Leakey and later collected by L. Kohl-Larsen. Although primitive hominid fossils were recovered during this preliminary work, they were either ignored or misidentified. Research began anew at Laetoli in the mid-through late-1970s, and approximately two dozen hominid specimens were recovered from sediments deposited in an arid upland savanna

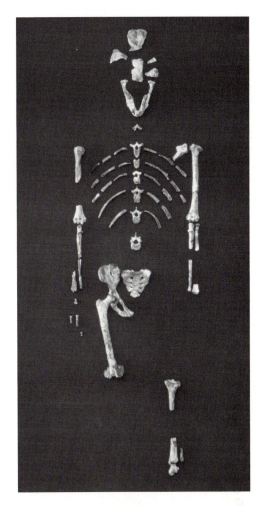

Figure 2
"Lucy" (AL 288-1)

Hadar, 1974. Cleveland Museum of Natural History.

environment. The collection of primitive hominid fossils includes portions of a juvenile mandible (LH 2 [LH-Laetoli Hominid specimen #2]), an adult mandible (LH 4), and an incomplete and fragmentary juvenile skeleton (LH 21).[14]

Are the fossil collections of Laetoli and Hadar related? Fortunately, one of Mary Leakey's assistants at Laetoli was paleoanthropologist Tim White. Because of his intimate familiarity with the Laetoli hominids, when shown the Hadar fossils White recognized that the Laetoli and Hadar hominids, although separated by approximately 300,000 years and 1,500 kilometers (1,000 miles), represented the same species. Johanson, who earlier suggested that the Hadar material represented two species,[15] was soon convinced that both sites sampled a single hominid species. Following their analysis of the material from

Hadar and a comparison with other early hominid fossils, Johanson, White, and Coppens announced in 1978 that these fossils represented a new hominid species named *Australopithecus afarensis*.[16] Not only was *A. afarensis* the earliest hominid species yet discovered, but also they concluded that it was ancestral to all other hominid species, including the other australopithecines (*A. africanus*, *A. robustus*, and *A. boisei*) and the *Homo* lineage. This simple conclusion has immense taxonomic and phylogenetic implications that continue to provoke intense debate (summarized in note 7).

Analysis and Interpretation

Taxonomy and phylogeny aside, what did these early hominids do? What information about the biology of this extinct species can the fossils from Hadar and Laetoli tell us? What did they eat? Can their reproductive and social behaviors be reconstructed? Although paleoanthropologists address these and other questions, we will focus on just two. First, do the fossil remains from Hadar and Laetoli represent only a single species? After all, at many other sites, multiple hominid taxa are present. Second, how did Lucy and her conspecifics walk?

Morphological Variation: How Many Species at Hadar?

Let's start with the number of species represented by the fossils from Hadar and Laetoli. Although Johanson and White concluded that these materials represent a single species, other researchers suggested that the amount of morphological variation found in this collection was too great for a single species and that the Hadar and Laetoli fossils sample two or more contemporaneous hominid species. How can we resolve this problem? First, we must learn why variation is a necessary prerequisite of evolution. Second, we have to be familiar with the factors that contribute to the amount of variation in living and fossil ape species.

Variety in form and behavior is a crucial element of evolution. We live with anatomical variation every day. How else do we distinguish among people? When I teach human anatomy to medical students, every group complains during dissection that the muscles, arteries, and nerves in their cadaver look different from the pictures and descriptions in anatomy texts. Why? Because no two humans are morphologically identical. We are all variations on a common theme. All humans have the same bones, muscles,

nerves, organs, and so forth, but their size, shape, and relationships differ. Most variation is a natural consequence of sexually reproducing organisms. Without variation, evolution by natural selection could not occur. Because no two individuals are behaviorally or anatomically identical, not all individuals are equally adapted to their environment. Some will have a slight edge. This advantage allows them to produce more offspring who survive to maturity. What initially was a rare or uncommon anatomical advantage may, over time, become prevalent in a species. This is evolution by natural selection. Not all diversity, however, affects our fitness, and some variation may be selectively neutral. Other factors contribute to the amount of variation in a population—age composition of the sample, for instance. Obviously, you look different today than when you were a child or than you will in twenty years. A fossil collection sampling a diversity of ages will appear heterogeneous.

Sex differences in morphology (sexual dimorphism) are another source of variation. Male and female humans do not look the same. Although the sexes differ in their primary reproductive roles and this is reflected in our reproductive anatomy, sexual dimorphism generally describes those anatomical differences associated with gaining access to and retaining a mate. In African apes (including hominids), males are generally larger than females. Male gorillas can weigh twice as much (or more) than a female. Male gorillas also look different from females. As the males mature, the normally black hair on their backs becomes gray or silver colored. This does not occur in females. Males also have much larger canine teeth than do females, and develop sagittal crests. Chimpanzee males are approximately the same stature as females but they weigh about 15 percent more. Except for this difference in muscle mass and noticeably larger canine teeth, male and female chimps look pretty much the same. Humans are very sexually dimorphic. Human males are taller, weigh more, and have a different distribution of fat and hair than do females. From available fossil evidence it appears that australopithecine males also were larger than females, to a greater degree than modern humans. Therefore, when estimating size variation from fossils, researchers must consider age variation, sexual dimorphism, and natural variety as contributing factors to the morphological heterogeneity in *Australopithecus afarensis*.

As informative as one fossil can be, numerous anatomical specimens are necessary to understand the scope of normal biological variation. In paleontological studies the fossil evidence for extinct animals is usually fragmentary. It cannot provide a complete picture of the biology and behavior of the long dead animals. In historical studies we must begin with what can be observed directly and only then extrapolate to the unknown. Therefore, anthropologists must be familiar with anatomy and its variation in humans and African apes. Fortunately, Don Johanson served as curator of the Laboratory of Physical Anthropology at the Cleveland Museum of Natural History (CMNH) in Cleveland, Ohio, when he addressed the species question at Hadar. The CMNH houses the Hamann-Todd osteological collection, which contains over three thousand well-documented (age, sex, cause of death, race) human skeletons and the largest collection of chimpanzee and gorilla skeletons in the world. These extensive collections provide direct evidence of the normal range of variation in living species.

Johanson and White, with their extensive experience in human and ape musculoskeletal variation, were well aware of the amount of normal variation that could be found in temporally diverse anatomical collections. The *A. afarensis* fossils represent a population of individuals that spanned more than six hundred thousand years in an ecologically dynamic habitat. Considering the above discussion, it is not unexpected that the Hadar and Laetoli fossils, although belonging to a single species, were not morphologically homogeneous.[17]

The first time I saw the Hadar fossils at the Ethiopian National Museum in Addis Ababa, I was impressed by the great range of size and shape of the specimens. Lucy's femur is much smaller than the largest femur from Hadar. Is this too much variation for a single species? First impressions suggest it is, but scientists must always question their initial assessments. Lucy is the centerpiece of the collection. Because of her completeness, she figures prominently in any comparison. However, with a height of only 1.1 meters, she is one of the smallest hominids ever discovered. Therefore, any comparison involving Lucy must take her short stature into account. The large proximal femur (AL 333-3) is also well preserved and is among the largest individuals from Hadar. It is natural to pick up the best preserved fossils to make a comparison (i.e., Lucy and AL 333-3), while ignoring the other more fragmentary, banged-up fossils. Quite simply, our natural bias toward the nicest specimens from Hadar causes us to compare the extremes in size. Any comparison that involves the largest and smallest individuals will necessarily overestimate the degree of size variation in a species. However, when all of the proximal femora from Hadar are examined, a continuum of small to large is seen with the best preserved specimens at the extremes. Independent analyses estimating sexual dimorphism by Owen Lovejoy and his colleagues and Henry McHenry[18] concluded that skeletal sexual dimorphism at Hadar only slightly exceeded that seen in modern humans. The early australopithecines were more dimorphic than chimpanzees and humans but much less so than modern gorillas and orangutans.

How Did "Lucy" Walk?

Considerable debate surrounds the manner in which *A. afarensis* moved around. Quite simply, did they walk upright on two legs like modern humans or was their locomotor pattern unlike any living species? Fortunately, we can reconstruct with some accuracy the locomotor behavior of this extinct species from their fossilized bones. Some authors suggest that the collection of fossils attributed to *A. afarensis* may represent the missing locomotor link between modern African apes and humans. Randy Susman, Jack Stern, and Bill Jungers (all of the State University of New York at Stony Brook) proposed that Lucy was anatomically adapted to both arboreal quadrupedality and terrestrial bipedality.[19] They suggest that the bipedal locomotion of *A. afarensis* was not like modern humans; Lucy and her type walked about with bent hips and knees. Not only is this an energetically expensive and uncomfortable way to get around (try it for a couple of minutes), but also it is inconsistent with the available fossil evidence. Although *A. afarensis* looked like a chimpanzee with small canines above the neck, below the neck the locomotor anatomy had evolved away from the primitive quadrupedal condition toward human-like bipedal function.[20] This species may be phyletically intermediate between humans and the ape/human LCA, but, like modern humans, it was fully adapted to terrestrial bipedality.

How do chimpanzees move around? Modern apes are among the largest arboreal animals alive today. They spend much time climbing in the canopies of trees as they feed or escape from enemies. Clearly, climbing is a major component of their daily activities and this is reflected in their anatomy. Although male gorillas rarely climb trees, they do, nevertheless, maintain the essential climbing adaptation seen in smaller apes. As you can imagine, a fall from a tree by so large an animal has severe consequences. Because even one fall can kill a large animal, selection has favored those who minimize the risk of falling by enhancing their anatomical adaptations to climbing. They display multiple anatomical specializations for climbing, reaching, and grasping. While moving about on the ground, chimps and gorillas use a unique quadrupedal locomotor style, known as knuckle-walking. When knuckle-walking, chimps and gorillas support themselves by resting their weight on the backs of their fingers. In the wild, they only infrequently walk bipedally on the ground. Apes are capable of this behavior (watch a trained chimpanzee at the circus), but it is energetically expensive for them. They do not demonstrate any anatomical adaptations to this method of progression.

What are the anatomical specializations that allow these large mammals to climb about in the trees? If we focus on the pelvis and the lower limbs in apes, we can identify several major and important morphological adaptations to arboreality, including an elongated ilium (a part of the hip bone), a stiff, inflexible trunk, a medially directed ankle joint, a mobile and abducted great toe, a flexible mid-tarsal joint in the foot, and absence of a bicondylar angle of the knee. Together, these anatomical specializations allow a large-bodied primate to climb into the highest portions of the canopy and traverse along the canopy in adjacent trees.

Many different aspects of the musculoskeletal system must be altered to evolve a terrestrial biped from an arboreal quadruped. Owen Lovejoy of Kent State University in Ohio has devoted much time to documenting these changes.[21] Bipeds, unlike quadrupeds, must support themselves on a single leg at some point during each gait cycle. To accommodate this functional shift, the musculoskeletal anatomy of the lower limb and hip must change. The human pelvis has a much shorter and laterally directed ilium. This changes the functional relationship of the gluteal musculature (muscles acting across the hip joint) and alters their role from that of extensors or thigh straighteners (as seen in other primates and quadrupeds) to that of trunk supporters or thigh abductors. Similar modifications are seen in the pelves of Lucy and in *A. africanus*. As Lovejoy and his colleagues—Jim Ohman of Johns Hopkins University and Bruce Latimer of the Cleveland Museum of Natural History (CMNH)—have noted, evidence of this muscular shift can be identified not only in the shape and external morphology of the hip and thigh bones but also in the internal bony organization of the femoral neck. Bone is a dynamic tissue that remodels (adds or removes bone, which modifies its internal or external shape) according to the direction and magnitude of the mechanical forces acting on it. Because of differences in mode of locomotion and orientation of their locomotor muscles, the way in which humans and apes transmit forces across their hip joint differs. Consequently, their bony anatomy differs as well. The

morphology of the internal bony structure and external surface topography in the proximal thigh bones of *A. afarensis* is similar to that of humans, thus suggesting that the extinct species walked bipedally like humans.

The knee of a striding biped is placed under the center of mass to support the body when walking. If you look at a standing person, you will notice that his or her hips are wider than his or her knees. Humans are knock-kneed. In contrast, the knee in quadrupeds is located directly beneath the hip joint. To verify this for yourself, notice that the thighs of a dog, cow, or gorilla, when seen from the front, are perpendicular to the ground. This angulation of the thigh in bipeds, known as the bicondylar angle, is a product of modifications in the distal end of the femur or thigh bone. Apes do not have this characteristic feature but, like all hominids, *A. afarensis* does.

The biped's foot is very different from that of a climbing ape. Bruce Latimer of the CMNH has carefully identified the many anatomical differences between apes and humans.[22] The ape foot is a grasping organ, more like our hands. In humans, the foot is best described as a propulsive lever. In apes, the big toe (hallux) is very mobile and abductable. This means that it diverges from the other toes and is not parallel to the remaining toes as in humans. Their hallux can be used for gripping and holding. To facilitate this grasping function, apes also maintain a greater amount of mobility between the ankle bones (mid-tarsal joint).

Humans propel themselves during bipedal walking by pushing against the ground. The foot, acting as a propulsive structure, is relatively rigid. This rigidity is maintained by the shapes of the tarsal (ankle) and metatarsal (foot) bones, ligaments, and muscles of the foot. When humans walk, they push off with the hallux. Apes, with the divergent, or thumb-like, position of their great toe, cannot transmit the propulsive force of walking in the same fashion as humans. Consequently, the bones of the big toe in humans, unlike those of chimpanzees but similar to those of *A. afarensis*, are large and robust. Therefore, the morphology of the bones of the foot is characteristic of and can be used to reconstruct the way animals walk. In each instance in which the function of the foot fossils from Hadar could be assessed, Latimer showed that *A. afarensis* used its foot as a propulsive lever, like humans, and not as a grasping structure like chimpanzees and gorillas.

Most quadrupedal animals use the hindlimb for propulsion or acceleration and the front limb for maneuvering and as a shock absorber. Bipeds must employ the hindlimb for all these functions. Not only must the hindlimb propel and support the body (as discussed earlier), but also the foot and leg must be adapted to absorb the repeated impacts of the foot striking the ground. Again, the anatomy reflects the function. Unlike apes, who have flat feet, humans have arched feet. Thus, not all of the sole of the foot contacts the ground during walking. This arch is maintained by both the shapes of the bones and the surrounding soft tissues. When humans walk, the arch deforms or straightens slightly. The deformations of the arches act like the shock absorbing springs in a car. They prevent the sudden jarring at impact that would ultimately lead to the deterioration of the joints and ligaments of the feet. That is why individuals with flat feet (less-developed or absent foot arches) were routinely rejected from military service. Flat-footed soldiers would soon develop painful and injured feet from the many long marches. In addition, humans and australopithecines, unlike other apes, have modified the shape and distribution of bone in their calcaneus (heel bones) to help dissipate the repeated shock of striking the ground during walking, thus preventing joint degeneration. Overall, the foot bones of A. afarensis show clearly that they had an arched foot, an adducted hallux, a less mobile mid-tarsal joint, and a human-like heel bone. The anatomy of the early hominid fossils demonstrates that A. afarensis walked bipedally.

But other data reinforce the anatomical conclusions. The site of Laetoli in Tanzania is famous for preserving a very rare and unusual fossil. Although an important series of fossilized bones was recovered there, the sediments include a 3.6-myo-volcanic tuff, which contains a series of footprint trails.[23] The ash from a volcanic eruption blanketed the savanna 3.6 million years ago, and many different animals walked, slithered, hopped, crawled, or ran across the ancient landscape that day and left their marks in the freshly deposited ash. The rain-moistened layer hardened and was soon covered by materials from another volcanic eruption, thus preserving the footprints. Unlike fossil bone collections that represent remains sampled over a very long period, these footprints represent a snapshot of just a few minutes of time. Significantly for anthropologists, three hominids, one larger and two smaller individuals, were walking across the savanna that day 3.6 mya. Interestingly, one of the smaller trails parallels the larger individual while the other small-footed individual carefully walked in the impressions left by the larger australopithecine. Does this represent a male and female walking side by side with their child following behind? Obviously, we can never know. But

the evidence for a modern human-like foot morphology and striding bipedal gait is unequivocal.

The preserved skeletal anatomy of the hip, knee, ankle, and foot (and other aspects not discussed here, i.e., upper limb, hand, vertebral column) in A. afarensis demonstrates that it was undoubtedly a terrestrial biped. In the anatomical specializations associated with locomotion found in A. afarensis, every one shows an adaptive response to upright, bipedal walking. This assessment is reinforced when the footprints from Laetoli are considered. A. afarensis, like modern humans, was behaviorally and morphologically adapted to terrestrial bipedalism. This does not mean that they could not or did not use the trees as a source of food or safety, merely that they had become adapted to life on the ground. If A. afarensis climbed the trees, they climbed them like modern humans. Why? Because they exhibit no anatomical specializations for arboreality.

The Search Continues

The search for A. afarensis continues throughout East Africa, especially in Ethiopia and Kenya. During the past fifteen years Hadar and two other areas in Ethiopia, known as Fejej and the Middle Awash, have produced fossils of A. afarensis. Fejej (pronounced Fedj-edj) is a hot, desolate area east of the Omo site in the southern part of the country. The site was originally discovered in 1989 during the Paleoanthropological Inventory organized by the Ethiopian Ministry of Culture.[24] Subsequent survey of the area by John Fleagle (SUNY at Stony Brook) and his associates yielded hominid teeth dated to about four mya.[25] Future surveys at Fejej should produce more early hominids.

The Middle Awash area, initially studied by Jon Kalb and associates during the 1970s,[26] is an extensive series of fossiliferous sediments along the Awash River about fifty kilometers (thirty-five miles) upstream (or south) of Hadar. Like Hadar, these sediments sample woodland environments associated with streams, swamps, and lakes. The Middle Awash deposits have yielded a series of cranial and postcranial remains dated to 3.4 and 3.85 mya. The first Middle Awash early hominid remains were found in 1981 by Tim White (University of California at Berkeley) and his colleagues in the adjacent dry stream drainages of Maka and Belohdelie.[27] In 1990, when fieldwork resumed, White and his fossil hunters were successful again and more 3.4 myo hominid fossils were recovered from Maka.[28] The Maka fossils, which include a mostly complete lower jaw, other mandibu-

Figure 3
AL 444-2

Hadar, 1992. Institute of Human Origins.
Photographer: Donald C. Johanson, Ph. D.

lar fragments, isolated teeth, a proximal femur, and a humerus, are morphologically similar to the Hadar and Laetoli finds yet are temporally intermediate. Berhane Asfaw, who described the 3.85 myo cranial remains from Belohdelie, concluded that they were very similar to the cranial fragments recovered from Hadar.[29] Therefore, the earliest appearance of *A. afarensis* can now be expanded by another two hundred thousand years. The Middle Awash finds serve to strengthen the links between the Hadar and Laetoli collections, extend the earliest appearance of *A. afarensis* in Ethiopia to 3.85 mya, and reinforce the idea that *A. afarensis* was a single, bipedal, widely distributed, sexually dimorphic species.[30]

Recent paleontological research at Hadar, led by Don Johanson and Bill Kimbel of the Institute of Human Origins (IHO), has continued to add more high quality fossils to the already extensive Hadar collections. Beside the usual assortment of teeth and mandibles (fifty-three new specimens discovered between 1990 and 1993) the IHO team has also recovered a partial arm and a virtually complete skull.[31] Previously, Hadar had not yielded a complete (or near complete) adult skull (cranium and mandible), but with the recovery of three myo AL 444-2 by Yoel Rak (an Israeli anatomist), that changed. This very large, presumably male, skull is a spectacular find. We can use the AL 444-2 skull to study the size and relationship between the face and the cranial vault, giving us insight into such factors as brain size and the chewing muscles in this early hominid species. Future research

at Hadar and other African sites will continue to refine our understanding of the evolution, ecology, anatomy, and behavior of this early hominid species.

In tandem with the increasing number of *A. afarensis* fossils being recovered, researchers are asking new questions, reanalyzing existing data, and using improved analytic approaches, including increasingly sophisticated biomechanical studies, computerized tomography imaging, and scanning electron microscopic studies, to examine the fossils. In addition, new techniques of aerial and satellite survey allow researchers to locate and prospect new fossiliferous areas.[32] Also, the many recent advances in geochronology give us a better understanding of the ages of the fossils we find. These new data and independent studies of previously recovered fossils and their context reinforce earlier assessments that *A. afarensis* was a single, upright-walking species that arose about four mya and lived in slightly to heavily wooded areas throughout Ethiopia, Kenya, and Tanzania for at least one million years. But so many other questions remain. What did they eat? How long did they live? What were the size and makeup of their social groups? Did they habitually make or use tools? Are bipedal locomotion and canine reduction linked together as part of an adaptive complex or did they arise independently? To date, the earliest australopithecines have been recovered only from sediments in the East African rift. Were they confined to this area or did they live outside this ecological zone? Why and when did *A. afarensis* become extinct? Did this lineage continue as the South African australopithecines, or the East African australopithecines, or as the *Homo* lineage that includes us? Clearly *A. afarensis* is an early hominid but is it the earliest hominid? Recently recovered fossils from the Aramis site in the Middle Awash suggest otherwise. With the announcement in 1994 of a new and older type of hominid, *Ardipithecus ramidus*, we have pushed back even farther the origins of our lineage to 4.4 mya and beyond.[33] Now we must search for more evidence of this newest early hominid. Unfortunately, deposits older than four mya are uncommon and only infrequently contain hominid fossils. But we will continue searching the Ethiopian badlands for our ancient relatives. Many long days of walking across the multicolored sediments still stand between us and the earliest hominids. With the hot sun and cloudy water, looking for our early ancestors isn't easy, but we, like many others, are anxious to continue. In East Africa, our past is lying at our feet. We just have to look.

Notes

1. Hominids are bipeds, meaning they walk on two feet (*bi* = two; *ped* = foot). All other primates are quadrupeds (*quad* =four) or use all four limbs during locomotion.

2. Raymond A. Dart, "*Australopithecus africanus*: The Man-Ape of South Africa," *Nature* 115 (1925): 195–199.

3. An endocast forms when sediments accumulate and harden within an empty braincase. This fossil retains the shape, size, and markings of the inside of the skull, allowing measurement of brain size and description of brain anatomy.

4. Dart named the newly described hominid from South Africa *Australopithecus africanus*, which means "southern ape of Africa" (*Austral* = south; *pithecus* = ape; *africanus* = African).

5. Many mammals, including all apes and monkeys, have four types of teeth. From front to back they are the incisors, canines (cuspids or unicuspids), premolars (bicuspids), and molars. Each tooth type has a characteristic shape and function.

6. The sagittal crest is a ridge of bone running from the front to the back of the skull and is formed by the enlargement of the chewing muscles (Temporalis muscle). This is commonly found in male gorillas, orangutans, and robust australopithecines.

7. Fred E. Grine, "Australopithecine Taxonomy and Phylogeny: Historical Background and Recent Interpretations," in Russell L. Ciochon and John G. Fleagle, eds., *The Human Evolutionary Sourcebook* (Englewood Cliffs, NJ: Prentice Hall, 1993), pp 198–210; Fred E. Grine, ed., *Evolutionary History of the "Robust" Australopithecines* (New York: Aldine de Gruyter, 1988).

8. Louis S. B. Leakey, "A New Fossil Skull from Olduvai," *Nature* 184 (1959): 967–970.

9. Louis S. B. Leakey, Phillip V. Tobias, and John R. Napier, "A New Species of the Genus Homo from Olduvai Gorge," *Nature* 202 (1964): 7–9. *Homo habilis means "handy man."*

10. Yves Coppens, F. Clark Howell, Glynn Ll. Isaac, and Richard E. F. Leakey, eds., *Earliest Man and Environments in the Lake Rudolf Basin* (Chicago: University of Chicago Press, 1976).

11. F. Clark Howell and Yves Coppens, "An Overview of Hominidae from the Omo Succession, Ethiopia," in Yves Coppens, F. Clark Howell, Glynn Ll. Isaac, and Richard E. F. Leakey, eds., *Earliest Man and Environments in the Lake Rudolf Basin* (Chicago: University of Chicago Press, 1976), pp. 522–532.

12. Donald C. Johanson, Maurice Taieb, and Yves Coppens, "Pliocene Hominids from the Hadar Formation, Ethiopia (1973–1977): Stratigraphic, Chronologic, and Paleoenvironmental Contexts, with Notes on Hominid Morphology and Systematics," *American Journal of Physical Anthropology* 57 (1982): 373–402.

13. Donald C. Johanson, C. Owen Lovejoy, William H. Kimbel, Tim D. White, Steven C. Ward, Michael E. Bush, Bruce Latimer, and Yves Coppens, "Morphology of the Partial Hominid Skeleton (AL 2881) from the Hadar Formation, Ethiopia," *American Journal of Physical Anthropology* 57 (1982): 403–452; Donald C. Johanson and Maitland Edey, *Lucy: The Beginnings of Humankind* (New York: Warner Books, 1981).

14. Tim D. White, "Additional Fossil Hominids from Laetoli, Tanzania: 1976–1979 Specimens," *American Journal of Physical Anthropology* 53 (1980): 487–504.

15. Donald C. Johanson and Maurice Taieb, "Plio-Pleistocene Hominid Discoveries in Hadar, Ethiopia," *Nature* 260 (1976): 293–297.

16. Donald C. Johanson, Tim D. White, and Yves Coppens, "A New Species of the Genus *Australopithecus* (Primates: Hominidae) from the Pliocene of Eastern Africa," *Kirtlandia* 28 (1978): 1–14.

17. William H. Kimbel and Tim D. White, "Variation, Sexual Dimorphism, and the Taxonomy of *Australopithecus*," in Fred E. Grine, ed., *Evolutionary History of the "Robust" Australopithecines* (New York: Aldine de Gruyter, 1988), pp. 175–192.

18. C. Owen Lovejoy, Kevin F. Kern, Scott W. Simpson, and Richard S. Meindl, "A New Method for Estimation of Skeletal Dimorphism in Fossil Samples with an Application to *Australopithecus afarensis*," in G. Giacobini, ed., *Hominidae: Proceedings of the 2nd Congress of Human Paleontology* (Milan, Italy: Jaca Books, 1989), pp. 103–108; Henry M. McHenry, "Body Size and Proportions in Early Hominids," *American Journal of Physical Anthropology* 87 (1992): 407–431; Henry M. McHenry, "Early Hominid Postcrania: Phylogeny and Function," in R. S. Corruccini and R. L. Ciochon, eds., *Integrative Paths to the Past: Paleoanthropological Advance in Honor of F. Clark Howell* (Englewood Cliffs, NJ: Prentice Hall, 1994), pp. 251–268.

19. Jack T. Stern and Randall L. Susman, "The Locomotor Anatomy of *Australopithecus afarensis*," *American Journal of Physical Anthropology* 60 (1983): 279–317; Randall L. Susman, Jack T. Stern, and William L. Jungers, "Arboreality and Bipedality in the Hadar Hominids," *Folia Primatologica* 43 (1984): 113–156.

20. C. Owen Lovejoy, "Evolution of Human Walking," *Scientific American* 256 (1988): 118–125.

21. Ibid.; C. Owen Lovejoy, "The Gait of Australopithecines," *Yearbook of Physical Anthropology* 17 (1974): 147–161; C. Owen Lovejoy, "A Biomechanical View of the Locomotor Diversity of Early Hominids," in Clifford Jolly, ed., *Early Hominids of Africa* (New York: St. Martin's, 1978), pp. 403–429.

22. Bruce Latimer, James C. Ohman, and C. Owen Lovejoy, "Talocrural Joint in African Hominoids: Implications for *Australopithecus afarensis*," *American Journal of Physical Anthropology* 74 (1987): 155–175; Bruce

Latimer and C. Owen Lovejoy," The Calcaneus of *Australopithecus afarensis* and Its Implications for the Evolution of Bipedality," *American Journal of Physical Anthropology* 78 (1989): 369–386; Bruce Latimer, "Locomotor Adaptations in *Australopithecus afarensis*: The Issue of Arboreality," in Yves Coppens and Brigitte Senut, eds., *Origine(s) de la Bipedie chez les Hominides* (Paris: Editions du CNRS, 1991), pp. 169–176.

23. Tim D. White and Gen Suwa, "Hominid Footprints at Laetoli: Facts and Interpretations," *American Journal of Physical Anthropology* 72 (1987): 485–514.

24. Berhane Asfaw, Yonas Beyene, Sileshi Semaw, Gen Suwa, Tim White, and Giday Wolde-Gabriel, "Fejej: A New Paleoanthropological Research Area in Ethiopia," *Journal of Human Evolution* 21 (1991): 137–143.

25. John G. Fleagle, D. T. Rasmussen, S. Yirga, T. M. Bown, and Fred E. Grine, "New Hominid Fossils from Fejej, Southern Ethiopia," *Journal of Human Evolution* 21 (1991): 145–152.

26. Jon Kalb, Clifford Jolly, Assefa Mebrate, Sileshi Tebedge, Charles Smart, Elizabeth B. Oswald, Douglas Cramer, Paul Whitehead, Craig B. Wood, Glenn C. Conroy, Tsrha Adefris, Louise Sperling, and B. Kana, "Fossil Mammals and Artefacts from the Middle Awash Valley, Ethiopia," *Nature* 298 (1982): 25–29; Jon E. Kalb, Elizabeth B. Oswald, Assefa Mebrate, Sileshi Tebedge, and Clifford Jolly, "Stratigraphy of the Awash Group, Middle Awash Valley, Afar, Ethiopia," *Newsletter of Stratigraphy* 11 (1982): 95–127.

27. Tim D. White, "Pliocene Hominids from the Middle Awash, Ethiopia," *Courier Forschunginstitut Senckenberg* 69 (1984): 57–68.

28. Tim D. White, Gen Suwa, William K. Hart, Robert C. Walters, Giday Wolde-Gabriel, Jean deHeinzelein, J. Desmond Clark, Berhane Asfaw, and Elisabeth Vrba, "New Discoveries of Australopithecus at Maka in Ethiopia," *Nature* 366 (1993): 261–264; Henry Gee, "Why We Still Love Lucy," *Nature* 366 (1993): 207.

29. Berhane Asfaw, "The Belohdelie Frontal: New Evidence of Early Hominid Cranial Morphology from the Afar of Ethiopia," *Journal of Human Evolution* 16 (1987): 611–624.

30. Leslie C. Aiello, "Variable but Singular," *Nature* 368 (1994): 399–400.

31. William H. Kimbel, Donald C. Johanson, and Yoel Rak, "The First Skull and Other New Discoveries of Australopithecus afarensis at Hadar, Ethiopia," *Nature* 368 (1994): 449–451.

32. Berhane Asfaw, Cynthia Ebinger, David Harding, Tim D. White, and Giday Wolde-Gabriel, "Space Based Imagery in Paleoanthropological Research: An Ethiopian Example," *National Geographic Research* 6 (1990): 418–434.

33. Tim D. White, Gen Suwa, and Berhane Asfaw, "*Australopithecus ramidus*, a New Species of Early Hominid from Aramis, Ethiopia," *Nature* 371 (1994): 306–312; Giday Wolde-Gabriel, Tim D. White, Gen Suwa, Paul Renne, Jean deHeinzelin, William K. Hart, and Grant Heiken, "Ecological and Temporal Placement of Early Pliocene Hominids at Aramis, Ethiopia," *Nature* 371 (1994): 330–333; Tim D. White, Gen Suwa, and Berhane Asfaw, "*Australopithecus ramidus*, a New Species of Early Hominid from Aramis, Ethiopia: Corrigendum," *Nature* 375 (1995): 88.

Suggested Readings

Aiello, Leslie C., and M. Christopher Dean. *An Introduction to Human Evolutionary Anatomy*. Academic Press: London, 1990. A summary textbook presenting comparative and functional analyses of human, ape, and fossil hominid anatomy.

Ciochon, Russell L., and John G. Fleagle. *The Human Evolution Sourcebook*. Englewood Cliffs, NJ: Prentice Hall, 1993. An extensive collection of readings covering many different aspects of human evolution during the past four million years.

Johanson, Donald C., and Maitland Edey. *Lucy: The Beginnings of Humankind*. New York: Warner Books, 1981. An entertaining firsthand account of the discovery, analysis, and announcement of *Australopithecus afarensis*.

Lovejoy, C. Owen. "Evolution of Human Walking." *Scientific American* 27 256 (1988): 118–125. A clearly written analysis of hominid locomotion focusing on *Australopithecus afarensis*.

White, Tim D., Donald C. Johanson, and William H. Kimbel. "*Australopithecus africanus*: Its Phyletic Position Reconsidered." *South African Journal of Science* 77 (1981): 445–470. A formal and thorough analysis of the phyletic relationships of the australopithecines, especially *Australopithecus afarensis*.

White, Tim D., Gen Suwa, William K. Hart, Robert C. Walters, Giday Wolde-Gabriel, Jean de Heinzelein, J. Desmond Clark, Berhane Asfaw, and Elisabeth Vrba. "New Discoveries of Australopithecus at Maka in Ethiopia." *Nature* 366 (1993): 261–264. The announcement and preliminary description of some newly discovered *Australopithecus afarensis* fossils from the Middle Awash region.

The Natural History and Evolutionary Fate of *Homo erectus*

Andrew Kramer

lthough scientists who study human evolution are popularly perceived as constantly being involved in rancorous debates, these paleoanthropologists would unanimously agree that we *have* evolved from more primitive predecessors. *Homo erectus*, a hominid species that flourished for over one million years in Africa and Asia, is generally regarded as humanity's immediate ancestor. However, there is still plenty of controversy surrounding the question of how (and even if) *Homo erectus* evolved into *Homo sapiens*.

In this chapter I present the remarkable story of the discoveries of and the ideas surrounding the original *Homo erectus* fossils. This leads into a discussion of how these early interpretations have influenced the present-day debates concerning the evolution of *Homo erectus*. Finally, I detail my own perspectives and contributions to the resolutions of these questions, and I conclude with some suggestions for future research.

Dubois's Ape-Man[1]

In the late 1800s the famous German naturalist Ernst Haeckel posited that a form of prehuman that bridged the evolutionary gap between apes and humans existed sometime in the distant past. Haeckel was even bold enough to name this hypothetical creature *"Pithecanthropus alalus,"* literally, "speechless ape-man." This idea fired the popular imagination and was the original source of the term *missing link*, a phrase coined by an American journalist at the time. In the early 1880s a young Dutch physician named Eugène Dubois, an anatomy assistant under Haeckel at the University of Jena, fell under the thrall of his mentor's evolutionism. In fact, Haeckel's ideas captivated Dubois so completely that he gave up his prom-ising medical career to devote himself full time to searching for the missing link!

Although Dubois's chances amounted to what was in all likelihood a million-to-one shot, he defied the odds and, amazingly enough, actually discovered what he had set out to find. Dubois decided to search for his fossils in what is today the island country of Indonesia, in southeast Asia. His decision was based on a combination of theoretical and pragmatic considerations. First, Haeckel thought that the gibbon was the closest living relative to humans, not the African apes as Darwin had proposed (correctly, it turned out). Therefore, because gibbons occupy the forests of mainland and island southeast Asia, Dubois logically concluded that the common ancestor of these apes and humans may have lived in this same region. The young Dutchman's decision to direct his energies to the area's islands, not to the mainland, was purely practical: What is today known as the Republic of Indonesia was the Dutch East Indies then.

Dubois enlisted in the Dutch colonial army as a health officer and arrived on the island of Sumatra in 1887. His paleontological research was eventually supported by the colonial government because much of the geological information he recovered was of economic value, such as sites that could produce potentially profitable mines. By 1890 Dubois had himself transferred to Java, and two years later he made the discovery that would rock the anthropological world. In September of 1891, near the village of Trinil along the banks of the Solo River, his team of convict excavators uncovered a long and low skull cap with protruding, ape-like brow ridges. The following August, only forty feet from the original find, a humanlike femur (thigh bone) was discovered that belonged, Dubois believed, to the same individual as the skull.

Dubois published his interpretations of these finds in 1894 and concluded that because the skull was intermediate in size between apes and humans he had truly found the missing link. Honoring Haeckel, and acknowledging the upright, bipedal gait suggested by the femur, Dubois named the fossil *"Pithecanthropus erectus"* ("upright ape-man").[2]

Upon his return to Europe in 1895, Dubois was plunged into the maelstrom of scientific controversy swirling around his finds. Although there were those who agreed with his missing link interpretation, including (not surprisingly) Haeckel, there were others, led by the renowned German pathologist and anthropologist Rudolf Virchow, who dismissed Dubois's fossils as nothing more than an extinct, giant gibbon. The acrimony of these exchanges may have been more than Dubois could take, for he became less and less involved in the public debates over the following years. Legend has it that he ultimately signaled his complete withdrawal by burying the fossils beneath the floorboards of his dining room and leaving them there unstudied for the next twenty years! Although Dubois's final thoughts concerning the status of *"Pithecanthropus"* currently remain a contentious topic,[3] it is acknowledged by all that his discoveries set the stage for those that followed during the succeeding decades.

Species, Species, and More Species

Beginning in the 1920s and continuing through the 1930s, fossils found in China demonstrated that Dubois's find was not unique. The remains of ancient hominids that were remarkably similar to *"Pithecanthropus"* of southeast Asia were recovered in a cave now known as Zhoukoudian, approximately thirty miles from Beijing. Davidson Black, an anatomist at the Peking Union Medical School, placed those specimens into a new genus and species, *"Sinanthropus pekinensis"* ("Chinese man of Peking"). Black created the new name in 1927 on the basis of a single molar tooth, and although the skulls that were found later in the same cave were much like *"Pithecanthropus,"* there was no effort at the time to consolidate the Javan and Chinese fossils into the same genus, much less the same species (see Figure 1).

This lack of consolidation reflected the "splitting" mentality that was pervasive throughout paleoanthropology until the 1960s. Almost every new hominid fossil that was discovered, despite its resemblance to the Javan and Chinese forms, was given at least a new species, and often a new genus, name

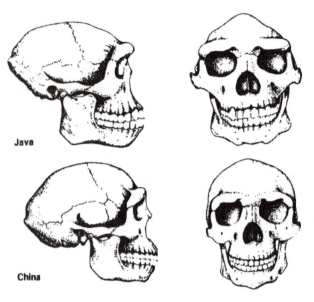

Figure 1
***"Pithecanthropus"* from Java and *"Sinanthropus"* from China**

Today both are considered to be representatives of *Homo erectus*. Note how they share relatively large brain cases that are long and low, projecting brow ridges, jutting lower faces, and the lack of a chin.

reflecting less the realities of biology and more the egos of the discoverers and namers. This trend is well illustrated by the treatment of the fossils discovered in Africa during the middle decades of the twentieth century. The genus names proposed for these specimens, such as *"Telanthropus," "Atlanthropus,"* and *"Tchadanthropus,"* were biologically meaningless labels that served only to clutter the taxonomic landscape.[4]

The lone voice in the wilderness during this "age of splitters" belonged to the famed German paleoanthropologist Franz Weidenreich. A refugee from Hitler's holocaust, Weidenreich published minutely detailed monographs describing and interpreting the finds from Zhoukoudian. He also reproduced extremely accurate casts and molds of these fossils. The scientific world owes a debt of everlasting gratitude to Weidenreich for these scholarly activities because the original Chinese fossils were mysteriously lost during World War II. In 1940 Weidenreich was the first to suggest that the proliferation of names given to the Javan and Chinese fossils was hindering the understanding of human evolution:[5]

Those terms which are generally used to designate different human types involve the idea that each one represents a more or less divergent genus without generic connections. In order to avoid this incorrect interpretation, the time has come . . . to eliminate all those names which may lead to some misunderstanding in this regard.[6]

Weidenreich observed that *"Pithecanthropus"* and *"Sinanthropus"* were not different enough from modern humans (*Homo sapiens*) to be placed into separate genera, and they were not different enough from one another to be considered separate species. Therefore, Weidenreich concluded that both could be accommodated by the name *Homo erectus*, recognizing that the Javan and Peking hominids belonged to the same early species of humanity, and their differences were no greater than those seen between modern humans living in southeast Asia and China today. Weidenreich truly was a visionary. He was decades ahead of his time in his recognition of the ubiquity of normal, intraspecific (within species) variation among fossil hominids and its importance in any reconstruction of human evolution.

Weidenreich's perspective became increasingly popular in anthropology over the following decades. Particularly persuasive arguments that *Homo erectus* was the appropriate taxonomic assignment for the Chinese and Javan fossil hominids were made by the American evolutionary biologist Ernst Mayr in 1950, and by the British paleoanthropologist W. E. LeGros Clark in 1955.[7] The 1960s and 1970s signalled the ascendancy of the "lumpers," who, unlike the "splitters" of the first half of the century, tried to bring paleoanthropology into line with the rest of modern biology. These researchers were much less inclined to name new fossil hominid genera and species and believed that *Homo erectus* could accommodate the variation present not only in the Javan and Chinese forms but also in similar fossils discovered later in Africa. Most anthropologists at this time viewed *Homo erectus* as humanity's immediate predecessor, a fossil species occupying an intermediate position on the unbroken evolutionary continuum between modern humans and the earliest African hominids, the australopithecines.

These ideas held sway throughout the 1970s and 1980s, as exemplified by the writings of such scholars as F. Clark Howell and William Howells, and continue to be championed today by Philip Rightmire.[8] However, in the mid-1980s an alternative viewpoint was presented concerning the taxonomic and evolutionary affinities of *Homo erectus*. Researchers such as Peter Andrews, Chris Stringer, and Bernard Wood sug-gested that the differences between the Asian and African forms of *Homo erectus* were significant enough to separate them into different species.[9] The Asian fossils would remain in *Homo erectus* while the African hominids would be placed into a new species, alternately called *Homo ergaster*,[10] or *Homo leakeyi*.[11] These paleoanthropologists employed cladistics, an analytical approach that determines evolutionary relationships based on the presence or absence of certain traits shared between groups of fossils. Their analyses isolated what they perceived to be unique features shared by the Javan and Chinese fossils that were absent not only in the East African representatives of *Homo erectus*, but also in modern humans. They concluded that Asian *Homo erectus* went extinct and that the African form was the sole ancestor of modern humans.

Was Homo Erectus a Dead End?

Is this "neo-splitting" position justified? Was Asian *Homo erectus* simply a doomed twig on the bush of human evolution, leaving no descendants among modern people? Or is it more likely that these archaic hominids were an integral part of the human evolutionary tree that significantly contributed to the origins of modern Asians? Before the latter two questions can be addressed, the first must be resolved, because the "resplitting" of *Homo erectus* bears directly on the issue of this fossil species' influence upon the evolution of modern *Homo sapiens*.

After the first wave of publications claiming that *Homo erectus* in Africa was a different species from its Chinese and Indonesian cousins, other scientists turned a critical eye on the features that were supposedly unique to the Asian hominids. For example, Günter Bräuer and Emma Mbua studied African and Asian *Homo erectus*, and later hominids from these continents and from Europe as well. They demonstrated that the characteristics supposedly unique to Asia were not confined to Asian *Homo erectus*, but were also present in varying frequencies in the fossils from both Africa and Europe.[12] I became interested in the problem of "lumping" versus "splitting" for a variety of reasons. As a graduate student at the University of Michigan I was trained by professors who were decidedly "lumpers." These scholars emphasized the importance of factors that could produce significant variation within species, such as sexual dimorphism (size and shape differences between adult males and females) and polytypism (geographic variation). My professors argued reasonably that these intraspecific factors had to be eliminated first as potential sources of variation in fossil samples before the presence of multiple species could be claimed. During the latter half of my graduate studies and the beginning of my professional career, from the mid-1980s through the early 1990s, it seemed to me that paleoanthropology was slipping "back to the future"—more and more publications were trumpeting the reality of new species that were split from other well-established taxa. I decided to investigate whether or not this trend was warranted with respect to the splitting of African from Asian *Homo erectus*. However, unlike other researchers, I chose to examine this question quantitatively by comparing skull measurements instead of the osteological (bony) features that were being argued over by the cladists.

My research compared *Homo erectus* with a sample of modern humans (made up of over 2, 500 individual skeletons from all over the world) and another sample composed of various fossils representing 2 to 3 different hominid species (called the mixed hominid sample).[13] The modern human sample was chosen because it exemplified the nature and degree of variation to be expected in a single but geographically variable hominid species. The mixed hominid sample was used to depict the variation present in a sample composed of multiple fossil hominid species. If my comparisons showed that *Homo erectus* was most similar in its magnitude and pattern of variation to the mixed hominids, then this would support the cladists' conclusion that *Homo erectus* included more than one species. However, if *Homo erectus* proved to be no more variable than modern humans, then this would support the "lumpers'" position that it was a single species.

The results of these comparisons would be quite important to the reconstruction of later human evolution. If there were multiple species of *Homo erectus*, this would support a very "bushy" view of human evolution, with many origins and extinctions of regionally isolated hominid species. This perspective would indicate that modern humans probably arose relatively late in the Pleistocene epoch from a geographically restricted area, such as Sub-Saharan Africa. In this scenario, the descendants of east African *Homo erectus* (*Homo ergaster*) were the sole ancestors of modern humanity. In contrast, if the results indicated that *Homo erectus* was indeed a single species, this would support a human evolutionary "tree," whose "trunk" was composed of *Homo erectus*, gradually growing into *Homo sapiens* around the world.

Most people think that science is objective. This objectivity may sometimes be illusory, however.

People bring biases and preconceived notions to everything they do, and scientists are no different. It is important to acknowledge these biases whenever possible. As one can easily tell by the foregoing discussion, I was predisposed to reconfirming that *Homo erectus* was a single species. But I did take precautions in my study not to make this a foregone conclusion. For example, the *Homo erectus* sample that I used was chronologically as broad as possible, dating from 1.8 million to less than 500, 000 years old. Because of their great time-depth, these fossils were potentially much more variable than the modern humans, who were sampled from a single point in geological time. This comparison, then, predisposed my study to conclude that *Homo erectus* was significantly different from *Homo sapiens* and therefore was composed of more than one species. In effect, I bent over backwards to prevent my conclusions from being predetermined by my biases.

In my analyses I used eight skull measurements that were common to all three samples (*Homo erectus*, the mixed hominid group, and the modern humans). I examined each of the variables individually and in combination, but the results of these preliminary investigations were not sufficient to resolve the *Homo erectus* species problem. Whether or not the fossils attributed to *Homo erectus* belonged to one or more species was ultimately a statistical question: What is the probability that the variation present in a fossil sample (such as *Homo erectus*) could be found in a sample taken from a single species (such as *Homo sapiens*)?

To answer this question I used a randomization procedure that is ideal for solving problems such as these. This procedure uses a computer to generate many random samples of a particular reference species (in this case, modern humans). The variation in these samples is then compared to that present in a fossil sample (in this case, *Homo erectus*) to determine whether or not the variation in the fossils is greater than the variation in equivalently-sized samples randomly drawn from a known single species, such as *Homo sapiens*. If the variation in the fossil sample exceeds the variation in 95 percent or more of the randomized modern human samples, then it is likely that the fossil sample is composed of two or more species. On the other hand, if a significant percentage (defined as greater than 5 percent) of the randomized modern human samples are more variable than the fossils, this provides evidence that the fossil sample represents a single species.

Let me illustrate this technique with the following example (see Figure 2). One of the eight measurements that I recorded was the greatest width of the brain case, formally known as *maximum cranial breadth* and abbreviated as XCB. This measurement could be taken on all 8 of the fossils in the mixed hominid sample, on 16 of 19 *Homo erectus* skulls, and on all 2, 533 of the modern humans. How variable XCB was in the two fossil samples was determined by calculating the coefficient of variation, known more simply as the CV. To begin with, was the CV for XCB in the mixed hominid fossil sample greater than expected for a single species, such as modern *Homo sapiens*? This was answered as follows: First, eight skulls were randomly drawn by the computer from the modern human sample and their CV for XCB was calculated. Only eight human skulls were taken because that was the number of fossil specimens present in the mixed hominid sample. After the CV was calculated, the eight skulls were returned to the human pool and the computer randomly drew eight more and calculated this new sample's CV. The computer repeated this process one thousand times, generating one thousand CVs for one thousand different eight-skull samples. Finally, the CV for XCB in the mixed hominid sample was compared to the modern human CVs generated by randomization. The extremely high CV of the mixed hominid sample exceeded 99. 8 percent (998 of the 1, 000) of the randomized modern human CVs, a result confirming the presence of multiple species in the mixed hominid sample.

In contrast, the randomization procedure told a different story regarding variation in *Homo erectus* (see Figure 3). This time the computer drew one thousand samples of sixteen skulls each from the modern human pool—sixteen skulls each because the *Homo erectus* sample included sixteen individual fossil specimens. When the CVs of the randomized samples were compared to the *Homo erectus* CV it was revealed that most (81 percent) of the randomized modern human CVs for XCB were greater than or equal to the relatively low *Homo erectus* CV for XCB. This result strongly supports the retention of *Homo erectus* as a single species because variation in these fossils is usually exceeded by the variation present in samples drawn from the known single species, modern *Homo sapiens*. The other results from my study corroborate this conclusion.

The fact that the *Homo erectus* sample, whose members were separated from each other by thousands of miles and by over one million years, was generally less variable than randomly drawn modern human samples directly counters the claims of the "neosplitters." Those who think that African *Homo ergaster* is a species distinct from Asian *Homo erectus* would expect that the reproductive isolation necessary to produce

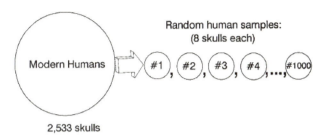

Final Tally of Random Sample CVs:

	Less than Mixed Fossil Hominids	Greater than or Equal to Mixed Fossil Hominids
	998	**2**

Figure 2

The randomization procedure randomly draws, with replacement, one thousand eight-skull samples from the modern human sample and determines the coefficient of variation (CV) for maximum cranial length (XCB) for each sample. The CV for XCB in the eight mixed hominid skulls is then compared to the one thousand CVs of the one thousand random modern human samples. Because 99. 8 percent of the modern human CVs are smaller than the mixed hominid fossil CV, it is likely that this fossil sample includes at least two species.

two species would result in the development of significant differences between the two forms. Instead, I showed that African and Asian *Homo erectus* shared a level and pattern of variation most similar to modern humans, and that their differences could be best explained by polytypism: geographic variation within a species. Thus, this evidence suggests that *Homo erectus* was, like us, a far-flung species that developed regionally distinct forms that were never reproductively isolated enough from each other to evolve into separate species.

The larger question remains: What became of *Homo erectus*? Did this species gradually transform into modern humans around the world, or did only one geographically constrained population of *Homo erectus* provide humanity's ancestry while the rest were doomed to extinction?

Homo Erectus and the Origins of Modern Humans

The debate about modern human origins has been raging in paleoanthropology for the last decade. In its most basic form, the controversy can be stated as two

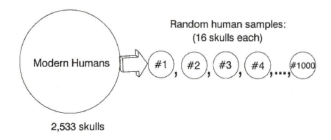

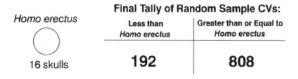

| Final Tally of Random Sample CVs: | |
Less than *Homo erectus*	Greater than or Equal to *Homo erectus*
192	808

Figure 3

The randomization procedure randomly draws, with replacement, one thousand sixteen-skull samples from the modern human sample and determines the coefficient of variation (CV) for maximum cranial length (XCB) for each sample. The CV for XCB in the sixteen *Homo erectus* skulls is then compared to the one thousand CVs of the one thousand random modern human samples. Because 81 percent of the modern human CVs are larger than the *Homo erectus* CV, it is likely that the *Homo erectus* sample includes only one species.

polar opposites: replacement versus multiregionalism. The replacement view, supported by Stringer, Andrews, and their colleagues, states that modern humans evolved relatively recently (one hundred thousand to two hundred thousand years ago) in Sub-Saharan Africa and subsequently spread around the Old World, replacing all of the indigenous, archaic human populations that they encountered.[14] In contrast, multiregionalism, espoused by Milford Wolpoff, Alan Thorne, David Frayer, and their co-workers, contends that archaic hominids from throughout the Old World (not just in Africa) contributed to the evolution of their local modern successors.[15] Both of these hypotheses produce very different predictions concerning the evolutionary fate of Asian *Homo erectus*: Replacement suggests that the Javan and Chinese hominids had nothing to do with the origins of modern humans in those regions while multiregionalists maintain that these fossil hominids are part of an unbroken genetic continuum linking Asia's ancient past to its present.

I decided to test these predictions with data I collected during my dissertation research. The fossils I studied are a group of hominid mandibles (lower jaws) from the site of Sangiran in central Java that date

to approximately one million years ago. Initially I was intrigued by these jaws because of their variability: Some were as huge as the biggest australopithecine mandibles while others were quite a bit smaller, as is typical for *Homo erectus*. My studies of the anatomy and measurements of these fossils led me to conclude that they all represented *Homo erectus* and that their great size variation could be best explained by sexual dimorphism.[16] Later I realized that the morphology of these mandibles could provide some important additional information bearing on the origins of modern humans.

The Sangiran mandibles are among the oldest *Homo erectus* fossils found outside of Africa and as such provide an excellent test case of the polarized predictions generated by the replacement and multiregional models. I compared the Javan jaws to samples of modern human mandibles from Kenya and Australia to explicitly test the following expectations.[17] According to the replacement hypothesis, the two modern human samples should display much more in common with one another, when compared to the fossils, because the Kenyans and Australians presumably share a relatively recent African ancestor that had nothing to do with one million year old Javan *Homo erectus*. In contrast, multiregionalism suggests that the Sangiran hominids' ancestry to modern humans in the region, such as Australian Aborigines, would be reflected in the number of features shared between the Sangiran and Australian jaws that are not found in the mandibles of modern Kenyans.

Most previous studies of modern Asian origins have generally presented varying lists of morphological features to promote either the replacement or the multiregionalism models. For example, Wolpoff and his colleagues support the multiregional position by noting numerous skull features that are shared between Middle Pleistocene (≈ two hundred thousand to five hundred thousand years ago) Javan hominids and recent Australians that are absent in early modern humans from Africa.[18] Critics of this interpretation contend that these morphological similarities are due either to cultural practices of cranial deformation or parallelism (independent evolution of the same features by ancient Javans and recent Australians).[19]

Little has been done to actually quantify these similarities and differences, particularly with respect to the earliest *Homo erectus* specimens from Java. Therefore, I used a statistical test to determine which of the two predictions would be borne out by the data. If the statistics showed that the modern humans from Kenya and Australia shared more features in common when compared to the fossils, this would support the replacement model. If the Sangiran and Australian jaws were demonstrably more similar to each other than either were to the Kenyans, then multiregionalism was a more likely explanation. Fisher's Exact Test of Independence is an analytical tool that can be used to answer these types of questions.

Fisher's test determines whether trait frequencies between two samples are significantly different (i.e., whether the differences are unlikely to have occurred by chance). For example, suppose that "Feature A" is present in all (100 percent) of the fossil jaws, in 90 percent of the Australian mandibles, but in only 20 percent of the Kenyans. Fisher's Exact Test of Independence would show that the frequency of "Feature A" is statistically indistinguishable when the Sangiran and modern Australian mandibles are compared, but that the frequencies are significantly different when the Australians are compared to the Kenyans. This was the predominant finding in my study. Of the sixteen mandibular features analyzed by Fisher's test, thirteen displayed insignificant differences in the Sangiran and modern Australian comparisons. In contrast, nine of sixteen trait frequencies were statistically different in the comparisons between modern Australians and Kenyans.

If the replacement model is closer to the historical truth, then the similarities between the ancient Javans and modern Australians could not be simply explained by an ancestral-descendant relationship. A more tortuous explanation involves the independent evolution of these similarities twice: once in the *Homo erectus* fossils and a second time among the modern Australians. Although the small size of the fossil sample tempered my conclusions with caution, my results clearly provide more support for the multiregional hypothesis—namely, that early *Homo erectus* from Java did contribute to the evolution of modern Australian Aborigines.

Where Do We Go from Here?

The evidence discussed in this chapter establishes that *Homo erectus* was a single, hominid species that evolved into *Homo sapiens* throughout the Old World over the past million years. Ironically, the very fact that modern *Homo sapiens* is the product of this gradual transformation has spurred calls for the "sinking" of *Homo erectus*! Wolpoff, Thorne, Jan Jelinek, and Zhang Yinyun have recently published a paper arguing that because there is no obvious morphological gap in the direct evolution of *Homo erectus* into *Homo sapiens* the former species should be formally "sunk" into the latter.[20] The authors maintain that *Homo erectus* could only be retained as a separate species if the fossil record indicates that the origin of *Homo sapiens* was the result of a branching speciation event, whereby the ancestral species (i.e., *Homo erectus*) ceased to exist by dividing and producing two descendant species. I agree with Wolpoff and his colleagues who do not see any evidence of such branching evolution in modern human origins. *Homo sapiens* appears to have a much greater time-depth and much more morphological variability than traditional views would assume.

Is this interpretation justified? Given the evolutionary species concept that Wolpoff et al. employ in conjunction with the evidence from the fossil record, their logic is unassailable.[21] But does their argument illuminate or obfuscate evolutionary relationships in labeling both big-browed, smaller-brained ancient hominids and high-browed, bigger-brained modern humans as *Homo sapiens*? This point will be debated for years to come. Most scholars would agree, however, that the label is not important in and of itself. The reconstruction of evolutionary patterns and relationships should remain our primary focus.

To that end I hope that future research on *Homo erectus* will concentrate on the regional patterns of evolutionary change leading to the emergence of *Homo sapiens*. Was the tempo of this evolution gradual throughout or was there a period of acceleration that could be used to mark the transition, thereby rendering the boundary between these two species less arbitrary? Although questions such as these may be answered by applying new quantitative methods to old data, the age old battle cry of paleoanthropology will certainly continue to ring out across our ancestral homelands: more fossils, more fossils!

Notes

1. Much of the information in this section comes from C. Loring Brace, "Tales of the Phylogenetic Woods: The Evolution and Significance of Evolutionary Trees," *American Journal of Physical Anthropology* 56 (1981): 411; C. Loring Brace, *The Stages of Human Evolution*, 4th ed. (Englewood Cliffs, NJ: Prentice Hall, 1991); F. Clark Howell, "Thoughts on Eugene Dubois and the 'Pithecanthropus' Saga," *Courier Forschungsinstitut Senckenberg* 171 (1994): 11.

2. Eugène Dubois, *Pithecanthropus Erectus: Eine Menschenähnliche Uebergangsform Aus Java* (Batavia: Landersdruckerei, 1894).

3. Compare, for example, Brace, "Tales of the Phylogenetic Woods," with Stephen J. Gould, "Men of the Thirty-Third Division," *Natural History* (April 1990): 12.

4. The following are the references for original works in which these genera were named: *"Sinanthropus"*—Davidson Black,"On a Lower Molar Hominid Tooth from Chou-kou-tien Deposit," *Palaeontologica Sinica Series D7* (1927): 1; *"Telanthropus"*—Robert Broom and John T. Robinson, "New Type of Fossil Man," *Nature* 164 (1949): 322; *"Atlanthropus"*—Camille Arambourg, "L'hominien fossile de Ternifine (Algérie)," *Comptes Rendus de l'Academie des Sciences (Paris)* 239 (1954): 893; *"Tchadanthropus"*—Yves Coppens, "L'hominien du Tchad," *Comptes Rendus de l'Academie des Sciences (Paris)* 260D (1965): 2869.

5. Franz Weidenreich, "Some Problems Dealing with Ancient Man," *American Anthropologist* 42 (1940): 375.

6. Ibid., p. 383.

7. Ernst Mayr, "Taxonomic Categories in Fossil Hominids," *Cold Spring Harbor Symposium on Quantitative Biology* 15 (1950): 109; W. E. LeGros Clark, *The Fossil Evidence for Human Evolution* (Chicago: University of Chicago Press, 1955).

8. F. Clark Howell, "Hominidae," in Vincent J. Maglio and H. B. S. Cooke, eds., *Evolution of African Mammals* (Cambridge, MA: Harvard University Press, 1978), pp. 154–248; William W. Howells, "Homo erectus—Who, When, and Where: A Survey," *Yearbook of Physical Anthropology* 23 (1980): 1; G. Philip Rightmire, *The Evolution of Homo erectus: Comparative Anatomical Studies of an Extinct Human Species* (New York: Cambridge University Press, 1990).

9. Peter Andrews, "An Alternative Interpretation of the Characters Used to Define *Homo erectus,*" *Courier Forschungsinstitut Senckenberg* 69 (1984): 167; Christopher B. Stringer, "The Definition of Homo erectus and the Existence of the Species in Africa and Europe," *Courier Forschungsinstitut Senckenberg* 69 (1984): 131; Bernard A. Wood, "The Origin of *Homo erectus,*" *Courier Forschungsinstitut Senckenberg* 69 (1984): 99.

10. Originally named by Colin P. Groves and V. Mazak, "An Approach to the Taxonomy of the Hominidae: Gracile Villafranchian Hominids of Africa," *Casopis pro Mineralogii a Geologii* 20 (1975): 225.

11. Originally named by G. Heberer, "Über einen neuen archanthropinen Typus aus der Oldoway-Schlucht," *Zeitschrift für Morphologie und Anthropologie* 53 (1963): 171.

12. Günter Bräuer and Emma Mbua, "*Homo erectus* Features Used in Cladistics and Their Variability in Asian and African Hominids," *Journal of Human Evolution* 22 (1992): 79.

13. Andrew Kramer, "Human Taxonomic Diversity in the Pleistocene: Does *Homo erectus* Represent Multiple Hominid Species?," *American Journal of Physical Anthropology* 91 (1993): 161.

14. Christopher B. Stringer, "The Emergence of Modern Humans," *Scientific American* 263 (1990): 98; Christopher B. Stringer and Peter Andrews, "Genetic and Fossil Evidence for the Origin of Modern Humans," *Science* 239 (1988): 1263.

15. Alan G. Thorne and Milford H. Wolpoff, "The Multiregional Evolution of Humans," *Scientific American* 266 (1992): 76; David W. Frayer, "Testing Theories and Hypotheses about Modern Human Origins," in Carol R. Ember, Melvin Ember, and Peter N. Peregrine, eds., *Research Frontiers in Anthropology: Advances in Archaeology and Physical Anthropology* (Englewood Cliffs, NJ: Prentice Hall, 1995).

16. Andrew Kramer, "A Critical Analysis of Claims for the Existence of Southeast Asian Australopithecines," *Journal of Human Evolution* 26 (1994): 3; Andrew Kramer and Lyle W. Konigsberg, "The Phyletic Position of Sangiran 6 as Determined by Multivariate Analyses," *Courier Forschungsinstitut Senckenberg* 171 (1994): 105.

17. Andrew Kramer, "Modern Human Origins in Australasia: Replacement or Evolution?" *American Journal of Physical Anthropology* 86 (1991): 455.

18. Milford H. Wolpoff, Wu Xinzhi, and Alan G. Thorne, "Modern *Homo sapiens* Origins: A General Theory of Hominid Evolution Involving the Fossil Evidence from East Asia," in Fred H. Smith and Frank Spencer, eds., *The Origins of Modern Humans: A World Survey of the Fossil Evidence* (New York: Alan R. Liss, 1984), pp. 411–483; Milford H. Wolpoff, "Multiregional Evolution: The Fossil Alternative to Eden," in Paul Mellars and Chris Stringer, eds., *The Human Revolution: Behavioural and Biological Perspectives on the Origins of Modern Humans* (Edinburgh: Edinburgh University Press, 1989), pp. 62–108; Milford H. Wolpoff, "Theories of Modern Human Origins," in Günter Bräuer and Fred H. Smith, eds., *Continuity or Replacement: Controversies in* Homo sapiens *Evolution* (Rotterdam: Balkema, 1992), pp. 25–63.

19. Erik Delson, "One Source Not Many," *Nature* 332 (1988): 206; Stringer and Andrews, "Genetic and Fossil Evidence for the Origin of Modern Humans," p. 1267; Christopher B. Stringer, "Replacement, Continuity, and the Origin of Homo sapiens," in Günter Bräuer and Fred H. Smith, eds., *Continuity or Replacement: Controversies in* Homo sapiens *Evolution* (Rotterdam: Balkema, 1992), pp. 9–24.

20. Milford H. Wolpoff, Alan G. Thorne, Jan Jelinek, and Zhang Yinyun, "The Case for Sinking *Homo erectus*: 100 Years of Pithecanthropus Is Enough!" *Courier Forschungsinstitut Senckenberg* 171 (1994): 341.

21. An "evolutionary species" can span a considerable amount of geological time and is formally defined as a single lineage of ancestor-descendant populations that maintains its identity from other such lineages and has its own evolutionary tendencies and historical fate. In contrast, the traditional "biological species" has no time depth and is defined as a group of actually or potentially interbreeding individuals who are reproductively isolated from other such groups.

Suggested Readings

Howells, William W. *"Homo erectus*—Who, When, and Where: A Survey." *Yearbook of Physical Anthropology* 23 (1980): 1–23. State of the art in 1980 on the distribution, taxonomy, and evolution of *Homo erectus*; today a bit dated.

Rightmire, G. Philip. *The Evolution of* Homo erectus: *Comparative Anatomical Studies of an Extinct Human Species.* New York: Cambridge University Press, 1990. State of the art today in book length, by the acknowledged leading expert on the subject.

———— *"Homo erectus*: Ancestor or Evolutionary Side-branch?" *Evolutionary Anthropology* 1 (1992): 43–49. State of the art today in easily digestible article length.

Wu, Rukang, and Lin Shenglong. "Peking Man." *Scientific American* 248 (1983): 86–94. A fascinating and lively look at the excavations and interpretations of the most famous Chinese *Homo erectus* site.

Testing Theories and Hypotheses about Modern Human Origins
David W. Frayer

The study of human evolution has always had a reputation for being a contentious subject. There is a long history of debates about the general course of human evolution, the details of the evolutionary process, the authenticity of the fossils, the reliability of their dates, and even the relevance of the fossils themselves for answering evolutionary questions. In some respects paleoanthropology is no more acrimonious than research on crickets or about black holes, but the academic battles in paleoanthropology are more often reported in the popular literature, making it seem like there is constant bickering about ideas and theories. In another respect, the "bone wars," as one journalist called them,[1] often persist because there is incomplete information due to a spotty and fragmentary fossil record. Even if paleoanthropologists wanted to reach an agreement on some issues, the incompleteness of the fossil record often allows it to be read in multiple ways and these inevitably lead to controversy. Still another source of troubles is the inability to frame hypotheses in ways that allow unambiguous testing and refutation. This is important since the primary mechanism for resolving scientific disagreements is through rejecting hypotheses on the basis of available data. Unlike some ongoing debates in paleoanthropology, however, the development of specific, testable hypotheses combined with an adequate fossil record has recently allowed the resolution of two contradictory theories about modern human origins.

Paleoanthropology has had a decades-long debate about the emergence of modern humans in the Old World. This debate has involved two different models. One model is that modern humans in each area are descended from the long line of fossils who preceded them in the area, which is evidenced by anatomical continuity within regions across time. Combining aspects of local selection, migration and gene exchange, and the effect of genetic isolating mechanisms, this theory is called multiregional evolution.[2] The other theory, previously labeled the Noah's Ark model,[3] contends that modern humans originated in one place, then spread throughout the Old World, displacing all the original inhabitants.[4] It is important to recognize that this spread of modern humanity was not the first wave of people out of Africa; both sides of the debate agree that the earliest humans left Africa about one million years ago. But, as its name implies, the Noah's Ark model argues for another, much more recent wave in which resident populations were displaced by new immigrants. It was not until the late 1980s that the debate over the two contradictory models really heated up. The heat was generated not by paleoanthropologists or by new fossil discoveries, but by molecular geneticists who claimed they had answered once and for all the question of modern human origins. Their resolution had nothing to do with the fossil record, but with patterns of variation in DNA. The hypotheses and predictions about the fossil record proposed by the new genetics-based theory were so fundamentally at odds with the multiregional model that it became possible to test unambiguously the two models of human origins.

The genetic solutions for the timing and appearance of modern humans appeared in two separate publications in the prestigious journal *Nature*. The first article by Wainscoat et al.[5] reviewed geographic variation in a genetic system known as the β-globin gene cluster. This set of genetic loci is supposedly nonfunctional, a crucial consideration since evolutionary forces (such as natural selection) can have major confounding effects in reconstructing ancestor-descendant relationships and in calculating the rate at which they diverged. Wainscoat and his colleagues studied eight geographic groups (represented by samples from Africa, Britain, Cyprus, India, Italy, Melanesia, Polynesia, and Thailand) and argued that "all non-African populations share a limited number of common haplotypes (a set of closely linked genetic loci) whereas Africans have predominantly a different haplotype not found in other populations."[6] According to their interpretation of the patterns of genetic variation in the samples, Wainscoat et al. speculated that (1) there was a small founding population for all living humans, (2) the population that gave rise to all living humans derived from Africa, and (3) the replacement occurred relatively recently (~100,000 years ago). The article by Wainscoat et al. coincided with the release of the box office hit "Out of Africa," and within a short time their interpretation was dubbed the "Out of Africa" theory.[7] Even though a few geneticists expressed doubts about the conclusions,[8] the scientific implications of the article were in tune with the Noah's Ark model and some paleontologists felt this particular version of human origins was strengthened, if not finally confirmed.

Before the article had time to really settle in, it was eclipsed by a much more influential publication by the geneticists Rebecca Cann, Mark Stoneking, and Allan Wilson. This article, which also appeared in *Nature*, bolstered the Noah's Ark model and boldly proclaimed that humans could trace their origins to "one woman . . . who lived about two hundred thousand years ago, probably in Africa."[9] Besides asserting a recent African origin of all living humans, the argument traced the ancestor to a single female, dubbed "Eve" by Wilson. While the β-globin gene cluster results created only a minor puff in human paleontology, the Eve hypothesis hit the field like a cyclone, setting the stage for an often rancorous, five-year debate about recent human origins. The conclusions of the genetic argument and the ensuing debate between the "Eveists" and the "multiregionalists" have been widely reported in the popular media, with articles on modern human origins appearing as cover stories in *Newsweek, U. S. News and World Report, Time*, a *Nova* documentary, and numerous popular science and newspaper accounts on the Eve theory. There is also a book[10] aimed at the popular audience that focuses on the debate and I recommend it to readers of this article. Like no other issue in human paleontology, this debate was recounted in the popular literature, so that in the early 1990s many people outside anthropology have heard about the Eve debate.

Besides the scientific implications, a few researchers suggested there were social consequences stemming from the recent origin of modern humans. With the publication of the β-globin gene cluster results, the narrow variation in this gene complex suggested to some that the human species went through a population crisis and that "[hu]mankind was an endangered species during an important part of its evolution."[11] With the publication of the molecular genetics results, Stephen Jay Gould (one of the leading evolutionary scientists and popularizers of modern biology) pondered in a lead article in *Newsweek*: "it makes us realize that all human beings, despite differences in external appearance, are really members of a single entity that's had a recent origin in one place. There is a kind of biological brotherhood that's much more profound than we ever realized."[12] Gould neglected to note that the Eve model involved a total replacement of one group of humans by another *without* admixture. The Eve theory did not allow interbreeding between the resident and invading groups, which means that the descendants of the original wave of settlers across the Old World would have been fully replaced by the invaders. As Milford Wolpoff once noted, this theory might be better named the "Cain" theory in that "[t]his rendering of modern population dispersals is a story of 'making war, not love,' and if true its implications are not pleasant."[13] Thus, in addition to claiming to solve the riddle of human origins, the Eve theory purportedly told us something about modern human nature, drawing all of us closer together due to our recent common genesis, however unpleasant the implications of the population replacement. Whatever the case, an important consequence of the Eve theory was that it led to very specific predictions about patterns of past variation and these could not be confused with the predictions of the multiregional model. Consequently, with the strictures imposed by the genetic analyses it was possible to test the Old World fossil record against the predictions of the two competing models.

The Essentials of the Debate

While argument over the Noah's Ark and multiregional models preceded the genetics results, several things triggered the relevance and intensity of the debate after 1987. Most important were the implications drawn from the molecular genetics. These data were viewed as sophisticated, technical information that could give an independent, unbiased assessment of what to expect in the fossil record. Some molecular geneticists were quick to point out that their data were qualitatively superior to the fossil record, and there was a certain amount of hubris among some molecular geneticists who felt the genetic data provided "objective information," while interpretations in the fossil record were riddled with subjective assessments.[14]

Another factor in the debate was the publication of new dates for sites in Western Asia and South Africa where some paleoanthropologists argued the earliest modern *Homo sapiens* fossils were found. Supporters of the Noah's Ark model often looked to the Near East for the origin of modern Europeans at two sites (Skhul and Qafzeh) in the Mount Carmel area of northern Israel. Some even called these fossils "proto-Cro-Magnoids" stressing their unique links to the early Upper Paleolithic populations of Europe and their distinctiveness from European and Near Eastern Neanderthals. Initially, it was thought these two sites were dated around thirty thousand to forty thousand years ago, which made the replacement coincide with the last evidence of Neanderthals in Europe. However, at about the same time the molecular estimates for the origin of modern humans were being published, new electron spin resonance and thermo-luminescence dates were appearing for Skhul and Qafzeh.[15] These more than doubled their estimated antiquity and greatly affected the debate, in that there was now a long temporal overlap of so-called "modern" and archaic human forms. For some, due to the contemporaneity of Near Eastern Neanderthals and the so-called "proto-Cro-Magnoids," this meant that two different species of humans lived side by side for a very long time, then eventually the archaic forms were totally replaced by the "modern" Near Eastern forms. For others, the dates of the Skhul and Qafzeh samples were questioned as was the "modernity "of the sample. In addition, a series of anatomical descriptions and new dates were published for fossil human material from the South African sites Border Cave and Klasies River Mouth.[16] For some, fossil material from these two sites was also considered anatomically modern and the dates indicated an antiquity of about one hundred thousand years.

These factors set the stage for a debate on the origins of modern humans. While it's doubtful that any of the participants anticipated an imminent resolution, in 1993 the Eve theory was refuted. To understand the debate and appreciate how it was resolved, it is necessary to review the crucial aspects of the two competing theories and contrast their nonoverlapping predictions about the fossil record.

The Eve theory was based on patterns of variation in mitochondrial DNA (mtDNA) among individuals representing different geographic areas. Mitochondrial DNA is a special type of DNA found outside the nucleus and is associated with energy metabolism in the mitochondria. Several important biological principles about mtDNA made it an attractive tool for attempting to unravel evolutionary relationships.[17]

The complete genetic makeup of mtDNA is relatively short (compared to nuclear DNA) and was fully sequenced so it was possible to make loci by loci comparisons, looking for links among different individuals. This information was used to reconstruct geographic relationships.

Mitochondrial DNA is only inherited through the maternal line (there is no paternal contribution in humans), so in effect it is cloned from one generation to the next. This is significant since during gamete production nuclear DNA is recombined, mixing maternal and paternal genes. Thus, tracing genetic similarities through generations in nuclear DNA is complicated by the "pollution" of the father's genes, while in mtDNA the maternal generations pass along basically unaltered genetic sequences, except for occasional mutations. This characteristic of mtDNA greatly facilitated its use in reconstructing evolutionary phylogenies.

Mutations accumulate more rapidly in mtDNA (compared to nuclear DNA) and this accumulation is presumed to occur at a constant rate, estimated at a 2 to 4 percent change per million years. This rate, coupled with the patterns of geographic variation, led to the estimate of a two-hundred-thousand-year-old "mother of us all."

Finally, it was assumed that no selection operated on mtDNA and that mutations were neutral, causing no change in an individual's fertility or survivorship. This is important since the rate of incorporation of new mutations can be affected by natural selection. The operation of natural selection on mtDNA would markedly (and fatally) affect the regularity of the molecular clock's ticking, reducing the two-hundred-thousand-yearold estimate to a guess.

Using these assumptions, Cann, Stoneking, and Wilson[18] studied the mtDNA variation drawn from 147 individuals and through a statistical program known as PAUP (Phylogenetic Analysis Using Parsimony) reconstructed human phylogeny.

Based on their statistical analysis, they rooted the phylogenetic tree in Africa, due to the finding that both "primary branches lead exclusively to African mtDNAs." Also, since there was a very narrow range of variation in non-African mtDNA, they argued there was no input of ancient, non-African mtDNA in the formation of the modern sample. This meant that the African replacement was complete and did not involve hybridization between the African invaders and the resident, native populations they replaced.

The multiregional evolution model, formulated by Alan Thorne, Xinshi Wu, and Milford Wolpoff,[19] is also based on patterns of worldwide variation. Instead of proposing a major disjunction across the Old World fossil populations, these paleoanthropologists argued that humans were descended from their forerunners in the region, not uniquely from an immigrating group. In many respects this model was an updated version of ideas first developed by Franz Weidenreich in his "polycentric theory."[20] Weidenreich's model was constructed after a long career of studying human fossils from Europe and Asia. His initial work in human paleontology was a reconstruction of an early Neanderthal skull from Ehringsdorf in Germany. He later was involved in the discovery and description of the important middle Pleistocene Chinese human remains from Zhoukoudian, and was well acquainted with the fossil material from Indonesia and with morphological variation in recent populations across Eurasia to Australia. Based on his familiarity with this material, Weidenreich saw regional patterning in certain morphological features. For example, he noted the high incidence of shovel-shaped incisors in fossil and living Asian populations. From these observations, he proposed that human evolution proceeded in each region of the world as an unbroken evolutionary stream and that the living inhabitants of each region exhibited morphological features that could be traced back into the distant fossil record of each region. Rather than a single place for the origin of modern humans, Weidenreich argued for separate geographic centers. In these places populations developed their own morphological features, leading to the inter-regional differences typical of populations today. However, the evolutionary changes did not occur in total isolation; gene exchange and migrations always occurred and all human populations remained members of the same species worldwide.

Multiregional evolution combined Weidenreich's perspective with an updated accounting of the fossils, especially those from North Asia, Indonesia, and Australia. It also incorporated the concept of "center and edge." This was an idea proposed by Alan Thorne,[21] who argued that patterns of variation relate to the geographic position of human populations. For example, those populations near the center of the species' range exchange genes with groups on all sides and maintain high levels of population variation. Those that are more peripheralized (1) take on unique features because they lack the magnitude of gene exchange typical of populations at the center and (2) are more likely to experience genetic drift (random changes) because of their relative isolation. This concept can be used to account for the morphological differences, say, between Europeans and aboriginal Australians. In a geographic sense, both regions are marginal or peripheral areas and at least in prehistoric times both were isolated at opposite ends from the center of the geographic range of *Homo sapiens*. Because of this isolation, genetic drift (or random factors) would increase variation between the native European and Australian populations. In addition, distinctive patterns of natural selection would operate to differentiate the populations since, given the ecological, climatological, and cultural differences between the two regions, human biology would respond in different ways to meet the specific fitness requirements. Consequently, Europeans and Australians have a constellation of features that differentiate them and that can be used to trace their evolution within their own region. Despite these differences, however, there was sufficient gene flow across the whole human range to maintain species integrity. In short, multiregional evolution proposes that geographic regions have chronologically deep human lineages in which unique features develop over time. These unique features serve to unite the fossil and extant humans in an evolving sequence that can be differentiated from other evolving sequences in other regions.

From these brief sketches of the Eve and multiregional theories, it should be apparent that they have contradictory predictions about the mode of origin for modern *Homo sapiens*. The Eve model requires complete replacement outside of Africa and a major break in the evolutionary sequence within a region. Thus, if the Eve theory is correct, the fossil record should reflect clear evidence of an Old World-wide replacement in the late Pleistocene. Following the assumptions of the Eve model, the replacers would have originated in Africa about two hundred thousand years ago, so the earliest modern populations everywhere should resemble the earliest modern populations from Africa, if indeed such fossils exist. Moreover, the replacing fossils would not be expected to resemble the resident populations, since the interpretation of the mtDNA data by the Eveists does not allow for mixing of the invading (Eve) and resident (original) populations.[22] Just the opposite, the multiregional theory hypothesizes the persistence of ancient traits through time since this model assumes that the ancestors of a particular region contribute to the formation of the descendants. Thus, the multiregional view predicts that the fossil record will not show an abrupt appearance of new (modern) human populations, but that ancient morphological features typical of the region will persist in the later populations.

The Fossil Test

Using these unambiguous, nonoverlapping predictions about ancient and recent patterns of geographic variation, it is possible to test the two models. This was the topic of a recent article by myself and four colleagues: Geoffrey Pope, Fred Smith, Alan Thorne, and Milford Wolpoff.[23] In our approach we followed the Popperian view of science, that hypotheses cannot be proven correct, but only refuted. We tested the basic predictions outlined above against the fossil record. It is not possible here to go through all the evidence we reviewed for Africa, Europe, Western Asia, North Asia, and Australasia, but for the full account, consult our detailed article in *American Anthropologist*. By now it should be obvious that since the Eve theory requires total replacement everywhere throughout the Old World, finding evidence for continuity of anatomical traits from ancient to modern populations *even in one region outside Africa* is sufficient evidence to refute the Eve hypothesis.

We started our review with an examination of the fossil record of Australasia (Southeast Asia and Australia), which has an extensive prehistoric sequence spanning probably more than seven hundred thousand years. Figure 1 shows four skulls, all of which are probably males. The skull (Sangiran 17) on the bottom is the most complete Middle Pleistocene skull from Java. Some of its distinctive features include a low flat frontal, large browridges that are continuous from side to side and project anteriorly, a well-developed torus (bony ridge) at the back of the skull, an extensive nuchal plane (the area below the torus where numerous muscles at the back of the neck attach to the skull), thick cranial bones, and a large face marked by massive zygomatics (cheek bones) and large teeth. The skull in the left middle (Willandra Lakes 50) is the oldest known human skull from Australia, probably about sixty thousand years old. Its cranial features clearly resemble Sangiran 17. The forehead is low and flat, the brows are massive, the posterior projection of the skull has a well-demarcated nuchal plane, and the bones of the vault are extremely thick. While there is no face, it is hard to imagine anything but a massive one associated with WLH 50. The

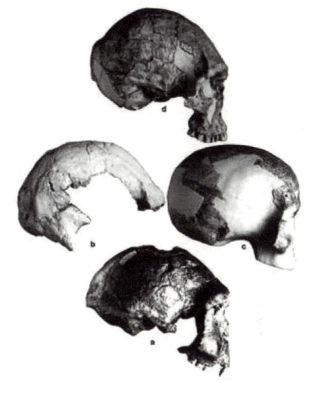

Figure 1

top skull is Kow Swamp 1 from the late Pleistocene of Australia. Kow Swamp 1 shows all the regional features found in the earlier two skulls (for example, it has a very flat frontal), but is clearly more modern in features such as skull height and reduction of the brows. Three skulls do not show all the anatomical variation in the Australasian sequence, but they do demonstrate the basic pattern for change within the region, linking morphological patterns across time in Australasia.

The other skull is Border Cave 1, a specimen from South Africa identified by the Eve supporters as a representative of the early modern populations that left Africa and replaced all other groups.[24] It does not take a specialist in human paleontology to recognize the fundamental anatomical differences separating Border Cave 1 from the three Australasian skulls. If the Eve replacement theory is correct, we would expect Border Cave 1 to differ from one of the oldest specimens from Australasia (Sangiran 17), because the Border Cave 1 fossil is much more recent. We might also expect Border Cave 1 and WLH 50 to differ substantially, since some might argue that WLH 50 predates the total replacement in Australia. However, since Kow Swamp 1 could only be descended from the Eve group, there should be some resemblance between it and Border Cave 1. But, Kow Swamp 1 continues the morphological pattern found in the earlier skulls from the region. It does not particularly resemble Border Cave 1 and, since descendants resemble their ancestors, Border Cave 1 is a poor candidate as the precursor of native Australians. While these Australasian skulls represent only a portion of the entire variation of the region, the pattern they show typifies the general evolutionary relationships over time. It is clear from Figure 1 that the skulls on the top, left, and bottom form the more likely evolutionary sequence. To insert populations resembling the Border Cave skull with a completely different morphology requires that the descendant populations take on the exact same constellation of features that uniquely typify the populations they totally replaced. Our analysis concluded that there is no major break in the Australasian sequence that would provide evidence for the sudden appearance of modern *Homo sapiens* invading from Africa. Rather, regionally restricted features persist over time; if the African Eves did invade and replace all the resident groups in Australasia, they left no trace of their features in the populations they would have founded. Thus, although the fossil evidence does not prove multiregional continuity, it directly contradicts the Eve predictions.

This problem of similarity between ancient and modern populations in Australasia did not go unnoticed by some Eve supporters. To interpret these observations in a way compatible with the Eve theory, Stringer and Andrews reached for an explanation which is unacceptable to most anthropologists: "Perhaps, Australia was a special case where local differentiation, cultural practices, or pathologies led in some cases to apparent evolutionary reversals."[25] Such an unfortunate conclusion is, perhaps, not surprising since an earlier definition of modern *Homo sapiens* by Stringer[26] defined modern humans on the basis of European features and, when applied to native Australians, about one-third of these modern people[27] were excluded from the category of *Homo sapiens*! Yet, rather than recognize the anatomical connections over time which unequivocally refuted the Eve hypothesis, Stringer and Andrews relegated native Australians to evolutionary throwbacks. In addition to the perpetuation of this deplorable stereotype about native groups and their lifeways, there is no biological reason to suspect that "local differentiation, cultural practices, or pathologies" would produce a convergence of identical traits which, according to the Eve hypothesis, were lost due to a total population replacement by an invading group. Stop for a moment to consider the

evolutionary trail that would have to be hypothesized in the Australasian sequence to make it consistent with the Eve theory.

1. There is an initial colonization of the Southeast Asian archipelago by around one million years ago.
2. Human groups migrate over sea to Australia, perhaps by sixty thousand to eighty thousand years ago. These earliest Australian fossils bear little resemblance to the fossil African Eves, but strongly resemble the earlier fossils from the same region.
3. A replacement of all the region's original inhabitants occurs either before the colonization of Australia or after it. The African immigrants (who have left no currently known fossils in Australasia) with their geographically distinct features do not interbreed with the resident populations. Moreover, they are able to swamp and totally replace the native groups (even though there is not a shred of archaeological evidence for the introduction of a new technology associated with the earliest modern Australians). Note here that even the European immigration to Australia with its accrued benefits of the Industrial Revolution and the intent and action to eliminate the native peoples did not succeed in completely replacing the native Australians.
4. Finally, in recent times, modern native Australians carry specific anatomical features that plainly link them to past populations of the region. These identical features evolve a second time, transforming the African Eve morphology back to the basic pattern typical of populations before the invasion. Visually this convoluted sequence can be traced by following the sequence a-c-d up the right side of Figure 1. If this sequence represents reality, it is important to note that there are no skulls found in middle-to late-Pleistocene times in Australasia that even remotely resemble the morphology typical of the African Eve Border Cave 1 individual. Consequently, besides having to construct some questionable and objectionable explanations for the links between the past and present variation, the Eve model requires an immigrant population (with origins in Africa), for which no biological or archaeological evidence exists. On the other hand, if one follows the a-b-d sequence in Figure 1, there is no necessity for speculating about a total population replacement or about the reappearance of anatomical features in the immigrating groups. Rather, native Aus-

Table 1

Incidence of Shovelling (Percentages) in Chinese, European, and African-American Samples

	Sample Size	*No Shovel*	*Trace*	*Semi-Shovel*	*Shovel-Shaped*	*Total*
Chinese[a>]	651	8.3	1.4	23.2	67.1	100.0
Europeans[a]	1000	62.5	28.5	7.4	1.6	100.0
African-Americans[a]	807	51.0	35.0	9.9	4.1	100.0

[a] From Hrdlicka.[30] Represents an average for males and females and for central and lateral incisors.

tralians could be seen as developing out of long-term change of the region's inhabitants, along with gene flow from other areas.

Clearly, in Australasia the basic predictions of the Eve theory are violated. These effectively refute the Eve hypothesis, since the Eve theory requires a complete, total replacement in all populations across the Old World. Even so, it is reasonable to ask if Australia is the exception to a general pattern with substantial evidence for replacement elsewhere around the Old World. Or, do other areas also show the persistence of ancient traits in late Pleistocene and Recent populations? As my colleagues and I have argued,[28] evolutionary sequences throughout the Old World provide undeniable evidence for some degree of continuity from ancient to modern populations. If one examines the fossil record for East Asia, there is overwhelming evidence for the persistence of specific cranial, facial, and dental features through time. One example will suffice. Table 1 reviews data for the incidence of shovelling in maxillary incisors for large samples of modern Chinese, Europeans, and African-Americans. Shovel-shaped incisors are defined by the existence of ridges along the margins of the central and lateral incisors in the upper jaw. According to some recent research,[29] there are details of incisor shovelling that are unique in East Asians compared to those of European or African descent. But, even ignoring these trait distinctions, there are unmistakable differences in frequency that distinguish the three groups. As is clear from the table, shovelled incisors exist in high frequencies in Chinese populations: 90 percent of the Chinese sample has marked shovelling (semi-shovel + shovel-shaped), while these categories reach less than 15 percent in European and African-American samples.

This is not a new observation, since this trait is often used as an important feature in modern forensic cases to identify suspects of Asian descent. Indeed, this regional trait is found in the initial founding pop-

ulations of China, where the earliest human teeth show distinct shovelling of the upper incisors. As in the Australasian case, it is important to recognize that modern patterns of anatomical variation extend into the deep past, and traits typical of ancient populations persist through time. In addition to incisor shovelling there is a constellation of features that appear early and are unique to East Asia.[31] Most of these would have had to evolve a second time if the Eve theory were correct—and that is hard to believe.

Even in Europe where the traditional view has held that Neanderthals were totally replaced by invasions of "modern" *Homo sapiens*, there is considerable evidence for the persistence of anatomical features through time.[32] These unique European features link the Neanderthal and Upper Paleolithic samples and run completely contrary to the Eve predictions, unless in yet another area, unique features would have evolved again in a replacing population that wiped out all the original inhabitants who possessed exactly the same features. It is difficult to accept repeated evolution of the same trait in one area, but a model that requires this type of origin for important sets of traits in every geographic area across the Old World is beyond the range of scientific possibility.

The African Evidence of Modern *Homo Sapiens*

The persistence of traits across long stretches of time is not the only prediction of the Eve hypothesis that is refuted by the fossil record. There is also no evidence for the early appearance of a modern *Homo sapiens* population in Africa. Remember that this is a fundamental prediction of the Eve hypothesis, since it is argued that the sole source of mtDNA in living people today is derived from an African population that differentiated around two hundred thousand years ago. It is reasonable to ask then if there is evidence for the appearance of a modern population in Africa. It might be that such a population has not yet been found in the fossil record. But this is not an acceptable premise, since we are required to work with the fossil record as we know it. Otherwise, if we relied on the unfound and unknown, anything would be possible. Hypotheses cannot be refuted on the basis of discoveries that have yet to be made! If so, there would be no scientific basis for any theory of human evolution. Some workers have identified fossils from Klasies River Mouth and Border Cave (South Africa) as the ancestors of us all. Much of the Border Cave material will always be without provenience due to the excavation procedures; for example, the most complete skull (Border Cave 1) was discovered when a farmer was digging for bat guano in the cave sediments. Beyond this, there are severe problems in accepting the rather fragmentary specimens from these sites as representing a modern population.[33] For example, three of the four mandibles from Klasies River Mouth Cave lack a chin, a feature that everywhere in the world is considered a mark of modernity. Moreover, even if the dates of Klasies are correct (eighty thousand to one hundred thousand years), an equally well-developed chin is found in the Tabun B mandible from Israel, which may be older by as much as fifty thousand years. There are numerous other features of the so-called "anatomically modern" *Homo sapiens* specimens from Africa which belie a modern classification.[34] While it may be true that some modern traits occur in a few specimens from South Africa, the same can be found in other areas in the world.[35] The fact is that there are a series of archaic features also present, and these disqualify the material as constituting a modern population.

The Genetic Refutation

From our analysis of the fossil record, we were able to reject the most basic predictions of the Eve theory,[36] which represents a clear refutation of the Eve hypothesis. But as it turns out, the Eve hypothesis is also rejected by the very genetic data on which it was based. This refutation comes from a detailed analysis by Alan Templeton,[37] an expert in phylogenetic analysis and creator of some of the statistical procedures used in the analyses of the mtDNA which culminated in the Eve theory. In his analysis of the original mtDNA data (which were provided by Stoneking), Templeton demonstrated that (1) the "geographic location of the common ancestor is ambiguous," (2) the date of the ancient Eve is "extremely ambiguous but is likely to be considerably more than two hundred thousand years ago," (3) the patterning in phy-

logenetic trees of mtDNA variation is a consequence "of a few recent population expansions of limited geographic range "along with some "geneflow throughout the entire time period tracing back to the common mitochondrial ancestor," and (4) mtDNA and nuclear DNA provide no evidence for a "single source population for all genetic variation."[38] Templeton's results are consistent with other analyses,[39] which taken together demonstrate that the genetic underpinnings of the Eve theory are shaky at best. In fact, instead of being an objective, accurate rendering of the course of human evolution, many unsupportable presumptions about the molecular data were made that directly affect the reliability of the conclusions based on the molecular data.

Conclusion

Coupled with the evidence from paleoanthropology, the undoing of the Eve theory of human origins is now total. The genetic basis on which it rested has collapsed and the fossil record, which represents the real remains of individuals who existed in the past, unambiguously contradict each of the basic predictions of the Eve theory. The ultimate measure of progress in science is the ability to refute hypotheses and then move on and attempt to refute others. The death of the Eve theory does not prove that the theory of multiregional evolution is necessarily correct. But, as Templeton concluded in his review of the mtDNA evidence, "all humans represent a single long-term evolutionary lineage with regional subdivision and always have throughout the entire period marked by mtDNA." This is multiregional evolution and this theory should now be the focus for refutation.

Notes

1. J. E. Ferrell, "Bone Wars," *Image, The San Francisco Examiner*, August 23, 1987, pp. 14–35.
2. Milford H. Wolpoff, Wu Xinshi, and Alan G. Thorne, "Modern *Homo sapiens* Origins: A General Theory of Hominid Evolution Involving the Fossil Evidence from East Asia," in Fred H. Smith and Frank Spencer, eds., *The Origins of Modern Humans: A World Survey of the Fossil Evidence* (New York: Alan R. Liss, 1984), pp. 411–483; Milford H. Wolpoff and Alan G. Thorne, "The Case against Eve," *New Scientist* 22, no. 1774 (1991): 33–37; Alan G. Thorne and Milford H. Wolpoff, "The Multiregional Evolution of Humans," *Scientific American* 266, no. 4 (1992): 76–83.
3. William W. Howells, "Explaining Modern Man: Evolutionists versus Migrationists," *Journal of Human Evolution* 5 (1991): 477–496.

4. William W. Howells, *Getting Here* (Washington, DC: Compass, 1993).

5. J. S. Wainscoat, A. V. S. Hill, A. L. Boyce, J. Flint, M. Hernandez, S. L. Thein, J. M. Old, J. R. Lynch, A. G. Faust, D. J. Weatherall, and J. B. Clegg, "Evolutionary Relationships of Human Populations from an Analysis of Nuclear DNA Polymorphisms," *Nature* 319 (1986): 491–493.

6. Ibid.

7. Eugene Giles and Stanley H. Ambrose, "Are We All Out of Africa?" *Nature* 322 (1986): 21–22.

8. Ibid.

9. Rebecca L. Cann, Mark Stoneking, and Allan C. Wilson, "Mitochondrial DNA and Human Evolution," *Nature* 325 (1987): 31–36.

10. Michael H. Brown, *The Search for Eve* (New York: Harper and Row, 1990).

11. J. S. Jones and S. Rouhani, "How Small Was the Bottleneck?" *Nature* 319 (1986): 449–450.

12. John Tierney, Lynda Wright, and Karen Springen, "The Search for Adam and Eve," *Newsweek* (January 11, 1988): 46–52.

13. Brown, *The Search for Eve*, p. 229.

14. Allan C. Wilson and Rebecca L. Cann, "The Recent African Genesis of Humans," *Scientific American* 266 (1992): 68–73.

15. H. P. Schwarcz, R. Grün, B. Vandermeersch, O. Bar Yosef, H. Valladas, and E. Tchernov, "ESR Dates for the Hominid Burial Site of Qafzeh," *Journal of Human Evolution* 17 (1988): 733–737; C. B. Stringer, R. Grün, H. P. Schwarcz, and P. Goldberg, "ESR Dates for the Homonid Burial Site of Es Skhul in Israel," *Nature* 338 (1989): 756–758.

16. G. P. Rightmire and H. J. Deacon, "Comparative Studies of Late Pleistocene Human Remains from Klasies River Mouth," *Journal of Human Evolution* 20 (1991): 131–156.

17. Cann, Stoneking, and Wilson, "Mitochondrial DNA and Human Evolution," pp. 31–32.

18. Ibid.

19. Wolpoff, Wu, and Thorne, "Modern *Homo sapiens* Origins: A General Theory of Hominid Evolution Involving the Fossil Evidence from East Asia."

20. Franz Weidenreich, "The Skull of *Sinanthropus pekinensis*: A Comparative Study of a Primitive Hominid Skull," *Palaeontologia Sinica* n.s. D, no. 10 (1943).

21. Alan G. Thorne and Milford H. Wolpoff, "Regional Continuity in Australasian Pleistocene Hominid Evolution," *American Journal of Physical Anthropology* 55 (1981): 337–349.

22. Chris Stringer and Peter Andrews, "Genetics and the Fossil Evidence for the Origin of Modern Humans," *Science* 239 (1988): 1263–1268.

23. David W. Frayer, Milford H. Wolpoff, Alan G. Thorne, Fred H. Smith, and Geoffrey G. Pope, "Theories of Modern Human Origins: The Paleontological Test," *American Anthropologist* 95 (1993): 14–50.

24. Chris Stringer, "The Emergence of Modern Humans," *Scientific American* 263 (1990): 98–104.

25. Stringer and Andrews, "Genetics and the Fossil Evidence for the Origin of Modern Humans," p. 1267.

26. Michael H. Day and Chris B. Stringer, "A Reconsideration of the Omo Kibish Remains and the erectus-sapiens Transition," in Henri deLumley, ed., *L'Homo erectus et la Place de l'Homme de Tautavel Parmi les Hominidés Fossiles*, vol. 2 (Nice: Louis-Jean Scientific and Literary Publications, 1982), pp. 814–816.

27. Milford H. Wolpoff, "Describing Anatomically Modern *Homo sapiens*: A Distinction without a Definable Difference," *Anthropos* (Brno) 23 (1986): 41–54.

28. Frayer, Wolpoff, Thorne, Smith, and Pope, "Theories of Modern Human Origins: The Paleontological Test."

29. Tracy L. Crummett, "A New Handle on the Shovel," *American Journal of Physical Anthropology*, supplement 12 (1991): 64.

30. Ales Hrdlicka, "Shovel-Shaped Teeth," *American Journal of Physical Anthropology* 3 (1920): 429–465.

31. Geoffrey G. Pope, "The Craniofacial Evidence for the Emergence of Modern Humans in China," *Yearbook of Physical Anthropology* 35 (1992): 243–298; Wolpoff, Wu, and Thorne, "Modern *Homo sapiens* Origins: A General Theory of Hominid Evolution Involving the Fossil Evidence from East Asia," pp. 424–436.

32. Frayer, Wolpoff, Thorne, Smith, and Pope, "Theories of Modern Human Origins: The Paleontological Test"; Milford H. Wolpoff, "The Place of the Neandertals in Human Evolution," in E. Trinkaus, ed., *The Emergence of Modern Humans. Biocultural Adaptations in the Later Pleistocene* (Cambridge: Cambridge University Press, 1989), pp. 97–141; Fred H. Smith, "The Neanderthals: Evolutionary Dead Ends or Ancestors of Modern People?" *Journal of Anthropological Research* 47 (1991): 219–238; David W. Frayer, "Evolution at the European Edge: Neanderthal and Upper Paleolithic Relationships," *Préhistoire Européene* 2 (1992): 9–69.

33. Rachel Caspari and Milford H. Wolpoff, "The Morphological Affinities of the Klasies River Mouth Skeletal Remains," *American Journal of Physical Anthropology* 81 (1990): 203; Fred H. Smith, "Models and Realities in Modern Human Origins: The African Fossil Evidence," *Philosophical Transactions of the Royal Society of London*, series B 337 (1992): 243–250.

34. Smith, "Models and Realities"; Frayer, Wolpoff, Thorne, Smith, and Pope, "Theories of Modern Human Origins: The Paleontological Test."

35. Frayer, Wolpoff, Thorne, Smith, and Pope, "Theories of Modern Human Origins: The Paleontological Test."

36. Ibid.

37. Alan R. Templeton, "The 'Eve' Hypotheses: A Genetic Critique and Reanalysis," *American Anthropologist* 95 (1992): 51–72.

38. Ibid.

39. P. Darlu and P. Tassy, "Roots (A Comment of the Evolution of Human Mitochondrial DNA and the Origins of Modern Humans)," *Human Evolution* 2 (1987): 407–412; Laurent Excoffier and André Langaney," Origin and Differentiation of Human Mitochondrial DNA," *American Journal of Human Genetics* 44 (1989): 73–85; David R. Maddison, "African Origin of Human Mitochondrial DNA Re-examined," *Systematic Zoology* 40 (1991): 355–363.

Suggested Readings

Brown, Michael H. *The Search for Eve.* New York: Harper and Row, 1990. A detailed account of the genesis and debate about the Eve theory before its resolution in 1993. The book also gives a feel for the personalities involved in the debate with sketches and interviews of some of the main scientific participants.

Lewin, Roger. "The Mitochondrial Route to Human Origins." *Mosaic* 22 (1991): 46–55. A concise review of the basic premises of the Eve and multiregional views by one of the world's premier science writers.

Stringer, Chris, and Peter Andrews. "Genetics and the Fossil Evidence for the Origin of Modern Humans." *Science* 239 (1988): 1263–1268. The first attempt by the "Eveists" to integrate evidence from mtDNA and the fossil record. The article ended with the statement that "paleoanthropologists who ignore the increasing wealth of genetic data on human population relationships will do so at their peril"—an ironic statement given the recent evidence for the misinterpretations of the molecular data.

Thorne, Alan G., and Milford H. Wolpoff. "The Multiregional Evolution of Humans." *Scientific American* 266 (1992): 76–83. A detailed, popular statement about the multiregional model from two prominent paleoanthropologists.

Wilson, Alan C., and Rebecca L. Cann. "The Recent African Genesis of Humans." *Scientific American* 266 (1992): 68–73. A detailed, popular statement about the Eve model from two of the originators of the molecular basis for Eve.

Wolpoff, Milford H., James N. Spuhler, Fred H. Smith, Jakov Radovcic, Geoffrey G. Pope, David W. Frayer, Robert Eckhardt, and Geoff Clark. "Modern Human Origins." *Science* 241 (1988): 772–773. A succinct, one-page response to the Stringer and Andrews article on modern human origins in *Science*. This was the opening round in the scientific debate about modern human origins.

When and How Did Humans Populate the New World?

William J. Parry

An Old Dispute

For almost five hundred years, European and American scholars have wondered about the origins of the native people (or "Indians") of the Americas. They had somehow reached the New World before Columbus, but when? How long had they been there? Where did they come from? Or had they always been there?

Philosophers, clergy, and scientists debated this topic for centuries. Lacking any direct evidence, they were forced to rely on speculation and guesswork. The famous American writer Washington Irving, in a satirical piece published in 1809,[1] summarized many of the most popular theories: that the Native Americans were descendants of Israelites, Vikings, Chinese, Egyptians, Celts, Phoenicians, Romans, Africans, or people from the mythical lost continent of Atlantis; that they came by land or by water via Greenland, Siberia, or Antarctica; or even that they had come from the moon!

As Washington Irving sadly noted,

It is an evil much to be lamented, that none of the worthy writers . . . could ever commence his work, without immediately declaring hostilities against every writer who had treated on the same subject. . . . If . . . these learned men can weave whole systems out of nothing, what would be their productions were they furnished with substantial materials![2]

In subsequent years, our knowledge of this topic has grown, even if the tone of the debate has not improved much. The development of archaeology in the United States during the nineteenth century was largely in response to this controversy, as early archae-ologists attempted to discover when and how and from where did the ancestors of the Native Americans first colonize the Americas.[3]

AGREEMENTS AND DISAGREEMENTS

Almost all modern anthropologists would agree that the ancestors of the Native Americans came from eastern Asia, and that they first crossed from Siberia into Alaska during the last Ice Age, at least twelve thousand years ago. Once in Alaska, they moved south, eventually spreading throughout North and South America. The best evidence for this migration is not archaeological but biological. Studies of DNA, blood groups, tooth shapes, and other genetic traits clearly show that all modern Native Americans are biologically related to each other, and to the native peoples of eastern Asia.[4]

There are basically two major areas of controversy. First, how many migrations were there? Are all Native Americans descended from one single band of immigrants, or did several different groups migrate into the Americas at different times? Second, how long ago did the *first* migrants enter the New World?

From archaeological research, we know that humans had settled in what is now the United States sometime before 11,600 years ago. There are a number of discovered sites that yield traces of these "Paleoindians" (early Indians); when dated by radiocarbon dating,[5] they all turn out to be about 11,500 to 10,500 years old.[6] Because some of the first evidence of these Paleoindians was found near the town of Clovis, in New Mexico, they are often referred to as the "Clovis people." Their handiwork is relatively easy to recognize, because they made a very distinctive style of spearpoint. These "Clovis fluted points" are finely flaked and symmetrical, with a characteristic groove or "flute" running up each face.

The Clovis people lived near the end of the Pleistocene epoch (the "Ice Age"), at a time when the climate was distinctly colder than today. Most of what is now Canada was then covered with glaciers, thick sheets of ice. In order to reach the interior of North America, the earliest immigrants would have had to thread their way between (or around) these massive barriers of ice and snow.

During the peak glaciation, about seventeen thousand to thirteen thousand years ago, it was probably impossible to cross Canada.[7] So the first immigrants might not have been able to reach the United States until sometime after thirteen thousand years ago, in which case the Clovis people were probably the first immigrants.

However, it is physically possible for people to have crossed at an earlier date, sometime before seventeen thousand years ago. In that case, the Clovis people would *not* have been the first Americans. Rather, they might have been the descendants of pre-Clovis immigrants, or the descendants of a separate group of later migrants. This is the crux of the controversy: Is there any evidence of pre-Clovis people in the Americas, or were the Clovis people the first immigrants?

Why Is This an Interesting Question?

Archaeologists, like everyone else, are motivated by many complex feelings. Almost all of us went into archaeology because we enjoy doing fieldwork, and more importantly, we want to satisfy our intellectual curiosity. We want to know what really happened in the distant past, and it's thrilling to be able to answer a question that no one else has been able to answer before. But many arguments begin from less altruistic motives, as Washington Irving pointed out. Sometimes we compete with each other, seeking older or more spectacular finds, or attacking someone else's theories (and defending our own), not to discover the truth, but to make ourselves look superior to our colleagues.

This has been a particular problem in seeking the First Americans. We could call this the "Guinness Book of Records" syndrome: Every archaeologist wants to find the *oldest* site in the Americas, just for the sake of the recognition that would come from making a record-setting discovery. But why should anyone else care? What difference would it make if

the oldest site turns out to be twelve thousand years old, fourteen thousand years old, twenty thousand years old, or one hundred thousand years old?

In fact, it makes a big difference, because the answer that you give to the question "How old is the oldest site in the Americas?" determines how you will answer a whole series of other questions about how humans behave in general. The first peopling of the Americas provides us with a unique case study of how people behave in certain situations. We begin with two large continents, teeming with animal life but devoid of humans. When the first humans arrived in this New World, what did they do? How did they react to this new situation? What impact did they have on the environment? The answers to all of these questions depend on first determining exactly *when* they first entered the Americas.

Let me mention just two examples. First, we know that the Clovis people, who were living in North America shortly after twelve thousand years ago, hunted a variety of large animals, including mammoth and mastodon (extinct varieties of elephant), wild horse, camel, caribou, and an extinct variety of bison. Except for the caribou, all of these animals became extinct between eleven thousand and ten thousand years ago.[8]

If the Clovis people were the first humans in the New World, then they might be responsible for these mass extinctions. As soon as they arrived in Americas, they started hunting animals that had never before seen humans (and maybe didn't know how to defend themselves). Within a thousand years, all of these animals were gone. Some archaeologists have concluded that the Clovis people killed off nearly all of the large animals (or "megafauna") in the Americas.[9]

On the other hand, if the Clovis people were *not* the first settlers in the Americas, then the animals must have coexisted with humans for thousands of years. In that case, it is unlikely that human hunting can be blamed for the extermination of the animals, and we must seek a different explanation. It has been suggested that environmental change might be the cause: The climate was rapidly warming around ten thousand years ago, and perhaps the animals couldn't adjust.[10]

A second question focuses on human population growth and expansion. The earliest Clovis sites that we know of, in the northern Plains of the United States, have radiocarbon dates no earlier than 11,600 years old.[11] A Clovis site in Nova Scotia, on the east coast of Canada, dates to about 10,600 years ago.[12] The site of Fell's Cave, at the very southernmost tip of South America, yielded a radiocarbon date of 10,700 years old.[13] If the Clovis people were the first inhabitants of the Americas, then they must have spread incredibly rapidly, even explosively, since they had reached the farthest shores of North and South America within one thousand years of their first entry into the continental United States, migrating through diverse environments to reach those points. On the other hand, if the Clovis people were *not* the first inhabitants of the Americas, then their population might have increased and spread much more slowly, and it may have taken tens of thousands of years to populate the two continents. We know that it is possible for human populations to increase and expand very rapidly, under certain special conditions,[14] but we won't know if that was the case for the first Americans, unless we can determine when they first entered the New World.

If the Clovis people were the first, arriving no more than twelve thousand years ago, then they had a profound impact on the Americas. It would appear that their populations grew explosively, expanded rapidly, and had a massive impact on the natural environment, culminating in the destruction of most of the large animal species that inhabited the New World. On the other hand, if some pre-Clovis people were the first inhabitants, arriving more than seventeen thousand years ago, then their populations and their impact on the environment would seem to have been much less.

What Is the Evidence?

In order to discover whether the Clovis or the pre-Clovis people were the first inhabitants of the Americas, we must carefully weigh the evidence on both sides. If we want to know what really happened, it is not enough to support one side or the other just because we wish the theory to be true, or we are friends with the people who support the theory, or because a majority of our colleagues believe it and we want to be on the winning side. You do not discover truth in science just by taking a vote.

Unfortunately, much of what has been written on the first peopling of the Americas borders on pseudoscience. Some scholars who claim to have discovered very early sites have been slow to publish their actual data and evidence. Rather than let the rest of us decide for ourselves whether or not they have proved their claims, they just say, "Trust us. Take our word for it." When you ask them to show you proof that their claims or interpretations are correct, some of them respond with personal attacks, saying that anyone who doubts them is narrow-minded and dog-

matic, or jealous and elitist.[15] This may be a good way to gain sympathy, but it's a bad way to discover scientific facts.

One of the difficulties I had in writing this summary is that so few of the claims for pre-Clovis occupations are backed up by published data. As of this writing (June 1993), not a single one of the sites that I will be discussing has been described in print in enough detail that I can really be sure that their claims are valid. I had to rely on the incomplete information found in brief preliminary reports, popular articles, and in one case the first volume of a planned multi-volume series (the other volumes not yet published).

In theory, it should be easy to prove that the Clovis people were not the first inhabitants of the Americas. All you would need is a single site that had indisputable evidence of human occupation before twelve thousand years ago; that would be sufficient to prove that there were pre-Clovis people in the Americas. On the other hand, it would be very difficult to prove that there *weren't* any pre-Clovis people, even if this were the truth. Just because you haven't been able to find any pre-Clovis sites, even after a long search, doesn't mean that one might not be discovered somewhere tomorrow. After all, there are still many places where we haven't looked, so it's almost impossible to prove that there are *no* pre-Clovis sites anywhere. We might think that pre-Clovis sites are unlikely, but we really can't prove it.

However, many people do claim to have discovered pre-Clovis sites, and thereby proven that the Clovis people were not the first to arrive in the New World. What sorts of evidence would be needed to demonstrate a pre-Clovis occupation? There are three basic points that need to be established, before a site can be accepted as valid evidence for pre-Clovis inhabitants.

The first point that must be demonstrated is that humans did in fact occupy the site—that the traces found there were left by people, not by wild animals or natural forces. The best evidence would be actual human skeletal remains. However, no human skeletons more than eleven thousand years old have yet been discovered in the Americas.[16] If human bones are not present, then there must be some other clear evidence: artifacts (tools and implements) and features (hearths, pits, and other constructions) of unquestionable human manufacture.

The second point that must be established is the age of the site. If a site is to provide evidence for pre-Clovis occupation, not only must it be shown that humans lived there; they must also have lived there more than twelve thousand years ago. Radiocarbon dating is the most commonly used technique (see note 5), but there are also many other ways of establishing the age of a site.[17] Ideally, it would be most convincing if several independent techniques all point to the same date.

Third, and most important, the archaeologist must demonstrate a valid *association*. This is the key to almost all archaeological inferences. In other words, are the dated materials really related to the evidences of human occupation? Were all of the materials deposited together at the same time, or have materials of different age been mixed together? Perhaps genuine tools, of relatively recent date, have been accidentally inserted into natural features of much greater age.

It can be very difficult to determine whether or not the items found in an archaeological site are really associated. A lot depends on the archaeologist's experience, ability to distinguish subtle changes in the soil that might mark some disturbance or discontinuity in the deposits, and the amount of care taken in excavating and precisely recording the locations and relationships of all finds.

Much of the debate surrounding pre-Clovis sites focuses on the question of association. It can be difficult to tell from a written report whether or not the archaeologist has correctly observed and interpreted the relationships among the finds. It is doubly difficult when, as is the case with almost all of the claimed pre-Clovis sites, the archaeologist doesn't bother to tell you exactly what was observed in the field, and why he or she concluded that certain materials were associated.

To illustrate the arguments that surround most pre-Clovis sites, I focus on several specific examples. Each of these has been claimed, at one time or another, to represent the definitive proof of pre-Clovis settlement in the Americas. But each of these is also deficient in at least one of the key points: Either the evidence for human presence, early dates, or the association of the two has been disputed.

THE CALICO SITE: HUMAN PRESENCE?

The Calico site, located in the Mohave Desert of California, is perhaps one of the most famous of the claimed pre-Clovis sites. It owes much of its notoriety to the involvement of Louis Leakey, the famed investigator of Olduvai Gorge in Africa. Late in his life, Leakey turned his attention to the Americas, determined to find traces of Early Man here, just as he had in Africa. The endorsement of such a famous scholar put Calico on the map.[18]

Excavations at Calico began in 1964 and still continue, at least on a small scale, thirty years later. There is no dispute about the great age of this site. Originally believed to be more than seventy thousand years old, it has now been shown to be about two hundred thousand years old.[19] The Calico site is located in an ancient alluvial fan—a mass of mud and gravel that slid down the side of a mountain. This gravel includes many chunks of flint. Not surprisingly, many of these rocks are broken, since they must have clashed against each other when they flowed down the slope. However, the excavators claim that there are some humanly produced stone tools mixed in with this mass of naturally broken rocks. After decades of excavation that have uncovered millions of broken rocks, they have identified about three thousand that they believe were *possibly* flaked by humans. From those three thousand they selected three hundred that they consider to have *probably* been of human manufacture. Of those three hundred there are about thirty that are considered to be crude but unmistakable tools made by humans.[20]

Except for the crude stone "tools," there is no other evidence for a human presence at the site: There are no human skeletons, no animal bones, and no convincing features. Thus, the entire claim for pre-Clovis occupation at Calico hinges on whether or not the broken rocks were fractured by humans (as opposed to natural forces). Several investigators have measured a sample of the specimens, and compared these measurements to naturally broken rocks and to genuine tools from other sites. Based on their measurements, one group of archaeologists has claimed that all of the specimens are natural,[21] while another group claims that their measurements prove that some specimens are humanly worked.[22]

The biggest problem with the Calico site is the way the evidence was collected. In principle, one of the worst sins that scientists can commit is to bias their data by selectively discarding any observations that don't fit their preconceived theories, in order to alter the final results. This is considered to be a form of scientific cheating only slightly short of outright fraud.[23]

In essence, this is what was done at Calico, by selecting a small number of "good" specimens and ignoring the vast majority that clearly were not tools. Even Louis Leakey's wife Mary, a noted archaeologist in her own right, was critical:

> However meticulous the excavation, he was still arguing in a completely unscientific way. . . . To me, it was the treatment of the finds that was most shocking. . . . [The excavator] sorted

through each heap [of stones] and selected certain pieces as possibly pleasing to Louis. Later, whenever Louis happened to be in California next, he would take certain pieces from the selection kept for him and pronounce them to be artifacts.[24]

My own opinion, and I think the consensus of most other archaeologists, is that all of the stones from Calico are naturally fractured and that none of them were worked by humans. There are some good criteria for distinguishing stone tools from natural rocks if you have an unbiased sample to study.[25] But it's impossible to tell if a single rock is a tool or not, when that rock has been singled out from an otherwise random assortment just because it is the one in a million that happens to look like a tool.

There are a number of other claimed pre-Clovis sites that have been the center of similar controversies. They are clearly very ancient, and in some cases have fossil animal bones as well as broken rocks, but none have human skeletal remains or definite cultural features. In each case, the only evidence for a human presence is broken rocks (or broken animal bones) that are interpreted as crude tools manufactured by humans. A few of the best-known examples are the Texas Street site in California, the recently reported Pendejo Cave site in New Mexico, Richmond Hill in Belize (Central America), Pikimachay Cave in Peru, and Pedra Furada in Brazil.[26]

The most spectacular example is Monte Verde, in Chile. This site has multiple occupations, of which the two earliest are claimed to be pre-Clovis, dating about thirteen thousand and thirty-three thousand years ago. Most, if not all of the stone "tools" that are associated with these early layers appear to be naturally fractured rocks. The excavators concede this point, but still claim that they were *used* as tools by humans, even if not deliberately manufactured.[27]

Because of its setting in a wet location, Monte Verde is exceptional in having pieces of preserved wood and other organic materials. In one area, a number of logs were found, lying in roughly rectangular arrangements, that the excavators interpret as the remains of wooden houses. Many archaeologists find this evidence very impressive, although a few skeptics have suggested that the logs are just natural dead trees, and don't provide convincing evidence of a human presence.[28] Until a detailed final report—with clear illustrations—is published, it is difficult to evaluate the claims made for this site, so it is best to suspend judgment for the time being.

THE LEWISVILLE SITE: DATING?

When the Lewisville site was excavated in Texas in 1956 it appeared that it would finally prove the presence of pre-Clovis populations in North America. The presence of humans was unquestionable: There were simple but definite stone tools (choppers and scrapers), features (hearths), and bones from extinct animals (some burned, in the hearths). Several radiocarbon dates from the hearths were all greater than thirty-seven thousand years old.[29]

The only objection to Lewisville was that one of the stone tools was a Clovis point. By definition, it could not be a pre-Clovis site, and it was thought impossible that a Clovis site could be thirty-seven thousand years old. Therefore, the Clovis point could not be associated with the dates. Some archaeologists suggested that the Clovis point was accidentally (or even fraudulently) introduced into the site from somewhere else. Others suggested that none of the stone tools was really associated with the dates, but that materials of different ages were mixed, and that the "hearths" were natural formations.

Curiously, no archaeologists ever questioned the accuracy of the dates—only their association. After the excavation, the site was flooded by a reservoir, and could not be reexamined. This situation changed in 1980, when a drought lowered the water level and exposed the site once again. Reexcavation yielded more hearths and stone tools. Additional samples were taken from the hearths for new radiocarbon dates. When these samples were closely examined in the laboratory, however, it was discovered that they were not wood charcoal. Rather, they were lignite (soft coal)—the fossilized remains of plants that had died many tens of thousands of years ago.

Evidently, the native people who occupied the Lewisville site dug coal out of the ground and used it for fuel in their hearths. The radiocarbon dates tell us when the plants died, but do not tell us that they were burned in the hearths many thousands of years later (see note 5). Lewisville is apparently a Clovis site, probably dating to about eleven thousand years ago. It is an authentic site, but the dating was wrong.[30]

MEADOWCROFT ROCKSHELTER: DATING AND ASSOCIATION?

Many archaeologists believe that the Meadowcroft site, located in western Pennsylvania, provides the most convincing evidence for pre-Clovis occupation in the Americas. This site is protected by an overhanging cliff (or "rockshelter"), which makes it an attractive place for humans to camp. Eleven distinct layers of debris were distinguished by the excavators, representing almost continuous occupation over the past several thousand years. The deepest layer in the site, Stratum 1, produced several radiocarbon dates ranging from twenty thousand to thirty-one thousand years ago. It is believed that these samples represent naturally occurring charcoal (perhaps from forest fires), and are not the result of human activities.

The oldest evidence for human occupation is found in Stratum 2a, which has radiocarbon dates ranging from 8,000 to 19,600 years ago. All of the dates from the bottom third of this layer are from before 12,800 years ago, which points to a pre-Clovis occupation. This same layer also had a number of unquestionable stone tools, including a spearpoint (shaped like a Clovis point but lacking the distinctive "flutes") and a number of chipped knives and scrapers, as well as animal bones and even two small fragments of human bone.[31] The evidence of a human presence at the site is unquestionable. The only real weakness in the evidence from Meadowcroft is that the radiocarbon dates are not independently supported by any other evidence that the site is very ancient. In particular, all of the plant and animal remains are of forest-dwelling species that still live in the vicinity of the site today, such as acorns and flying squirrels. This is surprising, because thirteen thousand to seventeen thousand years ago the climate would have been very different: It was much colder then, and forests probably would have been restricted to small, protected locations. Yet no extinct or arctic animals were found at Meadowcroft.

This has led at least a few archaeologists to question the dating of the site. Some have argued that the charcoal samples might have been contaminated by coal, which occurs naturally around the site. In this case, the radiocarbon dates would be wrong, just like the case of Lewisville. However, the excavators of the site have argued emphatically that this is not a problem at Meadowcroft.[32]

The other objection that has been raised does not question the accuracy of the dates, but rather their association with the human occupation.[33] Since it is conceded that at least some of the early dates represent naturally occurring deposits (even if not coal), it is possible that all of the dated charcoal samples represent natural events such as forest fires. Perhaps Stratum 2a contains material of different ages that have been mixed together. It is a typical problem in caves or rockshelters that the deposits become mixed and churned by animal burrows, falling rocks, and so on. However, the dates from Meadowcroft are so consistent—the deeper within the level, the earlier the date—that it does not appear that mixing has been a very serious problem.

In my opinion, the best way to settle this question would be to radiocarbon-date the two fragments of human bone. Unlike the charcoal, there can be no doubt that the bones are associated with human presence. If either of these two bone fragments turned out to be more than twelve thousand years old, then that would conclusively prove the presence of pre-Clovis people in the New World. Unfortunately, this has not yet been done, so the association of the early dates and the human remains has not been absolutely proved. The question of associations at this site must remain moot for the time being, since a detailed, final descriptive report has not yet been published.

Conclusion

In order to discover when and how the first people came to the Americas, it is not enough just to list the claims that have been made on either side of the controversy. We should always ask, "What is the evidence?" How can we decide which claims are true? A scientist does not rely on other people's opinions, or on second-hand accounts (like this chapter) that claim to report what other people have said. Rather, we should go back to the original publications, and see if the facts really support the claims that have been made. As one of the proponents of the pre-Clovis theory has very correctly pointed out,

> It is clear that in the current controversy about the circumstances of the initial settlement of the Americas, a reader must follow the basic principle of good scholarship. Never rely on secondary sources for basic information. Always go to the original sources, read them carefully and thoroughly . . . and judge the matter for yourself.[34]

Notes

1. Washington Irving, "Showing the Great Difficulty Philosophers Have Had in Peopling America," in *Diedrich Knickerbocker's History of New York* (New York, 1838), pp. 244–249.
2. Ibid., pp. 247–248.
3. Edwin N. Wilmsen, "An Outline of Early Man Studies in the United States," *American Antiquity* 31 (1965): 172–192; David J. Meltzer, "The Antiquity of Man and the Development of American Archaeology," in Michael B. Schiffer, ed., *Advances in Archaeological Method and Theory* 6 (1983): 1–51.
4. Joseph H. Greenberg, Christy G. Turner II, and Stephen L. Zegura, "The Settlement of the Americas:

A Comparison of the Linguistic, Dental, and Genetic Evidence," *Current Anthropology* 27 (1986): 477–497.

5. Radiocarbon dating is based on the fact that all living tissues contain minute amounts of naturally occurring radioactive isotopes. These radioactive isotopes decay at a constant rate, so by measuring how much radioactivity remains in a sample of organic material (such as wood charcoal, bone, etc.), we can estimate how many years have elapsed since the organism died. There are several limitations. First, the date is an estimate, and may be off by several hundred (or even thousand) years. Second, it cannot date things that are more than about forty thousand years old (it can tell us that they are *more* than forty thousand years old, but not how much more). Third, it only tells you the date that an organism died. It doesn't tell you when that organism was used by humans. That is, if you date a piece of wood charcoal, it tells you when the tree died, *not* when the wood was actually burned in the fireplace. And it can't be used at all to date things that were never alive, like stone tools. For more details, see a textbook such as: Colin Renfrew and Paul Bahn, *Archaeology: Theories, Methods, and Practice* (New York: Thames and Hudson, 1991), pp. 121–129.

6. Robson Bonnichsen and Karen L. Turnmire, eds., *Clovis: Origins and Adaptations* (Corvallis: Center for the Study of the First Americans, Oregon State University, 1991).

7. Knut R. Fladmark, "Times and Places: Environmental Correlates of Mid-to-Late Wisconsinan Human Population Expansion in North America," in Richard Shutler Jr., ed., *Early Man in the New World* (Beverly Hills, CA: Sage, 1983), pp. 13–41.

8. David J. Meltzer and Jim I. Mead, "Dating Late Pleistocene Extinctions," in Jim I. Mead and David J. Meltzer, eds., *Environments and Extinctions: Man in Late Glacial North America* (Orono: Center for the Study of Early Man, University of Maine, 1985), pp. 145–173. The "wild horses" that now roam the Great Plains were introduced by the Spaniards in the 1500s, and are not descended from the native wild horses of the Ice Age.

9. Paul S. Martin, "Prehistoric Overkill: The Global Model" in Paul S. Martin and Richard G. Klein, eds., *Quaternary Extinctions: A Prehistoric Revolution* (Tucson: University of Arizona, 1984), pp. 354–403; Larry D. Agenbroad, "Clovis People: The Human Factor in the Pleistocene Megafauna Extinction Equation," in Ronald C. Carlisle, ed., *Americans before Columbus: Ice-Age Origins* (Pittsburgh, PA: University of Pittsburgh, Department of Anthropology, Ethnology Monographs 12, 1988), pp. 63–74.

10. Ernest L. Lundelius, Jr., "What Happened to the Mammoth? The Climatic Model," in Ronald C. Carlisle, ed., *Americans before Columbus: Ice-Age Origins* (Pittsburgh, PA: University of Pittsburgh, Department of Anthropology, Ethnology Monographs 12, 1988), pp. 75–82.

11. George C. Frison, *Prehistoric Hunters of the High Plains*, 2nd ed. (San Diego, CA: Academic Press, 1991), p. 25.

12. George F. MacDonald, *Debert: A Paleo-Indian Site in Central Nova Scotia* (Buffalo, NY: Persimmon Press, 1985), p. 53.

13. Junius B. Bird, *Travels and Archaeology in South Chile* (Iowa City: University of Iowa Press, 1988).

14. Harry L. Shapiro, *The Pitcairn Islanders* (New York: Simon & Schuster, 1962), pp. 208–210.

15. John R. Cole, "Anthropology beyond the Fringe," *Skeptical Inquirer* 2 (Spring/Summer 1978): 62–71; John R. Cole, "Cult Archaeology and Unscientific Method and Theory," in Michael B. Schiffer, ed., *Advances in Archaeological Method and Theory* 3 (1980): 1–34.

16. R. E. Taylor et al., "Major Revisions in the Pleistocene Age Assignments for North American Human Skeletons by C-14 Accelerator Mass Spectrometry: None Older Than 11, 000 C-14 Years B. P.," *American Antiquity* 50 (1985): 136–140.

17. Colin Renfrew and Paul Bahn, *Archaeology: Theories, Methods, and Practice* (New York: Thames and Hudson, 1991), pp. 101–148.

18. Louis S. B. Leakey et al., *Pleistocene Man at Calico* (Redlands, CA: San Bernardino County Museum, 1972).

19. J. L. Bischoff et al., "Uranium-Series and Soil-Geomorphic Dating of the Calico Archaeological Site, California," *Geology* 9 (1981): 576–582.

20. Ruth D. Simpson, Leland W. Patterson, and Clay A. Singer, "Lithic Technology of the Calico Mountains Site, Southern California," in Alan Lyle Bryan, ed., *New Evidence for the Pleistocene Peopling of the Americas* (Orono: Center for the Study of Early Man, University of Maine, 1986), pp. 89–105; Herbert L. Minshall, *The Broken Stones: The Case for Early Man in California* (Van Nuys, CA: Copley Books, 1976), pp. 30–40.

21. James G. Duvall and William T. Venner, "A Statistical Analysis of the Lithics from the Calico Site (SBCM 1500A), California," *Journal of Field Archaeology* 6 (1979): 455–462.

22. Leland W. Patterson, Louis V. Hoffman, Rose Marie Higginbotham, and Ruth D. Simpson, "Analysis of Lithic Flakes at the Calico Site, California," *Journal of Field Archaeology* 14 (1987): 91–106.

23. Alexander Kohn, *False Prophets: Fraud and Error in Science and Medicine* (Oxford: Basil Blackwell, 1986), pp. 3–4.

24. Mary Leakey, *Disclosing the Past: An Autobiography* (Garden City, NY: Doubleday, 1984), p. 143.

25. Martin F. Hemingway and Dick Stapert, "Early Artifacts from Pakistan? Some Questions for the Excavators," *Current Anthropology* 30 (1989): 317–318.

26. David J. Meltzer, "Pleistocene Peopling of the Americas," *Evolutionary Anthropology* 1 (1993): 157–169.

27. Tom D. Dillehay, "The Cultural Relationships of Monte Verde: A Late Pleistocene Settlement Site in the Sub-Antarctic Forest of South-Central Chile," in Alan Lyle Bryan, ed., *New Evidence for the Pleistocene Peopling of the Americas* (Orono: Center for the Study of Early Man, University of Maine, 1986), pp. 319–337.

28. Thomas F. Lynch, "Glacial-Age Man in South America? A Critical Review," *American Antiquity* 55 (1990): 12–36.

29. Dennis Stanford, "Pre-Clovis Occupation South of the Ice Sheets," in Richard Shutler Jr., ed., *Early Man in the New World* (Beverly Hills, CA: Sage, 1983), pp. 65–72.

30. Ibid., p. 70.

31. J. M. Adovasio et al., "Paleoenvironmental Reconstruction at Meadowcroft Rockshelter, Washington County, Pennsylvania," in Jim I. Mead and David J. Meltzer, eds., *Environments and Extinctions: Man in Late Glacial North America* (Orono: Center for the Study of Early Man, University of Maine, 1985), pp. 73–110; R. C. Carlisle and J. M. Adovasio, eds., *Meadowcroft: Collected Papers on the Archaeology of Meadowcroft Rockshelter and the Cross Creek Drainage* (Pittsburgh, PA: Department of Anthropology, University of Pittsburgh, 1982).

32. J. M. Adovasio, J. Donahue, and R. Stuckenrath, "The Meadowcroft Rockshelter Radiocarbon Chronology 1975–1990," *American Antiquity* 55 (1990): 348–354.

33. Dena F. Dincauze, "The Meadowcroft Papers," *Quarterly Review of Archaeology* 2 (1981): 3–4.

34. Ruth Gruhn and Alan L. Bryan, "A Review of Lynch's Descriptions of South American Pleistocene Sites," *American Antiquity* 56 (1991): 342–348.

Suggested Readings

Canby, Thomas Y. "The Search for the First Americans." *National Geographic* 156 (September 1979): 330–363. Somewhat out of date, but beautifully illustrated.

Fagan, Brian M. *The Great Journey: The Peopling of Ancient America.* New York: Thames and Hudson, 1987. A general overview.

Fladmark, Knut R. et al. "The First Americans." A series of fourteen articles in *Natural History* (November 1986–February 1988). An excellent selection that covers all aspects of the controversy.

Meltzer, David J. "Pleistocene Peopling of the Americas." *Evolutionary Anthropology* 1 (1993): 157–169. Excellent but technical summary.

Wolkomir, Richard. "New Finds Could Rewrite the Start of American History." *Smithsonian* (March 1991): 130–144.

Were Early Agriculturalists Less Healthy Than Food-Collectors?

Mark Nathan Cohen

The study of the Neolithic Revolution—why prehistoric people switched from hunting and gathering to agriculture and how that switch affected human lives and human health—has generated a good deal of controversy in recent years. The controversy may now be moving toward a new synthesis, but opinion remains divided.

Until recently, consideration of the early history of human health was largely implicit in discussions that focused explicitly on technology and on human economic choices. Prior to the mid-1960s, the study of the origins of agriculture focused on when, where, and how the principle of plant and animal domestication was discovered and on when and how that understanding diffused to other regions. Research focused on identifying the original "hearths" of invention; and controversy revolved around the number of places in which agriculture had been invented "independently" (that is, without diffusion of crops or the concept of planting seeds from other regions).[1]

Archaeologists and botanists did not ask, however, why domestication and agriculture, once invented, were adopted as a way of life by human populations. That is because, in the earlier view, the answer seemed obvious: Agriculture was simply assumed to provide a better and more reliable diet than hunting and gathering and to promote better health; to permit larger numbers of people to gather permanently in one place; to provide increased leisure time; and to underwrite construction of the great architectural landmarks which distinguish incipient civilization.[2]

In the mid-1960s three things dramatically altered our perception of the origin of agriculture. First, agricultural economist Ester Boserup offered a new model of economic growth in human history. Second, anthropologist Richard Lee presented a description of life among contemporary hunter gatherers that seemed to fit well into Boserup's model. Third, anthropologists such as Morton Fried and Marvin Harris reexamined our understanding of the basis of civilized wealth and monumental construction.

Boserup,[3] studying the evolution of agricultural systems, suggested that growing population—rather than technological invention—had been the primary stimulus to economic growth in human history. She argued that simple technology such as shifting or impermanent cultivation was actually the relatively efficient technology of small and dispersed human populations; and that technological "progress," such as the adoption of continuous cultivation of permanent fields, the use of the plow, and irrigation, was actually technological accommodation to high density population, often with declining rather than increasing returns for labor. In short, she suggested that simpler technology often represented the most efficient use of labor, while advanced technology represented the efficient use of space. Boserup allowed us to think of the simple technology of small groups as a small-scale, low-density adaptation rather than as "primitive."

Lee[4] provided a description of a group of contemporary hunter-gatherers, the !Kung San of the Kalahari Desert in southern Africa, a group with very simple technology. The San, by his description, did not farm but actually enjoyed considerable leisure time, worked relatively little and enjoyed relatively good nutritional returns. Lee pointed out that they understood the principle of planting crops but could not be bothered to do so (in apparent accord with Boserup's model). He suggested that in return for labor averaging about 20 hours per week for adults, San enjoyed diets of about 2,100 calories (technically, kilocalories) per person per day combined with a healthy intake of protein, vitamins, and minerals. Further study of the San by Truswell and Hansen[5] and by Howell[6] suggested, moreover, that they enjoyed relatively good health and nutritional status and had a life expectancy at birth of about thirty years (roughly the average length of life, balancing the deaths of infants and children with the deaths of older adults, some of whom died in their sixties and seventies). This figure, although low by twentieth-century European and American standards was reasonably good compared to many eighteenth- and nineteenth-century European populations; and it compared favorably with many Third World populations such as India until well into the twentieth century.[7] Apparently, such food collectors were not necessarily the least healthy nor the shortest lived of human groups.

Anthropologists Fried[8] and Harris,[9] meanwhile, argued that the great monuments of civilization should not be considered primarily as evidence of technological sophistication and affluence but rather as evidence of the coercive power of political elites who could control very large amounts of human labor. The economic surplus necessary to underwrite the building of a pyramid resulted not from a simple ability to produce more food (since even !Kung San could apparently do this if they wanted to) but from political organization, which forced people to get more and to concentrate their surplus production. The social engineering to build a pyramid was at least as important as the mechanical engineering. It was the emergence of this coercive power, they argued, rather than any technological advance, that marked the origins of civilization.

In response to the work of Boserup, Lee, Harris, and Fried, a number of archaeologists began to ask why hunting and gathering societies (now considered relatively "affluent,"[10]) ever adopted agriculture at all, since agriculture seemed to offer no obvious advantages. Many concluded that some sort of stress such as changing climate or changing sea level would have been necessary to force populations to give up a successful hunting and gathering lifestyle; and several archaeologists[11] concluded, following Boserup, that an imbalance between population and resources (caused either by resource decline or growing human population) was the stimulus to economic change. Some new theories also argued that political incentives and coercion, artificially increasing the demand for production, might have been the stimulus for agriculture.[12]

Most of these theories, however, suggested that human populations, like all animal populations, were normally self-regulating and did not normally out-

grow the "carrying capacity" of their resources (the capacity of their resources to regenerate themselves).[13] Therefore, they suggested, the imbalance which necessitated the adoption of agriculture had to be a local and temporary phenomenon distorting an otherwise well-regulated equilibrium. However, recent work in the emerging field of biology called "sociobiology" has questioned whether such "self-regulation" has ever existed in the biological world and has, in my opinion, effectively eliminated this issue from discussion.[14]

In 1977, I proposed that human populations might commonly, if slowly, outgrow their resources (or at least their preferred resources, since human groups always seem to have some less desirable resources in reserve). According to this theory,[15] population growth would slowly force groups to modify their behavior and to make more and more economic and dietary compromises in much the same manner that slow inflation gradually forces people in the modern world to change their buying habits. I suggested that the adoption of agriculture was only one in a long sequence of such adjustments to population growth. This sequence also included the later intensification of agriculture, as Boserup had suggested, as well as the earlier adoption of aquatic hunting and fishing, the adoption of tools for hunting small game, and the adoption of grindstones for processing wild seeds and nuts. (The last three developments marked the Mesolithic or "broad spectrum revolution" that preceded the origins of agriculture in most regions of the world.)[16] Each of the steps leading to the adoption and later intensification of agriculture represented diminishing economic returns, I argued.

In short, I argued that slowly growing human population had forced gradual expansion of a relatively elastic resource base with ever diminishing returns for labor. An alternate theory proposed by Brian Hayden[17] also suggested that population and food technology grew in an interactive manner and had tracked one another very closely in human history; but Hayden argued that technological development was the main stimulus to growth and that the new technologies added increasing efficiency and greater certainty to the food quest.

Meanwhile, the conclusions of Boserup and Lee were being challenged from several perspectives. Some anthropologists and agricultural historians argued that empirical measurements of efficiency and the observed sequence of agricultural development in different parts of the world often did not follow Boserup's predictions.[18] Other workers with the !Kung San and their neighbors called into question both their "affluence" and their authenticity as representatives of an ancient lifeway. Wilmsen,[19] for example, suggested that San dietary intake fell well below Lee's estimates, at least seasonally. Further study suggested that the San actually were relatively inefficient foragers.[20] And it was suggested that they devoted a lot of their time to leisure because of extreme seasonal heat and dryness. It was also suggested that hot, dry seasons placed severe limits on the numbers of children that a family could rear and thereby contributed to the apparent leisure of parents in less stressful and more productive seasons.[21] Schrire[22] and others argued also that the !Kung San were not pristine remnants of an ancient way of life but creations of twentieth-century political conditions in South Africa and therefore their lives had little if any meaning for studying the human past.

In an effort to sort out the meaning of the !Kung San data, I undertook a review of published data on the health and nutrition of other contemporary hunter-gatherers. I studied more than forty additional hunting and gathering societies from all of the world's continents for which at least some comparable data were available.[23] For the purposes of this review, I argued that groups like the !Kung San, even if they were not pristine remnants of ancient life, might nevertheless act as twentieth-century experiments in hunting and gathering lifestyle through which we could evaluate certain aspects of the health and nutrition of hunter-gatherer groups. For example, whether or not contemporary hunter-gatherers were "pristine," we could use them to evaluate the potential for obtaining a balanced diet by foraging in various environments; the amount of labor involved in obtaining and processing various foods; and the impact of group size and nomadism on the transmission of infectious disease.

The comparative data[24] suggested that modern hunter-gatherers are indeed commonly well nourished in qualitative terms (vitamins, minerals, protein) although calories may be in short supply at least on a seasonal basis. Anemia was very infrequent in such groups. Diseases like kwashiorkor or marasmus (protein and protein-calorie deficiency), pellagra (niacin deficiency) or beri beri (thiamine deficiency), which plague modern poor populations world-wide, essentially do not occur among hunter-gatherers (until they are forced to adopt modern diets). In short, although they are occasionally hungry, modern hunter-gatherers are conspicuously well nourished by modern Third-World standards. Moreover, the !Kung San, living in a desert, far from being the most affluent, seem to be relatively impoverished in comparison to

other hunter-gatherers. Groups such as the East African Hadza, living in game-rich areas, seem to be far more affluent and also better models for prehistoric hunter-gatherers who chose similarly rich environments in which to live.[25]

The data also suggested that small group size and the mobility which characterizes hunters seems commonly to act to protect them against parasites of various types. This relative freedom from parasites contributes to the good nutritional health of hunter-gatherers since parasitic infestation typically robs the body of nutrients in a variety of ways.[26]

In particular, intestinal parasites spread by human feces are rare among hunter-gatherers populations who tend to move on before feces accumulates and who therefore suffer relatively little diarrhea. Perhaps most important, hunter-gatherers seem to suffer relatively little of the diarrhea of infancy and early childhood that contributes so heavily to the death of children in the modern Third World.[27]

The comparative data also suggested that contemporary hunter-gatherers are at least as successful as most historic populations in rearing children to adulthood. On the average, such groups seem to lose about 20 percent of their children as infants and about 40 percent of children overall before they reach adulthood. These figures are comparable to what was true for most of Europe in the eighteenth and nineteenth centuries and significantly better than European and American cities at the beginning of the twentieth century. Adult life expectancy is not as great in most hunter-gatherer groups as Howell suggests for the !Kung. But overall life expectancy at birth averages twenty-five years or so in these groups, a figure which is still moderate by historic standards.[28]

Two relatively new lines of inquiry contributed further to the debate in the 1980s. First, optimal foraging research[29] stimulated once again by a movement in biology and involving the precise measurement of time, work, and returns for labor has resulted in the careful reevaluation of the different foraging and hunting techniques with results that are of interest to the present discussion. Several such studies suggest that, as long as large game animals are to be found with reasonable ease, big game hunting is a far more efficient activity (measured in caloric returns per hour of work) than other foraging strategies. One study suggests that hunters in rich environments can *average* 7,500–15,000 calories per hour of work.[30] Other studies suggest that once a large animal has been encountered, it can be harvested and converted to food at the rate of 15,000 to 45,000 calories per hour of work. In contrast, many of the more recent resources associated with the mesolithic or broad spectrum revolution such as small game, shellfish, and small seeds can be harvested at rates of only about one thousand calories per hour even after they are located, even with the best and most "modern" stone or iron age equipment.[31]

These caloric studies strongly support the argument that economic changes leading up to the adoption of agriculture were motivated by necessity, not progress. The implication is that prehistoric foragers are likely to have focused more heavily on big game when they were available and to have turned increasingly to secondary resources such as shellfish, small seeds, and small game not because of technological advances but only because choicer resources, particularly large game animals, became scarce. The data also suggest that nutritional health is likely to have declined over this time span rather than improved. A further implication is that modern hunter-gatherers who often rely heavily on the low-return resources may not be as well nourished as their (and our) prehistoric forebears. Most simple agricultural systems average about three thousand to five thousand calories per hour of labor suggesting that they are less efficient than big game hunting but more efficient than "broad spectrum" foraging. This may explain why agriculture began only after the broad spectrum revolution in most parts of the world.

The second major new line of evidence which emerged during the 1970s and 1980s was the development of paleopathological techniques for the direct assessment of prehistoric health from the study of archaeological skeletons, mummies, and feces. Research techniques that had previously focused on the analysis of pathological individuals or the history of specific diseases began instead to provide quantitative, statistically based descriptions of whole populations which could, with caution, be used to compare the health of human groups from different periods of prehistory.[32]

Paleopathology can assess the presence and frequency of some specific, chronic diseases such as syphilis and tuberculosis in the skeleton. (When mummies are found their preserved soft tissues permit diagnosis of a far wider range of illnesses.) Paleopathology can also assess some specific nutrient deficiencies such as iron deficiency anemia. But it can also be used to assess a number of chronic but nonspecific indicators of nutrition, health, growth, and the disruption of growth, which permit the comparison of general health between populations.

In 1982, paleopathologist George Armelagos and I organized a conference of paleopathologists for the express purpose of evaluating the significance of the adoption of agriculture for human health.[33] We asked paleopathologists working in twenty-two regions of the world to use standard paleopathological indicators to assess health trends of populations prior to, at, and after the adoption of agriculture. Although each region of the world is subject to unique historical patterns we hoped that common trends shared by various regions would tell us something about the overall health of hunter-gatherers and farmers.

I had hoped that the data would display clear declines in health *prior* to the adoption of agriculture in support of my population-pressure model of agricultural origins. In this respect the data were disappointing. Fragmentary archaeological samples most often did not permit us to recognize more than one population that had existed prior to the adoption of agriculture in any region. The few comparisons that could be made were limited by small sample size and imperfect preservation. However, throughout the Old World where preagricultural samples are available (India, the Middle East, Mediterranean Europe, Northern Europe) the data suggest that people did get *smaller* before the adoption of agriculture. In at least one region (the Mediterranean) the trend in stature is combined with other signs of declining nutrition. Since decline in stature itself is often used as an index of declining nutrition in other historical contexts, this may be an indicator of declining nutrition among prehistoric groups. I consider this the best explanation of the trend. However, various authorities suggest that declining stature is, instead, an indication either of changing climate or of changing human activities.[34] In any case, few data from this period suggest that preagricultural human beings are making "progress" in health or nutrition. One population from Peru, however, counter to my expectations, does display an increase in stature and in other indications of health and nutrition prior to the adoption of agriculture.[35]

The comparison of prehistoric farmers with their hunting and gathering forebears provided much more interesting results. In most regions of the world, early farmers, living in larger and more sedentary communities than their ancestors, also displayed higher rates of infection in the skeleton (or preserved tissues or feces.) In particular, periostitis, the non-specific infection of bone surfaces usually attributed to staphylococcus or streptococcus infection, is almost invariably more common after the adoption of sedentary farming. A comparison of mummies from Peru suggested that intestinal infection also increased after the adoption of farming.[36] The same conclusion was suggested by comparison of human feces from different periods of prehistory in the American southwest.[37] Treponemal infection (yaws) also seems to be more common after the adoption of farming (its venereal form, syphilis, seems to be a much more recent affliction, rarely if ever being diagnosed with certainty in human groups of any region before the age of Columbus). Tuberculosis is almost entirely confined to relatively recent populations living in large urban aggregates, which do not occur in the absence of agriculture.[38]

Farmers also almost invariably displayed more frequent anemia than earlier hunter-gatherers in the same region. There is some controversy about the source of the anemia. One possibility is that it reflects iron deficiency resulting from farmers' dependency on cereal crops such as maize (corn), which are poor in iron and actually tend to inhibit iron absorption.[39] A more likely possibility is that it reflects the secondary loss of iron to parasites such as hookworm, malaria, or tuberculosis, all of which become more frequent when large sedentary aggregates of people are formed.[40]

Other signs of malnutrition such as retarded growth among children or premature osteoporosis (loss of bone) among adults also seem to be more common after the adoption of agriculture. Farmers also displayed higher rates of imperfections in the enamel of teeth (enamel hypoplasia and Wilson's bands) thought to be a permanent record of severe episodes of poor health in childhood.[41] This suggests, contrary to popular expectation, that prehistoric hunter-gatherers may have been *better* buffered against stressful episodes than their descendants.

The data, unfortunately, cannot be used to assess changing life expectancy. A cemetery may not be an accurate reflection of the community from which it is derived.[42] Immigrants and emigrants skew the age distribution in a cemetery, the former adding older individuals to the cemetery who were not born locally, and the latter subtracting older local individuals. Moreover, if a population is growing rapidly, each cohort (annual crop) of babies is larger than the last and the cemetery will have a disproportionately large number of young people—producing an apparent increase in infant and child mortality even if the actual risk of dying as an infant or child has not changed. A population that is declining and producing fewer babies each year will show the opposite effect. The available data, therefore, cannot be used to show a decline in life expectancy associated with the origins of agriculture as I anticipated; but neither do they provide evidence of the improvement in life expectancy archaeologists once took for granted as a concomitant of human progress.

Overall, these data seem to me to be a fairly substantial body of evidence in support of the hypothesis that the adoption of agriculture resulted in a decline in human health. This conclusion has been challenged, however, by individuals who question the value of skeletal samples.[43] These authors point out that skeletons in a cemetery may not be a true reflection of a once-living population. (As simply one example, skeletal lesions or scars of disease take time to form, so the number of lesions in a skeletal population *might* reflect not the number who were ever sick but the number who survived the illness long enough for the lesions to form. By this argument, a high frequency of pathology in a cemetery *might* perversely be an indication of relatively good health!)

Paleopathologist Alan Goodman has responded to this argument[44] by pointing out, among other things, that enamel hypoplasia do occur in living populations in proportion to deprivation and poverty, suggesting that they are a reliable and direct indicator of health stress. My own response[45] is to point out that several different lines of evidence can often combine to bolster conclusions when no single line of reasoning is sufficient. (It is this cross-checking of one kind of evidence against another that is the real hallmark of science.) For example, archaeological skeletons regularly display an increase in frequencies of infection with the adoption of large sedentary communities associated with farming. This might, as the critics suggest, be a misleading artifact of skeletal samples. But the increase in infection with large groups and sedentism is in accordance with standard modern epidemiological expectations based on knowledge of the life cycles of parasites. Moreover, the same increase is displayed over and over again when contemporary hunter-gatherers are settled in large communities. It seems reasonable to conclude, then, that the increase in infection with the adoption of farming is historic fact and not a mere artifact of skeletal sampling.

Similarly, anemia becomes more visible in skeletal populations after the adoption of farming. But we also know that anemia is infrequent in contemporary hunter-gatherers and that rates of parasitism (the most probable explanation of anemia for most populations) increase with farming. Again it seems reasonable to conclude that the increase in anemia is a matter of historic fact.

Similarly, dental defects indicating disrupted growth in children become more common in skeletal populations after farming. But observations on living groups suggest that weanling diarrhea—which is thought to be a major cause of such dental defects—also increases with sedentism suggesting that the prehistoric trend is real and not the product of a sampling error. Similarly, tuberculosis, which occurs only in relatively recent, dense, sedentary populations in the archaeological sequence is also primarily a disease of cities in the modern world, suggesting that we are not being misled about its prehistoric distribution.

In short, data from a variety of sources seem to be converging on a new way of viewing the origins of agriculture and other episodes in human history. Taken together, evidence from paleopathology, from ethnographic studies of contemporary huntergatherers, epidemiology or knowledge of disease mechanics, and optimal foraging research all suggest that human health declined with the adoption of agriculture—and these data also suggest more generally that much human "progress" has been a matter of diminishing returns for all but privileged groups and classes.

One final point needs to be made. One of the problems with our initial ideas about agriculture is that some of the basic assumptions—such as that agriculture represents "progress" (or indeed that human history as a whole has been about "progress")—were never tested. All ideas, no matter how plausible or how much in accord with prevailing beliefs, should be tested in many different ways.

The idea of "progress" is itself nothing more than an hypothesis that was created by scientists and scholars like ourselves who were working from similar data (although generally from *less* data and never from more data than are now available). If it is to be believed, the hypothesis of progress must be supported by empirical evidence from contemporary populations or skeletons, like any other competing hypothesis. At present it is not supported and I believe it has less actual empirical evidence in support than the alternative hypothesis offered here. I think it is time to change our thinking and our assumptions about what happened in history.

Notes

1. Jack R. Harlan, "Agricultural Origins: Centers and NonCenters," *Science* 174 (1971): 168–174.
2. V. Gordon Childe, *Man Makes Himself* (New York: Mentor, 1950).
3. Ester Boserup, *The Conditions of Agricultural Growth* (Chicago: Aldine, 1965).
4. Richard Lee, "What Hunters Do for a Living, or, How to Make Out on Scarce Resources," in Richard B. Lee and Irven DeVore, eds., *Man the Hunter* (Chicago: Aldine, 1968), pp. 30–43; Richard Lee, "!Kung Bushman Subsistence—an Input/Output Analysis," in A. P. Vayda, ed., *Ecological Studies in Cultural Anthropology* (New York: Natural History Press, 1969), pp. 47–79.
5. A. S. Truswell and J. D. L. Hansen, "Medical Research among the !Kung," in Richard Lee and Irven DeVore, eds., *Kalahari Hunter-Gatherers* (Cambridge, MA: Harvard University Press, 1976), pp. 166–195.
6. Nancy Howell, *Demography of the Dobe !Kung* (New York: Academic Press, 1979).
7. Mark N. Cohen, *Health and the Rise of Civilization* (New Haven, CT: Yale University Press, 1989).
8. Morton H. Fried, *The Evolution of Political Society* (New York: Random House, 1967).
9. Marvin Harris, "The Economy Has No Surplus?" *American Anthropologist* 61 (1959): 189–199.
10. Marshall Sahlins, *Stone Age Economics* (Chicago: Aldine, 1968).
11. Lewis R. Binford, "Post-Pleistocene Adaptations," in Lewis R. Binford and Sally Binford, eds., *New Perspectives in Archaeology* (Chicago: Aldine, 1968), pp. 313–341; Kent V. Flannery, "Origins and Ecological Effects of Early Farming in Iran and the Near East," in P. J. Ucko and J. W. Dimbleby, eds., *The Domestication and Exploitation of Plants and Animals* (London: Duckworth, 1969), pp. 73–100; J. T. Meyers, "The Origins of Agriculture: An Evaluation of Hypotheses," in Stuart Struever, ed., *Prehistoric Agriculture* (Garden City, NJ: Natural History Press, 1971), pp. 101–121.
12. T. D. Price and J. A. Brown, eds., *Prehistoric Hunter-Gatherers: The Emergence of Cultural Complexity* (Chicago: Aldine, 1985).
13. V. C. Wynne-Edwards, *Animal Dispersion in Relation to Social Behavior* (Edinburgh: Oliver and Boyd, 1962).
14. Edward O. Wilson, *Sociobiology* (Cambridge, MA: Harvard University Press, 1975).
15. Mark N. Cohen, *The Food Crisis in Prehistory* (New Haven, CT: Yale University Press, 1977).
16. Kent V. Flannery, "The Origins of Agriculture," *Annual Review of Anthropology* 2 (1973): 271–310.
17. Brian Hayden, "Research and Development in the Stone Age," *Current Anthropology* 22 (1981): 519–548.
18. Brian Spooner, ed., *Population Growth: Anthropological Implications* (Cambridge, MA: MIT Press, 1972).
19. Edwin Wilmsen, "Seasonal Effects of Dietary Intake on the Kalahari San," *Federation Proceedings* 37 (1978): 65–72.
20. Kristen Hawkes and James F. O'Connell, "Optimal Foraging Models and the Case of the !Kung," *American Anthropologist* 87 (1985): 401–405.
21. Nicholas Blurton-Jones and P. M. Sibley, "Testing Adaptiveness of Culturally Determined Behavior: Do Bushman Women Maximize Their Reproductive Success?" in *Human Behavior and Adaptation*, Society for the Study of Human Biology, Symposium 18 (London: Taylor and Francis, 1978), pp. 133–157.
22. Carmel Schrire, "An Inquiry into the Evolutionary Status and Apparent Identity of San Hunter-Gatherers," *Human Ecology* 8 (1980): 9–32.

23. Mark N. Cohen, *Health and the Rise of Civilization* (New Haven, CT: Yale University Press, 1989).

24. Ibid., pp. 184–192.

25. James Woodburn, "An Introduction to Hadza Ecology," in Richard B. Lee and Irven DeVore, eds., *Man the Hunter* (Chicago: Aldine, 1968), pp. 49–55; James F. O'Connell, Kristen Hawes, and Nicholas Blurton-Jones, "Hadza Scavenging: Implications for Plio/Pleistocene Hominid Subsistence," *Current Anthropology* 29 (1988): 256–263.

26. Cohen, *Health and the Rise of Civilization*, pp. 63–64.

27. Ibid.

28. Ibid., pp. 100–102, 195–204.

29. Bruce Winterhalder and Eric A. Smith, eds., *Hunter-Gatherer Foraging Strategies* (Chicago: University of Chicago Press, 1981).

30. Stuart Marks, *Large Mammals and a Brave People* (Seattle: University of Washington Press, 1976).

31. Rhys Jones, "Hunters in the Australian Coastal Savanna," in David Harris, ed., *Human Ecology in Savanna Environments* (New York: Academic Press, 1981); P. Rowly-Conwy, "The Laziness of the Short Distance Hunter," *Journal of Anthropological Archaeology* 38 (1984): 300–324; Roderick Blackburn, "In the Land of Milk and Honey," in Eleanor Leacock and Richard B. Lee, eds., *Politics and History in Band Society* (Cambridge: Cambridge University Press, 1982), pp. 283–306.

32. Jane Buikstra and Della Cook, "Paleopathology: An American Account," *Annual Review of Anthropology* 9 (1980): 433–470.

33. Mark N. Cohen and George J. Armelagos, eds., *Paleopathology at the Origins of Agriculture* (New York: Academic Press, 1984).

34. David Frayer, "Body Size, Weapon Use, and Natural Selection in the European Upper Paleolithic and Mesolithic," *American Anthropologist* 83 (1981): 57–73.

35. Robert Benfer, "The Challenges and Rewards of Sedentism: The Preceramic Village of Paloma, Peru," in Mark N. Cohen and George J. Armelagos, eds., *Paleopathology at the Origins of Agriculture* (New York: Academic Press, 1984), pp. 531–555.

36. Marvin J. Allison, "Paleopathology in Peruvian and Chilean Populations," in Mark N. Cohen and George J. Armelagos, eds., *Paleopathology at the Origins of Agriculture* (New York: Academic Press, 1984), pp. 515–530.

37. Carl Reinhard, "Cultural Ecology of Prehistoric Parasites on the Colorado Plateau as Evidenced by Coprology," *American Journal of Physical Anthropology* 77 (1988): 355–366.

38. Cohen and Armelagos, *Paleopathology at the Origins of Agriculture.*

39. Mahmoud El Najjar, "Maize, Malarias, and the Anemias in the Pre-Columbian New World," *Yearbook of Physical Anthropology* 28 (1977): 329–337.

40. Patty Stuart Macadam and Susan Kent, eds., *Diet Demography and Disease* (Hawthorne, NY: Aldine de Gruyter, 1992).

41. Jerome Rose, Alan Goodman, and Keith Condon, "Diet and Dentition: Developmental Disturbances," in R. I. Gilbert and J. Mielke, eds., *The Analysis of Prehistoric Diets* (New York: Academic Press, 1985), pp. 281–306.

42. Lisa Sattenspiel and Henry Harpending, "Stable Populations and Skeletal Age," *American Antiquity* 48 (1983): 489–498.

43. James W. Wood, George R. Milner, Henry C. Harpending, and Kenneth Weiss, "The Osteological Paradox: Problems of Inferring Prehistoric Health from Skeletal Samples," *Current Anthropology* 33 (1992): 343–358.

44. Alan Goodman, "On the Interpretation of Health from Skeletal Remains," *Current Anthropology* 34 (1993): 281–288.

45. Mark N. Cohen, "Comment," *Current Anthropology* 33 (1992): 358–359.

Suggested Readings

Cohen, Mark N. *The Food Crisis in Prehistory.* New Haven, CT: Yale University Press, 1977. The first comprehensive statement about the impact of population growth on prehistoric populations.

———. *Health and the Rise of Civilization.* New Haven, CT: Yale University Press, 1989. A readable summary of theory and evidence concerning the impact of civilization on human health.

Lee, Richard B., and Irven DeVore, eds. *Man the Hunter.* Chicago: Aldine, 1968. The modern classic description of hunting and gathering.

———. *Kalahari Hunter-Gatherers.* Cambridge, MA: Harvard University Press, 1976. The most concentrated discussion of the life and health of the !Kung San.

Marks, Stuart. *Large Mammals and a Brave People.* Seattle: University of Washington Press, 1976. A description of a modern African hunting economy.

Maya Hieroglyphs: History or Propaganda?

Joyce Marcus

The Maya—an American Indian group that numbers four million people and speaks some twenty-eight related languages—occupy parts of Mexico, Guatemala, Belize, El Salvador, and Honduras. In ancient times they were one of the most highly advanced peoples of the Americas. At the peak of their political power, between A.D. 300 and 800, they occupied large cities and proclaimed the exploits of their rulers in a complex system of hieroglyphic writing.

Maya writing is found on thousands of carved stone monuments, painted pottery vessels, and objects of jade, bone, and shell.

The earliest examples appeared on stone by A.D. 300, while the most recent appeared in "books" of painted deerskin around A.D. 1500.

Maya hieroglyphs have been studied by a wide variety of scholars for more than a hundred years. These studies reveal that the field has passed through many stages, during which researchers have repeatedly changed their opinions on the content of the ancient texts. Often, in fact, later scholars have returned to positions taken by earlier scholars. Such returns are sometimes called pendulum swings, and they are typical of science as a whole. Frequently one generation takes a position on a question; their immediate successors counter that by taking the opposite position; and the next generation returns to the original position.[1]

In this article we use the study of Maya hieroglyphs as an example of how science undergoes such pendulum swings. In particular, we ask the question: "What is the subject of Maya inscriptions? Is it astronomy and myth? Is it history? Or is it political propaganda?"

From 1830 to 1920: Maya Writing Is History

In 1839 an American lawyer named John L. Stephens decided to explore the Maya ruins of Mexico, Guatemala, and Honduras. He took with him Frederick Catherwood, an accomplished artist who was to draw all the sights they would see. Both Stephens and Catherwood were already world travelers, with Stephens's earlier trips having resulted in two best-selling books—*Incidents of Travel in Egypt, Arabia Petraea, and the Holy Land* and *Incidents of Travel in Greece, Turkey, Russia, and Poland*.

Those Old World adventures predisposed Stephens to develop a comparative perspective, one that took note of the similarities and differences among Old and New World civilizations.[2] In particular, Stephens compared Maya stone sculpture and hieroglyphic writing to those of Egypt, suggesting that both civilizations had depicted kings and recorded history.

Stephens's views were shared by a later Maya scholar, Herbert J. Spinden, who in 1913 agreed that the subject of Maya texts was history:

> In addition to what is now known we may expect to find in the Maya inscriptions some hieroglyphs that give the names of individuals, cities, and political divisions and others that represent feasts, sacrifices, tributes, and common objects of trade as well as signs referring to birth, death, establishment, conquest, destruction and other such fundamentals of individual and social existence.[3]

From 1920 to 1960: Maya Writing Is Astronomy, Myth, and the Philosophy of Time

New and influential Maya scholars such as Sylvanus G. Morley and J. Eric S. Thompson emerged during the 1920s and 1930s. Unlike Stephens and Spinden, Morley and Thompson believed that Maya texts contained astronomy, myth, cosmology, and philosophy.[4]

The human figures seen on many stone monuments were thought to be priests and astronomers rather than kings. The fact that some figures wore long robes or loose dresses only reinforced the notion that they were priests, perhaps the leaders of an ancient theocracy or "government headed by gods." In 1950 Thompson forcefully disputed the views of earlier scholars when he wrote," It has been held by some that Maya dates recorded on stelae [freestanding stone monuments] may refer to historical events or even recount the deeds of individuals; to me such a possibility is well-nigh inconceivable."[5]

Why did Thompson and others of his generation come to this conclusion? It had to do with the portion of Maya texts that could be translated at that time. Maya inscriptions often include dates, given in an ancient calendric system that the Indians of Mexico had invented hundreds of years earlier. By the 1940s different correlations linking the Maya dates to our calendar had been worked out, and both Morley and Thompson were proficient at such correlations. They had also determined that some Maya monuments give data on various planetary cycles, including those of Venus and the moon. Despite the fact that he himself had catalogued 862 of the noncalendric hieroglyphs, Thompson could not translate most of them.[6] Deprived of what we now know to be the main subject matter of the inscriptions, Morley and Thompson concentrated on the calendric and astronomical portions of the texts. Small wonder they saw the hieroglyphic inscriptions as "impersonal," and considered the Maya "obsessed with time." This view was only reinforced when it was discovered that the Maya were making calculations that involved millions of years and were recording events that took place thousands of years ago in our calendar.[7]

Thus, despite the fact that scholars of the period from 1920 to 1960 could read more of the inscriptions than could Stephens and Spinden, the limited portions of the text that could be read led them away from history. That situation lasted until 1958–1960, when two major breakthroughs took place.

From 1960 to 1990:
A Return to History

In the late 1950s two scholars, working independently, returned to the "historical" position advocated by Stephens and Spinden. One scholar was Heinrich Berlin, a German emigré to Mexico; the other was Tatiana Proskouriakoff, a Russian emigrée to the United States.

Palenque

Piedras Negras

Copán

Aguateca and
Dos Pilas

Seibal

Figure 1
Emblem Glyphs of Five Maya Cities

(Redrawn from Marcus, 1976, Figures 1. 7, 4. 11)

Berlin's breakthrough came while he was studying hieroglyphs on the stone coffin of a ruler buried in the Temple of the Inscriptions at Palenque, a Maya city in the jungles of southeastern Mexico. Here, for the first time, Berlin identified the personal names of Maya rulers and their relatives.[8] He also noted that the last hieroglyph in each name phrase at Palenque usually had the same compound structure. He called it the Palenque Emblem Glyph (see the upper left of Figure 1 for one of the Palenque emblem glyphs, and see the lower right of Figure 5 for a variant).

Berlin then turned to texts at other Maya sites, where he found that rulers' name phrases ended with a similar hieroglyphic compound, but with a different central element; he suggested that the final glyphic compounds referred to different cities (see Figure 1).

Berlin concluded that these different emblem glyphs functioned as rulers' titles, dynastic names, or place names.[9] Subsequent work has shown that these glyphs are compounds of a ruler's title plus the name of a place—for example, "Lord of Palenque"—and therefore do provide geographic references.

Proskouriakoff's breakthrough was the demonstration that Maya texts, just as Stephens and Spinden had suspected, recorded important events in the lives of rulers. She reasoned that the calendric phrases were the dates of rulers' births, accessions to the throne, and deaths. Initially, Proskouriakoff concentrated on Piedras Negras, a Maya city in northwest Guatemala, which she chose because its monuments were numerous and had been conveniently erected at five-year intervals.[10]

Proskouriakoff began by dividing the dated monuments into seven consecutive series. She noted that

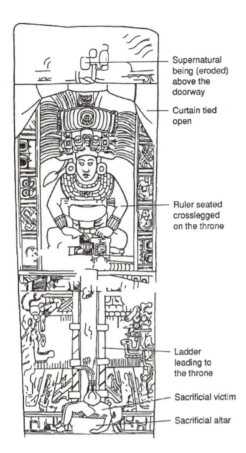

Figure 2
Monument at Piedras Negras, Guatemala,
Displaying the Ascension Motif

(Redrawn from Marcus, 1992, Figure 10. 14)

Figure 3
Hieroglyphs Referring to Major Events
in the Life of a Maya Ruler

(Redrawn from Marcus, 1976, Figure 1. 2)

each series began with the same pictorial motif: a human being seated cross-legged on a throne set in a niche or doorway, with a ladder leading up to it. Proskouriakoff called this scene the Ascension Motif (see Figure 2).

In the accompanying texts she noted one hieroglyph that was consistently associated with a date falling in the five-year period before the erection of the monument; she called this the Inaugural Date, and suggested that it marked the day the ruler ascended to the throne. Proskouriakoff also noted that each of the seven series began with a still earlier date that fell some twelve to thirty-one years before the Inaugural Date; she suggested that this might refer to the ruler's date of birth (see Figure 3).

Proskouriakoff went on to identify the hieroglyphs associated with Maya women, rituals of sacrificial bloodletting, and the capture of one Maya lord by another in battle.[11] Thanks to her, we now know that the robed figures considered to be priests by Morley and Thompson were in fact royal women.

While some admirers have described Proskouriakoff's breakthrough as a single stroke of brilliant intuition (like the lightbulb going on over a cartoon character's head), she herself considered it to be the result of logic and deduction. She said that she had relied on earlier work—including that of Spinden and Morley, who had already noted that the Piedras Negras monuments bearing the Ascension Motif were separated by time intervals "no greater than a human lifetime."[12] Thus Spinden's and Morley's earlier work allowed Proskouriakoff to start her study with a testable hypothesis—that each monument displaying the Ascension Motif marked the beginning of a new ruler's reign.

We need to remember that most breakthroughs in research are not gained in an instant through luck or intuition. Most are the hard-won products of combining past work with new questions and fresh approaches. New research may follow past work or contradict it, but it will always be affected by it in some way.

The Altar Q Story

To see how our interpretations of Maya writing have changed over the last 150 years, let us follow one carved stone monument through the whole process.

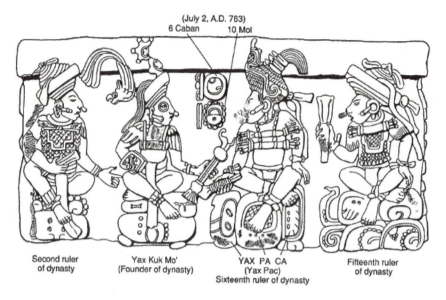

Figure 4
The West Side of Altar Q, Copán, Honduras

(*Redrawn from Marcus, 1976, Figure 4. 48*)

That monument is Altar Q at Copán, an ancient Maya city that once had ten thousand inhabitants.

Copán lies at 1,968 feet above sea level in a fertile, green valley in western Honduras. Supported by cornfields stretching along the floodplain of the Copán River, the city of Copán was built of blocks of greenish volcanic tuff quarried from cliffs flanking the valley.

Altar Q, a striking monument carved from a block of such tuff four feet seven inches square, sits today beneath a protective roof in front of Copán's Temple 16. The altar's layout reveals a very careful plan that paid particular attention to symmetry. It is four-sided, and its flat top bears thirty-six units, or blocks, of hieroglyphs. Around its sides are sixteen human figures—four to a side—each seated on a hieroglyphic compound (a glyph block containing several glyphs). The faces of all sixteen individuals are directed toward the west side of the altar, which is the principal side. On that side, the two main protagonists face each other (see Figure 4).

Between the faces of these two protagonists are two glyphs in the Maya calendar—6 Caban 10 Mol—that correspond to July 2, A.D. 763 in our calendar. That date is repeated several times at Copán, and so are the tenth, twentieth, thirtieth, and fortieth anniversaries of the same date. From the frequency of its use, we are given a clue: This was a very important date in the history of Copán.

TIMELINE OF ALTAR Q

1. In 1840 John L. Stephens found Altar Q. Given his comparative perspective on ancient civilizations, he concluded that "beyond doubt [its texts] record some event in the history" of the Maya.[13] Stephens was the first to conclude that the two figures facing each other on the west side of the altar were the protagonists and suggested that the other fourteen were following those leaders. He perceptively suggested that the hieroglyphic compound on which each figure sat might refer to that individual's name and political office, and he pointed out that one of the two protagonists was holding a scepter.

2. In the 1930s an astronomer named John Teeple studied Altar Q.[14] Because Mayanists at that time believed that the hieroglyphic texts dealt with astronomy and cosmology, he concluded that the sixteen figures were ancient Maya astronomers attending an astronomical congress. Suspecting that these Copán astronomers had produced the most up-to-date computation of the length of the tropical year, Teeple compared Altar Q to "a group photograph of the Copán Academy of Sciences taken just after their sessions." This position was supported by J. Eric S. Thompson and most other Mayanists of the 1920–1960 era.[15]

3. Following the breakthroughs of Berlin and Proskouriakoff, the individuals on Altar Q suddenly became historical figures again. By 1974 Mayanists

such as Tatiana Proskouriakoff, David H. Kelley, and I suggested that one of the two main protagonists was a Copán ruler whose hieroglyphic name was Yax "Sun at Horizon."[16] We also agreed that this ruler was inaugurated on July 2, A.D. 763, and that the protagonist on the left was handing him the scepter of office (see Figure 4).

The discovery (or rediscovery) that Maya inscriptions dealt with real historic figures greatly speeded up the process of analysis. Soon linguists like Floyd Lounsbury were at work on the actual pronunciation of the glyphs, combining their efforts with those of archaeologists (David Kelley and Peter Mathews) and an art historian (Linda Schele).[17] The decipherment of Stela 3 from the site of Piedras Negras, Guatemala, provides an example of such multidisciplinary approaches. As a student of Proskouriakoff, I used her approach to translate the entire inscription glyph by glyph.[18] Victoria Bricker, a linguistic anthropologist, then showed how each glyph might have been pronounced by the ancient Maya.[19]

By the 1980s most scholars working on the Maya were in agreement that Altar Q recorded a sequence of sixteen consecutive Copán rulers, all but one seated on his hieroglyphic name. Most also believed that one of the protagonists on the west side of the altar was the sixteenth ruler in the sequence, whose name could finally be pronounced *yax + pa + ca*, or Yax Pac ("First Dawn").[20] Lord Yax Pac was shown facing to his right, where he looked upon the glyphs that gave the date of his inauguration. Handing him the scepter of office was the other protagonist, a ruler named Yax Kuk Mo' or "Blue-green Quetzal Macaw." His headdress supplies the hieroglyphs of his name, and he sits on the hieroglyphic compound meaning *ahau*, "hereditary lord."

The 1990s: Maya Writing Is a Combination of Propaganda, Myth, and History

The 1990s is a period of real irony, because the breakthroughs of 1958–1960—which returned us to an historical perspective on Maya hieroglyphs—now threaten the notion that Maya writing is history. So many Maya texts have now been translated that we can no longer defend the notion that the Maya were only recording true events in the lives of their rulers. They were also employing heavy doses of political propaganda.

Altar Q is a prime example of such a combination of history and propaganda. Because the two protagonists, Yax Pac and Yax Kuk Mo', are shown facing each other, we might assume that they were contemporaries. We might also assume that we are witnessing an historic event during which Yax Kuk Mo' passed the scepter of office to his successor, Yax Pac.

In fact, Yax Kuk Mo' was *not* Yax Pac's immediate predecessor in office; he was the *first* in the sequence of sixteen rulers, ostensibly the "founder of the dynasty." Based on other monuments at Copán, it appears that Yax Kuk Mo' actually ruled ca. A.D. 430, some 333 years before Yax Pac's inauguration.[21] Thus the west side of Altar Q cannot record an actual historic event, since Yax Kuk Mo' would have been long dead by the time Yax Pac received his scepter of office. Having discovered this fact, our curiosity is aroused. Let us see what else we can discover about these rulers of Copán.

We turn first to the text on the upper surface of Altar Q, expecting it to feature Yax Pac, the ruler who commissioned it. Instead, the hieroglyphic text features the deeds of Yax Kuk Mo', who is proclaimed the founder of the dynasty. We learn that the monument was carved in A.D. 775 (twelve years after Yax Pac's inauguration), and that the two featured accomplishments of Yax Kuk Mo' took place in A.D. 426, some 350 years before Altar Q was carved. Why, we wonder, would Yax Pac devote so much space on his own altar to the accomplishments of a long-dead predecessor?

We turn now to a stone bench in Temple 11, another building at Copán. This bench was carved in A.D. 773—two years before Altar Q—and also commissioned by Yax Pac. On the bench we see twenty seated figures, divided into two groups of ten, one of whom is Yax Pac himself. Who are these figures, and how do they relate to the sixteen on Altar Q? Since Yax Pac always refers to himself as the sixteenth ruler in his dynasty, who are the additional four people on the Temple 11 bench?

Finally, we turn to Stela 8 at Copán.[22] This is a freestanding stone monument carved in A.D. 783, on the twentieth anniversary of Yax Pac's inauguration to the throne (see Figures 5 and 6). In its text, Yax Pac discloses for the first time that his mother was a royal woman from the ancient Maya city of Palenque, 265 miles northwest of Copán. Nowhere on this monument, nor on any commissioned by Yax Pac, is the name of his father given. Now our curiosity is heightened even more. Who was Yax Pac's father? If he were one of the sixteen members of the dynasty founded by Yax Kuk Mo', would he not be mentioned by Yax Pac? And why are there no monuments recording Yax Pac's father's marriage to the royal woman from Palenque?

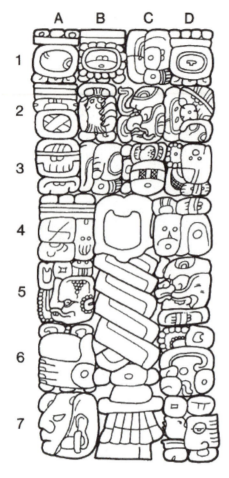

Figure 5
Hieroglyphic Text on Stela 8 at Copán

(*Redrawn by J. Klausmeyer from Schele and Freidel, 1990, p. 331*) Read across line 1 (A1–D1), then across lines 2 and 3. Then read down from A4–A7 and D4–D7.

	A	B	C	D
1	6 Caban July 2, A.D. 763 (his accession to the throne)	10 Mol	Forward count to	a day 9 Ik
2	and a month 15 Zip (5 days after his 20th anniversary)	His autosacrifice was performed by	ruler's title	Yax Pac
3	sky title	royal title	2 units of 20 years	celebration event
4	(he is the) 16th ruler in the sequence			a royal title
5	lord of Copán,			title
6	offspring of a female,			in the royal line of
7	the royal woman			Palenque.

Figure 6
Translation of the Stela 8 Text, Giving Yax Pac's Claim that His Mother Was from Palenque

Let us now summarize the evidence we have. In A.D. 763 a ruler named Yax Pac ascends to the throne of Copán. In A.D. 775 he dedicates Temple 16 at Copán, and he has Altar Q set in front of it. On the upper surface of the altar he orders the carving of a long inscription concerning the accomplishments of Yax Kuk Mo', a ruler preceding him by more than 333 years. On one side of the altar he orders a scene in which Yax Kuk Mo' hands him the scepter of office, and on the other sides he shows other members of the dynasty founded by Yax Kuk Mo'. At no point on any monument does he establish his biological relationship to any of the other rulers on the altar. Finally, on the twentieth anniversary of his inauguration he commissions a stela, on which he reveals that his mother was a royal woman from a city 265 miles away.

In my opinion, we are dealing with political propaganda. Yax Pac had Altar Q carved not to record an historic event, but to legitimize his right to a throne to which he had ascended twelve years earlier.[23] He achieved this by showing himself receiving the scepter of office from a long-dead heroic king whose exploits were recorded on top of the altar. He claimed royal bloodlines through his mother, but never mentioned his father nor proved his descent from the heroic king. This is the kind of propaganda one might expect when there was a break in Copán's dynastic succession. Perhaps the previous ruler had died without heirs; or perhaps Yax Pac—emphasizing his mother's royal credentials—had managed to wrest the throne from the legitimate heir.

Other Examples of Propaganda

The Altar Q story is only one case of Maya history manipulated for political purposes. Three carved stone monuments from the Pasión River drainage of western Guatemala provide an equally interesting story, one that combines war, astronomy, propaganda, and history.

The story begins at the Maya sites of Dos Pilas and Aguateca, two cities so closely allied that they used the same emblem glyph (see Figure 1). In the eighth century A.D. two monuments alleging the same series of events were erected at both cities. The stela at Dos Pilas displays superior carving, has a longer hieroglyphic text, and is twenty-two feet high. The stela at Aguateca was carved more hurriedly, has a shorter text, and is 9-½ feet high.[24]

Both monuments mention three events from an eight-day period in A.D. 735. The first event, on November 29, has been interpreted as a battle with Seibal, another city in the Pasión River drainage. The second event, on November 30, has been translated as the "decapitation" of the defeated lord of Seibal. The third event, on December 6, has been interpreted as "the adorning of the prisoner."

On both monuments, the defeated lord of Seibal (whose name was "Jaguar-paw Jaguar") is shown beneath the feet of the Dos Pilas ruler. The lord of Seibal has ropes tied around his arms, is bent over in a posture of submission, and is carved at much smaller scale than his standing captor (see Figure 7). Given their translation of the November 30 event as a "decapitation," some Mayanists—following the 1960–1990 framework, which views all Maya texts as "history"—have concluded that the Seibal ruler was defeated and killed by his Dos Pilas rival. In celebration of this military victory, the Dos Pilas ruler erected a twenty-two-foot stela at Dos Pilas and a smaller version at the allied city of Aguateca.[25]

Let us turn next to the city of Seibal. Among its monuments are carved stone steps that record the date October 30, A.D. 747, an event that took place twelve years after the alleged battle. To our surprise, we read about the same Seibal ruler we saw tied up on the stelae at Dos Pilas and Aguateca as the loser in an important ritual ballgame. Such ballgames have been interpreted as mechanisms of "conflict resolution," deadly serious contests designed to eliminate the need for war by resolving disputes between neighboring cities. Some scholars now think that the Seibal ruler was sacrificed following that ballgame, rather than twelve years earlier. But if we find yet another monument showing the Seibal ruler alive and well

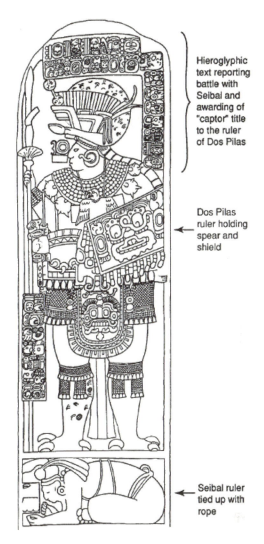

Hieroglyphic text reporting battle with Seibal and awarding of "captor" title to the ruler of Dos Pilas

Dos Pilas ruler holding spear and shield

Seibal ruler tied up with rope

Figure 7
Stone Monument from Aguateca

(*Redrawn by Kay Clahassey from Graham, 1967, Figure 5*) The monument shows the ruler of Dos Pilas standing above the cramped body of his prisoner, the ruler of Seibal.

five years after the ballgame, will we be forced to revise our thinking again?

What is going on here? Was the Seibal ruler really captured? Was he decapitated or not? How could he participate in a ballgame twelve years after he was killed by the lord of Dos Pilas? Were any of the hieroglyphic claims true, or was it all propaganda?

One answer is that we are seeing two different versions of history, each publicly displayed by one of two rival cities. Dos Pilas claims that its ruler defeated (and may have sacrificed) the lord of Seibal in A.D. 735. Seibal claims that its ruler not only survived the battle, but played in a ballgame in A.D. 747. Each city has its own political agenda. This situation is analogous to the daily press releases put out by both the Iraqi government and the U.S. Pentagon during the early stages of the 1991 Persian Gulf War. Both sides agreed there was a war going on; that part was history. Each side claimed it was winning; that part was propaganda.

In my opinion, there probably was a battle between Dos Pilas and Seibal, and that was history. The Seibal lord was, however, probably not decapitated or sacrificed; that was propaganda fomented by the Dos Pilas ruler. If we had only the Dos Pilas version of the events, we might have believed their story; but once we read Seibal's version, we could see the conflict between the two versions.

In the case of the Maya, we may even have reason to question the specific dates of some battles. Thanks to the work of Floyd Lounsbury, David Kelley, and Mary Miller,[26] we know that the ancient Maya followed the behavior of the planet Venus and used it as an important augury, or predictor of success, in warfare. November 29, A.D. 735—the alleged date of the battle between Seibal and Dos Pilas—coincided with the appearance of Venus as the Evening Star. October 30, A.D. 747—the alleged date of the Seibal ruler's participation in a ritual ballgame—coincides with what astronomers call the inferior conjunction of Venus.

The ancient Maya wanted us to believe that such battles were all timed to important astronomical events, and many probably were. Because some battles were reported seventy or more years after the fact, however, there was always the opportunity to assign auspicious dates to them retroactively. The latter possibility is hard to rule out for the following reason: We have other Maya texts that link both historical and mythical events to astronomical cycles thousands of years in the past, indeed so far in the past that they may not have happened at all.[27]

The Prospects for Future Study

I argued in a recent book that Maya hieroglyphic texts were not really history, but a combination of history, myth, and propaganda.[28] Maya writing was controlled by the ruling elite, and while it was based on real persons and events, it was biased and distorted in ways that suited the current needs of those rulers.

Maya studies are now divided into two opposing theoretical camps: those who think that the Maya were writing unmanipulated history, and those who believe that the inscriptions included large doses of royal propaganda. The first group are humanists who believe that the texts can be used to write a straight-forward history of the Maya. The second group, to which I belong, are social scientists who believe that the texts provide material for an analysis of Maya rulers' political goals, strategies, and agendas. What we hope to gain from the texts is an understanding of what Maya rulers wanted their subjects, their fellow nobles, their allies, and their enemies to believe. We do not believe they were trying to write impartial history.

One reason we believe this is that it was true of every other early writing system of the ancient world. The neighbors of the Maya—the Aztec, Mixtec, and Zapotec Indians of ancient Mexico— also used heavy doses of propaganda, mixing mythological and legendary events with historic ones in order to present their rulers in the best light.[29]

So, too, did the elites of Old World civilizations. The ancient Egyptians, like the Maya, portrayed their rulers as giants standing on the crumpled bodies of their enemies.[30] Were their military victories all "true history"? No. Egyptologist John Wilson has shown that five different pharaohs, spanning a period of 1,600 years, claimed to have executed the same Libyan noble prisoner in the presence of his wife and two sons. The hieroglyphic names of those Libyans, including the names of the wife and two sons, are duplicated exactly.[31] Nothing could be clearer than that later Egyptian pharaohs simply repeated the identical conquest claims of earlier rulers, much as Copán's Yax Pac used the surface of Altar Q to recite the accomplishments of the much earlier ruler Yax Kuk Mo'.

Over the next decade, many scholars will understandably devote themselves to translating more of the undeciphered Maya glyphs, to correcting past mistakes in translations, and to improving our understanding of how glyphs were pronounced. A major new frontier for Maya studies, however, will be the use of these ancient texts to understand broad anthropological issues. We need to know how rulers bolstered their position with strategic political and marital alliances; how their territories expanded and contracted; how major and minor lords interacted; and how subjugated towns battled for independence from the larger cities that controlled them.

We will not be able to achieve those anthropological goals as long as we continue to treat every Maya ruler's text as gospel, failing to recognize it as the biased, self-serving claim that it was. It is ironic that at the dawn of Maya studies 150 years ago, John L. Stephens pointed us in the right direction when he compared Maya writing to that of Mesopotamia and Egypt. Ask scholars in those two regions whether the texts they study are history or propaganda, and they will unhesitatingly answer, "both."

Notes

1. Joyce Marcus, "Lowland Maya Archaeology at the Crossroads," *American Antiquity* 48 (1983): 454–488.

2. John Lloyd Stephens, *Incidents of Travel in Central America, Chiapas, and Yucatan* (New York: Harper and Brothers, 1841).

3. Herbert J. Spinden, *A Study of Maya Art, Memoir VI of the Peabody Museum of American Archaeology and Ethnology* (Cambridge, MA: Peabody Museum, Harvard University, 1913), pp. 94–95.

4. Sylvanus G. Morley, *The Ancient Maya* (Stanford, CA: Stanford University Press, 1946); J. Eric S. Thompson, "Maya Chronology: Glyph G of the Lunar Series," *American Anthropologist* 31 (1929): 223–231; J. Eric S. Thompson, *Maya Hieroglyphic Writing* (Washington, DC: Carnegie Institution of Washington, Publication 589, 1950).

5. Thompson, *Maya Hieroglyphic Writing*, p. 155.

6. J. Eric S. Thompson, *A Catalog of Maya Hieroglyphs* (Norman: University of Oklahoma Press, 1962).

7. Sylvanus G. Morley, *An Introduction to the Study of Maya Hieroglyphs* (Washington, DC: Bureau of American Ethnology, Bulletin 57, 1915), pp. 114–129; Thompson, *Maya Hieroglyphic Writing*, pp. 314–316.

8. Heinrich Berlin, "Glifos nominales en el sarcófago de Palenque: un ensayo," *Humanidades*, vol. 2, no. 10 (Guatemala City: University of San Carlos, 1959), pp. 1–8.

9. Heinrich Berlin, "El glifo 'emblema' en las inscripciones mayas," *Journal de la Société des Américanistes de Paris* 47 (1958): 111–119.

10. Tatiana Proskouriakoff, "Historical Implications of a Pattern of Dates at Piedras Negras, Guatemala," *American Antiquity* 25 (1960): 454–475.

11. Tatiana Proskouriakoff, "Portraits of Women in Maya Art," in S. K. Lothrop, ed., *Essays in Pre-Columbian Art and Archaeology* (Cambridge: Harvard University Press, 1961), pp. 81–99; Tatiana Proskouriakoff, "Historical Data in the Inscriptions of Yaxchilan, Part I," *Estudios de Cultura Maya* 3 (1963): 149–167; Tatiana Proskouriakoff, "Historical Data in the Inscriptions of Yaxchilan, Part II," *Estudios de Cultura Maya* 4 (1964): 177–201.

12. Herbert J. Spinden, "Portraiture in Central American Art," in F. W. Hodge, ed., *Holmes Anniversary Volume* (Washington: J. W. Bryan Press, 1916), p. 446; Morley, *The Ancient Maya*, Plate 66.

13. Stephens, *Incidents of Travel in Central America, Chiapas, and Yucatan*, p. 140.

14. John E. Teeple, *Maya Astronomy* (Washington, DC: Carnegie Institution of Washington, Publication 403,

Contributions to American Archaeology, vol. 1, no. 2, 1930).

15. Thompson, *Maya Hieroglyphic Writing*, pp. 205, 317.

16. Proskouriakoff, "Historical Implications of a Pattern of Dates at Piedras Negras, Guatemala," p. 468; David H. Kelley, "Glyphic Evidence for a Dynastic Sequence at Quiriguá," *American Antiquity* 27 (1962): 332–333; Joyce Marcus, *An Epigraphic Approach to the Territorial Organization of the Lowland Classic Maya* (Ph. D. diss., Harvard University, 1974), pp. 173–180; Joyce Marcus, *Emblem and State in the Classic Maya Lowlands: An Epigraphic Approach to Territorial Organization* (Washington, DC: Dumbarton Oaks, 1976), pp. 139–143.

17. Daniel G. Brinton, "The Ancient Phonetic Alphabet of Yucatan," *American Bibliopolist* 2 (1870): 143–148; Benjamin L. Whorf, "The Phonetic Value of Certain Characters in Maya Writing," *Papers of the Peabody Museum of American Archaeology and Ethnology* 13 (Cambridge: Harvard University, 1933); Yuri V. Knorozov, *The Writing of the Maya Indians*, trans. Sophie Coe, Peabody Museum of Archaeology and Ethnology, Russian Translation Series, vol. 4 (Cambridge: Harvard University, 1967); David H. Kelley, "Kakupacal and the Itzas," *Estudios de Cultura Maya* 7 (1968): 255–268; Floyd G. Lounsbury, "Pacal," p. ii, and Peter Mathews and Linda Schele," Lords of Palenque—The Glyphic Evidence," pp. 63–76, in Merle G. Robertson, ed., *Primera Mesa Redonda de Palenque, Part I* (Pebble Beach, CA: Robert Louis Stevenson School, 1974).

18. Joyce Marcus, "The Origins of Mesoamerican Writing," *Annual Review of Anthropology* 5 (1976): 62–63.

19. Victoria R. Bricker, *A Grammar of Mayan Hieroglyphs* (New Orleans: Middle American Research Institute, Tulane University, Publication 56, 1986), pp. 192–198.

20. Floyd G. Lounsbury, "The Names of a King: Hieroglyphic Variants as a Key to Decipherment," in William F. Hanks and Don S. Rice, eds., *Word and Image in Maya Culture* (Salt Lake City: University of Utah Press, 1989), pp. 73–91; Linda Schele and David Freidel, *A Forest of Kings* (New York: William Morrow, 1990).

21. Linda Schele, "The Founders of Lineages at Copán and Other Maya Sites," *Copán Note 8* (Tegucigalpa, Honduras: IHAH); William L. Fash, *Scribes, Warriors, and Kings: The City of Copán and the Ancient Maya* (London: Thames and Hudson, 1991), pp. 79–83.

22. Sylvanus G. Morley, *The Inscriptions at Copan* (Washington, DC: Carnegie Institution of Washington, Publication 219, 1920), Plate 32; Marcus, *Emblem and State in the Classic Maya Lowlands: An Epigraphic Approach to Territorial Organization*, p. 145; Schele and Freidel, *A Forest of Kings*, pp. 330–331.

23. Joyce Marcus, *Mesoamerican Writing Systems: Propaganda, Myth, and History in Four Ancient Civilizations* (Princeton, NJ: Princeton University Press, 1992), pp. 256–257.

24. Ian Graham, *Archaeological Explorations in El Peten, Guatemala* (New Orleans: Middle American Research Institute, Tulane University, Publication 33, 1967), p. 14.

25. Ibid., pp. 9–19; Stephen D. Houston, *Hieroglyphs and History at Dos Pilas* (Austin: University of Texas Press, 1993).

26. F. G. Lounsbury, "Astronomical Knowledge and Its Uses at Bonampak, Mexico," in Anthony F. Aveni, ed., *Archaeoastronomy in the New World* (Cambridge: Cambridge University Press, 1982), pp. 143–168; David H. Kelley, "Maya Astronomical Tables and Inscriptions," in Anthony F. Aveni, ed., *Native American Astronomy* (Austin: University of Texas Press, 1977), pp. 57–74; Mary E. Miller, *The Murals of Bonampak* (Princeton, NJ: Princeton University Press, 1986).

27. Floyd G. Lounsbury, "Maya Numeration, Computation, and Calendrical Astronomy," in C. C. Gillispie, ed., *Dictionary of Scientific Biography*, vol. 15, Supplement 1 (New York: Scribner's and Sons, 1978), pp. 759–818; Floyd G. Lounsbury, "A Rationale for the Initial Date of the Temple of the Cross at Palenque," in Merle G. Robertson, ed., *The Art, Iconography, and Dynastic History of Palenque, Part III: Proceedings of the Segunda Mesa Redonda de Palenque* (Pebble Beach, CA: Robert Louis Stevenson School, 1976), pp. 211–224; Floyd G. Lounsbury, "Some Problems in the Interpretation of the Mythological Portion of the Hieroglyphic Text of the Temple of the Cross at Palenque," in Merle G. Robertson, ed., *Third Palenque Round Table 1978, Part 2* (Austin: University of Texas Press, 1980), pp. 99–115; Schele and Freidel, *A Forest of Kings*, pp. 244–254; Thompson, *Maya Hieroglyphic Writing*, pp. 314–317.

28. Marcus, *Mesoamerican Writing Systems: Propaganda, Myth, and History in Four Ancient Civilizations*.

29. Ibid., pp. 143–152.

30. Bruce Trigger, "The Narmer Palette in Crosscultural Perspective," in M. Gorg and E. Pusch, eds., *Festschrift Elmar Edel 1979* (Bamberg: Kurt Urlaub, 1979), pp. 409–416.

31. John A. Wilson, "The Royal Myth in Ancient Egypt," *Proceedings of the American Philosophical Society* 100 (1956): 439–442; Jean Leclant, "La'famille libyenne'au Temple Haut du Pepi Ier.," *Le Livre du Centenaire 1880–1980* (Cairo: Institut Français d'Archéologie Orientale, 1980), pp. 49–54.

Suggested Readings

Fash, William L. *Scribes, Warriors, and Kings: The City of Copán and the Ancient Maya.* New York: Thames and Hudson, 1991. A comprehensive overview of recent excavations and newly discovered texts from Copán, the city of Altar Q.

Henderson, John S. *The World of the Ancient Maya.* Ithaca, NY: Cornell University Press, 1981. A well-balanced synthesis of major topics in Maya archaeology.

Marcus, Joyce. *Mesoamerican Writing Systems: Propaganda, Myth, and History in Four Ancient Civilizations.* Princeton, NJ: Princeton University Press, 1992. This book develops a typology of four different types of propaganda and then applies it to the Maya, Zapotec, Mixtec, and Aztec writing systems.

Sabloff, Jeremy A., and John S. Henderson. *Ancient Maya Civilization in the Eighth Century A.D.* Washington, DC: Dumbarton Oaks, 1993. A recent synthesis of Maya civilization during its heyday, from A.D. 700 to 800.

Sabloff, Jeremy A. *The New Archaeology and the Ancient Maya.* New York: Scientific American Library Series, 1990. Discusses the necessity of formulating questions before conducting research and the importance of establishing a good fit between evidence and interpretations.

Sharer, Robert J. *The Ancient Maya*, 5th ed. Stanford: Stanford University Press, 1994. An up-to-date and highly informative overview of Maya archaeology.

Stephens, John L. *Incidents of Travel in Central America, Chiapas, and Yucatan.* Reprint, New York: Dover Paperbacks, 1969. This adventure story is set in the mid-nineteenth century, with Stephens and Catherwood leading us on a trip to discover Maya ruins covered by jungle.

The Concept of Race
in Physical Anthropology
C. Loring Brace

"Race" as a Social Construct

The reader of an essay such as this will normally expect it to start with an acceptable anthropological definition of what "race" is considered to be. For many it will come as something of a surprise, then, to hear that "race" is whatever people think it should be, but that it has no basic biological reality. Since "race" holds such a prominent place in life in America and has done so since before the country gained its independence over two centuries ago, the reader can be forgiven for thinking that the statement that "race" does not exist amounts to a bit of academic double-talk or verbal sleight-of-hand. The practicing physician will query rhetorically, "What do you mean, race does not exist? I see it in my clinic every day!" One can be forgiven for being suspicious that the denial of the reality of "race" is just another manifestation of post-modern relativism where reality is defined as whatever people choose to believe and has no objective identity.

Actually, what is thought of as "race" is in fact a manifestation of cultural relativism, and each group will perceive it in a different way. In Hitler's Germany, Jews and Gypsies were perceived as distinct "races," while the English have often thought of the Irish and the French as racially distinct. Americans, on the other hand, use the term to apply to what they perceive as larger groupings such as Africans or Asians and assume somewhat simplistically that a single label can encompass the spectrum found in each continent. Europeans would agree that these qualify as "races," but they then go on to make finer discriminations under that term.

In saying that "race" does not exist as a biological category, I am not saying that human biological differences do not exist. These do, and can be produc-

tively studied, but only after the concept of "race" is rejected as a starting point. I shall return to that point later on. At the moment, it should be noted that the concept is relatively recent and basically did not exist prior to the Renaissance. It is of some interest to reflect that neither the concept nor any word that could be used to designate it is present in the Judaeo-Christian Bible. One could say that, of course, the Biblical accounts describe a relatively restricted portion of the Middle East, although the scope covered actually ranges all the way from the Mediterranean up the Nile to Ethiopia.

There is no trace of a "race" concept in the extensive accounts in Egyptian hieroglyphics even though sub-Saharan Africans are represented in the accompanying illustrations. The "Father of History"—Herodotus (ca. 484–420 B.C.), described his travels all the way from the Black Sea north of Greece southwards and up the Nile to Nubia, but never used a term that could be construed as "race" even though some of the translations insert that word where the original Greek used *anthropoi* or sometimes *ethnea*, "people."[1] The medieval Venetian traveler, Marco Polo (1254–1324) went all the way from Italy to China by way of the "Silk Road," and came back via Southeast Asia and the Indian peninsula. However, when he wrote about his travels and the people he encountered, he never used anything that could correspond to the concept of "race."[2] The same thing was true for the even more widely traveled medieval Arabic geographer, Ibn Battuta (1304–1377), who not only duplicated Marco Polo's west-to-east span but added a perspective that ran from the Atlantic coast of Europe southwards across the Sahara to Timbuktu in sub-Saharan Africa.[3]

The big change in the perception of how people differ from place to place came in the Renaissance.

Prior to that time, travelers such as Herodotus, Marco Polo, and Ibn Battuta got from one place to another over land on foot or on horseback, one day at a time, and what they saw was the gradation of one population into the next without any discernible break. That means of seeing the world changed dramatically in the Renaissance because of the development of ocean-going ships that could set off from the shores of one continent and arrive at those of another without seeing anything in between. As a result, the sailors and their passengers perceived a world in which the people at the port of embarkation and the port of arrival appeared categorically different.

The marine technology and navigational skills that made such long-distance voyaging possible accompanied the emergence of the Renaissance in Europe and made possible the feats of Christopher Columbus, Vasco da Gama, and others. It also meant that European perceptions of other people were of categorical distinctions instead of the borderless gradations that were seen by Herodotus and his medieval successors. The modem phenomena of the jet plane and the television camera have simply reinforced the view that the world is inhabited by categorically distinct people. If this categorical picture of human differences was a construct that emerged from the circumstances of Renaissance Europe, it was still largely a vicarious view since it did not arise from the direct perceptions of the majority of the populace but rather from the second-hand reports of those who had actually been the travelers.

All that changed as a result of European colonization of other parts of the globe, in particular the western hemisphere. Colonization involved the actual movement of people from one relatively small segment of the world, western Europe, to other places such as the southern tip of Africa, Australia, and particularly to the western hemisphere. The western Europeans were then installed immediately adjacent to the indigenous populations whom they perceived as being categorically distinct.

The western hemisphere was particularly important in the construction of this categorical view of human differences because the Europeans had come from a relatively restricted region at the northwestern edge of the Old World. As it happened, the Native Americans with whom they came in contact had also come from a relatively restricted area but at the northeastern edge of the Old World, although no one knew this at the time of first contact. As near as we can tell, the movement of northeast Asians into the New World does not go back much more than 15,000 years, and that is not a long enough stretch of time for significant biological differentiation to have taken place.

There is no gradation in skin pigment among the Native Americans from the Arctic to the equator—unlike virtually all of the continuously occupied parts of the Old World. European immigrants, wherever they went in the western hemisphere, perceived the indigenous people as being categorically distinct from them in essentially the same sort of way.[4]

Subsequently, the European-derived population imported slaves by the thousands from a relatively restricted section of West Africa. The western hemisphere, then, presents a picture of people from three separate portions of the Old World, artificially brought together, and left to contemplate the meaning of their perceived distinctions. As such, it is the worst possible model to use in an effort to make sense out of the normal circumstances of human biological variation. At the same time, the issue of the meaning of those differences had an immediacy that was true for no other large segment of the world. Such has become the unwitting power that America has upon the way the world thinks about things that the concept of "race" that was reified by the circumstances of the settling of the western hemisphere is now being accepted as a matter of course in many parts of the world—China for example—where it had not previously existed.

The Biological Nature of Human Variation

Curiously enough it is the biological part of anthropology that has been slow to accept the implications of the previous section.[5] Actually, the realization that human populations grade into each other without break and that "race" is a completely arbitrary appellation was articulated before the outbreak of World War II,[6] and this was the basis for the approach taken by the late Ashley Montagu in his most significant contribution, *Man's Most Dangerous Myth: The Fallacy of Race*.[7] This was an important first step in showing that the concept of "race" has no biological basis, but there was one more development that was necessary before that realization could be nailed down. This was the development and application of the concept of "cline," defined as "a gradation in measurable characters."[8]

Ironically, although that idea was proposed by Julian Huxley—one of the two who influenced Ashley Montagu to realize that the concept of "race" was biologically indefensible—Huxley never fully realized why the treatment of clines provided the final demonstration of the nonexistence of that category. This was because he lacked the information demonstrating that clines are distributed without any relationship to each other in a species without reproductive boundaries. In the decade after Ashley Montagu's book was published, studies in field biology involving deer mice, leopard frogs, butterflies, red-eyed towhees, the American marten, and others showed that the traits under separate genetic control within each species had distributions that were completely unrelated to each other. Early in the 1950s, this led to the demonstration that the category of *subspecies* simply could not be used for forms that were reproductively continuous over large areas.[9]

Within another decade, it was realized that, since *Homo sapiens* also is a continuously distributed species without reproductive barriers between adjacent groups, the same logic should apply to the nature of human variation. This led one biological anthropologist, Frank Livingstone, to declare that "There are no races, there are only clines."[10] He had come to this understanding by noting that the distribution of hemoglobin S, the cause of sickle-cell anemia when present in the homozygous (SS) condition, is related to the distribution of a particular kind of malaria. When present in the heterozygous condition (AS), it conveys an ability to survive that particular form of malaria.[11] The distribution of the gene for hemoglobin S, however, is completely unrelated to the distribution of skin color, and if one tries to combine the manifestations of both in a single region, one can make biological sense of neither one. Add a third trait to the picture with a distribution unrelated to the others, and the pattern made by the intersection of those genetically separate traits becomes completely senseless. Adding further traits simply erases all indications of any pattern whatsoever. The only way to understand the biological meaning of the distribution of those traits is to treat the distribution of each one separately and compare it to the distribution of the selective force to which it represents a response.[12]

Skin Color

At this point, it will be instructive to look at the distributions of a few human traits that are inherited in straightforward fashion and for which there is enough information to build up a world-wide picture. Actually I am going to restrict the portrayal to distributions in the Old World since the western hemisphere has not been inhabited long enough for many adaptive traits such as tooth size and skin color to have developed much in the way of differential gradients. The first such trait to be considered is skin color since it is so closely linked in the minds of the public with what is assumed to be "race." Skin color is produced by the

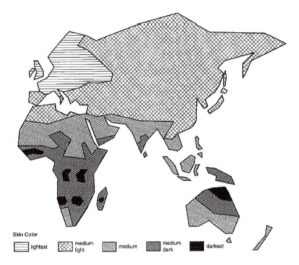

Skin Color

☐ lightest ▨ medium light ▨ medium ▨ medium dark ■ darkest

Figure 16–1
The Distribution of Variation in Intensity of Human Skin Color in the Old World

pigment melanin, which blocks the penetration of the most damaging part of the ultraviolet component of sunlight. In high doses, ultraviolet rays with wave lengths between 280 and 320 millimicrons (UV-B) can penetrate to the lower levels of the epidermis and can contribute to the development of skin cancer. There is obvious survival value to the presence of melanin in the skin of the inhabitants of the tropics.[13]

The significance of maintaining epidermal melanin away from the tropics is of less evident importance, and it is not surprising to find that skin pigment tends to decrease in proportion to the distance of a given population from the equator. The reason for increased skin pigmentation in the tropics is clear enough, but why it should reduce to the north and the south is not agreed upon. One theory has it that the reduction allows enough UV penetration so that Vitamin D can be synthesized. Heavy pigmentation could lead to Vitamin D deficiency and rickets during growth in areas such as the north where the annual UV dosage is far less than in the tropics. Others have noted that enough Vitamin D is synthesized and stored for further use during the summer no matter what the amount of skin pigment so that there is no particular advantage to depigmentation in the north. Another theory suggests that when selection for skin pigment is relaxed, as it is in the north where the chances of UV-induced cancer are small no matter how little pigment there is in the skin, the accumulation of chance mutations affecting pigment production will result in an eventual failure to produce a full tropical amount of epidermal melanin.[14] The distribution of human skin pigment in the Old World is shown in Figure 16–1 (on page 47).[15]

As can be seen, there is a general association of skin color differences with latitude, but it is far from perfect. The maximum pigmentation occurs among tropical populations who have long been resident at the latitudes where they are now found. The greatest amount of depigmentation occurs where people have resided farthest away from the tropics for the longest period of time. The slightly lesser amount of depigmentation of people in the north temperate portions of Eastern Asia may be because they have not been resident at that latitude for quite so long as their counterparts at the northwestern edges of human habitation. Certainly the lack of fully tropical amounts of pigmentation of people in the tropics at the southeastern edge of the continental Old World—Southeast Asia—is because the current inhabitants have only come south from temperate latitudes within the past few thousand years.[16]

I have already mentioned that there is no pigment cline in the New World, so it is apparent that the 15,000 years or so that the western hemisphere has been occupied is not enough time for a pigment gradient to have developed in place. In Australia there actually is a north-south pigment cline with the darkest skin occurring in the tropical north. That gradient, however, is nowhere near so marked as the gradient from the Equator in Africa to the southern tip of the continent, and it is apparent that the 60,000 years that Australia has been occupied is long enough to have produced the beginnings of a north-south pigment cline, but nowhere near long enough to have produced the kind of differences that you get ranging north from the African tropics to Spain, a latitude change comparable to the tropics to southern Australia. The time needed to have produced a spectrum such as that from West Africa to Spain would have required nearly 200,000 years, which is more than three times as long as Australia has been occupied.[17]

Tooth Size

If we are keenly sensitive to differences in human skin pigment, we are less so to differences in the size of the human dentition. Yes, we are aware that Africans tend to have larger teeth than Europeans, but it is not the uppermost impression in our minds when we compare the physical appearance of people from both places. If it has taken nearly 200,000 years to produce the differences in skin color that we see in the world today, the modern condition represented by the teeth we have has taken over 100,000 years to produce. No one has teeth as large as the common human ancestor had 130,000 years ago, but the reductions that have

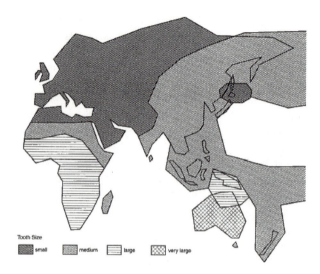

Figure 16–2
Human Tooth Size Differences in the Old World

taken place during the past 100,000 years have proceeded faster in some places than in others. Throughout most of the two million years of the Pleistocene, our ancestors ate things as they found them, namely raw. When teeth wore out, that was it and life came to an end as it does today for aged elephants whose last teeth have worn to useless stumps. Now, of course, we cook things to mush or puree them in machines that reduce things to drinkable consistency. In the past, however, teeth had to last a lifetime, and they had to have enough durability to reduce the toughest of uncooked food substances to swallowable consistency.

Starting in the glacial period before the most recent one, that is, over 200,000 years ago, the control of fire enabled people to become permanent inhabitants of the temperate zone. Part of that use of fire of course was to keep people warm. Unlike wolves, bears, horses, deer, and the like, people are restricted by the tropical physiology they have inherited from their primate ancestors, so survival in the temperate zone in the face of increasing glacial chill was only possible with the warmth provided by clothing and the hearth. As creatures dependent on the products of the chase, there was the added problem of eating something that was left over from a recent hunt when it had frozen solid. The Pleistocene cow, or auroch, was quite a large animal, and it was unlikely that a given band of human hunters could have consumed the whole thing at a single sitting. A day later, its icy remains would have defied mastication without some remedial treatment. The answer was the development of cooking.

While the control of fire had become a human universal well over 200,000 years ago, its use in the preparation of food was essential for survival in the northern stretches of human habitation (especially as glacial conditions intensified), in a fashion quite unlike that practiced farther south. This has been referred to as "obligatory cooking."[18] While this did indeed make it possible to eat what had previously been frozen, it had another incidental consequence. It meant that the food being eaten required less chewing before it could be swallowed, and this in turn meant that there was a reduction in the amount of tooth substance required to last a person throughout life. Relaxation in the selection maintaining tooth size meant that mutations affecting dental dimensions could occur with impunity, and, since the average mutation interferes with the development of the structure it controls, that structure—simple tooth substance in this case—can be predicted to reduce in the course of time. The argument is the same as the argument for the reduction of skin pigment among those people who have longest resided in areas where the selective forces maintaining skin color are less than in those regions subjected to the maximum amount of ultraviolet radiation. Both skin color and tooth size reduction are examples of evolution by entropy.

The maximum amount of dental reduction in the world, then, should occur in those areas where cooking has longest been used for the preparation of food. The archaeological record shows that this first occurred in a stretch running from the Middle East to the Atlantic shores of Europe, and it is not surprising to realize that the people in that area today, and their relatives just to the north, have the smallest teeth relative to body size of any of the peoples of the world. A simple version of the world distribution of human tooth size can be seen in Figure 16–2.[19]

Eventually the advantages of cooking spread elsewhere in the world. The spread to the south was not needed to thaw previously frozen food, but it was discovered that it made it possible to use as food something that had turned bad by being left out in the tropical heat for several days. It even made it possible to eat things that would have been indigestible raw: wheat, rice, yams, and the like, thus opening up a vast realm of potential foodstuffs that had previously been unavailable for human sustenance.

Cooking got into Australia last, and it is no surprise to discover that aboriginal Australian (non-European) teeth are closer to the size of the average human Pleistocene ancestor than are those of any other people in the world, and the farther south in Australia one goes, the less reduced are the teeth. Finally, the invention of pottery in the heart of those areas that first developed agriculture completely eliminated the

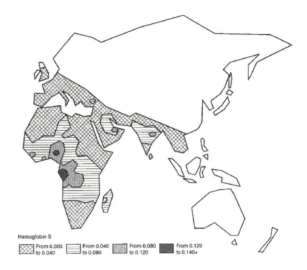

Figure 16–3
The Distribution of Hemoglobin S

selective forces maintaining any tooth substance at all. Yes, it is nice to be able to chew what we refer to as "toothsome" morsels, but, in the absence of teeth, sustenance can be ingested in the form of soups that need no chewing whatsoever. The smallest teeth in the world today occur among those in the area where pottery was first invented and has been in use for the longest period of time—the Near East.

Sickle-Cell Anemia

We can perceive differences in skin color and, to a lesser extent, tooth size, but there are many ways in which humans differ that we cannot see directly. Amongst these are differences in hemoglobin, a molecule whose principal function is delivering oxygen from the lungs to the tissues where it is used for metabolic purposes, and then taking the product of metabolism, carbon dioxide, back to the lungs where it is released into the atmosphere in exhaled breath. In addition to its primary role in oxygen transport, the hemoglobin molecule can affect the red blood cell that contains it.

One inherited hemoglobin variant, hemoglobin S, will tend to crystallize after it gives up its oxygen, and the crystals align themselves within the surrounding cytoplasm of the red blood cell as long stiff rods. These can change the shape of the softly rounded blood cell to an angular pointed affair that reminded microscopists early in the past century of miniature sickles: the famous "sickle-cells" of sickle-cell anemia. Those stiff, sickle-shaped cells get stuck in the capillaries at the peripheries of the circulatory system preventing blood from flowing through. The body, in response, dissolves the cells to restore circulation at the expense of the loss of those sickled cells, and the loss of red blood cells is what constitutes anemia— thus, sickle-cell anemia. The process also dumps immature malaria parasites into the plasma where they are sought out and destroyed by disease-fighting white blood cells before they can spread their infection to other red blood cells. This then reduces malaria although it does not eliminate it from the system.

The phenomenon of sickle-cell anemia was first identified by clinicians in the United States and noted to occur amongst Americans of African ancestry. Inevitably, sickle-cell anemia was regarded as an African disease and it is still thought of by many physicians and the public at large as an African "racial" marker. As it happens, although much of the sickle-cell anemia in America did come over with the Africans who were brought in as slaves, the genes that were responsible for the presence of that condition in Africa were not of African origin, ultimately having been brought in from the Middle East by traders down the African east coast or by caravan routes across the Sahara.[20]

Sickle-cell anemia is a single gene trait, and one needs to inherit the gene for hemoglobin S from each parent in order to show a full-scale manifestation of the phenomenon. Such a person is homozygous, which means having a double dose of the S gene (the SS condition), and that person has greatly reduced chances for survival. A person with one gene for normal hemoglobin and one gene for abnormal hemoglobin is a heterozygote exhibiting the AS condition. A homozygous normal is AA. In spite of the fact that the sufferers from sickle-cell anemia tend to have a sharply reduced life span and usually do not have children, the frequency of the gene is maintained from generation to generation in certain parts of the world. The reason is that the AS condition allows its possessors to survive attacks from a particularly mean kind of malaria. They are not immune to malaria, but they have a much greater chance of surviving it than do AA people.

As it happened, when West Africans adopted agriculture a couple of thousand years ago, the changes in settlement patterns and the hewing out of farm lands from what had been forest altered conditions to such an extent that that particularly noxious kind of malaria flourished and became a major threat to human survival. When hemoglobin S was introduced, then, it achieved relatively high frequencies in a relatively short period of time among the people who

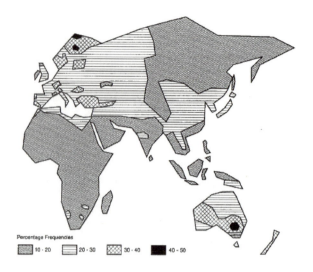

Figure 16–4

The Percentage Distribution of the Gene For Blood Group A in the ABO System

already lived there. Figure 16–3 shows the distribution of the gene for hemoglobin S in the middle of the twentieth century.[21] Like the distribution of skin color and tooth size, it follows the distribution of the selective force to which it represents an adaptation, but that selective force does not have the same distribution as the selective forces that control those other traits, and none of them coincide with either a given locale or what constitutes "race" in the popular sense of the term. There are many other forms of abnormal hemoglobin, and some of them are systematically distributed in conjunction with the distribution of other kinds of malaria.

The ABO Blood Group System

The final clinally distributed trait I am going to consider is another one that we cannot see but which we all know about, namely the ABO blood group system. This is controlled by three genes at a single locus found on the long arm of chromosome 9. Every person inherits one gene from each parent. If one has an A from both parents or an A from one and an O from the other, one tests as A since O is recessive. Likewise, whether one is BB or BO, one tests as B since B is also dominant over O. If one has an A and a B, one tests as AB. To test as "O," one needs to be homozygous for the O gene, namely, OO. This is all very well known since it is vital information for blood transfusions. O is the universal donor and can be given to people with any of the other genes, but neither A nor B can be given to an O individual. This is

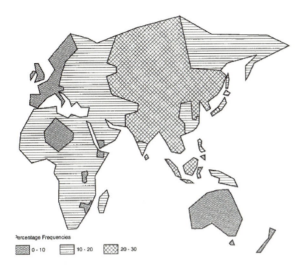

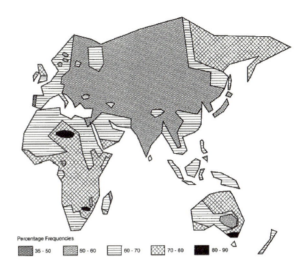

Figure 16–5
The Percentage Distribution of the B Gene
in the ABO System

Figure 16–6
The Percentage Distribution of the O Gene
in the ABO System

essential medical information, but there has been much less interest in why there are differences in the ABO system in the first place. There has been some suggestion that the different genes have something to do with the resistance or susceptibility to different diseases, but this is not well worked out. The system is inherited in simple and straightforward fashion, and the distributions of the A, B, and O alleles (i.e., genes that fit at the same locus on the chromosome) are well known, as shown in Figure 16–4 (on page 44), Figure 16–5, and Figure 16–6.[22] Once again, the distributions are evidently completely unrelated to the distributions of the traits plotted in Figures 16–1 through 16–3, and only confusion would result from having to force them all into a single interpretive framework.

Regional Features

One could present many more traits in the format offered earlier, and none of them would show the same kind of distribution. Likewise, none of them can be associated with a particular region of the world. Yes, there are latitudinal changes in features such as skin color, but that is not the same as restricting a given feature to a particular segment of geography. That is because the selective forces that govern their distributions are not themselves restricted by local geography. However, there are human features that can be associated with particular regions. We can recognize particular nuances of cheek bone and eye opening formation as recalling the inhabitants of the Far East, or ear shape in Africa, or aspects in the shape

of the nose as being peculiarly characteristic of Europe. Unlike the traits dealt with previously, however, there is no adaptive value in those nuances of eye, ear, and nose morphology. The only thing we can say about them is that they tend to resemble what can be seen in the regions from which the ancestors of those people came.

It seems evident that if traits can be identified with a particular region, then they have no adaptive significance, and no regional manifestation is either better or worse than any other. Clearly such regional traits are inherited, but they are just the inherited nuances of what was there and nothing else. At most this constitutes what I have labeled "family resemblance writ large."[23] As Marco Polo and Ibn Battuta recognized, those resemblances grade from one region to another without any break and are unrelated to survival capabilities. It is only when we see representatives out of context that we categorize them with "racial" labels, and these can only prevent us from a full understanding of the nature of human biological variation on a world-wide scale.

Notes

1. Herodotus, *The Histories*, 4 vols., with an English translation by A. D. Godley (Cambridge: Loeb Classical Library, Harvard University Press, 1920).
2. Marco Polo, *The Travels of Marco Polo, the Venetian*, the translation of Marsden revised, with a selection of his notes, Thomas Wright, ed. (London: H. G. Bohm, 1854).

3. Mohammed, In Allah Ibn Battuta, *Travels in Asia and Africa*, translated by H. A. R. Gibb (New York: R. McBride, 1929).

4. C. Loring Brace and A. Russell Nelson, "The Peopling of the Americas: Anglo Stereotypes and Native American Realities," *General Anthropology 5* (1999): 1–7.

5. C. Loring Brace, "The Roots of the Race Concept in American Physical Anthropology," in Frank Spencer, ed., *A History of American Physical Anthropology, 1930–1980* (New York: Academic Press, 1982), pp. 11–29; C. Loring Brace, "Region Does Not Mean Race: Reality vs. Convention in Forensic Identification," *Journal of Forensic Sciences* 40 (1995): 171–175.

6. Julian S. Huxley and Alfred C. Haddon, *We Europeans: A Survey of "Racial" Problems* (London: Jonathan Cape, 1935).

7. Ashley Montagu, *Man's Most Dangerous Myth: The Fallacy of Race* (New York: Columbia University Press, 1942).

8. Julian S. Huxley, "Clines: An Auxiliary Taxonomic Principle," *Nature* 142 (1948): 219–220.

9. E. O. Wilson and William L. Brown, Jr., "The Subspecies Concept and Its Taxonomic Application," *Systematic Zoology* 2 (1953): 97–111.

10. Frank B. Livingstone, "On the Non-Existence of Human Races," *Current Anthropology* 3 (1962): 279.

11. Frank B. Livingstone, "Anthropological Implications of Sickle Cell Gene Distribution in West Africa," *American Anthropologist* 60 (1958): 533–562.

12. C. Loring Brace, "A Non-Racial Approach toward the Understanding of Human Diversity," in Ashley Montagu, ed., *The Concept of Race* (New York: The Free Press of Glencoe, 1964), pp. 103–152; C. Loring Brace, "A Four Letter Word Called 'Race'," in Larry T. Reynolds and Leonard Lieberman, eds., *Race and Other Misadventures: Essays in Honor of Ashley Montagu in His Nineteeth Year* (Dix Hills, NY: General Hall, 1996), pp. 106–141.

13. Ashley H. Robins, *Biological Perspectives on Human Pigmentation* (Cambridge, England: Cambridge University Press, 1991); Nina Jablonski and George Chaplin, "The Evolution of Human Skin Coloration," *Journal of Human Evolution* 39 (2000): 57–106.

14. The Vitamin D argument is outlined in Jablonski and Chaplin, see Note 13. The effects of mutations under conditions of relaxed selection are presented by Brace in "A Four-Letter Word Called 'Race'," see Note 12.

15. Figure 16–1 is updated from Figure 3 in "A Four-Letter Word Called 'Race'," see Note 12.

16. Charles Higham, *The Archaeology of Mainland Southeast Asia: From 10,000 B.C. to the Fall of Angkor* (New York: Cambridge University Press, 1989); Matthew Spriggs, "The Dating of the Island Southeast Asian Neolithic: An Attempt at Chronometric Hygiene and Linguistic Correlation," *Antiquity* 63 (1989): 587–613.

17. Maciej Henneberg and C. Loring Brace, "Human Skin Color as a Measure of Time in situ," *American Journal of Physical Anthropology Supplement* 30 (2000): 177.

18. C. Loring Brace, *The Stages of Human Evolution*, 5th ed. (Englewood Cliffs, NJ: Prentice Hall, 1995).

19. A selection of the data used to construct Figure 16–2 is summarized in C. Loring Brace, Shelley L. Smith and Kevin D. Hunt, "What Big Teeth You Had Grandma! Human Tooth Size, Past and Present," in Marc A. Kelley and Clark S. Larsen, eds., *Advances in Dental Anthropology* (New York: Wiley-Liss, 1991), pp. 33–57.

20. Frank B. Livingstone, "Who Gave Whom Hemoglobin S: The Use of Restriction Site Haplotype Variation for the Interpretation of the Bs Gene," *American Journal of Human Biology* 3 (1989): 289–302.

21. The distribution pictured is adapted from Walter F. Bodmer and Luigi Lucca Cavalli-Sforza, *Genetics, Evolution and Man* (San Francisco: Freeman, 1976).

22. Figures 16–4, 16–5, and 16–6 are simplified from the information provided by A. E. Mourant, Ada Kopec, and Kazimiera Domaniewska-Sobczak, *The ABO Blood Groups: Comprehensive Tables and Maps of World Distribution* (Springfield, IL: C. C. Thomas, 1958).

23. In "A Four-Letter Word Called 'Race'," in Note 12, p. 136, reprinted in C. Loring Brace, *Evolution in an Anthropological View* (Walnut Creek, CA: AltaMira Press, 2000), p. 320.

Suggested Readings

Brace, C. Loring. *The Stages of Human Evolution*, 5th ed. Englewood Cliffs, NJ: Prentice Hall, 1995.

Brace, C. Loring. *Evolution in an Anthropological View*. Walnut Creek, CA: AltaMira Press, 2000.

Hannaford, Ivan. *Race: The History of an Idea in the West*. Baltimore: Johns Hopkins University Press, 1996. The extraordinary recency and subjectivity of the concept of "race" is eloquently documented.

Montagu, Ashley. *Man's Most Dangerous Myth: The Fallacy of Race*, 6th ed. Walnut Creek, CA: AltaMira Press, 1997. An update of a classic in the field and the last word on the subject by its original author, also available in a college edition.

Nandi: From Cattle-Keepers to Cash-Crop Farmers

Regina Smith Oboler

As one travels northwest from Nairobi, Kenya, through lush farmland dotted with herds of dairy cattle, the terrain slopes gradually upward to the edge of the Great Rift Valley. Here the view stretches off seemingly to the ends of the earth. Winding down to the valley floor, the road continues across arid plains and finally descends toward Lake Nakuru—pink around the edge with thousands of flamingoes—and Nakuru town. Climbing the other side of the Rift Valley, the road levels off slightly but keeps ascending through the Tinderet Forest, crossing the equator near Timboroa Summit at an altitude of over 10,000 feet. Here begins a gradual descent across the Uasin Gishu Plateau—bleak, windy, chilly, and often overcast—to the town of Eldoret, and the home territory of the Nandi. The road into Nandi District descends gently from an altitude of over seven thousand feet through rolling grasslands, crossing marshes filled with crested cranes before reaching Kapsabet, the District Center.

It is lush and green here, unlike the arid plains of the Rift Valley. It rains every month. During the main dry season in January and February it doesn't rain daily; as much as two weeks can pass with no rain. During the height of the rainy season in July, it can stay overcast and drizzly for days at a time. During most of the year, the day dawns bright and sunny, but rain clouds roll in predictably during the mid-afternoon. After a downpour, it clears again for the last few hours of daylight.

South and west of Kapsabet, the countryside becomes broken into more distinct and frequent hills and valleys with rocky outcroppings, until one reaches the Mau Escarpment in the west and the Southern Nandi Escarpment in the south. The edge of the Southern Escarpment, between 5,500 and 6,000 feet in altitude, overlooks another part of the Great Rift Valley. One can stand on the edge and look out at a part of Lake Victoria and sugar plantations on the surrounding plains more than a thousand feet below.

It's hard not to be affected by the grandeur of the physical environment, and to expect that the inhabitants will match it. And the Nandi are impressive: physically tall and fit, dignified in demeanor, though friendly, exuding self-confidence and fierce pride in their warrior heritage. The international track and field community knows these people very well, since they produce a disproportionate number of world-class distance runners, the best known of whom is Kipchoge ("Kip") Keino.

East Africa is known for aggressive cattle raiding. A popular myth among the Nandi is also found among the Maasai and other traditional pastoralist warrior peoples: "At the beginning of the world, God created cattle and gave them to our people. However, as time went on, many cattle wandered into the wrong hands. Though it is a serious crime to steal a cow from one of our own people, raiding others for cattle is simply restoring them to the ownership that God intended." Modern East African countries no longer permit cattle raids, but as a symbol this ethos is still alive. A young man, leaving home in 1976 on a track scholarship to an American university, was presented a spear and shield by his father's older brother and told: "In the past our young men raided with spears and shields; today you raid with pens and papers, but with the same goal—to bring wealth to our people."

The Nandi were among the most feared warriors of East Africa during the nineteenth century. "Nandi" is said to be a name of recent origin derived from the Swahili word for "cormorant," *mnandi*. This fish-eating, diving bird was a metaphor for Nandi warriors to the Swahili inland traders (East African coastal people of mixed African and Arab ancestry): like the cormorant, Nandi swept down from the heights to strike suddenly at their prey, the peoples of the plains. The Nandi came forcefully to British attention in the late 1800s as the bane of attempts to lay rail and telegraph lines; warriors repeatedly swooped down the Escarpment to steal iron and wires. The Nandi became famous among African peoples for the tenacity of their resistance to British rule; they were finally subdued only after a massive "punitive expedition" against them in 1905.

Economy

Cattle have been central to Nandi life and economy for as long as anyone remembers. Fresh and preserved milk (*mursik*) were dietary staples. Nandi slaughtered sheep and goats, particularly on special occasions, but like other African pastoralists, they rarely slaughtered cattle. They added animal protein to their diet by bleeding cattle and mixing the blood with milk. This was done by tying a strap around the animal's neck so a large vein stood out, shooting an arrow into it so that it didn't go all the way through, then withdrawing the arrow and allowing the blood to flow into a container. The animal was damaged little, and could "give blood" again in a month to six weeks. This practice has now been all but abandoned. With limited pasture, people keep only plow oxen and dairy cattle, and cannot afford to weaken animals whose productivity has clear economic value.

However, the traditional economy did not depend only on cattle. Because of rich topsoil and plentiful rainfall, Nandi District is excellent farmland and the Nandi have always been farmers. Before the colonial period, the staple crop was eleusine, or finger millet, cooked into a hard porridge and eaten with a variety of green leafy vegetables. Crops were cultivated near homesteads, and most cattle were taken to graze in distant pastures by the neighborhood young men. It is said that during grain shortfalls women took sheep and goats to the lowland villages of neighboring ethnic groups to trade for grain. To what extent the Nandi consciously *chose* to concentrate on herding instead of producing grain is debatable.

During the colonial era, hybrid maize, which produces well at high altitudes and with heavy rainfall, replaced eleusine as the staple. Eleusine is still grown for dietary variety and as a component of local beer.

Because the colonial government believed privatization of resources was the best route to economic development, land was divided into individual holdings with private titles beginning in 1954. Today Nandi live on small individual farms (averaging about twenty acres in the northern part of the district). Each family grows crops and grazes cattle on its own land. Most families produce a surplus of maize for the market, and tea is also a common cash crop.

Cattle continue to be important in the modern economy. The Nandi have an incredibly rich vocabulary describing cattle—anatomy, physical features, variations in color, and so on. Much conversation time was devoted to cows and their merits. This is still a popular topic, but the emphasis now is different. People no longer try to maximize the size of their herds; instead, they try to maximize milk production. Kenya Cooperative Creameries, the government sponsored dairy, buys milk daily and processes it into a wide variety of products including ultra-pasteurized "shelf-milk" and tinned butter and cheese. These products are exported to other African countries. Most Nandi families' major source of income is production and sale of maize, milk, and tea in varying combinations. Few traditional zebu cattle remain in Nandi; they have been replaced by "upgraded" cattle, a mix of traditional and European strains valued for resistance to disease, or Holstein-Freisian dairy cattle, valued for high milk production. Bulls have largely been replaced by artificial insemination. In 1976–1977 the government Veterinary Service agent who drove around the countryside in a yellow VW Beetle offering insemination from an array of purebred varieties was known as the "bullman."

Field Situation

I first arrived in Nandi in 1976 as a young doctoral candidate in anthropology, armed with research fellowships from the National Science Foundation, the National Institute of Mental Health, and the Woodrow Wilson Foundation. My husband Leon, then a graduate student in film and photography, accompanied me. Our goal was to study social change and gender roles. As a student I had spent years preparing to do research. On one level, I was elated that the time had finally come, that I had passed my doctoral exams, that I had succeeded in snagging several sources of research funding, that after a long struggle with Kenyan government bureaucracies over research clearance, I had finally received it. On another level, I was terrified. That there were no longer any ordinary obstacles meant that there were no longer any excuses.

What was left to do was to get in there, find a place to live, adjust to lack of heat and running water and the presence of daily rain, learn to communicate with these people in their own language, make friends, and learn everything it was possible to learn about their lives and their culture—all in eighteen months or so. How could anyone possibly do it? Yet I knew that my professors had all managed somehow. My major professor had been younger than I, and a single woman among a "stone age" people in Highland New Guinea who had barely been contacted by outsiders. I would be in a setting where almost every community contained a handful of English-speakers (English was the language of high school education), where there were stores with batteries for my tape recorder and radio, where not far from whatever area I ended up in there was a district center with electricity and running water—and I had Leon for company and moral support. With such luxurious fieldwork conditions, only a real wimp would complain!

We chose as our research site a sublocation north and slightly west of Kapsabet, on the edge of a forest. This was a recently settled area, typical of other Nandi communities in many ways, slightly different in some. Household heads were younger on average than elsewhere, and as a group they had a notably forward-looking attitude. Several men worked hard to get us to settle in their community. Why? I'm not sure I ever totally understood. Pride in community and the wish to publicize it played a part, as did curiosity about the new and exotic (us). They also asked us to teach in their self-help secondary school, since the students 'English would profit by having native speakers as teachers. For us, it was a perfect way to pay back the community for its help.

One day in June of 1976 we moved into a round, mud-walled, thatched house in a family compound near the sublocation "center" (a group of shops and a tree where old men heard legal cases). It was a very small house—we later built a bigger one—and half the neighborhood turned out to watch us move in. They marvelled at the incredible collection of stuff "Chumbek" (Europeans) always bring with them. We thought we were travelling light, but between trunks full of clothes and office supplies, tables, typewriter, books, paper, stove, lanterns, and more, it was a squeeze. Fortunately, a traditional Nandi house has a storage loft, or *tabut* (for drying firewood), just under the thatched roof, above head level. We planned to buy a four-foot wide mattress in Nairobi and have a bed built to fit it. However, a Nandi friend convinced us that this extravagance would be seen as another bit of white people's insanity, and take up too much floor space. So the two of us ended up sleeping for eighteen months in a three-foot wide bed—a real hardship only at the end of our stay, when I was seven months pregnant.

Our host family was headed by Jacob (a pseudonym, as are all names used here for Africans), an enterprising young man about six years older than my husband. Jacob seemed never to sit still. He was famous in the community for his boundless energy—always dashing from place to place, involved in dozens of schemes and projects. One of his money-making projects was buying surplus cattle and driving them through the forest to sell to butchers in neighboring Trans-Nzoia District. Through enterprise and thrift, Jacob had saved money and acquired any land that became available for sale near his original small holding, so that when we arrived he was one of the larger land-holders in the area. We interacted with the family and the community as if Leon were Jacob's younger brother, though we weren't formally adopted. That first day, after we unloaded the furniture, Jacob took Leon off to get acquainted, while Rael (Rachel), his wife, helped me organize our domestic life. She was younger than Jacob, about my age, a large, pleasant, extroverted woman with a ready smile and a directive, no-nonsense, take-charge manner. In another cultural setting, Rael might have been a politician—but among the Nandi this is an almost exclusively male role. The public demeanor of many Nandi women is subdued and submissive, but while Rael chatted easily and got along with everybody, I hardly ever saw her behave submissively except to Jacob, her father, and some of the older men. Though Rael spoke Swahili, she insisted from the first that I speak Nandi as much as possible. Much of my knowledge of the subtleties of Nandi culture came from the hours I spent in her smoky kitchen shed gossiping with local women.

A Nandi compound is a collection of houses, some close together, some further apart, that face each other across an open space and are connected by a network of pathways. The house belonging to Jacob, Rael, and their children, with their kitchen shed and granary, was the center of our compound. About twenty to thirty yards to one side of their house stood the house of Jacob's widowed mother. Our house faced "Kogo's" (grandma's) house across a wide pasture. Ultimately we had two houses, one split in half to accommodate our two field assistants, recent school-leavers from other communities. Behind Jacob's house was a maize field; at the far end of that was the house of Jacob's sister Marta, who was permanently separated from her husband. From Marta's, a path led to the home of one of the men who convinced us to settle in the community. The nearest neighbor on the other side was about thirty yards from our house, across a fence. The main road formed the third boundary; the nearest neighbors on the fourth side were on the next ridge, a fifteen-minute walk down a hill, across the river, and up the other side.

Gender: Early Learning Experiences

The group of men who first recruited us to the community became Leon's "age-mates" and close associates. The first day we settled in, they came in the late afternoon to invite him to go to the river to bathe. A huge group of neighborhood boys trooped along after them (I assumed just for the novelty of seeing what a *chumbindet*, or white man, looked like naked). The next day I heard from Rael that Leon had neighborhood approval on two important counts: that he was circumcised (the mark of male adulthood among the Nandi, who practice adolescent circumcision); and that he didn't shiver in the cold water. Throughout the day, other women congratulated me on my husband's ability to tolerate cold water. I tried to remain sanguine, though the reaction inside my own mind was, "Say *what*!?" I dutifully wrote it down in my field notes, figuring that eventually it might make sense.

In time, I pieced together that the house and hearth are women's domain; the shade tree where gatherings take place (*kok*) is men's domain; it's effeminate to hang around the hearth too much; it's manly (in a climate where it rains a lot and due to the altitude can get quite cold) not to mind exposure to the elements; therefore, real men don't shiver. This sequence of associations seems bizarre at first, but upon reflection it is no more so than our own cultural notions of what is or is not suitable for "real men." The Nandi believe a woman can make her husband weak-willed and subject to her control by feeding him polluting bodily substances (*kerek*, discussed later) or ground-up grass crabs. Inability to stand cold and frequent shivering are the outward signs of such poisoning.

The day after we moved in, I also got to bathe in the river and do laundry along with Rael and her friends. There was a spot at the river where a waist-deep pool of water collected. Rocks ringed this pool, shielding it from the view of anybody on the pathway, and this was the community bathing place. There was a signalling system (hanging clothes on the outer edge of the rocks) and an elaborate system of rules designed to protect everyone's modesty. However, the

Nandi definition of whose modesty needs protecting from whom—in other words, which categories of people may be unclothed in front of one another—differs markedly from our Euro-American expectations. Married women bathe together; children bathe with them. Unmarried, uninitiated women are permitted to bathe together with young men of the warrior age-set or with married women. Young people of both sexes do not undress in front of men of their fathers' age-set—and there are still more complications. I, along with the other married women, was expected to undress without compunction in front of anyone defined as a "child." The problem was that boys are "children" as long as they remain uncircumcised, which can be as old as sixteen or eighteen. In practice, older boys generally joined the young, unmarried men, but that first day one of the "children" present was Rael's thirteen-year-old son who was taller than I. It was difficult for me to take my clothes off in the presence of this strapping youth, but it was excellent practice in cultural relativism. "Relax," I kept telling myself. "It's no big deal. It doesn't mean the same thing here as it would at home. The other women aren't bothered. . . "

Another shock about gender norms—though one we had already dealt with during our stay in Nairobi—was the expectation of intimate touching between members of the same gender. Shortly after our arrival in Nairobi, a Kenyan couple from our research institute invited us to dinner. Over drinks, I sat with Georgia on one bench, and Leon sat with John on the other. "Have another drink," Georgia said brightly as she draped her arm around my shoulders, stroking my arm, and leaning close across me to fill my glass. On the other side of the table, I noted that John's hand was on Leon's thigh as he inquired about his favorite authors. On the North American continent, we'd be enacting a swingers' seduction scene—but in Kenya, this body language has no such meaning. In fact, the ideas that connect touching and sexuality are almost the opposite of Euro-American norms. A naive American visitor to Nairobi could easily assume that it's a gay paradise on the basis of numerous same-sex couples strolling the sidewalks hand-in-hand. This would be totally wrong. The Kenyan attitude toward homosexuality is less tolerant than North Americans'. Holding hands or touching intimately in public is a way of declaring the absence of any possibility of a sexual relationship. If people are sexually interested in each other, they will refrain from touching. Husbands and wives are never seen touching in public. This restraint in touching each other was one of the most difficult things for us to get used to in the field situation—much more difficult than walking hand-in-hand with our same-sex friends.

The public dominance of husband over wife and the wife's overt submissiveness were more difficult to get used to, especially for me. One shows one's husband "respect," and never corrects, contradicts, shows anger, argues with him, or tells him what to do. One is also expected never to complain or say anything negative about a husband to anyone else, unless there is a very strong grievance. Husbands are also supposed to "respect" and refrain from complaining about their wives, but they are freer to contradict them, order them around, and even shout at them if there is provocation. As we became more intimately acquainted with several couples, we could see that behind the scenes their relationships were not as inegalitarian as this public façade made it seem. At any rate, I had difficulty keeping the public façade in place with never a crack, and I wondered if Leon's cronies secretly pitied him for being married to such a shrew. Since I intended to study gender roles, it was lucky that some of the cultural differences that initially presented themselves most forcefully concerned gender. But there was still much to learn.

Male and Female in Nandi Culture

Toward the end of our fieldwork, when I became pregnant with our first child, I confided to Rael that I was really hoping for a girl. "No, Gina!" she exclaimed. "Don't tell anybody that! It's an insult to your husband. For him, you must hope for a boy, even though there's always a special love between mothers and daughters." As in so many world cultures, males in Nandi are the preferred sex at birth. However, the preference is only slight. The ideal family includes sons and daughters. Sons continue the line of descent, but the bridewealth received when daughters are married enables their brothers to marry in turn.

Clearly, parents have different expectations of sons and daughters. Girls wear dresses; boys dress in shirts and shorts. Both sexes have major work responsibilities, but the tasks they are usually assigned are different. Girls are expected to care for younger children and help with weeding fields and domestic chores, such as fetching water and firewood. Boys herd cattle and help with plowing, and perform miscellaneous errands and tasks. Boys' chores take them further from the compound and give them more scope for independent action. Boys *may* care for children, and girls *may* herd cattle, if no child of the ideal age and sex is available. However, families try to arrange things so that a child of the appropriate sex is available, and this in part accounts for the widespread custom of fostering.

Every household needs a *cheplakwet* (child nurse) and a *mestowot* (herdboy). So essential are these roles that a newly married couple not living in an extended family will "borrow" children from other relatives or friends to fill them. Many Nandi adults I interviewed spent time as foster children. Some must have had positive experiences, but most children seem quite distressed at being taken away from their mothers and familiar surroundings. This is reflected in their evaluation of the experience; "cruel uncles" figure in many life histories and in folklore. The fostering family is responsible for feeding and clothing the child, and in the modern setting for paying school fees.

Until recently, boys were much more likely than girls to attend school. A daughter leaves her family for another at marriage; a son remains and the family benefits from any increased earning potential he gains through education. In 1976, surveying 241 adults, I found that most men (72 percent) had completed more than the equivalent of 4th grade, most women (63 percent) had completed only 4th grade or less, and 24 percent of men, but only 11 percent of women, had attended high school. Nowadays, with primary education free, boys and girls are educated at the primary level in equal numbers. Boys are still more likely to pursue secondary school and higher education, though the gender gap in education is narrowing.

Though Nandi mothers denied that male and female babies are inherently different at birth, substantial adult gender differences in basic character traits are acknowledged. Men are said to have greater physical endurance; to be *korom*, "fierce" (courageous in confronting enemies or wild animals—women must also be courageous and stoic in childbirth and in coping with injury or grief); to be more intelligent, foresightful, and decisive; to be more inclined than women to forgive without holding a grudge.

Women are seen as more empathic than men, more capable of feeling "pity" (*rirgei*, "cry together"). These differences are believed to be learned, but are also thought to be set in place and reinforced by initiation.

Adolescent initiation, especially of boys, is one of the most central Nandi institutions. Boys and girls are initiated between the ages of twelve and eighteen, most often fourteen or fifteen for girls and fifteen or sixteen for boys. The central feature of the process is male circumcision or female clitoridectomy. The mere thought of such operations makes my American students gasp and shudder. Yes, they are extremely painful, and they are meant to be. The initiates are expected to be brave, quiet, and unemotional throughout. Initiation is thought of consciously as a test of the courage and toughness needed for warfare (though it is now a thing of the past) or childbirth.

It's worth digressing for a moment to discuss the issue of clitoridectomy, genital surgery involving the excision of all or part of the clitoris, and sometimes part of the external labia as well. This is a customary operation in many Subsaharan African societies, not to be confused with "infibulation" (practiced in northern Sudan), the partial sewing shut of the vaginal opening.

Clitoridectomy has been in the news in the last several years, with concerned Westerners increasingly urging the UN to pressure its African member states to ban what is viewed as a "barbaric, primitive" custom hazardous to women's health that denies them sexual pleasure. (It is argued that women are kept sexually faithful to unloving husbands by being kept from experiencing orgasm.) Certainly, there is partial truth in this criticism; deaths from infection and hemorrhage have occurred. I would point out, however, that these potential complications are also present for male circumcision, without producing any comparable international outcry. Initially, I struggled to keep my cultural relativism about me while confronting a people who, I was sure, robbed women of their sexuality. However, as I talked with women about the subject I discovered that they didn't see it this way. Nandi women, even those with sexual experience before and after clitoridectomy, insisted that their sexual pleasure was unimpaired, and acted amused at my belief that the quality of their sex lives should be affected. Since orgasmic response in women increases with age, perhaps these women have the clitoris removed before they are really aware of what they will be missing. However, there is another feasible interpretation.

Though I don't mean to be an apologist for clitoridectomy, I think that Western critics should consider the possibility that African women know what they are talking about and whether (because of "phantom limb phenomenon" or some other mechanism) it may be that women are *not* robbed of pleasure. Physiological research is needed before we can conclude anything. In many societies with clitoridectomy, wives' sexual infidelity is common. So clitoridectomy does not prevent adultery, contrary to the Western interpretation. The importance of abolishing clitoridectomy should be decided by African feminists (they have mostly not seen it as their highest priority). In any case, the ritual that includes clitoridectomy is usually an important focus of women's solidarity that may not be replaced easily.

Clitoridectomy has been illegal in Kenya for several years. Prior to this, Christian missionaries had been preaching against the practice for many years with some success. At the time I was in the field in 1976 about twenty percent of women in their twenties and thirties, primarily those with secondary education, but also some with higher levels of primary education, had refused to have the operation. Some women who had been traditionally initiated told me that they didn't see that they had gained anything much from it and wouldn't choose it again if they had the choice.

Girls' initiation takes place individually or in groups of two to four, in the family compound. The girls are outfitted in a standard costume for the occasion: a red skirt, men's white dress shirt, tie, a tall helmet, crossed bandoliers trimmed with colobus monkey fur and beads, knee socks, and athletic shoes. Many of these elements are associated either with the traditional dress of warriors, or with contemporary roles (e.g., the military, athletics, business) associated with men. Though women direct the ceremony, costuming is in the hands of male specialists. (Gender role reversals are seen in both female and male initiation. They include aspects of initiates' dress, men carrying water for the women, and, during girls' initiation, women attacking men physically with sticks.)

The ritual begins in the late afternoon. The girls dance through the night, accompanied by a group of younger girls. Guests visit throughout the night, and a crowd assembles in the morning, after dawn. The initiates distribute small gifts (candy, cigarettes, and so on) to the guests, and then a group of initiated women moves away from the main crowd and forms a circle in which the operation is performed. If the girl shows courage, the older women break from the circle and dash toward the crowd, whooping and ululating, to congratulate the male members of the families and drape them with *sinendet*, a ritually important plant. Singing, dancing, and celebrating continue all day. The initiates are secluded in neighboring compounds for several weeks, and are not to be seen again until their marriages are arranged.

Male circumcision is an important mark of both adult status and ethnic identity. Nandi ridicule ethnic groups whose men are uncircumcised. Male initiation is a community-wide event with larger numbers of initiates (ten to fifteen) than in female initiation. Men of the next older age-set supervise the process, which in many ways resembles fraternity pledging. Beginning in the morning, the boys have their heads shaved, are forced to behave submissively, are harangued and verbally abused, are made to perform "women's work" such as carrying water and firewood, and to sing and dance before the assembled crowd. At intervals, they are taken into a secluded grove for "secret instruction."

As sunset approaches the boys appear for the last time, and women friends and family members tie scarves around their necks as tokens of their moral support, since women may not be present at the actual circumcision. During the night the boys undergo minor tortures and physical hazing, building up to the operation itself in the pre-dawn hour. The women of their families sit up all night waiting around bonfires in the public ceremonial space. Just before dawn, some of the circumcision "instructors" reappear to return the headscarves and drape the women in *sinendet*. At a ceremony I attended, some women refused to accept the tokens until they were assured that their sons had been as brave as they could possibly have been. Moments later, as the first rays of the sun appeared above the horizon, all those assembled dropped to their knees facing it and sang a traditional Nandi hymn. The boys—now young men—remain together in seclusion until their wounds have healed, receiving instruction in traditional lore.

For young men, initiation marks the onset of a period of social freedom and intense sexual activity. Traditionally, this would also have been a time of high risk-taking as the new warriors went out on cattle raids to prove their mettle and began to amass their own herds. Today, very often, they are students, and otherwise exempt from adult responsibilities. In the late nineteenth century, the young men of each neighborhood slept in a communal barracks, often accompanied by their lovers, girls not yet old enough for initiation. These couples were free to engage in all forms of sex-play except actual penetration without any social stigma—girls were expected to be technically virgin at the time of their initiation. At present, young men have their own huts in their parents' compounds, and there is no disapproval of young uninitiated women spending nights in their boyfriends' huts.

Social and Political Organization

For men, initiation marks the entry into one of seven age-sets (*ibinda*, pl. *ibinwek*). The names of the age-sets are always the same, and rotate through time: Kaplelach, Kipkoimet, Sawe, Chuma, Maina, Nyongi, and Kimnyigei. At any time there are four sets of

elders, the "senior warriors," the initiates, and a set of boys. When all in the oldest age-set have died, its name comes back into use as the name of the set of the new initiates.

All men who are circumcised within a certain period of time belong to the same age-set. Since age at circumcision varies, at the margins of age-sets there may be some overlap of ages, with the oldest members of a junior set being older than the youngest members of the next senior set. The age-set members move as a unit through the life-cycle (like "The Class of 1998" moving from freshmen to sophomores, juniors, and seniors). During the 1800s there was a huge centralized ritual in which every Nandi man moved on to the next status: initiates became senior warriors, senior warriors became elders, senior elders "retired" from active life, and a new age-set began for boys about to be initiated. Immediately afterwards, the new warriors would launch a series of raids as a way of proving themselves.

The colonial government banned this event, fearing it would lead to military uprisings, and after independence it never made a comeback. Informal discussions among elders of different locales now produce consensus on which age-set is being initiated.

There is a strong sense of solidarity within age-sets, and a tendency for the members to act as a unit in taking on activities such as community improvement projects. The idea of unity is especially strong among those men who were initiated together in the same ceremony (called a *mat*, or "fire"). They are likely to have strong bonds of friendship for their whole lives, and provide mutual aid and support. I once went with a young Nandi man to visit another young man. When we arrived he was not at home, and his door was closed. My friend walked in, and decided since his shirt was dirty to trade it for a clean one he found inside. I expressed surprise, but he responded, "Why should I not take anything I need? He's my age-mate. I am free to take whatever he has." It is said that in the past it was common and condoned for a man to have sex with his age-mate's wife.

Relations among members of different age-sets are controlled by definite rules of etiquette. Men of younger sets defer to men of older sets. Sons should not belong to the age-set adjacent to that of their father, but to the next lower one. Familiarity between members of these age-sets is avoided. A man may not marry his age-mate's daughter, nor a woman her father's age-mate.

There are no age-sets for women, and no one I interviewed remembered hearing that they had ever existed, though they exist or are reported to have existed among several peoples related to the Nandi. Groups of women around the same age are often referred to as "Wives of . . ." with the name of a men's age-set.

The Nandi have extended families and clans with animal totems. Descent or membership in a family or clan is traced patrilineally (through males only). The clans' only function is the regulation of marriage. Certain clans do not marry members of certain other clans, though ritual elders told me that the pattern of marriage rules is continually shifting, depending on what inter-clan marriages have been successful in the recent past. The kin term system is basically the Omaha type common in patrilineal societies: the term "father" is used for all men of the same generation within a person's own descent group, the term for "sibling" for patrilineal relatives of one's own generation, and one's mother's patrilineal kinsmen of all generations are called by a single term. One of the most interesting aspects of Nandi terminology is the rich vocabulary for different kinds of relatives by marriage, since relationships with close in-laws are much more important than distant "blood" relationships.

Marital residence is patrilocal; that is, a bride moves in with her husband's family. Communities are not, however, based on kinship. Traditionally, families could move into any locality where they would be sponsored by people already living there—relatives, in-laws, age-mates, or others. Now with private land-ownership, people move into communities where they can buy land.

Traditionally, the local community (*koret*), consisting of several hundred people, was the most important unit of day-to-day life, the site of ceremonial and economic cooperation and dispute settlement. The term for the community's council of elders, *kokwet*, is used for both the council and the territorial unit, which might be called a "neighborhood." In the modern political scheme, several such units make up a sublocation, with a government-appointed subchief. Sublocations combine to form locations, each with a chief. The unit immediately larger than the kokwet was the *pororiet*, called a "regimental area "because its warriors formed a single fighting unit. The pororiet council, which made decisions about matters of concern to the local communities, such as warfare, circumcision, and planting, was made up of representatives from each kokwet council, and two representatives each from the warriors and the Orkoiyot.[1]

The Orkoiyot was a religious/political figure—a kind of chief, though his power was more ritual than political. This hereditary office created some political

centralization for all the Nandi for a short time, probably no longer than from a bit after mid-nineteenth century to the British Conquest. The main function of the Orkoiyot was to coordinate military activities and sanction cattle raids. Warriors planning a raid would ask the Orkoiyot (who was believed to foresee the future) to predict its outcome. They would stage the raid only if he predicted success, and thank him with a gift of captured cattle. In Nandi tradition the family of the Orkoiyot descended from powerful Maasai *ilai-bonik* (ritual experts with paranormal powers), who immigrated to Nandi and were absorbed into the Talai clan. However, the Maasai also believe that their ilai-bonik came from elsewhere, perhaps from Nandi, so the Nandi story may not be based on fact.

Prior to the emergence of the Orkoiyot as a political figure, the term *orkoiyot* was used to denote any man thought to have paranormal powers including the ability to foretell the future, to see things happening at a distance, to disappear and reappear somewhere else, and to control the weather and the health and fertility of humans and animals. The ability was thought to run in families and to be patrilineally inherited by men only. The institution of the Chief Orkoiyot was based on this model writ large. The *orkoiik* (plural of orkoiyot) of the Talai clan were believed to be more powerful than others, and people feared them because of the harm they could do to those who resisted their will. Talai men often had several wives because of the practice of "naming wives." A Talai stated his desire to marry a certain woman, with the implied threat to curse any other man who might try to win her. This abuse of power was resented by non-Talai. Other Nandi were not completely cowed, however, and there are stories of Orkoiik who displeased their constituencies being put to death—in one case, for example, an Orkoiyot erroneously predicted success for a raid in which many Nandi lives were lost.

Most Nandi still believe to some extent in the power of the Talai. One young Talai man told me that though his father and grandfather definitely could use Talai powers, he couldn't because of his Western education. In another case, a girl broke up with her Talai boyfriend, and he threatened (not jokingly) to curse other men she might take an interest in. Another highly educated man told an anecdote about his sister, who married into the Talai. She was astounded and upset one day when she couldn't find her first son, an infant not yet crawling. Her mother-in-law said, "Didn't you know? That's what Talai babies do— come and go as they please." Non-Talai are ambivalent in their feelings about the Talai. On the one hand, there is still some resentment over their past abuse of power. On the other, the Talai Orkoiyot who rallied the Nandi to resist the British is viewed as a glorious historical figure, and his descendants and those of other famous orkoiik bask in reflected glory.

Religion

There were a variety of minor supernatural beings in traditional Nandi cosmology, but most worship focused on a single deity called Asis or Cheptalel (and other names) . Nandi believed that ancestral spirits continued to exist after death, but they were relatively unimportant in human affairs.

Missionaries have long been active in Nandi District. Since the Nandi were monotheists for all practical purposes, it was not difficult for them to assimilate Christianity into their beliefs. "Jehovah" is equivalent to Asis; that God had a son was news, but not hard to accept. More difficult to accept were teachings concerning sexuality, polygyny, initiation, and similar issues. Most Nandi Christians are Roman Catholics, though many are also adherents of the Africa Inland Church. The Africa Inland Mission, with ties to Baptists and Methodists, translated the Bible into Nandi in 1925. Some Nandi are Anglicans and Seventh Day Adventists. Nandi are less likely than neighboring ethnic groups to join African independent churches. In 1977 over sixty percent of household heads in the community I lived in were at least nominal Christians. Most Nandi continue to believe that certain people can "bewitch " others, primarily through envy.

Marriage

For women, marriage took place shortly after initiation and for the most part still does. The average age at marriage for women in my census was 17.8. Young men, following initiation, spent a period of about twelve to fifteen years as warriors, and did not marry until most of this time had elapsed. Today, with peace, men's average age at marriage is younger, in the early twenties.

Ideally, a girl in seclusion following initiation waits for people to come seeking her as a bride on behalf of a young man. This is known as coming for "engagement" (*koito*). This group, the "engagement party," contains both women and men, including the prospective groom's parents, uncles, aunts, and older siblings, and close friends and relatives, at least some of whom know both families well. On the second visit, the girl's family makes sure to also have relatives and friends assembled, and the two groups get down to negotiating details of the proposal. There is no formal marriage contract, but information on such matters as how many cattle the groom has or stands to inherit, where the couple will live, and so on, is sought. The exact amount (which varies only slightly) of the bridewealth to be paid, in cattle, sheep and goats, and money, is also negotiated. Women in the engagement parties negotiate almost as actively as the men.

Ultimately, the bride must observe the prospective groom from behind a screen, and it is the responsibility of the father's sister to ensure that she finds the man acceptable. If she really dislikes him, she can hold out against the arrangement; however, girls are sometimes pressured into accepting less than ideal matches. In reality, when a girl is initiated her marriage may already be arranged, at least informally (after talks between the two mothers). Romantically involved couples can arrange in this way to be married, and this is becoming more popular.

Marriages between people whose families live in the same community are common. Sisters, in particular, try to marry men who live near each other, so that they will be able easily to turn to each other for assistance. There is a term, *lemenyi*, for men married to sisters, and this relationship is supposed to be close and supportive. Friends and age-mates sometimes try to arrange to marry sisters, and thus become lemenyi.

Nandi men and women expect that the husband will be the dominant partner. In public, wives behave submissively toward husbands, though often private behavior is more egalitarian. Marriage is usually a fairly harmonious give-and-take, though even a wife who has a lot of influence with her husband will ask his permission to do anything out of the ordinary. The husband has the right to punish the wife physically for "misbehavior," in particular for public disrespect. A Nandi college student told me that he did not like this aspect of his culture, but admitted that he might have to buy into it. "It depends on what *she* does. If she does certain things, I will have to beat her or people will lose respect for me." Both men and women spend more social time with same-sex friends than with their spouses, but socializing as couples is becoming more common among younger, educated people.

The payment of bridewealth by the groom's to the bride's family is the central act that creates a marriage among East African pastoralists. Nandi bridewealth is lower than most, at five to seven cattle, one or a few sheep and goats, varying amounts of cowrie shells (an item sometimes omitted now), and cash generally equal to the value of a cow. When families negotiate bridewealth, specific animals are indicated by name, and attention is paid to the history of their social exchange. It is important to include at least one cow from the bridewealth given for the groom's father's sister, or its progeny. If the groom's full sister is married, an animal received as her bridewealth is given. At the wedding feast, the animals are displayed so that the bride's brothers can come later to take them away.

The cattle given as bridewealth for a daughter should be used for the marriages of, or inherited by, *only* her full brothers. Each of a man's wives is the founder of a separate genealogical unit called a "house," and holds cattle separately from any other wives. At her marriage, a woman is given some of her husband's cattle to serve as the basis of her "house-property" herd. This herd also includes animals her relatives give her as wedding gifts, and grows through natural increase, further allocations from her husband, the addition of cattle she can sometimes acquire herself, and bridewealth given for daughters. In any decisions concerning house-property cattle, a wife must consult with her husband; he also is not supposed to sell, give away, or do anything with them without consulting with her. A husband, however, usually has cattle that have not been allotted to the house of any of his wives, and these are his to do with as he pleases. While husbands therefore have greater property rights than wives, they do not have complete control of family property. Nandi women told me that wives have the right to go to any lengths to prevent their husbands from taking their house-property cattle. In one instance, the wife took her complaint to the community elders and stopped the sale of her cow.[2] In some other African "house-property" systems, husbands have greater freedom to dispose of their wives' cattle.[3]

Cattle that husbands inherited were traditionally allocated as house-property in equal numbers to all wives. Today, this norm has been extended to forms of property such as land and money. Cattle gained in raids belonged to the husband, and this has been extended to cover cattle a man buys with money gained through wage labor. Many families sell low-milk-producing African cattle from the house-property herd and use the proceeds *plus* the wage-labor earnings to replace them with European dairy breeds. It is not always clear what rights each partner has in the new animals, and this has the potential to create conflict between spouses.

As in most African societies, marrying more than one wife was a mark of status for a Nandi man. Many men now claim that as Christians they have no intention of marrying second wives. Analysis of census data shows, however, that with age controlled, Chris-

tians are only slightly less likely to be polygynists than Nandi traditionalists. With private land ownership, it is becoming difficult for a man to provide adequate land inheritance for the family of more than one wife. Seventeen percent of married men in my census were polygynists. (For Nandi District as a whole, the figure could be closer to twenty-five percent.) Wives have no right to object to their husbands' marrying other wives, and some desire it. As in other societies, relations among co-wives may be friendly, neutral, or hostile, depending on individual personalities. I have observed physical battles between co-wives, and I have also seen them spring to one another's defense in conflicts with their mutual husband. Nandi folk-wisdom says that jealousy between co-wives is inevitable, and that their husband should arrange, if possible, for them to live far apart.

Traditionally, a marriage was not considered irrevocable until after the birth of the first child. After that point, divorce was commonly considered to be impossible. There was a divorce procedure, but no one could give any hypothetical circumstances under which it might be used. A Nandi woman, once married, is forever the wife of the man who first married her, and all children she bears are considered his children, even if she has not seen him for years. A widow is not free to remarry; if she has further children, the father is considered to be her original husband, and it is his property that her sons inherit. A young widow is expected to practice the levirate, cohabiting with a kinsman of her husband, who begets children regarded as those of her dead husband. Though this is the "respectable" thing to do, it is not required. A widow might, rather, take lovers of her own choice. Not being able to divorce an unbearable husband or legitimately remarry seems like a great infringement of a woman's freedom. However, the other side of the situation is that once-in-a-lifetime marriage gives her and her children exceptionally strong rights in her husband's property.

The Nandi also practice woman-woman marriage. Such marriages are about three percent of all marriages, and this incidence does not seem to be declining. Though each married woman holds a separate fund of property and is expected to become the founder of a "house," only sons, never daughters, may inherit property. If the house has no male heir, its property goes to sons of co-wives or of the husband's brother, but this is a very distasteful alternative. What to do? The Nandi solution is for the heirless woman to become the "female husband" to a younger woman, and "father" to her children; the sons of the younger woman become the heirs of the house. Once when I asked a man something about his father he told me, "The woman who married my mother was my father. She acted just like any other father." (Note that the father-child relationship is normally distant.) The culture insists that the female husband becomes a man. She must discontinue sexual relations with men. Though she has no sexual relationship with her wife, she has all the other rights of a husband. Her wife should cook for her and do all the domestic work. Outside the home, there is considerable ambiguity about whether female husbands in fact act like men in ways they claim are permitted to them, such as participating in political meetings and attending male initiation. Some female husbands did make a point of frequenting the "men's side" in the local beer hall (there are no longer beer halls since sale of African-style beer is now illegal.) It might be more accurate to see female husbands as occupying an ambiguous gender status, while they and others go to great rhetorical lengths to argue that they are in fact men.

Another alternative when there is no heir for house property is for a daughter of the house to "marry the center-post." She thus becomes like a daughter-in-law rather than a daughter. She remains at home and takes lovers, and her sons are the heirs.

Childbirth usually takes place at home, attended by local midwives, though some women now go to the hospital in the District Center. Women in labor are expected to be very stoic. I watched a young woman give birth without even a whimper, though pain was etched clearly on her face. In another instance, a woman behaved in a cowardly way during labor, and this became the subject of amused gossip and a lot of teasing for a long time afterward. Childbirth is "women's business," and men are expected to stay away from the house at this time, waiting nearby with other men for news of the birth. In the nineteenth and early twentieth centuries, it is said, the father would not resume living in the house for months, and would not touch the child or have sex with the mother again until the child was weaned and could walk. Fathers thus had very little intimate contact with young children; older children were expected to treat their fathers with respectful formality. The father-child relationship was important, but not warm and close. With regard to cross-cultural variation in men's participation in child-rearing, the Nandi were probably toward the extreme nonparticipation end of the spectrum.

Part of the reason for this distance between fathers and children was the belief in *kerek*, a mystical substance that was thought to emanate from infants and nursing women and was ritually polluting to men. Informants gave me contradictory information about sources of the pollution: the child's urine or feces, or

the mother's milk. In any case, close contact with either the mother or the child could make the father (and perhaps other men) lose skill with weapons, become weak-willed and indecisive, and shiver in the cold. Wives could cook for their husbands while nursing only after going through a lengthy process of ritual washing with river sand and cow-dung, and returning home without touching their bodies or clothes; the *cheplakwet* (child nurse) held the baby until after the mother cooked. If an unweaned child touched an object in the house, it was traded to a childless neighbor for a similar object. A favorite anecdote of old women was how their husbands used to spy on them to make sure they were thorough enough in their ritual washing. Some people now claim that all this was merely superstition, not real; others argue that kerek, though real, became a matter of less concern with the introduction of soap, which dissipates it very effectively. In any case, men now rarely hesitate about having contact with children, and most people say this is a positive change. It is also true that births are now spaced much more closely and families are larger; men's fear of kerek was probably a mechanism that helped to keep the birth rate down, even though the Nandi ideal was always to have as many children as possible.

Division of Labor

All family members have a part in the process of production. Men clear ground for planting and initially break it, in the past with iron-bladed hoes, today with an ox-drawn plow. It takes a team of two men to plow, one to drive the oxen with a whip, and one to hold the plow. The only instance of a woman plowing that I ever saw was Rael helping a man she hired to plow a field for vegetables she was growing to sell. Most people rent a tractor for a second round of plowing, and this is a source of cash for households in the community that own tractors (five in 1977). All ages and sexes plant and harvest, usually in cooperative work groups larger than one household. Cultivation during the growing cycle is done by both sexes, and women spend slightly more time at agricultural activities than do men. Cattle herding is mostly done by children, but women (more than men) also participate. Women and children do most of the milking.

Most men try to find some sort of full-time or part-time employment, but jobs are not plentiful in rural areas. Many men not formally employed, however, engage in some kind of entrepreneurial activity: agricultural contract labor for large landholders, cattle trading, charcoal making, dredging sand from rivers to sell for making concrete, and so on. There are also some skilled artisans with shops in the local center, for example, a tailor and a bicycle repairman. Only a few women engage in such activities or have jobs. Profit from the sale of cash crops—maize, tea, and milk—goes to male household heads, who are supposed to use it for the benefit of the household. Women often grow vegetables for sale, or sell chickens and eggs. Women are said to "own" chickens (sometimes called "the cattle of women"), vegetables, and the afternoon milk, which is for family consumption. (Morning milk, which belongs to men, is marketed through the Kenya Co-operative Creameries.) Women's biggest source of cash in 1976–1977 was brewing and selling maize beer. In the 1980s a ban on selling beer cut off this income source.

Changes

Each return to Nandi sees more changes: individualized kerosene-powered water pumps, generators, an occasional television, new roads, telephone service in rural village post offices, even the possibility of rural electrification in the not-too-distant future. Changes on the social level occur too, as greater educational opportunities bring new ideas. Which are "good" and which "bad" depends on one's personal perspective. Increasing incorporation into the cash economy has brought material wealth to many Nandi, especially as the Nandi are land-wealthy by rural Kenyan standards and live in an agriculturally rich area. The corollary, however, is a growing gap between rich and poor, as some prosper more than others. Improved medical technology has lowered infant mortality—something women often mention as an improvement over the "old days." But less infant death means population growth and increasing land shortage (so far less acute in Nandi than in many other areas). In terms of gender, the idea of companionate marriage has taken hold among the educated elite, but women may be losing the right to independent control of

property. Nevertheless, some things will not change. I expect that the land will always be beautiful, and the people always warm, friendly, and proud of their distinct Nandi heritage.

Notes

1. G. W. B. Huntingford, *The Nandi of Kenya: Tribal Control in a Pastoral Society* (London: Routledge &Kegan Paul, 1953), pp. 34 –35.
2. Regina Smith Oboler, *Women, Power, and Economic Change: The Nandi of Kenya* (Stanford, CA: Stanford University Press, 1985), p. 120.
3. Thomas Hakansson, "Family Structure, Bridewealth, and Environment in Eastern Africa: A Comparative Study of House Property Systems," *Ethnology* 28 (1989): 117 –134.

Suggested Readings

Krige, Eileen Jensen. "Woman Marriage with Special Reference to the Lovedu: Its Significance for the Definition of Marriage." *Africa* 44 (1974): 11–36. Good account of a South African society with a different kind of woman-woman marriage.

Obbo, Christine. "Dominant Male Ideology and Female Options: Three East African Societies." *Africa* 46 (1976): 371–384. Describes some ways women use traditional norms and institutions, including woman-woman marriage, to gain autonomy.

Oboler, Regina Smith. "Is the Female Husband a Man? Woman/Woman Marriage among the Nandi of Kenya." *Ethnology* 19 (1980): 69–88. A more thorough description of the Nandi institution.

———. "Nandi Widows," in Betty Potash, ed. *Widows in African Societies*. Stanford, CA: Stanford University Press, 1986, pp. 66–83. More on Nandi widows' status. The book also includes good articles on widows in other African societies.

Orchardson, Ian. *The Kipsigis*. Nairobi: East African Literature Bureau, 1961. A good, short ethnography of a society related to the Nandi and very similar in many ways.

Abelam: Giant Yams and Cycles of Sex, Warfare, and Ritual

Richard Scaglion

This article describes sex, warfare, and ritual in a New Guinea tribe. For the Abelam, sex, warfare, and ritual all have to do with giant yams, single specimens of which may be over ten feet long. Members of this tribe decorate and display these enormous yams, talk to them, exchange them, and organize much of their lives around them. However, this article is also about anthropological theory.

Now, many of my students' eyes glaze over at the mere mention of "social science theory." However, theories aren't really as complicated as they sometimes seem. A theory is actually nothing more than an idea or mental plan for analyzing or thinking about the things that interest you. It's a framework to help you organize these variables. If a theory helps you to better predict and understand human behavior, then it's a heuristic, or "good," theory.

Further along in this article we'll be looking for some theories to help us understand some basic questions about the Abelam. Why do the members of this New Guinea tribe abstain from sex for six months while they grow their giant yams? Why do they engage in sometimes violent warfare, but then agree to a truce every year so that enemies can visit each other's villages to measure and inspect the giant yams? Why do they have feasts and ceremonies together, and then try to kill one another? What's going on here?

The Abelam people, who are the subject of our ethnographic inquiry, live in the East Sepik Province of Papua New Guinea. I've done my fieldwork among the Samukundi, a subgroup of the Abelam who speak a distinct dialect and live in the Prince Alexander Mountains, a sometimes rugged mountain range near the north coast of the island of New Guinea. These

particular Abelam live in a dense tropical rain forest. They clear patches of it to build their villages and grow their gardens. Their main foodstuffs are yams, taro, bananas, and sweet potatoes. However, they grow a wide variety of other crops, and gather still more products from the forest. They supplement their garden produce by hunting and by keeping pigs and chickens.

Some of my beginning students seem to think that tribal people have to work very hard to eke out a meager existence. A common misconception is that tribal people all live miserable lives, often on the verge of starvation. Such is certainly not the case with the Abelam, who are well fed and comparatively well nourished. I once did a time-allocation study among the Abelam,[1] measuring how they spend their time. Among my findings were that Abelam like to sleep a lot: They average about nine hours and twenty-four minutes each day. On the other hand, the daily workload on average is about three hours a day spent gardening and one hour a day spent hunting. Abelam would consider an American eight-hour workday to be cruel and unusual punishment. Abelam always have enough to eat, and have plenty of time left over for a very rich religious and ceremonial life.

Historical Background

The history of European relations with the Abelam is relatively short. As nearly as I can estimate,[2] the Samukundi Abelam were first "contacted" by European labor "recruiters" in the 1920s. Neligum, the village in which I do most of my fieldwork, was preparing for an initiation ceremony for its young men one quiet afternoon when suddenly two white men (thought at the time to be spirit people) burst upon the scene, shooting off guns, which the Abelam had never before seen. In the ensuing confusion, the whites captured a young man, trussed him up like a pig, and carried him off to work on a plantation. He returned after several years, full of marvelous stories of the new world he had seen.

However, the Abelam weren't to participate very much in this new world for quite some time. A few government patrols passed through their territory now and then, but quickly left. A little gold was found in some streams in the Prince Alexander Mountains in the late 1930s, sparking a brief flurry of mining activity and the establishment of a government patrol post at Maprik in Samukundi territory in 1938, but the deposits weren't very rich and the patrol post was abandoned during the Second World War.

Elderly Abelam tell some fascinating stories of these days, however. The most interesting to me is always the story of the first airplane that landed at the newly constructed Maprik airstrip. People were working in their gardens when they heard a strange sound, *brrrrr* . . . , like a giant insect. They looked up and saw this weird thing, like a great bird, in the distance. The bird got closer and closer. It swooped around, flying in circles over Maprik. People laughed, people cried, people ran off into the jungles in fear. What the heck was this thing?

A few brave Abelam who happened to be near Maprik saw the bizarre creature land. Imagine their utter amazement when a hole in the side of the thing appeared and out stepped a person! Well, a white spirit being to be more exact. This was Ray Parer, a pioneer of early aviation in New Guinea.

After the disruptive events of the Second World War, which saw some fighting between Japanese and Australian troops in Abelam territory, the Abelam were left pretty much to themselves for several decades. The patrol post at Maprik was reestablished, and government patrols revisited Abelam villages from time to time, but Abelam lives were little changed from the precontact era. However, the government was gradually suppressing tribal fighting, and, in 1973, a government Local Court was established. In 1974 I arrived as a young anthropologist, seeking to study how the Abelam would react to these introduced courts.

While I was pursuing my graduate studies in the United States in 1973, I had been looking for a fieldsite where I could study the relationship between recently introduced Western law and a tribal legal system. A friend of mine, Peter Huber, an anthropologist who had recently returned from New Guinea, had told me

a little about the Abelam people. On the way back from his own fieldwork, he had visited their area. He told me that a Local Court was just then being established. He said that the people had large ceremonial houses, truly colossal yams, and "looked interesting." It seemed to be a likely place to do the sort of research I had in mind for my Ph.D. thesis.

Ethnographic Background

I began to do some research on the Abelam people to see what was known about them. The earliest mention of them by name that I could find was by the famous anthropologist Margaret Mead in her book *Sex and Temperament in Three Primitive Societies*. In describing the culture of the Plains Arapesh, who were distantly related to the Mountain Arapesh whom she had studied, Mead gave a thumbnail sketch of the Abelam tribe I planned to live with:

> As the mountain people look to the beach for all their new inspirations, the Plains Arapesh look to the neighbouring Abelam tribe, a gay artistic head-hunting people, who occupy the great treeless grass plains of the Sepik Basin. From the Abelam the Plains Arapesh have borrowed the style of their tall triangular temples, which rise seventy or eighty feet above the square plaza of the big villages, temples with sharply sloping ridge-poles and brilliantly painted facades. And with the Abelam and other plains people, the Plains Arapesh share the practice of sorcery, through which they terrorize their mountain and beach neighbours.[3]

Not a very flattering profile, I thought . . . a bunch of happy-go-lucky headhunters who were sorcerers to boot! "Gay headhunters" seemed like a terrible oxymoron to me. How happy can headhunters actually be? Oh well, I thought, I planned to study the Abelam of the mountains, not the plains. Perhaps they were different.

As my research continued, I discovered that there were actually three major dialect groups of Abelam: the Mamukundi, Kamu-kundi, and Samukundi. The Kamukundi people were the Plains or Wosera Abelam of whom Mead had spoken. This group had been previously studied by anthropologist Anthony Forge[4] and also by a human geographer, David Lea.[5] The Mamukundi Abelam, more similar to the mountain-dwelling Samukundi whom I hoped to study, had been previously described by anthropologist Phyllis Kaberry,[6] whose works I studied carefully. One passage in Kaberry's writings caught my eye: I read how headhunting was carried out only

> . . . on a limited scale, since only the heads of important men were taken. These were left in the stream till the flesh had rotted; the skulls were then painted, the eye-sockets were decorated with orange berries, and they were placed in the *house-tamberan* [the tall temples described by Mead], where they constituted ritual objects in one of the stages of initiation. They were supposed to endow those initiated with strength for fighting.[7]

This made me feel somewhat more secure. After all, I wasn't an important man (I reasoned); therefore, it was unlikely that my head would end up in an Abelam ceremonial house imbuing any Abelam initiates with strength. Or so I hoped.

The Ethnographic Present

Thus far in this essay I have touched upon various periods in the Abelam people's history of contact with Europeans. All of this history has been seen firsthand by Abelam people I've interviewed. Indeed, I heard the story of "first contact" from Mambil, the man who was captured by the labor recruiters, as well as others who witnessed the events of that day. Since that time, there have been dramatic changes in Abelam society. Mambil, now deceased, was a *matukulaa* (stone axe)—the Abelam name for someone who grew up before the introduction of steel tools. Mambil's son, my friend Tusais, uses steel tools and uses them well. He's an accomplished carpenter. Mambil's grandson uses books as his tools. He's a lawyer. Thus, Abelam society as it exists today consists of people with radically different world views. In fact, Abelam society was never an unchanging entity. According to Samukundi tradition, ancestral populations lived on the plains before moving into the mountains. Apparently, taro was the staple crop before yams were adopted. Abelam people have always been a dynamic and changing society, adapting constantly to both environmental and social changes.

How then do ethnographers write a single ethnographic profile of a people like the Abelam? One strategy is to use a theoretical construct called the ethnographic present. Very simply, the ethnographer picks a single moment in time, typically the time of first fieldwork. The ethnography is then written in the "timeless" present tense, whether or not the behavioral patterns being described are still going on. In

other words, the ethnographer picks a single "slice of time" and tries to understand how the society operates at that moment in time.

This strategy for analyzing cultural patterns was popularized by the British structural-functionalists of the early 1900s, epitomized by A. R. Radcliffe-Brown and his students. These anthropologists were interested in knowing what structures were present in society at a moment in time, and how those structures worked or functioned. They were particularly interested in kinship structures and other forms of social organization, since anthropologists were then beginning to realize that tribal societies are organized very differently from complex society. They used an "organismic analogy" for societies: that the parts of societies have particular functions and work together like the organs of biological organisms. This theoretical approach is *synchronic* (at a moment in time) rather than *diachronic* (through time).

For the purposes of this essay, I'll begin by using an ethnographic present of around 1974, the time of my first fieldwork. By this time, Abelam society was already altered from what it had been immediately before contact. For one thing, although enemy heads were still to be seen in the haus tamberans (temples), headhunting was no longer actively practiced. As one of my informants confided to me, "We were never very interested in headhunting anyway, certainly not as much as those Eastern Abelam were. We only took their heads to make them mad. We didn't bother to take the heads of our other enemies." Chronic warfare and raiding had been eliminated by the government, although specific conflicts often precipitated fights and raids in the "traditional" style. The "culture of warfare" was still very much alive. A few other practices, such as burying people in the floors of their houses, had been outlawed by the government, and indeed had been abandoned. Otherwise, the behavioral practices described here, including the growing of ceremonial yams and the consequent cycles of sex, warfare, and ritual were not significantly different from what they had been immediately before contact.

THE PROBLEM

I originally set out to study the interaction between introduced law (the newly established Local Court) and customary law. I wanted to know what elements of Western introduced law the Abelam would accept, and which they would reject. I quickly realized that this problem would make for a very short Ph.D. thesis, because the Abelam categorically rejected *all* aspects of the introduced law.

Essentially, the Abelam saw the Local Court as a foreign institution, completely at odds with their own practices of dispute resolution. In their own villages, they settle quarrels in village meetings (which legal anthropologists call "moots") that may last several days. In these meetings, people have ample opportunity to express their feelings, and a solution is often reached by consensus. A communal meal and an equal exchange of yams or shell money symbolically seals such an agreement, to which all present are witness.

The government courts, on the other hand, consisted of a judge from outside of Abelam society who did not understand their customs. There was little "bargaining," only a unilateral judgment. As a result, Abelam did not bring their civil disputes to the Local Court, and only appeared there when they had been charged with tribal fighting or some other offense. As a result of this, I began spending most of my time in Neligum Village observing daily life and looking for a new "problem" to study.

One thing immediately became clear to me: Large, ceremonial yams were then the central focus of Abelam life, and perhaps still are. This seems like a good time to begin the "ethnographic present" narration of this essay. You may have noticed that, in the above paragraph, I used the past tense for behavioral patterns that do not now exist (for example, there is no longer a total rejection of introduced courts, and some Abelam now bring their civil disputes to court). I used the present tense for ongoing patterns (for example, Abelam still use village meetings to settle disputes). However, the extent to which yams are still the focus of Abelam life is hard to judge. For most of the older generation, yam growing and yam taboos are still of paramount importance. However, the younger generation has developed other interests. Consequently, I will now begin to describe things as they were in 1974 in the "ethnographic present," thus relieving myself of the burden of making judgments about the current state of affairs of Abelam society (about which I am much less familiar).

Ceremonial yams are grown in special gardens only by adult men. Once harvested, the very best specimens, which have attained truly gigantic proportions, are decorated and displayed at yam festivals, where they are the focus of a great deal of ritual attention. Men from "enemy" villages come to measure and inspect these yams. After the displays, yam growers give away their best tubers to their worst enemies and rivals as part of a competitive exchange process. When an Abelam man gives a tuber to a rival, it obligates the rival to grow a yam of equal or higher qual-

ity to be given in return. Until the rival can grow such a yam, his status continues to drop relative to that of the donor. Thus, to a large extent, male status, prestige, and power are dependent on the quality of the ceremonial yams that they grow.

Women's status and, indeed, the status of entire kinship groups, also rises or falls at these yam festivals. Yam displays are accompanied by elaborate feasts prepared for the visitors from rival villages. Preparing more food (especially high quality food, such as pork) than the visitors can eat and giving them more than they can carry off increases the status of the group holding the festival. Thus, women can display their own skills at such events, and can impress their own female rivals with the quantity and quality of the food they have produced and prepared.

These yam festivals are truly spectacular events that may last for days on end. They are accompanied by considerable singing, dancing, feasting, and revelry. Men parade on ceremonial grounds with spears, chanting songs full of veiled metaphors that insult their rivals. There are ritualistic spear fights. Tempers sometimes flare, and actual fights sometimes break out. Every night, singing, drumming, and dancing last until dawn. In the late night hours, young people often engage in rather casually concealed sexual liaisons.

These festivals were virtually constant events during the early part of my fieldwork. The festivals last for several months, with various groups taking their turns at displaying their yams. One day, shortly after the group with which I was living had taken their turn and displayed their yams, one of my Abelam friends asked me how I had liked the festival, and how Abelam life compared with American life." Well, "I replied," the festivals remind me a lot of American television: lots of sex and violence."

"Oh," replied my Abelam friend, "we're not always like this. During the yam growing season, we never fight, and there is a total taboo against sex for everyone."

"How long is the yam growing season?" I asked.

"Six months," he replied.

"You mean nobody in this entire society has sex for six *months*?" I asked.

"That's right," he said.

Anthropologists distinguish between *ideal culture*, which is what people *say* they do, and *real culture*, which is what they *actually* do. For example, most Americans would describe our standard cultural marriage practice as "monogamy" (one person married to one other person) while an anthropologist might describe our practice as "serial monogamy" (one person married to one other person *at a time*, with several partners likely over the course of a lifetime). I thought something like this might be at work with my informant's assertion. People might claim that there was a total taboo against sex for six months, but I doubted that they would actually practice it.

However, as my fieldwork continued, I noticed something rather startling. I had been in the field for some six months. I had attended most of the major life crisis events, such as funerals, weddings, boys' initiation ceremonies, girls' first menstruation ceremonies, and so on. But I had never attended a birth ceremony, and, to my knowledge, there had not even been a birth in the village during that time.

After gardens had been cleared and the yam growing season began in earnest, I noticed a dramatic change in the "feeling" of the village. Whereas before people had been friendly, somewhat loud, outgoing, flirtatious, and obvious, people were now acting shy, reserved, quiet, and innocuous. The taboos against fighting and sex, practices thought to adversely affect yam growth, were in force. Something else became obvious: A great many of the women in the village were pregnant, and I soon became aware of many of the births I had been anticipating. A "baby season" was in full swing!

As I began to search for a theoretical framework to help me understand some of these relationships, I thought of an important article that had been written by Donald Tuzin, an ethnographer who had worked with the nearby Plains Arapesh, who also grow ceremonial yams. In this paper[8] Tuzin took a symbolic approach to analyzing the importance of yams. A symbol is something that "stands for" shared cultural understandings, which may have no direct natural link to the symbol itself. For example, the American flag "stands for" shared cultural understandings about the country, about its values, history, freedoms, etc. that have no intrinsic link to the actual pieces of cloth that comprise it. Just like the American flag, which is a very complex symbol, Tuzin showed how yams represented complex shared cultural understandings about fundamental and meaningful aspects of Arapesh life.

I realized that the same was true of Abelam yams. For Abelam, yams are imbued with extraordinarily complex symbolism. Perhaps most important is that yams form a link between people and their ancestors. Yams are propagated vegetatively. This means that particularly fine tubers are stored and allowed to sprout, then are cut up and used as "seed" for the next year's crop. So people are planting the "same" (that is, genetically identical) yams as their ancestors, since

yams are passed down from parents to children. Furthermore, yams never "die," but are (actually and metaphorically) "reborn" each year.

I often translate the Abelam word *gwaalndu* as "ancestral spirit," but it means much more than this. It also means something like "soul substance" or "life force." Abelam believe that, just as individual tubers die but the yam is reborn, so individual human beings die, but gwaalndu lives on and is reborn within the clan. Yams symbolize these complex religious beliefs.

Tuzin also took up other aspects of yam symbolism: Yams symbolize the body. People decorate and adorn yams in a manner linked to the adornment of the human body. Yams have pedigrees. When a young couple is married, they each bring their own family's yam "lines" to the marriage, where they are symbolically "joined" by being planted in the same garden. Yams are linked with the psychology and mythology of these people, and, in fact, permeate all aspects of life.

I began to better understand the reasons for the taboos. Yams are thought to have souls. They are sentient beings that have a sort of extrasensory perception. They can "feel" things. They appreciate tranquility, and can perceive social discord. Various other things, defined as "hot" activities, upset their serenity. Yams can "sense" an act of sexual intercourse, because it is "hot." Fighting is "hot." The killing and butchering of animals is also "hot," so there is a taboo against these activities while yams are growing.

Some of these beliefs may seem rather odd to you, as they did to me at first. But the Abelam firmly believe them. Once I expressed some doubt as to whether having sexual intercourse would really affect yam growth." Do you grow yams in America?" an Abelam friend asked me.

"Sure we do," I replied.

"And do Americans abstain from sex while they are growing these yams?" he queried.

"I doubt it," I said.

"How long are your yams?" he asked.

"Oh, about eight or nine inches," I answered.

"See!" he said in an amused tone.

Considering that Abelam yams are more than ten times longer, I couldn't very well argue with his logic!

As I pondered these kinds of issues, I began to wonder about the functions of these beliefs. What did this complex of beliefs do for these people? After all, I reasoned, people aren't stupid. Unless these beliefs made some sort of sense, they would probably have been abandoned long ago. And Abelam invest such physical and emotional energy in planting, tending, harvesting, displaying, and thinking about their yams! Certainly yam beliefs seemed to synchronize and structure many aspects of Abelam society, including the timing and intensity of warfare and the timing of human births. What else did they do? I began to consider another theoretical paradigm or model to help guide my thinking: *functionalism.*

In 1922 anthropologist Bronislaw Malinowski published a book entitled *Argonauts of the Western Pacific.*[9] In it he analyzed the Kula Ring, a complex set of trade networks linking the Trobriand Islanders with their neighbors. The kula are special shell valuables. Malinowski showed the importance of the exchange of these valuables for these islanders, and the complex ways in which this trade functioned. For example, through the secondary utilitarian bartering that accompanied it, kula trading helped to distribute specialized products throughout the ecologically diverse islands that comprise the ring. I started to think about Abelam yam beliefs in similar terms.

THE RITUAL CYCLE

I began by considering what I knew about the yam "cycle." The yearly cycle begins with a formal ceremony called *waapike yapevu,* "blowing on the yams." Exchange partners (rivals) from other villages come to symbolically "breathe life "into the planting material that has been displayed. This reminds me of a coin toss before a football game, or the opening instructions in a boxing match. Boxers shake hands, then try to beat each other senseless. Why are these niceties necessary? Very simply, I think that rivals are demonstrating their reacceptance of the structured rules of yam rivalry. Although yam exchanges are competitive, often angry affairs, men achieve their status by beating their rivals in a "fair fight" with structured rules. The mutual obligation of participating in these ceremonies underlines the fact that everyone has agreed to "play by the rules."

For the next month or two after this ceremony (which usually takes place in August or September), men begin to clear and burn the special yam gardens in preparation for planting, and the taboos begin. Yam growers spend much of their time in the gardens during this time. They only visit with a few trusted friends. They generally eat only at home, for fear of indirect pollution. After all, who could know if the food preparer had had sexual intercourse? If so, the food would become "polluted," the grower would ingest some of it, and the yams would suffer. Even something simple, like lighting a cigarette on a fire, can have adverse consequences. What if a sexually incontinent person had stepped over the fire, thus polluting it? A yam grower could ingest the pollution and ruin his yams! Social conflict is to be avoided at all costs while yams are growing. People must put aside their differences in the interests of the yams. Hostilities must be repressed. People must act in calm, mild, balanced ways. If a neighbor's pig enters someone's garden and eats his produce, the garden owner must control his anger. I once saw such an incident. A pig had eaten several of a yam grower's very best tubers. The man sat down on a rock at the edge of his garden and cried. But he never became overtly angry. He couldn't kill the pig, because that would have been a "hot "action. He never even mentioned the incident to the pig owner. To do so might have precipitated an argument.

At the end of the dry season, gardens are cleared, and yams are planted at the beginning of the wet season. Once planted, the yams are lovingly cared for. Growers spend considerable time arranging the vines on trellises, digging around and inspecting the tubers, and backfilling with rich, fertilized soil. Towards the end of the wet season, when yam growth is completed, yams are harvested according to individual inclination. Although the first yam festivals may not be held for another month or so, the rigid taboos become slightly relaxed as people worry less about the possibility of indirect pollution affecting the yams. Visiting again becomes common.

After all the yams are harvested, the yam festivals begin, usually around March. After a few months of yam festivals, equally elaborate male initiation ceremonies are held in some villages. There are four basic stages of initiation. Each moiety[10] in a village takes turns initiating the young males of the other moiety in collective, spectacular ceremonies held every few years. Sacred ritual objects are displayed to initiates in the haus tamberans mentioned earlier. Costumed dancers with towering headdresses adorned with colorful feathers perform on the ceremonial ground in front of the temples. These ceremonies are accompanied by the same sort of visiting, feasting, and social dancing that accompany the yam festivals. After the frenzy of this "ritual season" abates, the waapike yapevu is again held, gardens are cleared for yam planting, and the cycle begins again. Various elements in this ritual cycle are illustrated in Figure 1.

CONSEQUENCES OF THE RITUAL CYCLE

As I thought more about this ritual cycle, I made a list of some of things that the cycle seems to "do" for the Abelam:

1. Interpersonal conflicts are channeled into socially patterned, nonviolent forms.
2. Interpersonal conflicts are regulated and synchronized.
3. Warfare is synchronized and circumscribed.
4. Human births are synchronized.
5. Age cohorts are structured and synchronized.

How these things work is as follows. Yam exchanges and physical violence or warfare are often seen by Abelam as alternative ways to deal with social conflicts. One frequently hears statements like, "Some people fight with spears, others fight with yams." I once witnessed a case in Neligum Village in which one man was threatening to get his spears and kill another man. As the first man strode off to gather up his weapons, the other man shouted after him, "You talk about fighting, but your yams are inferior!" This put the first man in an extremely awkward position. If he got his spears and ran the other man through, he would just be proving his rival's point that he really was a violent man, and that his "hot" blood no doubt prevented him from growing admirable yams. The only way to really answer this challenge was for him to present his rival with a huge yam, thereby proving his yam-growing prowess. The potential fight never occurred, and the incident ended in the institution of a competitive exchange relationship between the two. Thus, through yam exchange, conflict was redirected into a socially approved, nonviolent channel.

Conflict is not only redirected by yam growing, but it is also regulated and synchronized. As I mentioned

Figure 1
Abelam Ritual Cycle

Seasonality of Related Variables

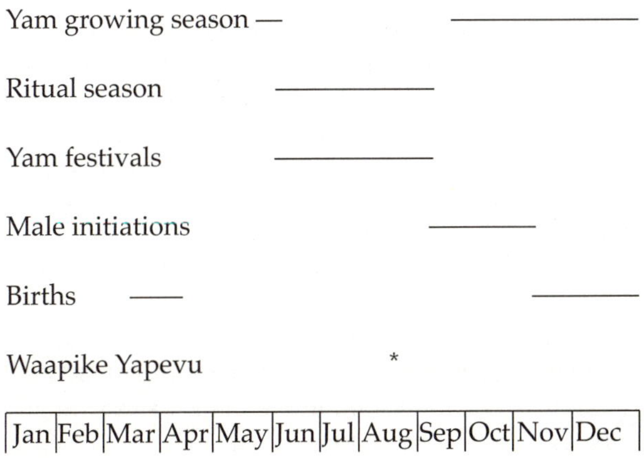

Yam growing season —

Ritual season

Yam festivals

Male initiations

Births

Waapike Yapevu

| Jan | Feb | Mar | Apr | May | Jun | Jul | Aug | Sep | Oct | Nov | Dec |

before, Abelam are quite serious about their yam taboos, and conflict is relatively rare during yam-growing. For the inevitable few problems that do arise and must be resolved, the Abelam use a different management style than they would otherwise employ.[11] During the yam growing season, mediators seek to bring about an immediate settlement by stressing areas of agreement. In the interests of the yams, most litigants are willing to compromise, at least temporarily. However, resentments sometimes remain, and, during the ritual season, mediators encourage catharsis by emphasizing areas of disagreement and exploring the full range of the dispute. This way, they allow people to "blow off steam," air all the issues that are bothering them, and come to a lasting agreement. I have seen many disputes that were brushed aside during the yam growing season emerge again during the ritual season. However, by now some months have passed, tempers have cooled, and people can be more reasonable.

Warfare, of course, cannot take place during the yam growing season without endangering the yams of all of the hostiles, so it rarely if ever occurs for these six months. However, even during the ritual season, the expression of warfare is regulated by yam beliefs. During yam festivals, male initiation ceremonies, and waapike yapevu, enemies must cooperate with one another by suspending hostilities and visiting one another's villages to measure and inspect yams, feast together, deliver yams, blow on each other's planting materials, and so on. Thus, the actual time available for warfare is quite limited. In other words, warfare is kept in check by the yam cycle.

Previously, I mentioned the "baby season" that I had observed. Counting back nine months from these births, it became obvious that virtually all of these conceptions would have occurred during the yam festival period, just after the six month taboo on sexual activities had ended. Since the Abelam do not practice any form of birth control, it seemed that my informant had been right, and that people really didn't have sex for six months! To further check this, I collected a small sample of twenty-nine birth months, analyzed the sample, and confirmed the existence of a pronounced birth season.[12] I realized something else, too. For most of the six-month period that sexual taboos were in effect, many of the women in the village were in their third trimester of pregnancy, were actually giving birth, or were recovering from their deliveries. Suspending sexual activities during these times didn't seem so strange as I had first imagined.

The clustering of births had another interesting

and, in my opinion, rather beneficial result for the Abelam. I myself was one of those unfortunate American children born in the cut-off month for attending school. This meant that my parents were forced to make the decision either to send me to school early, or to hold me out for a year. School officials felt that I was intellectually ready for school, but they weren't sure that I was socially ready. My parents decided to send me early, which caused me problems all through school. I was always the youngest in my class. I was somewhat of a discipline problem in the first few years of elementary school (and possibly far beyond). I hated dating in my senior year, because I still wasn't old enough to drive. But for the Abelam, all of the babies born in a particular year are virtually the same age. Thus, age cohorts are very discrete. In Abelam they are collectively called a *tembu*, a garden section. People of the same age cohort form very close bonds; they can "substitute" for one another in all sorts of social situations. Symbolically, the display of yams during the festivals is a time to reflect on both kinds of tembu: on the year's "harvest" of both yams and children.

SELF-REGULATION OF A SYSTEM

By now I was thoroughly intrigued with Abelam yam growing. It permeated so many aspects of Abelam life, it seemed an obvious focus for my Ph.D. thesis.[13] Having thought about some of the functions of the yams cycle, I began to consider another theoretical approach: cultural ecology. Cultural ecology is concerned with the relationship between people and their environments. In a nowclassic study entitled *Pigs for the Ancestors: Ritual in the Ecology of a New Guinea People*, Roy Rappaport described the ritual cycle of the Tsembaga Maring people as a "self-regulating system." He stated:

> . . . Tsembaga ritual, particularly in the context of a ritual cycle, operates as a regulating mechanism in a system, or set of interlocking systems, in which such variables as the area of available land, necessary lengths of fallow periods, size and composition of both human and pig populations, trophic requirements of pigs and people, energy expended in various activities, and the frequency of misfortunes are included.[14]

He described one particular ritual, the *kaiko* ceremony, as a sort of thermostat that kept all of these variables (the system) within tolerable limits. I realized that I could easily analyze Abelam yam growing

in this way too. I thought of Abelam yam growing as a sort of "pressure cooker valve" that relieved pressure and thus regulated some of the variables in the Abelam ecological system.

The Abelam had moved up into the mountains from the plains, where they found a lush environment ideally suited to yam growing. They had an appropriate technology, life was good, and their population began to rise. Now if we hold land constant for the moment, increased population density has several effects. For one thing, studies have shown that when people are crowded together, conflict usually rises. For one thing, since Abelam families need a minimum number of pigs, the pig population would rise, and, with land held constant, pigs would cause more and more damage to gardens, which would in turn cause a rise in the rate of conflict between pig and garden owners. Also, with an increasing population, the hunting of wild game, such as marsupials and cassowaries would increase, thus reducing their numbers.

Ritual yam exchanges can act to correct all these imbalances. As conflicts precipitated by increasing population density escalate, more and more competitive yam exchange relationships are created, since these yam exchanges are one of the most common ways of handling conflicts. This makes people pay even more attention to yam growing and be even more serious about the taboos. This reduces social conflict, particularly disputes about sexual jealousies and sexual behavior, which are the most common causes of Abelam conflict.[15] Whenever yams are exchanged, pork must also be given. So more yam exchanges means more pork, which of course means fewer pigs, thus the pig population is reduced and conflicts over pig depredations to gardens are lowered. Furthermore, the more serious people are about yam exchanges, the more strictly they adhere to prohibitions against hunting wild game, a "hot" activity. This creates a shortened hunting season, giving the wild game populations a chance to recover.

Yam growing can even act to adjust people/land ratios and thus reduce population density, which was the starting point for this analysis. When Samukundi Abelam wish to grow truly splendid yams, they clear virgin forest, since this land is known to be particularly good for yam growth. Later the land is given over to ordinary garden use. Thus, increased population pressure can increase conflict, which can increase yam exchanges, which can expand the amount of cultivated land, which can decrease the people/land ratio, which can relieve the population pressure and result in a balanced system once again.

Discussion

In the roughly twenty years that I've been studying Abelam culture, I've had occasion to use quite a few theoretical models to help me understand or think about various aspects of Abelam behavior. If I were to continue with the sort of analysis that I sketched out in the last section, I might consider employing a cultural adaptation model. Cultural adaptation is the idea that, as a result of a process of selection through time, societies will develop complexes of behavioral patterns that are adapted to their natural and social environments. I might want to think about what happened to the Abelam as they moved from the plains to the foothills, and why plains Abelam seem much less psychologically invested in yam growing than are mountain Abelam. Could it be that an increased interest in yam growing was a response to their changing environment? How would this have worked? To answer these questions, I would have to abandon the ethnographic present, and return again to the sorts of historical considerations that opened this paper.

There are all sorts of other theoretical frameworks that I could consider in thinking about this essay. No doubt some of you have noticed that I am male, and that Abelam ceremonial yam growing, the focus of this essay, is a male activity. Women play an important part in these activities, of course. Women take pride in their husbands' yams, because it shows that they, too, have rigidly followed the taboos. Women grow the crops that are eaten and distributed at feasts, they rear pigs that are slaughtered and distributed with the yams, they prepare food for feasts, they also maintain sexual continence in the interests of the yams. However, I was not able to observe the activities of women in as great detail as I could for the men.

Feminist anthropologists have made the very valid point that this state of affairs was all too common in the early days of anthropology when most ethnographers were men. Fortunately, the Abelam have been studied by at least four female ethnographers, including the previously mentioned Phyllis Kaberry, Brigitta Hauser-Schäublin,[16] Diane Losche,[17] and Barbara Huber-Greub.[18] Their work has helped provide a gender-balanced ethnography of the Abelam people. Yet it would be very difficult for any one ethnographer to provide such a picture. Abelam practice a fairly strict division of labor, which often keeps males and females working apart. Especially during the yam growing season, when contact between the sexes could lead to dangerous sexual temptations, the sexes are often segregated. It would not be appropriate for

an ethnographer of either sex to be spending time with the opposite sex during this period. A focus on gender and the anthropology of women can help us understand these sorts of relationships between ethnographers and the people they study.

Another possible way for you to think about this essay is by employing a body of theory called postmodernism. Postmodernism is concerned with, among other things, the acquisition, classification, production, and control of knowledge. After all, knowledge is power, particularly in the contemporary (computer-dominated, postindustrial, postmodern) world. Who decides what needs to be known? Who decides what knowledge needs to be disseminated? For what purposes?

Anthropologists employing postmodern theory have been concerned with analyzing the task of writing ethnography. Can an ethnographic profile, such as the one you've just read, really be objective? In the words of Michel de Certeau, how do anthropologists authorize themselves "to speak in the name of the 'real'?"[19] In writing this essay, I have had to make certain decisions about how I would present the Abelam to the outside world. What were my motivations? What were my reasons for studying the Abelam in the first place? How did I choose what to present in this essay, and how to present it? Postmodernism provides a useful theoretical framework to think about these sorts of issues.

There are many other theories that could be explored depending on one's interests. Marxist analysis, for example, initially focuses on the mode of production of a society, which is taken to be of paramount importance. Once the mode of production and control of the means of production are understood, other aspects of society are related to this and can often be explained as consequences. Using this theoretical framework, the primary Abelam concern with yams is not at all surprising, since yam growing is their major means of production. The fact that the religious system is related to (or, perhaps, results from) the mode of production also follows.

I hope that I've made the point that, while there are occasionally rival theories that can't both be true, most theories aren't mutually exclusive. Theories are just formulations of apparent relationships or underlying principles of certain observed phenomena that are only partially verified. If theories were totally proven, they wouldn't be theories, they'd be laws. So we have to keep experimenting with theories.

I believe that good social scientists are open minded enough to employ different modes of analysis for different problems. Theories should be judged by how useful they are in helping us understand human behavior and how accurate they are in predicting it. If they do those things well, they're "good" theories, and we should continue to employ and modify them. If they cease to be very useful to us, we should be dispassionate enough to abandon them.

Notes

1. Richard Scaglion, "The Importance of Nighttime Observations in Time Allocation Studies," *American Ethnologist* 13 (1986): 537–545.

2. Richard Scaglion, "Kiaps as Kings: Abelam Legal Change in Historical Perspective," in Deborah Gewertz and Edward L. Schieffelin, eds., *History and Ethnohistory in Papua New Guinea* (Sydney: Oceania Monograph no. 28, 1985), pp. 77–99; and Richard Scaglion,"Reconstructing First Contact: Some Local Effects of Labor Recruitment in the Sepik," in Nancy Lutkehaus et al., eds., *Sepik Heritage: Tradition and Change in Papua New Guinea* (Durham, NC: Carolina Academic Press, 1990), pp. 50–57.

3. Margaret Mead, *Sex and Temperament in Three Primitive Societies* (New York: Mentor Books, 1950), p. 20.

4. J. A. W. Forge, "Art and Environment in the Sepik," *Proceedings of the Royal Anthropological Institute* (1965), pp. 23–31; J. A. W. Forge, "Marriage and Exchange in the Sepik: Comments on Francis Korn's Analysis of Iatmul Society," in R. Needham, ed., *Rethinking Kinship and Marriage* (London: Tavistock, 1971), pp. 133–144; J. A. W. Forge, "The Golden Fleece," *Man* 7 (1972): 527–540 (originally the Malinowski Memorial Lecture delivered at the London School of Economics and Political Science, March 7, 1971); and J. A. W. Forge, "Style and Meaning in Sepik Art," in J. A. W. Forge, ed., *Primitive Art and Society* (London: Oxford University Press, 1973), pp. 169–192.

5. David A. M. Lea, *Abelam Land and Sustenance* (Ph.D. diss., Australian National University, 1964); David A. M. Lea, "The Abelam: A Study in Local Differentiation," *Pacific Viewpoint* 6 (2) (1965): 191–214; David A. M. Lea, "Access to Land among Swidden Cultivators: An Example from New Guinea," *Australian Geographical Studies* 7 (1969): 137–152; and David A. M. Lea, "Stress and Adaptation to Change: An Example from the East Sepik District, New Guinea," in N. C. Brookfield, ed., *The Pacific in Transition* (London: Edward Arnold), pp. 55–74.

6. Phyllis M. Kaberry, "The Abelam Tribe, Sepik District, New Guinea: A Preliminary Report," *Oceania* 11 (1940–41): 233–258, 345–367; Phyllis M. Kaberry, "Law and Political Organization in the Abelam Tribe, New Guinea," *Oceania* 12 (1941–42): 79–95, 209–225, 331–363; and Phyllis M. Kaberry, "Political Organization among the Northern Abelam," *Anthropological Forum* 1 (3–4) (1966): 334–372.

7. Phyllis M. Kaberry, "The Abelam Tribe, Sepik District, New Guinea: A Preliminary Report," *Oceania* 11 (1940–41): 240.

8. Donald F. Tuzin, "Yam Symbolism in the Sepik: An Interpretative Account," *Southwestern Journal of Anthropology* 28 (3) (1972): 230–254.

9. Bronislaw Malinowski, *Argonauts of the Western Pacific: An Account of Native Enterprise and Adventure in the Archipelagoes of Melanesian New Guinea* (London: George Routledge and Kegan Paul, 1922).

10. A moiety is one of the divisions of a society that results when that society is divided, normally on the basis of descent, into two halves.

11. Richard Scaglion, "The Effects of Mediation tyles on Successful Dispute Resolution: The Abelam Case," *Windsor Yearbook of Access to Justice* 3 (1983): 256–269.

12. Richard Scaglion, "Seasonal Births in a Western Abelam Village, Papua New Guinea," *Human Biology* 50 (1978): 313–323.

13. Richard Scaglion, *Seasonal Patterns in Western Abelam Conflict Management Practices* (Ph.D. diss., University of Pittsburgh, 1976).

14. Roy A. Rappaport, *Pigs for the Ancestors: Ritual in the Ecology of a New Guinea People* (New Haven, CT: Yale University Press, 1968).

15. Scaglion, *Seasonal Patterns in Western Abelam Conflict Management Practices*, p. 146.

16. Brigitta Hauser-Schäublin and J. Hauser-Schäublin, *Wir und unser Dorf: Die Kinder der Abelam in Papua Neuguinea* (Basel: Lehrmittelverlag des Kantons Basel-Stadt, 1980); Brigitta HauserSchäublin, *The Abelam: People of Papua New Guinea* (Boroko: National Cultural Council, 1980); Brigitta Hauser-Schäublin, "Schweinefleisch und Totenseele: Zur Bedeutung des Schweines in der Kultur der Abelam, Papua-Neuguinea," *Verhandlungen der Naturforschenden Gesellschaft Base* 94 (1983): 335–365; and Brigitta Hauser-Schäublin, "Ritueller Wettstreit mit Feldfrüchten: Yamsfeste im Sepik-Gebiet, Papua-Neuguinea," *Verhandlungen der Naturforschenden Gesellschaft Basel* 97 (1987): 87–102.

17. Diane Losche, "Gardens, Gods, and Body Language," *Australian Natural History* 20 (9) (1982): 301–311; and Diane Losche, *Male and Female in Abelam Society: Opposition and Complementarity* (Ph.D. diss., Columbia University, 1982).

18. Barbara Huber-Greub, *Kokospalmenmenschen: Boden und Alltag und ihre Bedeutung im Selbstverständnis der Abelam von Kimbangwa* (East Sepik Province, Papua New Guinea, Basel: Ethnologisches Seminar der Universität und Museum für Völkerkunde, 1988).

19. Cited in Ivan Brady, "Speaking in the Name of the Real: Freeman and Mead on Samoa," *American Anthropologist* 85 (1983): 908.

Suggested Readings

Kaberry, Phyllis M. "The Abelam Tribe, Sepik District, New Guinea: A Preliminary Report." *Oceania* 11 (1940–41): 233–258, 345–367. The first published description of the Mamukundi Abelam, and a good overview of Abelam culture.

Scaglion, Richard. "Ethnocentrism and the Abelam," in P. DeVita, ed., *The Humbled Anthropologist: Tales from the Pacific*. Belmont, CA: Wadsworth Publishing Company, 1990. This article describes some of the author's experiences while living with the Abelam.

———. "Samukundi Abelam Conflict Management: Implications for Legal Planning in Papua New Guinea." *Oceania* 52 (1981): 28–38. The article describes the conflict management practices of the Abelam, and how they are related to yam growing.

———. "Seasonal Births in a Western Abelam Village, Papua New Guinea." *Human Biology* 50 (1978): 313–323. An analysis of the Abelam "birth season."

Tuzin, Donald F., "Yam Symbolism in the Sepik: An Interpretative Account." *Southwestern Journal of Anthropology* 28 (3) (1972): 230–254. A careful and detailed symbolic analysis of the importance of ceremonial yams for the Ilahita Arapesh, the near neighbors of the Abelam.

On Cross-Cultural Research

Carol R. Ember and Melvin Ember

Cross-cultural researchers use information from different societies to try to arrive at general principles and general explanations. Their most important assumption is that comparison across cultures is possible, that across the wide diversity of cultures there are patterns of belief and behavior that are similar and explainable in similar ways. Why do cross-culturalists make this assumption? Mainly it is because we can predict much of the variation that has been observed cross-culturally. But our confidence that there are common explanations is also a matter of faith, which derives from our optimistic belief that even if social science has failed to find an explanation yet, it is only because we have not looked or thought hard enough yet.

In contrast, there are those who believe that cultures are so diverse and unique that they can only be described in their own terms. From this point of view, comparison is a waste of time because general explanations cannot be found. No general explanations are possible if there are no similarities across cultures. But cross-culturalists do not deny the uniqueness of each culture. Uniqueness and similarity are always present at the same time. What you see depends on how you look. If you focus on uniqueness, you may observe snowflakes and notice that each one has a unique structure; if you focus on similarity, you may observe that all snowflakes are roughly hexagonal and all melt when their temperature exceeds 32 degrees Fahrenheit at sea level.

Consider the following statements about sexuality in three different cultures:

1. The Mae Enga in the Western Highlands of Papua New Guinea believe that "... copulation is in itself detrimental to male well-being. Men believe that the vital fluid residing in a man's skin makes it sound and handsome, a condition that determines and reflects his mental vigor and self-confidence. This fluid also manifests itself as his semen. Hence, every ejaculation depletes his vitality, and over-indulgence must dull his mind and leave his body permanently exhausted and withered."[1]

2. "The Nupe men [of Nigeria], certainly, make much of the physically weakening effects of sexual intercourse, and teach the younger generation to husband their strength...."[2]

3. "... the milk avoidances of the Nilotes [Shilluk of the Sudan] are dependent on fear of contamination associated with the sexual act.... Only small boys herd the cattle and milk them, for once a boy has reached maturity there is the danger that he may have had sexual contact, when if he milked, or handled manure, or even walked among the cattle in their pens, he would cause them to become sterile.... If a man has had sexual relations with his wife or another he is considered unclean and does not drink milk until the sun has set the following day."[3]

Taken at face value, these three statements about male sexuality are each unique. Indeed, no statement about anything in a particular culture, sexuality or any other aspect of life, will be exactly like a corresponding statement about another culture. But there are also similarities in these statements that suggest a continuum of variation in regard to the degree to which males in a society believe that heterosexual sex is harmful to their health. It seems as if both Enga and Nupe males think that heterosexual sex is harmful. It is not so clear what Shilluk males think, because the statement quoted refers to harm to cattle and avoidance of milk, not to the health of males. But suppose we framed the question a different way and asked if people in a particular culture believed that heterosexuality (even with legitimate partners) brought some harm or danger. In regard to this question, we would say that all three of the cultures mentioned had such a belief. The important point here is that similarities cannot be seen until we think about *variables* (things or quantities that vary along some dimension). There is no right or wrong conceptualization; the researcher may choose to focus on any aspect of variation. But once researchers perceive similarity, they can perceive difference. Consider the following statements:

4. For the Cuna of Panama, "the sexual impulse is regarded as needing relief, particularly for males, and as an expression of one's *niga*, a supernatural attribute manifested in potency and strength. On the other hand it is considered debilitating to have sexual relations too often, for this will weaken one's *niga*."[4]

5. Of the Bedouin of Kuwait, "It [sexual intercourse] is the one great pleasure common to rich and poor alike, and the one moment of forgetfulness in his daily round of troubles and hardships that Badawin [Bedouin] or townsmen can enjoy. Men and women equally love the act, which is said to keep man [sic] young, 'just like riding a mare.'"[5]

The Bedouin beliefs contrast most sharply with the beliefs in the other cultures, because heterosexual intercourse appears to be viewed by them as purely pleasurable, with no negative associations. The Cuna seem somewhere in the middle. While they view sex as important, they appear to believe that too much is not good. Mixed beliefs are not a problem if the variable is conceptualized as a continuum with gradations. So, in a cross-cultural study conducted by Carol R. Ember of a variable labeled as degree of men's fear of sex with women, four scale points were identified: societies that had only negative statements about heterosexuality were considered high in men's fear of sex with women, those that had an equal number of negative and positive statements were considered ambivalent, those that had *mostly* positive statements were considered relatively low in men's fear of sex with women, and those with *only* positive statements were considered as lacking men's fear of sex with women. While the variable at issue does not capture everything that might pertain to beliefs about heterosexuality (in all their uniqueness), it does capture some distinguishable similarities and differences across cultures.[6]

What Is the Question?

Once cross-cultural researchers identify the trait or pattern they are interested in predicting and explaining, they begin to ask a variety of questions about it.[7]

One is a descriptive question, dealing with the prevalence or frequency of a trait. How common is the belief that sex is dangerous to one's health? What proportion of societies have it? A second kind of question deals with the causes of a trait or custom. The following are examples: Why do some societies have the belief that heterosexual sex is harmful? Why do some societies insist on monogamous marriage, whereas most allow polygyny (multiple wives)? Why is war very frequent in some societies and less frequent in others? A third kind of question deals with the consequences or effects of a particular trait or custom. This kind of question may be phrased broadly: What are the effects of growing up in a society with a great deal of war? Or a consequence question may be phrased much more specifically: What is the effect of polygyny on fertility? A fourth kind of question, which is not that different from the second or third types, is the relational question. Rather than hypothesizing about causes or consequences, a researcher may simply ask if a particular aspect of culture is associated with some other aspects. Is there a relationship between type of marriage and level of fertility? Is more war associated with more socialization of aggression in children?

Of the four types of questions, the causal or why question is the most challenging because such why questions rarely specify what the researcher needs to do. (Consequence questions may be equally unspecific, but often particular possible effects are specified in advance.) The descriptive question tells the researcher what to count in a representative sample of societies. If you want to estimate the frequency of monogamy versus polygyny, then you need to establish what each society allows and make a count of each kind of society. The specific consequence and relational questions usually specify a set of concrete things to look at. If you want to know whether type of marriage has an effect on or is related to fertility, then you know you need to measure both variables. But a causal question or unspecific consequence question does not tell the researcher exactly where to look for causes and effects. It only specifies what scientists call the *dependent* variable (the variable to be explained in the causal question) or the *independent* variable (the variable that may have effects in the consequence question). Exactly which possible variables may be causes or effects is something the investigator has to decide on, often as suggested by some theory.

We like to think of the causal question as analogous to the format of a detective story. After a crime is committed the detective may know a lot about the crime, but not "whodunit "or why. Finding the solution usually entails hypothesizing about suspects and their possible motives and opportunities, eliminating the implausible possibilities, and concluding who is probably the culprit. Similarly, in science, the pursuit of causes involves the testing of alternative explanations or theories that specify why something is the way it is or how it came to be that way. The researcher who chooses to investigate a causal question needs to identify plausible explanations or theories that could be tested, and to decide on a strategy (for collecting and analyzing data) that could falsify or disconfirm explanations. Although these requirements may suggest that the researcher who searches for causes may need to act differently from other kinds of researchers, this is not really the case, as we shall see.

The Cross-Cultural Research Strategy

The basic strategy in testing any kind of cross-cultural relationship is the same, whether the relationship involves presumed causes, consequences, or just an association or correlation of an unspecified nature. To illustrate this, let's consider what we ourselves did in a study designed to investigate why people in some societies go to war more often than in others.[8] We started where most researchers do, looking to see what is suggested in the literature about warfare. One of the theories we decided to test is the idea that people fight when their populations begin to press on their supply of resources. According to this theory, when people do not have enough of a resource, they supposedly look to take it from those who do have enough. This idea about the possible link between war and resource problems ("population pressure") has been discussed in anthropology mostly by ecological anthropologists such as Andrew P. Vayda and Roy Rappaport.[9]

Does this relationship hold true for most societies? We undertook a cross-cultural study to try to find out.[10] Our first step was to reduce the idea that population pressure causes war to a simple relationship that should be true if the causal theory is correct. If it is, societies with greater population pressure should be more likely to engage in war (should have war more frequently) than societies with little or no population pressure. Notice that the prediction (or more formally the "hypothesis") has almost the same form as the theory we stated above, but it differs in a fundamental way—the hypothesis simply predicts an association between variables (population pressure and war) but says nothing about causality. It merely

says that the presumed cause and the presumed effect should generally co-occur. This is the fundamental assumption of cross-cultural research, but it is an assumption shared widely by researchers in other fields. Suppose we were testing the idea that smoking causes lung cancer. One hypothesis is that smokers, compared with nonsmokers, have a significantly higher rate of lung cancer. If smoking causes lung cancer, the two variables should be statistically associated. If they are not, we are obliged to be skeptical about a causal link between smoking and cancer. So, cross-cultural research is not very different from research in epidemiology, which looks for correlations between disease outcomes and predictors in an individual's background or environment. Just as in epidemiology, however, research should not stop with the establishment of a correlation or association. Discovering a correlation is only the first step. Causal theories need also to be tested in other ways—experimentally, if possible, and by historical studies (looking at change over time)—to see if the presumed causes antedate the presumed effects. The testing for a correlation or association is an important first step because a test that reveals no significant correlation means that the underlying theory probably has no predictive value. And if a theory is not predictive, it has no causal or explanatory value. Historical studies are much more difficult and time consuming than correlational studies. So it is more efficient to test causal theories by first looking to see if the predicted nonhistorical associations truly exist.

To test for a correlation we have to find ways to measure the variables involved in objective and systematic ways. Most cross-culturalists use data collected by ethnographers to measure the variables in question. An ethnography is a descriptive account of the life of a group of people at a particular time and in a particular place. Usually the ethnographer is a trained anthropologist or other social scientist who uses a combination of methods to arrive at a picture of life in that community or society. In anthropology, participant observation and informal interviewing are almost always used; these methods of data collection may be supplemented by formal interviewing, testing, and systematic behavior observations. Almost always, the ethnographers writing cultural descriptions have not collected information with any cross-cultural comparison in mind. This means that they may or may not describe the information we are looking for and they may or may not use the methods that we deem the most suitable. In a very real sense, then, the ethnographic record limits the kinds of comparisons cross-culturalists can make. If ethnographers often describe what we are looking for, we can use ethnographic information to make cross-cultural tests. If there is little or no ethnography to use in a test, the theory will have to be tested in other ways. Later in this chapter we describe primary field comparisons in which researchers deliberately collect the information they need.

Designing measures that can be used to test theories is not that straightforward a process. Most theoretical variables are abstract constructs; researchers have to try to find a way to measure something that is observable.[11] Let's take the idea of population pressure. How can we measure population pressure on resources? As many anthropologists are aware, it is difficult to say exactly how many people could be supported in a particular territory because that depends mainly on the available technology. A society could increase the carrying capacity of its territory by improving its extractive and other technology. Population size may also depend on the weather. One year's crop may be good, and the visiting ethnographer may think that there is no pressure on resources. But another year, if the weather is bad, many may starve. The availability of resources can vary a lot from year to year. No one has yet devised an adequate measure of carrying capacity for one society, let alone for a cross-cultural sample. But we could know that a population has gone beyond its resources, without knowing how many people might be supported in that territory. According to Liebig's law of the minimum,[12] populations should adjust to the carrying capacity of their minimum years. If they have not, famines or serious food shortages should occur from time to time. For our study of war, we devised three different measures of resource (mainly food) scarcity. One was the amount of chronic or regularly occurring scarcity; the second was the number of reported famines in a twenty-five-year time period; and the third measure was the number of natural disasters that destroyed food supplies in a twenty-five-year time period. Coders were instructed to read the ethnographic materials on a particular culture and decide which of four ordered categories best fit that case on each of the three measures. Two coders separately read the ethnographic materials for each society, and we used only those societies for which the two coders' scores did not differ much.

And how did we measure frequency of warfare? First, we needed to define warfare appropriately because war as we know it in the world of modern nation-states is very different from the warfare described in the ethnographic record. For one thing, most societies in the ethnographic record lacked spe-

cialized fighting forces and formal military leaders.[13] Second, the wars were not usually organized on behalf of the entire society or even a major section thereof; in about 50 percent of the societies known to anthropology, the largest territorial unit involved in warfare was the village or other small community. So warfare as we defined it was any socially organized armed combat between members of different territorial units (communities or aggregates of communities). We asked our coders to read ethnographies and assess how often wars occurred in the society (or language group) according to a five-point ordinal scale ranging from less often than once every ten years to "constant" or occurring at any time of the year.[14]

The reader may wonder why we did not use more precise measures of warfare. For example, why didn't we use the exact number of months in a ten-year period that people were involved in warfare? The answer is that ethnographers rarely give us precise quantitative information on war frequency. They are more likely to say that war is rare or constant or occasional. If a scale is too precise, such that most cases cannot be measured, it is useless for cross-cultural comparison. But even imprecise scales can provide enough variation to allow us to find a relationship if one exists. Consider the relationship between height and weight. Of course we would want a researcher to use the best scale and the best ruler around. But imagine that you were in a place with neither a scale nor a ruler. You could line people up in order by height, so you would know who was the tallest and who was the shortest and the relative heights in-between. And you could probably rig up a seesaw or balance and use a set of stones to see how many "stones" people weighed. Chances are that even with such a crude measure you would find that taller people are generally heavier than shorter people. Researchers must sometimes be content with imprecise measures. A measure that rank-orders cases is better than no useable measure at all.

Cross-cultural researchers must also decide what societies to include in the sample. No one can examine all cultures; even if one could, the labor and time costs involved would not justify doing so. The most important operating principles in a scientific test of a hypothesis are: (1) to choose a sample that is representative of some universe of societies to which the researcher wants to generalize the results; and (2) to use a large enough sample so that the results are likely to be true for the larger universe of cases. As yet, there is no complete list of the world's cultures from which to sample, so researchers could sample from one of the following published cross-cultural samples including (from largest to smallest): a computerized concordance containing lists of societies in eight different cross-cultural samples; the "full" Ethnographic Atlas; the "summary" Ethnographic Atlas; the World Ethnographic Sample; the Atlas of World Cultures; the Human Relations Area Files (HRAF) Collection of Ethnography; the Standard Ethnographic Sample; the Standard Cross-Cultural Sample; and the HRAF Probability Sample Files.[15] Most of these samples contain bibliography (or pointers to bibliography) and some coded information on traits of interest to a variety of researchers. The HRAF Collection of Ethnography is different in that it contains no precoded data, but full texts indexed by subject matter and grouped by culture for the rapid retrieval of particular kinds of information. The important point about all of these lists is that they were not designed to support any researcher's pet idea or theory. In contrast, a set of cases chosen from a researcher's own personal library would be scientifically suspect.

What is a large enough sample? Statisticians have worked out formulas for calculating the size of the representative (random) sample that is needed to obtain a significant result (one likely to be true). The samples needed are usually much smaller than you might imagine. If a relationship is strong, a random sample of twenty to thirty is sufficient. While most people assume that "bigger is better," bigger samples require much more time and effort and expense—and they may not yield much more information or accuracy than a small random sample. Political opinion polls are a case in point. Samples of a few hundred to a few thousand people in the entire United States can often yield quite accurate predictions of elections.

Types of Cross-Cultural Comparison

The examples we have discussed so far are all from worldwide cross-cultural comparisons. But there are also other kinds of cross-cultural comparison. We can classify cross-cultural studies in terms of three dimensions: (1) whether the sample is worldwide or limited to a particular geographic area; (2) whether the comparison employs data collected by others (secondary data—e.g., from ethnographies, censuses, histories) or the data were collected in the field by the investigator (primary data); and (3) whether the data collected for each case were from the same (synchronic) time period or from two or more (diachronic) time periods. While eight combinations of these three dimensions

are possible, diachronic comparisons of any kind are quite rare as yet.[16] Worldwide cross-cultural comparisons using synchronic ethnographic information are the most common so far in anthropology. Some of the other social sciences compare across nations, which is a narrower type of cross-cultural comparison. Economists, sociologists, and political scientists also generally use secondary data when they study large samples of nations, but the data they use are not generally ethnographic; the measures are not based on cultural information collected by anthropologists or other investigators in the field. Rather, the data used in cross-national comparisons may be based on censuses and other statistics (crime rates, gross national product, etc.) or on historical documents. Cross-cultural psychologists are most likely to collect their own (primary) data, but their comparisons tend to be limited; often only two cultures are compared.

Before we turn to the advantages and disadvantages of the different types of comparison, let us first examine some of the other differences between cross-cultural and cross-national research. Cross-cultural research is broader in scope than cross-national research. The cross-national study compares countries, large populations that are politically unified. The cross-cultural study compares all types of society, from small hunter-gatherer societies with bands of fewer than seventy-five people and total populations in the hundreds to large societies dependent on intensive agriculture with cities and populations in the millions. As we noted earlier, about half of the societies known to anthropology had no political unification beyond the local community when they were first described, so many of the cultures studied by anthropologists are a lot smaller in scale than the countries studied in cross-national comparisons. The unit of study for an anthropologist is typically a population that lives in a contiguous geographical area and speaks a language not understood by its neighbors. (Anthropologists often call such a unit a society; its shared behaviors, beliefs, and values comprise its culture.) In contrast, the unit of analysis for a cross-national study is a politically defined country, which may be mostly one culture in the anthropological sense (e.g., Japan), or may include many different cultures. For example, Nigeria contains hundreds of cultures (e.g., Hausa, Yoruba, and Ibo). This is not to say that multicultural countries do not develop their own "national cultures," sets of distinctive customs including an official or national language. Still, it is important to realize that the units in a cross-national comparison often consist of more than one society (and culture) in the anthropological sense.

Advantages and Disadvantages of Different Types of Comparison

The major advantage of a worldwide comparison is its generalizability—a relationship found in such a comparison is likely to be applicable to the whole world. But when a researcher compares a lot of societies from different parts of the world, she or he is unlikely to know much about each society. If an explanation turns out to be supported (that is, if the hunch seems to pay off), the lack of detailed knowledge may not be a problem. However, if the cross-cultural test is disconfirming, it may be difficult to come up with an alternative explanation without knowing much about the particular cases. Because most anthropologists have regional specialties, the regional comparativist is likely to know somewhat more about each society in a within-region comparison. Narrowing the scope of a study to a region may mean you know more about the cases, but such narrowing decreases the chance that the results will apply to the whole world. The findings of a regional comparison may or may not be generalizable to the rest of the world; the only way to find out is to conduct tests using data from other world regions.[17] Of course, even a regional comparativist may not know all the cases in the region; that depends mostly on the size of the region. If the region is as large as North America, the comparativist is likely to know less about the cases than if the region is the American Southwest. Fred Eggan advocated small-scale regional comparisons, which he called "controlled comparisons," because he thought they would make it easier to control on similarity in history, geography, and language.[18] The presumption was that the researcher could then readily discern what accounts for some aspect of cultural variation within the region. However, similarity of cases within a region (in history, geography, language) may be a major drawback; if there is not sufficient variability in the aspect of culture the researcher is trying to explain (as well as in the presumed causes), it would be difficult or impossible to discern what the phenomena at issue may be related to. For example, suppose that almost all the cases in a region share beliefs about sexuality being somewhat harmful. It would be difficult or nearly impossible to be able to figure out what this belief is related to, because you could not tell which of the other regularly occurring practices or beliefs in the region might explain the sexual beliefs. Only if some of the cases lack what you are trying to explain might

you see that the causes are generally absent when the effect is absent.

It may seem preferable to collect primary data (from a series of fieldwork sites) because the researcher then has control over how the raw data are collected.[19] But the logistics of cross-cultural comparisons using primary data are formidable in time and expense. It is much more expensive to send fieldworkers to a series of sites than to retrieve and analyze data that have already been published—and it is difficult to maintain comparability across all the field sites. If a researcher has some confidence that the information needed is already available in published form, comparisons using secondary data are much easier and cheaper than comparisons using primary data. A primary comparison, of course, is the only way to compare if the information needed is not available in the literature.

Why haven't many diachronic studies been done yet? After all, if cross-culturalists are interested in cause and effect, it is important to know if the presumed causes preceded the effect. Perhaps the most important reason few such studies have been done is that diachronic data on a given case are not often easily available. Most societies studied by cultural anthropologists lacked native writing, and so there are usually no historical documents for earlier time periods. Reconstructions of prior time periods depend, then, upon oral history and the piecing together of occasional scattered documents from travelers, traders, missionaries, and other early visitors. In addition, while many cultures have been studied by different ethnographers at different times, ethnographers often have different substantive interests and their visits are unlikely to be neatly spaced out at regular intervals. It is no wonder, then, that most comparativists think it is more efficient to test causal theories first against synchronic data; if a theory has merit, the presumed causes and effects should generally be associated synchronically.[20]

The Validity of Cross-Cultural Research

Most cross-cultural research makes use of ethnography. Concern is often expressed about the quality of the data provided by ethnography and, therefore, the validity of cross-cultural studies that use ethnographic data. Some cross-culturalists, like George Peter Murdock, took the position that there is a great deal of "robustness "in the cross-cultural method. Murdock was not concerned with possible errors in ethnography because he thought they were uncommon and therefore unlikely to be threats to validity. In contrast, Raoul Naroll was quite concerned about possible errors in ethnography and proposed data quality controls to test for systematic errors that might lead to the acceptance of false hypotheses.[21] Since cross-culturalists cannot redo ethnography, Naroll proposed ways of analyzing the effects of data quality after the fact. He recommended that researchers rate the presumed quality of the ethnography they were reading by taking note of such things as whether the ethnographer had a command of the native language, how much time was spent in the field, and so on. Then he recommended that researchers look to see if those data quality factors were significantly associated with the variables in the tested hypothesis. If they were, Naroll suggested that the data quality control factors be tested as alternative explanations of the results.

Research over the past thirty years suggests that Naroll was too worried about the possibility of errors in ethnography affecting the results of cross-cultural hypothesis tests. Of the many studies done by Naroll, his students, and others looking for data quality effects, very few have found that a data quality factor accounts for some result. Accordingly, some cross-culturalists now recommend testing only for those data quality factors which, according to strong reasoning, are likely to affect results.[22] They also recommend that researchers develop a more direct coding of data quality that could be done while retrieving information from ethnographies to measure variables. For example, if a researcher is coding for sex ratio, a high score for data quality would be given to an estimate based on census data for a large population; estimates based on less quantified information would be given lower data quality scores. Researchers could then see if results were stronger (as they should be) using only the high quality data.

Another major reason some have for questioning cross-cultural findings is referred to as "Galton's Problem." In 1889, Francis Galton, in response to hearing a presentation of the first cross-cultural study (by Edward Tylor), suggested that many of Tylor's "cases" were duplicates of one another because they had similar histories, and therefore his results were suspect because the sample was inflated.[23] More recently, Raoul Naroll and his students have considered "Galton's Problem "a serious threat to cross-cultural research. Naroll and others devised several methods to test for the possible effects of diffusion and historical relatedness.[24] The concern behind these methods was that statistical associations could not be causal if they could be attributed mostly to diffusion (cultural borrowing) or common ancestry. Some cross-culturalists who were worried about Galton's Problem tried to solve it by making sure that their samples contained only one culture from a particular culture area (an area of related languages and cultures).

How serious is Galton's Problem? Cross-culturalists disagree. Most think it is a serious problem. Others like ourselves think not, because a random sample of cases is the best way to avoid sampling bias. Also, the sample cases in most cross-cultural studies usually turn out to speak mutually unintelligible languages, which means that the speech communities involved have been separated for at least a thousand years. If two related languages began to diverge a thousand or more years ago, many other aspects of the cultures will also have diverged. Therefore, such cases could hardly be duplicates of each other.

Until recently, whether or not you worried about Galton's Problem made a big difference in how you would do a study. Naroll's tests for the possibility of diffusion were quite time consuming to carry out; probably for this reason, most cross-culturalists altered their sampling strategy so as to eliminate multiple cases from the same culture area. Recently, however, mathematical anthropologists have developed statistical solutions and computer programs that treat the proximity of societies (in distance or language) as a variable whose influence can be tested in a multiple regression analysis. (This is called testing for spatial autocorrelation.)[25] Whether or not a researcher agrees that Galton's Problem is a problem, the recent mathematical and computer solutions do not require a special sampling strategy, nor do they require expensive, time-consuming controls. All you have to do, if you worry about Galton's Problem, is test statistically for the possibility that proximity accounts for your results.

Cross-cultural researchers disagree about the seriousness of Galton's Problem and how to deal with it. And of course they often disagree about causal interpretations. But with all their disagreement, they agree on the necessity of doing cross-cultural research in order to arrive at universal explanations. Only a cross-cultural test gives us the opportunity to discover that a theory or explanation does not fit the real world of cultural variation and therefore should be rejected.

Notes

1. M. J. Meggitt, "Male-Female Relationships in the Highlands of Australian New Guinea," *American*

Anthropologist 66, no. 4, part 2 (1964): 210. Most ethnographers describe a culture as belonging to a particular time and place. Anthropologists refer to that time as the "ethnographic present." Meggitt was describing the Mae Enga as of the 1950s.

2. S. F. Nadel, *Nupe Religion* (London: Routledge & Kegan Paul, 1954), p. 179. Described as of 1934–1936.

3. C. G. Seligman and Brenda Z. Seligman, *Pagan Tribes of the Nilotic Sudan* (London: George Routledge & Sons, 1932), p. 73. Described as of 1909–1910.

4. David B. Stout, *San Blas Cuna Acculturation: An Introduction* (New York: Viking Fund Publications in Anthropology, 1947), p. 39. Described as of 1940–1941.

5. H. R. P. Dickson, *The Arab of the Desert: A Glimpse into Badawin Life in Kuwait and Sau'di Arabia* (London: George Allen & Unwin, 1951), p. 162. Described as of the 1930s–1940s.

6. Carol R. Ember, "Men's Fear of Sex with Women: A Cross-Cultural Study," *Sex Roles: A Journal of Research* 4 (1978): 657–678. This cross-cultural study tested four theories about why some cultures were high in men's fear of sex with women. Note that women's beliefs about men were not studied at the time because so few ethnographies reported women's beliefs.

7. The next four paragraphs are adapted from Carol R. Ember and Melvin Ember, *Guide to Cross-Cultural Research Using the HRAF Archive* (New Haven, CT: Human Relations Area Files, 1988), pp. 5–6.

8. Carol R. Ember and Melvin Ember, "Resource Unpredictability, Mistrust, and War: A Cross-Cultural Study," *Journal of Conflict Resolution* 36 (1992):242–262.

9. See, for example, Andrew P. Vayda, *War in Ecological Perspective* (New York: Plenum, 1976); and Roy A. Rappaport, Pigs for the Ancestors (New Haven, CT: Yale University Press, 1967).

10. Our cross-cultural research did find support for the notion that population pressure makes war more likely. However, chronic pressure on resources did not seem to predict more war; the strongest predictor in our study (Ember and Ember, "Resource Unpredictability, Mistrust, and War") was unpredictable shortages of resources caused by natural disasters. But our results suggested that people with a history of unpredictable disasters fought more or less constantly, not just when the disasters occurred or right after.

11. For a more advanced treatment of measurement issues, see Carol R. Ember, Marc H. Ross, Michael Burton, and Candice Bradley, "Problems of Measurement in Cross-Cultural Research Using Secondary Data," *Behavior Science Research* ("Cross-Cultural and Comparative Research: Theory and Method/Special Issue") 25 (1991): 187–216.

12. As described in E. P. Odum, *Fundamentals of Ecology* (Philadelphia: Saunders, 1959).

13. Keith Otterbein, *The Evolution of War* (New Haven, CT: HRAF Press, 1989).

14. Ember and Ember, "Resource Unpredictability, Mistrust, and War"; Carol R. Ember and Melvin Ember, "Warfare, Aggression, and Resource Problems: Cross-Cultural Codes," *Behavior Science Research* 26 (1992): 169–226.

15. For a more complete discussion of sampling issues in cross-cultural research, see Melvin Ember and Keith F. Otterbein, "Sampling in Cross-Cultural Research," *Behavior Science Research* ("Cross-Cultural and Comparative Research: Theory and Method/Special Issue ") 25 (1991): 217–233. The samples discussed here are as follows: Carol R. Ember, with the assistance of Hugh Page, Jr., Timothy O'Leary, and M. Marlene Martin, *Computerized Concordance of Cross-Cultural Samples* (New Haven, CT: Human Relations Area Files, 1992); "Ethnographic Atlas," published in the journal *Ethnology* from January 1962 to April 1968; George Peter Murdock, "Ethnographic Atlas: A Summary," *Ethnology* 6 (1967): 109–236; George Peter Murdock, "World Ethnographic Sample," *American Anthropologist* 59 (1957): 664–687; George Peter Murdock, *Atlas of World Cultures* (Pittsburgh: University of Pittsburgh Press, 1981); "Human Relations Area Files (HRAF) Collection of Ethnography" (nearly fifty years of annual installments distributed to member institutions); Raoul Naroll and Richard G. Sipes, "A Standard Ethnographic Sample: Second Edition," *Current Anthropology* 14 (1973): 111–142; George Peter Murdock and Douglas R. White, "Standard Cross-Cultural Sample," *Ethnology* 8 (1969): 329–369; and Robert O.Lagacé, ed., "The HRAF Probability Sample: Retrospect and Prospect," *Behavior Science Research* 14 (1979): 211–229.

16. For more discussion of the different types of comparison, see Melvin Ember, "The Logic of Comparative Research," *Behavior Science Research* ("Cross-Cultural and Comparative Research: Theory and Method/Special Issue") 25 (1991): 143–154.

17. For more discussion of regional comparisons, see Michael L. Burton and Douglas R. White, "Regional Comparisons, Replications, and Historical Network Analysis," *Behavior Science Research* ("Cross-Cultural and Comparative Research: Theory and Method/Special Issue") 25 (1991): 55–78.

18. Fred Eggan, "Social Anthropology and the Method of Controlled Comparison," *American Anthropologist* 56 (1954): 743–763.

19. For more discussion of primary field comparisons, see three chapters in *Behavior Science Research* ("Cross-Cultural and Comparative Research: Theory and Method/Special Issue") 25 (1991): Allen Johnson, "Regional Comparative Field Research," pp. 3–22; Robert L. Munroe and Ruth H. Munroe, "Results of Comparative Field Studies," pp. 23–54; and Robert L. Munroe and Ruth H. Munroe, "Com-

parative Field Studies: Methodological Issues and Future Possibilities," pp. 155–185.

20. This point has been made before by J. W. M. Whiting, "The Cross-Cultural Method," in Gardner Lindzey, ed., *Handbook of Social Psychology*, vol. I (Reading, MA: Addison-Wesley, 1954), pp. 523–531; Keith F. Otterbein, "Basic Steps in Conducting a Cross-Cultural Study," *Behavior Science Notes* 4 (1969): 221–236; Raoul Naroll, Gary Michik, and Frada Naroll, *Worldwide Theory Testing* (New Haven, CT: Human Relations Area Files, 1976).

21. George Peter Murdock, "Major Emphases in My Cross-Cultural Research," *Behavior Science Research* 12 (1977): 217–222; Raoul Naroll, *Data Quality Control: A New Research Technique* (New York: Free Press, 1962).

22. See the discussion of recommendations in Ember, Ross, Burton, and Bradley, "Problems of Measurement in Cross-Cultural Research Using Secondary Data."

23. Edward B. Tylor, "On a Method of Investigating the Development of Institutions Applied to the Laws of Marriage and Descent," *Journal of the Royal Anthropological Institute of Great Britain and Ireland* 18 (1889): 245–269; Francis Galton, "Comment on Tylor," *Journal of the Royal Anthropological Institute of Great Britain and Ireland* 18 (1889): 270–272.

24. Raoul Naroll, "Data Quality Control in Cross-Cultural Surveys," in Raoul Naroll and Ronald Cohen, eds., *A Handbook of Method in Cultural Anthropology* (Garden City, NY: Natural History Press, 1970), pp. 927–945.

25. For some newer treatments of Galton's Problem, see Burton and White, "Regional Comparisons, Replications, and Historical Network Analysis," for references.

Suggested Readings

Burton, Michael L., and Douglas R. White. "Regional Comparisons, Replications, and Historical Network Analysis." *Behavior Science Research* ("Cross-Cultural and Comparative Research: Theory and Method/Special Issue") 25 (1991): 55–78. Reviews the history of within-region cross-cultural studies, their advantages, and newer solutions to Galton's Problem.

Ember, Carol R., and David Levinson. "The Substantive Contributions of Worldwide Cross-Cultural Studies Using Secondary Data." *Behavior Science Research* ("Cross-Cultural and Comparative Research: Theory and Method/Special Issue") 25 (1991): 79–140. Provides an overview of the major findings of cross-cultural research through 1990.

Ember, Carol R., Marc H. Ross, Michael Burton, and Candice Bradley. "Problems of Measurement in Cross-Cultural Research Using Secondary Data." *Behavior Science Research* ("Cross-Cultural and Comparative Research: Theory and Method/Special Issue") 25 (1991): 187–216. After reviewing basic measurement concepts, reviews the problems of measurement using secondary data at each stage of the research process. Strategies for minimizing measurement error are suggested.

Ember, Melvin. "The Logic of Comparative Research." *Behavior Science Research* ("Cross-Cultural and Comparative Research: Theory and Method/Special Issue") 25 (1991): 143–154. Discusses the logic of the various comparative research strategies and points out how they can contribute to the scientific understanding of the variables and constants of human culture.

Ember, Melvin, and Keith F. Otterbein. "Sampling in Cross-Cultural Research." *Behavior Science Research* ("Cross-Cultural and Comparative Research: Theory and Method/Special Issue") 25 (1991): 217–233. Reviews existing cross-cultural samples against ideal characteristics and makes recommendations about practical choices.

Munroe, Robert L., and Ruth H. Munroe. "Comparative Field Studies: Methodological Issues and Future Possibilities." *Behavior Science Research* ("Cross-Cultural and Comparative Research: Theory and Method/Special Issue") 25 (1991): 155–185. Discusses design, measurement, and analysis strategies in primary comparisons.

Naroll, Raoul. "Data Quality Control in Cross-Cultural Surveys" and "Galton's Problem." In Raoul Naroll and Ronald Cohen, eds. *A Handbook of Method in Cultural Anthropology*. Garden City, NY: Natural History Press, 1970, pp. 927–945, 974–989. Raoul Naroll increased attention to two important issues—data quality and Galton's Problem in cross-cultural research. Although many cross-cultural researchers do not advocate his solutions, it is important to understand how Naroll perceived the problems.

Do Apes Have Language?

Jane H. Hill

Thirty years ago, the answer to the question "Do apes have language?" was obviously "No." Hockett and Ascher, in a famous essay, laid down the terms of "the human revolution": Human language has a unique combination of "design features" that differentiates it from all other animal communication systems.[1] Today, new information about wild and captive great apes suggests to many scientists that the human revolution was not so revolutionary after all. In this chapter I will try to show why most linguists still believe in some version of a "revolution," despite evidence for a capacity for language in great apes. In my review of this evidence I focus on chimpanzees: *Pan troglodytes*, the common chimpanzee, and *Pan paniscus*, the pygmy chimpanzee or bonobo.[2]

The common ancestors of humans and chimpanzees may have lived as recently as five million years ago, and we share about 99 percent of our genetic material.[3] Wild chimpanzees live in complex social groups, make and use simple tools, and communicate through intricate systems (which are by no means completely understood) of sounds, gestures, and other means. These systems exhibit individual variation and local dialects. Young chimpanzees need several years to acquire the range of communicative and other behaviors characteristic of their home group.[4]

Captive chimpanzees have learned to use signs based on American Sign Language, the language of the Deaf community in the United States. Other chimpanzees have learned to use artificially constructed signs. In both cases, the animals use their signs to communicate with one another and with human companions, and come to use novel combinations of these signs.[5] A few chimpanzees have learned signs from conspecifics, without obvious human intervention.[6] This evidence suggests that chimpanzee intellectual potential includes something very much like the human capacity for "language."

The Subsystems of Language

In order to see why the question "Do apes have language?" remains controversial in the face of this exciting new evidence, we must understand that linguists do not consider human "language" to be a single unitary phenomenon. Instead, linguistic knowledge and behavior in humans is the result of the interaction of many different subsystems. While parts of these subsystems are probably learned by children (for instance, they have to learn the words specific to their language), other components are almost certainly part of the genetic makeup of speakers, and emerge during maturation as they are triggered by environmental stimuli. Linguists do not all agree on the most theoretically profitable way to distinguish the major subsystems of human language. Here I will review chimpanzee linguistic accomplishments in terms of five major clusters of systems: (1) pragmatic systems; (2) conceptual systems; (3) phonological systems; (4) syntactic systems; and (5) discourse systems.

Pragmatic Systems

Linguists often separate the linguistic code itself from the encoded messages. These messages come, not simply from the material stuff of the code, but from inferences that listeners must make about speakers' purposes: whether a string of code is intended to question, to command, to promise, to joke, or simply to inform. Pragmatic systems constrain these inferences.

The most fundamental pragmatic inference is that the speaker is a meaning-producing being who is speaking a language. The philosopher Daniel Dennett states that humans, in interpreting the utterances of children, assume an "intentional stance."[7] Consider our interpretive position when a tiny baby cries and grabs for the breast. We do not assume that the crying and grabbing are "about" the breast. Instead, we take them to index the child's inner state, hunger. But when a little child sees an apple and says [bab oo],[8] we take this to be "about" something that is outside the child: the apple. We hear the sequence as a "name," a communicative act dominated by the pragmatic function called "reference." Whether or not apes, like children, can "refer "has been intensely controversial.

Many ape-language researchers feel that the "intentional stance" is the most useful position from which to interpret the utterances of sign-trained chimpanzees, just as it is for early child speech. They argue that when these chimpanzees make a sign glossed APPLE, they "mean" apple in the same sense that we think the child "means" apple. They are using their signs to "refer," even when they want the apple, just as the pragmatic function of reference is technically present when the child wants the apple. This is controversial because many scientists argue that in interpreting animal behavior we should assume the intentional stance only as a last resort, when other interpretations fail.

Why do we assume the intentional stance in interpreting the first words of children? First, while the child who says [bab oo] may be asking for the apple, we know we will soon hear her use this "word" even when she does not want the fruit. We expect her to use this sequence of sounds to designate apples of many shapes and colors (or even to make the mistake of using the sign for pears or pomegranates), and we know that soon she will be able to mention apples even when there are no apples, or pictures of apples, in her presence (so-called "displacement"). Ape language researchers argue that all of these behaviors also appear in chimpanzees, albeit at a lower frequency than in children. For instance, Kanzi, a male bonobo in Sue Savage-Rumbaugh's laboratory, sometimes uses lexigrams (artificial symbols accessible on a computerized board) for food and then turns down the proffered reward. Kanzi began to use the lexigram keyboard without prompting from human trainers (he was present while his mother was being trained). He plays with the lexigram board by himself when no human is present. A second bonobo, Panbanisha, has also shown these behaviors. Chimpanzees have been observed to use ASL signs when alone; Washoe enjoyed naming pictures in magazines and books, and often preferred to do this by herself.[9]

An important argument for the capacity to "refer" in chimpanzees is that they, like the human child, sometimes spontaneously generalize, for instance, signing APPLE for similar fruits. This suggests that their internal state includes a "representation," a mental category "roundish, reddish fruit." Additional strong evidence for such a mental category is that chimpanzees can learn that a category like APPLE can be subsumed under a more inclusive category, FOOD. Sue Savage-Rumbaugh taught two common chimpanzees, Sherman and Austin, to sort food items and simple tools into separate bins. She then taught them lexigrams for these items, and, finally, taught "generic" lexigrams for FOOD and TOOL. Sherman and Austin learned to sort the "specific" lexigrams alone, without any stimulus objects, by lighting up either FOOD or TOOL on their computer display. Savage-Rumbaugh claims that this means that the lexigrams were signs for mental representations: Thus, Sherman and Austin were "referring."[10]

If we take a conservative position, assuming the "intentional stance" toward chimpanzee signing only as a last resort, what other accounts besides "reference" are available? One is that the signs of chimpanzees, like the hunger cry of the human baby, are not "about" anything outside the animals, but are about their interior physiological (not mental) states. In the presence of a stimulus item, the chimpanzee experiences desire for food or play, and learns that making a sign will cause that desire to be satisfied. The sign could be associated with the food or toy as a "paired associate," an automated response instilled by conditioning.

The most famous example of such conditioning is an experiment by the great Russian psychologist, Ivan Pavlov, who trained dogs to salivate at the sound of a bell. Training took the following form: First, whenever a bell was sounded, food was presented to the dogs, who salivated in reaction. Less and less food was presented when the bell was rung, until the food was absent altogether. But the dogs continued to salivate when they heard the bell. Knowing this history, we do not want to claim that the salivation was a "sign" for the bell, or an "answer" to its call.

Imagine a chimpanzee who has repeatedly, over many trials, been shown an apple and asked to make a certain sign that the experimenter thinks of as "the sign APPLE." When the chimpanzee succeeds in making the sign, she is given a reward.[11] This reward "reinforces" the behavior. The reward is gradually withdrawn, but the chimpanzee continues to make the sign when an apple is shown. How is this different from the case of Pavlov's salivating dogs?[12]

Even Savage-Rumbaugh's "sorting" experiment with Sherman and Austin is vulnerable to this criticism. These results were achieved by training in many stages. First, real food and real tools were sorted; then the chimpanzees were taught to match food items, tools, and lexigrams. Then the stimulus objects were gradually withdrawn (photographs of the objects were used in an intermediate stage) until only the lexigrams remained. The "generic" lexigrams were first introduced as labels on the bins that had been used in sorting; after several trials the bins were removed. The possibility thus remains that what happened to Sherman and Austin was a particularly intricate version of Pavlov's classic training regime, and not training in "meaning" or "categorization." However, while remaining cautious, most scholars now believe that the weight of the evidence does support the claim that chimpanzees share with humans the pragmatic capacity for reference, even though instances of "pure" reference may be rarer among chimpanzees than children.

Another important controversy over the "intentional stance" involves repetition. Herbert Terrace and his co-workers found that a very high frequency of the signs and sign sequences used by the chimpanzee Nim were repetitions of signs used by his trainers. They took this to be evidence that Nim was merely "imitating" the trainers, and was not producing signs and sentences of his own.[13] Human children also repeat the utterances of conversational partners, but researchers assign diverse pragmatic functions to these repetitions, of which "imitation" is only one. Adopting the same standards of pragmatic interpretation used by child-language researchers, Patricia Greenfield and Sue Savage-Rumbaugh found examples of many of the same functions in the "repetitive" utterances of both common and pygmy chimpanzees. For instance, they interpreted the following sequence, produced by Kanzi and his caretaker Rose, as "choosing an alternative." The lexigrams are glossed in capital letters. Rose is also speaking English, shown in small letters.

Rose: You can either PLAY or watch TV.
Kanzi: TV (Kanzi watches after Rose turns it on).[14]

Phonological Systems

Phonological systems organize the physical realization of speech. In deaf and hard-of-hearing humans, physical realization is accomplished through gesture (for this reason we can see that the term "phonology," from Greek *phóné* "sound," may now be a misnomer). In hearing people, speech produced through sound begins to dominate from the first year of life. Phonological systems include principles for the timing, types, and sequences of movements of the speech-production organs (diaphragm, lungs, vocal cords, tongue, lips, etc., or, in the deaf and hard-of hearing, the hands).

Chimpanzees share very little of the human anatomical and perceptual substratum for sound production.[15] Chimpanzee hearing is most acute at different frequencies from those where humans hear best. The shape of the chimpanzee oral cavity and the musculature of the tongue make it impossible for them to articulate human consonants. The chimpanzee soft palate cannot be raised to close off the nasal cavity. The relative lack of flexion in the chimpanzee vocal tract, and the high position of the larynx, means that chimpanzees cannot imitate the vowels of human languages. Perhaps most important, chimpanzee sound production is very closely tied to their emotional state, and it is very difficult for them either to suppress sounds, or to produce them on command.[16]

One of the great breakthroughs in the exploration of chimpanzee linguistic capacity occurred when Allen and Beatrix Gardner showed that Washoe, an infant common chimpanzee, could be trained to use gestural signs from American Sign Language.[17] American Sign Language (ASL) as used by humans definitely is constrained by a "phonological" system: The meaningful signs of ASL are made up of meaningless elements, including hand position relative to the body, hand shape, and motion of the hand. Workers with ASL-trained chimpanzees use these standards for scoring sign production, and native ASL speakers can interpret the signs.[18] But the chimpanzees exhibit many deviations from human ASL standards, and it is not clear what principles shape these.

The "lexigrams" used by chimpanzees trained by Savage-Rumbaugh are made up of combinations of a dozen meaningless elements (straight lines, open circles, solid circles, squiggles, etc.), but the algorithm for combining these to construct meaningful elements—any combination of these elements that can be distinguished by chimp vision can occur—is not at all like the constraints on phonological systems in human languages, where certain components are never combined with one another (this is true in both sign and oral languages).

In summary, the systems of communication used by chimpanzees are probably not, strictly speaking, "phonological," even though superficially they may seem to satisfy the criterion of "duality of patterning" (meaningful signs are made up of meaningless components) proposed by Hockett as one of the "revolutionary" design features of human language. This is not trivial, since Philip Lieberman argues cogently that the speed of communication permitted by the phonological substratum in human language (whether spoken or signed) is an important reason why language can be used effectively in reasoning:

Large amounts of information can be packaged within the span of human short-term memory.[19]

Conceptual Systems

Human knowledge includes much that is not encoded through language: It is "unspoken."[20] Conceptual systems specify the categories of human thought and knowledge that can be represented in language, making these accessible to other linguistic systems. Conceptual systems specify the possible propositions about these categories, and the logical relations into which they can figure.

Like humans, chimpanzees know many things. We are concerned here, however, not with knowledge in general, but with "conceptual structure," the principles that sort knowledge so that it is available for "linguistic" purposes. Thus, we restrict ourselves to considering the evidence for chimpanzee conceptual systems that is revealed when they use signs.

Sign-trained chimpanzees can acquire vocabularies of up to at least 168 signs (the number recorded for chimpanzee Moja).[21] However, in comparison even to quite young human children, these sign repertoires are very small. Before age three, human children go through a "vocabulary explosion," going from under one hundred words to over a thousand in a very short period. The large size of the lexicon of a typical three-year-old, let alone an adult human, means that this system must have a complex internal structure; it is unlikely that all of this vocabulary could be acquired and stored if it were organized as a single long list. This internal structure is one aspect of the human conceptual system. The small vocabularies of sign-using chimpanzees, though, may be listlike. Is there any evidence to the contrary?

First, as noted above, chimpanzees often spontaneously extend the meaning of signs to novel cases, evidence for the creation of conceptual categories. Preferred word orders may give evidence for conceptual structure. Kanzi showed a decided preference for sequencing lexigrams for transitive actions like BITE or CARRY before the entity acted upon, with twenty-nine examples of this type compared to six of the reverse order.[22] However, this was also the order preferred by Kanzi's human caregivers, so it may not project an event-entity distinction for Kanzi himself, given the small number of signs involved. ASL-using chimpanzees apparently respond to questions as if their signs were organized in conceptual categories. For instance, they respond to WHO questions with names of persons and chimpanzees, and to WHERE questions with signs like HOME or OUT.[23] Chim-

panzees can sort objects for color, number, shape, and other attributes.[24]

An ingenious alternative account has been proposed for one famous case of sorting: Savage-Rumbaugh 's claim that Sherman and Austin were able to sort lexigrams into abstract conceptual categories (FOODS and TOOLS). Robert Epstein suggests that Sherman and Austin depended on food-related physiological responses (transferred in training from the literal foods to the lexigrams for them) to correctly sort "foods" from "tools." Most of the mistakes they made in sorting tools on early trials involved assigning tools that were used in food preparation, like pans, juicers, and knives to the FOOD category (Sherman and Austin were even accustomed to licking some of these items). This pattern of errors is accounted for neatly by Epstein's conjecture.[25] However, this "physiological" account is not available for many other kinds of chimpanzee sorting behavior, or for vocabulary generalizations that do not involve food items.

In summary, the evidence thus far suggests that chimpanzee "conceptual structure" may overlap at least partially with that of humans. Chimpanzee fluency with signs offers an opportunity to explore concepts that chimpanzees form by themselves, rather than to train chimpanzees in concepts provided by humans. For instance, we could see Sherman and Austin's early category "food and tools used to prepare food" not as a deviation from a human category, but as evidence for a concept in chimpanzee intelligence, suggesting, for instance, that "termites" and "termiting sticks" may go together for wild chimpanzees in a way that they do not for humans.

Syntactic Systems

Syntactic systems restrict the possible meaningful combinations of the elements of the linguistic code (most linguists distinguish morphology, the principles for the formation of words from smaller elements, from syntax, but morphology is not relevant for our purposes here). Thus, in English, "Jane raised Eric" has a different meaning from "Eric raised Jane." Syntactic systems are the reason why, if someone says, "The boys knew that the girls thought a lot of one another," he means that the girls liked other girls, not the boys. Some syntactic constraints yield distinctions that seem quite arbitrary: We can ask, "What are you eating with?" but not "What are you eating and?"[26]

In the early years of modern syntax linguists often spoke of syntactic "rules," a way of thinking about these systems that was a carryover from traditional grammar. Many linguists now no longer speak of "rules" (except loosely), preferring to think of syntactic systems as a set of "principles" that limit the kinds of combinations of elements that are meaningful.

Most linguists feel very confident in drawing a sharp qualitative line between the syntactic systems of human languages and the combinations of elements seen in chimpanzee signing. As with vocabulary, human children seem to cross some sort of great syntactic divide before they are three years old. In the earliest stages of acquisition, human children utter only one word at a time. Then, for a few months, they make two-word combinations. Some time before they are three years old, they suddenly begin to produce long and complex utterances.[27] Instead of "No night-night!" we hear, "Harold no wanna go night night now!" By age three children control a wide range of construction types, and the difference between the syntactic abilities of a six-year-old and those of an adult is subtle indeed.

Sometimes the relationship between syntactic constraints and spoken utterances is rather subtle. For instance, consider one theory about the constraints that yield meaningful word order. Human-language sentences are made up of phrases. The structure of each phrase includes a "head" and a "complement." The major lexical categories—nouns, verbs, prepositions, and adjectives—can function as heads of phrases. Human languages seem to come in two types: "head-final" languages, where heads follow their complements (like Japanese) and "head-initial" languages, where heads precede their complements (like English) . A second important underlying principle is that every noun must have an abstract property known as "case." Verbs and prepositions can assign case—but only to nouns that are in their phrases, not to other nouns. In English, the result of the interaction of the principle "heads are initial" with the principle "nouns must have case" is that a noun that follows a verb is understood as the object of that verb. In Latin, the case requirement is satisfied by case "inflections," markers on the nouns themselves. Therefore, in Latin an object need not be adjacent to the verb, and so-called "free word order" is permitted.

Many scholars think that Greenfield and Savage-Rumbaugh's analysis of word order patterns produced by the bonobo Kanzi provides the strongest evidence for syntactic competence in chimpanzees. While workers with chimpanzees who use ASL have reported many sign combinations used by these animals, only in the case of Kanzi has a complete record been published. By the time Kanzi was five-and-a-half years old, analysis of his two lexigram sequences

showed that he had acquired from his trainers a preference for the order "action-object," as in BITE BALL. He had also invented two new preferences (which the researchers call "rules"). The first is "place gesture after lexigram," as in CHASE (gesture toward dog), where the dog is supposed to chase Kanzi. The second is "order expressions for action in the order in which they will be performed, " as in CHASE HIDE and HUG BITE.[28]

Are these preferences syntax? One problem is that Kanzi's order preferences are statistical, not categorical. Human syntactic word order, except in the very earliest stages of language acquisition, is notoriously not a quantitative matter. "Kanzi bite" is one English sentence; "bite Kanzi" is another. (In the early stages of child language, we do see order variation; researchers interpret this to mean that the children are not yet sure whether their language is of the "head-final" or "head-initial" type.)

A more serious problem for a "syntactic" interpretation is the incorporation of gestures into Kanzi's combinations. The gestures that Kanzi uses are like those used by wild chimpanzees. Laura Pettito, studying two deaf children learning sign language, found that they had trouble learning how to use the ASL words for "me" and "you," even though the signs (pointing to self and pointing to addressee, respectively) are not arbitrary, and even though the children had been using pointing gestures for several months prior to the emergence of "real words." Her results suggest that prelinguistic gesturing by human children (which is probably evolutionarily related to gesturing by chimpanzees) is "discontinuous" with both verbal language and the linguistic gestures of ASL.[29]

Lois Bloom's work also suggests that Kanzi's gestures are not "linguistic" and so should not be part of a syntactic analysis. Bloom analyzed videotapes of thirty children who had just begun to use words. The analysis showed that the frequency of expressions of emotion (or "affect") exhibited a "dip" before a child said a word, and rose to a peak immediately after the word. This is Bloom's interpretation:

> We are interpreting the dip before the word as the time during which the mental activity associated with the experience and expression of emotion is, essentially, suspended. This is the time the child uses for the cognitive work that saying a word involves. . . . The peak in affect expression comes after having said the word, when the child's cognitive resources are now free once again for constructing the representations associated with feeling states.[30]

The order of Kanzi's gestures, which are probably part of the chimpanzee system with its "emotional" foundation, in relation to his lexigrams can be accounted for in Bloom's terms. Kanzi's "emotional "gestures follow his lexigrams because at that point his" cognitive resources are . . . free once again" for emotional expression. This is not a "syntactic" principle of word order, but instead exemplifies a different kind of constraint on human capacities, the kind that make it difficult for people to pat their heads and rub their stomachs at the same time.

Bickerton (1990) has suggested that we credit chimpanzees with "protolanguage," the system seen in one-and two-word stages of child language. For Bickerton, "protolanguage" is based on principles that are discontinuous with those that appear during the "syntax explosion" that emerges in the child between two and three years of age. Whatever the nature of this change, there is no evidence that chimpanzees, at any age, can be trained to go through it.

Discourse Systems

Finally, discourse systems organize our utterances into sequences and distinguish different types of sequences: lists from stories, call-and-response from conversation. Discourse systems organize the strategies of "economy" that allow us to summarize what has already been said ("Amy likes chocolate mint ice cream. So does Jane.") and the strategies of "iconicity" that sometimes seem to make sentences look like small diagrams of the world ("Ken has to change planes in Chicago and New York on the way to London," a sentence that names the cities in west-to-east order, is preferred to "Ken has to change planes in New York and Chicago on the way to London.").

Chimpanzee "discourse" is organized according to a few simple principles. Chimpanzees do not make lists, or tell narratives, or construct arguments. They can chain signs together to intensify requests, as in the sequence YOU ME SWEET DRINK GIMME,[31] and use repetition in many functions; my personal favorite is chimpanzee Tatu's ICE CREAM, ICE CREAM, ICE CREAM, ICE CREAM, ICE CREAM, ICE CREAM.[32] Greenfield and Savage-Rumbaugh suggest that chimpanzees observe an important discourse principle, the "strategy of economy": not mentioning what is unchanged in a situation, while mentioning what is new or changed."[33] Kanzi's preference to "order expressions for action in the order in which they will be performed" may exemplify the discourse strategy of iconicity, not syntax in the strict sense.

Conclusion

Many chimpanzee researchers believe that skepticism about their claims comes from ideological bias, the unquestioned assumption of human superiority. Such an assumption is unwarranted. Human language is not necessarily "superior." It is highly specialized, a bit like echolocation in bats and dolphins, or locomotion by brachiation in gibbons. From this specialization comes experiences that we humans value, like the pleasures of complex reasoning, poetic rhythm, stirring oratory, and good detective stories. But the role of language in whatever our success as a species may be is not obvious.[34]

Has research with chimpanzees shown that "apes have language"? My own answer is, "Some apes seem to share with humans some parts of some subsystems that play a role in human language." If researchers can show that this sharing is at the level of deep principle, not superficial resemblance, then we will have identified a component of our common evolutionary heritage, and will have greatly refined our understanding of what happened in "the human revolution."

Notes

1. Charles F. Hockett and Robert Ascher, "The Human Revolution," *Current Anthropology* 5 (1964): 135–168.
2. For work on gorillas, see F. Patterson, J. Tanner, and N. Mayer, "Pragmatic Analysis of Gorilla Utterances," *Journal of Pragmatics* 12 (1988): 35–54; and Juan Carlos Gomez, "The Emergence of Intentional Communication as a Problem-Solving Strategy in the Gorilla," in Sue Taylor Parker and Kathleen Rita Gibson, eds., *"Language" and Intelligence in Monkeys and Apes* (Cambridge: Cambridge University Press, 1988), pp. 333–355. For orangutans, see H. Lyn White Miles, "The Cognitive Foundations for Reference in a Signing Orangutan," in Parker and Gibson, eds., *"Language" and Intelligence in Monkeys and Apes*, pp. 511–539.
3. Mary-Claire King and A. C. Wilson, "Evolution at Two Levels in Humans and Chimpanzees," *Science* 188 (1975): 107–115.
4. Christophe Boesch and Hedwige Boesch, "Tool Use and Tool Making in Wild Chimpanzees," *Folia Primatologica* 54 (1990): 86–99; Jane Goodall, The Chimpanzees of Gombe (Cambridge, MA: The Belknap Press of Harvard University Press, 1986); Michael Tomasello, Barbara L. George, Ann Cale Kruger, Michael Jeffrey Farrar, and Andrea Evans, "The Development of Gestural Communication in Young Chimpanzees," *Journal of Human Evolution* 14 (1985): 175–186.

5. Researchers using American Sign Language signs have attempted to approximate the normal conditions for language acquisition in the child by assuming the role of "foster family" to infant chimpanzees: See R. Allen Gardner and Beatrix T. Gardner, "A Cross-Fostering Laboratory," in R. Allen Gardner, Beatrix T. Gardner, and Thomas E. Van Cantfort, eds., *Teaching Sign Language to Chimpanzees* (Albany, NY: State University of New York Press, 1989), pp. 1–28. Researchers using artificial signs have generally used operant-conditioning methods: See E. Sue Savage-Rumbaugh, *Ape Language: From Conditioned Response to Symbol* (New York: Columbia University Press, 1986). I do not undertake here a systematic review of the chimpanzee language experiments. I reviewed the first generation of work in Jane H. Hill, "Apes and Language," *Annual Review of Anthropology* 7 (1978): 89–112. For a good overview of the critical literature, see Joel Wallman, *Aping Language* (Cambridge: Cambridge University Press, 1992). One of the leading sign-language laboratories issues a quarterly newsletter intended for nonprofessional audiences, with many pictures and updates on research; information can be obtained from Friends of Washoe, Central Washington University, Ellensburg, WA 98926.

6. Roger S. Fouts, Deborah H. Fouts, and Thomas E. Van Cantfort, "The Infant Loulis Learns Signs from Cross-Fostered Chimpanzees," in Gardner, Gardner, and Van Cantfort, eds., *Teaching Sign Language to Chimpanzees*, pp. 280–292; Deborah H. Fouts, "Signing Interactions between Mother and Infant Chimpanzees," in Paul G. Heltne and Linda A. Marquardt, eds., *Understanding Chimpanzees* (Cambridge, MA: Harvard University Press, 1989), pp. 242–252.

7. Daniel Dennett, *The Intentional Stance* (Cambridge, MA: MIT Press/Bradford Books, 1987).

8. This is how my first child pronounced "apple." The vowel in the first syllable [a] should sound like the vowel in "cap." The vowel in the second syllable [oo] sounds like the vowel in "put."

9. See Roger S. Fouts and Deborah H. Fouts, "Loulis in Conversation with the Cross-Fostered Chimpanzees," in Gardner, Gardner, and Van Cantfort, eds., *Teaching Sign Language to Chimpanzees*, pp. 293–307; R. Allen Gardner and Beatrix T. Gardner, "A Cross-Fostering Laboratory," in Gardner, Gardner, and Van Cantfort, eds., *Teaching Sign Language to Chimpanzees*, pp. 1–28; E. Sue Savage-Rumbaugh, "Language Learning in the Bonobo: How and Why They Learn, "in Norman A. Krasnegor, Duane M. Rumbaugh, Richard L. Schiefelbusch, and Michael Studdert-Kennedy, eds., *Biological and Behavioral Determinants of Language Development* (Hillsdale, NJ: Lawrence Erlbaum Associates, 1991), pp. 209–234. Workers in Irene Pepperberg's laboratory reported this type of "private speech" from an African Grey parrot, Alex, who can say English words: Irene M. Pepperberg, Katherine J. Brese, and Barbara J. Harris, "Solitary Sound Play during Acquisition of English Vocalizations by an African Grey Parrot (*Psittacus erithacus*): Possible Parallels with Children's Monologue Speech," *Applied Psycholinguistics* 12 (1991): 151–178.

10. Savage-Rumbaugh, *Ape Language*.

11. I leave aside here the possibility that the trainer unconsciously "cues" the animal to make the correct sign.

12. Great importance was placed on the fact that the signs used by chimpanzees are "arbitrary": No property of the sign itself, only the decision of the researcher, determines what a sign means. However, arbitrary relationships have long been demonstrated in research with animals; animals like pigeons can easily learn to press a black button for seed, and a white button for water.

13. Herbert S. Terrace, Laura A. Pettito, Richard J. Sanders, and Thomas G. Bever, "Can an Ape Create a Sentence?" *Science* 206 (1979): 891–902.

14. Patricia M. Greenfield and E. Sue Savage-Rumbaugh, "Comparing Communicative Competence in Child and Chimp: The Pragmatics of Repetition," *Journal of Child Language* 20 (1993): 1–26.

15. Apes can apparently understand a good deal of spoken language, which suggests that the neurological and aural substratum is to some degree "preadapted" for human-style speech. Hopkins and Rumbaugh suggest that Kanzi, who has produced several vocalization types otherwise unattested in bonobos, may even be imitating human intonation: William D. Hopkins and E. Sue Savage-Rumbaugh, "Vocal Communication as a Function of Differential Rearing Experiences in Pan paniscus: A Preliminary Report," *International Journal of Primatology* 12 (1991): 559–583. (I thank Irene Pepperberg for calling my attention to this reference).

16. Linda E. Duchin, "The Evolution of Articulate Speech: Comparative Anatomy of the Oral Cavity in *Pan* and *Homo*," *Journal of Human Evolution* 19 (1990): 687–697; R. Allen Gardner, Beatrix T. Gardner, and Patrick Drumm, "Voiced and Signed Responses of Cross-Fostered Chimpanzees," in Gardner, Gardner, and Van Cantfort, eds., *Teaching Sign Language to Chimpanzees*, pp. 29–54; Goodall, The Chimpanzees of Gombe; Shozo Kojima, "Comparison of Auditory Functions in the Chimpanzee and Human," *Folia Primatologica* 55 (1990): 62–72; Philip Lieberman, *The Biology and Evolution of Language* (Cambridge, MA: Harvard University Press, 1984).

17. R. Allen Gardner and Beatrix T. Gardner, "Teaching Sign Language to a Chimpanzee," *Science* 165 (1969): 664–672.

18. Deborah H. Fouts, "Signing Interactions between Mother and Infant Chimpanzees," in Heltne and

Marquardt, eds., *Understanding Chimpanzees*, pp. 242–252; Beatrix T. Gardner, R. Allen Gardner, and Susan G. Nichols, "The Shapes and Uses of Signs in a Cross-Fostering Laboratory," in Gardner, Gardner, and Van Cantfort, eds., *Teaching Sign Language to Chimpanzees*, pp. 55–180.

19. Charles F. Hockett and Robert Ascher, "The Human Revolution," *Current Anthropology* 5 (1964): 135–168; Philip Lieberman, *The Biology and Evolution of Language*.

20. Here is a useful experiment that reveals "unspoken" knowledge. If you play a musical instrument well, or are good at some athletic endeavor (e.g., gymnastics or sprinting), try to explain your skill to someone else. Use only words: No demonstrations or touching the other person is permitted in the experiment!

21. Gardner, Gardner, and Nichols, "The Shapes and Uses of Signs in a Cross-Fostering Laboratory."

22. Patricia M. Greenfield and E. Sue Savage-Rumbaugh, "Grammatical Combinations in *Pan paniscus*: Processes of Learning and Invention in the Evolution and Development of Language," in Parker and Gibson, eds., *"Language" and Intelligence in Monkeys and Apes*, pp. 540–578.

23. Thomas E. Van Cantfort, Beatrix T. Gardner, and R. Allen Gardner, "Developmental Trends in Replies to Why Questions by Children and Chimpanzees," in Gardner, Gardner, and Van Cantfort, eds., *Teaching Sign Language to Chimpanzees*, pp. 198–239.

24. Tetsuro Matsuzawa, "Spontaneous Sorting in Human and Chimpanzee," in Parker and Gibson, eds., *"Language" and Intelligence in Monkeys and Apes*, pp. 451–568.

25. Robert Epstein, "'Representation' in the Chimpanzee," *Psychological Reports* 50 (1982): 745–746, cited in Joel Wallman, *Aping Language*, pp. 73–74.

26. Linguists use the asterisk or "star" (*) to mark sentences that are not syntactically well-formed (this is different from the kind of "ungrammaticality" people have in mind when they tell you not to use double negatives or say "ain't").

27. In expressing these stages in terms of "number of words" we are biasing our account toward kinds of human languages that have relatively short and simple words, like English. In languages like Eskimo or Mohawk, where words are as long and complex as sentences are in English, the "one-word" stage is often a "one-syllable" stage, and in the "two-word" stage the earliest complex words (words made up of multiple meaningful parts) appear.

28. Greenfield and Savage-Rumbaugh, "Grammatical Combination in *Pan paniscus*: Processes of Learning and Invention in the Evolution and Development of Language" and "Imitation, Grammatical Development, and the Invention of Proto-Grammar by an Ape," in Krasnegor, Rumbaugh, Schiefelbusch, and Studdert-Kennedy, eds., *Biological and Behavioral Determinants of Language Development*, pp. 235–258.

29. Laura A. Pettito, "On the Autonomy of Language and Gesture: Evidence from the Acquisition of Personal Pronouns in American Sign Language," *Cognition* 27 (1987): 1–52.

30. Lois Bloom, "Representation and Expression," in Krasnegor, Rumbaugh, Schiefelbusch, and Studdert-Kennedy, eds., *Biological and Behavioral Determinants of Language Development*, pp. 117–140.

31. Savage-Rumbaugh, *Ape Language: From Conditioned Response to Symbol*, p. 27.

32. Beatrix T. Gardner and R. Allen Gardner, "Cross-Fostered Chimpanzees II: Modulation of Meaning," in Heltne and Marquardt, eds., *Understanding Chimpanzees*, p. 240.

33. Patricia M. Greenfield and E. Sue Savage-Rumbaugh, "Perceived Variability and Symbol Use: A Common Language-Cognition Interface in Children and Chimpanzees (Pan troglodytes)," *Journal of Comparative Psychology* 98 (1984): 201–218.

34. For a review of possible adaptive functions of language, see Steven Pinker and Paul Bloom, "Natural Language and Natural Selection," *Behavioral and Brain Sciences* 13 (1990): 707–784. One aspect of human adaptation is, unfortunately, all too obvious: Human cultural strategies, especially the use of chimpanzees in medical research, endanger chimpanzees as a species: See Geza Teleki, "Population Status of Wild Chimpanzees (*Pan troglodytes*) and Threats to Survival," in Heltne and Marquardt, eds., *Understanding Chimpanzees*, pp. 312–353.

Suggested Readings

Bickerton, Derek. *Language and Species*. Chicago: University of Chicago Press, 1991. An exceptionally clear presentation of syntactic theory in relation to ape and child linguistic competencies.

Gardner, R. Allen, Beatrix T. Gardner, and Thomas E. Van Cantfort, eds. *Teaching Sign Language to Chimpanzees*. Albany, NY: State University of New York Press, 1989. Summarizes twenty years of research on teaching signs from American Sign Language to chimpanzees.

Hill, Jane H. "Apes and Language." *Annual Review of Anthropology* 7 (1978): 89–112. A brief overview of the first fifteen years of ape-language research.

Lieberman, Philip. *The Biology and Evolution of Language*. Cambridge, MA: Harvard University Press, 1984. A major summary statement by a leading researcher on the evidence for language in fossil humans; especially strong on chimpanzee anatomy.

Savage-Rumbaugh, E. Sue. *Ape Language: From Conditioned Response to Symbol*. New York: Columbia University Press, 1986. Reviews the history of research using artificial lexigrams, with clear presentation of methods.

Wallman, Joel. *Aping Language*. Cambridge: Cambridge University Press, 1992. This is the best summary of the criticisms of ape-language research.

Han: Pastoralists and Farmers on a Chinese Frontier

Burton Pasternak

There developed a perpetual antagonism, which demanded a decisive choice of every people and state that in the course of history overlapped the Great Wall Frontier, whether its founders were Chinese or non-Chinese—the choice between agriculture of a notably intensive form and nomadism of an especially dispersed form. Of the repeated attempts to create societies or states that could integrate both orders not one succeeded.[1]

When Han farmers first crossed the Great Wall in search of a better life, they found a setting where the climate was unmerciful, the land unyielding, and the local inhabitants unfriendly. Many eventually gave up and went home; only those prepared to alter their behavior were able to remain. This chapter is about their adjustment on the grasslands, and about their response to a government which has, especially in recent years, taken strong measures to shape their lives. It is about how tradition, politics, and economy have interacted to define life on the Inner Mongolian frontier.

Whether they speak Mandarin or some other dialect, Han have a common history and tradition. They use the same written language, and share many goals and values. Their way of life is rooted in intensive farming. They transfer population pressure to land, applying ever more labor and attention to squeeze marginal increments out of limited space. Male-headed extended families (consisting of two or more married couples) provide the workers.

The history of Han expansion testifies to the success of their adaptation. But there have been limits, areas inhospitable to their way. It was at just such a frontier that they drew a line of stone, a Great Wall, to mark the end of the "civilized" world. It was a frontier beyond which they could not long survive as Han, or at least that is what many believed.

The Chinese state endorsed an ideology that encouraged homogeneity. Pressures to sameness increased in post-1949 China, as the communist state extended its apparatus downward to influence and control all aspects of life. Never before had government so controlled where people lived, where they worked, what they might grow, what they could eat or buy, when they could marry, and even when and how many children they might have. People took their place in a hierarchy of groups. Throughout the country children learned Mandarin in school. Collectivization provided a common framework for the deployment of land and labor. By eliminating private property, regulating marriage, and stimulating class struggle within families, the state attempted to redirect orientations from family and locality to nation. Differences of wealth, life-style, and opportunity narrowed. People married, formed families, and even bore children in increasingly similar ways.

But older themes played on, along with their variations. In so vast and varied a country, with its multitude of climates, topographies, crops, and cultures, it could not have been otherwise. With the recent collapse of communes and restoration of family-based production, the potential for variation has increased.

We focus on Han adjustment on the Inner Mongolian frontier, but we are also interested in changes underway in rural China as it shifts from a socialist to a market economy. The world watches as the Chinese try another tack, and there is much at stake. If their efforts are successful, an elusive prosperity may come to China, and provide a model for others to modify and use. If the attempt fails, we may witness yet another monumental upheaval in China.

Our study is based on fieldwork in four communities conducted in collaboration with Janet Salaff, a sociologist at the University of Toronto, and Chinese colleagues from the Institute of Sociology at Peking University.[2] During the summers of 1988 and 1990, we crossed into northeastern Inner Mongolia. We visited two communities of people whose recent ancestors settled where they could use hoes, plows drawn by draft animals, and other familiar north Chinese tools and techniques. We then crossed the Great Chingan mountains to the west, entering vast grasslands that run to Outer Mongolia and Siberia, where we chose to study two communities of Han herdsmen. It is there that the homogenizing power of the Chinese state confronts a special challenge.

Did Han there become, over time, more like their Mongol neighbors than like Han who tilled fields at the fringes of the grassland? Or were pressures to uniformity so powerful that they overwhelmed differences of ethnicity and ecology? Our work will show how ecology and technology create diversity in China, how the nature of labor influences family formation and relations within families. It did so during the collective era and before, and now as the economy decentralizes and moves toward a market economy, we can expect even more varied local responses.

Farming and herding differ in fundamental ways. The nature of crucial resources and the timing and places of work determine the tasks assigned to women and men of different ages and influence the family structure and reproduction. Farmers can only work harder because they depend on an essentially unexpandable resource—land. Labor is intensive, but not uniform. Each phase of the farming cycle—preparation, planting, maintenance, harvest—calls for a special kind of effort, and there are marked peaks and troughs in demand. By farming near home, women can work alongside men, doing much the same tasks while still managing domestic chores.

The situation is different for pastoralists. Herds and flocks are expandable, and their managers may obtain great rewards. With sufficient grassland they can enlarge and diversify livestock, even cut hay for sale. The routine is more continuous and repetitive. Grazing, cutting hay, and most other pastoral work take place some distance from home. Women cannot do such work and at the same time milk the cows and run the household. The division of labor is thus sharper.

The ideal herdsman is an adult male. Strength and experience are important. Mistakes can menace generations of animals; therefore, youngsters contribute less than they do among the farmers, while old people have more to offer and remain self sufficient longer. An elderly couple would have a hard time plowing, building mounds, or harvesting on their own, so at about age sixty-five farmers gradually retire. They do not become idle even then. Old women free younger ones for work outside by looking after home and grandchildren. The elderly of both sexes lend a hand in the fields and process harvested crops when labor is badly needed.

Farming and herding differently shape family structure, the relationships of women and men and their access to education, the ages at which people marry and bear children, and even the number of children they have. The contrasts predate the commune and have outlasted it. Collectivization changed the way property and labor were used, and the state extended its control deeper, but differences rooted in ecology and technology have always precluded uniformity. We will explore these linkages in greater detail, tracing continuities and discontinuities. At the same time we will try to get some feel for important changes now taking place in rural China.

From Commune to Family Responsibility

After long discouraging private enterprise, the Chinese began to dismantle rural collectives in 1979. Communes had promised economic security and increased productivity through economies of scale, mechanization, and the deployment of mass labor. They promised to improve livelihoods and promote equality. But equality and production were in tension; the system designed to reduce disparities ultimately hampered development.

Collective life diluted risk, providing some protection against failure. But there was little incentive for hard work since everyone shared earnings. The disjointing of effort and reward weakened commitment. Large scale management was especially problematic in the herding area. When responsibility shifted from worker to worker, weakening the identification herdsmen had with particular animals, attention flagged and losses were considerable.

In the region we studied, abandonment of communes was complete by 1983. To encourage production with minimal state investment, the government now allocates land to individual families, encouraging them to adopt new ways to increase income. This change has brought increased activity and higher rural incomes, along with some negative changes. There is evidence that education, health care, and welfare, previously collective responsibilities, have weakened. There are questions about whether, as they move toward a market economy, the Chinese will be able to reconcile their longstanding commitment to equality with their desire for increased production. Under the family "responsibility system" the collective slogan "everyone eating out of the same big pot," has given way to "some will get rich first." Emerging differences within and between communities arouse tension.

Production could decline as land divides into plots too small to support machines. Fragmentation could also disturb an already precarious balance between people and land. Reports suggest that the unleashing of "get rich quick" attitudes and uncertainties about the duration of family responsibility contracts are encouraging people to despoil land and water for immediate profits. Farmers cultivate fragile hillsides without returning nutrients. Herdsmen think only of animal numbers, disregarding the effects on pasture. With the abandonment of communes, it is hard to restrain these depredations or mobilize to improve the environment.

There are also questions about how these changes will affect women. In some places low labor productivity draws men to new opportunities elsewhere, leaving women, the old, and the young behind to work the land. Will the burdens of women now expand to include new and greater obligations, including those associated with handicrafts, husbandry, or other ventures additional to farming and family reproduction? Our four communities provide windows through which to explore these issues.

The Setting

Inner Mongolia provides an exceptional setting in which to explore the way ecology shapes labor and, through it, marriage and family structure. We compare two modes of production, pastoralism and cultivation, each with subvariants—pure farming versus mixed cultivation—dairying, limited versus extensive pastoralism. Our laboratory, Hulunbuir League in northeastern Inner Mongolia, borders Heilongjiang province to the east, the (former) Soviet Union to the northeast, and Mongolia to the northwest. To the north, in the foothills of the Great Chingan range, is an area rich in minerals and forest. East of the mountains people farm (mainly maize, soybeans, wheat, potatoes, and sugar beets), or combine cultivation with limited dairying. Lush grasslands west of the mountains support sedentary and nomadic pastoralism (cattle and sheep).

Seasons are extreme, the winters cold and long, summers cool and short. In January the temperature dips to −7.6 degrees Fahrenheit (−22 degrees Celsius) in the cultivating area and −18.4 degrees Fahrenheit (−28 degrees Celsius) on the grasslands. Because the frost-free period is less than 135 days, farmers produce only one crop. Large scale cutting during the first half of this century left few trees; the loss has permitted erosion in the cultivating regions and threatens desertification on the grasslands.

Seasonal wind storms sweep through. Soils are sandy. Nature is capricious, periodically providing either too much or too little rain. Rivers and streams flood, destroying crops and eroding farmland.

The climate is a problem for herdsmen as well. Sudden changes can dramatically reduce animal numbers, denying their future contributions as well. Most dangerous are "white disasters," heavy or early snowstorms that threaten lambs and prevent sheep from pawing to grasses beneath. Then there are "black disasters," when snowfall is so light that there is little water for the animals and grasses are poor.

Inner Mongolia is one of China's poorest regions. In 1989 income per capita was only 478 RMB, compared to 602 RMB in rural China generally.[3] It was in part because of this that families in all of the sites we visited welcomed the shift to family production. Income has risen in recent years, but much of the region continues to be remote, undeveloped, and sparsely populated.

Although the 1990 census of Inner Mongolia indicated a large ethnic minority population, most of whom are Mongols, we focus on the Han. Their number has increased steadily to 80.6 percent of the population, 83.4 percent in Hulunbuir League. Centuries of cultural and political separation have left a legacy of ill will. A massive intrusion of Han after the turn of this century, and the associated displacement of pastoral peoples, magnified the problem. Conversion of grassland into farms in the earlier settled south ruined traditional grazing lands, prompting a pastoral retreat. Heavy-handed attempts to create a Chinese version of socialist uniformity during the Cultural Revolution brought the problem to a head, and distrust remains on both sides.

Doing Fieldwork in Inner Mongolia

Since 1979 the Chinese have permitted a limited number of foreigners to conduct local studies. There is an enduring distrust of foreigners in China, and to complicate matters we were working in a border region, where local sensitivities were particularly intense. Our colleagues from Beijing were concerned, especially during our second visit shortly after the Tiananmen massacre in 1989, about ongoing changes in China's distant heartland that might later color the political correctness of our visit.

If our hosts had to come to terms with our presence, we had to adjust as well. The pastoral sites were reminiscent of the early North American frontier. Problems of water, sanitation, climate, and isolation pose formidable challenges. They call for adjustments on the part of the local inhabitants as well as ourselves.

Water was one problem, both too much and too little of it. There are no pipes or sewers. Earthen roads are muddy and, during the rainy season, many impassible. Paradoxically, water is also a precious commodity, particularly on the open grassland. In Great Pasture Town, one of our sites, water is carted from a central well and stored in large jars that are all too quickly emptied. Bathing is episodic, a big treat from a small pan. We also had to contend constantly with the fine, windblown earth that covered everything, including our computers.

Conveniences everywhere were simple or absent. In the towns, we made use of all too frequently overwhelmed public outhouses and backyard pits. On the open grassland there were no designated latrines at all. For Mongols it is no problem, they simply squat under their long robes. But for trousered visitors it is more complicated on unobstructed plain, lacking rock or tree, where one can see for miles.

On the grassland, *yurt* encampments are far apart. We split up and moved about by tractor, sometimes by horse-drawn cart. We consumed large quantities of milk-tea, wine, dried sheep's milk cheese, mutton fat, and noodles during our stay on the grassland. Eating the Mongol way took some getting used to. Meat is boiled in a large pot, after which pieces, especially the choice fatty parts, are pressed on guests. The parts are quite recognizable—rib cage, lower jaw, etc. In the farming villages, we had water and a more varied diet, including vegetables. On arrival in Middle Village, in our honor, a dog was killed for us to eat. That took some getting used to, especially since we had seen someone blow-torch its fur. It was disconcerting to see one of the cadres (administrative workers) assigned to manage our visit removing the caps of beer bottles with the pistol he carried "to defend us."

For local officials, hosting outsiders in an uncertain political climate introduced an element of troublesome unpredictability. The Soviet border was only an hour away. Who would be responsible if the Russians chose to assassinate us to create a rift? We were not there to study Han-Mongol relations, but what might we say about them later? Would we portray local folk as backward? What if we wrote uncomplimentary things, or published controversial materials or pictures? What if unsuspecting townsfolk revealed aspects of local life, or of recent history, that might upset officialdom above? Our second visits were at a time of even greater uncertainty. The wrenching disintegration of socialist states, including Mongolia just across the border, ethnic tensions in Tibet and the Soviet Union, and events in Tiananmen Square combined to deepen sensitivities.

I can convey some sense of this by describing an event that took place during our first days at one site. We believed our way had already been prepared, but during a welcome dinner provided by the local leadership we learned otherwise. Our host, called from the room, returned ashen faced and soon conveyed the reason for his somber mood to one of our Chinese colleagues. When, after dinner, our Chinese colleagues conferred without us, we anticipated a storm.

Clearances for our project should have passed down through three chains of command—government, Communist party, and security. The security clearance had gotten stuck somewhere. We had been walking about talking to people for two days without clearance! Local officials suggested we return to the League capital on the next train. It took some doing to persuade them to let us send a Chinese colleague to clear the administrative block. We were allowed twenty-four hours to resolve the matter, during which we foreigners would confine ourselves to our rooms.

After the matter was worked out, our embarrassed hosts reminded us that the Soviet border was only an hour away, and that the region is normally closed to foreigners. They assured us that even if a local person should go fishing along the Russian border and come back empty handed, there would be many questions to answer. We were foreigners wandering without notice into the local middle school and other places. We were taking photographs of homes, including some rather picturesque (in their view shabby) Russian homes, which might create the "wrong impression." We were far from Beijing, and news reached here slowly. It was not easy to know which way the winds were blowing at any particular time. Better that we limit our conversations and visits to persons and places agreed on in advance. Sensitive issues having to do with the Cultural Revolution, family planning, Han-Mongol relations, or corruption had to be avoided so as not to threaten our local hosts or our

Chinese colleagues. Were we to write something unacceptable they would answer for it.

As a result, even where local people were eager to cooperate, it was not always possible to pursue issues our colleagues viewed as politically sensitive. Some people were eager to talk about birth control policies, but the simplest questions on these matters reminded our colleagues of American criticisms of their one child per family policy, so we had to pursue this topic in the most indirect fashion. We also had to stay clear of factional struggles and ethnic disputes, and deal with the manipulations of particular individuals. At one site, a young Mongol cadre new on the job suggested that his older colleagues might be harboring an American spy. To his mind I had all the requisites—a miniature radio, a computer, and a camera. It took a while and a few drinking bouts to ease his suspicions.

The restrictions, naturally frustrating, became less burdensome as time passed. At first, we were not to take pictures or casually visit people and, for our safety's sake (and theirs), we were not to swim in the river or ride horses. We were reminded not to cross certain bridges into townships for which we had no clearance. But once our presence was accepted and no longer a novelty, we wandered, visited, and photographed somewhat more freely.

Frontier Farmers

Tranquillity Village and Middle Village provide a baseline against which to measure changes that occurred when Han moved into areas less hospitable to cultivation. They were settled by parents or grandparents of the people we met, who came from impoverished regions across the line of stone to scratch some sort of living out of the dry, sandy earth. Life was hard, even during the era of collectives. As before, the commune depended heavily on the labor of everyone. But the scale of operation created serious problems here and in the pastoral communes. The collective consciousness that endless political campaigns had tried to evoke proved hard to sustain. Some people, content to live on collective allotments and vegetables grown on small private garden plots, put few hours and little energy into collective fields. Others had to work harder simply to maintain output and work-point value. Low productivity meant low work-point value, so even with hard work there was little difference between what top and bottom earners brought home.

Families no longer owned land or major implements, but the number of family workers still governed income. Families with several men earned most because cadres reserved the best-paying jobs for men.

To make a decent living, however, everyone had to do something; if there were not enough men, women or youngsters or older persons could substitute. Indeed, people claim that women did more during the collective period than before.[4]

In theory, women doing the same "heavy" jobs as men could earn as many work-points, but in fact they earned less. The assumption was that women are "not strong enough" to do the heaviest work, and that they work "less well." Since the leadership defined women's tasks as "lighter," they were assigned fewer points. Women's work days were also shorter because they had unremunerated household tasks to do. The fact that women worked fewer hours for lower wages only reinforced the traditional notion that men are "more valuable." Women often found themselves torn between farming and domestic work. A mother-in-law relieved a younger woman for work in the fields. Or a young mother might leave her infant in a nursery, in the care of older siblings, or even alone constrained on the family sleeping platform, a solution that sometimes had tragic consequences when unattended infants rolled off onto the floor. Because the women often worked far from home, nursing was inconvenient. A mother could not bring her infant to the fields, and having it brought to her when it cried or returning home to nurse it were impractical. This was a common problem without an easy solution, and a significant problem as well since nursing frequency is an important determinant of fertility. It is well known that frequent and longer nursing lengthens birth intervals and therefore lowers fertility.

After her sons married, a woman gradually reduced her outside work, and remained at home more to care for grandchildren and manage lighter household chores. Her daughters-in-law replaced her in the fields. Even retired, men and women did light field tasks, especially during periods of high demand. They could plant potatoes, pull weeds, turn compost, and help process the harvest. Essential characteristics of collective labor use—intensive use of all workers, minimal use of machines, and the general substitutability of labor—are still salient. The types and amounts of labor needed have changed, but these general features have endured.

By 1979 communes were in serious trouble. People were not eager to work for low wages, and value of the work-point had fallen so low that many were in debt. Rumors of plans to replace the commune only increased uncertainty and worsened morale. Toward the end of 1982 the countryside shifted to a new system in which collective land was given to households under long-term contract, the so-called "responsibility system." After years of collectivization, the family resumed its role as basic unit of production as well as consumption, but with an important difference. Land remains publicly owned; it still cannot be bought or sold and therefore cannot reconcentrate in fewer hands as in former times. Families may sink into poverty, but they cannot solve their problems by selling land.

Under the new system farmers contract to sell a certain amount of grain to the government at a set price. In return they enjoy the right to manage their land and dispose of the rest of their crop nearly as they choose. The average holding per person has remained the same since the system was put in place. In Tranquillity Village and Middle Village it is just under six *mu*, including garden plots.[5] This is so little land that no family can get rich on production alone.

The intention was to assign land by contract for at least fifteen years to encourage improvement. But family division, population growth, and erosion created problems. In Tranquillity Village two further redistributions took place before the original contracts expired, which contributed to substantial peasant insecurity. Farmers who had worked hard, carefully rotating crops and applying compost and chemical fertilizers, lost plots they had struggled to improve. With tenure uncertain, many are reluctant to invest time and resources.

The new system has also altered labor needs. Households are thrown back on their own resources. The family determines what, when, how, and where to plant; how to allocate labor, what sidelines to undertake, and with whom to cooperate, if anyone. People are eager to supplement earnings from sidelines in Tranquillity, and by raising a few milk cows in Middle Village. The ability to diversify depends heavily on the amount of labor a family has.

Villagers occasionally repeat the old adage, "Boys are precious, girls useless," but it has little substance in these farming villages. Indeed, the restoration of family-based production, and the development of new sidelines, increased the variety and value of women's contributions. By age seventeen or eighteen, all teenagers have acquired basic farm skills. Even children under fourteen can help, which is why parents short on labor sometimes end a child's schooling early. Nearly all children finish elementary school now; formal schooling is no longer a privilege of the few or limited to boys. However, while fewer than five percent of boys and girls (ages ten to nineteen) have had no formal schooling, most go no further than primary

school because additional education has little to offer youngsters destined to replace their parents.

It is not easy for a woman to combine domestic and outside work, especially if there are infants to care for. It is actually more important to have more than one woman in a household than more than one man. Women can make up for a shortage of men, but it is hard to make up for a lack of women. Women's work is held in lower esteem, so men avoid housework and are not trained for it. It is the multifaceted contribution of women that enables farmers to undertake sidelines without greatly cutting into farm work.

Since land cannot be enlarged and cultivation earnings are limited, sidelines provide an important supplement to income. In Tranquillity people gather and transport gravel, collect and sift construction sand, process grain, make potato noodles and bean curd, tend a few sheep, fish, and manage small grocery stores. Such sidelines contribute about nineteen percent of village income. In Middle Village, which is further from substantial markets, these sidelines are less common (only six percent of income). Most families (eighty-nine percent) raise a few dairy cows (average of four) on limited grassland, and they provide twenty-seven percent of village income. Dairying is a simple matter; there is no need to travel far, nor do men spend much time away cutting hay. Mostly they raise their animals in sheds, buying fodder from other places. Animals and stalls are close by, and so distract little from the fields.

Men tend sheds, women milk cows, and families often hire local cowboys to graze their cows. Because of the heavy demand for labor from farming, however, the division of labor by sex cannot be hard and fast. Women often work in the fields, and men occasionally help with the milking. When men are busy in the fields, women may help in the sheds. In Middle Village, as in Tranquillity, cultivation remains central.

Income and Its Distribution

Motivation and income improved once the responsibility system was in place. The view that modernization requires a freeing of initiative replaced older egalitarian notions at the foundation of collectives. But in a society that struggled to eliminate extremes of wealth and misery, even a modest increase in inequality causes concern. It has not yet turned to outrage in the communities we visited only because, while differences have widened, most have seen improvement and few have become poorer.

In 1987 the mean net income per person was 594 RMB in Tranquillity, 712 RMB in Middle Village. In both, just under 7 percent of households were below a "poverty line" officially defined as 200 RMB per person. Nineteen percent of households in Tranquillity, and 36 percent in Middle Village were "wealthy," earning over 800 RMB per person. The spread was about the same in both villages.[6] In general, families with more land enjoyed higher incomes. Grouping the communities, the "wealthy" farmed areas forty percent larger than the "poor."[7] Although cultivated area declined slightly in recent years, production has risen, thanks mainly to greater use of compost and chemical fertilizer.

Land and labor are not the whole story. Much depends on what families do with their capital and labor. Seventy percent of Tranquillity villagers have some sort of nonagricultural sideline, which contributed thirty-one percent of income for the wealthy compared to only ten percent among the poor. In Middle Village, dairying furnished twenty-nine percent of income for the wealthy, but only seven percent in poor households. Wages do not make a significant contribution to income (less than five percent) or to income disparity in either farming village. There are few jobs, and people who take them cannot easily manage farm work. Sidelines complement farming, starting and stopping in rhythm with peaks and slacks.

There is still little money for emergencies, let alone for saving or investment, and many costs are rising. It costs more to feed, dress, educate, and marry off children. At the same time, youngsters spend more time in school and contribute later. Further, many expenses once underwritten by the collective, like education and medical care, are now the family's burden. As incomes rise, people are tempted to acquire the consumer goods increasingly available. Thanks to dairying, many Middle Village homes are newer and of more substantial construction than those in Tranquility Village, but in both communities people spend more on housing.

Marriage is no longer so simple as during the more spartan years of Chinese communism. There has been a dramatic increase in cost, for bride as well as groom, especially since the shift to a privatized economy. Cadres tolerate greater display, and villagers spend more. In fact, getting children married is probably the heaviest burden any family must bear. Traditionally more costly for the groom, even the expense of marrying a daughter has increased, which is another indication of growing prosperity. It is interesting that some families are still content to accept compensation for a daughter's labor (bridewealth) without giving dowry in return; bridewealth without dowry is more common than the reverse, reflecting perhaps the importance of women's labor.

Children are costly even after marriage. At some point every family divides; sons move off to live on their own, taking a share of family assets. Ideally the share of each should be equivalent. Preparations have become more urgent in recent years because there is more to divide and because sons begin to live on their own sooner. On all fronts farmers work harder to achieve ever rising standards and expectations. No one would want to reverse that, but the situation does lead people to rethink older notions about marriage, family division, and family reproduction.

The New Herdsmen

In the farming area Mongols adopted the Han mode of farming and way of life. Because of their smaller numbers and the demands of cultivation, they live interspersed with the Han and have become culturally indistinguishable from them. Few can speak Mongol. They often intermarry and, like the Han, they favor early patrilocal marriage (bride joins her husband's family), two or three children, and "stem" families consisting of parents and one married son. As Han adapted to the grassland, they abandoned farming for a pastoral life, which now shapes what they do and value. They did not cease to be Han, however, and despite the homogenizing efforts of the state, they forged another kind of Han Chinese society.

In the pastoral region there are more Mongols and more marked cultural and political differences. Han and Mongols share public facilities and have many common interests, but at another level remain distinct subcommunities. We see this reflected in dress, speech, political competition, rarity of intermarriage, and occasional fights. More so than among the cultivators, people speak their own languages and marry their own kind. Their children go to separate schools where instruction is in their native tongues. Separate clinics treat according to distinct traditions.

There is an uneasy mix of traditions in Sandhill and Great Pasture. Mongols in town have homes like those of the Han, and like them grow vegetables in small gardens. They dress like Han, and most speak Mandarin in addition to their native tongue. Few Han speak Mongol, but they too eat beef and mutton rather than pork, drink milk-tea, and share a regional penchant for hard liquor. When they cut hay or graze animals on the open grassland they, too, live in yurts.

When Han first turned to pastoralism, dairying was more in keeping with their sedentary farming tradition. In Sandhill wages supplement dairying, and in Great Pasture many sell hay, raise sheep, or fish. Used to a more nomadic way, the Mongols have favored sheep. They rarely cut hay for sale and do not fish because these activities would interfere with shepherding. Just as cultivation forged similarities, so too has pastoralism encouraged convergence. Old specializations blur as Han add sheep and Mongols expand into dairying. Han shepherds add yurts, while Mongol dairymen acquire fixed residences in or near town, close to schools and milk collection stations. The size and structure of their families respond similarly to the needs of herding. Both marry later, are more often neolocal (couples live separately from kin), and have smaller, simpler families than Han and Mongol farmers. In these regards pastoral Han are more like Mongol herdsmen than like Han or Mongol farmers.

From Collective to Family Herding

Here, too, collective management ultimately turned out to be problematic. There was little incentive to carefully tend livestock, and cadres could not effectively control how people did their work. They allocated more points for harder and longer tasks, but there was little reason to work hard because one earned a day's wages no matter how well one performed. The problem was exacerbated during the Cultural Revolution (1966–1976), when cadres assigned points according to days worked regardless of difficulty. Herdsmen then had every reason to avoid the hardest work. Many animals were lost, and livestock numbers expanded slowly if at all. Much labor was also unused because then, as now, women and youngsters did little on the open range.

There were attempts along the way to allocate each household a couple of cows to raise. Inevitably they fared better than those in collective herds, but the leadership worried about encouraging family-level management under a socialist regime, so none of the experiments lasted long. The frequent policy reversals left a legacy of uncertainty that also reduced the benefits.

When the family became the basic unit of accounting, administrative responsibilities passed from commune to township, and brigades became villages. Families drew lots for cows and sheep expecting that they would pay for them over time. Not many Han were interested in sheep, but everyone wanted cows, which do not require long periods on the move far from home. Most Sandhill and Great Pasture Han lent their sheep to Mongol shepherds in exchange for meat. Pasture and grassland remain publicly managed and commonly shared. In Great Pasture, where it is more abundant, herds are larger and people cut large quantities of hay. There, cadres assign cutting areas to families annually in terms of the number of animals they have.

While they lost a good deal of power with demise of the commune, cadres still make many important decisions. They allocate land for home construction, collect taxes and fees, count livestock, resolve arguments and disputes, and pay stipends to demobilized soldiers. They supply veterinary services, assign fishing rights, manage pasture, and regulate seasonal flock movements and grass-cutting. They underwrite the cost of artificial insemination, and offer incentives to encourage flock development. But because they no longer have direct control over livestock, they have lost crucial power since commune days.

Forms of Pastoralism and the Division of Abor

In Sandhill and Great Pasture the shift from farming is complete. Grassland is now more abundant and herds are larger than in Middle Village. In 1988, most Sandhillers (eighty-three percent of households) had cows, an average of six. Three percent had more than fifteen. In Middle Village no family had a herd that large. Herds were larger still in Great Pasture. There, ninety-eight percent of Han families had cows, an average of fifteen, and fully fifty-one percent had more than fifteen. Now there are also differences in the way livestock are managed. Dairying is more intensive in Sandhill, the goal is more to increase milk yields by selective breeding (artificial insemination) and use of costly feed supplements than to enlarge herds. Great Pasture's pasture supports a larger number and variety of animals, and herdsmen have adopted a more extensive strategy. They are more interested in increasing animal numbers than in applying costly technologies.

Pastoralism has demanded adjustment of the Han way. Livestock require constant attention. There are periods of greater demand, but they are not as well marked as among the farmers, and there are no slack periods. The distances herdsmen travel and the need for skilled, experienced labor underlie sharper differences in the tasks of women and men, young and old. Even in collectives the division of labor is very sharp. Teams of men pasture collective livestock, a smaller group of women earn points milking them. Other women and a few older men work collective gardens during the short growing season. Some weave baskets at home, a brigade sideline. In Great Pasture men also dominate important supplementary activities—cutting hay and river fishing. Groups cut hay on distant pastures in summer. From spring through autumn others haul boats to the nearby river, and in winter go ice-fishing. Construction and transportation, too, are men's work.

Men earn points at a variety of tasks year round, but women and older men are "half labor," and their work is more limited. They often remain at home. For most tasks cadres prefer men. Maturity, experience, strength, and endurance are crucial because harsh weather, mismanagement, wolves, and disease can quickly decimate herds and flocks. Herdsmen have to know what they are doing, be able to lift heavy animals and other objects, and be prepared to spend long periods away from home, often in severe weather. Youngsters lack the necessary judgment, and women are inexperienced and in any case have to remain close to home to run the household and care for children.

With the collective gone, families depend more heavily on their own resources, and for the full range of tasks. Especially in Great Pasture, where larger herds spend more time in open pastures, and where men put more into cutting hay or fishing, dairying takes so much time and energy that neither men nor women can easily take regular additional employment or undertake unrelated sidelines. And since men all do their work at about the same time, just as women all milk at the same time, exchanges of labor between sexes and between families are not easy to arrange.

Sheep are risky and most efficiently managed in sizeable flocks (over two hundred), so only people with experience who are prepared to make a serious commitment find it worthwhile. Sheep need more substantial pasture and closer attention than cows; they must be moved often and watched constantly. Great Pasture Han were initially no more eager than Sandhillers to spend long periods on the open grasslands, so they, too, put the few sheep they obtained in the care of Mongol shepherds. But recently, as their selling price began to rise, a number of Han with sufficient family labor (men) have added sheep-herding to dairying.

Han shepherds have become the new nomads of China's northeastern frontier. Sheep, not assimilation to Mongol culture, encourage commonalities in behavior. Indeed, combining sheep and dairy cows from either direction requires substantial adjustment. Not only does the combination require lots of labor in

different places at the same time, but patterns of living must change.

Dairying is easier with sedentism and proximity to milk collection stations, while sheep pasture year round on open grassland and move over substantial distances. Shepherds change the location of their yurts and flocks six times a year.

While Mongols still prefer life in yurts on the open range, Han shepherds come from a sedentary tradition and still rely more heavily on dairying. They must have men on the range year round, but they prefer to leave their families and cows in town. Mongols adapt in the other direction, as they expand their dairy herds, by compromising mobility. Their women, elderly, preschoolers, and cows move among seasonal encampments close to town even while the men graze sheep elsewhere. The encampments are close enough to milk-collection stations to market milk, but too far for children to attend school. Some, even those without dairy cows, find temporary housing in town until schooling ends, or send children to live with kin in town, or in the Mongol school dormitory.

Among the herdsmen, each sex has different work to do. Men work hardest in winter, when cows are penned much of the time. Women are busiest during the summer peak milking time. But compared to farmers, the tasks men and women do, and when they do them, change little during the year. Men have principal responsibility for work away from home, and for tasks that demand great strength. In Great Pasture, they hitch up tank carts and haul water from the community well each day. Only they have the strength to free fully laden carts stuck in the mud. They cut, haul, and pile hay. They shovel cow pens and feed livestock in winter. Pasturing sheep through the deep cold of winter imposes heavy demands, and only men fish in the nearby river. Women and men classify all these jobs as "heavy work," largely the domain of men.

Women do most of their work within compound gates. They care for children, build and maintain fires, clean, cook, wash, repair and refill the padding in winter clothing, sew clothes, make shoes, garden, and put up vegetables. They milk cows in the courtyard. Women also convert cow dung into cooking fuel, shaping it into disks that they turn and dry in the winter sun, then pile for storage. They also make mud bricks used to fix houses. They do all this with bare hands in bitter cold.

On occasion, when there are not enough men, women and young sons help shovel the pens or pile straw, but most consider such work too taxing for them on a regular basis. In fact, there are few tasks for which women and men readily replace each other.

Local people explain that women are built differently, and they have more stamina. They can maintain long-term, low levels of energy. Doing "lighter" work, women spread their energy evenly over time. They are capable of short bursts of intense power, but men are believed to be more so.

A woman may provide temporary relief by watching sheep in deep winter, but relying too heavily on her could be costly. There is little room for error, especially with sheep. We often heard comments like, "What would happen if there was a sudden storm and the sheep began to scatter? How could an inexperienced girl handle that?" In any case, a woman should not remain on the open grassland through winter they believe. When the weather turns cold, a brother or hired shepherd must replace her.

Because the lines are more clearly drawn than among the farmers, men show even less willingness to do "women's work." Once home, they "rest." They may occasionally milk cows, even do housework, but only when female labor is really short. And while women might appreciate having men do more around the house, they are also convinced that the division of labor is natural and reasonable. By bolstering traditional concepts, the pastoral regime sustains a self-fulfilling prophesy. Once culturally defined capabilities become the basis of task assignment, people considered wrong for certain jobs are not trained to do them.

The assignment of work by age is also different from that among farmers. Youngsters are too inexperienced to do much until about age fourteen, later than among the farmers. They lead calves to nearby pastures at daybreak, and carry milk cans to the collection station twice a day. Girls help with milking. In general, people under twenty do not fully participate in herding sheep or cows, milking, cutting grass, or fishing. Like women, they may fill in but cannot replace men.

Because they start working later, not because education has anything more to offer, children among the pastoralists go to school longer than among the farmers. More attend junior high, and the farmer-herdsmen difference is especially marked for girls. Among the farmers, girls receive the least schooling, but among the herders they are even better educated than males; more go to middle school. That is because they do little, and because milking takes place before or after school.

At the other end of life, retirement for pastoralists comes later than among cultivators. An elderly couple can actually make a living on their own until they are quite old. They can reduce the number of cows they manage, and thus the amount of pen cleaning and winter feeding they do. They may hire a cowherd to pasture their cows. Their children cut the hay they need, or they can trade grass cutting rights for hay.

In Great Pasture, where dairymen make every effort to increase the number of cows they tend, haying is a major source of income in its own right. Much of it is transported to other regions of China or exported to Japan. But cutting grass on that scale requires expensive machines and an ample supply of men prepared to spend several months at a time on distant grasslands. There must also be men at home to pasture cows and handle routine dairying tasks. Families with large herds but not enough men to cut grass and tend cows often hire someone to pasture their animals during the haying season. Women, even young children, clean pens and do "men's jobs" at such times. If herdsmen add haying, then, they cannot easily raise sheep, take jobs, or undertake other sidelines as well.

Because they make a better living than farmers, have a sharper division of labor, and work continuously with livestock, often in distant places, herdsmen have little time for regular jobs or sidelines in fixed locations. Instead, they concentrate on expanding their herds and flocks, altering their mix. It is difficult even to combine different pastoral activities—to cut large amounts of grass for sale, manage a flock of sheep, and tend a herd of dairy cows, for example.

Income and Inequality: Herdsmen and Cultivators Compared

Herdsmen earn significantly more than farmers. Income decreases as we go from extensive pastoralism to pure cultivation. Tranquillity farmers earn the least notwithstanding their sidelines. Shed dairying provides greater advantage to Middle Villagers, and wages added to dairying yield still higher incomes in Sandhill. But Great Pasture households, with their extensive pastoralism and large scale haying, earn most. Their mean per capita income in 1987 was 1,156 RMB, compared to 811 RMB in Sandhill.

Privatization and diversification have increased income inequalities within and between communities. Great Pasture has the largest proportion of wealthy households and the widest income spread. Sandhill has the second largest proportion, and Tranquillity the lowest.[8] A good start in land or animals and abundant family labor are no guarantee of higher income. Household size and income are certainly related; larger families earn more, but only because more workers allow farmers to develop sidelines, and herdsmen to expand their herds, raise different sorts of animals, cut grass for sale, or fish. Only the number of *men* in a herding family is significantly related to income. That the number of *women* is also related to income among the farmers is further testimony to their more important and more varied role in the farming communities.

By allowing families to enlarge and diversify their enterprises, the new family responsibility system provided the basis for greater income inequality. Families that work harder, at a greater variety of tasks, see incomes rise. Inequality is on the increase, especially among the herdsmen, but there has also been a general rise in living standards. Contrary to direct predictions, there is no evidence yet of growing poverty in any of the sites we visited. This is especially clear if, in comparing communities, we keep in mind that income alone is not a sufficient indicator of wealth. It is especially imprecise for pastoralists because it does not consider capital assets (for example, savings, livestock, or machines). Animals are expendable as well as expandable capital; they represent wealth on the hoof.[9] The herdsman invests care, feed, and capital and, if all goes well, they multiply. Farmers also invest labor and capital, but their holdings do not grow.

Nor does income reveal differences in risk, or in ability to rebound from setbacks. Even herders with ample labor, livestock, and equipment experience difficult years. They may have to replace animals, or purchase and repair machines. As everywhere, marriages and funerals may produce negative incomes. Whereas even a small rise in expenses can throw a farm family into enduring debt from which it is difficult to recover, challenges for herdsmen are shorter term. They also adjust more easily to changes in labor availability. Land cannot be sold when labor is short and bought back later. But by adjusting the number and kinds of livestock they tend, herdsmen can make a living with few workers.

Economy and Family

It was not necessary that every commune family handle the full range of tasks; work teams drew from many families. In the farming area, there were ample opportunities for all family members to earn points, and the more members a family had, the more it could earn. It was particularly desirable to have more than one woman, one to handle domestic chores while the other earned points. In that sense collectivization encouraged a continuation of early patrilocal marriage, delayed family division, and enlargement of the family to stem form.

In the pastoral area family labor was not fully used, and because the most remunerative jobs were assigned to men, having more than one in the household was useful. There was no great need for more than one woman. Because the herdsmen did not need to mobilize as much labor as the farmers, and because their women played a smaller role, they could marry later and live more often in simple neolocal households.

Families all have more to do on their own now, but the farmers have greater short-term requirements, and more reason to cooperate seasonally with others. Such arrangements seem to work well only where a small number of families is involved and relationships are close enough to ensure reliability. Even so, people prefer to place primary reliance on the family, and therefore still favor early, patrilocal marriage, and stem families with one woman to work outside and another to work inside the home.

Family division is a bigger setback for farmers because it removes labor and can especially leave women in a bind, saddling them with simultaneous obligations at home and in the fields.[10] Small holdings become smaller and more fragmented since parents give land to sons who establish their own families. It is not easy to recover what is lost, or continue profitable sidelines after family division. It is important to preserve at least the stem family (parents and one married son) since it provides security for the elderly. This is of special concern now that families limit childbearing, people live longer, and rural folk still do not enjoy the pensions of urban workers. Moreover, there are fewer public services since dissolution of the communes.

Herdsmen, too, prefer patrilocal marriage and stem families, but they more often depart from those traditional forms. Early marriage is less pressing for them because adding a daughter-in-law early is less important, while holding a son longer is more important. Still, family division is less of a setback. A son takes livestock when he leaves, but animals multiply in a way land cannot. For that reason, even though herdsmen marry somewhat later than farmers, they divide their families sooner thereafter and more often live apart from kin (neolocally) when they marry.

In pre-Communist China, technological factors sometimes discouraged partition long enough to produce "joint" families, in which married brothers remained together. There is evidence, for example, that farming on the basis of rainfall rather than canals and cultivation of tobacco discouraged family division; the former because it put a premium on having a lot of men in the family, the latter because it increased the need for women. When families invested capital and labor in different enterprises, too, there were sound reasons to avoid partition.[11] By maintaining a single family, married brothers could economize labor and capital, shifting both from enterprise to enterprise to avoid hiring or borrowing. If they lived apart as separate households within a single property-owning family, they could avoid the strife that so often precipitated family division.

Under normal circumstances joint families were fragile and short-lived. Strife, especially among women, eventually triggered division. The custom of passing property from father to sons underlay conflicts between mother and daughter-in-law, and between sisters-in-law, all of whom depended on men for access to the family estate. A woman tried to exert some control first through her husband, and then through her sons. But sons' wives sought control through their husbands, trying to defend the interests of their conjugal units (husband, wife, and children if any) against those of other conjugal units within the larger family.

Once collectives took over productive resources and discouraged private enterprise, there was little reason to maintain joint families. In that sense, collectivization undermined some traditional sources of family complexity. Because policy now endorses family diversification, some predict an increase in the number of joint families, but for the present few resist inherent tendencies to divide. There are no technological reasons to discourage it, and family investment is likely to remain simple here because capital is scarce and markets distant and undeveloped. For cultivators and pastoralists alike, stem families suffice to diversify the household economy and integrate the elderly. It is also important to keep in mind that present families reflect earlier reproductive patterns capable of supplying personnel for large families. If strict family limitation continues, stem families are likely to remain the most complex form in which most people will have lived.

Because farmers need more women sooner, they have long married earlier than herdsmen, and are more likely to marry before legal ages. From 1950–1980 (when legal age was eighteen for women and twenty for men), seventeen percent of farm men (sites combined), and thirteen percent of the herdsmen married early. The difference was greater for women—twenty-two percent of the farmers were early, only eight percent of the herders. From 1981, when minimum ages were raised to twenty for women and twenty for men, forty-five percent of the farm men married early, compared to fourteen per-

cent for herders. Thirty-nine percent of farm women wed early, but only fourteen percent of the herders did.

Han prefer patrilocal marriage, a form of marriage which minimally produces stem families. However, marriage is more commonly patrilocal, and families more often stem, among the farmers. Herding households are simpler and smaller, only 4.5 persons compared to 4.9 for the farmers.

Older herdsmen are also more likely to live independently longer; 9.5 percent of pastoral households contain couples or individuals (mainly older people), compared to only 2.5 percent among the farmers. Whereas 61 percent of herding households contain people 65 or older, 84 percent of the farm households have them. Much of farm work would simply be too difficult for the elderly on their own. Without someone to share women's work, it would be particularly hard on a farm woman.

Pastoralists are also more likely to divide their families *at* marriage. Since they marry later, however, the event comes later, and despite that fact, they more readily recover. Farmers usually partition some time *after* marriage, and division reduces earnings all around. They therefore try to separate marriage and division, avoiding the latter as long as possible.

Family Reproduction

Throughout China the government has encouraged people to delay marriage and limit family size. Inner Mongolia has not escaped these efforts, although family planning has not been as strictly enforced as in interior China. Regulations should have levelled differences in age at marriage and number of children born, or at least altered behavior uniformly, but they have not. Parents continue to arrange marriages close to the legal thresholds, with little change in average age at marriage, although herdsmen still delay longer than farmers. Regulations limiting childbirth have had a greater impact on reproductive behavior, however. In all sites women have fewer children, but for all age groups farmers have more children than herdsmen. They exhibit higher fertility (measured by mean number of children born alive) despite *stricter* implementation of family planning regulations, and the difference predates family planning.

When infant and child mortality were high, many children increased the likelihood that enough would survive to assure care in old age. When collectives subsidized medical care and education, raising children cost less. Fewer children need be born now to be certain some will survive, but the cost of raising and marrying them have increased, especially among the herders. For these reasons couples, especially pastoral couples, are content to stop with two or three children, and would likely restrain childbearing beyond that even without state regulations. Indeed, family planning is probably tapping already-present inclinations to have fewer children. Had they been free to do so, women might have placed brakes on childbearing earlier. Present policy, propaganda, and enforcement empower them to do that.

While pastoralists and cultivators are no longer eager to have as many children as they can, neither are they prepared to stop with one. Herdsmen have more reason to avoid having many children, given their greater cost, longer school attendance, and later contribution, but even they have not embraced the one-child model urged by the state. During 1980–1988, when family planning regulations tightened, most children delivered were *not* firstborns (only seventeen percent), although people did have fewer later children than during the preceding decade. Only fifteen percent of births during 1980–1988 was a fourth or later child compared to fifty-six percent during the previous decade. Many mothers still have a second child (and even additional children), and they have their second child sooner than the state would like. Despite a requirement that couples wait four years to conceive, only six percent of women between the ages of fifteen and twenty-nine and only eleven percent of those between thirty and thirty-four waited that long.

Childbearing exceeds state recommendations in all sites, but the farmers have more children than the pastoralists. Longstanding differences in reproductive behavior, rooted in ecology and economy, have carried forward to the present. While there is no significant difference in the average number of children born to Han and Mongol herdsmen, Han herders have fewer children than Han farmers. This suggests that differences in economy and ecology are more important than ethnicity in this regard.

Earlier marriage may contribute to higher fertility, but it cannot be the whole story since farmers aged forty and over had more children but did *not* marry earlier. Farm women in every age group had more children during the first ten years of marriage. Differences in infant mortality, morbidity, and frequency of intercourse could also affect birth spacing. Unfortunately, our data cannot tell us whether the farmers had higher mortality.

Goiter was once common in Tranquillity, but it would hardly have *raised* fertility and was no problem in Middle Village. Venereal disease, endemic among grassland Mongols during the late 1930s and

1940s, came under control in the early 1950s. It is not clear how affected the Han were, but there is some suggestion in the literature that they were less so. The effect may have been minimal in our villages, however, since we find no difference in Han and Mongol parities (births), and lower herdsmen fertility persisted even *after* venereal disease was eliminated on the grassland.

Nor are differences in frequency of sexual intercourse important. Herdsmen do periodically leave for months at a time, but they visit periodically. Moreover, shepherding and hay cutting on a large scale are recent while lower fertility is not. What then might account for the long-standing difference in fertility (average number of children born by mother's age)? In all likelihood differences in nursing behavior, in turn a product of dissimilarities in the division of labor, are the main cause. In a natural fertility context (where people make no conscious effort to limit conception or childbirth) the more frequently and longer a woman nurses, the longer are her intervals to next conception and birth and, consequently, the lower her fertility. Farm women nurse less often than pastoral women, who are always at home. Thus, farming may encourage higher fertility as well as larger and more complex families.

Cowboys, Cultivators, and the Status of Women

The communist emphasis on mass participation brought large numbers of women into the labor force, and some suggest that it enhanced their leverage at home. Indeed, the collective, too, benefited from their contribution. If women enhance their value and voice by adding to income, then farm women should certainly be advantaged, especially in the new economy. There were fewer ways for pastoral women to earn work-points during the collective era, and they still largely confine themselves to milking and tending the home. It is unlikely that nonpastoral sidelines will develop to involve them.

But the connection between work and status is not straightforward. For one thing, women do not control their work, product, or income. Further, for a woman's labor to be considered "important" it probably must be visible and clearly linked to her efforts. But even when women have worked outside, their earnings have usually been delivered to the family head. Neither among farmers nor herders do people consider women's work "important" in the sense of being central to the household economy. When asked to specify the "most important" pastoral work, women and men mentioned grass cutting, fishing, or cleaning stalls, not milking. Even farm women's labor is seen as "lighter" or "domestic," and therefore not real labor. With the collective gone, women who once brought in work-points now work *for the family*, work too easily thought of as subsidiary. It is far from certain, then, that the reforms of recent years will enhance the value, influence, or autonomy of women. But no one has yet systematically measured the effect of outside work, and the clues we have are ambiguous, even contradictory.

Because they bring wealth or property when they marry, for example, farm women should have more influence. Everyone born is entitled an allocation of land. Granted to a person, it actually becomes part of a family estate controlled almost invariably by a male. When she marries, a woman's land flows back into community reserve and her husband's family requests an assignment on her behalf. Farm women thus enjoy a right to property that pastoral women do not. The community assigns herding women no animals, pasture, or grassland when they are born or marry. If property confers status or influence, then, pastoral women would be disadvantaged. However, in the minds of farm family members even the land a woman brings with her is not identified with her. She does not decide what will be grown on it, who will use it, or how it will be planted. We cannot simply assume, then, that it necessarily elevates her position.

Structural differences might even tip the scales the other way, to enhance the position of herding women. Recall that cultivators more often marry patrilocally. A farm woman is more subject to her mother-in-law's judgments and moods. Since pastoralists more often marry neolocally and live in conjugal families, we might expect that herding women would enjoy a greater measure of autonomy. Consider, too, the fact that herding women go to school longer, work and marry later, and bear fewer children, and that many are better educated than their husbands. Is it not possible that these characteristics, which derive from their *lesser* contribution, confer a measure of influence or self-fulfillment?

In fact, the educational advantage of pastoral girls does not lead to a better job or a better life. Most follow in the steps of their mothers. Indeed, the lower education of farm women, their earlier marriages, and their higher parities reflect their importance to the domestic economy. Nonetheless, it is doubtful that the earlier and more substantial input of farm women give them any great bargaining power. It may only make their lives more difficult.

Our unsystematic and limited observations in the field suggest that farm women do enjoy greater voice, but the matter is clearly complicated and deserving of further careful study.

Notes

1. Owen Lattimore, *Inner Asian Frontiers of China* (Boston: Beacon Press, 1962), p. 39.
2. Although the findings presented here summarize the findings of a more detailed analysis of the data by Salaff and myself (Pasternak & Salaff 1993), I hasten to relieve her of responsibility for this summary of our common work. For a full analysis of our data see Burton Pasternak and Janet W. Salaff, *Cowboys and Cultivators: The Chinese of Inner Mongolia* (Boulder, CO: Westview Press, 1993).
3. RMB or *renminbi* is a monetary unit equivalent to .172 US dollars as of December 1992.
4. During the Great Leap Forward (1958–1960), the leadership collectivized many domestic burdens in an unusual effort to draw women into the fields. For a brief (and unsuccessful) period of several months, even food preparation and child care were done in common.
5. One *mu* = .0667 hectares. Around five percent of land is kept in "reserve" for new household members. When people leave by death or marriage their land flows back to the reserve.
6. Gini scores, which summarize income distribution, were .34 and .32 for Tranquillity and Middle village respectively.
7. Poor households cultivated 21.5 *mu* compared to 30.1 for the wealthy.
8. Gini scores for Great Pasture and Sandhill were .42 and .31, respectively.
9. Han think of livestock as a form of capital; the more they have and the heavier when sold, the better. They may hold animals longer than sensible, not simply because they value size and numbers, but because they anticipate need for capital—perhaps to pay for a wedding, purchase a house for the new couple, or endow them with a herd of their own. Families with many animals are also better able to weather fluctuations in earnings or expenditures. But their "more is better" strategy can also be environmentally problematic, especially if it involves sheep, which are particularly hard on pasture.
10. For a cross-cultural study that highlights how incompatible labor demands encourage family extension, see Burton Pasternak, Carol R. Ember, and Melvin Ember, "On the Conditions Favoring Extended Family Households," *Journal of Anthropological Research* 32 (1976): 109–123.
11. For a more extensive discussion of these issues see Myron L. Cohen, *House United, House Divided: The Chinese Family in Taiwan* (New York: Columbia Uni-

versity Press, 1976); and Burton Pasternak, *Guests in the Dragon: Social Demography of a Chinese District, 1895–1946* (New York: Columbia University Press, 1983).

Suggested Readings

Cohen, Myron L. *House United, House Divided: The Chinese Family in Taiwan.* New York: Columbia University Press, 1976. A penetrating analysis of Chinese family development and the factors that influence it, based on Taiwan fieldwork.

Lattimore, Owen. *Inner Asian Frontiers of China.* Boston: Beacon Press, 1962. A comprehensive history of Han Chinese expansion into Inner Mongolia prior to the Communist period.

Pasternak, Burton. *Guests in the Dragon: Social Demography of a Chinese District, 1895–1946.* New York: Columbia University Press, 1983. This study, based on fieldwork and an analysis of household registers, explores the connections between technology, family organization, and demographic behavior (fertility, mortality, divorce, adoption).

Pasternak, Burton, and Janet W. Salaff. *Cowboys and Cultivators: The Chinese of Inner Mongolia.* Boulder, CO: Westview Press, 1993. A more extensive analysis of the data on Han herdsmen and farmers presented in this chapter.

Yanomamö: Varying Adaptations of Foraging Horticulturalists

Raymond B. Hames

The documentation of behavioral variation in cultural anthropology is key to scientific description and explanation. Early ethnographers were content to describe typical patterns of behavior to give readers an idea of what was expected or customary in a given culture. In order to understand variation in cultural practices, anthropologists who are engaged in cross-cultural comparison use individual societies as data points or exemplars of particular traits. While comparative or cross-cultural approaches have been enormously productive, they are not the only useful approach to a scientific understanding of cultural variation. Within each society, individuals or even whole regions may vary enormously in how they conduct their social, economic, and political lives. Accurately documenting this intracultural variation and attempting to associate it with explanatory factors is an important alternative approach. This is not to say that intracultural comparisons are superior to or in competition with cross-cultural approaches. In fact, I would expect them to complement each other. For example, one might demonstrate cross-culturally that warfare is strongly associated with a particular environmental variable. This then might lead us to test that proposition within a particular cultural group if that environmental variable had enough variation.

The goal of this chapter is to describe variation in Yanomamö economic activities at cross-cultural, regional, and individual comparative levels. I will first compare Yanomamö horticultural adaptation to other horticultural groups. The striking finding here is that compared to other horticulturalists the Yanomamö spend an enormous amount of time in the foraging activities of hunting, gathering, and fishing. In many ways they behave like hunters and gatherers, peoples without agriculture. I will then turn to a regional comparison of Yanomamö economic adaptations by comparing how highland and lowland Yanomamö adapt to the rain forest. Here we will find that highland Yanomamö are much more dedicated to a sedentary horticultural life than lowland Yanomamö. Finally, I will turn to an analysis of individual Yanomamö to describe how sex and age determine the division of labor and the amount of time that individuals work.

Demography, Geography, and Environment

The Yanomamö are a tribal population occupying the Amazonian border between Venezuela and Brazil. In Venezuela, the northern extension of the Yanomamö is delimited to the north by headwaters of the Erebato and Caura rivers, east along the Parima mountains, and west along the Padamo and Mavaca in a direct line to the Brazilian border. In Brazil, they concentrate themselves in the headwaters of the Demini, Catrimani, Araca, Padauari, Urari Coera, Parima, and Mucajai rivers. In both countries the total area inhabited by the Yanomamö is approximately 192,000 square kilometers. Dense tropical forest covers most of the area. Savannas are interspersed in forests at high elevations. In general, the topography is flat to gently rolling, with elevations ranging from 250 to 1,200 meters.

Area Exploited

The area village members exploit in the course of their economic activities is probably best characterized as a *home range*. Home ranges differ from territories because they are not defended, but like territories they tend to be used exclusively by a single group. This exclusiveness is not determined by force but by the following simple economic considerations. Important food resources tend to be evenly distributed in the tropical forest. When Yanomamö establish a new village they intensively exploit and deplete resources near the village. Through time, they must travel greater distances where higher return rates compensate for greater travel costs needed to reach areas of higher resource density. At a certain point they will begin to reach areas that are exploited by neighboring villages and if they were to travel still further they would begin to enter areas close to neighboring villages that have been depleted. At this point, it is not economic to travel further since the costs of gaining resources increases (more travel time) while resource density decreases. Thus the borders of home ranges are established with some overlap with the home ranges of adjacent villages. The point to understand here is that a village has near-exclusive use of its home range but that exclusivity is determined by economic factors and not by aggression or threat of aggression.[1]

Where warfare is intensive home ranges may become more like territories if enemy villages are neighbors. In such cases exclusive use of an area is maintained through aggression or threat of aggression. However, it is difficult to determine what is being defended. It may be that the Yanomamö want to keep enemies out of their foraging areas so that they may hunt and gather without the worry of meeting a raiding party; or it may be that a powerful village decides to press its advantage over a weaker neighbor by expanding its range into a neighbor's area to monopolize all the resources in the area. The way in which Yanomamö verbally rationalize their reasons for warring complicates this matter further. Yanomamö may claim that they go to war in order to avenge an insult, a previous killing, an abduction of a woman, or the illness-causing spells cast by a neighboring shaman. Therefore, Yanomamö explain war in terms of vengeance for harm caused by an enemy. The problem here is that neighboring villages invariably have members who have done one of more of the above to a neighbor or a neighbor's ancestor. Why some past wrongs are ignored or acted upon may be determined by economic (territorial) and political factors (opponent's strength or perceived threat). Further complexities of Yanomamö warfare are described in the section on conflict below.

We have little comparative data on sizes of the home ranges of Yanomamö villages. Differences in home range may be the result of ecological differences in resource density or the distribution of neighboring villages. The limited data we have indicate that home ranges vary from three hundred to seven hundred square kilometers, roughly a circular area with a radius of ten to fifteen kilometers. This radius is approximately the distance one can easily walk through the forest in less than a day.

DEMOGRAPHY AND SETTLEMENT PATTERN OF YANOMAMÖ VILLAGES

Although ethnographers have done extensive and excellent demographic research on some Venezuelan and Brazilian Yanomamö, a complete census for Venezuelan and Brazilian Yanomamö is lacking. Current estimates are 12,500 and 8,500 Yanomamö in Venezuela and Brazil, respectively, for a total of 21,000. However, the figures for Brazil may be significantly less because of epidemics and white-Yanomamö fighting caused by incursions of Brazilian gold miners starting about 1987. I discuss this problem later. In Venezuela and Brazil there are approximately 363 villages ranging in size from 30 to 90 residents each. But some Venezuelan villages in the Mavaca drainage may reach 200 or more. Napoleon A. Chagnon[2] provides evidence that warfare intensity is associated with village size: where warfare is intense, villages are large. People are forced to associate in large villages both to deter attackers and enable themselves to mount effective counterattacks. Population density ranges from about 6.7 square kilometers per person to 33.5 square kilometers per person.

Anthropologists consider stable settled life one of the important consequences of the agricultural revolution. Although the Yanomamö are agriculturists, villages are unstable in duration, location, and membership. A typical Yanomamö village (*shabono*) has the shape of a giant circular "lean-to" with a diameter of fifty meters or more depending on the number of people living in the village. Each house or apartment section of a village has a roof and back wall but no front or side walls. Individual family leantos are joined in a circle. When a Yanomamö sits in his hammock and looks left or right he sees his next door neighbor; if he looks straight ahead he sees a broad plaza and the dwellings of neighbors on the other side of the village. A village structure rarely lasts more than a few years before the roof thatch begins to rot and the entire village becomes filled with vermin. On such occasions, a new village may be constructed adjacent to the old one.

Aside from the reasons stated above, Yanomamö villages are relocated about every five years because of economic and political considerations.[3] The practice of shifting cultivation forces the Yanomamö to use extensive tracts of land. This is because garden land is used for only two to three years and then abandoned to the encroaching forest. Through time gardens become increasingly distant from the village. When gardens or easily accessible garden land become too distant, the village may move several kilometers to be in the midst of good garden land. Raiding provides a political cause for village relocation. When a village is repeatedly raided by a more powerful enemy, the entire village may be forced to relocate. Such moves are designed to put as much distance as possible between themselves and an enemy and may cause great privation due to loss of easy access to productive gardens.

HIGHLAND AND LOWLAND

There is good reason to suspect that there are fundamental differences in environmental quality for Yanomamö who occupy highland and lowland elevations. Defining a precise boundary between the highlands and lowlands is impossible at this point. However, I tentatively define highland populations as villages found in areas higher than 500 to 750 meters of elevation and occupying areas of highly dissected and hilly terrain with small fast flowing streams and occasional savannas. The lowland environment is flatter with slowly moving, larger streams and rivers. This highland-lowland distinction appears to have important implications for the fundamental economic activities of gathering, hunting, fishing, and agriculture.

General ecological research provides considerable evidence that plant biomass and diversity decrease with increases in altitude. Detailed ethnographic research on the Yanomamö points to a similar conclusion. For example, ethnobotanical research by Lizot[4] shows a greater variety of edible plants are available to lowland groups, more plants are restricted to lowland environments, and, on average, more edible plants are available on a monthly basis for lowland groups. In addition, the cultural geographer William Smole[5] notes a decrease in edible plants with increasing elevation. Although it cannot be positively concluded that gathering is more productive in lowland areas since plants differ enormously in food value, processing costs, density, and seasonal availability, available data show that the rate of return in gathering wild forest resources is much greater in lowland than in highland areas.[6]

It is well established that fish are more abundant and larger in the wider, slower moving rivers in lower elevations.[7] A comparison of sites reveals that groups living along large streams or rivers consume twice as much fish and other aquatic prey (frogs, caimans, and crabs).[8] In addition, these lowland groups gain fish at efficiencies two to three times higher than highland groups.[9]

The evidence on game density is less direct. However, it is my impression (based on Yanomamö statements and direct observation) and that of other Yanomamö researchers[10] that game animals are much less abundant in higher elevations. In terms of kilograms of game killed per hour of hunting, Colchester shows that the highland Sanema Yanomamö hunt much less efficiently than lowland Yanomamö.[11] Since both highland and lowland groups use the same bow and arrow technology and are equally adept hunters, it can be concluded that the greater hunting success of lowlanders is the result of greater game densities in the lowlands. A review of the ecological and biogeographical literature on altitude and animal biomass gradients suggests that huntable biomass declines with increasing elevation.[12]

We have no convincing comparative data to indicate significant differences between highland and lowland areas for agricultural pursuits. Agricultural productivity is a complex interplay of many factors such as soil quality, quantity and distribution of rain, and temperature extremes. It is clear, as I show below, that there are significant differences in garden size corresponding to a highland and lowland divide. What is not clear, however, is whether these differences are the result of environmental, economic, or socio-political factors to be discussed below.

Yanomamö Economics

Economically, the Yanomamö, along with most other tribal peoples living in the tropics, are classified as shifting cultivators because most of their dietary calories come from horticulture. However, a significant amount of time is allocated to the foraging activities of hunting, gathering, and fishing. In fact, as we shall see later, the Yanomamö allocate more time to foraging activities than they do to agriculture. Their dedication to foraging is greater than any other Amazonia group and any other horticultural group that we know of.[13] Given this huge investment in foraging activities it might be more accurate to refer to the Yanomamö as "foraging horticulturalists." In this section I describe the basic productive components of the Yanomamö economy.

TECHNOLOGY

Until the mid-1950s the Yanomamö relied on a locally produced "stone age" technology, which was dependent on local, nonmetal resources. For example, axes were made of stone, knives of bamboo, fish hooks of bone, and pots of clay. Since that time much of their traditional technology has been replaced by steel cutting tools (machetes and axes), aluminum pots, and other industrial items given or traded to the Yanomamö primarily by missionaries. The main impact of such introductions has been to reduce labor time and increase Yanomamö dependence on non-Yanomamö to satisfy these new needs.[14] In many instances the Yanomamö no longer possess the skills to make or use traditional technology such as clay pots or fire drills.

GARDENING

In shifting cultivation, forest is cleared with machetes, axes, and fire. The newly opened forest is then planted with plantains, root crops (manioc, sweet potatoes, and taro) and a large variety of plants that serve as relishes, medicines, and technology sources. After about two to three years of cultivation, the garden is abandoned to the encroaching forest. In most years Yanomamö add to the size of a current garden by clearing adjacent forest. As yields begin to diminish and weeding becomes time consuming, they cease to work old areas of the garden and let them naturally revert to scrub and, later, to forest. Men do nearly all the heavy work involved in clearing, such as slashing the undergrowth and felling large forest trees. Men and women work together to plant the garden and women are responsible for the nearly daily trips to the garden to harvest and weed.

There is considerable variation, as Figure 1 clearly indicates, in the amount of land under cultivation per capita in Yanomamö villages. Per-capita land cultivated in highland villages averages five times as much as in lowland villages, a difference that is statistically significant. There are at least two possible ecological and economic explanations for these differences. Garden land may not be as fertile in higher elevations, or basic crops may not be as productive because of the cooler temperatures in highland areas.[15] As a result, highlanders are forced to increase garden size to produce the same quantity of plantains as lowlanders. A second reason to cultivate less land in lowland areas is that foraging success (efficiency) is greater in lowland areas, therefore lowlanders may gain a larger fraction of their diet from foraging, which lessens their dependence on garden food.

There is a basic contrast in subsistence crops relied upon by highland and lowland groups that may have far reaching consequences in helping us understand their economic differences. Lowland groups rely on plantains and bananas as the basic subsistence crop while some highland groups rely more heavily on manioc, a very productive root crop. Where either crop is a staple, it contributes up to forty percent or more of all dietary calories. This difference leads us to ask why some highland groups depend on manioc and what impact dependence on one or the other has on the overall Yanomamö economy. Colchester suggests that manioc is a recent introduction from neighboring groups such as the Ye'kwana.[16] Where manioc has been introduced the Yanomamö have taken it up because it appears to be a forty percent more efficient source of calories than plantains. However, this alleged advantage may disappear since the comparative data on efficiency do not consider processing costs. Some varieties of manioc become poisonous ("bitter") soon after harvesting and must be detoxified. In addition, many varieties require a laborious process of peeling, grating, and baking before consumption. Plantains, in contrast, are easily peeled and quickly cooked by roasting or boiling. Chagnon makes an opposite argument by suggesting that manioc was aboriginal with the Yanomamö and it was replaced by plantains (an Old World crop introduced by the Spanish more than four hundred years ago) because plantains were a more efficient producer of calories.[17] Unfortunately, neither Colchester or Chagnon have quantitative data to back up their claims. Clearly, relatively simple research could help settle this issue.

Whether or not manioc or plantains are ancient or recent introductions, dependence on one or the other may have a strong impact on the Yanomamö economy. The key issue here is not one of efficiency but of reliable and predictable yield. Tropical forest peoples tend to rely on crops that can be harvested over a long time. In contrast to temperate horticulturalists, many tropical peoples who grow root crops or plantains do not harvest their entire field during a single harvest period and do not store the crop to tide them through seasons when crop growth is impossible or risky. Instead, tropical cultivators stagger-plant throughout the year so that what is needed can be harvested from the field every few days or week. For example, one can harvest manioc six, twelve, or eighteen or more months after it is planted. This allows the manioc cultivator considerable flexibility in insuring a steady and reliable yield. Plantains, in contrast, have much less flexibility. Although Yanomamö attempt to stagger-plant plantains to gain a reliable weekly or half-

Figure 1
Garden Land Per-Capita (m²) in Nine Villages,
and Lowland/Highland Contrasts

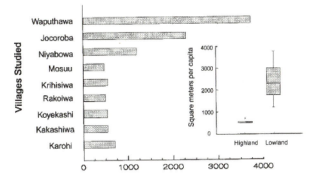

weekly yield, a variety of environmental factors thwart this strategy. Dry spells can hasten maturation while prolonged wet spells slow maturation. Also, heavy winds that accompany violent thunderstorms may blow down plantains with heavy maturing racemes (bunches). Yanomamö can salvage blown down bunches of plantains (if they're close to maturation) by hanging them in the village. When the plantains ripen there will be a momentary glut of food, but there will be a lack of plantains in the near future when they would have otherwise matured.

Heavy dependence on plantains by lowland groups may help us to understand their greater reliance on gathering compared to manioc producing highland groups. Since plantains are far less reliable than manioc, lowland Yanomamö may be forced to gather because of periodic underproduction of plantains. Evidence consistent with this idea is presented in Table 1. The only highland group on which we have time allocation (Sanema, in the table) shows that the average adult spends only twenty-six minutes each day gathering, which is the lowest figure in the table and fully one-half of the average time allocated to this task in lowland villages.

If manioc is more reliable than plantains we must ask why plantain-growing lowlanders do not grow more manioc than they currently do. Since lowland gathering is about twice as efficient as highland gathering, it may mean that unreliable plantain production is buffered by highly productive gathering. Since the overall work effort for the highland Sanema is essentially identical to the average level of work for lowland villages (see the Total column in Table 1), I suggest that this is clear evidence that plantain gar-

dening coupled with a high reliance on gathering causes no discernible hardship in overall work effort.

FORAGING

Foraging is the simple extraction of resources from the environment without any attempt to modify the environment (as agriculture does) to increase the yield of that which is harvested. Hunting, gathering, and fishing are the basic foraging activities. Foraging is the most ancient technique humans use to exploit the environment and an adaptation that humans share with all other animals. What is interesting about Yanomamö foraging is the large amount of time they allocate to it. As time allocation statistics in Table 1 indicate, Yanomamö allocate more than twice as much time to foraging as they do to gardening.

Given the amount of time the Yanomamö spend foraging on a daily basis, the term foraging horticulturalists might be an apt designation for their economic adaptation to the tropical forest. The logic of this designation is further reinforced by the Yanomamö practice of *waiyumö*, or trekking. Trekking is camping in the forest and subsisting mostly by foraging. It usually occurs in the dry season when there is an abundance of forest fruit and the dryness makes walking and camping out pleasant. The probable motivation behind most trekking is to save travel time by taking advantage of abundant vegetable resources distant from the village. However, trekking may also be stimulated by a shortage of garden food or the presence of powerful enemies. If the latter is the cause, then trekking is an adaptation designed for concealment against enemies. Treks may last a week to more than a month and normally include all village members. Dependence on wild resources is not total, since young men are sent from forest camps to gardens to harvest plantains if the wild resources are scarce.

HUNTING

Hunting is the main source of dietary protein for the Yanomamö. As we shall later see in the time allocation statistics, hunting is essentially a male activity with important social and ritual functions. Bows and arrows, which measure approximately two meters in length, are the main weapons of the hunt. The long arrow is not accurate beyond about thirty meters. This is of little significance in dense tropical forest where it is rare to have a clear shot at a greater distance.[18] Skills in locating game and stalking it to a short distance are abilities that differentiate good from poor hunters. Game sought ranges from 1-kilogram birds, to 25-kilogram peccaries, and to the occasional 175-kilogram tapir (the largest terrestrial animal in South America). Yanomamö quivers contain large lancelotate (spear shaped) tips for big game, poisoned pencil-shaped tips for monkeys, and harpoon points for birds and small terrestrial game. Because arrows are two meters long a hunter can carry no more than three arrows on a hunt; however, hunters carry a case which contains a repair kit of thread, resin, and a hand tool to repair damaged arrows.

Although most hunting is done by individuals or pairs, organized group hunts occur under two important circumstances. If a hunter discovers a herd of white-lipped peccaries (a distant relative of the pig weighing 20 to 30 kilograms), he carefully notes the location and immediately returns to the village to alert other hunters who return to cooperatively hunt the herd. To prepare for a feast (*reahu*) organized hunting parties travel great distances and may continuously hunt for a week in order to amass a large quantity of game to provide high quality meals for visiting allies on a variety of social occasions (reahu and *braiai* rituals). During these excursions hunters especially seek highly esteemed game, such as peccaries, turkey-like birds, and monkeys.

Gathering

The harvesting of wild plant resources is an activity that includes all ages and sexes and is commonly organized by families and groups of families. Important resources include honey, palm fruits, brazil nuts, palm heart, and cashew fruit. Men specialize in the risky task of climbing trees to shake loose fruit or to sever fruit-laden branches. The peach palm is especially important. It is planted in gardens but it only begins to yield several years after a garden has been abandoned and it continues to bear for a decade or more. The Yanomamö assert that peach palms are owned by those who planted them and it is not uncommon for disputes to arise over ownership. With the exception of the peach palm, the Yanomamö make little or no effort to harvest fruit trees or palms so they may be harvested on a sustained basis. The Yanomamö fell small, fruit-ladened trees to make harvesting easier, but never such forest giants as Brazil nut or cashew trees because of the enormous labor required.

Fishing

Most Yanomamö villages occupy areas between major rivers that are crossed by small streams. Fish found here are seldom larger than a few kilograms. Nevertheless,

fishing is widely and avidly pursued by all ages and sexes, especially in the dry season through hand catching, stream poisoning, and archery. In the dry season small streams begin to shrink, leaving fish in large ponds or cutoffs. The Yanomamö will use a vegetable poison to stun fish and cause them to rise to the surface where they can be grabbed or shot with a miniature bow and arrow. Women sometimes will jointly push a long, broad palm frond through the water to herd fish towards a bank where they can be trapped.

Marriage and Family

Yanomamö marriage rules prescribe that marriage partners ought to be cross-cousins. Ideally, mates are double cross-cousins, a result of the practice of sister exchange. Soon after their first menses, women typically marry men in their early twenties. Although women are required to reside in their husband's village after marriage (patrilocal marriage), a husband must initially live with his in-laws for several years and work diligently for them, performing what is known as bride service. This requirement may be relaxed for high status males. Polygyny (a man having more than one wife) is permitted; 10 to 20 percent of all males at any time are polygynists. Ideally, polygynists marry sisters (sororal polygyny) since the Yanomamö believe that sisters get along better. If a woman's husband dies she may be required to marry his brother (levirate marriage) and if a man's wife dies he may claim her sister as a bride (sororate marriage). Men and women average 2. 8 marital partners during their lifetime, with about 75 percent of those marriages ending as a result of divorce with the balance as a result of death of one of the partners.[19]

Monogamous or polygynous nuclear families are the rule among the Yanomamö. Deviations from this pattern occur when aged parents live closely associated with married children or when newlyweds dwell with one or the other's parents. Each family has a garden or gardens and is responsible for basic subsistence activities.

Political Organization

Each Yanomamö village is an autonomous political entity, free to make war or peace with other villages. Coalitions between villages are important: nevertheless, such coalitions tend to be fragile and ephemeral. Although the Yanomamö are an egalitarian people, age, sex, and personal accomplishments are important in status differentiation. Yanomamö men acquire high status through valor in combat, accomplished oratory, and expertise in shamanism. However, high status cannot be inherited—it must be earned. Mature men dominate positions of political authority and religious practice. Local descent groups play important roles in regulating marriages and settling disputes within the village.

The village headman is the dominant political leader and comes from the largest local patrilineage (a kin group whose members trace descent through male relatives). When a village is large or when two local descent groups are approximately equal in size, a village may have several headmen. The headman must rely on demonstrated skills in settling disputes, representing the interests of his lineage, and successfully dealing with allies and enemies. Styles of leadership vary: some headmen lead through practiced verbal skills while others resort to bullying. Concerted action requires the consensus of adult males. However, an individual is free to desert collective action if it suits him.

Villages range in size from about 40 residents to more than 200. As a village increases in size it has a tendency to break into two groups of approximately equal size, which form new villages. As villages become large, kinship relationships become weaker and village headmen are less able to amicably settle disputes.[20] In addition, local resources tend to be more quickly depleted, which causes an increase in work effort.[21] However, if warfare is intense village members are more likely to realize the value of large size as a deterrent against enemies and are more likely to tolerate irksome co-villagers and increased work loads.

SOCIAL CONTROL

Conflicts typically arise from accusations of adultery, failure to deliver a betrothed woman, personal affronts, stinginess, or thefts of coveted garden crops such as tobacco and peach palm. For men, if such conflicts move past a boisterous shouting match, a variety of graded, formal duels may occur. If a fight becomes serious, respected men may intervene to cool tempers and prevent others from participating. Frequently, duels end in a draw, which allows each contestant to preserve his dignity. For women, dueling is rare. Instead, a direct attack is made by the aggrieved woman using hands and feet or makeshift weapons.

CONFLICT

Warfare between villages is endemic among the Yanomamö. While the initial cause of a conflict may be frequently traced to a sexual or marital issue, conflicts are self-perpetuating since the Yanomamö lack any formal mechanisms to prevent aggrieved parties from exacting the amount of vengeance or counter-vengeance they deem sufficient once a conflict has started. The primary vengeance unit is the lineage, but coresident non-kin have some obligation to assist, since coresidence with a feuding faction is seen as implicit support of the faction by the faction's enemies. Most combat is in the form of stealthy raids. The goal is to quickly kill as many of the enemy as possible (who are frequently found on the outskirts of the other village engaging in mundane activities), abduct nubile women if possible, and return quickly home. While the primary goal is to kill mature men and their kin believed to be responsible for a previous wrong, unrelated co-villagers may be killed if there is no safe opportunity to kill primary targets. Endemic warfare has a profound effect on politics and settlement size and location. Each village needs at least one allied village it can call upon for assistance if it is overmatched by a more powerful enemy; and village size and distance between villages tend to increase with the intensity of conflict. Peace between villages may develop if conflict has remained dormant for a long period and there is a mutual need for an alliance in the face of a common enemy. It begins with a series of ceremonially festive visits. If old antagonisms do not flare, visits may lead to joint raids and intermarriage between villages that strongly solidify an alliance. Proximity of missions and government agencies has had little impact on warfare.

Major Changes

Over the last twenty years most Yanomamö have become totally dependent on outside sources of axes, machetes, aluminum cooking pots, and fish hooks and line. These metal goods have replaced much of their stone-age technology. Most of these items have come from missionaries as gifts and wages. Through mission-organized cooperatives, the Yanomamö recently have begun to market baskets and arrows and some agricultural products.

Missionary presence has also distorted the traditional Yanomamö settlement pattern. Yanomamö attempt to gain easy access to mission outposts by moving their villages near a mission. As a result, the normal spacing of about a day's walk between villages has diminished dramatically. For example, around the Salesian mission at Mavaca there are five

Table 1
Time Allocation in Eight Yanomamö Villages (Minutes per Day)[25]

Village	Hunt	Fish	Garden	Gather	Cook	Manufacture	Misc	Total	Source
Bisaasi	83	86	29	51	42	43	33	367	2
Hasubë	65	19	40	100	ND	ND	ND[a]	4	
Koyekashi	42	85	85	66	26	36	17	357	3
Krihi	32	108	32	54	26	58	65	375	2
Mishi	13	109	81	53	37	149	17	459	1
Rakoi	12	109	44	24	27	68	76	360	2
Sanema	70	15	52	26	59	118[b]	ND	350	5
Toropo	61	56	43	55	41	69	35	359	1
Yanomami	38	40	38	45	54	52	84	357	2
Mean	50	64	45	52	37	62	49	359	

Sources: 1 = Hames, 1989; 2 = Hames, b; 3 = Lhermillier, 1974; 4 = Good, 1989; 5 = Colchester, 1984.
ND = no data.
[a]total not given because of incomplete data
[b] technology and maintenance activities are combined and column mean ignores these figures

villages and numerous small settlements with a total population of about nine hundred people within one day's walk. This population density is unprecedented for the Yanomamö and has led to severe depletion of wild resources. In addition, a significant fraction of that population no longer lives in traditional round communal villages but rather in small settlements of two to three houses occupied by a few families. Despite these changes, missionaries have failed to gain significant numbers of Yanomamö converts to Christianity. The Yanomamö have enormous pride in their culture and have strong doubts about the authenticity or superiority of Christian beliefs.

However, the greatest change and threat to the Yanomamö are the thousands of Brazilian gold miners who have infiltrated Yanomamö territory in Brazil and who have again (July 1993) illegally entered into Venezuela and this time killed seventeen men, women, and children. The situation in Brazil is similar to the situation in the United States in the 1800s when whites expanded into the lands of Native Americans. Miners bring epidemics of measles and influenza that lead to high mortality rates among the Yanomamö. Gold processing pollutes streams with mercury, killing fish and ruining a village's water supply. And open warfare between miners and Yanomamö has killed numerous Yanomamö and disrupted village life.[22]

Time Allocation

In the West, we tend to think of work as something done away from the home for 40 hours a week. In subsistence-based tribal populations this sort of definition is as inadequate for them as it is for us. While it is true that the Yanomamö, for example, leave the village to travel to garden, forest, and stream to acquire resources, much work takes place in the village. But the same thing is true in the West. Driving to work, mowing the lawn, shopping for food, washing clothes, and all those other household chores that must be done are not what we would call leisure time activities. We do these tasks to maintain our material well-being. I believe that most of us would define leisure time activities as including dining out, going to the movies, visiting friends, and playing sports. Therefore, one can define work as all those other activities we must do in order to maintain or enhance our material existence. Clearly, adults in the West work more than 40 hours per week if we use this expansive definition of work. Researchers who have investigated time allocated to work in the West show that urban European and North Americans work on average 55 to 65 hours per week, or 7.8 to 9.3 hours per day, seven days a week.[23]

Table 1 presents time allocation data for adults in eight Yanomamö villages on a basic set of work activities. The table reveals that the Yanomamö work about 6 hours per day (360 minutes) or 42 hours per week. This is significantly less than the 55 to 66 hours of work in modern societies. Furthermore, if we compare Yanomamö and related simple tropical horticulturalists to other types of economies (hunters and gatherers, pastoralists, agriculturists, etc.) we find that they are among the most leisured people in the world.[24]

Although Table 1 shows little variation in overall labor time (mean 359, SD 7.88), there is considerable variation among villages in time allocated to various subsistence tasks. Much of the variation can be attributed to local conditions such as the season in which the researcher collected the data, the degree to which a village is associated with missionaries, or special environmental conditions. Nevertheless, the only highland site, Sanema, shows some interesting patterns. This village allocates the third-most time to gardening, the least time to fishing, the second-least amount of time to gathering, and the second-most amount of time to hunting. Gathering and gardening times are probably related, as I suggested earlier. Since the density of wild sources of plant food is lower in the highlands, foraging is not as productive, which leads highlanders to spend more time gardening. Related to this is the higher reliability of manioc gardening, which makes gathering less of an important alternative source of vegetable foods. Another way of expressing the contrasting dependence on foraging (hunting, gathering, and fishing) and gardening in highland and lowland locales is to note that the highland population spends the least amount of time foraging and has the lowest ratio of foraging time to gardening time (2.13:1.0 compared to a mean of 4.43:1.0 for the lowlanders).

The extremely low amount of time highlanders allocate to fishing and the relatively high amount of time they allocate to hunting are also related. Highlanders do little fishing because of difficulties exploiting steep and narrow highland streams. Since fishing and hunting are the only ways of gaining sufficient high quality protein to the diet and fishing is unprofitable, highlanders are forced to hunt more intensively.

Division of Labor

As Figure 2 indicates, women spend significantly more time in cooking, fishing, gathering, and in child care than men do, while men spend more time hunting than women. From what we know about the division of labor cross-culturally these differences in time allocation are not surprising. In all cultures hunting is either predominately or wholly a male activity. Although the data indicate that Yanomamö women do almost no hunting, some qualifications are necessary. Yanomamö women occasionally accompany men on hunting forays to act as spotters and assist in the retrieval of game. Rarely do they ever make kills while with men. However, they occasionally make fortuitous kills of their own while gathering or fishing. Such kills are made without the use of bows and arrows.

Although the data show no significant difference between men and women in gardening there are important differences in garden tasks performed. Men almost exclusively do the heavy work of felling large trees, slashing the undergrowth, and burning the resulting debris prior to planting. Both sexes share in planting, while the daily tasks of weeding and harvesting fall almost exclusively to women. The pattern of men doing tasks which are dangerous and/or take them far from home is consistent with Judith Brown's model of the division of labor.[26] Brown suggests that women tend to dominate tasks that are compatible with simultaneous child care. Such tasks are not dangerous, can be accomplished near to home, and can be interrupted and resumed with no loss of efficiency.

While Brown's model usefully captures much of the variation in the division of labor among the Yanomamö and other groups, it does not explain why women who are postmenopausal or otherwise unencumbered with intensive child care do not, for example, engage in hunting or tree felling. For dangerous and arduous activities such as tree felling, it is probable that models that focus on physical strength differences may be useful. Or perhaps task linkages are required to complement Brown's model.[27] However, lack of female participation in hunting may require yet another explanation. Hunting is a highly skilled activity that is not easily learned and requires frequent practice to maintain proficiency. On average, little Yanomamö boys spend sixty to eighty minutes per day playing with bows and arrows and spotting, tracking, and stalking small birds and other tiny game near the village. It may be the case that women don't hunt because they never acquired the skills necessary to become proficient hunters.

The question of whether men or women work more can only be answered if we have a reasonable definition of work. Generally, economic anthropologists define work as all of those activities required to directly maintain and enhance survival and reproduction. Thus, it includes rather obvious activities such as the provisioning and preparing of food, construc-

Figure 2
Male and Female Time Allocation
to Basic Economic Tasks

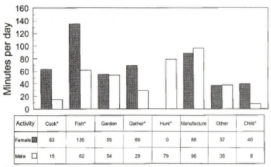

Activity	Cook*	Fish*	Garden	Gather*	Hunt*	Manufacture	Other	Child*
Female ▇	63	135	55	69	0	88	37	40
Male ☐	15	62	54	29	79	96	38	8

* Statistically significant difference at 0.05 level or better

tion and repair of tools and shelter, and the acquisition and management of fuel (or firewood, in the case of the Yanomamö). If we use this definition of work, Yanomamö women work about 12 minutes per day more than men, but the difference is not statistically significant. This finding is rather interesting since in the vast majority of horticultural tribal populations on which we have time allocation data, women work significantly more than men.[28] The only societies in which men work significantly more than women are hunters and gatherers. That Yanomamö men and women work approximately equally is therefore consistent with the point made earlier: that they can be best characterized as foraging horticulturalists since their time allocation patterns fall between horticulturalists and hunter-gatherers.

Some may consider this definition unnecessarily restrictive because it ignores a task that is critical for the long-term survival of the Yanomamö: child care. The tropical forest harbors many sources of environmental trauma that are very dangerous to infants and small children. Inside and outside the village there are stinging and biting insects, dangerous plant spines, and poisonous plants, snakes, and insects. Infants and small children are protected from these threats by being carried in slings much of the time and actively watched when they are set down.[29] While caring for infants and small children in this way may be pleasurable, it is also exhausting and difficult. And recall that I defined work as those things we do to enhance or maintain our physical well-being. Just as the Yanomamö labor to provide food for their children, they also physically care for them. In order to assess

the impact of child care on overall labor time differences, I must restrict my analysis to data I collected on four Yanomamö villages (Mishimishimaböwei, Rakoiwä, Krihisiwä, and Bisaasi) since none of the other studies collected child care data. When I include direct child care activities (carrying, feeding, nursing, holding, etc.),[30] female work time increases by 43 minutes per day while male work time increases by only 8 minutes per day. If child care activities are added to conventionally defined labor, then Yanomamö women work more than men.

STATUS AND THE ALLOCATION OF LABOR

The Yanomamö, like all people, exhibit strong individual differences in the amount of labor they perform that are independent of sex. Factors such as age, number of dependents, and marital status should logically help us to understand much of the variation. For example, one would expect that a married couple with numerous dependent children to labor more than newlyweds with no dependents. Such a prediction is based on a number of assumptions, such as each family is wholly responsible for supplying its economic needs and economic resources are freely available. While this latter assumption is correct for the Yanomamö, the former is suspect, as I will later explain. In this section I will examine the degree to which age determines individual labor time allocation.

CHILD LABOR TRENDS

On the basis of our own experiences we expect that the amount of work one does will increase with age and that it eventually begins to diminish when one retires or becomes physically incapacitated. We also tend to believe that childhood should be a carefree time with little in the way of work responsibilities—a time for play, exploration, and learning. An examination of Yanomamö time allocation data will allow us to evaluate all of these ideas; and, since the Yanomamö are relatively typical representatives of the tribal world, we can get a sense of whether our Western experience is in any way typical over the history of humankind.

Figure 3 shows the amount of time children from ages five through eighteen allocate to labor time activities.[31] As can be easily seen, labor time does generally increase with age. The rate of increase is uneven only because of small sample sizes in some of the age groups. Over the chart I have superimposed

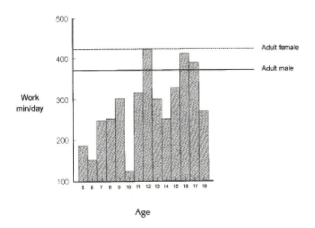

Figure 3
Labor Time of Children

adult male and female labor time. You will note in this graph that adult females work significantly more (421 min./day) than males (372 min./day). These figures differ from the ones given earlier in the ten-village comparison because they derive from the four villages I studied. I use this smaller data set here because it is the only one broken down by age. As the figure indicates, boys and girls begin to achieve adult labor time levels by the time they become teenagers.

The data presented seem to indicate that childhood is brief and children are quickly recruited into the family work force. To some extent these figures are an artifact of the method I used to collect time allocation data. If I could not observe someone when I was sampling behavior, I had to rely on reports of what they were doing. For example, someone would tell me that all the members of a particular family were in the forest gathering wild palm nuts or weeding the garden. When I was able to accompany families on their economic activities I found that children did work but not as hard or as constantly as adults: they worked about 40 to 80 percent as much as adults when, for example, a garden was being weeded. Nevertheless, the data tell us something important about work and family life that provides a strong contrast to what occurs in the urban West. Yanomamö children work alongside their parents and are important to the household economy. The family unit does not separate in the morning; children and adults do not go their separate ways to school and work only to rejoin each other in the evening. "School" for a Yanomamö child is in the context of the family economy where

they learn how to hunt, gather, garden, fish, and perform all the other activities necessary for them to become competent adults.

ADULT LABOR TRENDS

If we extend the analysis of time allocated to work across the entire life span we expect to see labor time increase to a point then decrease. This pattern, an inverted U-shaped curve, is evident for both men and women in Figure 4. However, the shapes of the curves are quite different. Male allocation of labor time begins at a lower level but increases rapidly until it peaks around age thirty-five and then rapidly decreases thereafter. Females, in contrast, begin at initially higher levels, ascend more slowly to a peak at age fifty and then decrease their efforts much more slowly. The last point is rather interesting since the curve shows that women at ages thirty and sixty work about the same amount of time. The factors that account for these patterns are quite complex. Women engaged in active child care (for example, nursing) work less than women who are not.[32] This fact probably accounts for female labor time peaking after menopause. Male labor time decreases quite rapidly after age thirty-five, but I am not sure why the rate of decrease is so much greater than for women. There are two interrelated possibilities. Since males have higher rates of mortality than women at all ages they may also have higher rates of decrepitude than women that is, their ability to do physically demanding labor may decrease more rapidly. Related to this trend is that as men become older they work more at relatively sedentary tasks such as manufacturing and the gardening tasks of weeding and harvesting, and work significantly less in hunting and clearing new gardens.

Conclusion

Since 1975 when Allen Johnson reintroduced anthropologists to methods for measuring time allocation, 33 studies of how people use their time have become increasing popular among anthropologists. In this chapter I have attempted to show some of the uses to which time allocation can be put by showing how it can elucidate fundamental ethnographic problems in intracultural variation. I showed that differences in environment between lowland and highland Yanomamö lead to differences in the allocation of time to basic economic activities. We found that highland

Figure 4
Work over the Life Span

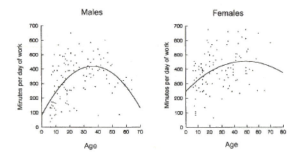

groups are much more tied to agricultural pursuits because of a lack of high-quality foraging resources. In the area of the sexual division of labor we found that men and women work nearly the same amount of time but allocate their efforts much differently. In addition, we found that if child care activities are included in labor time, then women work significantly more than men. Finally, I showed that time allocation patterns show significant patterns associated with age. Both boys and girls are quickly absorbed into the family's labor pool and adult male labor effort peaks earlier and declines more quickly than it does for women.

In closing I should note that time allocation studies are not simply restricted to the documentation of variation in work effort. Researchers now use the method to quantify patterns of social interaction such as how much time husbands and wives spend together, the size and composition of play groups among children, and patterns of cooperation among co-villagers. So long as ethnographers are interested in quantitative measures of variation in social life we can expect that time allocation studies will play a central role.

Notes

1. R. Hames, "The Settlement Pattern of a Yanomamö Population Bloc," in R. Hames and W. Vickers, eds., *Adaptive Responses of Native Amazonians* (New York: Academic Press, 1983), pp. 192–229.
2. N. Chagnon, *Studying the Yanomamö* (New York: Holt, Rinehart & Winston, 1974).
3. N. Chagnon, *Studying the Yanomamö*; R. Hames, "The Settlement Pattern of a Yanomamö Population Bloc."
4. J. Lizot, *Les Yanomami Centrau* (Paris: Editions de L'Ecole des Hautes Etudes en Sciences Sociales, 1984), p. 54, Table 2.
5. W. Smole, *The Yanoama Indians: A Cultural Geography* (Austin: University of Texas Press, 1976).
6. M. Colchester, "Rethinking Stone Age Economics: Some Speculations Concerning the Pre-Columbian Yanoama Economy," *Human Ecology* 12 (1984): 291–314.
7. M. Goulding, *The Fishes and the Forest* (Berkeley: University of California Press, 1980).
8. G. Saffirio and R. Hames, "The Forest and the Highway," in K. Kensinger and J. Clay, eds., *Working Papers on South American Indians #6 and Cultural Survival Occasional Paper #11*, joint publication (Cambridge, MA: Cultural Survival, 1983), pp. 1–52.
9. R. Hames, "Time, Efficiency, and Fitness in the Amazonian Protein Quest," *Research in Economic Anthropology* 11 (1989): 43–85. Anthropologists measure the efficiency of subsistence activities in kilograms of food gained per hour of work, or kilocalories of food gained per kilocalorie of work.
10. W. Smole, pp. 81 and 227.
11. M. Colchester, p. 300, Table 2; Hames, "Time, Efficiency, and Fitness in the Amazonian Protein Quest," p. 64, Table 6.
12. J. Eisenberg, "The Density and Biomass of Tropical Mammals," in M. Soule and B. Wilcox, eds., *Conservation Biology: An Evolutionary-Ecological Perspective* (Sunderland, MA: Sinauer Associates, 1980), pp. 35–55; J. Eisenberg, M. O'Connell, and V. August, "Density, Productivity, and Distribution of Mammals in the Northern Neotropics," in J. Eisenberg, ed., *Vertebrate Ecology in the Northern Neotropics* (Washington DC: Smithsonian Institution Press, 1979), pp. 187–207.
13. R. Hames, "Time, Efficiency, and Fitness in the Amazonian Protein Quest."
14. R. Hames, "A Comparison of the Efficiencies of the Shotgun and Bow in Neotropical Forest Hunting," *Human Ecology* 7 (1979): 219–252.
15. Data on Yanomamö garden size is from the following sources: E. Fuentes, "Los Yanomami y las plantas silvestres," *Antropologica* 54 (1980): 3–138; Smole, *The Yanamo Indians*, pp. 36–37; J. Lizot, "Economie Primitive et Subsistence:Essai sur Le Travail et L'alimentation Chez les Yanomami," *Libre* 4 (1980):69–113; and J. Lizot, "La Agricultural Yanomami," *Antropologica* 53 (1980): 3–93. Information on cultivated bananas and plantains can be found in N.W. Simmonds, *The Evolution of Bananas* (London: Longmans &Green, 1979).
16. M. Colchester, p. 301.
17. N. Chagnon, *Yanomamö, the Fierce People* (New York: Harcourt Brace Jovanovich, 1992).
18. R. Hames, "A Comparison of the Efficiencies of the Shotgun and Bow in Neotropical Forest Hunting."
19. T. Melancon, "Marriage and Reproduction among the Yanomamö of Venezuela" (Ph.D. diss., Pennsylvania State University, 1982). Cross-cousins are offspring of siblings of the opposite sex. For example, your father's sister's children are your cross-cousins

and so are your mother's brother's children. Double cross-cousin marriage is set up when two men marry one another's sisters. The Yanomamö prescribe that the offspring of such unions should marry. These people are double cross-cousins because (using the male as an example) a male is marrying a woman who is simultaneously his father's sister's daughter and his mother's brother's daughter.

20. N. Chagnon, *Yanomamö*, the Fierce People.

21. R. Hames, "The Settlement Pattern of a Yanomamö Population Bloc."

22. N. Chagnon, *Yanomamö: The Last Days of Eden* (New York: Harcourt Brace Jovanovich, 1993); N. Chagnon, "Covering Up the Yanomamö Massacre," *New York Times*, October 23, 1993; see also Saffirio and Hames, on the impact of road construction on Yanomamö economy, and N. Chagnon and T. Melancon, "Reproduction, Epidemics, and the Number of Kin in Tribal Populations: A Case Study," in N. Keyfitz, ed., *Population and Biology: a Bridge between Two Disciplines* (Liege: Ordina Editions, 1984), pp. 147–167, on the effects of epidemics spread by whites.

23. R. Hames, "Time, Efficiency, and Fitness in the Amazonian Protein Quest." Adult labor time is the average of male and female labor time.

24. Sources for time allocation data in Table 1 are as follows: Colchester, p. 299; K. Good, "Yanomami Hunting Patterns: Trekking and Garden Relocation as an Adaptation to Game Availability in Amazonia, Venezuela" (Ph.D. diss., University of Florida, 1989); Hames, "Time, Efficiency, and Fitness in the Amazonian Protein Quest"; A. Lhermillier and N. Lhermillier, "Vie Economique et Sociale d'une Unite Familliale Yanomami" (thesis, L'Ecole Pratique des Hautes Etudes, 1974); Lizot, "Economie Primitive et Subsistence."

25. Ibid.

26. J. Brown, "A Note on the Division of Labor," *American Anthropologist* 72 (1970): 1073–1078.

27. G. P. Murdock and C. Provost, "Factors in the Division of Labor by Sex: A Cross-Cultural Analysis," *Ethnology* 12 (1973): 206–212; M. Burton and D. White, "Sexual Division of Labor in Agriculture," *American Anthropologist* 86 (1984): 568–583. In their task linkage model Burton and White show that the sex that begins a task that has a series of steps is more likely to complete the subsequent steps. For example, if women harvest food they are more likely to perform the processing and storage tasks that immediately follow harvesting.

28. R. Hames, "Time, Efficiency, and Fitness in the Amazonian Protein Quest."

29. R. Hames, "Variation in Paternal Care among the Yanomamö," in B. Hewlett, ed., *The Father's Role: Cultural and Evolutionary Perspectives* (Chicago: Aldine de Gruyter, 1992), pp. 85–110.

30. Ibid.

31. The data reported here on the division of labor, male and female labor time, and child labor time are taken from data I collected in the villages of Mishimishimaböwei-teri, Rakoiwä-teri, Bisaasiteri, and Krihisiwä-teri in 1986 and 1987. The data set consists of seventy-three adult females and seventy-six adult males. Adults are defined as anyone over the age of fifteen years who is married or has been married.

32. Ibid.

33. A. Johnson, "Time Allocation in a Machiguenga Community," *Ethnology* 14 (1975): 301–310. See also the continuing series of studies of time allocation, in various societies, that are published by the Human Relations Area Files.

Suggested Readings

Biocca, E. *Yanoama: The Narrative of a White Girl Kidnapped by Amazonian Indians*. New York: E.P. Dutton, 1970. Helena Valero was captured by Brazilian Yanomamö when she was twelve years old. This book is the exciting account of her capture, problems in adjusting to Yanomamö social life, marriage to several Yanomamö men, and eventual release to missionaries.

Chagnon, N. *Yanomamö: The Fierce People*. 4th ed. New York: Holt, Rinehart & Winston, 1992. This is perhaps the most popular ethnography written in the last several decades. It is an introductory yet detailed ethnography of the Yanomamö with a special focus on kinship, social organization, and politics.

———. *Yanomamö: The Last Days of Eden*. New York: Harcourt Brace Jovanovich, 1993. A more personal and accessible account of the Yanomamö than Chagnon's standard ethnography listed above. It presents a lucid picture of what it is like to do fieldwork with the Yanomamö and some contemporary problems faced by the Yanomamö.

Early, J., and J. Peters. *The Population Dynamics of the Mucajai Yanomamö*. New York: Academic Press, 1991. This monograph describes Brazilian Yanomamö with a special emphasis on demography in relation to social organization. In addition, it presents a novel explanation of mother-in-law avoidance by the son-in-law, a moderately common cross-cultural phenomenon.

Lizot, J. *Tales of the Yanomami: Daily Life in the Venezuelan Forest*. Cambridge: Cambridge University Press, 1985. Jacques Lizot is a French social anthropologist who has worked with the Yanomamö for nearly two dozen years. He presents vignettes of Yanomamö life in novelistic fashion with stories of romance, vengeance, politics, shamanism, and women's lives.

Haitians: From Political Repression to Chaos

Robert Lawless

Haiti may be regarded as a predatory state run by an elite class that extorts its living from the masses. The institutional structures of government do not operate for the benefit of the people as a whole. Rather, the government largely serves the elite. Directly and indirectly, members of the elite depend on the government to make their living. Thus, in order to earn and increase their incomes, members of the elite have to stay in power. All members of the elite, however, cannot be in control at the same time, and so individuals, families, and groups must make alliances with those who manage the agencies of government.

The political repression seen in the succession of arrests, torture, and gross violations of human rights in Haiti represents the efforts of the elite to maintain itself economically at the direct expense of the poor. Their loss of power would result not only in the loss of control and prestige but also in the loss of income.

It is my view that the long Duvalier reign from 1957 to 1986 destroyed the traditional balance among the competing members of the elite and raised both the degree of violence of the state against the people and the techniques of stealing from the people to their highest levels in Haitian history. For example, although the Central Bank maintained a minimum of integrity and kept the Haitian currency tied to the U.S. dollar, all other state units and agencies were absolutely personal sources of household income for the Duvaliers and their cohorts. After the downfall of the Duvaliers in February 1986 the machinery of political repression had no traditional channels for its expression and devolved into a chaotic situation with no conventional, indigenous solutions currently in sight (as of the time of this writing in Spring 1994).

Laying the basis for such a thesis requires some knowledge of basic information about Haiti and also some knowledge of the history of Haiti.

Introduction

Located in the Caribbean Sea just 54 miles (90 kilometers) southeast of Cuba and part of the Greater Antilles, Haiti shares the island of Hispaniola with the Dominican Republic. Taking up the western third of the island, Haiti contains about 11,100 square miles (27,750 square kilometers)—approximately the size of Maryland. Its topography varies from a few flat, semiarid valleys to some densely forested, deeply dissected mountains and many semi-denuded, gently sloping mountains. About one-third of Haiti is at an elevation between 660 and 1,650 feet (200 and 500 meters) above sea level and about two-thirds is divided into three mountain ranges with the highest elevation, the La Selle Peak, at about 8,840 feet (2,680 meters).

The average annual temperature falls somewhere between 75 and 81 degrees Fahrenheit (24 and 27 celsius). The major changes in temperature are caused by changes in elevation. Starting at the capital of Port-au-Prince with an altitude of 130 feet (40 meters) and a mean temperature of 79, a perspiring person can walk up to nearby Petionville at an elevation of 1,320 feet (400 meters) and experience a mean temperature of 76, and the same person can continue up the road to an elevation of 4,785 feet (1,450 meters) at the vegetable center of Kenscoff with a quite enjoyable mean annual temperature of 65 degrees Fahrenheit.

Demographic information is difficult to come by, but an educated estimate would put the total population at about 6.5 million. Port-au-Prince has about 1.25 million people, and the second largest city, Cap-Haitien, has maybe 70,000. The important regional cities such as Les Cayes, Gonaives, Port-de-Paix, Jacmel, Jeremie, St. Marc, and Hinche have populations of only 10,000 to 50,000 at the most. Probably about 80 percent of the Haitian population lives in rural areas and subsists through farming.

Outsiders have traditionally misunderstood the language situation of Haiti. It has often been stated that the elite speaks French, and the masses speak some sort of degraded version of French called *patois* or Creole. Anthropological linguists wring their hands in despair at such notions. All languages that have been in use for more than a couple of generations are structurally and functionally complex enough to handle all the descriptive, emotional, and expressive needs of the people speaking the particular language. The language of Haiti, the language spoken by *all* Haitians, is properly referred to as Haitian Creole. For much of the modern history of Haiti, however, the official language of government, business, and education has been French, even though only about 8 percent of the people speak French consistently. The reason for the usage of French is that members of the educated elite have found that they can exclude the masses from competing for scarce jobs by requiring knowledge of the French language for positions in government and business.

The contrast between "Blacks" and "mulattoes" is a salient theme in Haitian history. A nineteenth-century writer, for example, pointed out that color distinctions were extremely important and he included an appendix with charts on color types in the Haitian population.[1] Even Leslie Manigat, a political science professor who was briefly president of Haiti in 1988, spoke in the mid-1960s at North American universities in terms of these color distinctions, saying:

> On the one hand, there has been the light-skinned elite, claiming to be ideologically liberal, in reality, politically autocratic, economically conservative, socially sectarian, and culturally pro-European. When in power, this elite has represented the interests of the urban, moneyed oligarchy. Against its traditional hegemony, on the other hand, there has been a coalition led by the dark-skinned elite. Although socially progressive because of the need to maintain solidarity with the middle classes and masses through the common denominator of color, this coalition was also politically autocratic, ideologically authoritarian, economically quasi-traditional, and culturally nationalistic.[2]

The "color issue" was nonexistent in the election campaigns leading up to the November 1987 aborted elections, in which Manigat was originally a minor candidate. Almost all families in Haiti can claim members whose skin color ranges from light to dark, but the idea of a society divided into a small sophisticated, Westernized mulatto segment and a large dangerous, Africanish Black segment does benefit some groups. In particular, the traditional power elite gains an advantage by presenting this picture of Haiti to the white world, that is, the mulatto elite can claim outside help in its efforts to rule the unruly masses.

Despite its political difficulties Haiti is internationally famous for its art and literature. In the 1940s Haiti burst into the consciousness of the art world with an astonishing display of paintings. Her artists justly deserved the worldwide attention they received for their so-called primitive or naive art.

Haitian writers initially focused on concepts of negritude foreshadowing the black power and anti-colonial post-World War II movements. Haiti's literary production is even more amazing in light of the high rate of illiteracy, probably around eighty-five percent. Fewer than half of the rural children attend school, and only about twenty percent of those complete the primary grades. Most of the literature is strikingly indigenous. Voodoo has been a major theme in many of the novels.

The current chaos, however, has closed down the traditional channels for the production of art and literature. Writers had usually depended on bookstores with small print shops to put out limited editions of their works, which were sold by the bookstores. These book stores and print shops have been virtually put out of business through losing their primary customers (because schools have been closed) and through harassment by army and police personnel, who see any printed work as anti-government. Artists had depended largely on the tourist trade to earn a living. The few hardy tourists who were not turned off by the AIDS scare are now thoroughly repulsed by the continuing chaos and perceived lack of safety in Haiti.

Religion

A cementing element of the Haitian population is religion. Although some of the population is nominally Roman Catholic and although Protestant missionaries have made considerable headway in the poorer rural areas of Haiti, the religion of Haiti is still Voodoo, a religion that focuses on contacting and appeasing immediate relatives, such as dead parents and grandparents, and ancestral spirits, who include distant, stereotyped ancestors.

Voodoo is an egalitarian religion with both men and women serving as priests presiding over ceremonies that include divination rites, which are used to find out the course of the future or the causes of various difficulties. It has healing rites in which a Voodoo priest interacts directly with sick people to cure them, propitiatory rites in which food and drink are offered to specific spirits to get into their good graces, and preventive rites in which ancestors are offered sacrifices to help head off any possible future trouble. Indeed, many Voodoo rituals can be seen as healing rites, since many of the rituals are performed at times of sickness and death. Much of Voodoo, then, can be seen as a folk medical system that attributes illness to the work of angry ancestors and that consists of ceremonies performed to appease those ancestors in order to cure illness.

The influence of Voodoo on politics has always been problematic since Voodoo is practiced largely on a household level and has no regional or national connections. Due to its egalitarian ideology, Voodoo has often been the target of repression by the government. Voodoo may, indeed, be the one aspect of Haitian life surviving quite well through the current period of chaos.

Health

Voodoo healers are a major part of the medical system of Haiti, though Western medicine has been available to the urban elite for several decades and is, indeed, available from a few rural clinics. For the most part, however, health and healing for poorer Haitians is handled by herb medicine, bone setters, injectionists, Voodoo rituals, and by a rich body of folk knowledge. The poorer masses, nevertheless, suffer many health problems of malnutrition and disease. The daily per capita food consumption is estimated at sixteen hundred calories, and measles, diarrhea, and tetanus kill many children before they reach their teens.

Tuberculosis is Haiti's most devastating disease, followed closely by malaria, influenza, dysentery, tetanus, whooping cough, and measles. Eye problems are endemic, with the chief causes of blindness being cataracts, scarring of the cornea, and glaucoma.

A ninety-two-page study released in September 1992 by the Permanent Commission on Emergency Aid, which represents over sixty nongovernmental development and democracy organizations in Haiti, said that the death rate has been rising and the health of the population dropping since the September 1991 military coup that ousted the democratically elected government. It also pointed out that there has been a deterioration in state services amounting to a descent into chaos, with the Departments of Public Health and Water totally mismanaged. The supply of drinkable water, for example, has dropped by fifty percent in the cities and twenty percent in the countryside. According to the report, "The situation is extremely critical and just waiting for cholera to strike."[3] Other problems include an increase in garbage in the streets (with only about twenty-five percent of the country's garbage being collected), a rise in the number of preventable illnesses, and a deterioration in mental health.

History

Haitian history is unique among Caribbean nations and, in fact, unique in the world; Haiti's slave uprising was the only one that grew into a modern nation. How Haitians view themselves and how the world views Haiti must always be filtered through the prism of this momentous historical fact.

SLAVE BEGINNINGS

Haiti became a slave colony of the French after Europeans, mainly the Spaniards, killed off the pre-Columbian Indian population on the island of Hispaniola through murder, diseases, and slavery. Then the Europeans looked toward Africa for the labor they needed to work the farms that were to become enormous sugarcane plantations. In 1502, just ten years after Columbus landed in Haiti, the Spanish governor brought the first black slaves to Hispaniola, and in 1505 sugar cane was introduced to Hispaniola from the Canary Islands. In 1697 Spain recognized France's claim to the western part of Hispaniola, to be known as the French colony of Saint Domingue.

INDEPENDENCE

The brutality and exploitation of the French resulted in many failed slave uprisings until, in August 1791, the slaves managed a major revolt that the plantation owners could not contain. By 1796 white supremacy was at an end, and Black rule was established under the leadership of Toussaint L'Ouverture, a charismatic ex-slave. In 1800 Napoleon sent twenty-eight thousand troops to retake the colony and re-enslave the Blacks, but by late 1803 the Haitians had defeated the French troops. On January 1, 1804, Jean-Jacques Dessalines, Toussaint's successor, proclaimed the independence of Haiti, an event that shocked the white world to its foundations. Haitians further goaded the white world by proclaiming Haiti as a symbol of redemption for the whole African race. For example, the first Haitian constitution designated Haitians of whatever color as "Black" (including those Germans and Poles who had been given Haitian citizenship), opened Haitian citizenship to all persons everywhere of African or Indian descent, and forbade whites to own land.

At the time of the Haitian Revolution fully two-thirds of the slaves had been born in Africa. By the end of the revolution virtually all the whites had been eliminated, and there were several massacres of the mulattoes. As a consequence, Haiti was ostracized by the white world. It was not until 1862 that Haiti's most important neighbor, the United States, recognized Haitian independence. Great Britain was one of the few nations that did have early diplomatic relations with Haiti, but it was in the writings of the English racists and anti-abolitionists that Haiti began to get its unwarranted bad press,[4] focusing largely on the savagery of these "African" Haitians and the barbaric practices of Voodoo—especially its alleged ritual cannibalism.

In actuality Haiti represents the only time in history when a slave population on its own suddenly faced the task of organizing a government and an economic system. The press on Haiti, nevertheless, focused almost entirely on the former prosperity of the French system in Saint Domingue in contrast to the poverty, ignorance, and disorder in independent Haiti—just as the press today largely emphasizes the destitution found in Haiti. Such depictions, however, neglect the fact that in colonial Saint Domingue only an extraordinarily small percentage of the population enjoyed the good life—and, indeed, even today only a small percentage of the Haitian population enjoys considerable wealth.

One of the crucial problems facing Haiti immediately after independence concerned access to the land previously owned by the French and how to maintain the agricultural productivity of this land. Initially the Haitian government attempted to reinstate the painful plantation system of colonial Saint Domingue. When these attempts failed because plantations were associated with slavery, land was, for the most part, simply distributed among the ex-slaves. As a result, from sixty to eighty percent of the farmers currently own their own land, though the plots are fragmented and small. The urban-based government has rarely shown a sustained interest in agriculture, and although the state owns land, nobody seems to pay much attention to it and peasants occupy most of it rent-free.

MODERN DEVELOPMENTS

Except for a brief period between 1915 and 1934 when it was occupied by United States Marines, Haiti has remained self-consciously independent. The twenty-three-year period after the occupation and until the election of François "Papa Doc" Duvalier as president saw increased feelings of nationalism and pride in the African heritage, a growth in trade and political interaction with other Caribbean nations, the development of peasant economic cooperation, the introduction of a progressive income tax, and, especially, the rise of a new Black middle class. In 1957 Duvalier won the presidency with a decisive margin as the self-proclaimed heir to these new developments.

In addition, Haitians have always taken a special interest in the affairs of Blacks throughout the world. In 1859 the Haitian government ordered a special requiem mass for the death of John Brown, the famous American abolitionist. In that same year the Haitian Secretary of State called for immigration to Haiti by "members of the African race, who groan in the United States" (quoted in DuBois)[5]. More than a hundred years later the Duvalier regime declared several days of national mourning after the assassination of Martin Luther King Jr. And two major thoroughfares in Port-au-Prince are named after John Brown and Martin Luther King Jr.

DUVALIER THE SENIOR

Widely regarded as a tool of the army by some and as a lackey of the U.S. embassy by others, Duvalier, instead, proved to be an extraordinarily astute politician; initially he gained the trust of the indigenous clergy, the peasants, and the urban proletariat, and then he brought diverse elements into his circle of advisers, including communists, North Americans, Haitian exiles, taxi drivers, Voodoo priests, and Black power intellectuals. To keep the army in control, he cut its funding and created an alterative volunteer militia loyal only to him, the organization that came to be known as the notorious *tonton-makout*—named after a character in Haitian folklore who stalks bad children and carries them off in his basket.

The first few years of Duvalier's rule were marked by several unsuccessful coups and invasions. In 1958 and 1959 invasions by Haitian exiles were thwarted, and in 1963 Clément Barbot, chief of the tonton-makout, attempted a major coup that was accompanied by a small guerrilla war and a number of bombings and shootings in and around Port-au-Prince. Also in 1963 an attempt was made on the life of Duvalier's children Simone and Jean-Claude. In April of the next year Duvalier declared himself president-for-life, and in August yet another invasion failed. In 1968 the National Palace was bombed but an accompanying invasion fizzled out. Duvalier's reprisals were swift, vicious, and widespread. The result of his campaign of oppression against opponents was increased isolation from the international community, which began to attribute all of Haiti's problems to Duvalier.

During the years of Duvalier's rule thousands of Haitian professionals fled to the United States, Canada, the Bahamas, the Dominican Republic, Venezuela, French Guyana, Africa, and France. During the rule of his son, from 1971 to 1986, thousands more from all classes fled to Florida. The Haitians who left greatly influenced politics back in Haiti. Those who went to the United States tended to have little patience with the traditional French-oriented elite. Haitians of all classes mixed extensively and intensively overseas, and the Duvalier brand of Black nationalism found little support among these upwardly mobile, welfare-conscious Haitian exiles.

DUVALIER THE JUNIOR

In January 1971, Duvalier announced that his son would succeed him as president-for-life, and in April of that year Duvalier died and was, indeed, succeeded by his nineteen-year-old son, Jean-Claude. The junior Duvalier closely tied the fortunes of Haiti to the United States—a relationship featuring private investments from the United States wooed by such incentives as no customs taxes, a minimum wage kept very low, the suppression of labor unions, and the right of U.S. companies to repatriate profits from their offshore plants. So, with the help of U.S. government agencies Haiti became economically dependent on its powerful North American neighbor. Also, with the aid of the international lending enterprise Haiti joined the ranks of the debtor nations for the first time in its history. And with the Reagan administration giving five times as much military aid to the dictatorship as had President Carter, the army in Haiti finally regained the power under the junior Duvalier that it had lost under the senior Duvalier.

In addition to the economic exploitation by the United States, Haiti suffered greatly from the oil crises of 1973–1974 and 1980. In addition, Hurricane Allen in 1980 devastated the coffee trees and ruined the production of coffee, one of Haiti's most significant exports.

Initially Jean-Claude did make some progressive changes under pressure from the Carter administration and its emphasis on human rights. By the end of 1979, however, Jean-Claude's administration had slid back toward repression as the Carter administration became occupied with other matters. Correctly reading the incoming Reagan administration's lack of interest in human rights, the Haitian government increased its control of political, press, and labor groups. Immediately following Reagan's election in November 1980, several hundred progressive Haitians were arrested and many were deported.

According to a study of the North American mass media, "The foreign media seemed confused by the attitude of the American government, and, understandably, could not present a clear picture of the enigmatic Jean-Claude. Some journalists, especially Americans, who had written about the hopelessness of François Duvalier's Haiti, began writing about the sudden improvement in Haiti after the death of Papa Doc. Others, especially Haitians, claimed that repression was just as bad under Jean-Claude as it had been under François."[6] Clearly Jean-Claude was not as politically astute as was his father. Some Haitians have emphasized to me that the beginning of his end was his elaborate wedding in 1980 to Michèle Bennett, the daughter of a mulatto business family. This event alienated many of the Black power followers of his father. At any rate, after fourteen years of rule by a second Duvalier and precious few, if any, economic gains, Haitians reached the end of their patience. In late November 1985 street protests began in towns throughout Haiti, and the violent police responses led to further protests. Despite these attempts at repression, some reshuffling at high levels of government, and a farcical "referendum" that gave Jean-Claude "99.98 percent" of the vote, the second of the Duvaliers could not hang onto power. Just a little over a year later, on the morning of February 7, 1986, Jean-Claude Duvalier fled to France. An era had ended. That morning the streets of Port-au-Prince were full of Haitians with tree branches symbolically sweeping away the evil spirits of the Duvaliers.

Later in the day it was announced that Haiti would be run by an interim government initially composed of a five-member council. Headed by Lt. Gen. Henri Namphy, it was pared down to three members six weeks later. A few days after the ouster of Jean-Claude the council abolished the widely hated tonton-makout, but the interim government did not pursue supporters of Duvalier except under intense public pressure. Namphy and others still in power obviously did not view the end of Duvalier as a revolution signaling the end of authoritarianism in Haiti.

CURRENT EVENTS

For several years Haiti limped along with various forms of the council, all of them inevitably run in one way or another by the army. With assorted groups jockeying for influence Haiti attempted to have presidential and National Assembly elections in November 1987 and presidential and National Assembly (and mayoral) elections in January 1988. Despite the indifference of the council to the public welfare, attempts to form a progressive government continued. The 1987 constitution is, in fact, a good example of an indigenous document created by progressive Haitians to solve the peculiar political problems that have arisen out of Haitian history. It was, of course, produced in opposition to the wishes of the ruling military-dominated council.

The referendum on the constitution, held in March 1987, represented the highest level of political participation by the Haitian general public since the elections that led to the installation of the Duvalier dynasty in 1957. Almost all Haitians that I have talked with regard the twenty-day period leading up to the referendum as the freest political period in living memory and the period in which cultural expressions reached their height. The constitution was published both in French and Creole. Several hundred thousand comic books and posters explaining the constitution were distributed throughout Haiti. Radio stations devoted many hours of their air time to the reading and discussion of the constitution.

After the overwhelming approval of the new constitution, various thugs, including those identified as former tonton-makout, began attacking institutions identified with the new democratic processes, such as radio stations and the elections offices. It seems that these attacks occurred because the military and other elite elements saw the involvement of the masses as a threat to their position, and preferred the appearance of chaos in the hope that they would be called back to power to restore order.

In the ensuing descent into disorder two presidential candidates were killed—one in front of a police station clutching a copy of the constitution. Another candidate refused to campaign because of the lack of police protection. A few days before the elections the polling headquarters was burned down, a popular radio station was set on fire, and arsonists screaming "Long live the army!" destroyed a large open-air market in Port-au-Prince.

On the morning of the November 1987 presidential and National Assembly elections, gunmen roamed the streets of Port-au-Prince firing at those going to vote and invading some voting sites killing several people. Haitians have told me that uniformed soldiers often joined in these attacks. Outside of Port-au-Prince the ballots were rarely delivered because the trucks had been hijacked, usually by soldiers.

At least thirty-four people were killed in these aborted elections, which the council cancelled later in the day. On the very next day a friend in Cap-Haitien wrote to me,

For many months, November 29, 1987, has stood out in the hearts and minds of Haitians as a day of hope. Yesterday it became a day of deception. Yesterday, we saw, in one day, our hopes and dreams for a democratic and free Haiti crushed. We feel we no longer have a hope that there will be a change in the country.

Another told me in Creole the same day over the telephone, "Kè-m grenn" (My heart is broken).

While the military council tried to control politics, social controls in the streets began breaking down. Starting soon after Duvalier's departure Haitians spoke to me about the lack of control in Port-au-Prince and Cap-Haitien and complained about the unprecedented frequency of crimes in these two largest Haitian cities. During the first week of October 1986 the opening of schools was delayed in Cap-Haitien because of rioting that included the sacking of the CARE warehouse and the main post office.

Personal violence that had been extremely rare in Haiti began occurring. Haitians were shocked by several rapes in Port-au-Prince in February and March 1987. One Haitian told me, "There were people so frustrated by what they saw as a worsening situation here that rioting and burning barricades was their only means of expression." A returning exile is quoted as saying, "We have no work, nothing to live on; the country is in ruins."[7]

After the 1987 elections were undermined by the army and aborted, the 1988 elections were controlled by the army and widely regarded as illegitimate. Leslie Manigat, the president installed from this 1988 election, attempted to finesse the army and was thrown out by the military after four months.

For a couple of years after 1988 there were a series of military coups, and then a legitimate election was held in December 1990. Scheduled first for November 4 and then postponed to December 16, this election was monitored by more than four hundred international observers, including former U.S. President Carter. Jean-Bertrand Aristide won the presidency in a landslide approaching 70 percent of the estimated 75 percent of the two million registered voters who cast ballots, and his election raised expectations both in Haiti and elsewhere in the Caribbean. For example, at Aristide's inauguration Jamaica's prime minister said that he sensed "a very great moment in Caribbean history after all the generations of struggle and tyranny."[8]

Installed in office on February 7, 1991, five years to the day after the end of the Duvalier dictatorship, Aristide was a thirty-seven-year-old charismatic priest who had been active in Haitian human rights movements for many years. At the time of his election he had escaped at least three assassination attempts, one by uniformed soldiers. He has an obvious and perhaps volatile appeal to many segments of the Haitian population, especially the peasantry and the urban poor.

While attempting to reorganize military policy, Aristide was ousted by the army a little over seven months after he took office. The Organization of American States declared the new government to be illegitimate, and in November 1991 the United States imposed an embargo on Haiti demanding that the army allow a democratically elected government to take its place. Aristide has lived since his ouster mostly in the United States negotiating with the United States, the Organization of American States, and various power brokers in Haiti for his return to what can only be some limited form of presidential power.

Part of the current chaos no doubt comes from heightened expectations. After the ouster of the Duvalier regime a very wide variety of urban and rural groups attempted to develop a progressive government. Even peasants in some of the most isolated areas of Haiti came to think of the government not only as the cause of problems (the shortage of drinkable water, for example) but also as the source of possible solutions to such problems.

Haitian Social and Economic Life

Since political repression has traditionally resulted from the elite's exploitation of the rural farmers, an understanding of Haiti must include knowledge about the peasantry. About sixty-five percent of the labor force works in agriculture and only about seven percent in manufacturing (with one percent in construction and twenty-seven percent in other sectors).

The greatest accomplishment of the early Haitian nation was total land reform. Changing the country from a collection of slave-worked plantations to a nation of land-owning Black peasants involved, as I have stated, dividing the land among the former field slaves and their descendants. After these rural farmers received their small subsistence plots they wanted nothing further to do with the government, which they had always seen as being responsive to the slave owners. And, indeed, until very recently—beginning ironically with François Duvalier's efforts to court rural support—they have regarded the government as having little relevance to their lives. Another result of the land reform is that—in striking contrast to the rest of the Caribbean and Latin America—the largely mulatto elite, descended from the former house slaves or freed mulattoes, retreated to the cities and, with no land to their name, made its living from taxing peasant markets and the nation's imports and exports.

PEASANT FARMERS

In addition to constantly attempting to deflect a parasitical elite, the Haitian farmers face many problems, perhaps the most immediate being how to cope with small, scattered plots that are subdivided each generation. In addition, farmers often denude the land of trees to make charcoal for cooking fuel, lack capital to buy fertilizer, seeds, pesticides, and farm equipment, and are always dealing with increasing soil erosion. Since 1983 farmers have also had to deal with the loss of their major livestock population due to the total pig eradication project carried out by U.S. and international agencies after the discovery of African Swine Fever.

The peasants, however, do endure. Most of the people of Haiti, in fact, can be found living in scattered huts in villages loosely tied together by well-traveled trade routes. They organize their lives around a cluster of households composed of loosely related residents serving a particular Voodoo spirit under the guidance of the oldest male member. In the past there were also regional centers that had considerable importance culturally and commercially. Since the 1915–1934 U.S. occupation, however, Port-au-Prince has become a more important city that now dominates the country.

In his classic study of the peasant farmers of Mirebalais in central Haiti the anthropologist Melville J. Herskovits described a scene that rings true even today more than half a century after his fieldwork there in 1934:

> The small cultivator holds the center of the economic stage. In the main he works his own land, inherited from his father or acquired through purchase.... The life of the Haitian farmer, though hard, is simple and self-contained. With but few exceptions, he supplies all his necessities.... The day's work begins at dawn, the women rising before the men to prepare coffee.... When finished with his breakfast, the

farmer goes to his field, where, except for the hottest hours, he works until sundown, his own meal being brought to him at about nine or ten o'clock in the morning. His wife meanwhile occupies herself with her household tasks, pounding grain in her mortar or working in her garden. . . . On market days she takes the produce of the family's fields to the town to sell. If she has young children, she cares for them while she does her other work, but when they are old enough, they help her about the house if they are girls, or, if boys, go with their father to the garden. From time to time, when house repairs are needed or there are implements to be mended, the man spends a day at home getting these odd jobs done.[9]

RURAL MARKETS

The involvement of Haitian peasants with the wider world is through marketing. And it is women who usually market and make marketing decisions. As Herskovits wrote,

> The woman, who is held to be more thrifty than the man, is thus the banker of the family. Her opinion is prized by her husband, and though a man has the legal right to dispose of a horse or a cow or his own land as he desires, in most households nothing would be done until the wife was consulted.[10]

The anthropologist Sidney Mintz has done the pioneering and still the best studies on Haitian markets, and he has pointed out that market women are "as typically Haitian as voodoo."[11] In fact, the market women and the bustling markets scattered all over the Haitian country are the very heart of the Haitian economy. These rural markets fill the roles of banks and warehouses; they operate as a socioeconomic network that moves the goods, as well as the gossip, that the people need in order to live materially and socially.

Haiti's primary products of coffee, sugar, rice, and cocoa have traditionally moved through these rural markets. Many Haitians also engage in part-time craft work, particularly in the manufacture of wood utensils, tools, and furniture. Haiti was, in fact, well-known for its fine mahogany carvings, and most of the products of the industrial arts were aimed at tourists. Due to the AIDS scare, however, the tourist trade declined drastically beginning in the early 1980s and declined to nearly zero following the sociopolitical instability after Duvalier's 1986 ouster.

NONRURAL MARKETS

In recent history there has been a market for products from light manufacturing in Haiti, which has consisted largely of shoes, soap, flour, cement, and domestic oils. The industries owned by foreign interests produced items such as garments, toys, baseballs, and electronic goods almost exclusively for the U.S. market. This small-scale industrialization has, however, always been a minor part of the Haitian economic scene and has not added much to the national economy since the purpose of it is to supply cheap labor that the U.S. corporations can exploit. In addition, the instability of the government since 1986 has resulted in a number of these foreign-owned industries leaving Haiti. Those that had not left before November 1991 did leave during the imposition of the U.S. embargo during that month.

FAMILY AND HOUSEHOLD

With the men in the fields and the women in the markets it may be stated—at the risk of oversimplification—that men handle the agricultural production and that women handle the produce of agriculture. The men who do the agriculture, however, usually do it for the women. In other words, the women depend on the men to have a product to sell, and the men depend on the women for domestic labor and marketing. The Haitian family structure, then, contains a great deal of gender complementarianism, as well as generational complementarianism; the children are seen as working for the parents. Growing out of these complementary roles and statuses is a complex system of mating, parenting, and day-to-day subsisting that is maintained through a variety of household arrangements.

Herskovits, in his classic anthropological ethnography, made the important clarification that "the word 'family' as employed in Haiti can be understood only in terms of a broader meaning than is given it in Europe and America. . . .; the Haitian 'family' includes a wide range of relatives. . . .; on the sides of both parents."[12] It is, in fact, relatively rare that the small group of people contained in a household acts on its own without consulting with a large number of relatives.

The plantation system and the institution of slavery throughout the eighteenth and nineteenth centuries certainly did not encourage slaves to develop a legally recognized family institution, and the urban orientation of the republic reinforced the tendency of the peasants to avoid legal and church marriages. Consequently a wide variety of households exists, such as long-term co-residing couples, unions without formal sanction, couples who do not live together, fathers who do not participate actively in rearing their children, as well as, of course, conventional church weddings. In addition, the same man may simultaneously marry, maintain a consensual union in a second household of which he is the titular head, and conduct one or more relatively stable extraresidential affairs in which the women head the household. Women also may legitimately enter several different kinds of unions. As it turns out, then, children may be born to a married couple, to a married man with another woman, to a couple in a consensual union, to a mother not in union with any man, and so forth.

Due to the great variety of households, inheritance can be a troublesome problem. In general, all children from all the varieties of marriage have equal rights of inheritance, but, in practice, residence, contacts, and personal feelings play important roles. Since both adults and children change residences frequently, children have a variety of temporary residential rights and come into contact with a relatively large number of adults who may discipline and train them. In general, a great deal of emphasis is placed on respect for adults, who are quick to use corporal punishment in enforcing that respect.

Living in Chaos

Current Reports

In March 1993 a student of mine made a trip from Port-au-Prince to the interior regional center of Hinche. The 750-mile trip used to take about 2 hours. Due to the deterioration of the roads in Haiti, however, it took him 6 hours. Coming into Hinche he was stopped at five different military checkpoints, and he, his driver, and his vehicle were searched at each checkpoint. Hinche itself had no electricity and no running water. The people were afraid to use the water from wells and streams because there was no sewage treatment. He was told many stories of arrests, tortures, and the disappearance of numerous townspeople. He also mentioned to me that, as a sport, soldiers often aimed their jeeps at people in the streets and sped toward them, apparently killing one little girl.

A February 1993 report from the Chicago Religious Task Force Delegation to Haiti stated that a Mennonite Central Committee worker was detained because he carried pamphlets about Haiti Solidarity Week, a celebration scheduled for February 7 through February 13, marking the February 7, 1986, fall of the Duvalier regime and the February 7, 1991, inauguration of Aristide. The worker had to stand by helpless as his Haitian guide was beaten.

The same report noted that Gonaives, a city where Dessalines declared Haitian independence and also a city where the first anti-Duvalier protests took place, was heavily patrolled by the army. Arrests, torture, and violence were rampant there.

In January 1993 representatives from over fifteen international organizations concerned with human rights and refugee issues in Haiti met in Port-au-Prince to attend the International Colloquium on Human Rights. Colloquium participants strongly condemned the human rights violations by the Haitian military regime. The colloquium estimated that since the September 1991 military coup approximately three thousand Haitians have been killed, six thousand injured, forty thousand have fled by boat, and up to four hundred thousand have been internally displaced.

Personal Consequences

A newsletter published in Haiti by a coalition of grassroots democratic movements recently detailed a typical story of a delegate who was elected to the National Assembly in December 1990. Samuel Madistin, the twenty-nine-year-old son of a Protestant minister, was to represent about forty thousand citizens in the Artibonite Valley. After only a few months in office, he found the government taken over by the army. He stated, "Today we are witnessing an unimaginable situation. People are arrested, taken to jail, sometimes beaten to death. They are gravely injured, they lose their eyes, they are forced to eat their excrement. These are all things we have been witnessing for the past twelve months."[13]

In March 1992 when the Assembly convened to vote on the "Washington Accord," a compromise agreement between the legitimate government and the de facto military government, Madistin and others who were going to vote in favor of it were taken out of the Assembly room and beaten by soldiers. Since then Madistin has apparently been blacklisted by the military and is in hiding.

Conclusion

The elite of Haiti has always made its living through their control of the state apparatus, a situation that one contemporary Haitian scholar calls "state fetishism."[14] The new Black middle class—largely a product, ironically, of François Duvalier's efforts to counter the old, mulatto elite—makes its living from mercantile, capitalist, and service enterprises. For the most part, this middle class has been politically neutral and socially silent throughout the recent upheavals.

Indeed, arguments about governance have mostly involved only a small number of members of the elite class. Although their college experiences may differ, members of the elite pretty much attend the same schools in Haiti and accept the same values. What divides them from the rest of the nation is the extremely unequal allocations of resources between rural regions (including the increasingly slum-like urban fringes) and downtown urban (and outer suburban areas); the elite is wealthy and the rest of the people are poor. Keeping the poor from claiming their fair share of the meager resources is what has led to sociopolitical repression. What divides the elite into seemingly arbitrary, and often competing, segments is their noncooperative efforts to gain individual and familial power.

This competition enjoyed a certain balance throughout most of Haitian history, but the supporting structure began, as we have seen, to collapse under Duvalier policies. At least four factors have recently come together that seem to lead to the chaos: (1) The various group and family elites have become increasingly smaller (with many members living abroad); (2) The resources of Haiti are increasingly limited, rural markets exhausted, and foreign aid virtually shut off; (3) The new Black, politically neutral middle class is trying to tap into these same finite resources (and expecting government services); and (4) The military has been left as the only existing instrument of government (and, for the most part, they neither desire nor are capable of governance).

My expectations for the future of Haiti are both optimistic and pessimistic. Haitians have survived incompetence, corruption, ignorance, the military, the greed of powerful neighbors, and even the machinations of their own elite; most of the them will probably survive the current chaos. How long, however, will they have to yearn for their freedom?

Notes

1. John R. Beard, *The Life of Toussaint L'Ouverture: The Negro Patriot of Hayti* (1853; reprint Westport, CN: Negro Universities Press, 1970).
2. Leslie F. Manigat, *Haiti of the Sixties: Object of International Concern* (Washington, D.C.: Washington Center of Foreign Policy Research, 1964), p. 33.
3. Staff Report (Port-au-Prince: CPAU, 1992).
4. James Franklin, *The Present State of Hayti (Santo Domingo): With Remarks on Its Agriculture, Commerce, Laws, Religion, Finances, and Population* (1828; reprint London: Cass, 1971); Charles MacKenzie, *Notes on Haiti: Made During a Residence in that Republic*, 2 vols. (1830; reprint London: Cass, 1971); and Spenser St. John, *Hayti: Or the Black Republic* (London: Smith, Elder, 1884).
5. F. E. DuBois, "Call for Immigration," in James Redpath, ed., *A Guide to Hayti* (1861; reprint Westport, CN: Negro Universities Press, 1970), p. 99.
6. Robert Lawless, *Haiti's Bad Press: Origins, Development, and Consequences* (Rochester, VT: Schenkman, 1992), pp. 160–161.
7. Annick Billard, "Haiti: Hope, Return, Disillusion," *Refugees* 39 (1987): 16.
8. Susana Hayward, "Priest Becomes Haiti's First Freely Elected President," *Gainesville Sun*, February 8, 1991, p. 5A.
9. Melville J. Herskovits, *Life in a Haitian Valley* (New York: Knopf, 1937), pp. 67–68.
10. Ibid., p. 125.
11. Sidney W. Mintz, "Markets in Haiti," *New Society* 26 (1963): 18.
12. Herskovits, *Life in a Haitian Valley*, p. 123.
13. Staff, "Profile," *Haiti Info* 1, no. 2 (1992): 2.
14. Michael-Rolph Trouillot, *Haiti: State against Nation: The Origins and Legacy of Duvalierism* (New York: Monthly Review Press, 1990), p. 9.

Suggested Readings

Aristide, Jean-Bertrand. *In the Parish of the Poor: Writings from Haiti*. Maryknoll, NY: Oris, 1990. A revealing book by the charismatic priest who was popularly elected as president of Haiti.

Bellegarde-Smith, Patrick. *Haiti: The Breached Citadel*. Boulder. CO: Westview, 1990. A brilliant account of modern Haiti by a Haitian-American.

Brown, Karen McCarthy. *Mama Lola: A Vodou Priestess in Brooklyn*. Berkeley: University of California Press, 1991. A sympathetic reading of Voodoo.

Laguerre, Michel S. *Urban Life in the Caribbean: A Study of a Haitian Urban Community*. Cambridge, MA: Schenkman, 1982.

Nicholls, David. *From Dessalines to Duvalier: Race, Colour, and National Independence in Haiti*. Cambridge: Cambridge University Press, 1979. A contemporary account of the ideology of the Haitian elite.

Roumain, Jacques. *Masters of the Dew*. New York: Reynal and Hitchcock, 1944. The most famous novel written by a Haitian.

Andean Mestizos:
Growing Up Female and Male

Lauris A. McKee

Ecuador, an ecologically and ethnically diverse country, is named for the equator, which crosses it a few miles north of the capital city of Quito (splendidly sited at 9,200 feet). The nation is one of the smallest in South America; its population is currently estimated at over eleven million and its land area is roughly comparable in size to the U.S. state of Colorado.[1] It borders the Pacific Ocean, and is divided into three major ecological zones by a double chain of mountains, the Andes, which run north to south.

In the 1980s the ethnic composition of the country was approximately forty to forty-five percent mestizos (Spanish-speaking persons of mixed Spanish and Native American descent), forty percent Indians (Quíchua-speakers, hereafter referred to properly as *runa*), ten to fifteen percent *blancos* ("whites," who claim exclusively Spanish descent) and five to ten percent *negros* ("blacks").[2]

Today, the runa population is declining due to acculturation and absorption into the mestizoized, Spanish-speaking majority.[3] Identification as a runa or a mestizo (which are *social*, not racial categories) depends on the language people speak in the home, the clothing they wear, and their community of residence.[4] Changing one's ethnic identity often is motivated by migration to urban areas to find work. The economic and social pressures to acculturate are encouraging the emergence of a mestizo majority.

Ecuador's major ecological zones are called the *Costa* (the Pacific coastal plains), the *Sierra* (the mountain highlands) and the *Oriente* (the eastern Andean foothills and the flat riverine basins of the upper Amazon region). The Sierra, the focus of this chapter, rises high above the tropical Costa and Oriente. The verticality of the landscape gives the country its special character, for the valleys of the inter-montane Andean region boast a climate of "eternal spring." The mountain chains are punctuated by nine massive snow-capped volcanoes, including the imposing Chimborazo (20,560 feet), Cotopaxi (19,642 feet), and Tungurahua (16,456 feet). The cold of their heights distinguishes Ecuador as the only country in the world where one encounters snow and frost at the equator.[5]

Fieldsites

The people I worked with live in four different communities in the valleys of the Sierra. There is considerable ecological variation among the sites. Patate lies in a lush, irrigated valley at an altitude of 7,400 feet. Patateños cultivate avocados, garden vegetables, vine and tree fruits, alfalfa, corn, and barley. Tumbaviro, situated at 6,888 feet, is the smallest of the communities. In its warm climate, sugar cane and corn are major crops and tropical fruits such as cheremoyas and guavas grow. In the mountains, descent or ascent of a few hundred feet make a difference in average daily temperatures and Mira (whose name evokes its panoramic view) at 7,708 feet is too cold to grow the tangerines that flourish in Patate, though it is famous for its beans and corn. Guaranda, above eight thousand feet, is colder yet, and the staple crops are potatoes, barley, wheat, corn, and broad beans (*habas*). Potatoes are grown in all sites, but assume more economic importance at higher altitudes. The populations in these towns and villages are predominantly mestizo, though, with the exception of Mira, each community also includes a runa constituency.

Guaranda, the capital of Bolívar Province, is a large town and a market center. The Saturday market attracts Coastal fishmongers, vendors of tropical fruits, pottery-makers from Cotopaxi Province, women herbalists from the Oriente selling medicinal plants, tree bark, and seeds, and local runas and mestizas marketing garlic, onions, chickens, eggs, potatoes, and "grains" (Ecuadorians class lentils, peas, chochos, and beans as grains along with wheat, barley, and oats). Manufactured clothing, plastic goods, pots and pans, tennis shoes, and rubber boots fill stalls along thronged streets, and women sell fried fish, grilled plantains, and fried or roasted pork to hungry shoppers. There are a few permanent stores in Guaranda, and the Provincial government, the schools, and the hospital are major employers.

The villages of Patate and Tumbaviro and the town of Mira, are located (respectively) in the Provinces of Tungurahua, Imbabura, and El Carchi. In these communities, food production, for subsistence or for the market, is the major occupation, and almost everyone is involved in some capacity in agriculture.

There are several small shops and a small weekly market. Most houses in Patate, Mira, and Tumbaviro have small *huertas* (gardens) in back, but unlike U.S. farmers, who generally live on their land, farm families live in the nucleated communities and walk out to their fields.

Except for the few haciendas which remain in these areas, small landholdings, (*minifundio*) prevail over large farms (*latifundio*). Rather than owning one large farm, the ideal in the mountainous environment is to own several small fields at different altitudes. The wisdom behind this strategy is expressed in English in the old adage that warns "don't put all your eggs in one basket;" for if crops on the south side of a mountain are hit by a battering hailstorm or a flood in an exceptionally hard rain, the crops on the mountain's north side may be spared. Both location and altitude are important, for most plant varieties thrive only in specific latitudinal niches. Food-crops produced for family consumption or for the market would be unduly limited if one planted in a single altitudinal niche.[6]

Work

The heaviest agricultural work is usually given over to men, but the whole family cooperates in sowing and harvesting. Tractors are virtually useless on precipitous Andean slopes, so preparing plots for planting entails arduous labor. The earth is broken with wide-bladed hoes or plowed by oxen if a family can afford to rent them and the terrain permits it. Sowing and harvesting are done by hand. In some steeply inclined fields near Patate and Guaranda, men harvesting grain with a hand scythe tie themselves to stakes pounded into the ground to secure their footing.

Landless men sell their labor as *peones* (agricultural workers hired by the day), or if they have some capital, may rent or sharecrop plots owned by absentee landlords. In the poorest families, *both* sexes engage in agricultural wage-work. The wage structure, however, is asymmetrical, with men's pay being higher (sometimes nearly double) that of women. Men also dominate the higher-paid jobs of fruit-tree pruning and pesticide spraying. The higher wage for spraying is offset by the health risk, for laborers are insufficiently protected and their skin and lungs absorb the poisons they apply. The father of a family I worked with in Mira coughed up purple phlegm after each day of spraying pesticides on potato crops. In a return visit two years later I found him dying in the hospital and his family unable to pay his bills.

Higher status "white-collar" jobs are available to both sexes, depending on their social class and education, though the most prestigious and best-paid jobs mainly are reserved for men. There are governmental and administrative offices in all communities, and secular as well as church-operated schools. Among the field sites, only Tumbaviro lacks a secondary school. Women teachers are well represented in the educational institutions, and some elementary classrooms are segregated by sex; in Patate, men teach the boys and women teach the girls.

In the home, women perform the hundreds of tasks requiring hand labor that are needed to maintain rural households in an unmechanized, pre-industrial country. They process and prepare food, make clothing, care for their children, tend animals, gather feed for guinea pigs and rabbits, shell corn for the chickens, and wash clothing and bedding in water so icy cold that within a minute or two their hands are aching.

Shopping for food, processing it, and cooking it is generally dominated by women. People say that men do not "know" how to cook, which really means that if a man does cook, he is ridiculed. The activity of food preparation is assigned by gender as are many other tasks, and the resulting division of labor creates mutual economic dependency between the genders. Men, prohibited from cooking, must marry, or failing that, live with their mothers, sisters, or other female relatives who will provide this service.

In all but the wealthiest families (usually those of hacienda owners) women engage in a number of cash-producing enterprises. They keep small *tiendas* ("stores") in the front rooms of their houses. They raise animals to sell their meat or their products, they may sew, cook, clean, or wash clothing for other families, or prepare food for public sale during fiestas or market days. In Mira, women earn money by knitting sweaters and caps. These are contracted to be sold in Quito, Europe, or the United States at twenty times the price paid the knitters.

Diversification is a major survival strategy for rural Ecuadorians. People diversify their investments in land, labor, and capital. They diversify and inter-crop the varieties of plants they cultivate and thus reduce the risk of failure incurred by monocropping.

They also diversify their social ties and commitments through *compadrazgo* ("ritual coparenthood"). Ties are created with others of similar status, (which strengthens an already warm relationship) or with people of higher status to instantiate a friendly relationship. In either case, they extend both their social network, and their obligations, for *compadres* have mutual expectations of social and economic support. Compadres of similar status are more likely to ask each other for labor-aid, whereas higher status compadres are asked to use their influence or their expertise on the behalf of a lower status family, who in turn offers labor-aid and gifts of food. A sentiment commonly heard is that a good compadre is more trustworthy than one's own kin.

The Natural Environment and the Communities

The Andes mountains dominate the landscape and the communities lying at their feet. Slopes near the field sites are marked by zig-zagging 'foot-roads' that ascend by paths too steep for motor vehicles. Landslides often block the highways, but they are rapidly cleared away. Mira and Guaranda each are connected by paved two-lane highways to larger Andean cities, but Patate and Tumbaviro are an hour's drive from the major roads. Water supply is a problem in the Andes, for rivers lie in deep ravines, and there are surprisingly few natural springs. Carrying water up from the rivers is exhausting work, but the government has made water supply a priority, and today all the sites have both piped water and electricity.

Each village and town has its own special character, but in all of them, most houses are built either of cinder block (*bloque*) or of *bahareque* (mud packed onto a structure of lashed cane supported at doorways, windows and corners by strong beams) construction. Roofs are of terra cotta tile or of corrugated plastic, though a few *chozas* (traditional Andean adobe-walled dwellings) still have thatched roofs.

Walls of adobe or cinder block enclose the house-gardens. If families keep pigs, their styes are in the garden. Chickens run free in the garden or the enclosed patio, and guinea pigs (*cuyes*), a source of food for special ritual or celebratory occasions, scurry in the shadows of dirt-floored kitchens. In those houses resembling "western" models in plan and construction, kitchens are floored with wood or cement, and the guinea pigs are banished to an exterior shed.

The scent of burning eucalyptus wood perfumes Ecuadorian communities, but wood is a scarce and expensive good, and is used strictly for cooking, not for heating dwellings, so houses are very cold on clear nights. Conversely, when the mountain mists lie above the rooftops, they prevent the escape of the heat accumulated during the day, and nights (and houses!) are warmer.

The economic status of families in the study communities varies widely. Rural populations often live precariously: hunger is a spectre that haunts the future, and death from respiratory and gastrointestinal diseases is an ever-present possibility. Ecuadorian infant mortality rates still remain very high.[7] But the poverty and malnutrition of the urban poor can equal that of the rural poor who at least can consume the food they raise. (Though the rains caused by the El Niño phenomenon of 1982–1984 destroyed crops, and hunger led to massive migration to urban areas.)

Poorer families often live in a single room, whose walls are black with the smoke of thousands of open wood fires. Higher-income families live in houses with sitting rooms, one (or many) bedrooms and kitchens with propane gas stoves and fitted cabinets. Older houses of both types may have large wood-fired ovens in the patio, where they roast pigs or bake bread. Bathrooms, rare in the 1970s, are becoming more common, and many families have at least a flush toilet, though the poorest families still use chamber pots and empty them into the garden for fertilizer.

This brief description gives the reader a mere glimpse of these communities, and does not convey the magic of each locale. The clarity of the sky and sun in high mountain landscapes, the menacing but beautiful mists that descend as evening falls, the bell-tones of frogs singing in the rainy season, the scent of eucalyptus, the vivid flowers sprouting from adobe walls. (On the less romantic side are the mud or dust of unpaved roads, the cold of unheated, barren houses, the scrawny, vicious dogs.) Neither are Ecuadorians well-depicted in such a brief work, and their humor, courage, beauty, ingenuity, hospitality, tenaciousness, and patience require much more than a chapter to describe.

There are considerable cultural and economic dissimilarities among social classes and ethnic groups in the Sierra. But in this chapter I am more interested in documenting the cultural similarities that provide bridges of understanding and meaning among these groups. Certain attitudes, beliefs, and practices that guide parental childrearing strategies are widely shared; for this reason it is possible to allude to something like a highland culture, at least in the areas studied. Of particular concern is how cultural conventions for raising children lead parents to bring up their daughters and sons differently.

Socialization

We look to socialization to understand how parents try to replicate their own culture. Through socialization, parents teach children about their future roles in the world, the behavioral codes of their society, and its particular belief systems. Though these codes vary with a child's age, ethnicity, class, and gender, in small communities there are remarkable consistencies and agreements concerning how to raise children. Of course, children are not passive recipients of these efforts to instruct them and to modify their behavior, so socialization becomes negotiation, as children assert their own views and preferences.

As I define it here, socialization is the outcome of caretakers' efforts to replace children's idiosyncratic expressions of biological urges and emotional responses with culturally approved modes of expression. The socialization process (the demands for change made on children) offers insight into the various ways a society constructs *childhood*. The "biological child" is only partially perceived; what people see instead is a baby who embodies the cultural vision of children's "nature." How rural Andeans perceive infants and children can be inferred from their caretaking of them, and the explanations they give for treating them as they do.

Many cultural standards and rules for behavior, and even for the *perception* of development, vary with gender. The "logic" of gender difference creates distinct sets of experiences for growing girls and boys, and thus ensures that the genders *are* different. All children, even non-kin brought into a family as indentured servants, are required to learn to control or modify their own impulses and to conform to expectations of gendered behavior, at least to the degree that they become tolerable members of the family subculture and acceptable members of the wider culture. To understand socialization practices, it is necessary to

understand the reasons motivating them. So let us consider the beliefs concerning the earliest moments in children's development.

Beliefs Concerning Fetal Development, Birth, and Infancy

CONCEPTION

To conceive a healthy baby the father should be healthy and sober. Women insist that insemination by a drunken man results in the birth of a mute or deformed child. Furthermore, a couple should have sex in the "normal" (missionary) position or they might conceive a damaged child. Although women know that good (or poor) nutrition during pregnancy has a significant effect on children's mental and physical development, in reality only the mildest infant deformities and mental deficiencies (called *taras*) are attributed to mothers' malnutrition or to their frustrated cravings for certain foods during pregnancy. In the majority of cases, an inebriated begetter bears the blame for the birth of a defective infant.

Men are not the only inseminators. The Rainbow (or *cuiche* in Quíchua) can also impregnate young women. They attract him especially if they wear brightly colored clothing, or if they urinate in a stream or an irrigation ditch. These pregnancies usually end in miscarriages, but frogs, snakes, and "insects" issue forth, not human infants.[8] The mountain deities also are viewed as potential impregnators who ravish women sleeping alone on the mountain. They beget albino children, whose white hair and skin announce the identity of their snow-capped genitor.[9]

PREGNANCY

Gender differences that prefigure traits attributed to adult women and men are said to be present in the unborn child. Male fetuses, by the second or third month, are thought to be fully developed (in utero, they resemble tiny, perfectly formed "babies"). At three months, they can "walk" in the womb (mothers can feel them move). The runa women in our study (together with other runa such as the Saraguro) believe that boys are fully formed homunculi (little "men") even at the moment of conception.[10] But girls are said to have a different ontogeny. Even by the end of the second trimester (the fifth or sixth month) the form of the fetal female is said to be "just a ball of flesh" (a *bola*) that resembles the "eye of an ox." (Some women state that they know this for a fact, for they have seen these forms in the remains of aborted fetuses.) Due to their unformed state, girls do not "walk " until the end of the second trimester.

Despite their tardy development, girls' gestation period is perceived as shorter: it most often is reported as eight and a half months, whereas boys' gestation lasts nine or more months. These perceived gender differences "explain" the differences in "strength" between the sexes, for girls' shorter gestation implies a congenital "weakness."

BIRTH

Today, many women give birth in local health clinics, or if they can afford it, travel to the provincial hospital to deliver their first children. However, the hospitals are associated with death and with loneliness due to separation from one's kin. There is a widespread conviction that in the urban *Maternidades*, venal nurses or doctors will switch babies, selling the boys women actually bore to rich clients for adoption, and replacing them with another woman's female infant.[11] The doctors and *obstetrices* (university-trained midwives) are opposed to the ancient custom of giving birth while squatting or kneeling (a position which utilizes gravity's force to speed a birth). For these and other reasons, home births are often preferred (in the mid-1980s, fifty-five percent of all infants in the Sierra, and seventy-eight percent of those in rural areas were born at home).[12]

Home-births are accomplished without anesthetics. No drugs are taken except an occasional *canelazo* (hot water flavored with cane alcohol, sugar, and cinnamon), but if labor is extended (which, if informants' memory is to be trusted, is the rare case), women may be fed egg whites beaten with sugar to give them strength and to "help the baby slide out." Women delivering at home may be attended by their husbands, by a midwife, or by female relatives. The treatments newborn infants receive vary among families. Often they are bathed in water mixed with a little cologne and their heads are washed, or they may simply be wiped clean with tepid water and dried with a soft cloth. In some families, newborns are not bathed for two or three days or until their navel cord dries and falls off. Generally, they are given a second bath after three days.

The navel cord is cut with a sharp piece of cane, though modern midwives use scissors or knives. Gender determines the length of the stump, which is important to the child's future reproductive role. The cord is left longer for a boy (the width of four or five adult-sized fingers) to make certain his penis will grow to a sufficient length. A girl's cord usually is cut a little shorter, but never *too* short, or she will have difficulty delivering her future children. But if the cord is cut too long, she will be over-sexed—in fact, she will possess the heightened degree of desire regarded as "normal" for men, but scandalous for women.[13] (These beliefs reveal an interesting ambiguity concerning the fixity of gender traits as these are culturally defined: people think the traits are innate [an essentialist view] but also think the traits can be altered depending on the treatments children are given.)

Once the cord is tied off, newborns are swaddled and may be given a little anise tea brewed with a tiny piece of onion to prevent colic. Some women nurse their babies for the first time within three or four hours after delivery; others wait from twenty-four hours to three days.

Infants of both sexes are generally swaddled shortly after birth. Mothers say they swaddle babies so their bodies and legs will grow straight and strong; they also think it prevents them from catching cold. Failure to swaddle leaves children weak and "limp" or bow-legged. It is customary to swaddle newborns from shoulders to feet until they are two to four months old; after this, and until six months, most mothers only bind babies from hips to feet, leaving the arms free. Babies accompany mothers everywhere, and when swaddled, are easier to carry and cry noticeably less compared to unswaddled infants.[14]

New mothers also undergo a kind of "swaddling." They are tightly wrapped in a cloth, from below the breast to below the buttocks. The wrapping is said to support pelvic bones, which women conceive of as weakened, having been 'opened' during the rigors of birth.[15] Wrapping the mother is also thought to hold her womb in place and help to prevent a new pregnancy.

The period following birth, called the *dieta del parto* (the "birth diet") is a syncretic combination of Hispanic practice and pre-Columbian belief. The dieta is a time of rest, seclusion, and recuperation that frees new mothers from exhausting labors such as planting, weeding, carrying heavy burdens, and laundering clothes in icy mountain waters. It also affords them the opportunity to adjust to their infants' rhythms for eating and sleeping and their modes of expressing needs.

In the ideal case, mother and infant remain indoors for forty to forty-two days. The seclusion period is identical to that prescribed in sixteenth century Catholic Spain (and other Mediterranean countries), where women's supposed ritual "pollution" from the blood shed in childbirth required seclusion and ultimately, purification by a priest.

In the Andes, women are not secluded due to "pollution," rather, the motive is protection from the sun's heat, which is believed to produce illness in mother and child. In the pre-Columbian pantheon, the Sun was a male deity. Today, informants do not personalize the sun (as they do the Rainbow), nor is it portrayed as especially hostile to women and infants. The power of its heat, however, is feared and respected and resonates with the Ecuadorian version of humoral medicine in ways that indicate that it is not merely a thermal force, but is also a supernatural force.[16]

During the *dieta*, the mother is heavily garbed and her head is covered. The room is darkened and if possible, a curtain or canopy is constructed for the bed, which prevents any vagrant sun-ray from reaching the bodies of the mother and her swaddled child. Following birth, the pair are in a delicate state (conceptually "hot"), and the sun causes a grippe (a 'flu') that can be fatal.[17]

Though women avoid the equatorial sun, other warmth is positively valued. The extra clothing women wear shields them and warms their backs; this is important for the infant's nourishment, for women agree that breast milk diminishes or disappears if their backs or "lungs" become chilled. Today, the *dieta* is reduced to a mere eight days for most rural women, some of whom complain about the abbreviated recovery period and rapid resumption of daily tasks that rob them of time to tend their newborns.

BREASTFEEDING

As recently as 1984, children in the rural Sierra were virtually universally breastfed.[18] But breastfeeding has had more than a nutritional function in Ecuador: the culture uses it to construct character traits "ideal" for each gender; thus, lactation varies with the child's sex. This practice is motivated by the belief that prolonged lactation enhances masculinity by increasing the amount of sexuality and aggressiveness a child displays at maturity. These traits are desirable in the male *character*, but are deplorable and even destructive if manifested in the female *character*. Thus, until recently, most mothers weaned daughters earlier than sons.

In Patate in 1976 mothers thought that eight months was the ideal age to wean girls, whereas twenty-four months was ideal for boys. When asked, however, for

the age at which they actually weaned each daughter and son, it resulted that the average age for weaning girls was 10.3 months, whereas the average for boys was 20.27 months. Girls' experience of breastfeeding, then, was relatively (and notably!) shorter.[19] The *belief* in the need for differential lactation is still professed today in Mira, Tumbaviro, and Guaranda, but it has little effect on practice except among those mothers who have three years or less of education.

This group of women still observes the old tradition, and they and their husbands offer two cultural scenarios to predict the fate of an overly breastfed, and therefore overly sexual and aggressive, daughter's fate. The first is that her strong drives will lead her to rebel against her parents and seek sexual partners before she is married. This notion is widespread in mestizo culture, and arises from a value on premarital chastity imported from the Spanish (and, indeed, circum-Mediterranean) cultural insistence on female honor. A woman, as bearer of the family honor, shames her entire family, but particularly her male relatives, if she fails to defend her virginity.[20]

The second scenario predicts that her strong sexuality will burden such a girl in the future with numerous pregnancies. Neither of these "fates" is viewed positively, so women are convinced that, even though it gives them pain, they do their daughters a favor by weaning them early, saving them from negative consequences in their future adult lives.

Of course, rules are made to be broken, as evidenced by Carmen, the mother of five children. She told me, "How sad I was to wean Zoila when she was so little, and she really missed the breast. So with my last baby, I just kept nursing her until she was almost two years old; don't you see how contrary she is?"

Let me emphasize that children are not weaned because their mothers think that beyond infancy, sucking as a nutritive modality is a bad thing. In the rural Sierra, sucking is viewed as a pleasurable way to consume many soft, sweet foods such as fruit and ice cream. When visiting people's homes, I often was offered a bowlful of tangerines to eat with the invitation, "*Chupe! Chupe!* (suck! suck!). On buses traveling to the city of Quito, ice-cream vendors hawk their wares at each major stop, and some win a laugh from potential customers by urging "*Chupe! Chupe!* Your mother taught you how!"

In rural areas, nursing is still an accepted public activity; mothers feel no compunctions about nursing their children in the marketplace, on the street, or on the buses. Sick children as old as six years are comforted by sucking on baby bottles filled with sweet liquids. Gender ideals, not prudishness about children sucking at the breast, provide the cultural motive for weaning, and breastfeeding does not carry the prurient sexual undertones it sometimes does in the United States.

Nevertheless, fewer highland women practice extended nursing today. The use of infant-feeding bottles is on the increase, because they allow mothers to leave babies at home with other caretakers. If women are exclusively breastfeeding, then they must carry children with them on their daily tasks. These often include hikes of two or three hours (round-trip) up and down the mountain to carry lunch to husbands, sons, or hired help working the fields or pasturing animals. Women say this prolonged exposure to the sun "heats" their breastmilk. The "hot" milk makes the child feverish and ill, and causes diarrhea. To prevent this, women express some of the milk and throw it away leaving the "cooler" milk for the baby. If babies stay home, women are less burdened on their journeys, and they believe their children are safest in the shelter of the house.

BREASTFEEDING AND SEX DIFFERENCES IN MORTALITY

Data from the first national Ecuadorian census in 1950 through the 1977 census registered significantly more *female* than male deaths among highland children between the ages of one and three years.[21] This is contrary to the pattern demographers expect to find. International vital statistics indicate that if there *are* sex differentials in children's mortality, *male* deaths usually predominate, as relatively higher mortality for males is recorded throughout infancy and childhood. When we find mortality ratios reversed, as, for example, in India or China, this generally indicates some sort of discrimination against females. Male-preference in these countries is reflected in elevated female mortality rates.[22]

It is important to note that child-mortality rates in Ecuador follow internationally "expected" patterns from birth to age one, in that male mortality is higher relative to female age-mates'. This is not surprising, for if most children are breastfed for at least one year, male mortality should show a "normal" pattern. It is when cultural practice intervenes that mortality rates depart from "normal" demographic patterns, and female deaths exceed males' remaining higher until age three. This suggests that differential access to breastmilk may be an important contributing cause of early female mortality.[23]

Why should breastfeeding (or the lack of it) be related to infant mortality levels? In the highlands, respiratory and gastrointestinal diseases are the leading causes of death among infants and young children. These factors interact with high levels of parasitic infestation in rural areas lacking potable water and effective sanitation. Human milk at all stages of lactation that have been studied continues to contain immunoglobulins and other antimicrobial factors that are particularly effective against respiratory and gastrointestinal diseases.[24] These immune factors especially aid and protect newborns, whose own immune mechanisms are not mature. An early switch to environmental foods may increase the probability that some weaned infants will succumb to disease.

My data suggest that until recently, sex differences in breastfeeding were widely practiced, and that this difference resulted in higher female mortality even though parents did not consciously seek that outcome. We might ask, however, why did the population want fewer girls? Population growth-limitation is one possible reason. The rate of population growth depends on the number of fertile women in a society. If the number of girls is reduced, prior to their reaching puberty, the rate of population increase is reduced. In a nation where agriculture has been the primary means of subsistence (and arable land is scarce), the ratio of person to land is a continuing concern. The relatively slower growth of population in this region in the past indicates that some sort of controls were imposed.

And, indeed, we are aware of a pre-Columbian practice that had similar (though surely larger) effects. The Inca ensured that hundreds of prepubescent girls would not reproduce by annually selecting the most beautiful nine-year-olds to be sequestered in *acllahuasi* (houses of the *aclla* which the Spanish invaders perceived as "convents"). There they learned to be master weavers, and though some of them may have been given in marriage, it appears that most remained celibate for life.[25]

Today population is increasing to the degree that Ecuadorians cannot grow sufficient food to feed themselves. (By 1971 an estimated 15 percent of food had to be imported.) If the taboo on prolonged breastfeeding for girls once checked population growth, it no longer does so. Both sexes are given infant-feeding bottles, sometimes from birth, but more commonly after three or four months of breastfeeding. Both sexes are weaned early in all but the poorest families. Germ theory still is not a prominent explanation for illness, but folk-medical practice determines (for example) that milk or the water for herbal teas is well-boiled before it is consumed. These are culturally developed rules that promote health. Bottles, however, are extra-cultural items, newly imported into child-care without time for an oral tradition concerning them to develop. So bottles are rarely sterilized; instead, they usually are rinsed in unboiled water, and often are not washed with soap.

Parents rarely give bottle-fed babies commercial infant formula: it is too expensive for the rural poor to afford. Instead, babies are fed *coladas* (fruit juices, milk, or water thickened with oatmeal or other grain flours) or weak, sugared coffee. A cornstarch, water, and sugar mixture is a popular milk substitute; it resembles milk, but it is virtually nutrition-empty. The Ministry of Health distributes *leche-avena*, a mixture of dried milk and oatmeal, to poor families with infants who qualify for aid, but this product is usually not reserved for the babies; rather, it is used to enrich the family's soups, and to improve the mother's diet so that she can nurse effectively.

Given alterations in infant-feeding practices, one could speculate that mortality patterns in Ecuador will change, though the direction of change is uncertain. One would suspect that if most infants continue to breastfeed for four months and then are weaned to the bottle, female mortality will remain more or less unchanged. Male mortality, conversely, should increase, and more closely approximate observed international ratios.

However, recent access to contraception may reduce overall fertility rates, and with fewer children, family diet may improve. Sanitation is another important factor affecting children's survival, and the national government has striven to bring potable water to rural communities. Easy access to water is a significant factor in reducing the incidence of illness, and as Ecuador becomes increasingly urbanized improved sanitation should lower infant mortality for both sexes. We can only wait and see.

FEMALE PREFERENCE

What I have said up to this point may suggest that parents do not value their daughters or treat them well. This, however, is not the case. Both parents dote upon daughters. When I asked women how many children they would like, and how many girls and boys there would be in an "ideal" family, I found they would like to have two to four children, and prefer a balanced sibling set comprised of a girl and a boy, or two girls and two boys. Most women prefer their first-

born child to be a girl who will be their aid and companion, though they state that men would prefer a son. If the last child in the family is a girl, she receives special preference from her parents and siblings sometimes even into adult life.

DEVELOPMENTAL STAGES

Folk perceptions of developmental stages vary somewhat among families. As long as children are still breastfeeding, they are considered *tiernos* (infants); from the time of weaning until around age five, they are *niños* (children). At age five, they begin to help in the fields, sowing and harvesting. Mothers say that at the age of twelve children begin to change significantly—they stop playing children's games and become young people (*jóvenes*). A girl becomes a *señorita* when she begins to menstruate.

TODDLERS

At the age of two years, children receive their first haircuts. Parents view the capacity for speech as innate but if a child's hair is cut before the age of two, (and some informants wait until six years) they are said to become *mudos* (mutes) in Mira and Patate, or (in Guaranda) to "lose their memory," so that they will never do well in school. This has nothing to do, mothers say, with a child's level of intelligence; only with the capacity to speak.

If children delay in talking or cannot speak clearly, then parents provide magical assistance. They give them strawberries, uvillas, or grapes to eat to help "loosen" the tongue and free the speech. The fruit must be left outside overnight (*enserenada*) before the child consumes it. No one explained why this treatment should be effective, but as strawberries resemble the human tongue, I supposed the cultural logic to be based in sympathetic magic (entities similar in appearance can have mutual effects). This is not, however, a completely satisfactory explanation for the efficacy of grapes and uvillas; their shape and texture have some resemblance to the tongue (but one might speculate that they also resemble the uvula).

Toddlers often are let to run bare-bottomed and their excreta is cleaned up after the fact. Parents are casual about toilet training until children are around age three, but then children are expected to inform their caretakers, who take them outside or provide them with a chamber pot. Mothers hold their babies away from their bodies—arms extended—and make a hissing sound to motivate them to urinate. "At nine months, they let you know, but up to three years they need help if they are to be clean." If children defecate in their clothing, one "training" strategy is to clean them by bathing them in cold water (in fact, this is a multipurpose punishment, which usually gets results).

A proper diet, of course, is necessary to health and development—but sometimes food also is applied externally to achieve a desired developmental result. A remedy for children who are late in walking is to rub their legs with avocado pulp. But tradition holds that if children younger than two years eat avocados, camotes (a tuber resembling the sweet potato), cheese, or the colostrum of cows, their speech development will be retarded and their mental functioning affected.

CHILDREN AND WORK

Young children give considerable aid to parents working in the fields, however, it is not expected that a child will always be obedient. When children ignore parents' orders, and they often do, there usually are few if any repercussions.

Relative to boys, girls are more often given regular tasks. Care of younger siblings is a major responsibility allotted to daughters, however, sons are recruited if there are no older daughters. Mothers view daughters as their helpers, and for this reason, most mothers prefer that their first-born child be a girl, so she can help them with later-born children. Indulgence of youngest children regardless of sex is customary, and youngest daughters may be liberated from many tasks. However, task assignment by gender can override this special status. In one observation, Sra. G. urged her protesting youngest child, Aida, to get out of bed and help her with the washing, repeating the maxim that she who rises early will receive God's help (*al que madruga, Dios le ayuda*); nevertheless, her son Segundo got to stay in bed another half hour.

This section has dealt with the generalized cultural context of children's development. Let me turn now to a subtle aspect of socialization—parental responses to touching—that shape gendered behavior and boys' and girls' *styles* of interacting with others.

TOUCH ME OR TOUCH ME NOT: DEVELOPMENT OF GENDER STYLES

This section explores how children in the village of Patate come to display nonverbal gendered behavioral styles when they are relating to others. It reveals how parents intervene in, and attempt to alter, children's spontaneous behavior patterns through their responses to children's touches—the child's attempts to make intimate physical contact with parents. In this way parents transmit crucial aspects of gender ideals shared in the family and common to the wider society. On the negative side, the replication of stereotypic behaviors maintains the status quo, and contributes to the entrenchment of sex inequality.

In Patate, parents try to shape their children's behavior to accord with their own categories and constructions of gendered behavior. Femininity and masculinity are publicly represented in expressive behavioral styles. These are enhanced by material accouterments such as garb or hair arrangement (which also are markers for social class). Dress and hairstyle are simple matters; they are easy to acquire or to abandon. But behavioral styles have a certain permanence: They must be learned so early in life that they are automatic and intrinsic to the motor-response repertoire of the person. It is true that some aspects of gendered style are purely idiosyncratic, or unique to individual families, but here I refer to broadly drawn behavioral configurations that are stereotypic in the wider society.

To illustrate, let me recreate certain macro-features of the early experiences of two children I will call Silvia and Roberto. I place them in the context of two real families who participated in this study, but Roberto and Silvia are composite figures whose behavioral story represents the patterns that emerged from observations of fifty-one children interacting with their parents.

Because I focus on gender-socialization, the children's stories are a necessarily reduced account of the families and village-world they inhabit.

SILVIA

Silvia was born to Rosa Chicaiza and Tomás Melo. She was born at home, and her mother reports that she gave birth alone, "without any help from anyone" except her husband, who held her while she delivered the baby. Rosa tends a little shop in the room of her house that fronts on the street. She sells sundries such as candles, matches, toilet paper, cane alcohol, three kinds of pisco (fruit-flavored alcohol), soap, sodas, bottled water, bread, candy, and tins of sardines. Tomás is the janitor and guardian of the *cantón's* administrative building (a canton is an administrative unit somewhat similar to the U.S. county). He also works as a carpenter whenever he has a client, and he spends some time almost every day in one of the family's *huertas* ("gardens").

When Silvia was an infant, Rosa bound her to her back in a soft *chalina* ("shawl") and carried her. She was her mother's small companion in all her labors: household chores, tending the store, or planting, weeding and harvesting the vegetables and fruits that grew in three small huertas and a half-acre *frutal* ("orchard") that Rosa and Tomás rented. Often, when Rosa cooked at the wood fire on the raised hearth, Silvia drowsed, so she put the swaddled baby into a little hammock slung from the house rafters, tying her securely in place, before the older children pulled on a rope that swung the hammock and rocked her to sleep.

Sometimes older sisters or brothers carried Silvia in the chalina, and when her aunts and their children visited, she was passed from one pair of arms to the next, because they all liked playing with the baby, but mainly she was in her mother's care.

As Silvia rode in the chalina, her senses brought her information about her mother. The texture and color of her clothing, the scent of her hair, the angles of her face when she glanced over her shoulder at Silvia, the variable nuances of her voice, her expressions of satisfaction or displeasure, her lively conversation with relatives as Silvia lay in her lap and nursed. These observations of her mother's activities and her siblings' play were Silvia's main sources of entertainment. But importantly, until she was a year old, her experiences of the world generally took place in the protected warmth and comfort of her privileged post on her mother's back.

Rosa responded to Silvia's slightest indication of discomfort by offering her breast. Usually she divined her baby's need from the first restless stirrings she felt against her body, so Silvia almost never needed to cry to signal hunger. Rosa fed her often and generously. At night, Silvia slept next to her mother where her hunger could be satisfied even while her mother continued sleeping.

When Silvia was eight months old, her grandmother suggested that she should be weaned. The doctor at the local clinic seconded this opinion. Breast milk, he said (falsely), had absolutely no nutritional value after a year, "It is like water!" In fact, Silvia was reaching an age where, as Patateños believed, continued nursing would damage her character. Rosa's own mother and older relatives had told her that to nurse a daughter too long was to court trouble—both for the child and her parents. People said that breastfeeding gives the weak sex (girls) too many of the qualities of the strong sex (boys). A girl nursed too long would become rebellious and her sexual drive would be too strong. This would cause her difficulty in finding a husband, and whether she did or not, she surely would have too many pregnancies; worse, she could become a *grosera* (vulgar and boy-crazy).

When Silvia was a year old, her mother decided that she really should wean her, and so she sent her away for a week to stay with her grandmother. By the time she returned, she had "forgotten" the breast, and her mother gave her coladas, cookies, or bread, foods she was fond of, to mitigate the loss of the breast. Although the baby was weaned, she was so young that Rosa still carried her, and Silvia enjoyed that accustomed pattern of physical closeness to her mother and other caretakers until she became a competent walker.

Walking was an exciting new skill, and it permitted her to explore the house and the patio on her own. Still, she repeatedly begged her mother to carry her, and though sometimes she was successful, her mother generally refused. This made Silvia angry, and she protested, but her mother drew her close, and she contented herself with remaining beside her mother, and watching or imitating her performance of her tasks, or she was given to her older sister to take out to the patio or the street where she could see interesting things.

By the time Silvia was three years old, she still wanted her mother to hold her and carry her, but was resigned to the hug or pat Rosa usually gave her instead. Rosa attempted to interest her in some activity that allowed Silvia to sit or stand close by her. Gradually, Silvia's efforts to make physical contact diminished to less than forty percent of all her behavior vis à vis her mother—she was weaned from the habit of continual contact with her.[26] Still, Rosa let her touch her as frequently as she did when she was two years old, and by age three, Silvia actually increased her touches to her mother by six percent. Rosa ensured Silvia's closeness to her would continue by answering most of her touches with a touch (increasing her touches by more than sixty percent of her daughter's touches).[27]

If touching rewards security-seeking, one can assume that touch-backs (returned touches) were highly gratifying to Silvia, and encouraged her to touch her mother yet again. Rosa liked her to be nearby, and Silvia liked this, too. In fact, if Silvia initiated a social exchange with her mother while being spatially distant from her, the probability that Rosa's response would be hostile increased. And if Silvia reacted with hostility to this treatment, her mother increased her own hostility to Silvia.[28] Rosa preferred, then, that Silvia be spatially close to her, and in relatively frequent contact. Here are some descriptions from field notes that describe Silvia's style of relating to her mother:

S. (age 4) is "helping" her mother wash clothes at the concrete tank in the yard. Her mother tells me she is worried that the wawa (baby) will catch cold; the day is cool and the water is icy, but she does not impede her in any way. For the two hours of my visit, S. stays near her mother and plays at washing; dipping articles of clothing or her headless doll in the water tank.

S. is tired after celebrating her fifth *onomastico* (the day of the Saint she is named for is celebrated as a "birthday"). Her uncle and aunt are visiting. They are offered coffee and bread, and the remnants of the birthday sponge cake. After eating, S. sits next to her mother, leaning heavily against her body and listening to the conversation. After a bit, she crawls onto her mother's lap, lifts her poncho and snuggles under it. She pokes her head out of the neck-opening under her mother's chin (she looks like a little marsupial) and listens a while longer, but her eyes begin to droop, and she falls asleep.

Both parents collaborate in establishing a pattern of frequent contact on the part of their daughter. When Silvia touched her father, he returned ninety percent of her touches with touch-backs.[29] Her father rewarded her security-seeking through touch even more strongly than did her mother, and we see that both parents encouraged Silvia's touches.

There are differences between them, however. Silvia's father is less concerned with keeping her near him. He gives her few rewards for mere proximity, but strong rewards for touching. In contrast, Silvia's mother wants her to stay close, and rewards her for remaining spatially near her, as she grinds hard white corn (morocho) to make soup or cuts up pumpkins to cook for pig-feed.

Her mother's encouragement of spatial proximity (and her father's absence during the day when he was away at work), kept Silvia and her mother close, and the hostility she showed her mother at age two (usually, when she refused to carry her), has diminished by age three and continues to diminish up to age six.

But the hostility Silvia expresses in her relationship to her father is patterned differently. Until the age of six Silvia shows less hostility to her father compared with the level boys display at the same age. But by the age of nine, her hostile reactions to her father increase. (Examples of hostile behavior taken from the observations are expressing displeasure [to], touches

to move out of the way, ignores, criticizes, derogates, resists or rejects, and so on.)

Silvia's hostility may signal the beginning of the "respect" relations (meaning an increase in social distance) that conventionally are observed between daughters nearing puberty and their fathers, for neither her spatial distance from him nor her hostility to him made her father reciprocate with anger or disapproval, and he continues to offer her touches whenever she signals a need for security.

ROBERTO

Like Silvia, Roberto was his mother's companion during the performance of her daily tasks, riding securely tied in the chalina. His parents, María Araujo and Samuel Caicedo, worked hard. His father farmed the family's fields with his older sons, and tended two cows and a calf. His mother earned money by slaughtering a pig each week and preparing it for sale in the market. One can buy two types of cooked pork there, *hornada* (the meat of pigs roasted whole in earthen ovens) and *fritada* (fried pork). María made fritada.

Her other tasks centered on the care of her large family. Mending clothes, washing them on a waist-high concrete rub-board and hanging them out to dry, grinding the morning coffee and the chili-pepper condiment for the family meals, preparing the lunches she carried up the mountain to her husband and sons in the fields, tending her chickens and guinea pigs and sweeping out the house and the patio.

Roberto's father, Samuel, also was a cobbler who could produce sturdy, though homely, leather shoes and boots. With buses now available to the city where more attractive shoes could be purchased, few clients came to his *taller* (workshop), and he spent most of his time in agricultural work.

Roberto rode on his mother's back as she trekked daily up the mountain, his weight added to the weight of the food she transported. His mother feared his exposure to the sun's heat during her long journeys, and she attributed Roberto's occasional bouts of grippe and diarrhea to the sun overheating his body, or to his consumption of "sun-burned" breastmilk. She took the precaution, when she nursed him in the field, to extract some of the 'burned' milk from her breast and throw it away; then she drank cold water to "cool" the rest of her milk before feeding the baby.

She never allowed him to crawl on the wood floor of the house or on the earthen floor of her dark kitchen, where free rein was given a rabbit and eight guinea pigs. Neither did he crawl on the patio, where clothes dripped on the lines and the chickens and an occasional errant pig left its ordure. "Crawling children put dirty things in their mouths, which can make them sick," she said. So until he walked strongly and well, Roberto was carried or put on the family bed or in the hammock to sleep. At night he slept between his parents, next to his mother and her nourishing breast.

On market day, Roberto went with his mother and, peering over her shoulder, he watched her serve up the luscious fritada to her regular customers, spooning it out of the big brass *paila* (skillet). The activity in the crowded, noisy market entertained Roberto: the bustle of shoppers carrying big wicker baskets piled with onions, tomatoes, plantains, avocados, or carrots, or purchasers tying hundred-pound bags (*quintales*) of potatoes or grain on the backs of paid carriers (*cargadores*). There were lively altercations between sellers and their hard-bargaining customers, sales pitches yelled into megaphones by itinerant merchants, and the butcher's curses at hungry dogs skulking hopefully around the tree stump that served as a butcher block.

When Roberto was around seven months old, his mother began to feed him a little soup or colada but she continued to nurse him long after Rosa had weaned her daughter Silvia. María says she plans to nurse her son until he is around two or two and a half years old. This will help her delay having another baby, and will give him a *caracter fuerte* (a strong character). This is a good thing for boys, she says, because "When they grow up, they need to be strong to dominate their wives and gain their children's respect."

By age two, Roberto runs and plays with his siblings, but discomfort, boredom, or tiredness brings him back to his mother to nurse and be held, and when he is done, he tries to get her to carry him. At two he is quite a burden, and since he was eighteen months or so, his mother has tried to "wean" him from being carried. Now that he is twenty-four months, she weans him from the breast as well. She puts Mercurochrome on her nipples to dye them red and tells him she is hurt. He finally stops demanding to nurse, and the transition is eased by the sudden availability of some of his favorite foods and baby bottles full of sweet liquids.

At age two, he continues to seek the comfort of his mother's body, however, and pesters her to hold him (his touches to her exceed the frequency of Silvia's contacts with her mother). But he finds that when he pulls on her skirt, or hits her legs, she ignores him. Even when he tries to stay near her, she pays him little mind, and though she is not hostile, neither does she assuage his need by offering touch-backs, such as Silvia received.[30]

This makes him angry, but if he is hostile to her, she reacts hostilely to him: she moves away and sharply reprimands him. So Roberto stamps his feet and screams and throws himself on the floor, but his mother doesn't pick him up; instead, she announces proudly to whomever is near, "What a temper! What a little *macho* he is!" If his father is at home, he may scoop Roberto up in his arms, while laughing with amusement at his tantrum, and carry him off to find something to interest him.

Roberto soon learns that his old pattern of contact with his mother that made him feel secure is no longer available to him, and touching his mother gains him few rewards.[31] If, however, he keeps his distance from her, and then initiates a social exchange, he finds that not only his mother but his father pays him a great deal of fond attention. His mother enjoys conversing with him, singing with him, and she is amused and delighted by his antics.[32]

Roberto's attempts to touch his father usually meet with success in that he is allowed to touch, though his father is significantly less likely to reward him by touching him back. Instead, he responds to him with a smile, a joke, or a question that continues the interaction. His father's use of means other than touch to express his approval and affection seems to inhibit Roberto's own attempts to touch him, which diminish over time. He finds that if he stays spatially close to his father, he receives more negative sanctions. But when he plays within sight of Samuel, but is spatially distant from him, his father watches him approvingly and is entertained by the things he does, (even when he makes noise or squabbles with his siblings).

By the age of three, Roberto actively seeks this focused attention.[33] Because his most rewarding interactions with his parents occur across space he must attract their attention rather than simply approaching them and touching them. (His attention-drawing behavior includes such actions as assaults, converses, marches, dances, threatens, inquires, shows to, makes noise, makes music, restrains [another], etc.) María also regards Roberto's high jinks as amusing; however, neither María nor Samuel reward Roberto's sisters for this sort of activity.

On a visit to the family, I note that Roberto (who now is three) commands the attention of everyone in the room the entire time he is present. He wants some money! He does not want to wash his face! He jumps up and down, and throws a ball around, imperiling the heads of all present. He demands to have his shoes, and cries when his mother says she cannot find them (they are hidden to preserve them for the coming fiesta), but he nags and argues until she gives in and gets them. Before he can wear them, his aunt has to sew them up because he has torn them. His mother describes him in his presence as *muy exigente* (very insistent) and as having a *caracter fuerte*.

By age five, Roberto becomes more hostile in his exchanges with his mother, and now, surprisingly, she does not answer with hostility, as she did when he was age two, but rather tries to placate him or accede to his demands.[34] In fact it appears that both she and Samuel expect Roberto to show a certain level of hostility. His father's attitude toward this behavior shows that he approves of it, but he also tries to limit its expression. When Roberto is less hostile in his behavior to Samuel, he receives significantly more positive reinforcement, but also more negative sanctions! We can interpret this mixed response as Samuel's involvement in shaping his son's hostility—ensuring that Roberto shows a certain level of aggressiveness and independence, while trying to keep their relationship positive.

If we analyze Roberto's and Silvia's patterned interactions with their parents over time, we find that the children are being socialized for two distinct non-verbal styles of interaction. Parents' treatments of the children differ with the child's sex. The kinds of treatment given also differ with the parents' sex. Both parents reward touches from their daughters (but not from sons), and reward their sons' attention-drawing behaviors (but not their daughters'). Mothers provoke children's anger and frustration when they wean them from the back, but tend to inhibit daughters' freedom to express that hostility while encouraging and approving their sons' outbursts. Fathers converge with mothers in supporting and rewarding this behavior and in rewarding a certain degree of aggressiveness in their sons.[35]

These strategies "situate" children in interactional space vis à vis these significant others. They also appear to inculcate gendered styles of approaching or distancing themselves from members of their own sex and their own families once they grow into adults. A brief look at the salient features of adult roles that have some relevance to these socialized behaviors may be helpful.

IDEAL MALE ROLES AND SOCIAL DISTANCE

The ideal traits cited in this section and the following one are often preceded by a "should." *Should* cues readers that they are confronting not a behavioral fact but a social norm or ideal. For example, men say a man should be wary of trusting others. In business dealings, his attitude should be aloof and skeptical. A man should convey the impression that it is dangerous to trifle with him, and should defend his own and his family's interests. (Because rural Andeans have been exploited by politically powerful elites for over four hundred years, this attitude has certainly been prudent, and has helped families to survive.) These statements portray an aloof, detached, tenacious, and suspicious persona. The male roles of husband and father, however, require a completely different set of attitudes: women say that men should be understanding, generous, and loving with their families.

Mestizo men and women agree that a husband is the *jefe* (boss; chief) of the household. Wives and children defer to him, and their relations with him are marked by respect and social distance. At meals, he is served first, and often eats alone, or in the company of his sons. He should avoid any attitude or action that indicates he is unduly influenced by his wife (henpecked husbands are ridiculed). Romantic behavior is acceptable for sweethearts, but public displays of affection between spouses are rare; even linking arms or holding hands causes comment.

Though this behavioral taboo serves many purposes, one of them is to enhance male solidarity, which conjugal devotion threatens. Peer efforts to weaken conjugal loyalty are evident at public fiestas where there is drinking and dancing. At these celebrations two or three men (usually married themselves) seek out recently wed male friends and, with jocular adamancy, drag them over to hapless unmarried women insisting that they dance together. The jokes and the accompanying leers of his friends indicate to the young man that this is his chance to break the "apron strings."

Drinking is a social activity to be done only with other people. Men's habitual social distance from others usually is disinhibited when they consume a lot of alcohol (and in Patate, if a man takes a drink, the usual end is inebriation, as toast after toast and shot after shot are formally exchanged). Inebriation excuses almost every antic. The sober-sides, aloof and distant during the week, after a few shots of pisco or trago, freely throws his arms around his male companions in warm embraces. He may even sing to them. If a fiesta is under way and he is well into his cups, he may dance with sensual abandon or clown hilariously for the amusement of the onlookers.

IDEAL FEMALE ROLES

The strong sanctions against affectionate demonstrativeness between married couples carries over into the household. In Patate, it is considered inappropriate for spouses to kiss or caress in front of their children, who, people say, would lose *respect* for them. However, touching and proximity as established, rewarding behavior systems socialized in childhood are permitted to women in other ways. We know little of its resonance with conjugal sexuality, but we can observe other outlets for affective touching. Mothers caress, kiss, and embrace their youngest children, publicly and freely; they carry them close against their bodies and embrace them in their sleep. Breastfeeding often appears to be a deeply satisfying activity for mothers as well as their children.

Recently married couples live matrilocally (with the bride's parents) in around a third of Patate families, so women often have a continuing, close relationship with adult daughters. Women's friendships are generally restricted to their kin, and they express their affection (through decorous touches) to their kinswomen or favorite *comadres* (co-mothers; godparents). They may sit close by each other, one resting her head on the other's shoulder, or holding her hand. They walk arm-in-arm together in the street.

But like their men, contradictions are built into highland women's roles. The loving mother and submissive wife often has another side: a "business" persona, premised on advancing her family's interests and the expectation that she must "defend" herself and her family against would-be exploiters. Most women are formidable bargainers who carry in their minds the "rock-bottom" prices for an incredible inventory of goods. Business dealings with non-kin call for a direct, assertive, even aggressive attitude, although women's joking and good humor mitigates this manner.

Often, women are their families' main support. They define a "good husband" as a man who contributes half his earnings to his family's needs (retaining the other half for his own entertainment). In contrast, women's earnings from their small business enterprises or wage labors is spent almost entirely on maintaining their families.

This chapter has moved from socialization of gender-stereotypical behavior to a description of adult behavior, implying that parents selectively reward gendered styles of interaction, and that early experience is connected in complex ways to adult behavioral outcomes. This view faces some opposition.[36] Still, even casual observations of children and adults in traditional communities might convince skeptics that parents do not simply sit back and "let nature take its course." Rather, they attempt to inculcate consistent responses in their children that result in engendered, enculturated modes of moving their bodies through

interpersonal space. Still, children also have minds, and they are active negotiators in parent-child exchanges. Each child's history is unique, and in that uniqueness lies the potential for cultural change.

Notes

1. *Proyecciones de la Población Ecuatoriana por Provincias, Cantones, Areas, y Grupos de Edad, 1982–1995* (Quito: Instituto Nacional de Estadística y Censos, 1985), p. 2.; Dennis Hanratty, ed., *Ecuador: A Country Study* (Washington, D. C.: Library of Congress, 1991), p. 54.
2. *Area Handbook for Ecuador* (Washington, D.C.: U.S. Government Printing Office, 1991), p. 83.
3. *Diario Hoy* (Quito, Ecuador, September 1993).
4. Ronald Stutzman, "El Mestizaje: An All-Inclusive Ideology of Exclusion, "in Norman Whitten, Jr., ed., *Cultural Transformations and Ethnicity in Modern Ecuador* (Urbana: University of Illinois Press, 1981), pp. 45–94.
5. Francisco Sampedro V., *Atlas Geográfico del Ecuador* (Quito: Offsetec, 1976).
6. John V. Murra, *Formaciones Económicas y Políticas del Mundo Andino* (Lima: Instituto de Estudios Peruanos, 1975), pp. 59–116.
7. As calculated by Roger Avery for children aged one year or younger in 1973, mortality per thousand ranged from a low of 16.8 in El Carchi Province to a high of 84.77 in Chimborazo Province. Source: Anuario de Estadísticas Vitale (Instituto Nacional de Estadística, 1973), Tabla 16, pp. 166–123. Compare this with the current U.S. infant mortality rate of 9.8 per thousand, and remember that our mortality rate is higher than that of 22 other developed nations. (*The New York Times*, April 16, 1992).
8. See *Evil Wind, Evil Air*, a documentary film directed by Lauris A. McKee. Distributors: Pennsylvania State Audiovisual Services.
9. *Compare Dario Guevara, Un Mundo Mágico-Mítico en la Mitad del Mundo* (Quito, Ecuador: Imprenta Municipal, 1972), pp. 89–90. For the role of mountain deities in contemporary runa cosmology in Peru, see Catherine Allen's discussion in *The Hold Life Has* (Washington, D.C.: Smithsonian Institution Press, 1988), pp. 41–44; and Billie Jean Isbell, *To Defend Ourselves* (1978; reprint Prospect Heights, IL: Waveland Press, 1985).
10. For the Saraguro, see Jim Belote and Linda Belote, "The Limitation of Obligation in Saraguro Kinship," in Ralph Bolton and Enrique Mayer, eds., *Andean Kinship and Marriage* (Washington, D.C.: The American Anthropological Association, 1977), p. 107.
11. Though this sounded far-fetched, in 1986, in Ecuador's neighbor, Colombia, newspapers revealed that a ring of medical professionals in certain hospitals in Bogotá, were stealing healthy newborns and

selling them to adoptive parents. The biological mothers were told their babies were stillborn.

12. *Encuesta Anual de Estadísticas Vitales* (Nacimientos y Defunciones) (Quito: Instituto Nacional de Estadística y Censos, 1986), p. 3. The Encuesta Nacional de Fecundidad reports for the nation as a whole, that in 1979, forty-nine percent of women gave birth at home, seventeen percent of these gave birth alone; five percent had medical assistance and twenty-seven percent were assisted by a midwife (Quito: Instituto Nacional de Estadística y Censos, 1979) p. 243.

13. Lauris A. McKee, "Ideals and Actualities: The Socialization of Gender-Appropriate Behavior in an Ecuadorian Village." (Ph.D. diss., Cornell University, 1980). This differs from practice reported for the runa community of Peguche in the 1930s where the cord was cut "about an inch from the body . . . there is no lore concerning it." Elsie C. Parsons, *Peguche: A Study of Andean Indians* (Chicago: University of Chicago Press, 1945), p. 44.

14. To swaddle a newborn, mothers first cover the umbilicus with a navel band made of crocheted white cotton thread, then the baby is diapered and placed on three layers of cloth (a cotton cloth, then a folded thick piece of wool topped by another cotton cloth). The baby is placed on these materials and mothers fold all three layers across the body and over the right arm, tucking the cloth under the left side of the body. This operation is repeated for the left arm, and the right side. The ends of the cloth are folded under the feet. Finally, while its arms and legs are held straight, the baby is wrapped about like a little mummy, with a long, crocheted white cotton strip. Swaddling was an Incaic as well as a Spanish custom. According to Garcilaso, the Incas bound their infants' bodies, including the arms, until they reached four months of age. *El Inca, Garcilaso de la Vega, Royal Commentaries of the Incas*, trans. Harold Livermore (Austin: University of Texas Press, 1966), p. 212.

15. Lauris A. McKee, "The Dieta: Postpartum Seclusion in the Andes of Ecuador," in Anna Cohn and Lucinda Leach, eds., *Generations.*(Washington, D.C.: Smithsonian Institution, 1987), pp. 205–211.

16. Ibid.

17. Lauris A. McKee, "Los Cuerpos Tiernos: Simbolísmo y Magia en las Prácticas Post-Parto en Ecuador," *América Indígena* XLII (1982): 615–628; and "Sex Differentials in Survivorship and the Customary Treatment of Infants and Children," *Medical Anthropology* 8 (1984): 91–108.

18. In 1982–1984, data from six field sites, Guaranda, Píllaro, Rayo, Mira, Tumbaviro, and Gualaceo showed that of 1,416 births reported, 92.5 percent of these mothers still nursed their babies in the early months of life.

19. The difference in actual ages of weaning is statistically significant (unlikely to be due to chance). B. Vasquez Fuller, "La Mujer Indígena," *América Indígena* 34 (1974): 664–675. Reports differential weaning in Otavalo runa communities as well—the custom is to nurse boys for three years and girls for two years. She does not state the ideal versus the actual ages.

20. See Julian Pitt-Rivers, *The People of the Sierra* (Chicago: University of Chicago Press, 1954); J.G. Peristiany, ed., *Honor and Shame: The Values of Mediterranean Society* (Chicago: University of Chicago Press, 1966); and J. G. Peristiany, ed., *The Fate of Schechem* (Cambridge: Cambridge University Press, 1977).

21. *Encuesta Anual de Estadísticas Vitales* [Nacimientos y Defunciones]1977 (Quito: Instituto Nacional de Estadística y Censos, 1977); *Serie Estadística 1967–1972* (Quito: Instituto Nacional de Estadística, 1974); *Anuario de Estadísticas Vitales 1973* (Quito: Instituto Nacional de Estadística); and *Tablas de Mortalidad por Sexos (1950–1962)* (Quito: Junta Nacional de Planificación y Coordinación Económica, 1974).

22. For mortality patterns, see Samuel Preston and James Weed, *Mortality Patterns in National Populations* (New York: Academic Press, 1976); and *Levels and Trends of Mortality since 1950* (New York: United Nations, 1982). For the effects of male preference, see E.M. Rosenberg, "Demographic Effects of Sex-Differential Nutrition," in R.F. Kandel, N.W. Jerome, and G.H. Pelto, eds., *Nutritional Anthropology* (Pleasantville, NY: Redgrave Publishing Co., 1980); Linda Ortmeyer, "Females' Natural Advantage? Or, the Unhealthy Environment of Males? The Status of Sex Mortality Differentials," *Women and Health* 4 (1979): 121–133; William Divale and Marvin Harris, "Population, Warfare, and the Male Supremacist Complex," *American Anthropologist* 78 (1976): 521–538; A. Kehoe and D. Giletti, "Women's Preponderance in Possession Cults: The Calcium Deficiency Hypothesis Extended," *American Anthropologist* 83 (1981): 549–561; Barbara Miller, *The Endangered Sex* (Ithaca, NY: Cornell University Press, 1981); M. Graham and A. Larme, "Food Allocation and Child Health in Rural Peru," paper read at the 91st Annual Meeting of the American Anthropological Association, 1992.

23. See Monica Das Gupta, "Selective Discrimination against Female Children in Rural Punjab, India," *Population and Development Review* 13 (1987): 77–100; L.C. Chen, E. Huq, and S.D. Souza, "Sex Bias in the Family Allocation of Food and Health Care in Rural Bangladesh," *Population and Development Review* 7 (1981): 55–70; Judit Katona-Apte, "The Relevance of Nourishment to the Reproductive Cycle of the Female in India," in Dana Raphael, ed., *Being Female: Reproduction, Power and Change* (The Hague: Mouton Press, 1975), pp. 43–48.

24. The anti-infective agents in human milk are associated with biologically meaningful differences in

morbidity and mortality in developing countries, at least throughout the first year of life. See A. Cunningham, "Breast-Feeding and Morbidity in Industrialized Countries: An Update," in D.B. Jelliffe and E.F.P. Jelliffe, eds., *International Maternal and Child Health* (Oxford: Oxford University Press, 1981).

25. Garcilaso de la Vega, *Royal Commentaries of the Incas and General History of Peru*, pp. 195–202.

26. Thomas Maretzki and Hatsumi Maretzki, *Taira: An Okinawan Village*, vol. VII of the Six Cultures Series (New York: John Wiley and Sons, Inc., 1966); John Whiting, "Environmental Constraints on Infant Care Practices," in R.H. Munroe, R.L. Munroe, and B.B. Whiting, eds., *Handbook of Cross-Cultural Human Development* (New York: Garland Press, 1981); and Billie Jean Isbell and Lauris McKee, "Society's Cradle: An Anthropological Perspective on the Socialization of Cognition," in John Sants, ed., Developmental Psychology and Society (London: St. Martin's Press, 1980), pp. 343–344. Also see Beatrice B. Whiting and Carolyn P. Edwards, "A Cross-Cultural Analysis of Sex Differences in the Behavior of Children Aged Three through Eleven," *Journal of Social Psychology* 91 (1973): 171–188. The authors find little differentiation between the sexes except for two styles of interpersonal contact. Rough-and-tumble play for boys and touching for girls show remarkable consistency across six cultural groups, and the authors suggest that they may be good candidates for essential sex differences. Their analyses of data from the Six Cultures Study inspired my own research into possible environmental antecedents for these two behaviors. Also see the following works, which indicate that environmental/social factors such as children's spatial distance from home or the types of tasks they are assigned have effects on cognitive styles and social behavior: Ruth Munroe and Robert Munroe, "Effect of Environmental Experience on Spatial Ability in an East African Society," *Journal of Social Psychology* 83 (1971): 15–22; Sarah Beth Nerlove, Ruth Munroe, and Robert Munroe, "Effect of Environmental Experience on Spatial Ability: A Replication," *Journal of Social Psychology* 84 (1971): 3–10; and Carol Ember, "Feminine Task Assignment and the Social Behavior of Boys," *Ethos* 1 (1973): 424–439.

27. This increase of touches is statistically significant.

28. Distance gains girls more negative responses from their mothers: though this finding does not reach significance, it indicates the trend in treatment. Two- and three-year-old children's frustration over refusals to carry them leads to the expression of a good deal of hostility to their mothers. Mothers significantly retaliate with more negative sanctions to two- and three-year-olds of both sexes.

29. Fathers significantly increase their touches to daughters by 90.5 percent of the proportion of times daughters touch them, regardless of the daughter's age. Daughters, as they grow older, show a signifi-

cant decline in hostile responses to mothers, but at age six their hostility to fathers increases, and by age nine they are marginally more hostile to father than sons are.

30. Mothers significantly reduce rewards dispensed as touches to their sons by the time sons are three years old, and boys have learned to reduce their touches to their mothers.

31. Two-year-olds, both male and female, spend a similar proportion of their time close to mother, but by age three the proportion of time in proximity to her significantly decreases for boys. Both age and sex predict children's distance from mothers.

32. Fathers significantly respond to sons' touches with a decreasing proportion of touch-backs.

33. To find security boys must take the initiative or increase their activity rates, such that they become the focus of their parent's attention. Independently of age, all boys in the sample perform significantly more attention-drawing actions than all girls.

34. This is a marginally significant trend, but is a point that should be pursued further, given mothers' encouragement of hypermale (*macho*) behavior in young boys. Fathers' reactions to sons' hostility are complex and contradictory. If sons behave less hostilely, fathers increase negative sanctions (in that they increase their hostile responses) but they also give sons significant positive rewards for less hostility. This apparent "double-bind" situation may be interpreted as true ambivalence: fathers want their sons to approximate male role-ideals and attitudes, which include a certain level of hostility to others. On the other hand, fathers do not wish sons to be hostile to themselves.

35. The histories of Silvia and Roberto are based on data from fifty-two randomly selected children (twenty-six girls and twenty-six boys) between ages two and nine. The children were matched on age, opposite sex, parents' education and socioeconomic status, and number of children in the family. One child's family moved away, leaving fifty-one children in the sample group. One child was selected in each family, and designated as the Central Figure for observation (CF). I recorded all the self-instigated interaction attempts on the part of female and male CFs, and their parents' responses to those attempts. Children were observed at a time of day when both parents were present. The observations of an hour's length were made on two different days. The last half-hour of each observation was coded in numerical sentences in accord with my adaptation of the APPROACH code developed by Bettye Caldwell, Alice Honig, and Ruth Wynn for their own extensive research. See their *Coding Manual for Approach: A Procedure for Patterning Responses of Adults and Children*. Coding Manual. American Psychological Association, ms. no. 2. These analyses have been bolstered by participant observation in twenty-two

families in other study communities during two years of additional research.

36. For example, see Richard A. Shweder, "Rethinking Culture and Personality Theory Part I: A Critical Examination of Two Classical Postulates," *Ethos* 7 (1979): 255–278.

Suggested Readings

Parsons, Elsie Clews. *Peguche: A Study of Andean Indians*. Chicago: University of Chicago Press, 1945. Parsons collected the data for this ethnography in the 1930s. Still, it is one of the few sources for information on child-rearing customs.

Whitten, Norman E., Jr., ed. *Cultural Transformations and Ethnicity in Modern Ecuador*. Urbana: University of Illinois Press, 1981. The chapters examine several aspects of Ecuadorian life and culture.

Harrison, Regina. *Signs, Songs, and Memory in the Andes: Translating Quechua Language and Culture*. Austin: University of Texas Press, 1989. A lyrical exploration of gender and Andean life through song and symbolic systems.

Suggested Videos

McKee, Lauris A. *Evil Wind, Evil Air;* and *New Life: Reproductive Beliefs and Practices in the Ecuadorian Andes*. These two films explore Ecuadorian ethnomedical beliefs and practices.

Rotuma: Interpreting a Wedding

Alan Howard and Jan Rensel

In most societies there are one or two activities that express, in highly condensed ways, what life is all about for its members. In Bali it is the cockfight,[1] among the Australian Aborigines the corroboree, in Brazil there is carnival. One might make a case for the Super Bowl in the United States. On Rotuma, a small isolated island in the South Pacific, weddings express, in practice and symbolically, the deepest values of the culture. In the bringing together of a young man and young woman, in the work that goes into preparing the wedding feast, in the participation of chiefs both as paragons of virtue and targets of humor, in the displays of food and fine white mats, and in the sequence of ceremonial rites performed, Rotumans communicate to one another what they care about most: kinship and community, fertility of the people and land, the political balance between chiefs and commoners, and perpetuation of Rotuman custom. After providing a brief description of Rotuma and its people, we narrate an account of a wedding in which we participated. We then interpret key features of the wedding, showing how they express, in various ways, core Rotuman values.

The Island and Its People

Rotuma is situated approximately three hundred miles north of Fiji, on the western fringe of Polynesia. The island is volcanic in origin, forming a land area of about seventeen square miles, with the highest craters rising to eight hundred feet above sea level. From the air, Rotuma appears a dark green jewel framed by a white garland of breaking surf in the midst of the vast blue ocean. On closer inspection one sees a far greater array of colors and hues; the dark green of coconut trees that cover much of the island are complemented by the softer tints of breadfruit trees, banana plants, and taro and yam gardens. The white sand beaches on parts of the coast are offset by black lava rocks from ancient eruptions. Tropical flowers and vines add even more variety to a kaleidoscopic landscape of living things. The island is nearly as beautiful up close as it is from afar, and one can understand why some early visitors confused it with paradise. But after one experiences the sometimes overpowering heat and humidity—Rotuma is only 12 degrees from the equator and has an average 140 inches of rain per year—and the ubiquitous flies and mosquitoes, illusions of paradise are likely to evaporate.

The island is divided into two parts joined by an isthmus of sand, forming a configuration about eight miles long and at its widest three miles across, with its lengthwise axis running due east and west. A packed sand road, reinforced in places with concrete strips, circles the perimeter of the eastern segment of the island and extends to coastal plains west of the isthmus. Villages and hamlets are scattered along the road, with occasional stretches of bushland in between. The interior of the island is heavily cultivated with gardens of taro, yams, cassava, bananas, pineapples, watermelons, and other food crops. A few people plant vanilla, cocoa, or kava as commercial crops as well. Kava is a plant of the pepper family, the roots of which are used to make a drink with mild narcotic properties; it is an essential part of Rotuman ceremonies at which chiefs and dignitaries are honored. Fruit trees abound: mango, papaya, orange. Rotuman oranges—wonderfully sweet and juicy—are justifiably famous in that part of the Pacific. Cattle and goats are tethered to coconut trees adjacent to plantations, and pigs are kept in stone-walled enclosures.

Linguists have long debated the place of the Rotuman language in the Austronesian family. Although sharing a significant portion of vocabulary with Tongan and Samoan, Rotuman has some unique characteristics that set it apart from others in the vicinity.

The current view is that an earlier form of the language was closely related to ancestral languages in western Fiji,[2] but that invasions from Tonga and Samoa resulted in a good deal of borrowing and innovation. The product is a language that is unintelligible to speakers of other Pacific tongues.

Politically Rotuma has been governed as part of Fiji for over one hundred years. When the paramount chiefs of Rotuma's seven districts ceded the island to Great Britain in 1881, for administrative convenience the British decided to incorporate it into the Crown Colony of Fiji, some three hundred miles away.

When Fiji was granted independence in 1970, the Rotuman people decided to remain a part of Fiji. They also decided to stay with Fiji, though not without controversy, following two military coups in 1987.

The total number of Rotumans enumerated in the 1986 census of Fiji was 8,652, of whom only 2,588 were resident on the home island. The remainder live mostly in Fiji's urban centers, where they are conspicuously successful in professions, government service, and private industry. Travel back and forth between Fiji and Rotuma is facilitated by weekly flights and cargo vessels that take passengers. A substantial number of Rotumans have also migrated to Australia and New Zealand, and they, too, make return visits on occasion. In addition to keeping in touch by mail and radio-telephone, Rotumans living in Fiji and abroad host visitors from the island and send remittances, household appliances, and other manufactured goods back home to enhance their kinsmen's standard of living.[3] For their part, those remaining on Rotuma frequently send gifts of produce, prepared foods, and Rotuman handicrafts to their relatives living away.

Culturally, Rotuma clearly falls within the Polynesian orbit. Titled chiefs are important to the social and political life of the island, and Rotuman values and custom show strong resemblances to other cultures of western Polynesia (especially Tonga, Samoa, Futuna, and Uvea). At the heart of the kinship system is the concept of *kainaga*, which in its broadest sense refers to all one's "blood" relations, that is, anyone who is descended from a common ancestor. In its restricted usage, kainaga refers to common rights in a specific named house-site. Rotumans say that each person ideally belongs to eight kainaga, corresponding to their great-grandparents' homes. At life-crisis ceremonies such as first birthdays, weddings, and funerals, relevant house-sites are gathering places where members congregate to prepare food and materials for the event. They then go as a group to make their presentations.

Also important for life-crisis events is the institution of name giving. Prior to the birth of a child, someone with a special relationship to one or both parents requests that the baby be named after him or her. Name givers may or may not be close relatives, but when accepted a special bond is formed between them and the newborn child. Name givers are expected to bestow special gifts on birthdays, Christmas, and other occasions, and to champion the causes of their namesakes. At weddings they play a special role, as we shall see.

Prelude to a Wedding

As recently as 1960, when Alan first began research on Rotuma, marriages were often arranged by parents without their children's direct involvement. Sometimes bride and groom met for the first time on their wedding day. Arrangements for such a marriage were formal and complex. They began with representatives of the young man seeking approval from the young woman's parents for the match. If her parents agreed, a more formal delegation was formed to approach the chief of the woman's district. In Rotuman, this event is called *süf hani*. The gravity of the proposal would be enhanced by each side's asking titled men, perhaps even their district chief, to represent them. To emphasize the seriousness of the request the young man's representatives would bring a gift of a whole pig cooked in an earthen oven and a small kava plant.

In turn, the young woman's kinsmen would feed the young man's representatives. The pros and cons of the prospective match would be discussed, and if agreed upon, preparations would begin for the next stage, *fai ran ta*, a ceremony at which the wedding date was set.

The following field notes, obtained by Alan from a participant in an arranged marriage in 1960, provides a sense of what these negotiations were like. The groom, Aisea, was a schoolteacher from the district of Malhaha; the bride, Ieli, was the granddaughter of Tokaniua, the paramount chief of Oinafa district. Aisea met Ieli during the Christmas "play" season[4] and decided he wanted to marry her. He went to Tokaniua and told him of his intentions.[5] Tokaniua was reluctant because of Aisea's reputation for drinking, but said he would accept if Aisea would change his ways. Aisea promised that he would.

When he left Oinafa, Aisea went back to his home in Malhaha and early the next morning told his father the news. Immediately Aisea's father went to the Chief of Malhaha (also named Aisea; we will refer to him as Chief Aisea) and informed him. This was necessary because Ieli, being a district chief's granddaughter, should be asked for by someone of chiefly rank. Chief Aisea decided on the best time to go *süf hani* to ask formally for Ieli's hand.

SÜF HANI: ASKING FOR A YOUNG WOMAN'S HAND IN MARRIAGE

All the sub-chiefs in Malhaha were called on to join the delegation. The only person of rank to stay behind was Aisea's brother, who remained to supervise the preparation of food for the delegation, who would have to be fed upon their return. In addition to Chief Aisea and five sub-chiefs, Aisea's namesake and one other untitled man joined the delegation; the latter was selected by Chief Aisea to carry the kava plant.

In keeping with Rotuman custom, the delegation left early in the morning. The district messenger from Malhaha had been sent earlier to Oinafa to inform Chief Tokaniua of the date and time of the delegation's arrival. (Each district has a formal position of messenger, responsible for communicating the paramount chief's desires and intentions vis-à-vis other districts.) When the *süf hani* delegation reached Oinafa they were greeted at the chief's house by Tokaniua himself. This was a sign of acceptance. If Tokaniua had not been there to offer them greetings, this would have been a bad sign—a note of disapproval. Even if a marriage does not directly involve the chief's family, if the bride and groom are from different districts, proper custom requires the chief of the young woman's district to receive the *süf hani* delegation, provided the union is agreeable to her family.

After the delegation was greeted by Tokaniua they were asked into the house and sat down. Already seated and waiting were Ieli's namesake and members of her kainaga. Tokaniua opened the meeting by welcoming the delegation and thanking them for coming. Then the oldest member of the groom's delegation, a man in his eighties by the name of Hanfakaga, began to talk and came straight to the point. He took the initiative because he was related to Tokaniua and therefore less restrained by barriers of respect. Hanfakaga talked very humbly about Aisea. His job was made more difficult by Aisea's reputation for drinking, but in any case humility is called for by custom.

The interaction between the two groups was essentially democratic, with each person speaking in turn. Generally the young man's delegation "talks down" his desirability as a husband and apologizes for his faults, while it is up to the young woman's side, provided they are disposed toward acceptance, to emphasize his good points. Eventually, after each person on both sides had their say, Tokaniua gave an official

acceptance on Ieli's behalf. If a verdict is in doubt the young woman's representatives may go into private conference in order to reach a decision, but the final answer can only be properly given by the chief. During all this time Ieli was not present, nor did she have any official say in the scheduling or form of the wedding.

Tokaniua then advised the Malhaha delegation to tell Aisea to come to Oinafa the next the day so that the chief could talk to him and Ieli together, to advise them and instruct Aisea when to go to the government station to post their marital banns (usually the day after such a meeting). He also gave the delegation a date for their next meeting, the *fai ran ta*, when the wedding date would be arranged. The date for the *fai ran ta* is discussed along with the other business of *süf hani*, but the final decision is made by the young woman's side and announced by the chief. After concluding their official business, tea and biscuits were served to all who were present, following which the Malhaha delegation returned home to inform Aisea and the rest of his kainaga of the good news.

FAI RAN TA: APPOINTING THE DAY

The same people who went on the *süf hani* formed Aisea's delegation for the *fai ran ta* expedition. One of the members provided the following account:

When we left Malhaha we had to take a kava plant. A special person, Kaitu'u, chosen by Chief Aisea, took the kava. [He was the same man appointed to take the kava for the *süf hani*.] Arriving at Oinafa at seven in the morning, we were welcomed at the chief's house by Chief Tokaniua and Ritia, Ieli's mother [the daughter of Tokaniua]. When we entered the house, some of Ieli's kainaga were already there waiting. We shook hands with them and sat down on some *apei* [fine white mats] that had been spread out for us. The first thing they did was serve us with a coconut each. We had to wait until Chief Aisea began to drink and then we each could drink. That is the Rotuman way.

After we finished drinking, Tokaniua gave the first speech. He's the one to date the wedding. He gave the date for the wedding as February 20, 1960. He asked us what we thought about it. Chief Aisea gave a speech and said that anything that Tokaniua and his kainaga think best is all right with us.

It didn't matter that we came early. We had to wait for all Ieli's kainaga to come before the meeting took place. Tokaniua gave his speech announcing the date before the "meeting" took place, that is, before all the kainaga had arrived. He should really have waited until all the kainaga were assembled before giving his speech. After they all arrived, Tokaniua told them he had already informed Aisea's contingent of the date set for the wedding. We had nothing further to say, simply to thank Tokaniua and Ieli's kainaga. Chief Aisea gave that speech. Then they thanked us. First Tokaniua gave a speech of thanks for Ieli's side and next Fakraufon, the Chief of Noatau, who is one of Ieli's relatives. They told us everything was all right.

After that they prepared breakfast. First the higher ranking chiefs from both sides ate breakfast together; the lesser ranking chiefs ate at a second sitting with other members of Ieli's kainaga. Right after breakfast we shook hands with all the members of Ieli's party and left. Ieli was not present at the meeting. We left at 10:00 A.M. When we arrived back at Malhaha (10:30), Aisea's father welcomed us and we entered the house and sat down on the regular floor mats. They prepared a breakfast for us—coffee, cocoa, bread, biscuits, butter, and jam—the same things we had in Oinafa. When we were eating Chief Aisea gave a speech telling Aisea's father and his family the date of the wedding. Only Aisea's family (including Aisea) were there. Aisea's father then gave a speech of thanks. After breakfast we left.

Soon after the date of the wedding had been set, each side would hold a meeting to decide who would be responsible for providing the various items such as pigs, apei, mosquito netting and bedding for the couple's bed, the bridal purse, and other paraphernalia required at a proper wedding. Usually relatives and friends would volunteer, but the man and woman designated to take charge of the preparations might assign specific tasks.

Maika and Susie's Wedding

Although in many respects life on Rotuma has not changed radically since 1960, some things have.[6] For one, arranged marriages of the type described above have all but disappeared. More open courtship is tolerated and youths are given more freedom in choosing their spouses. They also play a more active role in planning their weddings. Nevertheless, the form of

weddings has not changed significantly, and Rotuman rituals are still performed in conjunction with church and civil ceremonies.

The wedding we shall describe took place in the village of Lopta, district of Oinafa, on July 21, 1989. The groom, Maika, was from nearby Oinafa village. He was a policeman in the Fiji constabulary, assigned to duty at the government station on Rotuma. The bride, Susie, whose parental home is in Lopta, was employed at the Rotuman branch of the National Bank of Fiji, also situated at the government station. Maika was twenty-six years old and had been previously married and divorced. Susie was twenty-four and had never been married.

FAO TE: THE DAY BEFORE

The day prior to a wedding is set aside for preparations. A number of house-sites on the groom's side and bride's side are designated gathering places where kinsmen, friends, and neighbors bring their donations of food, mats, and other materials central to the wedding. Each grouping is referred to as a *sal hapa*, a 'part' of the bride or groom's kainaga. Although in theory there should be eight sal hapa on each side, in practice convenience and social relationships often change this. Almost all Rotumans are related to one another, some in multiple ways, so people can usually choose among several sal hapa. The choices they make are an indication of social solidarity, of who is getting along with whom at the moment.

Because we were living in the groom's village we participated in one of his side's seven sal hapa. In fact, six of the seven sal hapa were located in our village, the other was from the neighboring district of Noatau. Food and mats at each sal hapa location had been accumulating for several days previously. On this day, they would be taken to the groom's home, or to be more precise, the groom's father's home. The groom's father, Sautiak, is a greatly respected sub-chief, second in rank only to the paramount chief of the district.

From early in the morning we watched as pickup trucks full of food—taro, yams, squealing pigs, and noisy chickens—headed for Sautiak's place. At around 9:00 A.M. our sal hapa organized and made its way across the village to the gathering throng. The women carried mats in procession; those carrying apei headed the line, those with common mats followed. In deference to our curiosity over everything taking place, Jan was asked to head the parade and was given a quick lesson in etiquette concerning the proper way to carry a fine mat. Some excerpts from her diary give the flavor of the occasion.

When we got there we went in the front door and into the sitting room. Two or three women were in there—I recognized Manava sitting in the doorway. [Manava played the role of designated elder and announced each white mat brought indoors.] We all put our mats down and sat around and said a few words. Then Vera and another woman took the mats into the bedroom and the rest of us went out to the verandah where they were serving bread and tea. . . . I was trying to find Alan with the camera because another group was arriving with mats, followed by men with taro (carrying it in bunches with stalks and leaves upright). Marieta was calling out nonsense like, "Here we come," and afterwards she explained that she'd done it to liven things up—"What is this, a wedding or a funeral?"

I decided to ask Marieta how she was related (which sal hapa) and found out that more people can come than just sal hapa—Sautiak made an open invitation to everyone. . . . People were clustered in groups from Sautiak's house toward the beach, on mats, under trees, playing checkers and cards, talking, eating. The young men were singeing the hair off two pigs and then gutting them, preparing them for the next earthen oven. The smoke smelled awful.

Much of the day was spent preparing food for the wedding feast. A large number of pigs and several cows were slaughtered and cooked in earthen ovens, fashioned by digging large holes in the sandy soil, placing kindling wood inside, covering them with lava rocks, and lighting a fire. When the coals are red hot, whole pigs (gutted and cleaned), sections of beef, chickens, and tubers of various kinds were wrapped in leaves and placed inside. The contents were then covered with leaves, burlap bags and finally with earth. This is how the ceremonial food is prepared; it is allowed to cook from a few hours to overnight, depending on its size.

Preparing ceremonial food is the work of young men, and they were busy throughout the day. The young women spent much of their time setting out lighter food for the people who had gathered—tinned corned beef and tinned fish, tea, and biscuits. Cooked taro and yams were also served by the women. The work, and the festivities, lasted into the night.

The Wedding Day

Let us return to Jan's journal, amplified by our field notes, for an account of the wedding day:

We woke early, dressed in our wedding clothes, ate breakfast at 6:30, and Tarterani drove us to Lopta at 7:00 A.M. People had already gathered, the band was playing, and the female clown was at work. [At large, proper, Rotuman weddings the bride's side designates a woman to act as hostess and clown; she is formally in charge of the wedding, and is given a great deal of license to joke, mock, tease, and generally raise havoc. Her antics are a major source of amusement for everyone in attendance.] She was taunting people, especially the chiefs, and making them dance. She soon seized on Alan and me since we were going back and forth taking pictures. She snagged me and gestured for me to sit down on her chair. I did but then patted my lap for her to sit down. But she gestured for me to get up, and *she* sat down and I sat on her lap and then swung around and put my arms around her neck and laid my head on her chest. She got up, holding me, then sat down and I got up and left. A little later she ordered Alan to come to her and he ran to her with his arms open and sat/sprawled on her lap so they both nearly fell over. She pretty much left us alone after that but blew us kisses and announced that she wanted to take Alan home with her.

Semesi [a cousin of Susie's, at whose house the wedding feast was held] came up to us, saying he felt a little sick. He asked Alan to videotape the events of the day with his, Semesi's, camera. So I got charge of the still camera and photographed the clown and others dancing as we waited for the groom's side to arrive. (They were held up by a contingent from Faguta who were supposed to come to Oinafa for breakfast at 5:00 A.M. but didn't arrive till seven. We saw them as we left Oinafa. They had mats with matching yarn decorations—hot pink.) I sat with my friend Nina on the steps to the house, behind the *päega* [ceremonial seat made from a pile of common mats topped with a fine white mat and a colorful piece of cloth] where Susie was sitting. Nina advised some men who were hanging a white mat above the päega as protection against bugs dropping. But I spent most of the day running from side to side taking pictures.

[In Rotuman custom, the bride initially takes her place on a päega provided by her relatives. Then, prior to the formal arrival of the groom's procession, his side brings mats to form another päega on top of hers, but a fine mat provided by the bride's side is always placed on top of the pile.] We saw the groom's side assembling down the hill and walked down to greet them. After talking with various people for a while we went back up to the house to await their formal arrival. They finally came up the hill at about 9:30, led by Maika, who, because he is from a chiefly family, did not need an *'a su* to represent/precede him [At a proper wedding, the groom's procession must be led by someone from a high-ranking family; usually the district chief selects a close female relative to be *'a su*]. Maika and his best man wore their Royal Fiji Police uniforms.

Qwenda, the district chief's unmarried nineteen-year-old granddaughter, led the women bearing mats. So many mats were brought by the groom's side that there weren't enough women to carry them. I saw three or four men helping out. Then came the men with baskets of cooked food, pigs and cow, and finally the kava and sugar cane. All the food was set down across the road from the *ri hapa*, a temporary shelter built for the occasion to shield the day's dignitaries from sun and rain. (The only problem was that there was so much food it extended into the road, and every now and then a car or the bus had to get through!) A portion of the food they brought was already cooked and ready to serve; another portion was uncooked. The pile of uncooked taro, leaves and all, was covered with mats after it was laid out, along with a live, tied-up pig. The whole thing was topped by a fine white mat. [This food represents the groom's own garden, even though all the produce may have been donated by his relatives.]

When the groom's party got close they stopped and assumed a crouching position. A representative for the group then called out the traditional greeting, which was responded to by a representative from the bride's side. Maika then moved forward and took his place beside Susie. This was followed by speeches of greeting. A couple of other women from the groom's party unrolled bolts of cloth and hung them around the perimeter of the shelter. As soon as Maika sat down, members of his party came to congratulate the couple, one by one. Each would kneel or crouch in front of the päega to shake Maika's hand and kiss Susie's cheek, sometimes pressing an envelope into his hand or tucking a five or ten dollar note into her clothing.

As soon as things settled down, Fakrau brought a change of clothes (*osi*) and presented them on behalf of the groom's side to Susie, who quickly and unobtrusively changed on the spot.[7] (Later on, before going to church, Susie went inside the house to change into her wedding gown and veil.) After this, Fakrau draped and tied traditional Rotuman garlands (*tefui*) around Susie's and Maika's necks, then doused them with perfume. Concurrently, several young women from the groom's side moved about on their knees, dousing the chiefs, and others under the shelter, with perfume or sprinkling them with sweet-smelling powder (Johnson's Baby Powder is a favorite). After Fakrau had finished, a woman from the bride's side presented Maika and Susie with garlands and perfumed them.

As the time for the [Methodist] church service approached, Susie's uncle, Mekatoa, apologized that the church would be too small for everyone to attend the service. About 11:00 A.M. Sautiak's flatbed truck drove up to take the chiefs to the church. Alan and I realized that we should go too, because we were the designated photographers, and scurried to get on. Unfortunately it had rained a bit and although they put a mat down (the clown had called for the mat and had added in English, "Please," to the amusement of the crowd), it still puddled. Both Chief Maraf's wife Feagai and I got our dresses wet and dirty.

At the church we were asked to sit up with the chiefs from the groom's side, but in front of them (in deference to our roles as photographers). Our pews were on the right-hand side of the church facing across to another set of pews where the chiefs from the bride's side sat. While we waited for the bride to arrive some of the congregation sang. Maika and his best man sat waiting. When Susie came in (veiled) everyone rose.

There were prayers, the service, vows, exchange of rings, a brief kiss, and speeches by the various chiefs. Some of them talked about Susie's and Maika's life histories. I nearly fell asleep during Reverend Erone's sermon because it was so hot—I'd forgotten to bring a fan. At the end of the service, Alan climbed out the window so he could videotape the couple coming out of the church. I followed the couple and the District Officer, whom I bumped as we got out and missed getting a shot of the wedding party before they dissolved into a reception line. We rode back to the house, this time in the front of a truck. Tokaniua[8] brought the couple back to the house in his car, which was decorated with leaves, flowers, and ribbons.

Both sides presented mats to make a new päega in front of the one on which the couple already sat. Then the couple moved forward and sat on the new päega, and soon afterward they had the hair snipping ceremony. Susie's namesake came with a pair of scissors trimmed with colorful ribbons and passed them over her head. Maika did not participate in this ceremony, in which his namesake would have passed scissors over his head. Nor did he participate fully in the following ceremony, called *fau*, in which the bride and groom are wrapped in white mats. [This ceremony is performed only at big weddings, and only when the bride is young and virginal. Only fine white mats are used to wrap the bride, and the groom if he participates.]

Susie was wrapped in three or four large fine mats. Then groups of young men carried both of them (Susie and Maika), with much joking and laughter, from the bride's side to the groom's side of the shelter. Maika's white mat was simply tied with a sash and carried over, along with Susie's *'at fara*, which was tied with a blue ribbon. [The 'at fara is a small woven purse made specially for the bride. Although people now put money in it, in olden times it held a small container of coconut oil, a supply of turmeric powder, and a piece of soft native cloth to hang at the end of the bridal bed. We were told that the oil was for lubrication, the turmeric for medicine/antiseptic, and the cloth to clean up with following intercourse. Elisapeti Inia, a knowledgeable elder, told us that 'at fara translates as "to beg soul," and explained that the man begs for the woman's soul and she gives it to him in intercourse.] The 'at fara is carried by a representative of the highest ranking person from the groom's side, in this case the district chief's granddaughter, Qwenda. After the fau ceremony, Qwenda carried the 'at fara back to the central päega, preceding the couple and carrying it over her head for all to see.

Soon after this each side brought out the fine white mats for display—about thirteen from each side, not counting the ones used for the päega and for the fau ceremony. Then the kava ceremony was held and dinner was served to the honored guests, including us. We sat next to Kafoa, the catechist, and were served by Fani-

fau. It was very hot and I thought longingly of Fiji beer and ate only two bites of beef, a little taro, half a banana, and two globs of Rotuman pudding (made by baking a pounded starchy root, such as taro or yam, or banana, mixed with coconut cream and sugar). When we finally got home in the early evening we were so tired we could barely talk.

For most people the highlight of the wedding day is the feast, which begins with the ceremonial presentation of food and kava. When all the contributions of food (in coconut-leaf baskets) and kava roots are assembled in front of the shelter, the men squat and a spokesman announces quantities of pigs, cows, chickens, and baskets of taro, yams, etc. It is customary to greatly exaggerate the numbers involved, perhaps to enhance the prestige of the occasion.

After this announcement, food is distributed according to ceremonial protocol. Chiefs on Rotuma eat off low tables called *'umefe* (at feasts, everyone including chiefs sit cross-legged on the ground to eat). In times past there were carved wooden bowls unique to each chief. 'Umefe were symbolic of the chief's title. Even today, taking a chiefly title is referred to as "turning the 'umefe up," and relinquishing a title as "turning the 'umefe down." At contemporary feasts, low wooden tables have taken the place of these traditional food bowls. The tables are initially placed upside down. Only when food is about to be served are they turned upright. The designated elder calls out the names of persons in rank order, and the young men bring baskets of food to each table in turn. The first presentation of food is to the 'a su, and includes the best selections. The newlyweds are served next, then the chiefs. Visiting dignitaries are fit into the order depending on their status; a high-ranking church official is likely to be served before the chiefs, a lesser dignitary after them. Each table has a young woman in attendance. She lays a covering of banana leaves on the table, takes the food out of the basket, unwraps it, cuts or breaks it up into manageable chunks, and arranges them on the table. If something is missing, or if more food is needed, she calls to the young men who are distributing the food and they do their best to accommodate her.

Once the food has been distributed, the kava ceremony begins. Each bundle of kava roots has a spokesman who recites a short ceremonial speech relating heroic deeds, often in obscure language not understood by the audience. Once this part of the ritual is concluded, kava bowls are brought forward, attended by three young women each. One mixes the previously pulverized kava with water and strains it through a clean cloth, the second assists by pouring fresh water and filling cups, and the third acts as cup bearer. When the kava is ready a designated elder announces the persons to whom cups of kava are to be served. The order of serving reflects relative rank and is crucial; mistakes are likely to be deemed intentional insults by those who are passed over and in the past were grounds for war.

Following a Christian prayer said by a minister or priest, the meal starts when the 'a su begins to eat. The attendants fan the tables with woven pandanus fans to keep the pesky flies off the food. All the people eat with their hands, although knives are usually provided to cut up larger chunks of meat or starchy roots. Commoners eat away from the shelter, wherever a level patch of ground can be used. A "table" is prepared by laying down rows of banana leaves, upon which the food is set by the young men, but there are no attendants and all must fan the flies for themselves. During the meal, speeches are made by chiefs from both the bride's and groom's side, thanking everyone for their work and cooperation, and reminding the newlyweds of all the labor that has been expended on their behalf. It is a way of impressing upon them the seriousness of the commitment they have made to one another.

The feast concludes the formal rituals, but people may stay on for some time afterwards. Entertainment is always provided. In the past, the people from one village, or even a whole district, would be asked well in advance to prepare traditional Rotuman group dances. The songs accompanying such dances were composed for the occasion; they centered on the bride and groom and their families and praised the location of the wedding and associated chiefs and dignitaries. The dance group would bring some fine white mats to the wedding and would be given some in return, as a show of appreciation.[9] Nowadays it is more common to invite one of several local bands to play instead. Bands usually consist of four or five men, playing guitars and electronic keyboards with amplifiers. They, too, may compose songs to honor the occasion, but for the most part they play modern Polynesian-style music with Rotuman, English, or Fijian lyrics. Dancing to the music—in a kind of adapted disco style—is one of two main forms of entertainment throughout the day.

The other main form of entertainment is provided by the female clown. On the wedding day she generally dresses in flashy clothes and carries a stick, with which she mock-threatens people, or taps them to dance or do various chores. In her role as clown she is permitted to act in an outrageous fashion, such as ordering chiefs to dance, kneel, and otherwise humiliate themselves—actions that invert the usual social order. In turn, people tease her, and taunt her with insults that she quickly returns.

On the day of Susie and Maika's wedding, the clown was especially active. Her name was (perhaps fittingly, perhaps ironically) Kava, and she had been chosen, according to custom, by Susie's parents. Among the observations we made of interaction between Kava and the crowd on the wedding day were the following:

1) Kava danced almost every dance throughout the day, mostly in a humorous fashion, involving exaggerated motions, often having sexual overtones (though nothing explicit). She sometimes danced on her own, and sometimes grabbed one of the chiefs or other dignitaries and danced in a silly way with them.

2) People in the crowd teased Kava about being dirty and black (neither of which was really the case). One of our friends commented, after Alan's encounter with her (which involved a fair amount of physical contact) that it would require bathing in hot water that night to wash off the dirt; he jokingly promised to bring some Detol (disinfectant).

3) At one point a man handed Kava the jawbone of a pig. Apparently this was in reference to a standing joke between him and Kava. The story is that he had some time previously suggested to Kava that she get false teeth to replace her front ones, which had been extracted. Kava's response was, "Are you going to give them to me?" The man answered, "Yes." Apparently this developed into a standing joke, so that when the two met Kava would ask if he had the false teeth and he would answer, "No," or "Not yet." When he handed Kava the pig jaw at the wedding he apparently said, "Here's your teeth." She laughed and played with putting the jawbone up to her mouth, pretending to open and close it like false teeth, much to the crowd's amusement.

4) The wedding site was transected by the road, which was Kava's main "stage." She created several amusing incidents with passing traffic. When a bus came by she stopped it imperially and bellied up to it, as if it had hit her, and recoiled as though injured. She bantered with the driver for a few moments, then let him go on.

5) Dr. Panapasa [Chief Medical Officer on the island] at one point drove up in the Medical Department's vehicle and pulled right up to Kava. He then got out of the car and grabbed her arm, pulling her to the passenger's side, and pretended to push her in. He joked that he would take her to the hospital, or to a pigsty. She resisted and adopted a mock begging mode, falling to her knees and pleading not to be taken away. Dr. Panapasa relented and finally got into the car and backed away.

THE DAY AFTER

By custom, a married couple initially establishes residence with the bride's family, although practical considerations may dictate otherwise (in this case Maika and Susie took a cottage at the government station where both of them worked). In order to affirm their commitment to the groom's family, however, a day or two after the wedding the couple go ceremonially to his parents' home, along with a contingent of her relatives and friends. Formerly this took place the day after the marriage was consummated; a piece of white bark with the bride's hymenal blood was featured as proof that she was a virgin.

At the groom's home the couple are fed and entertained, and another marital bed is prepared for them. They generally stay for a few days before returning to the bride's family home. In this instance, Maika and Susie came to Sautiak's home in Oinafa on the day after the wedding. Jan's diary captures the mood of the gathering.

At about 5:00 P.M. we walked over to Sautiak's and were invited to sit under the canopy they had strung up in front of the house. The band was playing and people were dancing. After one dance, people (Vai, Mekatoa) started asking me to dance, and I asked Maika and Reverend Erone—it was fun. At six they announced dinner and we all shifted around; Susie and Maika and their päega were moved forward, her relations on the left, his (including us) on the right. Her relatives and the couple, being treated as the honored guests, were served on 'umefe; the rest of us just ate on banana leaves. We were served taro, pork, tinned corned beef, Rotuman pudding, and sugarcane. Tokaniua's wife cut me some nice pieces of pork off a big hunk they gave us and I actually found it quite tasty and still hot. I ate quite a bit (for me, especially compared to yesterday) and caught the eyes of a number of women, including Fanifau, looking on approvingly. Then we wanted to wash our hands so went in the side door to the kitchen. Inside, Torike told us to go have a look at the bridal bed made of mats—lovely with a ribboned mosquito net above. She pointed to a pile of mats in the living room, including five fine white mats which, she said, were *not* used in the wedding presentations.

We came out and sat down again. The nonchiefs from the bride's side were eating on banana leaves out on the grass; after they finished the groom's side was fed. Maika's close relatives were served last, and his parents told us later that they did not eat at all. Throughout the feasting people were making speeches, praising the couple, acknowledging the abundance of good will, and thanking all those who contributed. Alan made a speech praising both sides for creating such a grand event, and for contributing to the perpetuation of Rotuma custom.

The band started to play again and the dancing resumed. I danced with Tokaniua, Dr. Panapasa, Reverend Erone, and some little boys! They started asking me after I saw [three-year-old] Isimeli dancing with a group of small children. I went over and asked him to dance with me, making the gracious gesture I'd seen others making before the bride and groom—bowing and holding hands out, with palms up. He took me quite seriously and we danced. Alan said Maika and Susie loved it. After that the children surged up at each song, to ask people to dance; the little girls asked the little boys, and the little boys asked me, Susie, and Qwenda. Sometimes the whole group of children surged toward the couple and seemed to be inviting them en masse.

The adult dancing continued without incident, although there seemed to be a competition between the sides with regard to who could be more outrageous. The Lopta people, including Farpapau [a schoolteacher], Mekatoa [Susie's uncle], and Kava [who was still playing the clown, although here in an unofficial capacity] would dance in silly or provocative ways, and Sautiak [Maika's father], Kaurasi, and Vera [Maika's aunts] responded in kind. Farpapau was crawling between men's legs and rolling on the ground (carefully clutching her sarong). Mekatoa got me on a chain dance and clutched me tightly from behind, making faces and lifting me up.

There was lots of play around the couple's päega—people taking the bride or groom's places pretending to be the ones who had just gotten married (and by implication would occupy the bridal bed that night). It ended up with Alan and Kava rolling on the floor behind the päega. She had her legs wrapped around him from behind, and when he tried to get away she would let him get part way up, then draw him back down. People roared with laughter at the suggestive display, and someone came up and threw a mat over them, as if to afford them privacy. Someone else brought over an empty plastic bucket, which also set Kava off. She put it on her head like a hat. Then a woman came over and took it from Kava; she motioned as if the bucket were full of water and doused Alan and Kava with it, as if to cool their uncontrollable ardor.

After that, Tokaniua came over to make sure we understood it was all in fun. Of course we did. We danced until our feet and knees hurt [much of the dancing is in the Rarotongan fashion, requiring bent knees. It was wonderful—all together, old and young, dancing and sweating. The band had some trouble with static in their speakers but it didn't matter. Sometimes people even danced without music. They kept saying, "Too bad tomorrow is Sunday" [when such activity is prohibited on the Methodist side of the island]. After dinner Mekatoa said that the Lopta people would stay for three or four dances only. About an hour and a half later he said they would stay for only two or three more, but we went on until nearly midnight [when the Sunday taboo on partying begins]. When Alan and I left people thanked us profusely for participating so actively. At home we showered, took Nuprin for our aching knees, and fell into bed.

Susie and Maika stayed for two days at Maika's home, then were ceremonially returned to Susie's home in Lopta. Again a ritual presentation of pigs and mats was required. That day Jan's diary includes the following entry.

Tarterani dropped us off in Lopta and left, later bringing Qwenda and some of the Malhaha High School kids. We waited till everyone was assembled, then proceeded up the hill with mats (I carried one) and the ceremonial food. We deposited the mats in front of Susie and Maika and later someone cleared them away (there was one fine white mat, five or six Fijian-style ordinary mats, and five or six large Rotuman ordinary mats).

The band was playing between speeches, although there was sometimes a long time between songs and the dancing didn't get off the ground. One of the speeches was about both sides winning through the wedding. That was a nice ending to the mock competition that characterized much of the dancing.

The clown was still active and at one point danced with an Indian man who feigned pregnancy, making all sorts of lewd gestures; at another she was the pregnant one; and later she dressed in jeans, black tee shirt, and black plastic sleeveless raincoat with a baseball cap and swimming goggles. She also wore a belt of Fijian one dollar bills.

A group of men from the groom's side also made a valiant and sustained effort to get things moving—and the young men, who according to Joe [Qwenda's brother] had been drinking beer and rum, eventually showed up and joined in. The clown played with them, then jokingly told the bride's side that she liked the groom's side better.

Like everyone else, Alan and I were tired and it was hot so eventually we just sat. When dinner was to be served, one of the men gestured for Alan to go sit with the chiefs and honored guests. I just kept sitting with the women. Just before serving began Vamarasi took my hand and led me up to sit next to Alan. Then as the food was being set out, Reverend Erone told Alan to take Maika's place on the päega. Alan asked, "Why me?" and Erone said, "Because all the young boys are too scared." He said it was Rotuman custom for someone to relieve the bride or groom if they get too tired. Then he told me to go too. Maika seemed quite ready to be relieved of the spotlight, but Susie just shifted to one side. At first I was embarrassed to be sitting so high, especially when I realized the best food had been put in front of us. At one point a little girl (a niece of Susie's?) came and asked for some pork from her. The piece in front of her had been pretty well picked over whereas the one in front of me (originally served to her) was barely touched. I picked it up and put it in front of Susie. I just knew that etiquette wouldn't allow anyone to take it away from us even though we were "usurpers." The old lady who sat behind us kept fanning us as the honor of the *päega* required and I heard her say something to Alan about me having a good head and knowing how to behave properly *fak Rotuma* [according to Rotuman custom]. That was gratifying.

We talked with Susie a little bit and found she was going to work the next day. Then we left immediately after eating as it was all breaking up and a group was taking the couple to their home in Ahau.

Interpretation

Before we begin to examine the events described above for their cultural meanings there is one point we would like to make: there is no such thing as a "typical" wedding, in Rotuma or elsewhere. To describe an event as "typical" is to decontextualize it, to treat it as if it were unconnected to other events. In fact all such events are embedded in particular histories that color them and give specific meanings to their unfolding. In the case of Susie and Maika's wedding, a number of historical factors were involved. To begin with, the wedding was the culmination of a healing process between Lopta and Oinafa villages following some serious disputes. At the heart of the disputes was disagreement over visits by tourist ships, which discharged visitors on the beach at Oinafa.[10] The people of Lopta disapproved of the tourist incursions (which disproportionately benefitted residents of Oinafa village), and withdrew their cooperation from district activities. Maika's father, Sautiak, was one of the main advocates (and beneficiaries) of tourist visits; Susie's uncle, Mekatoa, led the Lopta resistance. Hard feelings prevailed for more than two years, so there were profound tensions in the air prior to the wedding. However, it was clear that everyone welcomed the opportunity for reconciliation—in fact, opposition to tourist visits had toned down quite a bit following the initial furor. Speeches at the wedding focused heavily on the importance of cooperation and on laying old grievances aside. At one point during the proceedings, Mekatoa, who was in the position of host, declared the formal rules of protocol—which act to keep the bride's and groom's parties separated—inoperative, since "we are all one family." As confirmation, the feast was served without the usual formalities.

Other factors contributing to the specific form of this wedding were Maika's status and the particular site at which it was held. As a member of a chiefly *kainaga*, Maika's parents chose not to have him repre-

sented by an 'a su selected by the district chief. This was a matter of choice, and constituted a political statement of sorts by his immediate family. The fact that Maika had been married before also was relevant, since it rendered two of the rituals irrelevant: the symbolic haircutting, and the wrapping in mats. These rituals are reserved for individuals who are in transition between unmarried youth to married adult, and since Maika had already been through them once they were inappropriate for him.

The choice of Semesi's house as location for the wedding also affected events. Had his house been nearer to the church, for example, vehicles would not have been needed to transport people back and forth, and the fact that the road transected the site affected arrangements in several ways. In fact choices must be made in connection with any wedding, giving each its unique flavor.

A Note on the Process of Interpretation

As should be evident by now, Rotuman weddings, like ceremonies everywhere, are rich in symbolism. Interpreting the meaning of these symbols is no easy task and is fraught with pitfalls. One can, of course, ask people involved what the various symbols mean, and receive some perfectly reasonable answers. For example, Rotumans will readily tell you that the importance of the 'a su is to elevate the event to a chiefly plane, taking it out of the realm of the ordinary. But ritual symbolism is largely unconscious, or at least unarticulated; it is therefore left to the ethnographer to make sense of it. Doing so requires a great deal of cultural knowledge: a familiarity with history, myths, language, and patterns of behavior. The task is made more difficult by the fact that key cultural symbols are polysemic; that is, they condense meanings from many different aspects of experience. They are also multivocal, suggesting different things to different people. Thus, the cross, for Christians, stands for a wide variety of beliefs, values, and institutions. It condenses an enormous array of historical and cultural meaning.

Another complication is the fact that rituals originating in one historical context are often perpetuated into another, changing the meaning of some symbols and robbing others of their initial significance. On Rotuma, most of the non-Christian wedding rituals had their origins in rites associated with ancestral spirits and Polynesian gods. Conversion to Christianity has certainly altered their significance in many important respects. Nevertheless, we believe that they remain meaningful, and that their current meanings resonate with their pre-Christian precursors. To put this differently, we believe that some of the most important values in pre-Christian Rotuman society remain vibrant today, and that holdover symbols and rites still signify those values, although their specific associations may differ. For these reasons we shall not try to interpret the wedding described above ritual by ritual, symbol by symbol. Rather, we shall proceed by articulating core values, then show how various aspects of the wedding reflect them. Fortunately in this instance we have an extraordinary resource to draw upon—the work of Vilsoni Hereniko, a Rotuman playwright-scholar who has recently completed a study of the role of the female clown at Rotuman weddings.[11] In the course of his analysis, Hereniko offers compelling explanations for much of the symbolism we witnessed; we make liberal use of his insights in our analysis.

VALUE 1: KINSHIP AND COMMUNITY

As are most Pacific societies, Rotuma is organized primarily on the basis of kinship relations. In any village most people are related to each other, sometimes in multiple ways. Chiefs are chosen on the basis of their kin connections to ancestral titleholders. Kinship considerations therefore serve to organize interhousehold cooperation, productive labor, and political activity. Reaffirming kin connections through exchanges of food and labor is central to being considered a person of good character. The fisherman coming back from an expedition is likely to share his catch with his neighbors/kinsmen; the woman who makes banana jam sends jars to selected households. If people need their house repaired or need help preparing for a family event, they can generally count on their village mates for assistance. When times are good and relationships strong, people look for things to do for one another; they use any excuse to hold an event that will bring people together, no matter how much work is involved.

Weddings are prime events for celebrating kinship relations and community cooperation. A wedding the size of Maika's and Susie's, involving around five hundred people, requires a great deal of effort and interaction. The men must spend much time in their gardens producing and harvesting taro, yams, and, if in season, pineapples and watermelon. In preparation for the wedding they gather pigs, and perhaps a cow or two, to be slaughtered and cooked in earthen ovens. The women plait mats, which is also labor intensive. To make an apei takes a skilled woman a

month or so of steady work. All of this effort, and the products that result from it, are donated to the wedding. The total value of donations adds up to thousands of dollars (a fine white mat has a sale value of up to 400 Fijian dollars, or about U.S. $268; a pig from 25 to 100 Fijian dollars depending on size; a cow around 400 Fijian dollars). Thus the formal presentations of food and mats at a wedding are announcements to the whole community of the work that has been done on behalf of the bride and groom. It is as if each mat unfolded and each basket of food presented symbolizes the willingness of the presenters to labor on behalf of those being honored. The speeches at a wedding focus on thanking all those who contributed, and impressing on the bride and groom the magnitude of effort expended on their behalf. The implication, of course, is that the couple are beholden to a great many people and owe it to them to make their marriage successful and fruitful.

Much of the time prior to the wedding is spent working with kin and neighbors on the preparations. The choice of with whom to work affirms certain relationships and possibly slights others. Which sal hapa one chooses to join—people usually have a number of kainaga with whom they could affiliate—is a statement about one's sense of closeness to various relatives. Working together, and especially sharing food at meals, signifies the very essence of kinship for Rotumans. Sharing in the preparation of the wedding, and participating together in the wedding feast, symbolizes the new relationship between the families of bride and groom, as much as the marriage itself.

The central role of namesakes in the wedding can also be seen as a way of impressing upon everyone that there is more involved in a marriage than simply joining two individuals or two families. In a very important respect namesakes represent broader kin rights and responsibilities—the fact that parents are not the only ones with a stake in the fate of individuals. By acting as surrogate parents in this context, namesakes thus render the occasion communal rather than familial in orientation.

The female clown can be understood in this light as well. She is technically in charge of the wedding, given that authority by the leading chief from the bride's side. The event is thus taken out of parental or familial control and transformed into one put on by the chiefs and wider community. As mistress of ceremonies she is responsible for facilitating interaction between the two sides, and for creating a jocular environment where all can enjoy themselves. By serving as a focus of attention, she relieves the bride and groom of the intensive scrutiny they might otherwise receive and involves a greater segment of the community in the activities of the day.

VALUE 2: FERTILITY OF PEOPLE AND LAND

The dominant theme in pre-Christian Rotuman religious rituals, and in supporting myths,[12] was securing from the gods and ancestral spirits abundance here on earth. Rites focused on ensuring fertility of the land and perpetuating the kainaga through the fertility of its people. The major religious figure in early Rotuma was the *sau*, an office occupied for periods ranging from six months (one ritual cycle) to several years. Men were chosen as sau by the leading chief on the island to represent the well-being of Rotuma. When not participating in specific rites the sau did little but sit and eat. Districts took turns hosting him, and each was obliged to feed him to satiation. It seems that the sau was seen as a temporary incarnation of the gods. To feed him was to feed the gods, in return for which they were expected to bring prosperity.

Ceremonial feasts were dedicated to the gods and involved sacrifices to them. Sacrifice is a way of feeding gods, of infusing them with life. The ultimate sacrifice, of course, is a human life. There is no evidence that Rotumans ever engaged in human sacrifice, but their myths make it clear that pigs are a substitute for human beings. (Reversing this equation, pre-Christian Fijians referred to humans eaten at cannibal feasts as "long pig.") It is not fortuitous, therefore, that pigs must be cooked whole for a ceremonial feast, for they would lose their essential quality as sacrificial animals if cut into pieces prior to cooking. In contrast to pigs, cows, which were introduced by Europeans, are not considered sacrificial animals and are butchered prior to cooking.

The formal presentations of food prior to the feast can be better understood in the light of this cultural concern for abundance. The food is assembled, drawing public attention to its volume, and the ritual calling out of exaggerated quantities is a way of further increasing the magnitude of the display. It is a way of demonstrating to the community the beneficence of the gods (or contemporarily, the Christian God). The food display is followed by the kava ceremony, which in ancient Rotuma was a ritual form of communion, aimed at obtaining divine blessings. Kava was conceived as originating in the realm of the supernatural, and hence as a drink of the gods. The chanted recitation prior to its being served traditionally tells the story of its arrival in Rotuma. That the words of the chant are not understood by most people serves to further mystify kava, enhancing its ritual potency.[13]

Finally, just prior to eating, Christian prayers are offered in thanks for the food to be eaten.

This central Rotuman concern for productivity of the land is matched by a concern for human fertility. Through the production of children, families prosper. Barrenness is regarded as one of the worst misfortunes that can afflict a Rotuman couple; it is considered a sign of divine disfavor. In pre-contact Rotuma, childbirth was dangerous for both mother and child, and with the coming of Europeans, introduced childhood diseases like measles and whooping cough took a terrible toll. This put an even greater premium on having children (and keeping them alive).

Many aspects of a wedding allude to the fact that the couple form a new breeding unit, one that can potentially contribute descendants to each of the kainaga represented (since they are all formed around ascendants of either the bride or groom). In many respects the bride and groom are treated like gods on their wedding day, perhaps because they are making a transition from a state of presumed barrenness to a state of presumed fecundity. Through marriage they are socially recognized as having the "god-given" capacity to create life. They are seated upon a fine white mat, itself a sacred symbol, and the shelter under which they sit with the chiefs is marked off as sacred by the rolls of cloth hung up by the groom's party following their arrival. (In earlier days fine mats were used.) Tiu Malo, a Rotuman who has written about marriage on the island, states that:

> This 'screening' of the *ri hapa* [shelter] symbolically creates a sacred atmosphere. The simple shed is now a temple, a holy place for the marriage rituals. Hence the *mafua* [spokesman] refers to entering the *su 'ura* [king's house, that is, a sacred or taboo place].

Several of the rituals symbolize the change in status of the bride and groom. The public change of clothes is one instance. The fact that the bride and groom are both given clothes by the other side underscores the claim each side has over the couple's potential offspring. Clothes are perhaps the pre-eminent symbol of cultural conformity. To publicly don the clothes someone else has given you is to symbolize your acceptance of a new role, and in this instance, a new set of relationships.

Another instance is the hair-snipping ceremony, in which the groom's namesake symbolically cuts the bride's hair and vice versa. In ancient times youths grew a long lock of hair until they were married, so the ceremony was conducted in earnest. Cutting the hair signified a shift in status from that of youth, with minimal responsibilities to the community, to that of an adult. It also signified community recognition of the couple's reproductive capabilities. Today, since youths do not grow a long lock, cutting is only symbolic, but the implication is the same.

The ritual that most dramatically symbolizes the couple's new status as breeders is the fau ceremony, in which bride and groom are each wrapped in fine mats and bound with cloth. They are then carried from the bride's side of the shelter to the groom's side, where the cloth binding is removed and they are unwrapped. There is much evidence to suggest that the act of wrapping the couple symbolizes the binding of spiritual powers in the service of fertility. The carrying of the couple from the bride's side to the groom's side dramatizes the legitimate claims the groom's family has (in addition to the bride's family) to the offspring of the union.

It should now be clear why Maika did not actively participate in these rituals. Having been married before, he had already made the ritual transformation from youth to adult. His reproductive capabilities had already been ritually bound; all that was necessary now was to transfer his virility to the service of his new wife and her family. This was sufficiently symbolized in other ways (for example, the wedding vows in church).

Apei are key symbols in many of the wedding rituals. They are carried by the highest ranking women and formally unfolded for all to see. The bride and groom's seat is topped with an apei, and an apei is placed above them as "protection." The uncooked food brought by the groom's side is covered with mats topped by an apei. The bride and groom are wrapped in apei during the fau ceremony. Furthermore, apei are given in gratitude to chiefs and other participants, such as the female clown, who contribute to the success of an affair. The bride's and groom's parents exchange mats, as do their namesakes. Ultimately, most of the apei presented at a wedding are redistributed among the main participants.

To understand the meaning of ritual transactions it is necessary to have a good sense of the importance of apei in Rotuman culture. One thing is clear—that apei are the most important traditional valuable. Apei are central to every ceremonial transaction, and are even used to influence political events. A request backed by the gift of an apei is nearly impossible to refuse, and an apei assures a plea for forgiveness will be accepted no matter how grievous the offense. Why should this be so? Vilsoni Hereniko has argued persuasively that traditionally apei were conceived by Rotumans as "woven gods." He cites several lines of evidence to support his assertion: that in a popular Rotuman myth malicious spirits are domesticated by capturing them in woven nets; that in earlier times women who were commissioned by a chief to make apei were granted license to act outrageously, like unrestrained spirits, until the task was completed; that an apei must be consecrated with a sacrificial pig (thereby transferring the life force of the pig into the mat). To give an apei is therefore equivalent in Rotuman cultural logic to a gift of life. Since the gift of life ultimately comes from the gods, an apei is comparable to a god, and has divine associations.[14]

The importance of apei at weddings becomes clear in the light of Hereniko's analysis. They represent the binding of life forces, derived from the gods, in the service of human reproduction.

The clown's paraphernalia and behavior also underscore the importance of fertility and reproduction. The stick she wields is more than a useful prop for pointing and threatening people. It also reminds spectators of the digging stick that men use to plant taro and cassava in their gardens, and hence to the production of food. However, its primary referent, according to Hereniko, is the male phallus and its procreative function in human propagation.[15] In addition, the clown's sexual banter and lascivious innuendoes draw attention to the theme of reproduction.

VALUE 3: POLITICAL BALANCE BETWEEN CHIEFS AND COMMONERS

The role of chiefs in Rotuman weddings is central. Chiefs elevate the status of events in which they participate; they lend dignity to any proceedings. By representing the bride's and groom's parties they transform a family occasion into an affair of state, implicating all whom they represent. But they do more than this, for in pre-Christian Rotuma chiefs were conceived as sacred beings—as conduits to the gods. Although the ultimate source of prosperity was thought to reside with the gods (including distinguished ancestors), it was the responsibility of chiefs to act as intermediaries, to influence them to act benignly. Conceptually the distinction between gods and chiefs was somewhat blurred, in fact, since chiefs were thought to be transformed into gods following their deaths. The presence of chiefs at a wedding therefore sanctifies the event, increasing the likelihood that the couple will be blessed with good fortune.

Because this is the case, the behavior of the female clown is something of a puzzle, for she is granted license to badger the chiefs, to order them around, to make them the butt of jokes. How can this be reconciled with the notion of chiefs as sacred beings?

To paraphrase Hereniko's compelling explanation: Rotuman weddings, like plays in the Western world, provide safe arenas in which forces potentially threatening to the well-being of society's members can be acted out, diffused, displaced, or resolved. Clowning, in the frame of a wedding, is an act of communication from the bottom up, from females to males, from the bride's kin to the groom's kin, and from commoners to chiefs.

The female clown at a Rotuman wedding communicates through inversion. Values of humility, respect, and restraint—cornerstones of Rotuman society—are inverted and replaced by their antithesis in her antics. Paradoxically, the clown's violation of Rotuman values reinforces them at the same time. For example, by dethroning the chiefs, she draws attention to the importance of their normal role. For Rotuman society to function submission to authority is necessary. The clown temporarily displaces the chiefs and assumes their power in a parodied form. If everyone in the community can submit to a clown, then submission to chiefs should be second nature.

Furthermore, in a society where the chiefs are men, the public portrayal of authority in female hands invites laughter, particularly when the exercise of chiefly power is displayed in its extreme form. As the clown is female but behaves as male, both male and female attributes are indirectly communicated. The conjunction in one individual of male aggressiveness and a presumed female lack of control results in chaos. The destructive and chaotic world portrayed by the female clown is the antithesis of harmony, testimony to the impracticability of a world in which folly reigns. The model that the clown holds up for scrutiny is therefore to be rejected. Through inversion, the clown affirms the complementary but different natures of chiefs and commoners, of males and females.

There is another message in the clown's outrageous behavior. The wedding frame is an opportunity for chiefs to be made aware of what it is like to be ordered about. The clown holds up a mirror to the chiefs, showing them how they will appear if they get too pompous. Her actions graphically remind them that although they may have divine sanctification for their positions, they are still mere mortals who depend on their fellow beings for their privileged status. A Rotuman wedding is therefore an arena in which chiefs learn the importance of humility.[16]

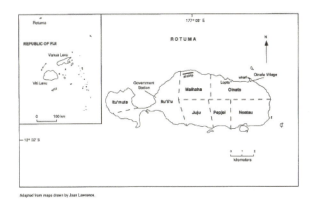

Adapted from maps drawn by Joan Lawrence.

PERPETUATION OF ROTUMAN CUSTOM

Legally one can get married on Rotuma simply by getting a license at the government station and by having the district officer or a justice of the peace perform a civil ceremony. In fact, many couples do just that, or have a simple ceremony at home performed by their priest or minister. By doing so they avoid large expenses and increased obligations. Therefore, full-scale weddings, like Susie and Maika's, play a special role in perpetuating Rotuman culture and are valued accordingly.

As in most Polynesian societies many key features of the traditional culture were suppressed or abandoned following European intrusion. Methodist and Catholic missionaries attacked customs associated with the ancestral religion; government officials undermined the traditional roles played by chiefs; imported goods replaced those of indigenous manufacture. The world was turned upside down, and like colonized people everywhere, Rotumans faced a future that could have stripped them of their unique traditions. But despite pressures to desist—missionaries and colonial officials often chastised Rotumans for "wasting" so much food and money on "useless" ceremonies—the people on this small, isolated island have persisted in adhering to those customs they see as central to Rotuman identity. Even the most cosmopolitan Rotumans recognize the value of an apei, the importance of a pig cooked whole in an earthen oven, the significance of the kava ceremony. They may criticize individual chiefs, but they support the institution of chieftainship. They value these customs regardless of personal beliefs because the customs have come to symbolize their unique cultural heritage.

In a full-scale Rotuman wedding feast, all of these key Rotuman cultural symbols are highlighted. When Susie and Maika got married, therefore, they not only celebrated their union. They celebrated Rotuman culture as well. They provided a setting for the entire community to affirm everything that is essential to their identity as a people.

Notes

1. Clifford Geertz, "Deep Play: Notes on the Balinese Cockfight," *Daedalus* 101 (1972): 1–37.
2. Andrew Pawley, "New Evidence on the Position of Rotuman," *Working Papers in Linguistics*, No. 56, Department of Anthropology, University of Auckland, New Zealand, August 1979.
3. For an account of Rotuman migration and its consequences for life on the island, see Alan Howard and Jan Rensel, "Rotuma in the 1990s: From Hinterland to Neighbourhood," *Journal of the Polynesian Society*.
4. For about six weeks during the holiday season, Rotumans stop nearly all serious work and engage in a variety of leisure activities. In the past, it was a prime time for courtship and continues to be so today.
5. If he were following Rotuman custom strictly, he would have asked an elder to speak to the chief on his behalf.
6. For a general overview of changes, see Alan Howard, "Reflections on Change in Rotuma, 1959–1989," in Anselmo Fatiaki et al., *Rotuma: Hanua Pumue (Precious Land)* (Suva, Fiji: Institute of Pacific Studies, University of the South Pacific, 1991), pp. 227–254.
7. Both sides present the couple with new clothes at this point as well as later on in the ceremony. Formerly, weddings took place over many more days, and these gifts of new clothes would be donned each morning and afternoon. Today, the couple changes less frequently; in this case, Maika wore his policeman's uniform throughout the day's activities.
8. This is not the Tokaniua who had been Oinafa district chief in 1960 but a prominent sub-chief who later succeeded to the title.
9. Tiu Malo, "Rotuman Marriage," in Anselmo Fatiaki et al., *Rotuma: Hanua Pumue (Precious Land)* (Suva, Fiji: Institute of Pacific Studies, University of the South Pacific, 1991), p. 72.
10. See Alan Howard, "Dispute Management in Rotuma," *Journal of Anthropological Research* 46 (1990): 263–292.
11. Vilsoni Hereniko, *Woven Gods: Female Clowns and Power in Rotuma* (Honolulu: University Press of Hawaii).
12. For interpretations of Rotuman myths along these lines, see Alan Howard, "History, Myth, and Polynesian Chieftainship: The Case of Rotuman Kings," in Antony Hooper and Judith Huntsman, eds., *Transformations of Polynesian Culture* (Auckland: Polynesian Society, 1985), pp. 39–77; and Alan Howard, "Cannibal Chiefs and the Charter for Rebellion in Rotuman Myth," *Pacific Studies* 10 (1986): 1–27.
13. Today most people do not know the traditional chants, and often substitute stories or recitations of their own. Even so, the words remain largely unintelligible, either because they are mumbled or because nonsense syllables are included. It appears that intelligibility would undermine the association of chanting with the mystified world of gods and spirits.
14. See Hereniko, *Woven Gods*.
15. Ibid.
16. Ibid.

Suggested Readings

Fatiaki, Anselmo, et al. *Rotuma: Hanua Pumue (Precious Land)*. Suva, Fiji: Institute of Pacific Studies, University of the South Pacific, 1991. A collection of essays, mostly by Rotumans, on various aspects of their society and culture. Includes an essay by Tiu Malo on Rotuman marriage.

Gardiner, J. Stanley. "The Natives of Rotuma." *Journal of the Royal Anthropological Institute* 27 (1898): 396–435, 457–524. A comprehensive account of Rotuman society in the nineteenth century.

Hereniko, Vilsoni. *Woven Gods: Female Clowns and Power in Rotuma*. Honolulu: University Press of Hawaii. A masterful analysis by a Rotuman playwright, combining the intuitions of a cultural insider with the theoretical insights of a sophisticated scholar.

Howard, Alan. *Learning to Be Rotuma*. New York: Columbia University Teachers College Press, 1970. An account of Rotuman childrearing practices and character development in the context of culture change. Includes an account of formal schooling on Rotuma and how it contrasts with indigenous socialization.

Howard, Alan. "History, Myth, and Polynesian Chieftainship: The Case of Rotuman Kings." In Antony Hooper and Judith Huntsman, eds. *Transformations of Polynesian Culture*. Auckland: Polynesian Society, 1985, pp. 39–77. A symbolic analysis of Rotuman myths focusing on the sacred role of chiefs, fertility, and the relationship between humans and gods.

Cherokee: The European Impact on the Cherokee Culture

William L. Anderson

At the time of European contact the Cherokees, one of the Five Civilized Tribes (Cherokees, Chickasaws, Choctaws, Creeks, and Seminoles) in the southeastern United States, claimed an area spanning 124,000 square miles and encompassing what would eventually become eight southern states. The area of Cherokee occupation included North Carolina, South Carolina, Georgia, Tennessee, and Alabama, and the Cherokees claimed hunting grounds in Kentucky, West Virginia, and Virginia.

The Cherokee population numbered from sixteen thousand to twenty-two thousand in 1700,[1] and was scattered throughout approximately sixty towns, which dotted the rivers and valleys of the Appalachian Mountains. For the most part the towns were located at the mouths of small creeks where clear water could be obtained. The larger streams or rivers into which the creeks emptied were used for transportation and for fishing. The towns were grouped in clusters, and the inhabitants of these clusters were interdependent, with a loyalty to each other that went above and beyond their loyalty to the greater Cherokee Nation.[2] These divisions and associated interests resulted from four basic factors: (1) geography or topography in which natural barriers such as the mountains separated one area from another; (2) linguistic divisions brought on by three different dialects;[3] (3) international politics—because each region had different neighbors, each had different allies and different enemies; and (4) economic self-interest—some areas were near trading posts that were in direct competition with other areas of the nation.

The Cherokee Culture

According to their traditions Cherokee men spent their time hunting, fishing, erecting public and private buildings, and making tools; women farmed, made clothes and pottery, wove baskets, cooked, and tended the children. Although tradition rigidly divided Cherokee work habits along gender lines, men helped clear fields for the crops and helped with harvesting when necessary, and women helped dress the skins of deer, their most important game animal. Cherokees followed a subsistence economy. They grew only what was needed and killed only what they could eat.

In the eighteenth century, visitors to the Cherokee country often reported that the men were lazy and the women overworked, but the visitors' observations were colored by the season of their journeys. They came to the mountainous habitations of the Cherokees in warm weather months, when the men's major task—hunting—had been completed and the women's major task—agriculture—was in full swing. The women were not slaves, as many Europeans pictured them, but in fact were extremely important and powerful forces in Cherokee tribal life. The basis of their significance lay in the matrilineal kinship system that the Cherokees and most other southeastern Indians followed.

In the matrilineal system a person traces his or her kinship through the mother's line, or clan.[4] There were seven clans in Cherokee society: Wolf; Deer; Bird; Paint; Long Hair, or Twisters; Blind Savannah; and Holly.[5] A person inherited clan membership

231

through his or her mother, and therefore the most important relatives were the mother, the mother's mother, the mother's brothers and sisters, and the individual's own brothers and sisters. The father belonged to a different clan (the clan of *his* mother). Although usually *informed* of events such as weddings, the father was never *consulted* because he was not in the children's kin group. Male-oriented tasks such as educating a boy in the hunt and deciding when he was old enough to go to war fell to the mother's brother, the maternal uncle, who was the closest male relative in the parental generation.

All seven clans were usually represented in each Cherokee town, and each clan had three major responsibilities: (1) each clan acted as a land-holding unit, assigning garden spots for the extended family; (2) each clan enforced marriage rules, such as which clan a person could marry into and what steps to take in preparing for a marriage; and (3) each clan resolved problems in an orderly fashion. Since the clan provided both protection against and restitution for crime, there was no need for a separate law-enforcement agency.

Perhaps the most important problem the clan was responsible for resolving was murder. Murder within the tribe called for clan revenge. If, for example, a member of the Wolf clan killed a member of the Deer clan, the Deer clan would have the right and the responsibility to kill the murderer. The victim's soul would be doomed to wander the earth and the Cherokee world would be out of balance until his murder was avenged. The murderer would not flee, because if he did the clan member most closely related to him would be killed in his place, nor would the clan of the murderer protect him. When the murderer was killed the anger would be forgotten and harmony would be restored. Although usually called *clan revenge*, this process would more aptly be called *privileged retaliation*. Privileged retaliation was more than just seeking revenge—it was a way to reestablish balance and harmony and maintain peace within the tribe. Perhaps if European society had practiced privileged retaliation there would have been no such thing as the feuds of the Hatfields and McCoys.

There was no privileged retaliation among different societies, however. If a Cherokee killed a Creek, for instance, whether it was intentional, an accident, or in self-defense, the Creeks would seek vengeance against any and all Cherokees. The whole Cherokee Nation would be held collectively responsible. Incidents such as this often resulted in intertribal war.[6]

Clan kinship was an extremely important part of Cherokee life. Clan membership came before Cherokee citizenship. If you were not a member of a clan then you had no rights and were in the same category as a slave. In the power structure clan membership came first, then the town, and then the society. The governing body of each town was the council. Men and women were equal participants in town council meetings.[7] As one observer put it, "the very lowest of them [thought] himself as great and as high as the rest, and everyone has to be courted for their friendship, with some kind of feeling and made much of."[8] The council meetings were nonconfrontational. Discussion was continued until a consensus could be obtained, or if none was possible, the decision was postponed.[9]

Town chiefs had no real power over individuals. They led their people more than they commanded them. Just as a woman could not be forced into a marriage she did not desire, a warrior could not be forced to go to war. Chiefs were selected for their ability to achieve a consensus. In each town or village there were two distinct governments and thus two different chiefs: a red chief and a white chief. The red chief conducted the town meetings in time of war and the white chief was in charge during peacetime. Usually the red and white governments were mainly divided by age. The white government was mostly composed of the older men and the red government was controlled by the young warriors.

Not until the eighteenth century was there a national chief who "ruled" the entire society. The national chief did not have as much power over individuals as did the clan, however. A good example of the power of the clan took place during the French and Indian War (1756–1763). In 1759 a Cherokee war party killed some English settlers in Carolina, in retaliation for members of their tribe who had been killed by Virginians. A number of Cherokee chiefs formed a delegation to go to Charleston to maintain peace, but the peace delegation was seized by the English and held hostage. The English then threatened to kill the hostages and launch an expedition against the Cherokees if the killers were not surrendered.[10] Despite the threat of war against the entire Cherokee Nation, only the clansmen of the murderers could turn them in; no chief could override the clan's authority. The clan refused to turn their men in, and thus began the Cherokee War of 1760–1761.

The Cherokees were opposed to any form of coercion. As one eighteenth-century observer put it, "They [couldn't] be compelled to do any Thing nor oblige[d] them to embrace any party except they Please[d]."[11] They were shocked when they saw European schoolmasters caning their students. If a Cherokee needed to be punished he or she was simply ostracized. Ostracism was one of the major sanctions utilized by the Cherokees to discourage antisocial behavior.[12]

Cherokee harmony was ceremoniously preserved each year with the Green Corn Ceremony. This festival celebrated a fresh beginning. Old wrongs (except murder) were forgiven, bad marriages were dissolved, stored food was discarded, and harmony and order were restored.

Although the Cherokee language did have three different dialects, their common language served as a unifying force. In addition, Cherokees shared a common belief system. At the very core of the Cherokee belief system was the concept of order. This order sought a balance and harmony with nature and other humans, along with subsistence in economic life and equality in social life. Europeans directly or indirectly affected every aspect of these beliefs, changing some and almost destroying others.

Culture Clash

From the very beginning contact between European culture and Cherokee culture had negative results. Indeed, the European impact on Cherokee culture was devastating, pervading the very essence of tribal life. The first adverse contact came shortly after the establishment of Charleston, when South Carolina issued permits for exporting several Seraqui (Cherokee) slaves captured by the Savannah Indians.[13] One of the earliest contacts with Europeans, then, resulted in some Cherokees being captured and deported to the West Indies. The colonists soon followed this incident with an attack on the tribe (some reports claimed the "visit" was to establish trade; others indicated that the colonists were looking for gold, or perhaps for more slaves). A few years later, in 1693, a Cherokee delegation went to Charleston seeking protection from their enemies who were capturing Cherokees and selling them into slavery.[14]

At this time the South Carolinians sought to establish trade with the Cherokees. The deerskins the Cherokees furnished were especially coveted because they hunted deer in the higher altitudes, so the deerskins were much thicker than those from the coastal plains and neighboring vicinities. Although commerce did begin between the Cherokees and the South Carolinians by the turn of the century, the Cherokees' contribution was insignificant until 1715, when Indian agents made a concerted effort to expand the Cherokee trade.[15]

The establishment of trade between the Cherokees and South Carolinians virtually turned Cherokee culture upside down.

Cherokee order began to disappear. The Cherokee concepts of balance, harmony, and equality were enormously affected by the supposedly innocent establishment of trade.

The slaughter of tremendous numbers of deer for the purpose of trade prevented the Cherokees from performing traditional rituals before they killed each deer. This action of killing deer without performing the necessary rituals altered the balance and harmony with nature required by Cherokee beliefs. According to their legend of the origin of disease and medicine, killing a deer without first asking permission through rituals threatened the hunter with crippling rheumatism.[16] Excessive hunting of certain animals skewed the balance with other animals and plants, and further eroded the balance and harmony with nature that the Cherokees had always strived to maintain.

The trade items needed most by the Cherokees were guns. (Although guns became the major hunting weapon, use of the bow and arrow persisted during the prerevolutionary period.)[17] Guns were useful in hunting, but more important, their enemies had guns; without guns the Cherokees were at a decided military disadvantage. The Cherokees found themselves in a Catch-22 situation: If they did not sacrifice their traditional hunting rituals and forget, at least temporarily, their balance and harmony with nature by killing more deer to obtain guns from the colonists, they would either be killed or enslaved by their enemies. When some Cherokee men chose to take this risk rather than increase their hunt to obtain European guns, Charleston responded by offering an enticing reward to the hunter who killed the greatest number of deer.[18]

The guns that the Cherokees received for their deerskins were called *trade* guns and were different from standard guns used by colonists.[19] Because the trade guns were lighter they were preferred by the Cherokees, but they also had a different size bore, requiring special shot. These guns were cheaply made and broke easily, thus insuring Cherokee dependency on the colonists. Guns facilitated the hunt and, together with the acquisition of horses, rapidly extended the Cherokee hunting range.[20]

Not only were Cherokees killing more deer than they needed, but also some Cherokees who were better hunters than others acquired more guns and trade items. Prior to European influence the Cherokees were buried with their prized possessions or their possessions were burned at their death. This practice was consistent with their belief in equality—it eliminated inheritance. But with European trade some Cherokees occasionally acquired unique guns and other items, and went against tradition by passing these items on to their relatives. As early as the mid-eighteenth century the noted Indian trader James Adair recorded that "the Cherokees of late years, by the reiterated persuasion of the traders, have entirely left off the custom of burying effects with the dead body; the nearest of blood inherits them."[21] As Cherokee burial rituals were modified, so too was the Cherokee belief in equality eroded.

The marriage of Cherokee women to white traders especially upset societal traditions. The women went to live in their white husbands' houses instead of following the Cherokee custom of husbands residing in their wives' houses. Although the Cherokee offspring of these unions inherited their mother's clan, they also took their father's name and inherited their father's material possessions, thus introducing the first real economic inequality into Cherokee society.[22]

Beliefs in equality and the matrilineal system were further eroded as the Cherokees began to acculturate. In September 1808 the Cherokee National Council enacted the first written law of their society. Primarily aimed at formalizing and expanding the Light Horse Guard, a Cherokee police force established in 1797, the law, written in English, enumerated the duties and responsibilities of that group. It stated that the Light Horse Guard was to "give their protection to children as heirs to their father's property."[23] At least by the turn of the century, then, the Cherokees had begun to abandon their traditional belief in matrilineal kinship in favor of white patrilineal inheritance. The 1808 law also suggested the abandonment of their belief in clan revenge (this suggestion was spurred by the killing of a Cherokee by a member of the Light Horse Guard in performance of his duties).[24] The existence of the Cherokee police force itself was an indication that the clan system was disintegrating. No longer was the clan able to fulfill its duties.

Although women had traditionally accompanied men on the hunt to help skin and cure the hides, hunting gradually became more exclusively a male occupation. As the hunt accelerated it became more dangerous, and this resulted in less participation by women in the hunt. Although this relieved Cherokee women of much hard work and danger, it also meant their exclusion from one of the most important phases of Cherokee life, which was a major factor in the declining position of women.[25] Because men were the hunters and trade concerned the hunt, women were initially ignored by the traders, which contributed to the decline of the women's influence in Cherokee society. In some respects, however, the trading economy, which contributed to the declining position of women

in politics and in the economy, simultaneously reinforced the cultural status of women:

> The removal of men from the villages and towns for long periods tended to preserve the aboriginal pattern of matrilineal land control and matrilineal descent in spite of increasing importance of deer hunting to the community . . . Women, therefore . . . served as the thread of cultural continuity from generation to generation and certainly were a powerful force of cultural conservatism.[26]

Europeans introduced new crops, which the Cherokees readily adopted. Among the more important ones were watermelon, sweet potatoes, and peaches, which were evident at least by the mid-eighteenth century. In most cases the Cherokees were selective in their adoption of European culture. For example, Cherokee women did not raise cattle, in part because cattle were viewed as a danger to garden crops, which were in the female domain, but also because cattle were seen as the "deer" of the colonists and thus were viewed as "male" cultured animals. Cherokee women did adopt hogs after mid-century because the hog was neither hunted nor herded, and it was not seen as part of the male domain. The horse, on the other hand, was associated with male pursuits such as hunting and warfare, and its use was adopted quickly by Cherokee males. James Adair noted that by the mid-eighteenth century "almost everyone [had] horses, from one to a dozen."[27] Horses enabled the Cherokees to exploit a far greater hunting range at a more efficient and successful pace than ever before. After mid-century, increased European population together with commercial hunting by the Cherokees seriously depleted the abundant game that once existed on Cherokee land. Adoption of both hogs and chickens helped ease the depletion of the meat supply. This adoption also gave the women some control over the meat supply, enabling them to maintain a meat supply even when the men were away on extended hunts.[28]

Prior to European contact, group hunting was common among the Cherokees, and was usually a seasonal occupation, but the Cherokee hunting process of the eighteenth century gradually became less of a group event. In fact, by the end of the Yamasee War in 1718 the movement was toward smaller hunting parties, and the smaller hunting parties were eventually replaced by individual hunters who were seeking the new commercial rewards associated with colonial fur trade.[29]

In addition, increased warfare, which came as a result of European contact, reduced the Cherokee population, which meant that fewer men were available for hunting. The increased warfare also made the hunting grounds dangerous. As a result, summer and winter hunting declined, especially in the more vulnerable frontier towns, because men were reluctant to leave their families unprotected.[30]

Hunting was no longer an activity performed solely for subsistence. When the Cherokees abandoned the traditional practice of killing only what they needed for food and clothing and started killing for a profit, the entire environment was exploited. Hunting became a year-round activity, with Cherokee men frequently going on long hunting expeditions that depleted the wildlife in the area.[31]

European contact and trade also affected Cherokee clothing, as Cherokee women applied European techniques in clothing manufacture to their native dress. They made short gowns of turkey feathers and tree bark, and petticoats of woven mulberry root bark. Although the Cherokees still used animal skins for clothing, these skins were altered to imitate European dress. For example, the women cut arm holes in deer skins to make them resemble European coats.[32]

European trade eventually made the Cherokees dependent on the colonists. In 1725 the head warrior of Tunissee told Colonel George Chicken, emissary of South Carolina's Governor Henry Middleton, that the Cherokees "could not live without the English trade."[33] Skiagusta, head warrior of Keowee, one of the Lower Cherokee Towns, made a statement lamenting this dependency:

> My people . . . [cannot] . . . live independent of the English. *What are we red people?* . . . the clothes we wear, we cannot make ourselves. They are made . . . [for] us. We use . . . [English] ammunition with which to kill deer. We cannot make our guns. They are made [for] us. Every necessary of life we must have, comes from the white people.[34]

This dependency seriously restricted Cherokee freedom, because any Cherokee action that was viewed unfavorably by the colonists brought the risk of economic coercion in the form of trade embargoes. If the Cherokees were cut off from supplies during a time of war the result would be deadly. By siding with the English in the Yamasee War, the Cherokees made themselves dependent on South Carolina. The Creeks blocked their potential trading paths to Florida, and the Choctaws blocked their paths to New Orleans.

The Cherokees lost their freedom of choice when they took the side of the English. The only open trading paths led to Charleston. The South Carolina government realized this, and they were able to use this as leverage to maintain some degree of control over the Cherokees.

As the Cherokees became dependent on trade goods their traditional craftwork began to decline. The decline in native craftsmanship may have also contributed to some of the estrangement between generations that was so noticeable among males in the eighteenth century. In the past, Cherokee boys had learned the craft of making tools and weapons from their male elders, but now this important bonding ritual between males from different generations was gone.[35]

Although there was a decline in native-made objects, they never disappeared completely. In fact, native industries were stimulated in some cases. For example, Cherokee basketry was in great demand by Charlestonian merchants. Also, the Cherokees were able to improve some of their crafts with the use of the tools they acquired through trade. The employment of iron tools obtained from the Europeans stimulated farming, canoe making, and house building.[36] European trade items were sometimes incorporated into Cherokee craft: Polychrome hand-painted delft sherds were often used as adornments, glass fragments were used as tools, and wineglass stems were substituted for quartz divining crystals.[37]

The English colonists affected the settlement patterns of the Cherokee tribe with the establishment of trading posts and factories in Cherokee territory. The Cherokees wanted the convenience of exchanging and buying goods, so they often relocated closer to trading posts. Habitation near a trading post was also considered a good strategic measure, and provided some Indians with protection from enemy tribes in the area.

Location near a trading post could bring prosperity to a tribe. For example, Tugaloo, the Lower Cherokee town where one of the first trading posts was established, became a very wealthy and secure town in the early part of the eighteenth century. Tugaloo was renowned throughout Cherokee territory for its wealth and economic activity. However, by mid-century Tugaloo and other Lower Towns were weakened by wars, disease, and the threat of attack from the colonists.[38]

Trade with the Europeans led directly to land cessions. The Cherokees were persuaded to cede some of the hunting grounds they did not frequently use. Then the colonists encouraged the Cherokees to obtain goods from traders on credit; these trade debts led to several land cessions in the eighteenth and nineteenth centuries.[39]

In addition to restricting residential and hunting areas, land cessions changed the Cherokee pattern of thought. Before European contact the Cherokees believed "old equals good equals honor." But in 1774, when the Cherokees, led by Attacullaculla, chose to cede an extensive amount of land to Richard Henderson, young Cherokee warriors under Attacullaculla's son, Dragging Canoe, felt that the old men had sold them out, and the principle of "old equals good equals honor" no longer applied. A schism developed, separating the Cherokee Nation along lines of age and status, with "amiable old men" in the older towns and "violent young men" establishing the Chickamauga towns.[40]

Even Cherokee dances and ceremonies were affected by the Europeans. The Booger Dance was instituted to ward off white people and their evils. The Green Corn Ceremony was influenced by European technology: In the second movement of the ceremonial dance an explosive noise was required to mark the interval between song and dance; in the precontact period this noise was produced by hitting a piece of hot charcoal with a stone club, but after the Cherokees acquired guns through trade they used guns for the explosive noise.[41]

European contact increased the frequency of warfare. Prior to contact Cherokees made war in retaliation or to gain captives to replenish their numbers. When war was waged in retaliation Cherokees usually killed the same number of enemy as their enemy had killed, and then withdrew. Europeans did not understand this concept, and on several occasions they called the Cherokees cowards for retreating in the middle of battle, when in fact the Cherokees were far from cowards—they were merely following their principle of killing the number of enemy equal to their previous losses. Most likely the Cherokees thought the Europeans were crazy because they seemed to want to kill everyone.

Europeans increased the frequency of war by inciting the Cherokees to attack other Indians.[42] On more than one occasion Cherokees raided enemy villages to obtain captives they could exchange for trade goods.[43] There was one incident in which the Cherokees attacked the Yuchi village of Chestowe under the persuasion of two traders—Alexander Long and Eleazer Wigan—who had a personal grudge against the village.[44] These events helped to cement some of the alliances and foster some of the animosities that dominated Cherokee affairs for the next fifty years.[45] Europeans seemed especially pleased when the Indi-

ans were fighting one another. As long as the Indians continued to fight one another, there was no threat of them joining forces to attack the colonists. For example, when the Cherokees sided with the Chickasaws against the French, the French retaliated by inducing other tribes, especially the Creeks, to attack the Cherokees.[46] Another example of Europeans pitching Indians against one another occurred in 1715, when Colonel Maurice Moore persuaded some Cherokees from the Lower Town of Tugaloo to wage war against the Creeks while the English fought the Yamasees. These Cherokees killed sixteen Creek ambassadors in the Tugaloo townhouse, violating the southern Indians' international law, which entitled ambassadors to safe conduct. Although only a few Cherokees were involved in the killings, this incident put the entire Cherokee Nation at war with the Creeks.[47] The killing of the Creek ambassadors embittered the Creeks, and their hatred of the Cherokees fanned the flames of war up to the 1750s.[48]

Cherokee politics were also affected by Europeans. Cherokees normally chose chiefs based on their ability to achieve a consensus among the people. Chiefs did not have the power to force individuals to do anything, and their influence did not extend past the borders of their towns. Europeans introduced a new requirement for Cherokee leadership. When Maurice Moore went to the Lower Towns he asked the Conjurer of Tugaloo, Charitey Haigey, to bring the Cherokee Lower Towns into the Yamasee War on the side of the English colonists. By turning to Charitey Haigey, the English colonists boosted his prestige as a headman, and through him they introduced the new requirement for leadership in the Cherokee Nation—the ability to negotiate with Europeans. Haigey, although spokesman and chief of Tugaloo, had previously had no power over his town except his ability to get the townspeople to reach a consensus of opinion, and certainly he held no power over any of the other Lower Towns. Maurice Moore helped change that. Charitey Haigey was the "first of a new breed of Cherokee leaders who based part of their influence on British favor."[49]

On at least two occasions Europeans interfered with the political process by actually appointing Indian leaders. The first of these occasions occurred in 1721 when thirty-seven Cherokee headmen visited Charleston to complain about trade. In an effort to organize trade among the Cherokees the first royal governor of South Carolina, Francis Nicholson, appointed one of the Lower Town chiefs—Wrosetasatow, also known as Outassatah—"Governor," or "Chief Commander" of the Cherokee trade with

South Carolina.[50] In November of 1723 a speech was sent to Governor Nicholson by Outassatah, who styled himself "King of the Lower Cherokees," and by Kureeroskee, who styled himself "Lord Chancellor," clearly illustrating the influence of the English colonists. These titles brought competition among Cherokees. After Governor Nicholson gave Outassatah his title, another Cherokee by the name of Konotiskee challenged Outassatah's position. Konotiskee claimed that the speech delivered by Outassatah was not "true talk." He also tried to persuade other Cherokees that he should be made king, and promised to travel to Charleston after Outassatah left.[51]

Perhaps the best example of Europeans directly appointing Indian leaders is that of an eccentric Scotsman, Alexander Cuming, who entered Cherokee territory in the spring of 1730. Cuming visited Moytoy, Chief of Tellico in the Overhill Towns of Tennessee, and proclaimed him "Emperor of all the Cherokees," a title Cherokees would later vie for, especially the chief of Chota.[52] This competition among Cherokees upset the entire political organization and increased factionalism among tribal members. Later, Cuming persuaded seven Cherokees to accompany him to England. Among the Cherokees who accompanied Cuming was Attacullaculla, or Little Carpenter.[53] The trip to England gave Little Carpenter added prestige, and started his career as perhaps the greatest eighteenth-century Cherokee leader.

European contact decimated the Cherokee population: Only a small percentage of Cherokee deaths came as a result of war; most deaths were the result of disease. Early Native Americans suffered their share of ailments before the arrival of Columbus, including tuberculosis, parasitism, and dysentery, but Indians had never known Old World diseases such as smallpox, measles, and diphtheria. What had been minor illnesses in Europe turned into killer plagues in the New World. Europeans had been exposed to these illnesses for centuries and had built up an immunity against them, but Cherokees and other Native Americans had no such immunity. There is evidence of at least five different smallpox epidemics among the Cherokees in the late seventeenth and eighteenth centuries—from 1697 to 1698, from 1738 to 1739, from 1759 to 1760, in 1780, and in 1783.[54] Certainly the most devastating of these epidemics was the one that lasted from 1738 to 1739, during which approximately seven to ten thousand Cherokees, about one-half of the total population, died. Cherokees tried traditional methods of purification—sitting in sweathouses and then plunging into icy streams. This practice only added to the number who died.[55] Those who survived small-

pox were horrified by their disfigurement, and often killed themselves rather than live in disgrace.

The 1738–1739 epidemic also had important consequences other than population losses. Towns were relocated because the Cherokees believed the English colonists had brought the disease deliberately.[56] Many of the Lower Towns, especially those on the Chatooga, Tugaloo, and Chattahoochee Rivers, which were closest to the English, were abandoned. The epidemic had a detrimental effect on Cherokee culture, because the elderly were among the most susceptible to this disease, and their unexpected deaths caused the loss of oral traditions. In addition, the epidemic upset Cherokee religious beliefs by undermining the power of the medicine men.[57] Traditionally, in times of illness Cherokees turned to their medicine men, whose successes were no doubt aided by the tremendous faith the Cherokees had in these individuals,[58] but the medicine men were unable to cure smallpox.

In 1785 the federal government pretended to be concerned with improving relations—by assimilating the red and white cultures—and launched a "civilization policy." The policy sought to transform Cherokee hunters into farmers, and was ultimately another way of arranging more land cessions from the Cherokees. If the Cherokees gave up hunting and spent their days in the fields, the vast Cherokee hunting areas would become surplus lands that the Cherokee would be willing to exchange for funds to support agriculture, education, and other "civilized" pursuits. As Ronald Satz so aptly stated, "Civilizing the Indian for their assimilation never took precedence over pushing them outside of the white settlement; it merely justified it."[59]

The "civilization policy" initiated almost total reorganization of the spiritual, social, and psychological world of the Cherokees. Even gender values changed. Unlike European women, Cherokee women had always been politically powerful. They had an equal voice in council meetings and were quite influential, due in part to the matrilineal kinship system. In the Cherokee legend of Kanati and Selu, Kanati, the man, was the hunter and Selu, the woman, provided the crops. This legend provided the basis for what became a well-defined division of labor along gender lines.[60]

By the end of the American Revolution, however, the once plentiful game in the Cherokee hunting grounds had diminished substantially, which changed the gender-based division of labor in the Cherokee villages.[61] In an attempt to become "civilized" in order to preserve their land, Cherokee men adopted farming and women turned to spinning and weaving. Therefore, women were gradually relegated to an inferior status, with no right to vote and with little control over family and land. This subordinate position of women was confirmed and popularized in the Cherokee Constitution of 1827.

By adopting white culture, the Cherokees hoped to gain the respect of the whites, which the Cherokees hoped would make them more capable of resisting U.S. demand for land cessions. For the Cherokees, then, acculturation was partly a defensive mechanism to prevent the further loss of land and extinction of their culture, the very goals whites hoped to achieve with acculturation. Consequently, the Cherokees, more than any other Native American tribe, embraced the tenets of the "civilization policy" and led the way by establishing schools and written laws. Intrigued and challenged by European written communication, Sequoyah, a Cherokee who was illiterate by white standards, invented a syllabary that enabled Cherokees to read and write in their own language. The Cherokees established *The Phoenix*, a national newspaper printed in both English and Cherokee. The syllabary of Sequoyah, besides being a tool of acculturation, was a powerful instrument of cultural retention, enabling the Cherokees to record culture that had formerly been dependent on oral transmission.[62]

European presence affected tribal government as well. By the early nineteenth century Cherokee political organization had become a combination of traditional elements and newer forms adopted in response to white contact. While some of the newer forms of government were directly borrowed from Europeans, most of the structure was composed of traditional forms of government that had been changed to meet new challenges. The Cherokees changed their political organization in order to create a system that the colonists could understand.[63]

In the early part of the eighteenth century the Cherokee town was the basic political unit, and there was no formal political organization beyond the town level. Within each town a council handled all political affairs, making decisions concerning relationships with other towns, other tribes, and Europeans. The council also dealt with internal policies regarding public buildings, communal agriculture, and public ceremonies. (Disputes between individuals and all cases of personal injury or property damage were, of course, affairs of the clan, not the town.) Various problems were discussed in council meetings until a consensus was reached. The Cherokees emphasized harmony and avoidance of conflict. If a conflict became unavoidable, a Cherokee was expected to withdraw emotionally and, if possible, physically.[64]

Although each Cherokee town acted independently of the others, to the point of having conflicting foreign policies, Europeans tended to treat the Cherokee tribe as a single political entity. Actions by one Cherokee town or even by a Cherokee individual often brought European reprisals against all Cherokees. Gradually, the Cherokees realized the need for centralization of power, and they organized a national tribal council modeled after the town council. However, the national council was unable to control the attacks on whites by groups of Cherokee warriors. This can be seen in incidents that occurred during the American Revolution, when the majority of Cherokees sought peace with the whites but the Chickamauga Cherokees continued to fight the whites (and did so until 1794). When the Chickamaugans attacked, whites retaliated without any regard as to which Cherokees they attacked. As a result, peaceful Cherokees often suffered the consequences of the actions of the Chickamauga. To heal the schism between the Chickamauga and the rest of the Cherokees a number of influential young warriors were eventually invited to join the national council.[65]

While the role of the original central tribal authority had been to deal with foreign affairs, internal matters had been left to the various towns.[66] But the establishment of a new national council saw the creation of laws that governed internal affairs. These early laws regulated horse stealing and inheritance, and abolished blood revenge, which was normally the domain of the town and the clan. The trend toward centralization of the Cherokee political system culminated in 1828 with the adoption of a constitution.[67] This constitution established a separation of powers and a bicameral legislature—all modeled after the government of the white colonists. The Cherokees were striving to deal with the colonists and win their praise, in hopes of saving remaining tribal land.

Acculturation and the appearance of missionaries made the factionalism and competition that existed among the various Cherokee villages even stronger. Many Cherokees disagreed with the attempt to imitate the whites even though the cause—to preserve their remaining land—was noble. Conversion to Christianity meant an unqualified rejection of all that was Indian and total assimilation to white values and behavior. Missionaries openly ridiculed traditional Cherokee beliefs. School children were forbidden to attend traditional ceremonies and were told that their parents and grandparents were wicked for practicing traditional Cherokee medicine.[68] Robert Berkhofer noted that the success of the missionaries sharply divided the traditionalists and the Christian Indians. In 1825 some newly converted Cherokees burned down the town council house, claiming it was "the Devil's meetinghouse." In retaliation some traditionalists threatened to burn down the mission school, and shortly afterward the headmen of the town asked the missionaries to leave.[69] In the early nineteenth century traditionalists held several Ghost Dances in an attempt to get Cherokees to stop and think about what they were doing. They wanted Cherokees to return to the old ways and follow tradition.

One other area in which the Europeans influenced the Cherokees was in the slavery system. Before they were exposed to the white plantation slavery system, Cherokees held their captives in a unique position. Enemy captives could be put to death by the Cherokees, adopted by a clan and given full rights just like any other Cherokee, or simply hold the precarious position of being a captive. Because they were outside the kinship system their lives were in constant danger. Slaves performed no real function in the Cherokee economy because the division of labor was according to gender, and the Cherokees had a subsistence economy, so they didn't need to improve the economy by producing more food. In fact, every year at the Green Corn Ceremony Cherokees burned all of their previous years' surplus.[70] However, with the advancement of the "civilization policy," black plantation-style slavery was introduced into Cherokee society. Plantation-style slavery, in turn, brought a series of laws controlling the activities of slaves, reflecting Cherokee adoption of white racial attitudes.[71]

Conclusion

The ways in which Europeans affected the Cherokees are endless. They influenced Cherokee politics and society and threatened the entire tribal belief system. European influence brought dramatic changes in population size, settlement patterns, and men's and women's traditional roles. Although some European influences were positive, such as showing the Cherokees that their culture could be preserved in written form, most were negative. Much is lost forever, but the Cherokees survive. Today there are more than two hundred thousand Cherokees—over ten times the number during the "removal" period in the 1830s when the Cherokees were forced to move to land west of the Mississippi. But the legacy of removal is still present today—the Cherokee Nation of Oklahoma and the Eastern Band of Cherokees in North Carolina are constant reminders of that grim period.

Today the Cherokees are increasingly taking control of their own destiny and becoming less dependent upon federal and state governments. Following the example of other Indian tribes, the Eastern Band recently secured the right to establish gambling on their reservation in western North Carolina. Much of the Eastern Band economy has been based on tourist trade during the summer months. It is hoped that this new enterprise will provide more year-round jobs for the tribe.

The Cherokees are in the midst of a major cultural revival. Cherokee arts and crafts are flourishing once again. Cherokee culture and traditions are being taught in elementary schools, high schools, and college classrooms, and the Cherokee language is being relearned by young and old alike.[72] In some areas, church services are conducted in Cherokee. IBM has created a typewriter script ball in the Sequoyah syllabary, and a computer program is being developed for the Cherokee language. Durbin Feeling, a Cherokee who is a language specialist, has published a Cherokee–English dictionary that will facilitate the learning of the Cherokee language. The revitalization of the Cherokee people is testament to their determination to recapture and preserve forever the culture of the Ani-Yunwiya—the Real People.

Notes

1. See Russell Thornton, *The Cherokees: A Population History* (Lincoln and London: University of Nebraska Press, 1990), p. 21; and Peter H. Wood, "The Changing Population of the Colonial South: An Overview by Race and Region, 1685–1790," in Peter H. Wood, Gregory A. Waselkov, and M. Thomas Hatley, eds., *Powhatan's Mantle: Indians in the Colonial Southeast* (Lincoln and London: University of Nebraska Press, 1989), p. 63.

2. John Philip Reid, *Law of Blood: The Primitive Law of the Cherokee Nation* (New York: New York University Press, 1970), pp. 11–12.

3. The three linguistic divisions were as follows: Elodi for the Lower Cherokee of South Carolina and Georgia; Kituwah for the Middle Cherokee of western North Carolina (the dialect of the present-day Eastern Band of Cherokees); and Adali for the Upper and Valley Cherokee of western North Carolina and Tennessee (the dialect of the Snowbird and Oklahoma Cherokees).

4. For one of the best detailed descriptions of the matrilineal system, see Charles Hudson, *The Southeastern Indians* (Knoxville: University of Tennessee Press, 1976).

5. The names of three of the Cherokee clans—Long Hair, Blind Savannah, and Holly—cannot be translated with any accuracy. For a different translation of these clan names see Mary Evelyn Rogers, *A Brief History of the Cherokees: 1540–1906* (Baltimore: Gate-

way Press, 1986), p. xiii.; and Emmet Starr, *Early History of the Cherokees: Embracing Aboriginal Customs, Religion, Laws, Folk Lore, and Civilization* (Oklahoma City: Printers Publishing Company, 1917), p. 9. According to Emmet Starr, originally there were six clans. When the Cherokees found a baby girl under a holly bush, they took her in and adopted her. When she grew up she married and had a large family, and in order to classify her descendants the Holly clan was created.

6.   Reid, *Law of Blood*, pp. 153–161.

7.   When the Cherokees visited Charleston and the colonial assembly they were shocked by the absence of women.

8.   William L. McDowell, ed., *Colonial Records of South Carolina: Documents Relating to Indian Affairs, 1754–1765* (Columbia: South Carolina Department of Archives, 1970), pp. 392–393.

9.   Duane Champagne, *Social Order and Political Change: Constitutional Governments among the Cherokee, the Choctaw, the Chickasaw, and the Creek* (Stanford: Stanford University Press, 1992), p. 281.

10. The Cherokees were retaliating for members of their tribe who had been killed by some Virginians. When restitution was not made, the Cherokees sought the restoration of balance by killing an equal number of Carolina whites. For the complete story see David H. Corkran, *The Cherokee Frontier: Conflict and Survival, 1740–1762* (Norman: University of Oklahoma Press, 1962), pp. 142–178.

11. McDowell, *Colonial Records of South Carolina, 1754–1765*, pp. 392–393.

12. Reid, *Law of Blood*, p. 241.

13. Verner W. Crane, *The Southern Frontier, 1670–1732* (Ann Arbor: University of Michigan Press, 1929), p. 40; William S. Willis, "Colonial Conflict and the Cherokee Indians, 1710–1760" (Ph.D. diss., Columbia University, 1955), p. 18.

14. Charles M. Hudson, "The Genesis of Georgia's Indians," in Harvey H. Jackson and Phinizy Spalding, eds., *Forty Years of Diversity: Essays on Colonial Georgia* (Athens: University of Georgia Press, 1984), p. 40. The enslavement of Indians declined after the Yamasee War (1715–1716), not for humanitarian reasons but because the Indian population had decreased and the trade in Indian slaves became less profitable. Also, perhaps because of vulnerability to disease, Indian slaves never brought as high a price as African slaves. In addition, Indians could escape and return home, whereas African slaves had no place to run.

15. Gary C. Goodwin, *The Cherokees in Transition: A Study of Changing Culture and Environment Prior to 1775* (Department of Geography Research Paper no. 181, University of Chicago, 1977), p. 95.
Historians often suggest that the Cherokees were a vital part of the trade with South Carolina by 1700, and were thus substantial contributors to the export business of Charleston in 1707 when Charleston reportedly exported 120,000 skins. However, in 1708 the South Carolina governor wrote to the Board of Proprietors, "The Cherokees are lazy and only average hunters, making trade with the tribe inconsiderable." Public Record Office, Colonial Office, Class 5, vol. 1264, fol. 152. Hereafter cited as PRO CO.
In 1717, 31 Cherokees brought in over 950 deerskins, while a second of 5 trading districts reported 770 deerskins. William. L. McDowell, ed., *Journal of the Commissioners of the Indian Trade 20, September 1710–1729, August 1718* (Columbia: South Carolina Department of Archives, 1955), pp. 186, 222.

16. James Mooney, *Historical Sketch of the Cherokees* (Chicago: Aldine Publishing Co., 1975), p. 83.

17. Willis, "Colonial Conflict and the Cherokee Indians"; Goodwin, *The Cherokees in Transition*, p. 142. The cost of a gun in 1716 was thirty-five skins, but by 1718 the cost had dropped to sixteen skins. See McDowell, *Journals of the Commissioners of the Indian Trade*, pp. 89, 269.

18. Willis, "Colonial Conflict and the Cherokee Indians," pp. 97–98.

19. By 1708 these "trade guns" were traded throughout the southeast, and in 1757 Edmund Atkin described the guns as the "cheapest guns, costing only ten shillings each." Willis, "Colonial Conflict and the Cherokee Indians," pp. 82–83.
The Indians preferred rifled guns, which were more accurate in time of war, but the colonists did not want the Indians to have equal firepower. Rifles also made larger holes in deerskins, so traders were forbidden to sell rifle-barreled guns. McDowell, *Colonial Records of South Carolina, 1754–1765*, p. 296; Katherine E. Holland Braund, *Deerskins and Duffels: The Creek Indian Trade with Anglo-America, 1685–1815* (Lincoln: University of Nebraska Press, 1993), p. 122.

20. Goodwin, *Cherokees in Transition*, p. 142.

21. Samuel Cole Williams, ed., *Adair's History of the American Indians* (New York: Promontory Press, 1986), p. 187.

22. Theda Perdue, *The Cherokee* (New York and Philadelphia: Chelsea House Publishers, 1989), p. 30.

23. Rennard Strickland, *Fire and Spirits: Cherokee Law from Clan to Court* (Norman: University of Oklahoma Press, 1975), p. 58. Other evidence of the adoption of white patrilineal inheritance can be seen in the will of Young Wolf, who divides his estate among his children. Payne Butrick Papers, Newberry Library, Chicago.

24. Strickland, *Fire and Spirits*, p. 58.

25. PRO CO, Class 5, vol. 377, fol. 3; Willis, "Colonial Conflict and the Cherokee Indians," p. 99; John R. Swanton, *The Indians of the Southeastern United States* Smithsonian Institution, Bureau of American Eth-

nology, Bulletin 137 (Washington, D.C. : U.S. Government Printing Office, 1946), p. 349.

Francis Jennings argues that the absence of men made it harder on the women while the men were gone, and the women had the prospect of more work when the men returned. Francis Jennings, *The Founders of America* (New York: W. W. Norton and Company, 1993), p. 203.

26. Carol I. Mason, "Eighteenth-Century Culture Change among the Lower Creeks," *Florida Anthropologist* 16 (1963): 73.

27. Williams, *Adair's History*, p. 242.

28. Daniel Lay, "Foods and Feeding Habits of White-Tailed Deer," *White-Tailed Deer in the Southern Forest Habitat: Proceedings of a Symposium at Nacoqdoches, Texas, March 25–26, 1969* (Nacoqdoches, TX: USDA, in cooperation with the Forest Game Committee of the Southeastern Section of the Wildlife Society and the School of Forestry, Stephen A. Austin University, 1969), pp. 8–9. While bear, beaver, fox, and raccoon populations suffered, deer herds completely disappeared from some areas. Part of the problem was the territorial nature of the white-tailed deer. When their food sources disappeared the deer did not move to other ranges; they starved or were hunted out.

29. Robert D. Neuman, "The Acceptance of European Domestic Animals by the Eighteenth-Century Cherokee," *Tennessee Anthropologist* IV (Spring 1979): 104. Neuman views the Cherokees' acceptance of cattle as marking the conversion from agricultural and hunting subsistence to full-time farming.

30. Goodwin, *Cherokees in Transition*, p. 142.

31. "Grant to James Glen (13 May 1752)," in William L. McDowell, ed., *Colonial Records of South Carolina: Documents Relating to Indian Affairs, May 21, 1750–August 7, 1754* (Columbia: South Carolina Department of Archives and History, 1958), p. 262; Goodwin, *Cherokees in Transition*, p. 142; and Willis, "Colonial Conflict and the Cherokee Indians," p. 97. In 1752 Ludovick Grant reported that the "[Cherokee] frontier towns . . . [were] not capable now in time of . . . general war to hunt to purchase ammunition, & merely to defend themselves from their enemies."

32. Goodwin, *Cherokees in Transition*, pp. 144–145.

33. "Journal of George Chicken," in PRO CO Class 5, vol. 12, fol. 21. Printed versions of Chicken's journal can be found in Samuel Cole Williams, ed., *Early Travels in the Tennessee Country: 1540–1800* (Johnson City: Watauga Press, 1928); and Newton D. Meerness, *Travels in the American Colonies* (New York: Macmillan Company, 1916) .

34. McDowell, *Documents Relating to Indian Affairs, 1750–1754*, pp. 453. Emphasis by the author.

35. Mason, "Eighteenth-Century Culture Change," p. 68. The absence of this learning situation also contributed to loss of respect for elders.

36. Willis, "Colonial Conflict," p. 275; M. Thomas Hatley, "Cherokee Women Farmers Hold Their Ground," in Robert D. Mitchell, ed., *Appalachian Frontiers: Settlement, Society, and Development in the Preindustrial Era* (Louisville: University Press of Kentucky, 1991), p. 49; and M. Thomas Hatley, *The Dividing Paths: Cherokees and South Carolinians through the Era of Revolution* (New York and Oxford: Oxford University Press, 1993), p. 33.

37. Michael Anthony Harmon, *Eighteenth-Century Lower Cherokee Adaptation and Use of European Material Culture* (Columbia: South Carolina Institute of Archaeology and Anthropology, 1986), pp. 45–46, 49, 69, 72.

38. Goodwin, *Cherokees in Transition*, pp. 115–116.

39. William L. Anderson, ed., *Cherokee Removal: Before and After* (Athens: University of Georgia Press, 1991), p. xv.

40. Fred Gearing, "Priests and Warriors: Social Structures for Cherokee Politics in the Eighteenth Century," *American Anthropologist* 64 (October, 1962): 60–61, 103–104. The most extensive account of the Chickamauga Cherokees can be found in J. P. Pate, "The Chickamauga: A Forgotten Segment of Indian Resistance on the Southern Frontier" (Ph.D. diss., Mississippi State University, 1969). The pressures of commercial hunting, the long periods spent in hunting camps, the ready supplies of rum, and the influence of lawless traders combined to further erode respect for traditional authority. Braund, *Deerskins and Duffels*, p. 131.

41. Frank G. Speck and Leonard Broom, *Cherokee Dance and Drama* (Norman: University of Oklahoma Press, 1951), p. 47; Goodwin, *Cherokees in Transition*, p. 143.

42. Theda Perdue, *Slavery and the Evolution of Cherokee Society, 1540–1866* (Knoxville: University of Tennessee Press, 1979), p. 23.

43. Alexander Moore, ed., *Nairne's Muskhogean Journals: The 1708 Expedition to the Mississippi River* (Jackson: University Press of Mississippi, 1988), p. 13.

In 1717 the Cherokees sold twenty-one Indian slaves to traders. McDowell, *Journals of the Commissioners of Indian Trade*, p. 186.

44. Perdue, *Slavery and the Evolution of Cherokee Society*, pp. 23–24.

45. John Phillip Reid, *A Better Kind of Hatchet: Law, Trade, and Diplomacy in the Cherokee Nation during the Early Years of European Contact* (University Park: Pennsylvania State University Press, 1976), p. 27.

46. Goodwin, *Cherokees in Transition*, p. 101.

47. Reid, *A Better Kind of Hatchet*, p. 70.

48. Reid, *A Better Kind of Hatchet*, p. 73.

49. Reid, *A Better Kind of Hatchet*, p. 62.

50. Duane King, ed., *The Cherokee Indian Nation: A Troubled History* (Knoxville: University of Tennessee Press, 1979), is mistaken when he states (p. xi) that Nicholson made the Chief "Emperor of the Chero-

kees." A committee of both houses of the colonial assembly recommended that since "Outassatah, King of the Lower Cherokees, being recommended to His Excellency at his first arrival, by the chief men and the deputies of the said Lower Nation, as the fittest person to be commissioned by His Excellency, to be Governor or Chief Commander of the said Nation [concerning trade], that the Cherokees be told that this government will look upon him as such." So Outassatah only received the title of Governor of Trade, and that was at the recommendation of other Cherokee headmen. See PRO CO Class 5, vol. 359, fol. 115–116.

51. PRO CO Class 5, vol. 359, fol. 115–116.

52. Originally South Carolina did not recognize the emperorship. However, fearing the influence of Christian Priber in establishing a centralized Cherokee state, and needing Cherokee assistance in King George's War, South Carolina issued a commission to Moytoy as Emperor in 1738. Corkran, *The Cherokee Frontier*, pp. 15–16.

53. "Journal of Alexander Cuming," in Williams, *Early Travels*, pp. 115–143.

54. Thornton, *The Cherokees: A Population History*, pp. 21–23, 28–34; Peter Wood, "The Impact of Smallpox on the Native Population of the Eighteenth Century South," *New York State Journal of Medicine* 87 (January 1987): 30–36.

55. William G. DeBrahm, who built Fort Loudoun in Cherokee country in Tennessee, believed that if the Cherokees "had not left off bathing . . . by their own notions, or by the advice of the Europeans " who were trading or garrisoned among them, the whole Cherokee Nation would have been wiped out in 1759–1760. Louis De Vorsey, Jr., *DeBrahm's Report of the General Survey in the Southern District of North America* (Columbia: University of South Carolina Press, 1971), p. 107.

56. The first use of biological warfare was evident in America during the French and Indian War, when a couple infected with smallpox were purposely put in a storehouse with blankets to be given to the Indians. This practice continued during the eighteenth century as an official policy of Sir Jeffrey Amherst, commander-in-chief of the British forces in America. See Russell Thornton, *American Indian Holocaust and Survival: A Population History since 1492* (Norman: University of Oklahoma Press, 1987), pp. 78–79.

57. Williams, *Adair's History of the American Indians*, pp. 244–247.

58. Goodwin, *Cherokees in Transition*, p. 107.

59. Ronald N. Satz, *American Indian Policy in the Jacksonian Era* (Lincoln: University of Nebraska Press, 1975), p. 2.

60. For the Kanati and Selu legend, see James Mooney, *Myths of the Cherokees: Nineteenth Annual Report of the Bureau of American Ethnology, 1897–1898* (1900; reprint, Chicago, IL: Aldine Publishing Company, 1975), pp. 242–250.

61. M. Thomas Hatley, "The Three Lives of Keowee: Loss and Recovery in Eighteenth-Century Cherokee Villages," in Peter H. Wood, Gregory A. Waselkov, and M. Thomas Hatley, eds., *Powhatan's Mantle: Indians in Colonial Southeast* (Lincoln: University of Nebraska Press, 1989), pp. 242–243. By mid-century Creek deerskins came to be preferred over Cherokee deerskins, and by the end of the eighteenth century the British industrial revolution, with its production of cheap cloth, caused deerskins to be in much less demand.

62. Raymond Fogelson, "Change, Persistence, and Accommodation in Cherokee Medico-Magical Beliefs," in William . Fenton and John Gulick, eds., *Symposium on Cherokee and Iroquois Culture* (Smithsonian Institution: Bureau of American Ethnology Bulletin 180, 1961), p. 216.

63. V. Richard Persico, "Early Nineteenth-Century Cherokee Political Organization," in Duane King, ed., *The Cherokee Indian Nation: A Troubled History* (Knoxville: University of Tennessee Press, 1979), p. 92.

64. Persico, "Early Nineteenth-Century Cherokee Political Organization," pp. 92–94.

65. Ibid., pp. 96–98.

66. Ibid., p. 106. The end of warfare and the adoption of plow agriculture resulted in a more scattered population, which weakened the town councils and paved the way for more complete centralized government.

67. Ibid., pp. 106–108.

68. William G. McLoughlin, "Who Civilized the Cherokees?" *Journal of Cherokee Studies* XIII (1988): 67.

69. William G. McLoughlin, *Cherokees and Missionaries: 1789–1839* (New Haven: Yale University Press, 1984), pp. 202–205.

70. For an excellent description of the position of captives before the development of plantation slavery, see Theda Perdue, *Slavery and the Evolution of Cherokee Society, 1540–1866* (Knoxville: University of Tennessee Press, 1979), pp. 3–49.

71. Theda Perdue, "Cherokee Planters: The Development of Plantation Slavery before Removal," in Duane King, ed., *The Cherokee Indian Nation: A Troubled History* (Knoxville: University of Tennessee Press, 1979), pp. 116–117.

72. In 1993 the state of Oklahoma began introducing Indian languages into the public schools.

Suggested Readings

Anderson, William L. *Cherokee Removal: Before and After*. Athens: University of Georgia Press, 1991.

Goodwin, Gary C. *Cherokees in Transition: A Study of Changing Culture and Environment Prior to 1775.* Chicago: University of Chicago, Department of Geography Research Paper no. 181, 1977.

Hatley, Tom. *The Dividing Paths: Cherokees and South Carolinians through the Era of Revolution.* New York: Oxford University Press, 1993.

McLoughlin, William G. *Cherokee Renascence in the New Republic.* Princeton: Princeton University Press, 1986.

Perdue, Theda. *The Cherokee.* New York: Chelsea House Publishers, 1989.

Reid, John Phillip. *A Law of Blood: The Primitive Law of the Cherokee Nation.* New York: New York University Press, 1970.

Chinatowns: Immigrant Communities in Transition[1]

Richard H. Thompson

I first met Betty Luk in 1976. Then thirty-five years old, she lived in a modest but pleasant apartment in downtown Toronto where she managed a precarious existence as a freelance writer. Independent, intelligent, and well educated, Betty fits well the image of the modern North American woman except for her Chinese ancestry. She, her two sisters, and brother are among the very small number of Canadian and U.S.-born children of Chinese immigrants before the 1950s. They attended public schools where Betty was an honor student, editor of the student newspaper, and prom queen. Although she and her siblings were the only Chinese students in the school, Betty recalls no traumatic experiences of ridicule or humiliation from white students. It was understood, however, that dating Canadian boys was out of the question. "They would be stigmatized," she said, "even though I had crushes on Canadian boys all the time." Betty had one long-term relationship with a Canadian-born Chinese boy whose parents ended the relationship fearing their son's promising future might be derailed by an unwanted pregnancy. Since then Betty has dated only Caucasian men though she has never married despite "several opportunities." Her circle of friends is exclusively white save for her siblings with whom she remains close.

Betty is typical of the first generation of Chinese born in North America. She cannot speak or read Chinese, is completely acculturated and successfully assimilated to Canadian culture and society, and spends little time in Toronto's burgeoning Chinatown.[2] "Sometimes," she says, "I'm not even aware that I am Chinese. It's funny—I look in the mirror and I'm reminded that I'm Chinese, but it's not a conscious thing all the time." Betty is nevertheless reminded that she is Chinese in her relationship with

her parents. She remembers being embarrassed by her parents' lack of fluency in English and ashamed of how their house looked compared to those of her friends. She recalls how her parents never praised her for doing well in school, nor ever said, "We're proud of you" or "We love you." Her parents were stern and reserved, not open and affectionate like Canadian parents. Unlike her parents, Betty values being open and straightforward but understands that they were "prisoners in a different society" who worked long hours in the family grocery store to make a better life for their children. Still, whenever Betty and her siblings have difficulty in relationships or in confronting personal problems, they attribute it to the "Chinese" in them.

Betty's brother Don, two years her senior and a supervisor with the postal service, has also never married despite constant pressure by his father to continue the family line. Mr. Luk wants Don to marry a Chinese woman, but Don does not want children and prefers to date Canadian women with whom he shares much more in common. Their elder sister, Eileen, did marry a Chinese-Canadian engineer but has recently divorced him and become involved in the women's movement. The youngest sister, Dorothy, married a Jewish boy after becoming pregnant, but they divorced after ten years of marriage and two daughters. Dorothy is deeply depressed by the divorce and thinks her Chinese upbringing and behavior patterns are responsible. "I do manifest Chinese patterns of submission," she remarked. "I am a low-profile person—I know how to be invisible. Playing the traditional Chinese wife role with Paul just didn't work."

Despite their successes, all of the Luk children trace their disappointments and difficulties to "the Chinese in us," even though their knowledge of Chinese culture has been gleaned mostly from books. They regard themselves as great disappointments to their parents who have continued to support them, sometimes economically as well as personally. The Luk children—educated, thoroughly anglicized, and seemingly well adjusted to Canadian life—still think of themselves as "marginal personalities" not fully at home in either the Canadian or Chinese worlds.[3]

The cultural gulf that separates the Luk children from their parents symbolizes the dramatically different circumstances faced by American- and Canadian-born Chinese from their immigrant parents. Mr. and Mrs. Luk are typical of how the first Chinese in North America were forced to live their lives. Mr. Luk was sixty-eight years old when I first met him, a retired green-grocer who maintained a comfortable living from rents on several buildings he owned in Toronto. His father had come to Canada in the early 1900s and, like the immigrants before him, left his family behind in China and sought his fortune in the gold mines of British Columbia. By this time the mining frenzy that had spawned the frontier boom towns of California and western Canada had subsided. Gold mining and newer industries such as canning, lumbering, and railroad construction were now in the hands of large companies who contracted Chinese and other immigrant labor, who were preferred over native whites because they worked reliably and performed rough and dangerous jobs.

After years of work in the mines in Nanaimo, British Columbia, the elder Luk sent for Mr. Luk, his middle son, who arrived in Victoria on the last ship carrying Chinese immigrants prior to the Immigration Act of 1923, which prohibited further Chinese immigration. Then fifteen years of age, Mr. Luk worked as a houseboy for a wealthy Vancouver family and was given the opportunity, rare at that time, to attend school. He left school after a couple of years, however, finding the language barrier too great to overcome and frustrated that the teachers made no attempt to teach him English. Like most of the early immigrants to North America, Mr. Luk speaks only broken English and associates almost solely with his Chinese-speaking friends.

In the late 1920s Mr. Luk left Vancouver for Montreal where, in partnership with another Chinese, he opened a grocery stand specializing in fresh produce. Hostility towards the Chinese in western Canada had caused many to either return to China or to migrate eastward where they found economic niches as petty entrepreneurs or workers in laundries, restaurants, and grocery stands where there was little competition

from whites. The same pattern had developed earlier in the United States due to anti-Chinese sentiment and legislation in California. In both countries, the Chinese were eventually excluded from citizenship and the vote, prohibited from owning farmland or gaining factory employment, and denied entrance into universities and technical and professional schools. Not wishing to arouse further hostility and denied participation in the U.S. and Canadian mainstreams, the Chinese moved to the growing cities where they found refuge and isolation in the form of ethnic enclaves that came to be known as "Chinatowns." To this day, even though all discriminatory legislation against the Chinese has been repealed, Chinese immigrants still pour into North America's cities where they continue to rely on Chinatowns for employment, housing, and other needs.

It was in Montreal that Mr. Luk met and married Mrs. Luk, a Canadian-born Chinese woman only several years his junior. Although Mrs. Luk was born in Canada, she was raised in the Chinatown community. Her father had worked for the Canadian National Railroad and later contracted with them to sell provisions as well as hire Chinese kitchen labor for the work crews. Because he had been classified a merchant, he was able to bring his wife to Canada, a "privilege" denied to other Chinese. Mrs. Luk's father disapproved of education for daughters and she was only permitted to complete primary school. She did learn some English, but after her school years she worked exclusively in Chinese businesses and today Chinese remains her primary language. Mrs. Luk, though Canadian-born, had her citizenship revoked upon her marriage to Mr. Luk, a Chinese "resident alien." In Montreal, and later Toronto, the Luks established a domestic pattern that was to continue until retirement. Mrs. Luk worked full time in the store tending to customers, paying the bills, and keeping the accounts. Mr. Luk ordered and picked up the produce and supervised their preparation and display. Like most other Chinese small business families, they lived in the back of the store, worked extremely long hours, saved money that was later invested in a larger business and real estate, and raised four children. They worked such long hours that the family did little together and the children gradually became estranged and isolated from their parents as they adapted to white Canadian society. Two generations of one Chinese family, each typical of the respective Chinese communities in which they lived, yet poles apart linguistically, culturally, and personally.

Chinatowns today are populated by Chinese quite different in background and experiences from either

Luk generation. There are thousands more living in the major Chinatowns of New York, San Francisco, Los Angeles, Toronto, Vancouver, and other large cities, which are now the main points of entry for recent Chinese immigrants.[4] Once small enclaves characterized by laundries, groceries, and restaurants scattered about the city and populated by men from rural China, Chinatowns today are thriving ethnic communities made up mostly of Chinese families emigrating from Hong Kong and other Chinese communities overseas.

It is useful to think of Chinatown history in three distinct periods; the "traditional community" spanning the years 1850 to 1945, the "transitional community" lasting from 1945 to 1965, and the "contemporary community" dating from 1965 to the present. Each period differs from the others in two ways: the characteristics of the Chinese themselves, and the American and Canadian policies and attitudes towards the Chinese. Understanding the relationship between these two factors is necessary for interpreting the Chinese experience in North America.

The Traditional Chinatown Community

Nearly all of the earliest Chinese immigrants came to North America, first to California and later to British Columbia, in the latter half of the nineteenth century. Initially, they came in search of the gold rush riches that led them to refer to the United States as Gum Shan ("gold mountain") where they panned already worked-out claims abandoned by whites for the few nuggets and dust that remained. The migrants were married men and young bachelors, most of whom migrated from two agricultural regions known as Sze-Yap (pronounced "say-yap"; literally "four districts") and Sam-Yap ("three districts") that surrounded the port cities of Canton (Guangzhou) and Hong Kong in southern China. Perhaps as many as sixty percent came from the single district of Toisan ("elevated mountain"), a rocky, mountainous coastal area whose agricultural output could support its population of over half a million only four months out of the year.[5] Because of this, many men from Toisan made yearly journeys to Canton and Hong Kong where they worked on the docks or as middlemen between merchants and the fast-growing number of foreign seamen who were now entering the port cities recently forced open by the British.[6] Through their contacts with these seamen they learned of gold discoveries in America and how to secure passage for the

three-month journey across the Pacific. Although the Chinese government prohibited emigration, peasants from Toisan and other poor districts in southern China had strong motivations to risk the journey to America. They were already accustomed to leaving their native villages many months of the year to supplement their family incomes through work in the city, and the opportunity to strike it rich in the gold mines of California, even if it meant several years away from village and family, was a sufficient economic lure to men already used to temporary sojourns.

Once men from a particular village or lineage became established in North America, they would occasionally return to China, usually to marry or visit the family they had left behind. Upon their return they might bring a teenage son or lineage "brother" with them. Immigration laws favored the migration of relatives already resident in North America provided the sponsor could guarantee work and living quarters for the new immigrant. This established a pattern of chain migration that led many villages in rural southern China to become known as "emigrant communities."[7] These were communities where most of the working-age men lived in North America and sent money (known as "remittances") to their families who remained. These remittances enabled Toisan to become the richest district in rural China with paved streets, electric lighting, and modern buildings and schools dotting its landscape.[8] The pattern of chain migration established more than a century ago continues today since immigration laws still favor the migration of relatives. In tracing the migration histories of two Chinese men who immigrated to Canada in the early 1900s, I discovered that thirty-five out of forty-four of their direct descendants were now citizens or permanent residents of Canada![9]

Very few Chinese struck it rich in the gold mines, of course, and most found themselves stranded in frontier mining towns with no money to return to China and few prospects for employment. Since the frontier populations of California and British Columbia contained few women, some Chinese made a living doing laundry and cooking, establishing the pattern of "women's work" that came to be the dominant economic adaptation of the traditional Chinatown community. As the mining towns went bust these Chinese moved to the growing cities of San Francisco, Sacramento, and Vancouver, where they established small hand laundries and cafes (the latter serving American, not Chinese, food in the beginning) that became the economic foundation of early Chinatowns.

Most Chinese in North America, however, found work constructing the Central Pacific Railroad in the

United States in the 1860s and 1870s, and the Canadian Pacific Railroad in Canada during the 1880s and 1890s. A shortage of white labor due both to the U.S. Civil War and small native-born populations led the directors of the large railroad companies (including Leland Stanford in California and Andrew Onderdonk in British Columbia) to recruit Chinese labor. The Chinese responded by the thousands, a situation that led to increased emigration from China. Their work on the railroads can only be described as heroic, and they were praised for their industry as they blasted through rugged mountain passes and worked in temperatures, both extreme heat and cold, that European workers disdained.

After the railroads were built, the Chinese found work as farm laborers, domestics, and workers in cigar and woolen factories, canneries, and fisheries.

As both the mining and railroad booms ended and Chinese gradually entered into other laboring occupations, they encountered increasing discrimination and anti-Chinese hostility by native whites, who found the Chinese convenient scapegoats for the economic problems facing the West in the latter nineteenth century. The Chinese made up ten percent of the populations of both California and British Columbia. Their Asian faces, lack of fluency in English, different modes of dress and culture, and lack of political power made them easy targets for groups such as Dennis Kearney's Workingmen's Party in California and the Knights of Labor in British Columbia.[10] These groups consisted of working-class whites, many of whom were European immigrants, seeking farmland and other opportunities in the expanding West. But land and railroad monopolies held a political stranglehold on the western economy made worse by serious recessions. The Chinese thus came to be seen as foreign competitors for scarce jobs and they were falsely accused of accepting "slave wages" that prevented whites from employment.[11]

Throughout the last three decades of the nineteenth century, the Chinese were subjected to looting, robbery, arson, and even murder, not to mention name-calling, periodic beatings, and other forms of harassment. Legislation discriminating against Chinese proliferated in the California and British Columbia assemblies. "Head" taxes ranging from fifty to five hundred dollars were levied on all Chinese entering North America. Chinese were prohibited from working on locally or state-funded public works projects and subject to other anti-Chinese ordinances. Most importantly, both California and British Columbia passed a series of exclusion acts designed to exclude the immigration of Chinese laborers and restrict Chinese immigration to officials, merchants, and students. What became known as "the Chinese question" dominated the politics of the West. Although many of the early exclusion laws were eventually vetoed or declared unconstitutional, both the United States and Canada succeeded in passing immigration acts that effectively halted Chinese immigration to North America.[12] These acts not only prohibited new Chinese immigration, but prevented Chinese laborers already in North America from sponsoring the immigration of their wives, children and other close relatives. Other laws were enacted at the local, state, and federal levels preventing Chinese from securing citizenship, owning farmland, and working in trades and factories where white labor predominated. Although several thousand Chinese merchants, officials, teachers, and students immigrated in the late nineteenth and early twentieth centuries, few Chinese came to North America during those years when immigrants from Europe were coming by the millions. The Chinese had been effectively shut out.

Chinese who were already resident in North America reacted to the violence and discrimination they faced in several ways. Many thousands (the precise number is not known) returned to China when jobs became scarce and anti-Chinese hostility increased. Many of those who stayed gravitated to the San Francisco and Vancouver Chinatowns, while others gradually migrated eastward to the urban centers of New York, Boston, Philadelphia, Montreal, and Toronto, where they established themselves in the laundry, restaurant, and grocery businesses that were now the accepted forms of Chinese employment. Such enterprises were relatively cheap to start up and protected the Chinese from direct competition with whites. Of greatest importance, however, the Chinese organized themselves into various associations both to protest their treatment by the United States and Canada and to unify and protect their economic and political interests.

These associations dominated the political, economic, and social organization of the early Chinatowns. They are referred to as family or district associations because membership in them was based on one's surname or district of origin in China. If your surname was Li or Wong, you belonged to the Li or Wong family associations; if you hailed from Toisan, you belonged to the Toisan district association. Such organizations had the effect of uniting all the Chinese in a city into a group of associations based on Chinese affiliations. These associations were grouped into a higher-level organization known in most cities as the Chinese Benevolent Association. The Benevolent Association was composed of the leaders of all the district and surname associations. It acted as a kind of government overseeing Chinese interests. It drafted specific regulations designed to prevent Chinese businessmen from direct competition with one another. Every business was required to register with the association and pay monthly dues based on their volume of business. The Benevolent Association was more than a business organization as it also undertook social welfare functions and fought against discrimination by the larger societies. The constitution of the Victoria, British Columbia, Benevolent Association is typical of those in other cities: "This association has been established in order to express our feelings of unity, to undertake social welfare, to settle disputes, to aid the poor and the sick, to eliminate evils within the community, and to defend the community against external threat."[13]

The Chinatown residents thus organized themselves into organizations that protected them from the often hostile U. S. and Canadian governments. These associations seem to have been modeled on organizations in China known as *hui guan* ("associations"). Hui guan were mutual aid and commercial organizations formed by peasant migrants to Chinese cities. Membership in a hui guan was based on one's surname, native village, or district. They were controlled by wealthy merchant leaders who possessed wideranging powers of judgment, arbitration and conciliation among association members and exercised powers of taxation, population registration, and political decision-making. Like the hui guan in Chinese cities, Chinatown family and district associations were dominated by the wealthiest merchants who exercised almost total social and legal control over their members, and who became the spokesmen for the Chinese in every North American city.[14]

Every large Chinatown also had fraternal and political organizations that coexisted alongside the family and district associations. The two most important of these were the Cheekungtong, known as "Chinese Freemasons" in English, and the Guomindang, or "Nationalist Party." The Chinese Freemasons was established in the 1860s and traced its origins to a secret society in China known as the Triads. Chinese without ties to the family or district associations often belonged to the Freemasons, an organization involved in gambling and other illegal activities in the early Chinatowns. It was not primarily a criminal organization, however, as it performed welfare functions similar to the other associations and came to be viewed as a legitimate and progressive institution in Chinatown politics.

The Guomindang is another early political association that played a prominent role in Chinatowns. It was established by Dr. Sun Yat-sen to overthrow China's last dynasty, the Qing, and establish republican government in China. Sun traveled to the United States and Canada establishing overseas branches of the Guomindang to provide financial support for his war effort. Leaders of the Guomindang in Chinatowns, usually the wealthy leaders of the Benevolent Association, received charters from Sun as "official spokesmen" of the Chinese government overseas; a move that enhanced their prestige and legitimacy. The Chinatown Guomindangs had their greatest influence during the Sino-Japanese War in the 1930s and 1940s when it mobilized all Chinese residents in North America to send money to Chiang Kai-Shek's Nationalist Army. The fact that China was an ally of the United States and Canada greatly enhanced the prestige of Guomindang leaders who often used their power to undermine rival political groups such as the Freemasons.

By the end of World War II, then, most Chinese in North America were concentrated in urban Chinatowns where an ethnic economy based on laundries, restaurants, and groceries had developed. Other businesses such as import-export emporiums sprang up to serve increasing numbers of tourists who found Chinatowns a source of Oriental exotica and cheap food. The Chinese were socially organized into a pyramid-like structure of family and district associations headed by wealthier Chinese merchant elites who regulated business, carried out welfare functions, and represented Chinese economic and political interests to the dominant societies. The position of the Chinese in North America during the traditional period can be described as an "internal colony."[15] They were legally confined to economic adaptations which reinforced ethnic solidarity. It was not unusual for Chinese who had lived in the United States for thirty or more years to speak little or no English since their contacts with the larger society were limited to transactions over a laundry or lunch counter. Although the Chinese were in North America, they were not of North America.

The Transitional Chinatown Community

Early Chinatowns were communities of Chinese men, not families, because immigration laws prevented men from bringing their wives and children with them. The bitterness felt by many is exemplified by a Chinese restaurateur who, when he related his story to me in 1976, had lived in Canada for sixty-two years.

I remember looking out over the dining room of our restaurant on a busy day in 1946. I counted one hundred old Chinese men sitting out there and just six women, four Chinese and two Canadian. And I thought to myself, if Canadian culture has a Christian spirit, how could they deny Chinese their families? The whole city of Toronto didn't have a dozen Chinese women in 1946. You know, they talk a lot about the Chinese gambling and all those things, but don't forget, this was all there was to do. I had family in China, but I couldn't bring them back with me. . . . I had been living here over thirty years and had contributed to the economy. I had worked hard and never asked the government for a nickel. And you know, because I didn't import thousands of dollars of goods from China . . . they wouldn't classify me as a merchant. And so I had to work hard all those years and I didn't have a family to help me. Canada never treated the Chinese very good then. Now it's different and my heart feels good to see so many Chinese families and women and children in Chinatown now. I have a son, a son-in-law, daughter-in-law, and wife here now and five grandchildren. Now that I'm old, I'm happy to see my family living in Toronto and they come and see me all the time. Now I think Canada is the greatest country in the world.[16]

The transitional period in Chinatowns dates from the end of World War II to the middle of the 1960s. During this twenty-year period the United States and Canada gradually dismantled the series of discriminatory laws that had been enacted against the Chinese. On December 17, 1943, President Roosevelt signed a law repealing all previous acts of Chinese exclusion, and four years later the Canadian Parliament followed suit by repealing the 1923 Chinese Exclusion Act. Other acts such as the U. S. War Brides Act, the Canadian Citizenship Act, and new immigration acts in both countries permitted the Chinese who had been resident in North America to become citizens and enter occupations and schools previously closed to them. Of greatest importance, however, were laws enabling the Chinese to sponsor their wives, children and, later, parents and other relatives to join them in North America. New Chinese immigration, however, was still strictly limited by both countries until the mid-1960s when discriminatory restrictions on Asian immigration were finally removed.[17] Chinatowns grew relatively little during this period as immigration was restricted to wives and children of

Chinese already resident and a small number of Chinese professionals who did not enter the ethnic economy.

This period of Chinatown history is characterized by two features: the reunification of Chinese families, and the gradual appearance of a native-born Chinese population who would successfully assimilate into the American and Canadian mainstreams. The Chinese were thus divided into two groups: the immigrant Chinese and the North American-born Chinese. Comparisons between these two groups in Canada show how different their circumstances were. Canadian-born Chinese integrated into the occupations and professions of Canadian society and attained incomes and educational levels equal to or higher than other Canadians.[18] This integration even extended to marriage where Canadian-born Chinese had lower rates of endogamy (marriage within the ethnic group) than did the British Isles, French, and Jewish origin groups.[19] This is the group typified by Betty Luk and her siblings. Chinese immigrants, on the other hand, remained confined to the Chinatown community, which consisted of lower paying and less prestigious occupations, primarily those associated with the traditional ethnic economy of laundries and restaurants. Their language remained Chinese and they had little formal education, factors that prevented them from assimilating into the larger society. For them, Chinatown remained an internal colony. But for the small, yet increasing numbers of U.S.- and Canadian-born Chinese, their successful assimilation produced a new image of the Chinese in North America. They were now regarded as a model ethnic community.

Chinatowns Today: The Contemporary Community

It is difficult to overstate the extent to which North America's Chinatowns today differ from those of the traditional and transitional periods. As a result of new immigration regulations of the mid-1960s Chinatowns have experienced explosive growth and the problems associated with such growth. The Chinese population of Toronto, for example, was about eight thousand in 1966, the year prior to Canada's removal of immigration restrictions against Asians. During my fieldwork in the late 1970s the population was estimated at 80,000 and a newspaper report from 1990 gives 250,000 as a reasonable count. While Toronto's Chinatown has perhaps experienced the greatest growth, other major Chinatowns in North America such as San Francisco, New York, Los Angeles, and Vancouver have Chinese populations of well over 150,000. Whereas Chinese immigrants to North America made up only one to two percent of the total number of immigrants from 1950 to 1960, they were nearly seven percent of the total during the 1970s and 1980s. Growth in the immigrant population has led to an increasing reliance upon and a tremendous expansion of the ethnic community.

More important than growth itself is the diversity which now characterizes Chinatowns. New immigration regulations in both the United States and Canada favor the immigration of family members of Chinese already resident. These "family class" immigrants are usually non-English speaking, working-class Chinese who must find jobs in the ethnic economy. Nearly eighty-five percent of all immigrants now come from Hong Kong, with the remainder emigrating from Taiwan, mainland China, or from other areas of Chinese settlement in Europe and Asia. Almost half of the Hong Kong emigres were born in China, primarily Guangdong Province, who made their way to Hong Kong after the Chinese revolution of 1949. Most, however, had lived in Hong Kong for many years prior to coming to North America, were thus familiar with an urban lifestyle, and usually took jobs similar to those previously held in Hong Kong. The language spoken in Hong Kong is Cantonese, which is now the predominant language of Chinatowns. About twenty percent of all immigrants, those who have achieved university educations in Hong Kong or Canada, are bilingual in both English and Chinese.

Recent Chinese immigrants thus differ greatly from the first sojourning immigrants who came from rural China. They immigrate as families who intend to make North America their permanent home. They are accustomed to the crowded urban lifestyle of North America's cities and expect their children to integrate successfully into the larger societies. Because of this, the family and district associations which were so important in traditional Chinatowns have decreased in influence. Recent immigrants now rely on social service agencies, churches, clubs, and other immigrant services to meet their needs. Occupations have expanded beyond the old laundry/grocery/restaurant niches that employed the early immigrants to include clerical and professional positions and factory work, the latter mainly in garment factories that employ thousands of recent immigrants.

THE CHINESE WORKING CLASS

The immigrant working class is distinguished from the other classes by their positions in unskilled and semi-skilled occupations in the Chinatown economy, and by their inability to speak, read, or write English. These immigrants must find jobs that require little knowledge of English and, as a result, are employed as garment workers, hotel domestics, or as waiters, cooks, cashiers, clerks, and other relatively low-paying and insecure jobs in Chinese restaurants or shops. Throughout North America, Chinese working-class families earn only sixty percent of the average income of Americans and Canadians as a whole, and the poverty rate for Asian-American immigrants is twice that of non-Hispanic whites.[20] They usually live in Chinese neighborhoods where housing is substandard, rents are high, and overcrowding is the norm. Their children attend public schools where many of the other children are Chinese, but where little attention is given Chinese language or culture.

Few working-class Chinese families take part in organized groups such as unions, ethnic associations, and cultural groups. Linguistic barriers inhibit association with non-Chinese workers, and their employment in occupations with little job security make such associations hazardous at best. Chinese workers are completely dependent on Chinatowns for jobs, housing, social services, and the like. The adults will live out their lives in a Chinese world, but place great pressure on their children to become educated and assimilated into North American society.

The case of the Pan family, whom I met in Toronto, is typical of the adaptations and sacrifices which working-class Chinese families must make. When I met the Pans in 1977 they lived in a small, four-room flat in downtown Toronto, which they rented for $130 a month. They had no car, a minimum of furniture, and no major appliances such as a washing machine. Their prize possession was a portable color television. Mr. Pan worked as a cook in a Chinese restaurant six days a week on the night shift from 5 P.M. to 1 A.M. Mrs. Pan also worked six days a week, but from 7 A.M. to 4 P.M. as a laundress in a downtown hotel. Their combined weekly income was about two hundred dollars. Like many Chinese families they were trying to save money for a down payment on a house, and they managed to save about one hundred dollars a month.

As is evident from their work schedules, Mr. and Mrs. Pan saw very little of each other. Mrs. Pan tried to sleep a few hours each evening after the children went to bed so she could spend some time with her husband when he came home from work. Mr. Pan also spent little time with his children since they were at school when he was at home. The children, two daughters aged thirteen and eleven and two sons aged ten and eight, were extremely self-sufficient. They arrived home from school two hours before their mother and while their father was asleep. The girls usually cooked supper for their father and did so with great delight since he had taught them how to cook. They also "mothered" the two boys, keeping tabs on them both at school and at home.

The children did very well in school. The girls especially spoke excellent English and were almost equal to their Canadian classmates in reading and writing. The boys also spoke good English, but were just learning how to read and write. At home, they usually spoke their native Fujian dialect, but increasingly the children conversed in English among themselves. Mr. and Mrs. Pan were very proud of their children's progress, but extremely anxious about several problems upsetting the household. The girls were becoming familiar with Canadian standards and saw how they stood out among their peers. Their clothes were out of style and they could not understand why their parents wouldn't buy them more. They were also beginning to view their family as quite "odd" in comparison to other families. The parents worried mostly about their sons, however, who were not learning as quickly as the girls and whose behavior they described as "wild." Nevertheless, the family is glad it came to Canada where, in the words of Mr. Pan, "There is always enough rice to eat."

The Pan family illustrates several patterns of working-class adjustments to Chinatown society. Like most families, both spouses work full time outside the home, most in laboring occupations in garment factories or restaurants.[21] The parents place extreme pressure on their children to succeed in school, since education has always been highly valued in Chinese culture. At the same time, however, the parents are ill-equipped to either help or monitor their children's progress. The extreme reverence for the family so characteristic of Chinese culture is both a blessing and a curse that children must psychologically navigate. Many children do succeed in school as evidenced by the large number of Asian-Americans who achieve college educations; forty percent as compared to twenty-three percent among non-Hispanic whites in 1990.[22] But twenty percent drop out of high school, never develop fluency in English, have inadequate skills to find anything but marginal employment, and usually have strongly negative feelings about their Chinese heritage. Many of these get involved in youth gangs and have resorted to criminal activities to make a living.[23]

Recent evidence indicates that Asian-American populations are experiencing the same divisions as other American groups: The rich are getting richer and the poor are getting poorer.[24]

The younger the children are when they come to North America, the easier it is for them to acculturate and assimilate. Chinese who come as teenagers, however, find it extremely difficult to learn English or do well in school since they are already fully enculturated in Chinese language and culture. Most of these students drop out of school and are forced to seek the same low-wage employment in the ethnic economy as their parents. Husband-wife relations are also strained by differing work schedules, the frustrations of adjusting psychologically and economically to a new environment, and the unique problems associated with child-rearing. They want their children to assimilate but regret their loss of Chinese language and culture. A survey conducted in Toronto on the "family cohesiveness" of Chinese as perceived by married women's perceptions of the quality of their family life indicated that 150 of 177 women interviewed rated "low" on family cohesiveness. The most significant factor contributing to low cohesion was a severe lack of communication and interaction among all members of the family stemming from linguistic barriers between parents and children and relatively little time spent together among spouses.[25]

In spite of these problems, most working-class immigrants I knew were happy to be in Canada even though they had to work much harder to make a living than they thought they would have prior to immigration. The relative safety and security of Canada compared to Hong Kong and better opportunities for their children were the reasons. Nevertheless, the Chinese immigrant working class is still an "internal colony" whose low-wage labor and long working hours in the factories and Chinatown sub-economy make considerable profits for their employers. The North American economies have benefitted greatly from these immigrants. Our "Made in U.S.A" clothes are economically competitive with those made in Taiwan, Hong Kong, Singapore, and other Asian sites because they are made by Chinese and other Asian immigrants who work very long hours for wages that non-immigrants would not accept.

THE CHINESE EDUCATED-PROFESSIONAL CLASS

One of the major changes distinguishing contemporary Chinatowns from the traditional and transitional periods is the presence of thousands of young, college-educated Chinese professionals who occupy key roles in the ethnic community as social workers, lawyers, counselors, and other "white-collar" employees. Many Hong Kong Chinese first came to North America as university students and achieved permanent immigrant status after graduation. These immigrants are unlike the educated North American-born Chinese in that they grew up in a culture (Hong Kong) in which both Chinese and English were necessary for educational success. They are bilingual and bicultural, knowledgeable about both Chinese and Anglo-European cultures, and do not experience the marginality of native-born Chinese.

Members of the educated class play important roles in Chinatown since they act as mediators or brokers between the Chinese working class and the institutions of American and Canadian society. Social workers, immigration and employment counselors, legal aid advisors, ministers, bank tellers, and other occupations in Chinatown require persons who can interpret the complexities of American life to Chinese-speaking immigrants. Effectively filling these roles requires an educated class that not only understands the Chinese immigrant community, but also has the education and training recognized by U.S. and Canadian universities. Because of this, their ability to speak and write in English is often equal to their abilities in Chinese, and their years of residence in North America, much of which was spent in university, has enabled them to learn and, in many cases adopt, the culture of North American society. This ability to interact effectively and creatively in both Chinese and North American contexts gives the educated-professional class its special distinction, and enables those of its members so inclined to assume influential and powerful roles in Chinatown. Chinese social workers in both the United States and Canada are a good example.[26] Their influence in Chinatowns is much greater than that of American or Canadian social workers for they are the primary interpreters of North American society to Chinese-speaking immigrants. The success of Chinese social services depends on their ability to articulate working-class needs to the state bureaucracies in order to secure funds to keep programs operating. Their jobs demand a knowledge of immigrant social problems, a great many of which stem from poverty and illiteracy in English.

The educated-professional Chinese have greatly altered the political landscape of Chinatowns. They have begun numerous community organizations that both stress and address the problems faced by recent immigrants in the areas of employment, housing, and schooling. They are "activist" in the sense that they sponsor voter registration drives, English language training, employee rights classes, and other activities designed to enhance the political participation and power of Chinese-speaking immigrants. They have also been leaders in organizing campaigns to protect Chinatown neighborhoods from development plans in Toronto, Vancouver, and New York that have threatened to displace needed services and housing for immigrants.[27] Such activism in support of working-class immigrants has brought Chinatown professionals into direct conflict with the traditional Chinatown leaders of the family associations. Recent immigrants have no use for the old associations so important to the early immigrants since their experiences and problems are so different. The associations have not recruited new members and thus remain the preserve of older immigrants rooted in the traditional Chinatown economy. In the Chinatowns of today, the professional class has effectively replaced the leaders of the Chinese Benevolent Association and other traditional associations as the spokespersons for the Chinese in North America. Their influence attests to the dramatic changes that have occurred in Chinatowns since the 1960s. The traditional associations were oriented inwardly to the special needs of a small entrepreneurial class who fought for removal of immigration restrictions and the reestablishment of family life in North America. Ironically, their successes in securing legislation that led to the influx of thousands of Chinese have also led to their own political and economic decline.

THE CHINESE BUSINESS CLASS

Despite the changes occurring in Chinatowns, Chinese businesses catering to tourists and immigrants alike remain the lifeblood of Chinatown communities. Although the hand laundries of the traditional community have disappeared due to the advent of home appliances and dry cleaning, restaurants retain their visibility as centerpieces of Chinese culture in North America. Next to the restaurants, however, are a wide array of new businesses not seen in previous times. Bookshops, gift shops, furniture stores, theaters, butchers, clothing stores, pet shops, beauty salons, Chinese groceries, real estate, automobile dealerships, professional offices, social service agencies, and more now crowd the Chinatown streets. A Chinese-speaking immigrant need never leave the confines of the community to meet his needs.

Chinese businesses are not only more diverse, but the scale of Chinese enterprise has greatly increased. In the traditional community, it was relatively inexpensive to start a laundry or small restaurant, but the cost of real estate and government regulations and restrictions have made it virtually impossible for any but the wealthy to establish a business. For many immigrants, however, the opportunity to start one's own business remains a dream. In every Chinatown small new businesses such as newsstands and tiny restaurants that represent the life savings of a few immigrant families crop up almost daily. Sadly, they are often out of business within a few weeks or months since they have neither the capital nor the credit to compete with the larger, more established businesses.

The Chinese business class is now dominated by a small, but wealthy and influential group of entrepreneurs, many of whom have recently immigrated from Hong Kong, London, Madrid, and other overseas communities where they established considerable fortunes. They have built multistory restaurants, shopping malls, and apartment complexes in Chinatown designed to attract tourists and upscale residents. They are viewed by the Chinese working class and their social worker allies as predators seeking to destroy housing and jobs. They are viewed as "businessmen first, Chinese second"; people who put profits ahead of their ethnicity and their responsibilities to the community. The businessmen, on the other hand, defend their actions by pointing to the number of jobs they provide Chinatown residents and the new businesses that attract tourists.

The "new entrepreneurial elite" with their business suits, car phones, and computers contrasts in both lifestyle and orientation with the "old merchant elites" who for years dominated the social and economic life of Chinatowns. This segment of the business class is represented by those successful Chinese of the traditional period who built their restaurants into large businesses and other enterprises that enabled them to gain considerable wealth. These older merchant elites controlled the family associations and the Chinese Benevolent Association, often to their own benefit, but they nevertheless saw themselves as representing the entire community. They were in the forefront of efforts to relax immigration and other restrictions against the Chinese and rightly viewed themselves as community leaders. The presence of the new immigrant business class has produced severe economic competition for these old elites whose economic resources pale in comparison. They consider themselves the guardians of "family business" who care about the Chinese community and thus also regard the new business class as predatory profit-seekers out to destroy the Chinese way of life. Toronto's most famous Chinese citizen and former leader of the traditional business elite summarizes their feelings:

You know . . . the old restaurants, we all know each other and we're friendly with one another. We know none could survive alone, so we cooperate. When the Sai-Woo opened twenty-five years ago all the rest of us went to their opening. We were anxious to see them do well because we knew them and we knew they came up the hard way.

But now this foreign money comes in and is so big that they can afford to take losses for two or three years. They say, "I'm not interested in your community. I don't care about the little man next door." And so they have price wars and pretty soon family business will be forced out.

You know, we fought hard for the immigration law and for the civil rights of the Chinese in Canada, but immigration has come too fast, too soon. Foreign money [from Hong Kong] comes in and they think they know how to do everything the Chinese way. All this new money has created a false sense of security, and the small people are being eaten up. . . , I'm no longer a spokesperson for the community. I don't know anyone anymore, and I can't represent a community I don't know.[28]

In many ways, this statement is a brief social history of the nature and extent of changes which have affected Chinatowns. Foremost among these perhaps is a "loss of community"—the feeling among longtime residents that Chinatown is no longer a smoothly functioning ethnic community based on the ethnic solidarity of the old associations. What this loss of community signals, however, is the passage of power from the older merchant elites to recently immigrated groups such as the new business class and the educated-professional class. The traditional structure of Chinatowns has been attacked on two fronts: economically by Chinese tycoons who compete for the tourist dollar, and politically by the educated class who now best represent the new working-class immigrants. For those Chinese who came to North America prior to the 1960s, modern Chinatowns are nearly as foreign as the new countries to which they came.

The Future of the Chinese in North America

Chinatowns today are best viewed as immigrant communities whose populations are mainly comprised of first-generation, foreign-born Chinese from Hong Kong, China, and other areas of Chinese settlement overseas. Their characteristics as ethnic communities thus reflect the diversity of the immigrants themselves, and the adjustments, hopes, and struggles that I have discussed. As the communities continue to grow, the Chinese will become increasingly dispersed geographically, a process that is already evident in the large metropolitan centers. Many smaller Chinatowns are thus springing up near the major ones as clusters of Chinese with particular origins, such as Taiwan, establish their own communities.[29]

Immigration has slowed appreciably since the mid-1980s, however, and if this trend persists Chinatowns will increasingly become communities of U.S.- and Canadian-born Chinese. Many of them will successfully integrate into the larger societies, but usually at the cost of losing—or never gaining—competency in Chinese language or an appreciation of Chinese culture.

Notes

1. Much of the data for this article is based on my fieldwork in Toronto, Canada's Chinese community during 1976–1977 and a subsequent stay in 1983. All names mentioned are pseudonyms.

2. Acculturation is the process of learning the language, attitudes, and habits of another culture. Assimilation is a social process that leads people from one cultural group to integrate into the occupations and statuses of another group.

3. The notion of "marginal personality" was developed by sociologist Robert Park to refer to the psychological and social conflicts experienced by persons who are caught between the demands of their native culture (e.g., Chinese culture) and a very different culture to which they are attempting to assimilate (e.g., American culture).

4. Most Chinese today immigrate to large urban areas where "major" Chinatowns offer them opportunities for housing and employment. Major Chinatowns are those with Chinese populations over one hundred thousand. There are also many mid-size and small Chinatowns scattered throughout North America's cities.

5. Betty Lee Sung, *The Story of the Chinese in America* (New York: Collier Books, 1967), p. 11.

6. Prior to the Opium Wars with Britain in the 1840s China had strictly regulated trade with foreign countries and did not permit foreign vessels to enter its ports. The British were victorious in these wars, however, and required China to open its ports for the opium trade and other goods. China was also required to grant a leasehold over Hong Kong to the British. This expires in 1997 and Hong Kong will revert back to China.

7. Chen Ta, *Emigrant Communities in South China* (London: Institute of Pacific Relations, 1940).

8. Sung, *The Story of the Chinese in America*, pp. 16–17.

9. Richard H. Thompson, *Toronto's Chinatown: The Changing Social Organization of an Ethnic Community* (New York: AMS, 1989), p. 174.

10. For a history of this period consult Elmer Clarence Sandmeyer, *The Anti-Chinese Movement in California* (Urbana: University of Illinois, 1939).

11. Sung, *The Story of the Chinese in America*, pp. 42–42.

12. In 1888 the United States passed the Scott Act, which prohibited any Chinese laborers from immigrating. Only those classified as merchants, teachers, officials, and students were permitted entry. Canada passed a law with similar provisions in 1923, which has come to be known as the Chinese Exclusion Act.

13. Harry Con, Ronald J. Con, Graham Johnson, Edgar Wickberg, and William E. Willmott, *From China to Canada: A History of the Chinese Communities in Canada*, ed. Edgar Wickberg (Toronto: McClelland and Stewart, 1982), p. 38.

14. For a description of the traditional segmentary structure in Chinese communities, see Lawrence W. Crissman, "The Segmentary Structure of Urban Overseas Chinese Communities," *Man, N.S.* 2 (1967): 185–204.

15. Michael Hechter, "Group Formation and the Cultural Division of Labor," *American Journal of Sociology* 84 (1978): 293–318.

16. Thompson, *Toronto's Chinatown*, pp. 105–106.

17. Although the Chinese are racially distinct from Europeans, the discrimination and prejudice the Chinese faced are best thought of as forms of "social intolerance" rather than "race prejudice." Although whites in California feared competition from Chinese labor, they did not couch their opposition to the Chinese in terms of racial ideologies of inferiority. The latter form of "race prejudice" has been reserved for Native Americans and African Americans. For a discussion of social intolerance and race prejudice see Oliver C. Cox, *Caste, Class, and Race* (New York: Monthly Review, 1959), pp. 392–393.

18. Thompson, *Toronto's Chinatown*, p. 117.

19. Warren Kalbach, *The Impact of Immigration on Canada's Population* (Ottawa: Dominion Bureau of Statistics, 1970), p. 340.

20. William P. O'Hare and Judy C. Felt, *Asian Americans: America's Fastest Growing Minority Group* (Washington, D.C.: Population Reference Bureau, 1991), pp. 6–7.

21. Mary T. Ling, "Values and Voluntary Associations: The Chinese Community in Downtown Toronto" (Unpublished ms., 1975).

22. O'Hare and Felt, *Asian Americans*, p. 8.

23. For a discussion of Chinese youth gangs, see Chialing Kuo, *Social and Political Change in New York's Chinatown: The Role of Voluntary Associations*, (New York: Praeger, 1977); and Bernard P. Wong, *Chinatown: Economic Adaptation and Ethnic Identity of the Chinese* (New York: Holt, Rinehart & Winston, 1982).

24. O'Hare and Felt, *Asian Americans*, p. 7.
25. Ling, "Values and Voluntary Associations."
26. For the roles that Chinese social workers play in Chinatowns, see Bernard P. Wong, "Elites and Ethnic Boundary Maintenance: A Study of the Roles of Elites in Chinatown, New York City," *Urban Anthropology* 6 (1977): 1–22; Richard H. Thompson, "Ethnicity vs. Class: An Analysis of Conflict in a North American Chinese Community," *Ethnicity* 6 (1979): 306–326.
27. Thompson, "Ethnicity vs. Class: An Analysis of Conflict in a North American Chinese Community."
28. *Ibid.*, p. 274.
29. For an analysis of a Taiwan immigrant community in Queens, New York, see Hsiang-shui Chen, *Chinatown No More: Taiwan Immigrants in Contemporary New York* (Ithaca, NY: Cornell University Press, 1992).

Suggested Readings

Barth, Gunther. *Bitter Strength: A History of the Chinese in the United States, 1850–1870*. Cambridge, MA: Harvard University Press, 1964. A good history of early Chinese settlement in the United States.

Chen, Hsiang-shui. *Chinatown No More: Taiwan Immigrants in Contemporary New York*. Ithaca, NY: Cornell University Press, 1992. A new study focusing on Chinese immigrants who establish communities apart from traditional Chinatowns.

Con, Harry, Ronald J. Con, Graham Johnson, Edgar Wickberg, and William E. Willmott. *From China to Canada: A History of the Chinese Communities in Canada*. ed. Edgar Wickberg. Toronto: McClellan and Stewart, 1982. The best general study of the Chinese experience in Canada.

Loewen, James W. *The Mississippi Chinese: Between Black and White*. 2nd ed. Prospect Heights, IL: Waveland, 1992. An interesting study of race relations comparing African Americans and Chinese in a rural Mississippi community.

Nee, Victor, and Brett DeBary Nee. *Longtime Californ': A Documentary Study of an American Chinatown*. New York: Random House, 1972. An excellent and poignant account of Chinese life in San Francisco's Chinatown.

Iroquois: The Tree of Peace and the War Kettle

Thomas Abler

They call themselves Hodenosaunee, meaning "people of the extended house." They saw their aboriginal homeland as a giant rectangular house, running from east to west with five hearths along its central corridor, one for each of the nations in their confederacy stretching from the Mohawk Valley westward through what is now upstate New York to the Genessee River. The confederacy became known to the English as the Five Nations but the French on the St. Lawrence River called them "Iroquois," and it is by this name that they continue to be known collectively. After their linguistic cousins, the Tuscarora, sought refuge among the Iroquois early in the eighteenth century (the Tuscarora had fled from their aboriginal homeland in North Carolina), the confederacy was frequently called the Six Nations.

Initial contact was established between the European invaders of North America and members of the Iroquois confederacy in the first decade of the seventeenth century. For the next two hundred years, the Iroquois were a dominant political force in northeastern North America. As a result, their diplomacy and oratory were translated and recorded by officials in colonial bureaucracies, their culture described by missionaries and travelers, their commerce sought by traders, their warriors recruited as allies and feared as enemies, and their leaders transported across the Atlantic to meet European monarchs. Before 1730 they were the subject of a major work (in French) comparing their customs to those of peoples of the ancient world and a history written by a British colonial official expounding their importance in the power struggle for control of trade and commerce with the Native Peoples of North America.[1] Thus the ethnohistorian has a rich record to examine in an attempt to understand the culture, the behavior, and the motivations of these remarkable people.

Iroquois culture did not die when, under intense pressures, they sold most of their lands to Americans and Canadians. A New York lawyer, Lewis Henry Morgan, working in collaboration with a young resident of the Tonawanda Reservation, Ely S. Parker, recorded a detailed description of Iroquois culture. The book that resulted, *League of the Ho-de-no-sau-nee*, [or] *Iroquois*, has been often hailed as the first ethnographic description of a native North American culture and continues to deserve careful reading. Since Morgan's pioneering work, a large number of anthropologists have worked in Iroquois communities, producing highly detailed descriptions of local variants of Iroquois culture. As a result the published record of Iroquois culture is indeed rich. Among native North American cultures, the length of the Iroquois bibliography is rivaled by few others, possibly only the Navajo and the Eskimo (or Inuit). This chapter, while built in part upon primary research which I have personally conducted in the documentary record of Iroquois history preserved in archives, owes a major debt to anthropological researchers (some of whom had Iroquois ancestry) and the communities that welcomed them over the 150 years since Morgan conducted his investigations among the Seneca of Tonawanda.[2]

The Iroquois and Their Neighbors

The eastern-most member of the Iroquois Confederacy were the Mohawk, who occupied a cluster of villages on the hills along the Mohawk River. To the west, near Woods Creek and Oneida Lake, the Oneida occupied a single village for most of the historic period. The Onondaga, whose central political role in the confederacy will be discussed below, resided near present-day Syracuse, New York. The Cayuga occupied a number of villages near the lake that now bears their name. Finally, as "Doorkeepers" of the Confederacy, the Seneca originally lived on lands west of the Cayuga to the Genessee River.

All of these nations spoke languages of the Iroquoian language family. Many of their neighbors also spoke languages of this family. Jacques Cartier encountered speakers of Iroquoian languages at Stadacona and Hochelaga (present-day Quebec City and Montreal) in 1535. These peoples had vanished by 1600. West of the Seneca were the Wenro and, across the Niagara River, the Neutral. South of Lake Erie were the Erie. North, between Lake Simcoe and Georgian Bay, were the nations of the Huron Confederacy, and to the west of the Huron, the Petun or Tobacco Nation (Khionontateronon). To the south, on the Susquehanna River, were yet another Iroquoian-speaking people, the Susquehannock. Far to the south, in what are now the Carolinas and Tennessee, lived the Tuscarora and Cherokee, who also spoke Iroquoian languages.

Other peoples surrounding the Iroquois spoke languages of the Algonquian language family. The Mahican lived east of the Mohawk. Several Algonquian groups lived in the Hudson Valley and New England. The Delaware occupied New Jersey, Delaware, and portions of Pennsylvania. The Algonquin (who gave their name to the language family) lived in the Ottawa Valley, and the Montagnais were hunting peoples north of the St. Lawrence River.

The Iroquois Confederacy has been and remains a focus both for members of the Iroquois nations themselves and for outsiders investigating the socio-political structure of the Iroquois. The oral tradition of the foundation of this institution will be outlined in detail below. Metaphor dominates Iroquois political expression, and the Nations of the Iroquois Confederacy saw themselves sitting in the shadow of the Tree of Peace, which was planted in a hole in which the weapons of war had been flung. The Tree of Peace, however, only cast its shadow on the members of the confederacy. Another metaphor was that of the War Kettle. Those who sat in the shade of the Tree of Peace had to defend, on occasion, that peace by waging war upon others. Thus the War Kettle was hung up, and members of the great Confederacy of the Iroquois went to war against belligerent neighbors. The kettle contin-

ues to be an important metaphor in contemporary Iroquois communities, but now it is a peaceful metaphor for hospitality.[3]

Settlement and Subsistence

Iroquois villages consisted of a large number of rectangular houses, known as longhouses, built of a framework of poles covered with slabs of elm bark. Each end, which might be rounded or square, had a door. An aisle four meters wide ran the length of the house and people used benches on either side for sitting and sleeping. Hearths or fireplaces were located every seven meters down the center of the aisle, each shared by two families who occupied the living spaces on opposite sides of the fire. Smoke from the fires, in theory, exited through smoke holes in the arched roof. These same smoke holes were the only source of external light for the residents. The houses were seven to eight meters wide, and the apex of the arched roof was seven meters or so above the floor. The length of the house varied with the number of families (and number of fireplaces) found therein. In the early historic period a house thirty meters long, with four fires and eight families, was the usual size, although houses three times that size have been reported.

There was considerable variation in village size, but in the seventeenth century most Iroquois lived in villages of more than fifty longhouses and well over one thousand inhabitants. There were, however, hamlets of only a few houses, usually near enough to a large village that the latter could be called to help, or sought as a refuge, in times of danger. At least some of the villages were surrounded by a palisade of sharpened logs, approximately seven meters in height. These palisades might be double or triple in thickness, with posts inclining toward each other and interlaced at the top. Platforms along the inside of the palisade near its top allowed village defenders to fire on attackers, throw boulders on them, and quench fires set by attackers in an attempt to destroy the timber wall. These defenses involved a great investment in labor, however, so very large villages, such as the principal village of the Onondaga, were left unfortified, possibly because the very number of fighting men residing therein deterred attack. Villages were also erected in defensive sites, and if physical barriers (i.e., a cliff too steep to climb) inhibited attack, no palisade would be erected in that sector. In times of peace, or when no invaders were anticipated, the palisade, if erected, would fall into disrepair. These fortifications were substantive enough, however, that the Dutch who were first to contact Mohawk villages called them "castles."

Whether palisaded or not, the longhouses of the village formed a compact cluster. Surrounding the village were the cleared fields which provided the bulk of the food consumed by the villagers. The Iroquois were an agricultural people, dependent upon the "three sisters"—maize (corn), beans, and squash—for their daily food. An alternate name for the "three sisters" has been translated as "the life sustainers."

The fields were cleared by males, girdling trees to kill them, then a year later felling them with a combination of fire and stone axes prior to the acquisition of the steel axe. Once the fields were cleared they were largely a female responsibility. To an extent the Iroquois practiced intercropping, for maize, beans, and squash would be planted in the same "hill," a mound of earth half a meter high heaped up to receive the seeds. After planting (the seeds for maize had been soaked in a poison to discourage consumption by crows), several stalks of maize grew from the top of the hill. The beans followed, twining themselves about the cornstalks. The squash, with its large, broad leaves, grew about the base of the hill, choking out any weeds which might grow there and compete with the food crops for nutrients. Many varieties of maize, beans, and squash (including pumpkins) were grown. A corn variety with red kernels was something of a gourmet treat, but low in productivity. Flint corn was by far the variety most commonly raised, valued for its properties as a flour. Maize was pounded into flour with a heavy wooden dumbbell-shaped pestle in a wooden mortar made by hollowing out a tree trunk. As such it was boiled as hominy or made into bread. Boiling its kernels in ashes would remove their husks and it was then made into soup. Corn soup remains a favorite dish among some contemporary Iroquois, although now made with pork rather than venison or bear meat.[4]

All of these crops stored well, providing sustenance from one harvest to the next. The Iroquois regularly tried to grow and store more than a single-year's consumption, since there was the danger of a poor year due to drought, frost, or insect pests. For a portion of the maize, the husks were stripped back from the ears and braided together forming a long string of ears, resembling somewhat the appearance of a bunch of bananas. These were hung from the rafters of the longhouses. The differing races of maize with their varied hues must have given the longhouse a spectacular appearance in the early fall. Another method of storing maize was to strip the kernels from the ear and store them in bark barrels or in underground storage pits beneath the benches at the sides of the longhouse. Elm bark structures, similar in construction to the longhouse, also served to store maize. Both squash (cut into strips) and beans were also preserved by drying.

The three sisters provided the bulk of the Iroquois diet, but other foods supplemented them. Another domesticated plant was the sunflower, valuable for its seeds and their oil. In addition, wild foods such as wild strawberries, other berries, maple syrup and sugar, nuts, mushrooms, roots, and greens added variety to meals and were used to flavor dishes made from maize. Meat and fish were eaten when available. At times (usually late winter) nearly the entire male population of a village would be absent hunting deer. While the venison was consumed, the deer hunt in times before the fur trade was made important by the fact that clothing was constructed from the tanned hide of the animal. Fowl were sources of meat and feathers. Expeditions would be organized to harvest large quantities of passenger pigeons. The meat of bears, with its high fat content, was valued. Bears taken alive as cubs were raised in a special pen within the village, to be slaughtered for food after two or three years. Some Iroquois with access to resources unavailable to others would trade them to neighbors; for example, the Oneida were a source of fish to the Mohawk.

The length of time a village could remain in one place varied with its population and surrounding habitat, but a dozen years seems to have been the minimum, and some sites were occupied for a longer period of time. Eventually, however, when houses fell into disrepair and fields became exhausted or pest-infested, it became more economical to build a completely new village in a new location than to continue to live in the old one. Most villages retained their old names when they moved, however.[5]

SOCIAL ORGANIZATION

Each of the nations of the Iroquois Confederacy were made up of from three to nine clans. The use of the term "nation" for a member of the Iroquois Confederacy has deep historical roots and continues in informal use, political rhetoric, and official designations (as the Six Nations Reserve in Canada and the Seneca Nation of New York Indians in the United States). In some publications these are referred to as "tribes." I see "nation" and "tribe" when used for Native Peoples of North America as synonyms. I see neither term as pejorative.

The clans were both exogamous, meaning one could not marry a member of one's own clan, and matrilineal, meaning one belonged to the clan of one's

Table 1
Clans of the Iroquois

Seneca	Cayuga	Onondaga	Oneida	Mohawk
Wolf	Wolf	Wolf	Wolf	Wolf
Turtle	Heron	Turtle	Turtle	Turtle
Bear	Snipe	Snipe	Bear	Bear
Beaver	Deer	Beaver		
Deer	Beaver	Ball		
Snipe	Turtle	Deer		
Hawk	Bear	Hawk		
Heron	Ball	Bear		
	Eel	Eel		

mother. Table 1 presents a list of clans for each nation. Three of these clans were found in all five nations while the remaining clans were found in two or three of the nations. The prohibition against marriage included all members of one's clan, regardless of village or nation. The clan names relate to birds and animals but are not always the common name for a species (even the "Ball Clan" may relate to the behavior of a young deer). Movements by Iroquois in the past two centuries, the possibilities for a clan to either die out or to split into two new clans, the incorporation of "foreign" elements (either other Iroquoian nations or outsiders), lack of understanding of ethnographers or their informants of distant communities, and other factors have all led to differences in detail on such lists of clans. Table 1 ignores these differences in detail but may therefore not be completely accurate, for many communities either today or in the past.

An aspect of clan membership was that one bore a clan name. Each clan had a finite set of names that were available to be assigned to members of the clan. These were not related to the clan eponym (many Iroquois names were in fact without meaning). They were, however, recognized as belonging to the clan. All infants born into the clan received one of its "baby names," not then in use, at either the Green Corn Ceremony or the Midwinter Ceremony. Upon maturity, the same individual would receive an adult name from the set of adult names not then in use. Thus every Iroquois bore a name used by clan members in generations past and destined to be used by clan members for future generations.

Each clan was composed of one or more matrilineages. Large clans were strongly represented in a number of villages. The matrilineage was essentially a local component of a clan. Its membership consisted of all people who could claim descent, through females, from the founding female ancestor of the matrilineage. Usually, the female core of the matrilineage was rooted in the village of their birth. Thus the core of the matrilineage was the group of matrilineally related women who lived out their lives beside each other in a single village and possibly in a single longhouse. Their brothers and sons might reside elsewhere, but all continued as members of the matrilineage of their birth, owing loyalties to that local unit of the larger clan. A single matrilineage might number as many of five hundred members. For a matrilineage to continue in time, however, its women had to bear daughters to replace themselves, and a matrilineage giving birth primarily to males faced reduction in size and possible extinction in later generations.

After marriage a male left his natal longhouse and moved to the longhouse of his spouse. The longhouse could be extended by building an addition to one end to accommodate the new family. Thus the residents of a longhouse consisted of a core of women related to each other either as mother-daughter, as sisters, or as daughters of sisters. Also living in the house were the husbands of these women and their unmarried sons. The association of the longhouse with the women of the matrilineage (who, in fact, were felt to own it) led to the clan symbol of the matrilineage to be painted above the door. Travelers would seek out a house with their own clan symbol over the door when visiting another village.

The matrilineages were also important in farming, since while fields could be individually owned, most seem to have been owned by the matrilineage. The women of the matrilineage cooperated in the planting and cultivation of the fields, and the results of the harvest would be stored inside the lineage longhouse.

Upon marriage, males remained members of the matrilineage of their birth. As outsiders in the house of their wives they retained strong ties to their natal homes. Such matrilineal-matrilocal societies usually feature a high incidence of divorce. The Iroquois appear to have been no exception. The tie between a woman and her mother remained stronger than that between the woman and her husband. Her children remained with her if her husband were sent home to his mother. In the extended family of the longhouse, however, the children of a divorced couple were not without role models to replace the absent father. Even if their mother did not remarry, husbands of her mother's sisters or her mother's maternal cousins resident in the matrilineage longhouse provided role models for the male children of the matrilineage.

A clan, which consisted of one or more matrilineages, among the western Iroquois was also linked to other clans in what anthropologists call a moiety organization. A society with moieties (from the French word for "half") is divided into two bodies, and each person must belong to one or the other. Among the Iroquois moiety membership was determined by clan membership. Within a nation certain clans are linked in one moiety while the remainder of the clans are linked to the second moiety. In Table 1 clans of the first moiety of each nation are separated by an asterisk (*) from the second moiety. In some communities the moieties are simply referred to as "sides" (since they sit on opposite sides of the fire). The Seneca speak of the animal clans (the Wolf, Turtle, Bear, and Beaver moiety) and the bird clans (the inclusion of the Deer clan among the bird clans bothers outsiders more than it seems to bother the Seneca). Among contemporary Onondaga, as in other Iroquois communities, the structure where religious festivals are held is called the Longhouse. The Onondaga "Mudhouse" is the adjacent building where foods are prepared for these festivities. Contemporary Onondaga moieties take their names from these buildings, the Longhouse moiety containing the clans Wolf, Turtle, etc., while the clans Hawk, Deer, etc., are found in the Mudhouse moiety.

Some have suggested Iroquois moieties, like clans, were exogamous, but best available evidence contradicts this.[6] Moieties did have socially significant roles, however. Lacrosse, at the intravillage and intranation level, involved competition between moieties. This was not simply a game, for it was believed a lacrosse match could cure illness and watching the game being played was felt to please the Creator. Seating, as practiced at certain events in the ceremonial cycle, was by moieties, and the moieties opposed each other in the bowl game at the Green Corn and Midwinter ceremonies. A moiety also buried the other's dead and consoled the opposite for its loss.[7]

Under the Tree of Peace

FOUNDING THE CONFEDERACY

The date of the establishment of the Iroquois Confederacy will probably always be uncertain. It does seem likely that it predated, possibly by as much as a century and a half, initial contacts of the Iroquois with Europeans. The elaborate oral tradition of the confederacy's founding exists in numerous variants. Here just the bare bones of this exciting story are presented.[8]

Deganawida was born to a Huron virgin on the Bay of Quinté on the Canadian side of Lake Ontario. Hearing of the endless wars of blood-revenge ravaging the peoples to the south of that lake, he determined to take a message of peace to those peoples. In the Mohawk country he converted the fierce cannibal, Hiawatha, to the cause of peace. (Those familiar with Longfellow's epic should be cautioned that the Iroquoian Hiawatha had his name stolen by the New England poet and attributed to the Ojibwa culture hero Nanabush. Longfellow's hero bears no relation to the Hiawatha of Iroquois tradition.) Some variants of the story suggest Deganawida had a speech impediment, hence Hiawatha became his speaker in councils. The Mohawk, Oneida, Cayuga, and Seneca pledged to join the Great Peace, but the Onondaga held out. Leading them was terrible sorcerer Thadodaho, with seven crooks in his body and snakes entangled in his hair. The Onondaga were persuaded to join with the recognition that Thadodaho was first (although still equal) among the confederacy chiefs, that the Onondaga would have more positions on the confederacy council than any of the other nations, that the Onondaga would be "firekeepers" for the confederacy whose council would regularly meet at Onondaga, and that the wampum keeper for the confederacy would be one of the Onondaga chiefs.

Wampum were cylindrical shell beads, white or purple in color. The former were made from the shell of the whelk, the latter from that of the quahog. They could be threaded into strings or woven into belts. Wampum had a sacred quality, for a speaker who held wampum demonstrated his sincerity. Belts and strings were exchanged at treaty negotiations and these served as a record of the accord reached in later years. Thus as wampum keeper for the confederacy the Onondaga preserved its diplomatic history.

The Great Peace was established at a council attended by fifty chiefs called by Deganawida. The fifty positions remain, and each individual on assuming the "antlers of office" (a metaphor for holding chiefly position) takes the name or title of his predecessor. Hence the names of the fifty founders of the confederacy continue. These Confederacy chiefs were strictly civil positions; as peace chiefs the members of the council were not allowed to go to war. There is an elaborate ritual for installing new chiefs, the Condolence Council, in which all fifty titles are recited. The recitation of titles follows the path through the longhouse from east to west.[9]

The number of chiefs varied from nation to nation. As mentioned above, the Onondaga had more than the others, fourteen, with Thadodaho first on the

Onondaga list. The Mohawk and Oneida each had nine positions. The Cayuga had ten. The Seneca, in historic times by far the largest of the five cantons, had only eight positions. However, the council deliberated until it came "of one mind," that is, reached unanimity, hence the number of chiefs was not particularly important.

CONFEDERACY CHIEFS AND MATRILINEAGES

The titles themselves were hereditary within matrilineages. The selection process is not completely clear, probably because of variation from place to place and through time. It is clear that the matron who headed the matrilineage (by a combination of seniority and competence) played a major role in selecting which male in the matrilineage would fill the position. The lineage matron held the wampum string that symbolized and validated the title. This same woman could remove an incompetent from office ("dehorn" him, that is remove his metaphorical "antlers" of office). While in theory the title could pass to any matrilineage male, the successor was usually a close maternal relative (brother or sister's son) of the previous title holder. It was not unknown to award the title to a minor who was the closest maternal relative of a deceased chief. While the minor bore the title, a guardian acted in his stead in councils until he attained maturity.

Not all matrilineages, and indeed not all clans, had representatives on the council of fifty confederacy chiefs. Both Mohawk and Oneida had nine chiefs, three chiefs for each of their three clans. The eight Seneca positions were divided evenly between the two moieties, but for the bird clans, three of the four were Snipe clan titles. Hawk held the other title; members of the Seneca Deer and Heron clans did not sit on the Confederacy Council. Of the animal clans moiety, the Beaver clan lacked a position and there were two Turtle clan positions. Data are not clear on Onondaga and Cayuga titles. Morgan recorded that the Turtle clan had five Onondaga positions, that Deer and Bear clans each had three, and the Onondaga Wolf, Beaver, and Snipe clans each had a single title. Morgan reported that among the Cayuga the Bear, Turtle, Heron, and Snipe clans each had two positions, Deer and Wolf each had one of the remaining two titles. The association of particular titles with many of these clans is contradicted by later fieldworkers. Morgan's listing may contain some error, but some titles clearly have been shifted from one matrilineage and clan to another in recent times. This was necessary if a matrilineage had no suitable candidate.[10]

The Confederacy Council was divided into two "sides" or moieties, one of which condoled the other upon the death of one of its chiefs and raised up his successor to the position. The Mohawk, Seneca, and Onondaga constituted one "side," sometimes referred to as the "elder brothers." The Oneida and Cayuga, as the "younger brothers," constituted the other "side." These moieties sat on opposite sides of the council fire, except for the Onondaga who as firekeepers of the Confederacy moderated the proceedings and sat separately. Issues were considered first by the Seneca and then by the Mohawk before being passed across the fire to the Oneida. They in turn passed the matter to the Cayuga. If both sides were "of one mind" the issue went to the Onondaga. The moiety division of the Confederacy Council was of importance in the Condolence Ceremony. When a Confederacy Council chief died and was replaced, the opposite moiety (e.g., the "younger brothers" if the chief were a Seneca) had the obligation to condole the bereaved moiety and raise up his successor. The grieving moiety's tears were dried and minds were cleared by the ritual in which the story of the founding of the Confederacy was recited, as were all fifty of the names of the Confederacy Council chiefs.[11]

In addition to the positions on the Confederacy Council, there were other chiefs recognized by the Iroquois. Some of the Confederacy chiefs had assistants appointed from their own matrilineage. In addition, individuals of exceptional merit would be recognized as chiefs, sometimes styled "Pine-Tree Chiefs" or "props to the longhouse." Since one could not wear the antlers of office and go to war, military leadership came from this last category. Only confederacy chiefs could vote in the Confederacy Council but at the local level, on issues of importance only to the village or nation, all chiefs seem to have been equal.

Throughout Iroquois history, outsiders have been lavish in their praise of the public oratory of Iroquois speakers in councils. The Iroquois themselves admired and valued those among them who could speak well. Politics and diplomacy for the Iroquois were a spectacular sport; major treaty negotiations would attract an audience of a thousand or more. A skilled speaker could exert influence despite other failings. The famous Seneca orator Red Jacket was burdened with a reputation for being a coward yet held sway over his contemporaries because of his intellect as expressed in eloquent speeches in councils.

One should also note the Iroquois were an egalitarian society. Chiefs did not accrue more wealth than others; indeed, they frequently had less in material goods than others because they would be called on for aid by those in want. It would also be best to characterize them as having influence rather than authority. As Morgan noted: "The government sat lightly upon the people, who, in effect, were governed but little."[12] Individuals or whole villages were known historically to follow policies contrary to those of the rest of the Confederacy or of their own nation. The nations themselves often acted in an independent fashion, making peace or war oblivious to the policies of their neighbors. Fenton has asserted the importance of the local village, noting that "power remained in the hands of local chiefs" rather than with the Confederacy Council.[13] The historian Allen Trelease observed:

> Many writers have waxed eloquent over this "forest democracy," but it might as easily be termed anarchy. If the voice of the warriors (and the women) prevented absolute rule by the oligarchic body of sachems, it also prevented the tribe from pursuing a resolute policy for any length of time. Tribal effectiveness was all too often diffused at the expense of factionalism or personal whim.[14]

I am of the view that the myth and ritual surrounding the Confederacy Council was very important for the *symbolic* unity it provided for the Iroquois even though the chiefs of the Confederacy Council could not force others to follow its formulated policy. It would seem that the myth and ritual surrounding the Confederacy were more important in ensuring peace and cooperation among the nations of the Confederacy than were the minimal authority and power of the fifty chiefs of the Confederacy Council.

The War Kettle

Although his intimate knowledge of the Seneca came nearly two generations after the Iroquois had seriously engaged in war, Morgan probably correctly characterized traditional Iroquois values about male activities: ". . . the life of the Iroquois [male] was either spent in the chase, the war-path, or the council-fire. They formed the three leading objects of his existence; and it would be difficult to determine for which he possessed the strongest predilection."[15] Although sitting in the shade of the Tree of Peace, members of the Iroquois Confederacy had frequent cause to hang up the War Kettle and to send young men off to fight.

Warfare was not simply a male preoccupation, though. It will be seen that just as they did in the selection and control of the Confederacy Council, women played a prominent part in the war complex.

Morgan has rightly suggested that fame could be achieved by military exploits, but it was not simply a quest for glory that led males to engage in combat. The motivation for military participation was tied to the "mourning war."[16] A key element in the mourning war was the loss of a member of a matrilineage. War provided a mechanism for filling that loss by returning with a prisoner to be adopted by the matrilineage or with a scalp in place of a prisoner.

It was the matron in the grieving matrilineage who initiated the war party. It was not members of her own matrilineage whom she sought to go to war to replace the loss, however. Instead the matron approached a warrior whose father belonged to the bereaved matrilineage. Men have an obligation to their *akato ni*, their father's kinsmen or matrilineage.[17] The matron of father's matrilineage controlled the military activities of a male. She could send him to war, to obtain a prisoner or scalp to replace a loss in her own lineage, or, alternatively prevent him from going to war. The Jesuit Joseph François Lafiteau noted that here "resides the advantage of having many men born in it [a matrilineage]. For these men . . . marry into different lodges [other matrilineages]. The children born of these different marriages become obligated to their father's lodge . . . [for] replacing them [who have died]."[18] It is interesting, and perhaps significant, that this society, which allocated so much authority to elder females in the war complex, gave that authority not to the mothers but rather the father's sisters of potential combatants.

An important goal in the conduct of war was the taking of captives. Men going to war carried with them a "prisoner tie," a specialized artifact with a broad band or collar (to be fastened about the prisoner's neck) with long, stout cords that were used to bind a prisoner's arms behind the back and wrists over the abdomen. The "prisoner tie" caused the prisoners a lot of pain and suffering. Fingernails were torn out and fingers amputated. Upon reaching the captors' home village the prisoners had to run the gauntlet, that is, run between two rows of villagers armed with clubs or other weapons. The prisoner would then be an adopted member of the matrilineage who had initiated his or her captor's participation in the raid. The lineage matron would decide the fate of the captive. Lafiteau notes, "The matrons to whom the captives are given are so entirely mistresses of the latter that the wish of the entire village could not save them if the former are desirous of throwing them into the fire nor could they be put to death if these women wish to grant them life."[19] Ritual execution through torture was one possibility. Ideally the torture victim was kept alive through the night to be scalped and have his heart torn out to greet the rising sun. Portions of the captive's body were then eaten.

A very large percentage of war captives, including most women and children, did not die at the torture stake. Instead they were adopted and incorporated into the matrilineage. Many of these individuals assimilated completely to the society of their captors. Even adult male captives were successfully assimilated. In the late seventeenth century the Seneca had at least eleven foreign nations incorporated within their populations while the Oneida had more captives and refugees than native-born in their country.

The "mourning war" may have impelled individual Iroquois males to go to war, but the wars themselves also reflected conflict between groups over resources. Conflict over deer-hunting territories seems to have sparked prehistoric conflict.[20] After the arrival of Europeans in North America, the fur trade, requiring access to European traders and a supply of the beaver pelts desired on the European market, sparked widespread and intense conflict. The result of these wars was the destruction by the Iroquois of many of their neighbors.

The Wenro were the first to fall, being driven from their territory, rich in beavers, by the Seneca in 1638. For the next decade Mohawks plundered furs from fleets traveling the Ottawa and other streams intent on trading with the French on the St. Lawrence. As conflict with the Huron intensified, large Iroquois armies destroyed Huron villages—three in 1647–1648 and two more by an army one thousand strong on March 16, 1649. The Onondaga were neutral in this war with the Huron. Panic spread through Huronia after the loss of two villages in the heart of their homeland in 1649; they burned the remainder of their villages and fled. Over the next year starvation probably killed more Huron than had ever fallen to Iroquois arms. The Petun were also forced to flee when their major village fell on December 7, 1649. With the Huron and Petun dispersed, removal of the Neutral would open all of southern Ontario to Iroquois hunters. The Neutral were attacked in the fall of 1650 and by 1652 they, too, were driven from their territory. It is estimated that an Iroquois army of 1,200 destroyed the principal Neutral settlement. Next came an attack on the Erie living to the south of Lake Erie. In 1654 the Erie suffered a major defeat to an invading force of some 1,200 to 1,800 Iroquois (the Onondaga

played a major part in the Erie war). Another nation ceased to exist because of Iroquois aggression.[21]

The Iroquois reached their apex of territorial control about 1675. As western Indians also became well-armed with firearms, they lost portions of newly conquered territory to these peoples. They did maintain a fearsome military reputation and continued to be a powerful military and diplomatic force in all of northeastern North America for another century.

The Iroquois were also caught up in the colonial rivalry between France and England. England and the Iroquois saw themselves tied together by a silver Covenant Chain. Despite the alliance, the Covenant Chain frequently became tarnished (one side had grievances about the actions of the other) and councils had to be held to polish the chain. The Mohawk, closest to the British administrative and trading center of Albany, New York, held most tightly to the Covenant Chain. The Seneca, who found trade with the French at Niagara attractive, were to fight beside the French and their allies against the British.[22]

Religion

THE CALENDRICAL CYCLE OF CEREMONIES

Our fullest documentation on Iroquois religion comes after its revitalization by the message of the prophet, Handsome Lake. Handsome Lake experienced a vision and began preaching his message in 1799; however, Handsome Lake's message was a combination of reform and conservatism, and those who follow his teachings preserve an annual cycle of ceremonies rooted in the year cycle of agriculture and other subsistence activities.

The calendrical ceremonies follow one another through the year (see the listing in Table 2). By far the two most important ceremonies are the Green Corn Ceremony in September and the Midwinter Ceremony in late January or early February. All other ceremonies currently last but a single day; both Green Corn and Midwinter are held over several days—at least four in the former and at least nine in the latter. At these two ceremonies the matrilineages announce the names of those born into the matrilineage over the past six months, as well as the adult names of those who have come of age in the same time period. Also in both these ceremonies the moieties play each other in the bowl game that symbolizes the contest of the Good Mind with his twin brother and grandmother for control of the earth.

While Green Corn cannot be regarded as a "typical" ceremony, an outline of the activities as recorded at the Coldspring Longhouse on the Allegheny (Seneca) Reservation provides an impression of the form of Iroquois ceremonialism. Over the course of the ceremony, one can note the performance of the "Four Sacred Rituals": the Feather Dance, the Thanksgiving Dance, the Personal Chant, and the Bowl Game.

The ceremonies could not begin until children were named. Thus, a preliminary day was necessary before the three formal days of the ceremony. After a general thanksgiving invocation and a Feather Dance, a speaker for each clan named the children born since the Midwinter ceremony (each is prompted by a matron of his clan). A Great Feather Dance was held and the assemblage was served corn soup.

Activities began on the next day (considered the first day of the ceremony) with runners circulating through the community to gather food for the day's festivities. The Feather Dance was performed, followed by the Women's Dance. Women carrying ears of the new corn led the latter. The adult names of maturing children were announced, and one such youth led the Great Feather Dance. The dancers circled counterclockwise in a line around two singers who straddled a bench. The singers struck the bench with large rattles made from snapping turtle shells, to accompany their singing.

Food was again collected for the second day of Green Corn, along with tobacco. The tobacco was burned in a communal thanksgiving rite. (The Iroquois believe burning tobacco is a way to communicate with the Creator.) The men sang their Personal Chants, and the Thanksgiving Dance (or Skin Dance) was performed. The leader of the Thanksgiving Dance carried a miniature bow and arrow, which recalled the encounter of the prophet Handsome Lake with Four Angels, whose speaker also carried a bow and arrows. The sacred activities were held in the morning, and the evening of the second day was devoted to secular, social dancing. Also at this time the moieties wagered on the outcome of the Bowl Game to be played the next day.

The third day of Green Corn featured the Women's Society rite honoring the life supporters—the three sisters of maize, beans, and squash. The Bowl Game was begun, contested between the two moieties. The Bowl Game, which represented the struggle between the Creator and his evil twin brother, and was the final ritual in the Green Corn Ceremony, often continued for several days.

The Bowl Game is one of the Four Sacred Rituals of the Iroquois, but its exact form varies from one community to the next. One form recorded by Morgan on the Tonawanda Reservation involves a contest over one hundred beans (other sources say 102), which serve as counters. Six peach stones are used as dice, being blackened on one side and light on the other. These were placed in a bowl, shaken, and the bowl struck on the ground. All of one color (either light or dark) won five beans; five of one color and one the opposite secured a single bean. All other throws lost and the bowl passed to the opposite moiety. When the hundred beans have been divided by winning throws between the two sides, then each winner takes the beans or bean from his opponent. The game ends when one side has amassed all the beans.[23]

THE MEDICINE SOCIETIES

The calendrical ceremonies focused upon the yearly subsistence cycle and the health of the community. Individual well-being, including mental and physical health, is also a dominant theme in the Iroquois view of their relationship to the world (including supernatural forces). The medicine societies cured illness and drove disease from the community. Medicine societies included the Society of Medicine Men (Shake the Pumpkin), the Little Water Society, the Dark Dance, the Bear Society, the Buffalo Society, the Eagle Society, the Otter Society, the False Face Society, and the Husk Face Society.

Of the medicine societies, most attention has been paid the False Face Society, probably because of their dramatic wooden masks (masks used by earlier generations are found in large numbers in museum collections). The False Faces cured individuals privately, performing with their masks and turtle-shell rattles. They also performed in public, at the Midwinter Ceremony. Each fall and spring they traveled through the community to cleanse it of sickness. Fenton described his encounter with the False Faces in the 1930s: "The company afforded a wild spectacle as they sped up the valley road in open Fords with their hair whipping in the chill winds; they grated their rattles on the car body and uttered their terrifying cries whenever they swerved to pass a stranger."[24]

The secret nature of the Little Water Society contrasts with the public performance of the False Faces. Nonmembers were barred from the ceremonial room, although they might, with permission, listen from an outer room. The rituals lasted from about 11:00 P.M. until dawn, the entire ceremony being conducted in the dark. Three sets of songs were sung and berry juice was served after each set. The songs relate to Good Hunter and the origin of the Little Water Medicine.

Table 2
Calendrical Ceremonies of the Iroquois*

Ceremony	Date
Bush	Within ten days of Midwinter
Maple	Late March / Early April
Sun	April
Thunder	April or in time of drought
Seed	Planting April / Early May
Strawberry	June
Green Bean	Early August
Corn Testing	Late August / Early September
Green Corn	Late August / Early September
Harvest	Late October / Early November
Midwinter	The new moon of midwinter— January or February

*Not all of these ceremonies are held in every community and some hold additional ceremonies not listed here.

Impact of Euro-American Contacts with Iroquoia

TRADE GOODS AND EPIDEMICS

Archaeological evidence reveals the Iroquois and their neighbors were using goods of European manufacture in the sixteenth century, but direct contact with Europeans did not occur until after 1600. From the earliest times, brass kettles and items made of iron and steel were in demand. As early as 1634 some Mohawk longhouses had doors of hewn timber (presumably shaped with steel axes) hung on iron hinges. Some garments were more comfortable when made with European woven textiles instead of native tanned leather. The same designs worked in porcupine quills or moose hair embroidery could be fashioned in glass beads. Even wampum became more abundant after European contact, since it could be manufactured on the Atlantic coast with steel drills. After 1640 firearms were a desired item for waging war; by 1680 they had become a necessity.

A less-welcome import from Europe were diseases. Smallpox killed large numbers of Iroquois, but even diseases such as measles were deadly to Native American populations who, never having experienced them, lacked immunity. Single epidemics were known to kill as much as half a village's population.[25] Adopted war captives replaced some of these losses, and Iroquois diplomacy encouraged refugee populations to settle among them, keeping up Iroquois strength.

An important part of the exchange of ideas that resulted from contact between the New World and the Old was an exchange of knowledge of domesticated plants and animals. Europeans adopted maize, beans, squash, tobacco, and numerous other plants from Mexico and South America. Native American populations were also not shy about adopting domesticates of European origin. Pigs adapted well to North American forests and pork was part of the Iroquois diet by 1675. Over the next century they began to plant cucumbers, onions, and watermelons in their fields and foster orchards of apple and peach trees. Cattle came to be found in Iroquois villages and horses eased the burden of gathering firewood from the forest.

The villages themselves, after 1700, changed from collections of bark-covered longhouses to single-family log cabins. As warfare grew more distant, palisades were abandoned and villages grew smaller, but in easy communication with each other. Smaller villages meant neither the fields nor sources of firewood within walking distance of the houses were exhausted, so the periodic relocation of villages characteristic of earlier times became unnecessary.

Women continued to garden and men to hunt, but men began to take up wage work as early as the mid-1700s—working as porters at the "carrying places" of the trade to the west.

At the outbreak of the American Revolution in 1775 there was considerable diversity among the Iroquois. For the most part the Onondagas, Cayugas, and Senecas had rejected attempts to convert them to Christianity. The Mohawks in the Mohawk Valley were members of The Church of England, taking Communion at Her Majesty's Chapel Among the Mohawks from a silver communion service presented to the Chapel by Queen Anne. Surrounded by non-Indians, Mohawk housing was identical to that of their neighbors. Native fashion dictated dress, but for the most part it was constructed of cottons and woolens purchased from traders. Even feathers used to ornament the hair (among men, shaving the head except for a small "scalp lock" at the crown was still a popular fashion) were sometimes ostrich feathers, imported by European traders from Africa. Many Mohawks were literate, either in Mohawk or English or both. When the Mohawk Chief Joseph Brant journeyed to London in 1776 to bring Mohawk complaints directly to the attention of the British government, he was at ease interacting with the British social and intellectual elite such as James Boswell, the biographer of Samuel Johnson. Brant's portrait was painted by George Romney, painter to Britain's aristocracy.

The more isolated western Iroquois nations, who

were not converts to the Christian faith, also had adopted log cabins for housing. Each community retained a large rectangular building used for council meetings and religious ceremonies. Known in English as longhouses, these structures continue as ceremonial centers in contemporary Iroquois communities practicing the traditional religion.

CONTEMPORARY IROQUOIS COMMUNITIES

Iroquois reservations and reserves are found in both the United States and Canada. While it is not a goal here to provide a detailed history of the Iroquois reserves and reservations, the following will note the location of contemporary communities as well as their origins.

Jesuit missionary activities in the second half of the seventeenth century, principally among the Mohawk, led to the initial movement of Iroquois from their traditional homeland. The French were anxious to remove their converts from proximity to English (and Protestant) influences. These converts settled on the St. Lawrence River and their descendants now occupy the reserves of Kahnawake (also known as Caughnawaga) and Kanesatake (Oka), both outside Montreal, and Akwesasne or St. Regis, which is found near Cornwall, Ontario. Although settled by Roman Catholic converts, these communities have remained so conservative regarding language that Mohawk has far more speakers today than any other northern Iroquoian language. Also, the traditional religion has been reestablished among a portion of the population of these communities. Gibson Reserve, near Georgian Bay in Ontario, was established in the nineteenth century by a faction from Kanesatake.

The remainder of the Iroquois continued to occupy their homeland until the American Revolution although the Seneca had expanded their settlements to the west into lands conquered in the Beaver Wars of the seventeenth century. The Tuscarora, who spoke a northern Iroquoian language but whose home had been the Carolinas, joined their northern cousins after being defeated by English colonists early in the eighteenth century. The Mohawks, like their Loyalist neighbors, were forced to abandon their lands in the Mohawk Valley during the American Revolution. In the American Revolution the Mohawk, Cayuga, and Seneca for the most part fought as allies to the Crown; the Oneida appeared on the side of the rebellious colonials. The peace treaty that settled that war established the boundary between the new United States and Britain's North American colonies north of Iroquoia, through Lake Ontario. Those who had maintained the Covenant Chain that bound them to the British Crown were forced to choose between migration to Canada or dealing with their recent enemies, the Americans. The Mohawk opted for the former. Some, under John Deseronto, settled on Lake Ontario's Bay of Quinté, founding the Tyendinaga Reserve. Others, led by Joseph Brant and accompanied by most of the Cayuga and portions of the other Iroquois nations, settled on the Grand River on lands that have become the Six Nations Reserve. The Six Nations Reserve in Ontario has four longhouses; other Iroquois communities with longhouses include Allegheny, Cattaraugus, Tonawanda, Onondaga, Oneida on the Thames (Ontario), Kahnawake, Akwesasne, and Kanesatake.[26]

Others were able to establish themselves on reservations in upstate New York. Those Onondaga who did not migrate to Canada remain in their ancestral home outside Syracuse, New York. The Seneca negotiated a complex series of land transactions but remain on three reservations, Allegheny, Cattaraugus, and Tonawanda, in western New York. The Tuscarora Reservation is near Lewiston, New York.

The Oneida attempted to remain in their ancestral lands, but pressures forced most to move, some to Wisconsin (near Green Bay) and others to Canada (near London, Ontario) in the 1830s.

Finally, there is in Oklahoma a settlement of Cayuga/Seneca who removed there from the Ohio country early in the nineteenth century.[27]

HANDSOME LAKE, THE PROPHET

Because of his role in bringing peace (and land cessions to the newly independent American States) following the American Revolution, Cornplanter, a Seneca chief, was given a personal grant of land by the state of Pennsylvania on the Allegheny River near its border with New York. A large number of kinsmen and followers lived there in a settlement known as Burnt House. There Handsome Lake, Cornplanter's half-brother and a Confederacy Council chief, experienced a vision and began to preach a doctrine of religious and social reform. Vices introduced by the Whites, especially alcohol, were to be shunned. Leaders who sold lands were subject to punishment in an afterlife. Aspects of traditional life were also subject to criticism by the prophet. The importance of the matrilineage (with frequent divorce) was subordinated to the importance of the nuclear family and marital stability. In religion the practices of the yearly ceremonial cycle and the Four Sacred Ceremonies were encouraged by Handsome Lake. He also attempted to suppress the medicine societies, but here he failed because of their crucial importance in maintaining physical and emotional well-being.

A quarrel with Cornplanter led Handsome Lake to leave Burnt House in 1803. He and his followers moved upriver to Coldspring on the Allegheny Reservation. Factional strife led Handsome Lake to move to another Seneca community, the Tonawanda Reservation. He was visiting the Onondaga Reservation, near Syracuse, New York, in 1815 when he died. His influence grew after his death and his teachings continue to be recited regularly at meetings in longhouses on reserves and reservations in Canada and the United States.

CHRISTIAN MISSIONARIES AND SCHOOLS

Mission activity converted many Iroquois to Christianity. Jesuits took Roman Catholic converts north with them in the late seventeenth century while the Church of England converted the remaining Mohawk over the next century. Samuel Kirland, a New England Protestant, was successful among the Oneida. Segments of other communities converted to Christianity in the reservation and reserve period.

Protestant missionaries had worked in earnest among the Iroquois since early in the nineteenth century. They met considerable resistance. The crusty Seneca orator Red Jacket voiced his opinion of the missions in the early 1800s. He argued that the missionaries' own people, not the Seneca, needed Christianity.

> Go, then, and teach the whites. Select, for example, the people of Buffalo. We will be spectators, and remain silent. Improve their morals and refine their habits—make them less disposed to cheat Indians. . . . Let us know the tree by the blossoms, and the blossoms by the fruit. When this shall be made clear to our minds we may be more willing to listen to you. But until then we must be allowed to follow the religion of our ancestors.[28]

Despite this opposition, the Protestant (Presbyterian, Methodist, and Baptist, for the most part) missions converted an increasing proportion of the Iroquois population through the years. Membership in a Christian church does not, however, prevent many Iroquois from attending traditional ceremonies in the longhouse or even participating in rites of the medicine societies.

Both missions and other agencies focused considerable energy on schools. Efforts were made to teach both spoken and written English, but "civilized" behavior was also emphasized. That is, the schools attempted to force their charges to learn the work ethic and gender roles espoused by American and Canadian society. Initially a few individuals achieved remarkable success. By 1850, for example, a Seneca, Maris B. Pierce, had graduated from Dartmouth, another Seneca, Ely S. Parker, was pursuing engineering, while the Cayuga Dr. Peter Wilson practiced medicine. A larger and larger portion of Iroquois communities were able to speak and write English; a majority of adults could do so by 1900. This success of school, though, led to a decline in the use of Iroquois languages, and since 1900 an ever-increasing portion of Iroquois speak and understand only English.

POLITICS, LAND, AND GAMBLING

When Joseph Brant and his followers moved to the Grand River in Canada after the American Revolution, they rekindled the council fire of the Confederacy there. They attempted to establish a Confederacy Council and in some cases, when a matrilineage that held a title on the Council was not represented, another matrilineage assumed the right to fill the position. Similarly, among those Iroquois remaining in New York, titles held by matrilineages that had emigrated were claimed by others who had remained behind. This meant the same title would be held by two individuals in different communities.

In many communities, both outside and internal pressures called for the replacement of the traditional matrilineal chiefs by a council elected by the community as a whole. In some places where this has happened, a faction continues to argue that traditional chiefs are the only legitimate government for the reserve or reservation. The politics of each Iroquois community is a complex issue which defies generalization, so only two examples will be mentioned. In 1848 a portion of the Seneca on the Allegheny and Cattaraugus Reservations in New York staged a "revolution" to remove the chiefs form of government and institute an elected President and Council. Only males were allowed to vote, but a vestige of female power was retained as land could not be sold (land sales by the traditional chiefs were a factor in the hostility against them) without the approval of two-thirds of "the mothers of the nation." For some time a number of chiefs and their supporters fought this move, but eventually the elective council was widely accepted. The Seneca titles on the Confederacy Council, which had been held at Allegheny and Cattaraugus, passed to lineages on the third New York State Seneca reservation, Tonawanda, where the chiefs form of government continues. In Canada, on the Six Nations Reserve, the Confederacy Council governed the community for over a century. They were ousted in 1924 by the Royal Canadian Mounted Police at the request of a faction on the reserve known as "dehorners" (because they desired to remove the antlers of office from the chiefs). A large segment of the reserve did not support this move and the conflict between supporters of the two forms of government continues generations after the institution of the elected council.[29] Loss of lands has been a perpetual concern of the Iroquois.

This loss continues. In recent years reserve and reservation lands have been taken for major projects such as the St. Lawrence Seaway, hydro-electric development on the Niagara River, and the Allegheny River Reservoir. Other "developments"—highways, power lines, bridges, and so on—have reduced the land base of Iroquois communities.

On the other hand, there has always been for many Iroquois groups agitation for the settlement of land claims. There are claims for lands taken without treaties or by treaties whose legitimacy is clouded. Some communities had pursued such claims for more than 150 years. Militant actions taken to push such claims have resulted in violence, as at Ganienkeh in northern New York in the 1970s and at Kanesatake outside Montreal in 1990.

Gambling has proven to be a divisive issue in several Iroquois communities. Many Indian reservations in the United States have established, with federal blessings, bingo operations on their lands. Large profits can be made by groups, such as the Oneida of Wisconsin, who develop them. Some Iroquois maintain that they remain sovereign peoples and that Canadian or American law does not apply within the boundaries of their reserves or reservations. Hence they argue that gambling operations more extensive than those allowed by federal, state, or provincial laws can be mounted in their communities. Others, many of them equally militant on issues of local sovereignty, oppose gambling casinos on moral or social grounds. Clashes between these groups have been violent, especially at Akwesasne, where conflict has led to arson and even killings.[30]

Conclusion

The Iroquois have had an impact on North American history far beyond what one might expect from their numbers. The metaphors of the Tree of Peace, the War Kettle, and the Covenant Chain were heard from beside council fires in western New York to the halls of government in Europe.

The Iroquois have also made their presence felt as Euro-American scholarship became aware of other cultural traditions. Beginning with the pioneering efforts of Joseph-François Lafiteau and Lewis Henry Morgan, the Iroquois have attracted continuous attention from scholars, both anthropologists and historians. The notes and bibliography for this essay are only a pale reflection of the quantity and quality of scholarly examination of Iroquois culture and history; many scholarly works, both readable and of high quality, have gone unmentioned.

Much of that scholarship, of course, has been dependent upon the vitality of the Iroquois themselves. Vast differences do exist between and within Iroquois communities with respect to acculturation to non-Indian ways. However, all manifest the cultural and social pride, even arrogance, that the Iroquois have exhibited since Deganawida, Hiawatha, and Thadodaho first sat in the shade of the Tree of Peace.

Notes

1. Joseph François Lafiteau, *Customs of the American Indians Compared with the Customs of Primitive Times*, ed. and trans. William N. Fenton and Elizabeth Moore (Toronto: The Champlain Society, 1974–1977), originally published as *Moeurs des sauvages amériquains . . .* (1724); Cadwallader Colden, *The History of the Five Indian Nations of Canada, Which Are Dependent on the Province of New York in America* (London: T. Osborne, 1774), 2 vols., first volume originally published in 1727. (Colden has been reprinted several times since the original publication.)

2. Lewis Henry Morgan, *League of the Ho-de-no-sau-nee,* [or] *Iroquois* (Rochester: Sage). This paper presents a synthesis that relies heavily on Morgan and on other works listed in the recommended readings found below. In the interests of space limitations, footnoting is less extensive than usual.

3. Both metaphors appear frequently in the historic literature. For the Tree of Peace, see the Deganawida legend paraphrased by Paul A. Wallace, *The White Roots of Peace* (Philadelphia: University of Pennsylvania Press, 1946). For speeches referring to the War Kettle, see Ruben G. Thwaites, ed., *The Jesuit Relations and Allied Documents* (Cleveland: Burrows Brothers, 1896–1901) vol. 27, p. 229, vol. 40, p. 169, vol. 41, p. 53. See also William N. Fenton, "Northern Iroquoian Culture Patterns," in Bruce G. Trigger, vol. ed., William C. Sturtevant, gen. ed., *Handbook of North American Indians, vol. 15 Northeast* (Washington, D.C.: Smithsonian Institution, 1978), p. 303.

4. Arthur C. Parker, "Iroquois Uses of Maize and Other Food Plants," *New York State Museum Bulletin* 144 (1910): 5–113; Frederick W. Waugh, "Iroquis [sic] Foods and Food Preparation," *Memoirs of the Geological Survey of Canada* 86 (1916). On the importance of women in agriculture and elsewhere, see Judith Brown, "Economic Organization and the Position of Women among the Iroquois," *Ethnohistory* 17 (1970): 151–167.

5. Thomas S. Abler, "Longhouse and Palisade: Northeastern Iroquoian Villages of the Seventeenth Century," *Ontario History* 62 (1970): 17–40.

6. Thomas S. Abler, "Moiety Exogamy and the Seneca: Evidence from Buffalo Creek," *Anthropological Quarterly* 44 (1971): 211–222.

7. Fenton, "Northern Iroquoian Culture Patterns," p. 310.

8. See Elisabeth Tooker, "The League of the Iroquois: Its History, Politics, and Ritual," in Bruce G. Trigger, vol. ed., William C. Sturtevant, gen. ed., *Handbook of North American Indians, vol. 15 Northeast* (Washington, D.C.: Smithsonian Institution, 1978), pp. 440–441, for a guide to published variants of the tradition of the establishing of the confederacy. More recently the tale has been published in Hanni Woodbury, ed. and trans., *The Iroquois League Tradition as Dictated in Onondaga by John Arthur Gibson* (Winnipeg: Algonquian and Iroquoian Linguistics, University of Manitoba, 1992).

9. William N. Fenton, "The Roll Call of the Iroquois Chiefs: A Study of a Mnemonic Cane from the Six Nations Reserve," *Smithsonian Miscellaneous Collections*, vol. 111, no. 15 (1950).

10. Fenton, "The Roll Call of Iroquois Chiefs," pp. 59–67; Shimony, "Conservatism among the Iroquois at the Six Nations Reserve," *Yale University Publications in Anthropology* 65 (1961): 58.

11. Tooker, "The League of the Iroquois," pp. 428–429; Fenton, "Northern Iroquoian Culture Patterns," pp. 310–311.

12. Morgan, *League*, p. 77.

13. William N. Fenton, "Locality as a Basic Factor in the Development of Iroquois Social Structure," *Bureau of American Ethnology Bulletin* 149 (1951): 52.

14. Allen W. Trelease, *Indian Affairs in Colonial New York: The Seventeenth Century* (Ithaca, NY: Cornell University Press, 1960), p. 22.

15. Morgan, *League*, p. 108.

16. Mourning War was applied to Iroquois militarism by Daniel K. Richter, "War and Culture: The Iroquois Experience," *William and Mary Quarterly, 3rd Series*, 40 (1983): 529; he derived the term from Marian W. Smith, "American Indian Warfare," *Transactions of the New York Academy of Sciences* 13 (1951): 348–365.

17. Fenton, "Northern Iroquoian Culture Patterns," p. 311.

18. Lafiteau, *Customs of the American Indians*, vol. 2, p. 99.

19. Ibid., vol. 2, p. 154.

20. Richard Gramly, "Dearskins [sic] and Hunting Territories: Competition for Scarce Resources in the Northeastern Woodlands," *American Antiquity* 42 (1977): 601–605.

21. See George T. Hunt, *Wars of the Iroquois: A Study of Intertribal Trade Relations* (Madison, WI: University of Wisconsin Press, 1940); Trelease, *Indian Affairs in Colonial New York*; Thomas S. Abler, "Beavers and Muskets: Iroquois Military Fortunes in the Face of European Colonization," in R. Brian Ferguson and Neil L. Whitehead, eds., *War in the Tribal Zone: Expanding States and Indigenous Warfare* (Santa Fe, NM: School of American Research Press, 1992), pp. 151–174.

22. Abler, "Beavers and Muskets"; Daniel K. Richter, *The Ordeal of the Longhouse: The Peoples of the Iroquois League in the Era of European Expansion* (Chapel Hill, NC: University of North Carolina Press, 1992).

23. For material on Handsome Lake, see Anthony F. C. Wallace, *Death and Rebirth of the Seneca* (New York: Knopf, 1969). For material on Iroquois ceremonialism see Morgan, *League*, pp. 182–225; William N. Fenton, "Tonawanda Longhouse Ceremonies: Ninety Years after Lewis Henry Morgan," *Bureau of American Ethnology Bulletin* 128 (1941): 139–166; Elisabeth Tooker, *The Iroquois Ceremonial of Midwinter* (Syracuse, NY: Syracuse University Press, 1970); Shimony, "Conservatism among the Iroquois at the Six Nations Reserve," pp. 140–191; and William N. Fenton, "The Seneca Green Corn Ceremony," *The New York Conservationist* 18 (October–November, 1963): 20–22, 27–28.

24. William N. Fenton, "Masked Medicine Societies of the Iroquois," *Annual Report of the Smithsonian Institution for 1940* (1941): 425; see also William N. Fenton, *The False Faces of the Iroquois* (Norman, OK: University of Oklahoma Press, 1987).

25. Dean R. Snow and Kim Lanphear, "European Contact and Indian Depopulation," *Ethnohistory* 35 (1988): 15–33.

26. Wallace, *Death and Rebirth*.

27. See the chapters on Iroquois nations and the Six Nations Reserve in Bruce G. Trigger, vol. ed., William C. Sturtevant, gen. ed., *Handbook of North American Indians, vol. 15 Northeast* (Washington, D.C.: Smithsonian Institution, 1978), pp. 466–536.

28. William L. Stone, *The Life and Times of Sa-go-ye-wat-ha, or Red Jacket* (Albany: Munsell, 1866), p. 291.

29. In addition to sources in the recommended readings, see Ralph W. Nicholas, "Factions: A Comparative Analysis," in Michael Banton, ed., *Political Systems and the Distribution of Power*, A.S.A. Monograph 2 (London: Tavistock, 1965), pp. 21–61.

30. See Lawrence Hauptman, *The Iroquois Struggle for Survival: World War II to Red Power* (Syracuse, NY: Syracuse University Press, 1986); Gail H. Landsman, *Sovereignty and Symbol: Indian-White Conflict at Ganienkeh* (Albuquerque, NM: University of New

Mexico Press, 1988); and Pierre Lepage, "Chronologie: La genèse d'un conflit à Oka-Kanesatake" *Recherches amérindiennes au Québec* 21 (1991): 99–110.

Suggested Readings

Fenton, William N. *The False Faces of the Iroquois*. Norman, OK: University of Oklahoma Press, 1987.

———. "The Roll Call of the Iroquois Chiefs: A Study of a Mnemonic Cane from the Six Nations Reserve." *Smithsonian Miscellaneous Collections*, vol. 111, no. 15 (1950). William Fenton has studied Iroquois culture and history for well over half a century. He is both a superb ethnographer and an excellent ethnohistorian. Among scholars his appreciation of Iroquois culture is unequalled. Although only two of his works are listed here, anyone with a serious interest in the Iroquois should consult his long list of publications.

Morgan, Lewis Henry. *League of the Ho-dé-no-sau-nee*, [or] *Iroquois*. Rochester, NY: Sage, 1851. This is still the best single book on Iroquois culture, although it is not without error with respect to Iroquois history (Morgan was not a good historian). It is also based almost entirely on research among the Seneca, so it is less accurate in description of the other nations of Confederacy.

Parker, Arthur C. *Parker on the Iroquois*. ed. William N. Fenton. Syracuse, NY: Syracuse University Press, 1968. Reprinted here are Parker's monographs: "Iroquois Uses of Maize and other Food Plants," "The Code of Handsome Lake, the Seneca Prophet," and "The Constitution of the Five Nations."

Shimony, Annemarie A. "Conservatism among the Iroquois at the Six Nations Reserve." *Yale University Publications in Anthropology* 65 (1961). Based on fieldwork conducted in the 1950s, Shimony's work is a thorough discussion of those Iroquois practicing the traditional religion on this large Canadian reserve.

Trigger, Bruce G., vol. ed., and William C. Sturtevant, gen. ed. *Handbook of North American Indians, vol. 15 Northeast*. Washington, D.C.: Smithsonian Institution, 1978. This volume contains numerous chapters on Iroquois culture, history, and prehistory. Especially noteworthy are "Northern Iroquoian Culture Patterns" by William N. Fenton (pp. 296–321) and "The League of the Iroquois: Its History, Politics, and Ritual"by Elisabeth Tooker (pp. 418–441).

Wallace, Anthony F. C. *Death and Rebirth of the Seneca*. New York: Knopf, 1969. The story of the prophet Handsome Lake and the impact of his message are detailed here.

Wilson, Edmund. *Apologies to the Iroquois*. New York: Farrar, Straus, and Cudahy, 1960.

Morocco: Adolescents in a Small Town[1]

Susan Schaefer Davis

She should marry him. . . . She's the one who knows him better. She went out with him so she understands him; they know about life. Parents don't know what's going on between them. Parents don't understand those things, they only know the old way of doing things. But we know the modern way of life.

Do readers expect Moroccan adolescent girls to talk like this seventeen-year-old? Or does "Morocco" call forth exotic images of palm oases in the Sahara, the Foreign Legion, and silent women in veils, or perhaps Bogart and Bergman in Rick's Cafe in wartime Casablanca?

Adolescents in Morocco in the mid-1980s resembled their American counterparts in some ways, and were quite different in others. I will illustrate this by describing Moroccan behavior and ideas on issues that are important to both groups. These issues include conflict with parents and degree of autonomy, and male/female differences in work, freedom, and relationships with each other. Young women's control of their own lives and how adolescents become adults are also important aspects of adolescence in Morocco.

Setting the Scene

Morocco is located on the northwest corner of Africa, a short trip across the Straits of Gibraltar from Spain. In climate and size, Morocco resembles California; there are chilly, wet winters and hot, dry summers. Beaches on the Mediterranean and Atlantic coasts give way to plains and mountain ranges, and finally desert in the far south. The population is Arab and Berber and almost completely Muslim.

These adolescents live in the small Arab town of Zawiya, located at the edge of an agricultural plain in the north central part of the country, about thirty miles from the city of Meknes. Living in a small town has important effects on the lives of these adolescents; they have somewhat less exposure to modern lifestyles and conveniences than city-dwellers but more than their cousins in isolated rural villages.[2] While no one of these three groups is typical, many Moroccans today live in small and medium-sized towns. Zawiya teens can walk two miles to the larger town of Kabar or take the train or bus to visit relatives in Rabat or Casablanca. They watch the government television station seen nationwide, and a few have cable TV. There are a primary school and junior high in town, and a mayor's office, post office, and police station, but no banks, hospitals, high schools, or restaurants. One can buy fruit, vegetables, and meat in several shops, and staples like oil, tea, and sugar, but most clothing and appliances are purchased in the larger town or at the weekly outdoor market. Zawiya has grown rapidly, from about five thousand in 1970 to twelve thousand in the mid-1980s. Many families moved into town from nearby rural areas, and that background reinforces traditional values.

Morocco is a constitutional monarchy led by Hassan II, a king with real power, whose father took over when the French left Morocco in 1956. He is assisted by a cabinet which he appoints and a popularly elected parliament. Local officials include an appointed mayor and an elected town council. Government employees staff many offices and the schools, and offer a model of white-collar jobs to which many adolescents aspire. Parents, on the other hand, work mostly in blue-collar service jobs, often related to agriculture, and many grandparents were farmers. The Moroccan economy is based in agriculture, with citrus fruits and cereals the main crops. Both oranges and wheat, as well as olives and vegetables, are grown near Zawiya. However, large landowners now control nearby farms and use mechanized equipment, and few local people work directly in agriculture; those who do are mostly day laborers. Some drive trucks to transport crops, some sell produce locally, and others work in jobs like construction or painting.

Zawiya families describe each other as well-off, average, or poor. The first group has members in a profession like law (who usually live in a larger city), the second white-collar workers, merchants, or others with a regular income, and the third has members who do manual work or who cannot find jobs. While incomes vary, Zawiya lifestyles are quite similar. Most residents live in concrete houses on unpaved streets, and until 1988 had no running water and had to carry their supply from seven outdoor taps. Yet nearly all households have electricity, and the majority have television. Thus while social classes do exist, and there is variation in total wealth, actual lifestyles do not vary as widely as they do in urban settings.

Most families in Zawiya consist of parents and children,[3] often with a grandparent or cousin added. While typical Arab families are thought to be extended, with grandparents, parents, and children all in one household, we found this rare in Zawiya. When it occurred, it was usually at the start of a marriage, while a couple saved money for their own home. Another Arab custom, cousin marriage, was also rare in Zawiya, where the majority of marriages were not to relatives, even in the parental generation.

Marriages arranged by parents are still the norm, although young people are having more input. The quotation I began with illustrates this tension; I had asked what a couple should do if parents opposed their marriage. In the past, a boy's parents looked for a wife for their son, and his mother would visit her family to observe their behavior and see the girl. She would report back to the son, the families would inquire about each other, and if all was satisfactory the marriage took place. The goal was a partnership between two economically similar and compatible families; romance between the bride and groom, who frequently did not know each other, was not a factor, although a strong bond often developed. There were also alternatives for dissatisfied young women: they could run away from a marriage that they opposed[4] or go back to their family if the relationship was intolerable. Today, marriages are still arranged by parents, but a young man may ask his mother to approach a certain girl's parents. Girls' families cannot initiate the process, but girls are asked whether they accept or not, and the girl often knows the boy (though she may not admit it). Dating is not accepted in Zawiya, which makes getting acquainted challenging, but young people do manage.

Zawiya's adolescents and their families live in a rapidly changing world. Grandparents farmed the land; their children may work in France, and Morocco is part of the world economy. Grandparents rarely saw a car; adolescents take trains to the capital. There used to be no electricity; now all watch television, which shows snow in Europe, something grandparents had only heard about, and *Dallas*, and men on the moon. Rural families lived in extended family groups: now each family lives alone, so most young women do not have to serve an exacting mother-in-law in residence. Only a few parents attended school;[5] most adolescents attended primary school and many go on. Boys and girls study together, and this, plus the walk to high school in town, gives young people a chance to get acquainted in ways that were less common in the past. Education also opens up white-collar jobs for both sexes, and in cities one sees office plaques for women doctors, dentists, and lawyers, something rare until the 1980s.

Margaret Mead thought rapid change between generations was one basis for the adolescent rebellion and conflict between the generations common in the United States. She did not find conflict in relatively unchanged Samoa, where parental knowledge and skills were still relevant for their children.[6] By Mead's standards, the rapid change in Zawiya should lead to intergenerational conflict. I will examine this below.

Data Collection

When I read an ethnography, knowing who collected the data and how helps me evaluate the results. Further, anthropologists (and others) now recognize the fact that there is no one "objective truth"; results are inevitably colored by the researcher and the methodology. A simple example is that my husband and I could not have gained the great cooperation we did with our research in Zawiya if I had not first been in the Peace Corps there and become an accepted part of the community. Later I did my Ph.D. research on women's roles in Zawiya.[7] People knew and trusted us from before, so they agreed to take part in our study of adolescence, answering personal questions and welcoming us into their homes.

Our study of Zawiya was part of the Harvard Adolescence Project, in which researchers collected comparable data in seven cultures.[8] We collected anthropological, sociological, and psychological data on about one hundred Zawiya adolescents and their families. The data included participant observation of adolescents and their families; this was facilitated by our living in a house in the neighborhood we studied. Because I first went to Zawiya in 1965 and had maintained contact since then, by 1982 my husband and I were seen almost as aunt and uncle to several local families. Our daughter was five in 1982, and having a child made us "normal," while setting up a preschool for her in our home put us into more contact with local families.

We first visited families and explained the study, asking their cooperation. We included young people from nine to twenty-one, and weighed, measured, and filled out a sociological questionnaire plus a school and family history for each of over one hundred young people. We gave psychological tests of cognitive development[9] and gender identity to about sixty, and did open-ended interviews on a group of about twenty with whom we had especially good rapport. Three-quarters of the interviews were with females, because I did most of them and had better rapport with girls. I returned in 1984 and updated these interviews, using a tape recorder in a private setting, and most of the material quoted below comes from these interviews. I asked young people what was important to them recently, what they hoped for in the future, how they had changed in the last two years, about their relationships and conflicts with parents, and about a personal dilemma and an imaginary one concerning marriage. My more general statements are based in observations of and interactions with families, and from conversations over a period of twenty years.

Adolescent Life

On the surface, adolescent life in Zawiya appears more tranquil than that in the United States. There are few angry exchanges with parents, and no slammed doors or "grounded" teens. If they are students, both boys and girls work hard; they see education as the path to a white-collar job with a good income.[10] For those of primary school age (under fifteen) in Zawiya, sixty-three percent of girls and eighty-two percent of boys attended school (and ninety-two percent had at one time); twenty-three percent of girls and forty-eight percent of boys were in high school. There is a large drop-off in attendance after primary school, partly because many fail the difficult final exam and also because older children can often help their families by working. The lower attendance of girls is mainly because they help their mothers at home; boys do not. Girls who are students bear a double burden, of housework and homework, unless they have an older sister who's already left school and helps at home. By sixteen, most Zawiya girls have the necessary skills to

run a household, including baking bread, cooking, washing by hand, cleaning, and child-care; in this way they are ahead of most of their American counterparts and often their city cousins.

In their leisure time, Zawiya teens watch television, including Egyptian, French, and American nighttime shows (including *Dallas*, *Little House on the Prairie*, and *The Incredible Hulk*) and Japanese and Disney cartoons in Arabic or French, and listen to cassettes of Arabic songs, Berber dancing, and Western reggae, rock, and country music. Boys and girls may study together at home, girls may go to a girlfriend's house to visit or embroider, and boys may play soccer or go to a movie in town. Walking to the high school in town and running errands or collecting water in Zawiya give boys and girls a chance to meet and talk. In general, girls stay closer to home and boys go further afield.

Adolescents and Conflict

We observed adolescents with their families and asked the interview group about conflicts with their parents, usually mothers, as well as their relationship in general. Most young people said their relationships were "good," although one boy and two girls said "so-so." I should explain that it is improper to discuss family problems with outsiders in Morocco, so that in general one wouldn't expect to hear a lot about conflicts. Yet the behavior we observed in families we knew well, the general relations between parents and teens, and the examples of conflict teens gave all support the idea that overt conflict is not common nor severe.

One thing that struck us immediately was the difference in American and Moroccan reactions when we said we were going to study adolescents: they reflected cultural expectations. Most Americans winced or groaned and said they didn't envy us, dealing with that age group. There was no such reaction in Zawiya, and only a few upper-class urban Moroccans responded that way.

I learned about ideal and problematic relations with parents when I asked what were the best and worst things that could happen between a teen and his or her parents. I made the question hypothetical so teens didn't feel they had to describe themselves. The best thing was usually to obey one's parents, and sometimes to give them money or gifts and take care of them. The worst was to disobey them, or to be seen speaking intensely to someone of the opposite sex, which would greatly upset parents and ruin their trust in you.

A few examples of conflicts give a clearer picture. I asked Majda, who was nineteen years old and had a primary education, about her relationship with her mother, and whether it had changed recently.[11]

> Our relations are good. We talk about my craft [embroidery]; I like talking about it. We talk about her family, my mother's family. We're on good terms, very good terms.

S. Has your relationship changed since you've gotten older?

> Well, since my brothers have been around there's some hassle. We keep squabbling, and one hits the other and so on. Sometimes my mother wants me to grab my brother and spank him. . . . He refuses to do his homework; he goes out or does something nasty. He gets her angry, so she tells me to hit him, and she curses: "May God do this to you, may God do that to you." She keeps on insulting me, but I really don't pay any attention to her, because it's him [the brother] who gets on her nerves.

In another family I observed a shouted argument between a girl of sixteen and her pregnant mother. The mother asked Fatiha to run down the street and buy some mint for tea, and Fatiha refused, saying she was tired and that her mother should go. After each giving the other several reasons why that one should go, the mother went. The interaction displayed a level of open disrespect for parents that was rare, but soon afterward the two were chatting in a friendly way; there appeared to be no aftermath.

Three young women told me that their relationship with their mothers was so good that in fact it was like she was not their mother; such relations seemed particularly relaxed. Aisha, an eighteen-year-old secondary student, said

> It is as if she were not my mother. That is, I am not inhibited by her or anything like that. She is like my sister or my friend. I tell her things. For example, I tell her what a guy says to me when I am on my way back [from school], and we laugh. . . . When I was still young, I used to be inhibited by her; I couldn't tell her a joke, for example. I couldn't tell her dirty jokes . . . now I can tell her. . . . About two years ago or so, we started talking about everything and laughing. . . . It's because I've grown up, and inhibition flew away.

Fatiha, who fought with her mother about fetching the mint, was a sixteen-year-old who had dropped out after primary school. She was one of the three teens who said they had "so-so" relationships with their mothers.

> Sometimes, when my mother insults me or hits me or does anything to me, I get upset really fast, and if I could find a knife I would stab myself or do something. . . . I cannot answer her back or raise my hand to her or anything. I just offer myself to her. I also feel like jumping off a cliff. . . . I cannot answer her back. Even if she beats me up, I don't cry; I hold back my tears, even if I feel pain. . . . I just keep quiet until I am by myself in a solitary place, and then I cry.

When I asked Fatiha what would be a bad thing to happen between a mother and daughter, she gave me a personal example that may sound familiar to Americans.

> For example, I tell my mother to dress up more. You know Mrs. S. [a neighbor]: she fixes her hair, changes clothes often and all the rest. But my mother looks older than Mrs. S., even though Mrs. S. is older. Mrs. S. is older than my grandmother, and my mother looks older than Mrs. S. My mother does not take good care of herself. Even though I tell her to fix her hair and change clothes, she doesn't want to; I don't know why. As for Mrs. S., you could take her for a girl.

Fatiha's mother's account makes the story even more familiar, when she complains that Fatiha wants to buy several new outfits monthly, and when the mother claims it's her turn "She always wants fancy clothes. She wants to dress well, but her parents do not matter."

Finally, when I asked Fatiha what nice thing could happen between her and her mother, she said "Nothing nice ever happens between us."

This last example should not overshadow the generally good relationships between young people and their parents. We did not see high levels of confrontation or tension between the generations. Yet Margaret Mead's work would lead us to expect many disagreements because rapid social change makes the knowledge and experience of parents often irrelevant to teens. They need to know how to study in school and get around on trips to the city, while their parents know when to plant wheat and how to churn buttermilk.

Several aspects of traditional Moroccan culture work to limit conflicts with parents. One is the respect for age that still predominates. Even very urban Moroccans are shocked at the idea of older relatives living apart in a "home," as they hear happens in America. Thus it is disrespectful to question or disagree with your parents because of their ages, and in addition, they deserve respect for raising you. Another factor is the greater importance of the family group in Morocco, as opposed to the importance of the individual and their autonomy in American culture. Moroccan teens often work toward goals that will benefit the whole family, such as completing their education so they can help financially, so there is not a family–individual conflict. Of course this is not always true; look at Fatiha and her mother competing for clothing. Yet there is usually agreement on family goals.

Additionally, parents and teens do not take passing conflicts too seriously, so there are few lasting hard feelings. And finally, when adolescents suspect their parents will disagree with something which does not seem too serious, they may just go ahead and do it. As Mohammed, a young man of eighteen who works in a trade said of his mother, "We always agree. Even if she says something I don't really agree with, I always tell her that what she says is right. Even if something isn't there and she tells me so, I tell her it's there. . . . For example, when I tell her I want to go somewhere, and she tells me not to go, I say O.K." This is related to respect, in not opposing parental views, and to less desire to prove one is autonomous and can do as one wishes.

Sex Differences

One of the most important determinants of an adolescent's life in Zawiya is whether they are female or male. The sexes do different kinds and amounts of work, have different degrees of freedom, and have different expectations and experiences in relationships with each other.

WORK AND FREEDOM

We wondered how adolescents felt about their lives, and one question which provided some answers was "Did you ever wish you had been born a boy (or girl—the opposite sex)?" The three males and about half of the eleven females we asked wished they had been born males, suggesting a preference for the male role.

Differences in workload and freedom were important factors in preferring the male role. Hayat is sixteen and has dropped out after finishing primary school. She says she prefers to be a girl, but her reasons lead her to see advantages for boys too.

In my opinion, it's better for me to be a girl. . . . Boys aren't good workers. They don't do housework, or anything else. He comes in and orders you to get him lunch. You get him lunch, then he asks "Are my clothes washed?" You get him his clothes. It's like he runs you. This is why it's better to be a boy. . . . [My brother] does nothing to help us. . . . He does nothing besides coming home to eat and grabbing his stuff to go to school. However, for a mother a daughter is far better. . . . She arranges things in the house for her. She helps her and gives her a hand. . . . But this is not the case for the boy. . . . A boy is free and responsible for his actions. He can go out at night, have fun with boys and bum around. Even if the girl is better than the boy, she doesn't enjoy complete freedom as does the boy. . . . If I'm late, [my mother] says "Why are you late? Why did you go to fetch water?" And she keeps yelling and asking for an explanation . . . even if it's just a little after sunset.

Boys often stay in school longer than girls, because they are expected to get jobs to support their own families and help out their parents. Most girls are expected to marry, and not to need much beyond primary education (though this is changing). Being in school usually means less housework, even for girls, and it provides much freedom of movement.

RELATIONSHIPS

Most marriages in Zawiya are still arranged by parents, and dating is seen as taboo, yet male-female relationships are one of the major concerns of Zawiya teens over the age of fifteen. The reader may find this strange, expecting a Muslim society to segregate the sexes and veil females, thus preventing contacts. While ideally there is very limited contact between unrelated people of the opposite sex (though buying vegetables is fine), this is far from reality. Boys and girls attend school together, girls are freer to run errands than their mothers were, and the town is larger so one is watched somewhat less closely. No adolescent girls wore veils (as some of their mothers did); as a friend said, their interest in veiling would match American girls' in wearing girdles.[12] In these changed conditions, there are few rules to follow; this may be one reason for so much focus on relationships. Boys and girls do get together, and activities range from joking and talking to kissing, and sometimes to petting and intercourse, though girls are very concerned with preserving their virginity. Yet none of this is acceptable, so that any contact between the sexes has a sexual implication: even talking is seen as leading to an intimate relationship.

At fourteen and just out of primary school, Farida is young to be interested in boys. Yet when I asked her "What's important to you these days? . . . . I want to know what you have on your mind, what preoccupies you most," her response was clear.

What interests us[13] is to see how girls meet boys, so that we learn too. We do want to start getting together with boys. However, if we do it now, we won't know what to do. . . . I want to learn to hold a discussion, how to become shrewd. . . . [My friend] watches girls from her own family and I from my family, and we teach each other.

Farida says she'll just watch, not ask questions, because her sister would be upset and say she was too young to have such ideas, which illustrates the social taboo, especially for girls. Boys too are interested: a young man of eighteen said a major topic of conversation with his best friend was girls they liked.

Amina was a young woman in her late twenties, whose age (and some degree of self-interest, though she was considered a good, respectable young woman) had given her a perspective on how things have changed in Zawiya in just one generation. I mentioned that parents would probably think it shameful if their daughter spoke to a boy.

Why is it shameful? Are her parents the ones who are going to do it? She *should* talk to him. In the first place, how would they know about it? They won't. . . . If she wants to talk to him, she'll just go to the well to bring water; are they going to follow her there? If she goes to the store and talks to him, are they going to accompany her? . . . . Just talking and fooling around is well-known in adolescence. There is nothing serious in that, nothing. . . . Listen, Susan, there is absolutely no girl on earth who would reach the age of thirty or twenty-four—the age of being asked for in marriage—without having felt the need at least to smile, talk, and laugh with a boy. . . . Now it is right; in the past it wasn't. It was shameful for a boy to talk to a girl. A boy would have one week to ask for a girl's hand, and marry her in ten or fifteen days.

Indeed, some young women and mothers described changing norms, based on their observations that being seen in public and meeting young men increased one's chances of marriage. Embarka, a thirty-five-year-old mother, told how she had thrown stones at neighbor women because she was so embarrassed when they joked about her own marriage. Yet for her daughter of sixteen:

Talk to her about marriage, she won't object. She'll like it. The [neighborhood] girls say they're late in getting married. . . . My cousin said "Look at the girls who move to town: they bring back a husband." A girl near us brought back a man just yesterday. She just went to Meknes . . . to visit her aunt . . . and now she's drawing up a marriage license. . . . [My cousin— in her early twenties] argued that because she and her likes are just staying home, nobody cares about them. . . . She does not go out. . . . She says she is always at home, always in the same blouse, always with her head covered. "Girls go out, they wear modern clothes, and go away and bring men, and we don't bring anything. That's why."[14]

Education has made contact between the sexes more possible by providing a place to meet, and requiring walks to and from high school in the larger town during which they can talk. Even those not in school are affected, because schoolgirls appearing in public make other girls less conspicuous than in the past, so girls running errands have become very common. Sixteen-year-old Hurriya, a secondary student, describes the settings in which couples meet and contrasts educated and uneducated girls.

Generally, educated girls prefer educated boys. They would like to get involved with the idea of marriage; they would like to finish their education together. And if they are successful they get married. Uneducated girls also find—with God's help—uneducated boys who spend time with them, but after taking advantage of them, they dump them. . . . They know these girls won't be adequate as their wives, and the girls waste their future with them. . . . [Educated girls] too are taken advantage of.

The ones who have a good life are educated girls. For example, they date a boy who has a motorcycle or something, and he gives her a ride to school. They have fun and all that. As for the girl who is not educated, she too finds an excuse to go out. She tries to run an errand or bring water or whatever: she finds tricks to meet her date. However, an educated girl has a lot of freedom. She can lie to her parents and say she'll be out of school at 5:00 while she actually leaves at 4:00. She makes a date with her boyfriend, and goes to Kabar [the nearby town] to take a walk. . . . Uneducated girls are always fearful. Even if she just stands with him here, she will be scared and will fear that her brother may show up or that her mother may see her.

Hurriya reveals another aspect of male-female relations: most girls want them to end in marriage, and most boys see them as temporary. This is closely related to Moroccan values, in which a girl should be a virgin at marriage, but premarital experience is encouraged for a boy. Young women risk their reputations by meeting with boys, because people suspect the worst. Yet they take this risk in the hope of marriage. Young men enjoy dating girls, but when it comes time for marriage, they, too, want a virgin, and a previous dating partner may now be considered "loose" even for kissing, and eliminated as a potential wife. Thus most couple relationships are very ambivalent: girls expect to be exploited, and boys distrust the girls for being the type to "go out."

Amina has lived through such a relationship:

Around their mid-teens, girls will date boys and have fun, but once they grow up and reach our age [late twenties], then that boy will have married another girl or just abandoned the one he dated. She will realize she was the victim of a disaster. She will have sacrificed herself. . . . It's like when you have a lamb you have raised; you care for it, and one day it just dies for no reason. It is the same situation as when a boy likes you; he speaks to you, he laughs with you, brings what you want—and some day later when he finds another girl, or when he improves his status and becomes rich, he doesn't care for you any more. You become like the lamb which died: a dead animal. Even if you love him, you are out of his heart. He doesn't think about you or care about you.

At nineteen, Majda too worries about male-female relationships. When I asked if she wanted to get married, at first she said yes, though not right away. But then she went on:

We see that nowadays marriage is not worth it. . . . Whenever I go to the women's center, I see wives fighting with their husbands. . . . I get all shaky when I see them. . . . They fight in the street [in front of city hall, where they file their complaints] while people are gathered around them. I hate that; it's what discourages me, it makes me pull back. I don't want to look ahead. I say to myself: "Look at those who got married first: they have achieved nothing. What will happen to me? Me, who doesn't yet know what God has in store for me. ". . . There are some who do take marriage seriously. They concentrate on it; they reach some kind of understanding. They have kids, they have furniture, and they don't use foul language in front of strangers. . . . If they disagree, they keep it to themselves. . . . Not like those who insult each other in public: that's just craziness. As the saying goes, "One rotten fish spoils the whole saddlebag full; one single fish makes the whole thing stink. ". . . That's what I said to myself: "Look at that one fighting with her husband— how can I get married after seeing that? " That's what pushed me to lose faith.

What do these vignettes show us about teens and their relationships in Zawiya? Although Zawiya's norms are still that there should be little contact between the sexes before marriage, the reality is quite different. Yet you've seen that these contacts are uneasy. While both sexes expect problems with each other, they also have romantic fantasies, fantasies which are fulfilled very briefly, if at all. Still, some young men do select a spouse after "dating" and have their parents make marriage arrangements. However, parents have veto power, both through the respect due them and because they finance the expensive wedding celebrations. A proper young woman cannot propose a possible husband, for it would indicate she knew him already. But she has more opportunity to get to know, and to accept or decline, the man her parents choose than in the past.

Female Power

If you began reading this with the stereotype of Arab or Muslim women as silent and submissive, totally dominated by men, hopefully you now have a different, more nuanced perspective. It's true that there are inequalities, that girls have more work and less freedom of movement than boys, but this doesn't mean they passively accept whatever the society or their male relatives declare they should. Think of what you've just read about relationships with the opposite sex, which according to social norms should not occur. At fourteen, Farida has a clear idea that she wants to talk to boys, and worked out a plan to do so. Amina feels strongly that she has a right to talk to boys, and Embarka and her cousin describe how important meeting them is in getting married. Hurriya's discussion of the different freedoms and fears of girls attending school and those who aren't shows that both groups defy social norms, even if uneducated girls are more frightened because they're more likely to be seen. It does seem unfair that girls take these risks because they are pursuing marriage, while boys are more concerned with a good time ... but it isn't any different from much of supposedly more egalitarian American society through the 1950s.

While some authors feel that many American girls "lose their voices" in adolescence,[15] that is, they lose the ability to say, or even know, what they want, I feel this is not true for these young women in Morocco. They know what they want and pursue it. There are some situations in which a woman, adolescent or adult, is expected to defer to males and she usually does, and this is one reason for the view of Arab women as submissive. Yet looking closely, you see women taking actions and making decisions which influence their lives, not turning this power over to others.[16]

A young mother in her early thirties gave a striking example of a friend who had clearly taken control of her life, using an especially daring method given social norms. We were discussing why a local young woman was unmarried, although she was very respectable; I asked what a girl should do who really wanted to marry.

> You know why: it's because she doesn't talk. She's too shy—she has to be talkative, to participate in this and that. She must have fun, talk to boys. . . . She starts [by] talking to one, dating him until a problem arises, either she gets pregnant or whatever, and she does marry him, by force. She warns him either to marry her or to face justice [the state can force marriages in some cases]. And he marries her. . . . It happens a lot ... for some it works, for others it doesn't. . . . I would say it does not work for the majority. Afterward their marriage becomes sour; they split.

Becoming an Adult

One goal of our research was to study whether "adolescence" was a life stage found everywhere, or perhaps an invention of Western psychologists. We asked if there was a special term like "teenager" used locally. Educated people had learned about "adolescence" (*assinn al-murahaqa*) in school, but there was no common term for adolescent in the local dialect of Arabic. Indeed, when I was going door to door explaining our research, I had to say we wanted to study "children who are not too young and not too old." Yet there were other terms related to this phase of life, with *rshed* and *blegh* referring to physiological changes, and *Taysh* and *khfif* meaning irresponsible behavior, often expected of teens.[17] Overall, however, there was no widely used term like "teenager" in Moroccan Arabic, showing that the concept of adolescence as a definite life stage does not exist in all cultures. This makes sense in cultures in which young people marry soon after they reach physiological maturity. As more Moroccans delay marriage, we predict that a stage of adolescence will be more widely recognized; it has certainly begun in upper-class urban families.

We did find a locally used term which helped us understand Moroccan ideas about adolescence and when that period ended: *'aql*. In the literary form of Arabic, *'aql* refers to reasonableness and intelligence; in the Moroccan Arabic spoken in Zawiya, it can mean mind, responsibility, thoughtfulness, or to remember. It is related to adolescence in that when people have fully developed their *'aql*, they are seen as mature people, not adolescents. We found "social sense" to be a good translation of *'aql*; a person with *'aql* considers all the consequences of his or her actions and reacts in a socially responsible and appropriate way. Someone without *'aql* would act on his or her own self interest, such as fighting with someone when angry, without considering first the broader implications. When people have fully developed their *'aql* or social sense, they are no longer seen as adolescents. In the past, marriage marked the end of adolescence. Now, with marriage age for females close to that in the United States (about twenty-one in rural areas and twenty-four in cities)[18] and males marrying later, *'aql* serves to mark the end of adolescence.

For example, my husband witnessed a fight between a young man and a customer who would not pay the price requested. The seller was near thirty, certainly old enough to have developed *'aql*. Yet his teenage male cousin, who witnessed the fight with my husband, was near tears with embarrassment and chagrin. The younger man was too young to intervene physically and knew his cousin was too old to display such socially inappropriate behavior. Such an angry emotional response indicated a lack of *'aql*; he should have been able to deal with the situation verbally. By fighting, he illustrated to the community that he did not yet have 'aql: he was not a fully adult man.

I asked Mohammed, age eighteen, if he had changed in the last two years. He had four years of primary school and now worked in a trade, and said he had changed. "Last year, you could say I was young and didn't have 'aql. I had just started a job, and I was still learning. Now, I've learned a lot." I asked why he felt he was immature before. "I didn't used to go to work [regularly].... I would just sit around.... I used to go around town.... [To] Kabar. I'd sit in places I like, for example a park, or go to someone's house ... or ride on a motorcycle, if there's one handy." He said he hoped to change even more and I asked how. "I shouldn't do anything that's not right. That's all. For example, in front of my parents, I should be very respectful. I should not do any embarrassing things.... They shouldn't hear anything bad about me, whether it happens in the street, at home, or at work."

Young women also develop a sense of 'aql as a mark of maturity, and in fact people in Zawiya expect females to develop it before males. In an extreme case, one person said girls develop 'aql by or in their teens, and males in their mid-twenties. This is partly related to girls' helping around the house; they learn to act responsibly very young, so that five-year-olds watch younger siblings. But females develop the full range of 'aql as social sense in their teens, and probably younger than their brothers. This is because of family expectations of girls, and the more diverse social settings in which males must learn to function.

The importance of 'aql in Moroccan culture, and the efforts adolescents make to develop it, are factors in the low amount of conflict between adolescents and parents. Young people are taught to try to understand all aspects of a situation, and to resolve problems in more subtle ways than open conflict.

Conclusion

I have described several issues that are important for adolescents, and shown how they are dealt with in Morocco. An eighteen-year-old woman in high school answered one of my questions in a way that includes all these issues. I had asked Aisha if she could give me an example of a personal dilemma she faced, a time when she was undecided about what to do.

There is a boy who wants to marry me but he is not working. But he wants to work. He told me he wants to marry me [after he gets a job]. Because he's not working, I didn't want to let

him see my mother and ask her for my hand. She will ask if he has a job, and he'll say, "No." So, I did not want him to come to my house. He is after me to start meeting and "talking," but I refused. People will see me with him and say, "That girl is bad." That's why I refused to meet with him. Now I am facing a dilemma these days: Should I let him see my mother and ask her, or should I tell him, "No," because my mother will say to him, "You are not working, so go away." I 'm still undecided. I've thought a lot about this....

I thought it through and decided no, I should not let him ask my mother. I told him, "Go find a job first. Then come back." He has been interested in me [following me] for four years. This is a long time. But he is not working.... He doesn't go to school.... He applied to go to Libya [to work], but he didn't succeed; they didn't answer his application.... His father is a butcher; he helps him sometimes.... Butchering is no good! ... It's dirty. But also because there isn't a lot of money in it.... He doesn't like it. He is not comfortable with it. He needs a decent job.... He knows what he wants to do, but he hasn't told me. I can't wait to spend time with him so that he can tell me.

S: If you spend time with him, will people gossip?

They will. He wants me to start going with him first, then he'll marry me. I refused.... If I decide to do what he wants and he doesn't marry me, he'll only take advantage of me.... That's why I refused to let him ask my mother until he finds a job.... I told him, "No." ... He said he'll try to find a job first and then tell my mother....

S: So you've made the right decision?

Yes.... Even if he asks her [now], this idea will not bear any result. I mean, nothing good will come out of it.... Because she'll tell him to go away.... She'll say, "You are not serious. You don't even have a job. "... He'll feel ashamed of himself if my mother refuses him because he has no job. I advised him not to go and face rejection that will make him feel bad. I told him he shouldn't go. Seriously, he needs to find a job first. Is he going to get married without money? ...

He agrees. He says he'll find a job . . . but when I saw him, he hadn't found anything yet. I told him to stop following me. When I go to school or come home, he waits for me. When I 'm home he keeps walking by my house, only because of me. His family knows about this. His mother knows that he wants me. . . . He told his family. . . . But then I noticed that his mother suggested to him that he should find a job. But he told her, "No, I tried and was unsuccessful." He refuses to work. He tells them he will start working only after he marries me. But I told him—I told his sister to tell him that he has to get a job first. I did that so that his family won't accuse me of keeping him from working, or say that he bums around because of me. . . . The heart of the matter is that I want him to work. Not only for me, but for his family as well. He is the eldest of his brothers and sisters. . . . I told him, "Work first, help your family, then get married." . . . If he does [get a job], I do want him.

I noted that there is little overt conflict between parents and adolescents in Zawiya, even though they may disagree on things because of rapid social change. If Aisha lived in the United States we wouldn't be surprised if she fought with her mother, arguing that she wanted to see the young man, even if they weren't going to marry.

Aisha handles the matter very differently for several reasons. Her society still values girls' reputations, and they can be ruined if a girl is often seen in public talking to boys. While many girls do meet boys, they try to "control the damage" by being discreet. This also limits conflict with parents because they are not aware of many actions they might disapprove. American adolescents might feel this is dishonest, and they would both be honest and assert their right to autonomy or independence by openly defying parental wishes. Moroccan society values interdependence, not autonomy, and Aisha's methods allow her to keep her relationship with her mother intact, while not totally denying her own wishes. Aisha also shows respect for her mother in that she appears to agree with the mother's [and society's] ground rules, that she should not get into a serious relationship unless a young man has a job. It is also respectful of Aisha not to openly see the young man because this would affect her whole family's reputation; people would say her mother couldn't control her.

I also mentioned that Zawiya teens are very concerned with female-male relationships, even though they are still socially taboo. Aisha's dilemma demonstrates this, and gives a flavor of what such relationships are like. Notice that Aisha says she can hardly wait to see her friend to hear what job he wants, but that she's decided not to see him until he gets a job, or people will talk—she's quite aware of the social taboos. So one wonders how she knows that he doesn't want to be a butcher, that he applied for a job in Libya but didn't get one, that he's told his family about her . . . if they don't even talk. In fact, they must have spent a fair amount of time together. The young man wants to speak to her mother so he can have the right to see her more openly, since they would be engaged, and perhaps to reserve her for himself; she was an intelligent and lovely young woman.

Aisha's dilemma also shows the kind of control that young women can have over their lives. The young man wanted to have a certain kind of relationship, but Aisha set her own terms. She decided it was not in her best interest to be seen with or engaged to someone without a job. She may have decided that this particular young man was risky because he had such a hard time finding work. His father's job of butcher is one of the better-paying local jobs, and he should have been able to work with his father or have the resources to find another job if he really tried.[19]

Finally, the way Aisha handles this relationship demonstrates that she has developed 'aql. She uses her "social sense" to evaluate the general consequences of her behavior; she doesn't just act on what she wants to do at the moment. While she wants to spend time with a young man, she does not talk to him openly because that would damage her reputation. She wants to marry him, but realizes that her mother would not give permission (usually the father is asked, but Aisha's parents are divorced) unless he has a job, and she herself knows that a jobless man is not a good prospect. If her mother turns him down, Aisha says he'll feel ashamed, and that could well influence his feelings toward her; that's another reason she advises him against asking now. An effect which she doesn't mention is that his request would make it likely for her mother to suspect a relationship, and thus watch Aisha's movements more closely, probably preventing the contacts they have now. And notice how Aisha told her suitor's sister that he should get a job first, so that his family won't blame her for leading him astray. Instead she's presented herself as someone who cares about his whole family's welfare; if she did marry him, this concern with the family would stand her in good stead.

You can see that adolescents in Zawiya, Morocco, resemble their American counterparts in some ways and are quite different in others. Moroccans are concerned with education and jobs as paths to a better life than that of their often uneducated parents, whose early lives were much different. They have conflicts with their parents, but they are less extreme and less common than much writing on American adolescents suggests. Although dating is condemned in the town setting, Moroccan teens are very interested in relationships with the opposite sex and pursue them to a much greater degree than their parents could. The content of these relationships appears quite different from much American experience, but the goals are similar to the United States in the recent past and for some today: most boys want to "score," and most girls want to catch a husband. The sexes lead quite different lives in Morocco, with boys freer and focused on their studies, while girls are more restricted and must do housework besides studying. Yet girls are not silent or subservient: they assert their views and claims, sometimes more clearly than their American counterparts.

Finally, the value Moroccans place on respecting elders, family interdependence, and developing 'aql or social sense helps young people negotiate the teenage years quite gracefully.

Notes

1. This chapter has a title very similar to a book my husband and I wrote on the topic: Susan S. Davis and Douglas A. Davis, *Adolescence in a Moroccan Town* (New Brunswick, NJ: Rutgers University Press, 1989). I use "adolescents" here to indicate that I will focus on individuals and their typical concerns, while the book covers the topic of adolescence more generally.
2. Morocco has gone from being predominantly rural to being nearly equally divided between urban and rural by the late 1980s.
3. We found an average of six children per Zawiya family in 1982, but nearly all the adolescents we interviewed said they wanted two children, a boy and a girl.
4. For an example of a Zawiya grandparent who chose her own husband after running away twice, see Susan S. Davis, "Zahrah Muhammad, a Rural Woman of Morocco," in Elizabeth Warnock Fernea and Basima Qattan Bezirgan, eds., *Middle Eastern Muslim Women Speak* (Austin, TX: University of Texas Press, 1977), pp. 201–217.
5. Under the French, there were few schools, so most parents did not have the option of education. Only

three of our sample of over one hundred parents had attended a Western-style school.
6. Margaret Mead, *Coming of Age in Samoa* (New York: William Morrow, 1928).
7. The Ph.D. has become a book: Susan S. Davis, *Patience and Power: Women's Roles in a Moroccan Village* (Rochester, VT: Schenkman Books, Inc., 1983).
8. The Project was directed by John and Beatrice Whiting and Irven DeVore at Harvard and supported by the William T. Grant Foundation and the National Institute of Mental Health (No. MH 14066 –06, 07, 08). Researcher-couples were sought, so we could gather anthropological and psychological data from both sexes. The other sites were an agricultural town in Romania, an Inuit village in the Canadian Arctic, an Australian Aboriginal community, a Muslim fishing village in hailand, a Kikuyu-speaking town in Kenya, and two Ijo sites in Nigeria. Books by Burbank (Australia), Condon (Arctic), Davis and Davis (Morocco), and Leis and Hollos (Nigeria) report the results.
9. Douglas A. Davis, "Formal Thought in a Moroccan Town," in J. Valsiner, ed., *Cultural Context and Child Development: Toward a Culture-Inclusive Developmental Psychology* (Toronto: Hofgrefe and Huber, 1989).
10. By the 1990s parents and youth had begun to realize that education alone would not guarantee a good job, and some were putting less energy and resources into study.
11. Ellipses (. . .) in a quotation indicate material skipped over. Comments in brackets [ ] are my own additions for clarification; names have been changed.
12. Kinza Schuyler, personal communication.
13. Farida uses the "royal" we, which several young people did at different points. It may be to distance herself from this perhaps embarrassing topic.
14. This same young woman now has a job outside Zawiya and wears modern clothes; can a husband be far behind?
15. See Carol Gilligan, *In a Different Voice* (Cambridge, MA: Harvard University Press, 1982); and Lyn Mikel Brown and Carol Gilligan, *Meeting at the Crossroads* (Cambridge, MA: Harvard University Press, 1992). My current research focuses on understanding why Moroccan girls and women keep their voices.
16. See Susan S. Davis, *Patience and Power* (Rochester, VT: Schenkman Books, Inc., 1983) for examples concerning older women.
17. See Susan S. Davis and Douglas A. Davis, *Adolescence in a Moroccan Town* (New Brunswick, NJ: Rutgers University Press, 1989), pp. 46 –59, for a more detailed discussion of these concepts.
18. Royaume du Maroc, *La nuptialite feminine au Maroc: Variations dans le temps et dans l'espace* (Rabat: CERED, 1987), p. 8.

19. In fact, she later married a civil servant, a much more reliable source of support.

Suggested Readings

Beck, Lois, and Nikki Keddie, eds. *Women in the Muslim World*. Cambridge, MA: Harvard University Press, 1978. A classic collection of thirty-three articles on Muslim women in different parts of the world.

Burbank, Victoria K. *Aboriginal Adolescence: Maidenhood in an Australian Community*. New Brunswick, NJ: Rutgers University Press, 1988.

Condon, Richard G. *Inuit Youth: Growth and Change in the Canadian Arctic*. New Brunswick, NJ: Rutgers University Press, 1987.

Csikszentmihalyi, M., and R. Larson. *Being Adolescent: Conflict and Growth, the Teenage Years*. New York: Basic Books, 1984. Reports activities of American adolescents.

Davis, Susan S. *Patience and Power: Women's Roles in a Moroccan Village*. Rochester, VT: Schenkman Books, Inc., 1983.

Davis, Susan S., and Douglas A. Davis. *Adolescence in a Moroccan Town*. New Brunswick, NJ: Rutgers University Press, 1989.

Leis, Philip, and Marida Hollos. *Betwixt and Between: Ijo Youth in Nigeria*. New Brunswick, NJ: Rutgers University Press, 1989.

Mernissi, Fatima. *Beyond the Veil: Male-Female Dynamics in a Modern Muslim Society*. Revised ed. Bloomington, IN: Indiana University Press, 1987. Describes the wider context of Moroccan gender relations, including historical and religious antecedents, which influence the adolescents in this chapter.

Youniss, J., and J. Smollar. *Adolescent Relations with Mothers, Fathers, and Friends*. Chicago: University of Chicago Press, 1985. Presents information on American adolescents.

Bakairí: The Death of an Indian

Debra Picchi

Peruare hanged by his neck from a tree in the garden. Yuka found him and cut his body down. Although Peruare was dead, Yuka ran back to the village to get help, as if believing the medical attendant could save the man. By the time he and the villagers returned, big scavenger birds soared above the corpse. The men shouted and waved their arms, but the birds did not retreat very far. A discussion ensued. Why had Peruare killed himself? Suicides were uncommon among the Bakairí. In fact, no one could remember a similar incident. What should they do?

Someone should inform the government agents. The Indians had worked with the other Brazilians long enough to know about their penchant for keeping records. Yet the Indians delayed, knowing these outsiders always complicated matters. The villagers wanted to sort things out first.

Someone asked, "What about his wife, Neude?" Yuka and the other men carefully kept their faces blank out of respect for dead Peruare. Yes, someone had to tell Neude. A few men agreed to remain in the garden with the body, keeping the birds at bay, while the others returned to the village.

The Bakairí

The Bakairí Indians live in central Brazil. They inhabit a reservation in the state of Mato Grosso, a rapidly growing part of Brazil. A hundred years ago only Indians and an occasional explorer or missionary passed through this region. Today the proliferation of towns, family-owned ranches, and agribusinesses is evidence of how extensively Brazilians have penetrated their country's interior.

When Europeans first arrived on the east coast of South America many indigenous groups either died from the effects of diseases brought from Europe or fled west into the forests. Mato Grosso, literally the "Big Forest," was one area where many Indians survived into the twentieth century in relative isolation. However, non-Indians eventually pushed into this part of Brazil, too, causing the indigenous peoples to relocate, or be relocated, onto tracts of land where the National Foundation of Indians (FUNAI), an organization very similar to the Bureau of Indian Affairs in the United States, took responsibility for them. FUNAI agents discouraged their migrations, monitored their health, and tried to teach them Portuguese. Today peoples such as the Bakairí continue to speak their own languages and practice traditional customs, while developing a growing awareness of how contact with non-Indians has irreparably changed their world.

Who are the Bakairí? To identify these Indians, we usually say they are Carib-speakers, Carib being one of the four major linguistic families of lowland South America. We also call them "riverine" Indians, as opposed to "foot" Indians. This signifies that they depend more on fish than on game for food, and that they travel by canoe on the rivers rather than on foot over land.

To identify them further we might say they were once part of the Xingu culture area. The Xingu River is a major tributary of the Amazon. Its headwaters lie in an isolated part of Mato Grosso. In the nineteenth century the German explorer Karl von den Steinen visited the region and discovered that at least ten different tribes coexisted in these headwaters, sharing common cultural traditions yet speaking different languages.[1] Today the Alto-Xingu, as it is called, has become even more linguistically and culturally complex because FUNAI designated the territory a reservation and relocated a number of different tribes there to protect them from harmful contact with Brazilian road builders.

The Bakairí used to live in the headwaters of the Xingu River, where they traded and intermarried with members of other tribes. Von den Steinen visited some of their villages along the Batovi and Kuliseu rivers and wrote about his observations. Later, however, in the late nineteenth and early twentieth centuries, a series of epidemics devastated the region's population, causing strife and panic. The Bakairí began to migrate out of the Xingu area, traveling southwest to the headwaters of the Paranatinga River. Agents from the Indian protection organization that preceded FUNAI eventually contacted them, and in 1918 they demarcated the Bakairí reservation.

The reservation is currently located in the municipality of Paranatinga. (A Brazilian municipality is similar to a county in the United States.) Its capital is the town of Paranatinga, which lies about 120 kilometers from the reservation. In 1979, when I began fieldwork with the Bakairi, it took about six hours, when the roads were at their best, for the FUNAI-owned truck to creep over the deeply scarred roads that connected the reservation to the town. At that time Paranatinga was a dusty village with dirt roads and small shops where we bought kerosene, cigarettes, aspirin, and staples such as coffee and sugar. I revisited Paranatinga in 1989. It still had narrow dirt roads, but some roads were also paved. And the shops, more numerous now, were stocked with various kinds of merchandise. I was also amazed to see a real restaurant with cloth-covered tables. It was amazing how rapidly the influx of newcomers transformed the region.

Paranatinga is located northeast of Cuiaba, the capital of the state of Mato Grosso, and west of Brasilia, the capital of Brazil itself. Researchers like me visit these towns to secure government authorization to enter Indian lands or to meet with other scientists. It is also easier to purchase gear for the field and do banking and telephoning in larger towns such as Cuiaba. The Bakairí, however, rarely travel to these larger, more distant cities. Not only do they lack the resources, but also they complain about the frantic pace they sense in these towns.

The following describes a mystery I stumbled upon while I did fieldwork with the Bakairí. It is "true" in that the events I describe really happened, although I changed the names to protect people. And it is a "mystery" in that I really do not understand what happened; I give readers a choice at the end of the story, allowing them to make up their own minds. In the process of showing how I heard about the puzzle and why I found the official explanation of it unsatisfactory, I provide a context that ultimately, I hope, informs people about Bakairí culture.

The Bakairí Reservation

The first thing that struck me when I arrived at the Bakairí reservation was the heat. I flew from Cuiaba to the reservation by small plane, landing on a dirt airstrip near the village. Cuiaba was hot, but the reservation felt a lot hotter to me. Maybe it was because the landing strip lay some distance from the cool forests and high banks of the Paranatinga River I could see in the distance. I climbed down from the plane onto the bleached lateritic soil that felt harder than concrete. The ground radiated heat back up onto my face while the sun beat down from above.

I remembered reading that the region's climate was classified as hot and semihumid. As was typical of places close to the equator, there were only two distinct seasons: the rainy and the dry. The rains occurred between November and March, and the dry season took place between May and September. Faced with the blinding, enervating heat of the dry season, I thought I would prefer the rains. My opinion changed, of course, when I experienced the red mud and copious mildew that accompanied the rains.

The landing strip lay close to Pakuera, the largest village in the reservation. Of the 430 or so people who lived in the Bakairí territory, about 170 belonged to this village. Another ninety Indians occupied Aturua, the second largest village, and the rest of the Indian population inhabited five other hamlets in the reservation. I later discovered that there were also about forty non-Indians living illegally in the reservation. FUNAI personnel clearly wanted them to leave because of the dangers of landless farmers invading and taking over the Indians' lands. However, they lacked the authority to force these people to move on.

Yuka, a heavyset man with a grown son standing by his side, approached me. He spoke gruffly without smiling, and I found him to be somewhat intimidating. Later I discovered that Yuka was, in fact, tough and aggressive. He had the courage to visit the capital of Brazil where he lobbied for his people in the offices of FUNAI. And he was extremely bright. He spoke Portuguese fluently, although he and his family spoke Bakairí at home, and he had served as headman, or *cacique*, of the Bakairí who lived in Pakuera. But Yuka could also be warm and concerned, as he was the time I got sick and needed help. And I noticed an impish sense of humor once in a while, especially around his wife, Beri.

Yuka invited me to live with him and his family, and I quickly and gratefully accepted. Choosing where to live when one does fieldwork is always a hard decision. By living with a family one runs the risk of inadvertently getting in the middle of warring political factions, but by living alone one misses opportunities to practice speaking the language and to join in family activities. I always preferred to live with families although I knew other anthropologists who felt strongly about remaining independent.

I followed Yuka down a lane lined with tall, fragrant mango trees. Since he spoke better Portuguese than I did, I was able to ask him who planted the trees. He said that when he was a child agents from the Indian Protection Agency reorganized the Bakairí village, arranging the houses in rows, rather than in traditional circles. At that time the agents also planted trees and bushes.

Although contemporary FUNAI personnel tried to be more sensitive about such Indian practices, Pakuera's houses still formed neat lines that ran on an east-west axis, intersecting at a point where the Bakairí built a men's house, the site of important ritual and political activities.

We arrived at Yuka's home, which was a square house with clay walls and a thatched roof, another deviation from tradition (the old-style homes were elliptically shaped and covered with thatched palm). Yuka explained that men and their male kin constructed a house by erecting a wooden frame, which they then covered with wet clay. Women gathered and dried palm thatch, which the men then arranged in thick layers on top. Later, when I observed young Jere building a home for himself and his wife, I noticed the festive atmosphere that pervaded the scene. The work group appeared to be enjoying themselves, laughing and joking with people who passed by, seemingly oblivious to the hard work they were doing.

Yuka's house was several years old, and he said that sometimes the roof leaked when it rained. Inside it felt cool and restful to me after the hot landing strip. Yuka told me to sit down, directing me to a chair of which he was clearly proud. A chair was a luxury, brought from outside of the reservation. Most Bakairí homes were furnished only with hammocks and an occasional stool or cured animal skin. Women made the hammocks of cotton from the gardens or of palm from the forests, while men carved the stools from hardwood, often making them in the shape of an animal such as an armadillo or a turtle. I glanced around the room and saw no such stool, but draped over an interior wall there were several hammocks, obviously pulled out of the way of daily traffic. I suspected people would sleep in them that night.

Beri, Yuka's wife, shyly entered the room. Her mother Alia followed her more slowly. Over the years that followed I became very fond of Beri. I admired her sense of humor, her concern for others, and her gentleness. I liked Alia, too, but she did not possess Beri's mildness, though she was a hard-working,

energetic person. The first day I met these two women I immediately saw a family resemblance. Both of them left their dark hair long and unbound, unlike some of the younger Bakairí women who cut their hair short, imitating Brazilian women they saw in Paranatinga. And they were both under five feet and relatively slight compared to some of the other Bakairí women, who were five feet or taller with more robust figures. Beri and Alia wore shiftlike dresses similar to those used by the Indian women in the Bakairí reservation. These dresses were simple to cut out and sew on a manual sewing machine or by hand. Women usually owned two or three such shifts so that they always had a clean one to put on, even after working in the garden.

Beri asked if I would "accept a *cafezinho*," a tiny cup of the strong, sweet coffee that is so popular in Brazil. The Bakairí acquired this custom from their Brazilian neighbors, who drank many such cups in the course of a day. I accepted the hot coffee, which I found refreshing even in the midday heat. An uncomfortable silence fell upon the group. Clearly it would take some time before we felt relaxed around each other.

At Home with the Bakairí

I tried to put Yuka's family at their ease by asking some general questions about who lived in the house. Yuka began by listing himself and his wife, Beri. I did not need to ask if he had only one wife. I knew that the Bakairí had previously practiced polygyny, the tradition of taking more than one wife, but the influence of the missionaries and, to a lesser extent, of FUNAI had discouraged this. Now the Indians were monogamous. Beri's father had lived with them until he died, but now just Alia, Beri's mother, remained from that generation. Additionally, a young daughter, now visiting Cuiaba, normally lived there, and Nai, their grown son, and his new wife Rea belonged to the household. Rea had recently found out that she was pregnant, and the family looked forward to the arrival of its new member with obvious excitement.

I was curious about Rea's presence in the household. Newly married couples tended to live with the wife's parents until the birth of their first baby, after which they sometimes set up their own households. Although not unheard of, it was unusual for couples to stay with the husband's family. The mystery appeared to be solved later in the week when a woman I thought was Rea's mother stopped by, in an advanced state of pregnancy, with two small children tugging at her dress. She was stressed and tired and asked Rea to watch over what I assumed were Rea's young sisters while she went down to the river to wash some clothes. I concluded that too many people were crowded into Rea's parents' home, so Nai and Rea had chosen to stay at Yuka and Beri's house, which seemed roomy by comparison.

Bakairí women could expect to give birth to their first child when they were between fifteen and nineteen years of age. They continued to reproduce for the next twenty to twenty-five years, having, on the average, about five children. Children were widely spaced, and it was not unusual for mothers and daughters to be pregnant simultaneously. Birth control as we know it was not available, but infanticide, the killing of unwanted or deformed infants, as well as "benign neglect," allowing children to die from lack of care, tended to keep the number of live children lower than expected.

Yuka counted six people living in his household. Later that month I visited each house in the village, introducing myself and doing a census at the same time. I found Yuka's household was only slightly above average in size, the mean being 4.88 ± .48 persons. I determined that the majority of households consisted of between three and six individuals, with a married couple making up the core of this unit.

After some casual conversation about my home and family in the United States, Rea, Beri, Alia, and I went down to the river. Three main rivers flowed through the reservation—the Paranatinga, Azul, and Vermelho. The Paranatinga River was the closest to the village, and it provided water for drinking, bathing, and washing clothes. The Indians also fished in the rivers and used the waters for transportation. They made their own canoes out of hardwood trees they found in the forests.

Alia and Beri chattered and laughed as they led me down the trail to the section of the river where the women bathed and filled huge cans with water. The men used a separate section, with a patch of trees dividing the two areas. To actually get to the water I clambered down a well-worn, rocky path that was slippery and steep the first time I attempted it. As I carefully picked my way through the rocks women in their sixties and seventies, with wet clothes and water cans balanced on their heads, barreled past me as if I were standing still. Once on the rocky beach I admired the green water and the huge trees that lined the river. It was quiet and peaceful, and the hum of the women talking as they worked and the shouts of the children playing contributed to my sense of tranquility.

We splashed around in the water for a while and then filled the cans with water to take back to the house. I offered to help, but the women agreed I had

to practice negotiating the path before I could carry things. So I helped Rea raise a heavy can to her shoulder, and then to her head. Later when I learned to carry water this way, I discovered getting the can up to the shoulder was the hardest part of the task. Once on the shoulder or head the weight was not difficult to manage because it distributed itself evenly.

We climbed up the path and walked the kilometer or so back to the house. It was already getting dark even though it was only 5:30. Being from a temperate climate, I was always surprised by the early sunsets close to the equator. My mental clock equated hot weather with long days; the nearly twelve hours of darkness in the tropics were unexpected.

Back at the house Beri helped me set up the hammock I brought from Cuiaba in the small area the family had generously vacated for me. Nai and Rea set up their hammocks close by, while Beri, Yuka, and Alia shared a space in another part of the house. It seemed we all had a modicum of privacy.

However, sounds carried easily in Indian homes. Walls reached only three-fourths of the way to the ceiling, allowing air to pass through, and, of course, soundproofed materials were unavailable. As I swung back and forth in my hammock, congratulating myself on a relatively painless beginning to a fieldwork session, I heard the murmur of Nai's and Rea's voices. Then silence fell. Not wanting to keep the family awake, I blew out the candle I had placed on the ground next to my hammock. But I lighted it again a few minutes later. I could have sworn I heard someone crying.

After a while I lay back down, deciding it must be Rea. She was the closest to my sleeping area, and it would not be unusual for a young girl, newly married and pregnant, to cry at night, especially when she probably felt homesick for her mother and sisters. After all, she received little or no support from her in-laws. Relations between the girl and them were cool and restrained in accordance with Bakairí traditions, which assumed that there would be less conflict if in-laws ignored each other. I thought no more about Rea's tears until later.

In the Gardens with the Bakairí

A few days later Beri, Alia, Rea, and I were carrying baskets slung over our shoulders. When the baskets were full, the basket straps went around our foreheads, supporting most of the weight of the potatolike manioc we harvested in the gardens. But for now the baskets were light, and we moved quickly down the path through the *cerrado*.

Cerrado, which resembled a dry prairie, covered most of the Bakairí reservation. The Indians used this land mainly for hunting, cattle raising, and, more recently, a modern agriculture experiment. They made their gardens in the rich gallery forest soils, which lined the banks of the major rivers. Some fields lay quite far from the village, but, on the average, the Indians made them about four kilometers from Pakuera. Locating these gardens was very difficult for the novice, as I was to find out when I did a land use census. But that day I was with Beri and her relatives, so we unerringly made our way to a section of tall forest that loomed before us. We passed through a green, tunnel-like strip of trees that divided the garden from the cerrado, and then we walked into an open space. The garden lay before us.

The Bakairí practiced both traditional subsistence methods and, to a lesser extent, modern agriculture, which FUNAI introduced in 1980. Traditional food production consisted of slash-and-burn horticulture in which a man asked his kinsmen to join him for a day or two to cut down the underbrush in a section of the forest. They then chopped down the trees, leaving the vegetation to dry out in the hot sun. A Bakairí man generally carved out of the forest a garden about four thousand square meters, or slightly under an acre, in size. His family depended on the crops from this field for several years, but since the household head cultivated a new area each year, they harvested food from several gardens simultaneously.

Garden clearing took place at the beginning of the dry season, when little rain fell. Several months later, around the beginning of September, the men began to scan the sky, anxiously trying to predict when the first rains would fall. They had to set fire to the dried-out vegetation and burn it all to ash before the rains began, but they felt compelled to wait until the last possible moment because prematurely burned fields would not burn completely. When this happened there was little ash—a natural fertilizer—for the crops. Also, a partially burned garden was hard to cultivate. Vines tripped people, and thorns cut into their skin. The need to weed was also greater in such a garden.

After the garden was burned the women joined the men in planting crops such as manioc, corn, beans, rice, and fruits such as melon, pineapple, banana, and sugar cane. The women also took responsibility for harvesting the crops, although men helped them as needed. They harvested the manioc tubers gradually, but the entire family turned out to harvest the rice and corn all at once because these crops could not remain in the field after they matured.

Beri and Alia planned to harvest manioc that day. But that did not stop us from eating some pineapple first. Beri chose a beautifully ripened fruit and cut huge slices from it with her machete, a tool both men and women kept close at hand. After I ate mine I explored the garden. Unlike the clean-cleared farmlands in the United States, Bakairí gardens seemed to the untrained eye to be a confused maze of plants, tree stumps, and branches. I really needed a machete to cut my way through the tangle of vines and weeds. I was grateful I had had the sense to wear a long-sleeved shirt and slacks, instead of shorts and a T-shirt.

I found the edge of the garden that bordered the river and was surprised to find a bank about twenty feet high. Disappointed, I told Alia I would be unable to bathe after working in the garden. She laughed and said I would not want to go swimming there even if I could. Anacondas rested in waters that were undisturbed by people. Anacondas were heavy snakes that grew up to thirty feet in length. They either crushed their victims or snapped their necks in order to incapacitate and then eat them. Although human adults were not usually in danger of being attacked by an anaconda lurking in the shadowy waters, I felt considerably less interested in having a swim after talking to Alia.

Beri and Rea were already digging up manioc with sticks and machete points. They quickly accumulated a pile, and before long we were stuffing manioc in our baskets and making plans to start the trip home. Beri and Alia accepted my offer to help this time, and Rea assisted me as I lifted the basket on my back and arranged the strap across my forehead. They gave me the lightest basket, I noticed, so the band did not cut into the skin as it might have. We left the garden in single file, trekking quietly through the green tunnel out onto the hot cerrado. It would take us over an hour to get back to the village.

Beri and Alia walked in front of me, and Rea followed behind. The two older women conversed in low tones. Since I did not yet speak Bakairí, I could not understand the words I occasionally heard. I let my mind wander until I suddenly heard fear in the voices of the women. I looked up and saw a cow standing in the path before us. Other cattle gathered in the area, peacefully grazing on the cerrado grasses. Beri and Alia were clearly agitated. They did not know how to force the cow off the path, and they could not go around it because of the other animals in the way.

After some discussion we decided to brandish sticks and machetes above our heads while yelling as loud as we could. Timidly at first, but then with more energy, we stamped our feet and waved whatever we had in our hands. I was convinced we must have looked like crazy fools, but after a while the cow languidly walked away. It showed no sign that we troubled it in the least, acting as if it were simply bored with the grass in that spot.

Beri and Alia started to laugh nervously. After congratulating ourselves on our bravery and quick thinking, we walked on. I asked about the cattle. Who owned them? Where did they come from? Alia explained that a long time ago diseases such as tuberculosis and syphilis killed most of the Bakairí. Agents from the Indian Protection Agency came to the tiny remaining village with a heifer. They showed the Indians the animal and said that any couple who had a child would receive one as a gift. Additionally, for the birthday of every child up to five years of age they would donate another heifer.

The Bakairí eventually responded to these incentives, and their population began to increase again. However, at first the Indians feared the cattle. Their huge size and horns terrified them. They did not understand how to milk the cows nor did they have a taste for milk. Being riverine Indians, they ate mostly fish during that early period and even had food taboos for many kinds of meat. By the time I began my fieldwork fifty years had passed, and the Bakairí were more or less accustomed to the cows. They ate beef whenever a steer was slaughtered, distributing the meat throughout the village. And they drank milk once in a while. Yet, as the incident on the trail showed, the alliance between the Indians and cattle continued to be somewhat uneasy.

A Bakairí Tragedy

Our small band continued walking through the cerrado, and Beri and Alia resumed their conversation. About fifteen minutes later I again heard a tremor of emotion in the women's voices. I looked up, expecting to see some more cattle, but there was nothing. The women appeared to be looking at a wall of trees to the west. There were expressions of dread on their faces. I asked what was wrong. I thought maybe they spotted a jaguar, an animal indigenous to the area as well as prominent in Bakairí myths. Beri lowered her voice and explained that four years ago a man named Peruare hanged himself in his garden. She raised her arm and pointed to a spot in the distance. His garden was located there, she said. Yuka discovered the body, and apparently the incident deeply disturbed him as well as the rest of the family.

I turned to Rea and found to my surprise that she was weeping silently. I asked her what was wrong, but she did not answer me. She lowered her head and walked on quickly toward Pakuera. I asked Beri and Alia why Rea was so upset, and they told me that Peruare was Rea's father. After some confusion, I sorted things out, discovering that the woman Rea called "Mother" was actually the sister of Rea's biological mother.

Taiwa bore Peruare four children before she died of malaria. Rea was the last one born and the only daughter. Of the three sons, one had died, one now lived in Cuiaba, and one lived in Pakuera but was bewitched. His name was Marce, and after Peruare's death he and Rea were raised by Tena, Taiwa's sister.

I thought Marce and Rea were lucky to have Tena. Maternal aunts were frequently perceived as comothers, and were even addressed with the kinship term "Mother" in societies that used what anthropologists called the Iroquois kinship system. Marce's and Rea's adoption by Taiwa's sister was also consistent with this model in that comothers were expected to share child-rearing responsibilities with their sisters.

Alia was making disapproving noises as she went on to tell me that Marce's and Rea's lives were difficult even before their father's suicide because of his remarriage to Neude, a beautiful woman who was considerably younger than Peruare. In fact, she was only sixteen when they married. According to Alia, Neude was unprepared to take on the responsibility of managing a household and raising nearly grown children. Additionally, she found herself interacting with stepsons who were her age. In fact, Claudio, the oldest son, was born the same year as Neude. Their proximity in age led to gossip, as people speculated about a possible sexual relationship.

Peruare and his family resolved this problem much as families do all over the world. Claudio simply left, moving out of the reservation to Cuiaba, and Rea and Marce spent more time at their Aunt Tena's. When Peruare died they moved their personal belongings there. Neude, with the one child she had by Peruare, returned to her father and mother's home. She quickly remarried.

By this time Beri, Alia, and I were hurrying after Rea toward the village we could now see in the distance. The sun was setting so we had little time to get home. I kept my head down, straining against the basket strap, but every so often I glanced up. The light-colored thatched roofs of the houses with their dry clay walls faded into the backdrop of trees. Smoke rose above the houses from the fires where women roasted manioc pancakes and fish.

Peruare's tragedy and his children's pain were far removed from the tranquil scene before us. It seemed so unlikely that a Bakairí Indian would commit suicide. No history or tradition of such a behavior existed, and I had come across no other account of such a case in the FUNAI agent's records or in the literature. It was inconsistent with what I knew of the Indians' culture. Perhaps I did not understand suicide, but I usually associated it with an atomized society in which people felt alone and unsupported. Either high pressure or despair factored into one's decision to die.

The Bakairí world contrasted sharply with this description. Each individual was highly integrated into the social system on the basis of many criteria. Although clans and highly developed lineages were absent, most belonged to large extended groups of kin. Family members provided each other with assistance, both on a regular basis and in times of special need. Individuals were rarely alone because they always had kin to keep them company.

Age and gender were two other factors that divided people into complementary groups. For example, the old were highly respected, contributing to society in such important ways as teaching young men to chant mask songs. And although females were considered subordinate to males, they performed tasks that the group recognized as important. No one person stood alone; everyone was part of at least several groups, each of which was valued for some reason. There were no "untouchables" in the Bakairí village.

It was an egalitarian world where gross discrepancies in wealth and power were absent. Everyone had equal access to resources such as land and technology. People did not even own their own gardens, but had the right to use the land only temporarily before rotating to another part of the territory. They shared their personal effects willingly, afraid of being called "stingy" in a society where being "good" meant being generous.

Furthermore, high-pressure situations or sources of despair also seemed foreign in the village. Men hunted, fished, worked in their gardens, watched their sons, and performed rituals that their grandfathers used years ago. Women bore children, washed clothes at the river, harvested food in the gardens, processed manioc, and also performed community rituals. Although I do not mean to describe a Shangri-La where everyone is always happy and at peace, it struck me that the Bakairí suffered less from the stress and anxiety associated with so-called modern living. Peruare's suicide sounded a jarring note in a musical score filled with playfulness and moderation.

We entered the village as dusk set in. I saw Yuka sitting in his chair in front of the house, exchanging affable greetings with the men and women who walked by. Rea was nowhere in sight. One thing was clear: Her tears at night were probably from more than just being a newly married, homesick girl. Her father's dramatic death four years ago and her brother's bewitching, whatever that meant, must have traumatized her. I realized, as I finally put the basket of manioc down in Beri's back yard, that these were additional dissonant notes I was hearing. I looked around me with concern, asking myself what other invisible currents I had missed.

In the Public Arena with the Bakairí

Time passed rapidly while I was with the Bakairí. The puzzle of Peruare's death continued to intrigue me, but other aspects of the Indian culture claimed my attention. At one point I set for myself the goal of trying to describe, as completely as I could, how the Bakairí were politically organized. I knew that the villagers informally chose headmen, or caciques. These leaders possessed limited powers that were mostly persuasive in nature. If, for example, they wanted the village men to clear grass and debris from the central plaza in front of the men's house, then they would begin to clear the area themselves, calling others to join them. If no one helped out, they had no authority to command or to punish those who did not participate.

Many Brazilians operated under the misconception that caciques controlled their people, erroneously believing that headmen actually exercised power over other Indians. This, of course, was not true. Probably the misunderstanding arose because headmen acted as information conduits, informing villagers about what was going to happen. This allowed the Bakairí to meet and discuss a plan of action. When they reached a consensus, they acted. However, to the Brazilians who were unaware of the middle part of the process, it appeared that the Bakairí were following orders.

For example, FUNAI wanted to vaccinate everyone against measles on a given day, when they planned to send in a plane with a medical team. They told the headman to gather the people in Pakuera, where they should wait for the arrival of the medics. Most of the Bakairí were there waiting for the plane when the team arrived, but it was not because the headman told them to be there. Rather, the Indians took medical treatment very seriously, and when the cacique informed them of the vaccination team's intentions, it did not require a great deal of discussion for the villagers to decide to cooperate.

Another example of how Brazilians misunderstood the headman's role concerned some squatters who lived illegally in the reservation. They arrived one day in the Bakairí village, telling a harrowing story of flight during the night from a rancher who threatened to kill them, rather than pay them for work they had done for him. The father and two of his grown sons helped the headman count cattle one afternoon. FUNAI needed to know the exact number of heads in the reservation for an annual census it was doing. Bakairí men and children milled about chatting and laughing as the process took place. At one point the headman suggested that one of the Brazilian adolescents move over to the other side of the field to make sure no cattle slipped by uncounted. The young man responded, "What the cacique commands, I do." The Indians laughed uproariously at such a notion, while the Brazilians stood there looking slightly perplexed.

A shaman was also an important figure in the village. He was a specialist who cured diseases or cast spells on enemies. A respected professional, he worked hard at his job, depending on knowledge learned during a lengthy apprenticeship. Central to the power of a shaman was his ability to call on a spiritual guide who was invisible to everyone except him. While other Indian shamans used hallucinogens in order to communicate with the spirits, Bakairí shamans used tobacco to bring on the trances in which they conferred with their spirit guides. Advice from the guide allowed the shaman to more effectively find the cause of the illness. During a curing session he used his spirit's help as he chanted, rocked, and massaged his patient's body. After he forced or coaxed the disease-causing agent out of its hiding place, he regurgitated the foul matter into his hand to show to his audience.

Later, when I told friends about my experiences with Bakairí shamans, they always asked me if shamanism "really worked." They contrasted it with Western medicine and doubted that it could help people get well. I was intrigued by the fact that the Bakairí never asked me a similar kind of question. That is, no one ever asked if Western medicine practiced by FUNAI medics "really worked," in spite of the fact that the Indians witnessed plenty of Western failures. For example, there were people in the village who were unsuccessfully treated for cancer, tuberculosis, and the Guillain-Barre disease, which was referred to as "French polio" at that time. I asked an older shaman about the spotty success rates of both Indian and Western models of curing, and he simply shrugged and said one worked in some instances, while the other worked under other conditions. Clearly he did not stay up nights worrying about it.

Bakairí curers, as well as the Bakairí people in general, lived comfortably in a dual world, accommodating conflicting world views that created cognitive dissonance in other societies. The belief in the existence of microbes was another example of the delicate balancing act these Indians perform. One month a FUNAI medical team came in to treat sick Indians. I was with a group of Bakairí women who were squatting on the ground preparing a meal outside one of the houses. A Brazilian nurse walked by, then stopped and spent some time explaining that it was not healthy to prepare food on a dirt surface. After some discussion she mentioned that "microbes," or tiny invisible things, lived in the dust and crawled on the food, which people then ate. The microbes caused illness in the bodies of their victims. I expected the Bakairí to laugh or to ignore the woman, but they absorbed what she said with little comment or disagreement. Later, when I discussed the matter further with them, I realized that at least half of what she told them was consistent with their own world view. The Bakairí, like many other indigenous people of the New World, had an explanation of disease and curing that involved invisible and dangerous items that lodged themselves inside the bodies of humans and caused disease and death. These dangerous items had to be removed in order for an individual to be cured.

However, one key difference distinguished Western and Bakairí explanations of disease. Western science did not ascribe a personal factor when explaining why a specific individual contracted a disease. For example, if I came down with the flu, it was not because a friend cast a spell on me after I missed a lunch date with her. On the other hand, the Bakairí model assigned primary importance to personal variables. A sorcerer psychically hurtled an invisible, disease-ridden object through the air at high speed to penetrate the body of the victim if an angry enemy paid the sorcerer to do so.

The nurse who advised the women not to prepare food on the ground did not speculate about the origin of the microbes. She assumed that it was understood that things such as bacteria and viruses naturally populate a world we can only access with microscopes, while the Indian women assumed no such thing. Disease emerged out of conflict between people. The dirt on the ground may or may not house such dangerous entities, according to these women. It all depended on one's enemies.

A shaman was not only a curer or sorcerer; he also exercised political power by using his skills to manipulate community events. Factions coalesced around him, tipping the balance one way or the other when conflict threatened to break into violence on the village plaza. Lino was a shaman when his brother, Tavio, was headman of Pakuera. Some villagers accused Tavio of stealing and then selling community cattle. People almost came to blows in front of the men's house, where such important issues were frequently discussed. Tavio, in shame and anger, took his wife, Jude, and retreated to the garden to save face.

He left Lara, his influential mother, Lino, his brother, and Veri, Jude's brother, to clear his name. Lino did not waste any time. He publicly recounted conversations with his guide in which the spirit warned that he would send a huge wind to blow his brother's enemies away. One rainy evening, when he talked about this, Lino dramatically raised his arm and pointed to black clouds that were rolling across the sky. He said the end would look similar to that unless he could persuade his guide to leave Tavio's detractors alone.

The metamessage in Lino's communiqué was clear. The supernatural had labeled Tavio's enemies as wrong and deserving of punishment, while Tavio was cast in the role of a misunderstood leader. Lino gained prestige because he was seen as the peacemaker. He was responsible for soothing an angry spirit who could have wreaked havoc in the village. Eventually the problem of the missing cattle was resolved, and Tavio returned home.

I tried to work with shamans like Lino, interviewing them about their beliefs and about what they do during their long apprenticeships. This was a complex area of Bakairí culture that required sophisticated control of the Bakairí language and worldview, things I felt I did not perfectly understand. However, I sat on the earth floor in Lino's house, plodding on with my questions, when Marce, Peruare's youngest son, entered the house.

Marce was in his midteens when his father died; when I first met him he was twenty. He seemed shy and gentle, with a quiet voice and serious demeanor. He was extremely thin, with small bones, lacking the physical development of most Indians. The active, hard-working lifestyle of the Bakairí resulted in muscular physiques in both the men and women. Marce looked frail in comparison.

Additionally, his skin was pale yellow, a color that I only saw when a young boy was in seclusion for a long period of time. As a boy passed through adolescence his father and uncles required him to remain in a specially partitioned section of the house. To strengthen the boy physically and spiritually his elders forbade him to speak above a whisper or to walk outside during the day. Above all he could not look at or be seen by people outside his immediate family. Because this seclusion period went on for months, the boy's bronze tan usually faded, and his skin acquired a creamy yellow shade that the Bakairí people considered beautiful.

Marce's entire presentation was much like a young man in seclusion. His skin, his frailty, his voice, and his avoidance of my eyes all suggested a person set apart. He spoke with Lino in low tones and then silently left. I asked Lino about him, and he told me that after the death of his father, Marce had tried to escape the whispers and stares of the villagers by going to Cuiaba to live with his brother Claudio. His transition to life in the capital of Mato Grosso was not successful. He began drinking, was unable to keep a job, and, finally, began a downward spiral that so concerned Claudio that he brought his brother back to the reservation, announcing to everyone that he was bewitched.

Tena, his aunt, speculated that someone in the city had taken possession of Marce's body and soul. She asked Lino to treat him, and he met with the young man, questioning him about his symptoms. Marce responded that he constantly had a headache, had no appetite, was weak and lethargic, and frequently felt confused and sad. Curing treatments hastily began.

I thought some North Americans might describe Marce's problem a little differently than did the Bakairí. A psychotherapist might conclude his father's sudden and violent death shocked and anguished him. He felt unable to cope with what was happening because there were few immediate family members left to support him. He confronted the additional stress of living in a small society. Such a world could be warm and caring, but when something unusual or dangerous occurred, victims like Marce, perhaps made into scapegoats out of fear, could not escape the intrusive and punishing gaze of the villagers. There was really nowhere to hide, and his desperate attempt to live outside the reservation proved how tough it must have been for him in Pakuera.

After my conversation with Lino I was certain I had learned a lot about the devastating impact Peruare's death had had on Marce. Yet I had also discovered something about shamans, I thought. Lino was not Marce's kinsmen, but he supported the boy and helped him as few others in the village had. He was not only Marce's healer, but also his friend. A thread of compassion ran through his actions, a quality that I had not, up to that time, associated with shamans. My study emphasized the side of shamanism that involved power and manipulation because, I thought, that would help me understand political events in the village. I had almost overlooked another, more humanistic dimension of the tradition.

Out Back with the Bakairí Women

Beri woke me up early one morning to let me know that Ivane, the daughter of Marti, had eloped to the gardens with Odi. I quickly threw on some khaki slacks and a fresh T-shirt and joined the other women in back of the house where they squatted around a fire. The sun had not risen but a gray light permeated the scene. Beri poured some coffee into a tin mug and handed it to me. Although she did not drink the beverage herself, she prepared it over the fire for me every morning, for which I was grateful.

Alia was torn between being irritated that she had not predicted the event and being gleeful that it had taken place. Clearly this was no painful tragedy. Even Odi's wife, who stormed home under the cover of darkness the night before, was reportedly more furious than sad about her husband's defection. Her family was keeping quiet, as was Marti's kin. No one wanted to trigger an open conflict before figuring out what Ivane and Odi planned to do.

The couple had been having an affair for some time. This was not uncommon in Indian villages. Many anthropologists have reported high levels of sexual activity among South American Indians, and the Bakairí were no exception.[2] However, the Indians considered an affair one thing, and divorce and remarriage something quite different. Affairs, if handled discreetly, affected only two parties, while divorces affected families and disrupted the entire village. Odi and Ivane's flight to the gardens signaled that they were taking the ultimate step. They were going to marry. They would remain in the gardens until Odi's wife had moved home and the village gossip died down. Then they would quietly return to the village to resume their daily routine as nonchalantly as possible. Under the best of circumstances, that would be the end of the story.

Alia muttered darkly about Marti's daughters and the trouble they caused. When I asked what she meant, she burst out angrily that Neude was Ivane's sister. Neude had many affairs while married to Peruare, and she had not been at all discreet. In fact, everyone knew when she became seriously involved with

Wito, the youngest son of Maka. The two were regularly and obviously together, something that caused Peruare great pain. It was clear, Alia said, that Peruare killed himself because he felt such anguish and humiliation over his wife's infidelities. She bitterly concluded her story by saying Ivane was no better. It must run in families.

Alia energetically slapped the manioc pancake that was toasting on the clay griddle over the fire. But I saw her lips trembling and knew she was distressed. Although Peruare had not belonged to Alia's age cohort, he was close to her in age and experience. When members of small societies like the Bakairí died, it was keenly felt by everyone. Death left huge gaps in people's lives, even though they said they tried to "forget the sorrow."

The sun rose as we squatted there eating manioc pancakes. I thought about Peruare's death. Was it possible that he killed himself because of Neude? It seemed unlikely to me because so many Indian men and women were having extramarital affairs that it was practically the norm. It would have been a gross overreaction on the part of Peruare to hang himself over a wayward wife. Even if he had thought that Neude was going to leave him for Wito, that still would not lead to suicide. He would simply remarry as he had when Taiwa, his first wife, died.

Alia continued to complain about Marti and her girls. She said that she had not raised her daughter Beri to behave in such an ugly fashion, and neither for that matter had Lara, whose girls were also well-behaved. I tried to remember Lara, mentally reviewing the rough map of the village I sketched during my first month in Pakuera. Lara was a women in her sixties or seventies who lived with her many daughters and sons at the west end of the village. I recalled that at first I confused her with Marti, who occupied the central part of the village near the men's house.

Suddenly I realized that another powerful old woman inhabited the eastern part of the village. Her name was Maka, and she was Wito's mother. She was one of the few Indians in the village who had white hair, but she was still strong and able to influence her five sons and three daughters, all of whom were married with children.

Lara, Marti, and Maka—these were three powerful women leading three powerful village factions consisting of sons and daughters and their spouses and children. At that point I had been with the Bakairí long enough to know that some individuals consistently took certain predictable positions regarding issues affecting the village. Was it possible that the village factions did the same?

For example, Joi, one of Maka's sons, aggressively supported the mechanized agricultural project promoted by FUNAI agents. He was an articulate and public advocate of the practice of modern agriculture in the cerrado. His brothers and the husbands of his sisters, as far as I could remember, all held similar positions. They voted as a block.

I thought about the agriculture project. It was considered to be the salvation of the Bakairí by some and the bane of Bakairí existence by others. In 1980 FUNAI transported a tractor to the reservation and supplied the Bakairí with rice seed and chemical fertilizers. They instructed the Indians to clean clear the land, plow it with the tractor, plant and fertilize the seeds, and harvest the rice using modern harvesting machines. The goal, they explained to the Indians, was to sell the crop to middlemen in Paranatinga, who would in turn take the harvest to markets in the cities. FUNAI hoped the Bakairí would use the cash proceeds to purchase more fertilizer, seeds, and diesel fuel. It seemed simple enough.

The project only produced about fifty percent of the anticipated harvest that first year. FUNAI and the Indians hoped to harvest about 1000 sacks of rice, but only 450 sacks were filled. The Bakairí worked hard, but a number of obstacles stood in their way. Their lack of know-how, the absence of technical support from FUNAI, equipment malfunctions, and early rains all conspired against the initial success of the Bakairí's project. During subsequent years FUNAI support dwindled as the organization itself underwent reform. Yet, the Indians managed to harvest quite respectable amounts of rice from time to time. For example, one year they cultivated only 25 hectares, but harvested 680 sacks of rice. This was substantially more than the 450 sacks they managed to squeeze from the 50 hectares they originally plowed.

One of the controversies among the Bakairí about the project concerned how it affected village life. Some Indians pointed out it reduced the people's reliance on traditional gardening and increased their dependency on FUNAI. A study I did while in the village tested this hypothesis. The data I gathered indicated that since the modern agriculture project was introduced, fewer household heads made traditional manioc gardens in the gallery forest.

In 1981 16.9 percent (10 of Pakuera's 59 households) did not make traditional gardens in the gallery forests along the rivers. In 1989 48.8 percent (20 of 41 households) lacked gardens. Although I discovered that the reasons for not making gardens varied, people who did not have them turned to FUNAI or other organizations for food or cash in order to sur-

vive. It seemed the critics of the project were right about the dependency issue, at least.

When I reviewed my field notes I identified many village issues on which Maka, Lara, and Marti's factions differed. Some were trivial and simmered in the background, but others led to public conflict and threats of violence. In fact, sometimes, under the cover of darkness, men fought each other with knives, and the losers fled to their gardens to heal their wounds before FUNAI agents discovered internal disputes the Indians wanted kept secret.

Was it possible that the death of Peruare had more to do with village politics and conflict between factions than with Neude's affair with Wito? Suicide seemed highly improbable, which left accidental homicide or murder. I needed to know if there was a possible motive. Subsequent conversations with Alia and Lino led me to conclude there were plenty of reasons, both new and old, for Peruare to come to blows with members of one of the factions. For example, Peruare was not a member of a strong kin faction. In fact, he had few relatives in the village. Many anthropologists have reported how vulnerable Indians were to accusations of witchcraft and general persecution if they lacked kin to defend them.[3]

Additionally, Peruare advocated a more traditional lifestyle. He, like many of his generation, felt uncomfortable with the recent changes in the reservation. He avoided traveling in the truck, did not own a radio, and rarely left the reservation. He kept to himself, not even cultivating friendships with FUNAI agents, potential allies in a village where he counted few friends.

Villagers such as Yuka and Lino described Peruare as detached and quiet. He did not laugh or joke with people, which probably did nothing to increase his popularity among the Indians, because the Bakairí valued a good sense of humor. He was apparently somewhat intense, which was also problematic because one needed "thick skin" in the village, where the rub of daily interactions took its toll.

Although I did not identify a specific issue that might have precipitated a violent altercation, I was satisfied that, given the Bakairí cultural context, Peruare's personality would have increased the likelihood of a confrontation, then a fight, and finally his death. I could imagine a variety of scenarios, but there was one that seemed likely given the location of his body. He was probably alone in his garden, without help from the few kin he had, when a man or a group of men came by to visit, as was common among the Bakairí. Etiquette dictated that Peruare offer them some fruit and then chat with them cordially before going on with his work. However, he was noted for his taciturnity, so he probably ignored his guests until they teased or jeered at him. Then, provoked, he probably attacked them, or was perhaps attacked by them. The fight took an unfortunate turn, and Peruare lay dead. The fact that he was strung up from the branch of a tree suggested to me that more than one man was eventually involved. I figured that if the altercation was originally between only two men, the visitor could have panicked and run for help from a kinsman when he realized he had killed Peruare.

But how would I find out the truth? I could not ask Lino or Tavio, two important village leaders who surely knew what happened. They were the brothers-in-law of Wito, Neude's current husband. (Jude, who was Wito's sister, was married to Tavio.) And no one in Marti's faction wanted to discuss this possibility because the truth directly affected Neude. FUNAI officials did not possess all the facts because the Bakairí took care about what they reported and did not report to these officials. Although the courts could not prosecute and send Indians to prison because they were wards of the state, the Bakairí claimed FUNAI inflicted indirect kinds of punishment on them when they committed transgressions.

As the months passed I occasionally made an observation about Peruare's death to members of Yuka's household or to other Bakairí. But I made no further discoveries. People consistently said he killed himself. If I pointed out that Bakairí did not commit suicide, they responded, yes, wasn't that odd?

Epilogue

Almost ten years later I visited Pakuera again. I stayed in Yuka's house and enjoyed seeing Beri's wide smile and Alia's unaltered pace. Yuka and Nai were both considerably heavier than they had been when I first met them, probably because of the dietary changes that followed increased contact with Brazilians. The adoption by some Bakairí households of the Brazilian method of frying rice in pork fat before steaming it had done nothing to improve the health of the Indians.

Rea looked great. She and Nai still lived in Yuka's house, but now there were three extra mouths to feed. Beri and Alia spent an enormous amount of time fussing over the children. When I did a census during my previous fieldtrip I noted that couples whose children were grown frequently adopted or "borrowed" children from other village families. Although children were useful in that they performed important chores around the house, the Bakairí gave every appearance of doting on them. I suspected Beri and Alia worked

hard to convince Nai and Rea to remain with them instead of building a new house close by.

Rea seemed quiet but content. I did not hear her crying at night, and the bouts of sudden weeping no longer occurred. I was relieved her life has assumed a kind of placid normalcy. After all the upset during her formative years, it must have been a relief for her to live without tragedy for a while.

Rea told me that Marce married a young woman named Yeda. It was probably not a coincidence that Yeda was relatively unknown in the village. I am certain he sought a companion who did not know all the details about his family. They lived with Yeda's parents in a homestead located several miles from Pakuera. I visited the place on my first field trip and found that it was a lonely place that the Brazilians might have called *triste*, or sad, but maybe Marce needed the quiet and solitude.

My second day in the village I woke up and looked out the window to see Marce sitting on the neighbor's stoop, looking as thin as he had a decade ago. I went out and greeted him. I asked him about his headaches and weakness, and he said he thought he was still bewitched. Lino and he continued to work on the problem. He explained to me that an Indian being bewitched was different from a non-Indian being sick and being treated by a doctor. It took a long time to cure an Indian. I told him that I agreed. I wished him luck, and sincerely meant it.

Notes

1. Karl von den Steinen, *Entre os Aborigenes do Brasil Central* (São Paolo, Brasil: Departamento de Cultura, 1940).
2. Thomas Gregor, *Anxious Pleasures: The Sexual Lives of an Amazonian People* (Chicago: University of Chicago Press, 1985).
3. Robert Murphy, "Deviance and Social Control I and II," in Patricia Lyon, ed., *Native South Americans* (Boston: Little, Brown & Co., 1974), pp. 195–208.

Suggested Readings

Chagnon, Napoleon. *Yanomamö: The Fierce People*, 3rd ed. New York: Holt, Rinehart & Winston, 1983. Although many are not convinced that the Yanomamö people are, in fact, as fierce as the title of the monograph suggests, most readers agree that Chagnon has done an excellent job of describing a remarkable people.

Harner, Michael. *The Jívaro: People of the Sacred Waterfalls.* New York: Anchor Books, Doubleday, 1972. Harner's book is still one of the most vivid accounts of head-hunting and what to do with the head after it is cut off the body. Additional chapters on how the Jívaro see life after death are also excellent.

Murphy, Yolanda, and Robert Murphy. *Women of the Forest*. New York: Columbia University Press, 1974. Mundurucu society divides women from men in many profound ways that are both different from and similar to North American society. The ramifications of this division, as described by the two anthropologists, will intrigue and surprise readers.

Stearman, Allyn MacLean. *No Longer Nomads: The Sirionó Revisited*. New York: Hamilton Press, 1987. This is a restudy of the Sirionó, who were originally described in Allan Holmberg's 1950 *Nomads of the Long Bow: The Sirionó of Eastern Bolivia*. It is worthwhile and poignant reading because it shows what frequently happens to hunting and gathering bands when they are settled into villages by state governments and missionaries.

Werner, Dennis. *Amazon Journey: An Anthropologist's Year among Brazil's Mekranoti Indians*. Englewood Cliffs, NJ: Prentice Hall, 1990. This is great reading for those who are interested in learning in more detail what it is like to do fieldwork with Brazilian Indians. It also explains the different lifestyles that evolve when certain groups alternate living in large villages with living in "trekking" groups.

Nimpkish: Complex Foragers on the Northwest Coast of North America
Donald Mitchell

The lower reaches of the Nimpkish River, from the outlet of Nimpkish Lake to Broughton Strait, are a 7-kilometer (4.4 mile) stretch through which pass some of the largest runs of Pacific salmon on the central British Columbia coast. Upwards of 250,000 fish annually enter these waters now and it is likely their numbers in earlier times were even greater. Some, like the pink, chum, and coho salmons, spawn in gravels on the river's floor; others, like the sockeye and spring salmons, move on through the lake to ascend and deposit their eggs in its feeder streams. No one lives here now, but in the thick forest that lines its banks and on a grassy bluff near its mouth lie the remains of settlements belonging to the Nimpkish people. While they now dwell nearby, across Broughton Strait on Cormorant Island, a few generations ago Nimpkish existence centered on this river and it was here they lived for much of the year. This chapter focuses on life at that time, specifically between late eighteenth century contact with Europeans and late nineteenth century resettlement at Alert Bay.

In those years, the Nimpkish were but one of some twenty-five politically autonomous local groups whose territories lay on northern Vancouver Island and the adjacent mainland, within North America's Northwest Coast culture area. Anthropologists have long referred to this set of local groups collectively as the Kwakiutl—sometimes, Southern Kwakiutl to distinguish them from linguistic relatives to the north. More recently, acknowledging that the term "Kwakiutl" properly applies to but one group, the "Southern Kwakiutl" have encouraged use of the name Kwakwaka'wakw—meaning "those who speak Kwakwala," the language shared by all twenty-five local groups.

Nimpkish territory included the Nimpkish River valley as far inland as the head of Nimpkish Lake (beyond which were the Nenelkenox, one of the rare inland groups of the Northwest Coast), a few kilometers off the Vancouver Island shore to either side of the river's mouth, an adjacent cluster of small islands lying to the northeast, and fishing grounds stretching several kilometers to the north into the waters of Queen Charlotte Strait. There were extensions to this home territory by rights of seasonal access to more distant streams. Most Nimpkish went each year to the Kingcome River (90 kilometers or about 56 miles away by water and home of the Tsawataineuk), some to the Klinaklini River (141 kilometers or about 88 miles away and within Awaitlala territory),[1] to fish for eulachon. And when the salmon were running, members of other local groups joined the Nimpkish at their river fishery for a share of its exceptional harvest.

The Environment and Population

The principal land area occupied and used by the Nimpkish is a narrow coastal plain lying between the mountains of northern Vancouver Island and the protected waters at the head of Queen Charlotte Strait. In elevation, their offshore islands are an extension of this plain. Nimpkish Lake, however, is steep-sided and extends fjord-like deep into the mountainous interior. These mountains provide some protection from the prevailing moisture laden westerlies and leave an only moderately wet territory in an otherwise very damp part of the continent. Immediately west of the mountains, in Nuuchahnulth (Nootka) territory, annual precipitation in some places averages over 500 centimeters (196 inches). Here, it is around 150 centimeters (59 inches). Snow falls each winter, but little accumulates as it soon dwindles with the winter's rain and frequent warm spells.

Dense forests of hemlock, Douglas fir, and cedar clothe the land from shore's edge to high on the mountain slopes. The canopy of mature evergreen forests of this type blocks light and curbs growth of an understory, with the result that the woods themselves, though carpeted in mosses and ferns, are largely devoid of wildlife. However, summer fires periodically sweep through the timber, forming large tracts of brushland over which deer, elk, and black bear forage. In such areas and along the margins of streams and lakes, trailing blackberries and shrubs like salal, huckleberry, cranberry, and salmonberry thrive.

Large land mammals in the area included deer, elk, bear, cougar, and wolves. Near those mainland locations to which the Nimpkish seasonally traveled were grizzly bear and mountain goats. Along the shore or in the woods were smaller mammals like river otter, raccoon, mink, and marten. Sea mammals to be found in their territory included harbor seal, sea lions, porpoise, killer whale, and the occasional gray whale.

Birdlife is plentiful. There are summer resident ducks, geese, and swans and a wide range of migrating shorebirds and waterfowl both spring and fall. A small population of diving birds winters in Broughton Strait.

Unquestionably, the most important Nimpkish resources were to be found in the sea, on its beaches, and seasonally in its tributary rivers. The sea held such fish as halibut, herring, ling cod, rock cod, perch, and sculpin. To the rivers came five species of salmon (spring, sockeye, chum, coho, and pink) and steelhead and to selected mainland rivers, eulachon. On or in the beaches were littleneck, butter, and horse clams, cockles, mussels, snails, barnacles, sea urchins, sea cucumbers, and crabs.

As resources for the region's human occupants, two important characteristics of many of the economically significant plants and animals were their cyclical (seasonal) availability and nonrandom (geographically specific) distribution. In addition, many resources (including the critical runs of salmon and herring) were unpredictably variable from year to year. The effects of the first two characteristics were met by seasonal moves to specific locations to harvest resources as they became available and by adoption of preservation and storage techniques that permitted stockpiling for lean seasons. The unpredictable nature of certain resources was accommodated partly by the preservation technology, partly by trade, and partly by the common practice of intergroup feasting. The

Nimpkish were fortunate in that their river had runs of salmon that were both large and relatively stable. Other Kwakwaka'wakw without direct access to the resources of this river might experience the occasional very lean year.

The number of Nimpkish supported by this environment at or before contact was likely under two thousand. Captain George Vancouver, who visited the area in July 1792, estimated there were about five hundred in Xwulk, a village at the mouth of the Nimpkish River, but at that time of year others may well have been in residence at either of two settlements further upstream. A Hudson's Bay Company estimate put the figure for the Nimpkish in 1838 at about 1,990. By 1883 their numbers had fallen to 190,[2] a reduction brought about almost entirely by the disastrous effects of disease—most notably smallpox.

The Annual Subsistence Round

Kwakwaka'wakw local groups each consisted of a number of extended households that traditionally gathered in winter at a common village but during the rest of the year might be found at any of a number of settlements within or beyond the home territory. We will follow the moves and activities of one of these Nimpkish house groups during a typical year.

The winter season (which we treat as the final chapter in the annual round) was brought to a close with the appearance of the year's first abundant and important resource: the herring. As early as February or March, vast schools of Pacific herring approach the beaches to spawn. The exact choice of beach is not predictable, but there are areas of greater likelihood, and to one of these our house group, in company with many others who had the right to exploit this resource, would travel. One likely area is in the islands across Broughton Strait, where the seasonal settlement of Ksuiladas was situated. For the move, their house at Xwulk, the winter village, was dismantled, leaving only the heavy posts and beams of the framework. The large split cedar planks forming the roof and walls were loaded and lashed crossways on pairs of big cedar dugout canoes to form platforms for passengers and possessions and up to four of these affairs for each household, accompanied by smaller canoes, would be paddled, on a favorable tide, across the strait and through the islands to Ksuiladas. Here, the cargoes were unloaded onto the beach at one of the three small coves to the north and south of the settlement (it extended right across the narrow island) and the planks were set up on a log framework similar to that at the winter village.

From this base, parties traveled out each day in the small canoes to search for and observe herring. Once the probable spawning beaches had been determined (the water is whitened by discharged milt), preparations were made for the harvest. Previously cut evergreen boughs were thrust into the beach at low tide to form a miniature temporary forest. When the herring came inshore with the rising tide, they deposited many of their eggs on these branches, and as the spawn was one of the major desired herring products, harvesting consisted simply of gathering the heavily laden branches. The other product was the herring themselves. These were taken by paired fishermen, one at the stern paddling the small canoe through the school of fish, the other at the bow plying a device known as a herring rake. It was a thin, narrow strip of wood, about 1.5 meters (5 feet) long, and for about half the length of one narrow edge set with 4–5 centimeters long slender bone points about 3 centimeters apart. Sweeping it through the water like a paddle, but edgewise, the fisherman twisted his body as he carried through on the stroke and shook off into the canoe any herring that been impaled. Fish and eggs were taken back to Ksuiladas where they were dried by wind and sun on a pole framework or by heat and smoke high in the rafters of the house.

While some stayed in this settlement at the end of the brief herring season, our group, members of the Tsetsetlwalagame descent group ("the famous ones"), moved on as they had the right to fish for eulachon at the head of Knight Inlet. Many others went to Quaee on the lower reaches of the Kingcome River where their descent groups held similar rights.[3] Those who remained at Ksuiladas took halibut from banks in nearby Queen Charlotte Strait and hunted for porpoise or seal in the same waters. Halibut are locally available all year round but most effectively caught in late April and early May before the growth of a brown, scummy weed on the ocean floor hides the baited hooks from the fish. The halibut fishing apparatus consisted of a long line at the end of which were a weight and, tied to the line a little way above this, a short, horizontally floating wooden pole. Suspended from each end of the pole by lengths of leader were large baited hooks.[4] Halibut are big fish (they average around 16 kilograms or 35 pounds but may attain over 200 kilograms or 440 pounds) and were processed by filleting into very thin sheets of flesh and hanging the pieces over pole frames in places where wind and sun could combine to dry the flesh, such as on the two rocky points jutting out from Ksuiladas' south beaches.

The move to the eulachon fishery was similar to that described for the shift from Xwulk to Ksuiladas:

Planks were again removed from their frameworks, strapped onto pairs of big dugouts, and loaded with boxes containing the possessions of this mobile household. The long trip up Knight Inlet must be accomplished as quickly as possible for winds can blow here very strongly and along its high and steep shores there are few places to shelter. With luck, a following wind would help them along the way, but a head wind, accompanying the steady down channel current, could make the going tough for the paddlers and their awkward craft. The destination was Tsawitti, a stretch of the Klinaklini River estuary and one of the few locations along the whole Northwest coast to which come the eulachon—a diminutive smelt of such exceptionally high oil content it has earned the common name of "candlefish." Tsawitti saw an annual gathering of households from many local groups and there they set up residence in closely neighboring villages.

The spawning eulachon were taken in large fine-meshed nettle-twine bag nets or captured in baskets at the apex of wicker V-shaped fences set in the river shallows. These fish were mostly valued for their oil, which was extracted by a combination of putrefaction and boiling. Large wooden vats (sometimes dugout canoes would be pressed into service) were filled with water and partially rotted fish and brought to the boiling point by the addition of hot stones. The oil was skimmed from the surface and stored in tightly fitted wooden boxes or containers made from kelp—a large seaweed whose bulbous end and long stem are hollow—which after filling would be coiled in boxes.[5]

By May, or before if the eulachon came early, our group would reassemble its twin-hulled vessels and, now laden with processed oil, move off down the inlet on a return voyage to the Nimpkish River. Some of the oil was subsequently transported in canoes to the head of Nimpkish Lake and then packed over a rough trail that led to the west coast of Vancouver Island. Here it was traded to Nuuchahnulth groups, in whose territories no eulachon ran.

On the return to the river from the eulachon fisheries, the Nimpkish took up residence at Xwulk, Udzolas, and Gwadzi. Planks were set up on the standing house frames and from these bases the inhabitants engaged in a varied set of summer pursuits. Beaches on nearby Broughton Strait were dug for clams and seaweed was gathered from along the shore. Berries were picked and, like the seaweed, dried for later use. Some villagers owned plots of land at Kagis, on a low islet in the river estuary.[6] Here, they tended and eventually harvested crops of cinquefoil and clover roots. But from mid-summer until late in the fall, the main activity was catching and processing salmon. First to come are the sockeye. Over one hundred thousand pass by the lower Nimpkish River settlements, with the run beginning in May but peaking in July. Lesser quantities of pinks, coho, and spring follow—peaking in August and September—after which comes the large and important run of chum. They appear first in October, crest in November, and are through by mid-winter.

Some fish will be taken with harpoons as they mill about before starting upstream, but most are captured with great efficiency at weirs and in traps constructed along the lower reaches of the river. Of several kinds of traps used by the Kwakwaka'wakw, two are known to have been employed in the Nimpkish River. One was a composite device. Part was a post-and-pole compound with a V-shaped entryway on the downstream side of the trap terminating in two long baskets that became packed with fish swept there by the current. Between the baskets and downstream from the V 'd entry was a U-shaped rock trap with a sloping wooden ramp at its entry to make it difficult for fish to escape. Near the outlet to Nimpkish Lake was a large pole compound with a low rock wall as its downstream side. Fish would leap the rock barrier but be stopped by the wooden fence. Fishermen speared the salmon from a canoe moored to posts at one end of the trap.[7]

This was a period of intensive work for all and each segment of the house group had its designated tasks. In general, men attended to the traps and speared or netted fish, while women processed them for storage. The latter was by far the more time-consuming task. Children helped, and slaves could be pressed into service, but given the size of the Nimpkish River fish runs and the effectiveness of the traps, the limiting factor in producing dried salmon for storage still must have been not "catching" labor but "processing" labor. Each fish had to be gutted, its head and backbone removed, and body split lengthwise to the tail. The flesh on each side piece was then scored with a sharp knife to permit easy penetration of air and smoke. The paired body pieces were hung on pole frames and allowed to dry. As the season advanced and rainy days grew more frequent, this drying moved indoors. The prepared fish were hung high in the rafters where hot air and smoke could finish the process. When ready, they were packed in boxes for winter storage.[8]

As summer moved into fall, some attention turned to trapping deer and elk. Deer, it was said, were so bold and plentiful they came right into the villages among the houses. Log deadfalls set along the game trails would trap unwary animals even as the people continued to work at the river.

During the fall, some Nimpkish traveled to camps on the lake from which the men went out each day with guns (as early as 1792 there were reportedly two or three per house),[9] spears, and perhaps bows and arrows to hunt deer and elk. Women and children would gather and dry the last of the season's berries.

For much of the period before the historic move to Alert Bay, when the fall's work was done, all would settle for the winter in their large plank houses at Xwulk, although there are traditions of an earlier period when the upriver villages were also occupied at this season. Perhaps this was so before the nineteenth century population decline was well advanced. The plank dwellings served as shelter for their inhabitants and also as storage places for the household's supply of food. Of course, through the winter the occasional deer or elk might be shot, there were cod and wintering seabirds to be taken in Broughton Strait, some steelhead would be running in the river, and clams and other shellfish were available at nearby beaches. But the focus of attention now was on ceremonial activities within the houses. The great feasts accompanying these affairs drew not on the little fresh food that could be gathered in this cold, wet season's few hours of daylight, but on those dried and smoked provisions they had earlier worked so hard to assemble.

Their strong dependence on accumulated resources at this season could conspire with a lower than average fall harvest of salmon and comparatively short shelf life for dried salmon to produce serious late winter shortages. The people then looked forward with some concern to the first green shoots of spring and a hopefully early return of the herring and eulachon.

Material Culture

One reflection of the mild but wet climate was the clothing. For much of the year, men would wear nothing, women, a simple apron. Either might don a loose-fitting robe or blanket when it grew cool and a woven cape and conical hat if they wished to keep off the rain. Year round they went barefoot.[10]

In part, the form of the dwellings also reflected the climate's wet and temperate nature. Their houses were commodious and airy, even drafty, each providing a large sheltered area for its inhabitants to work and rest. The permanently erected supporting framework of cedar logs consisted of substantial upright posts and heavy beams. When villagers were in seasonal residence, the roof and sides were clad in wide split cedar planks. Inside were a raised earthen perimeter platform bearing the sleeping and storage chambers and a sunken central court that served as a work area for the house. There were no windows and light entered through cracks between the wall planks and openings in the roof through which smoke also escaped. In size, these houses were commonly around nine meters square although in later years some of fifteen to eighteen meters dimension were not unusual.

Although the foregoing were enduring characteristics, during the nineteenth century, many other aspects of style and construction changed quite dramatically. As depicted by the earliest European visitors to record such details, in the 1790s[11] wall planks were positioned horizontally in clapboard fashion, held in place between widely spaced pairs of tall, thin poles. Short ropes joined the poles ladderlike between each plank, providing a sling in which the board rested. This arrangement allowed for easy dismantling of the walls for the regular seasonal moves. At this time, the common roof style was a single pitch (shed roof) form, high at the front and sloping to the back, although the engraving in Vancouver's *Voyages* on which our information is based shows that low-pitched gable-roofed structures were also present at Xwulk. It is not certain where the door was situated, but it at least seems not to have been in the side facing the water. Some houses (Vancouver says they were the homes of the "principal people") had large decorated front panels. Although smaller, the resemblance of this early form of Nimpkish house to dwellings of the Salish and Nuuchahnulth is obvious.

The fashion then shifted towards a form that was more like houses of the northern coast.[12] Low-pitched gable roofs became the norm, and wall planks might be either attached horizontally as before, or repositioned vertically with their upper ends set into channels cut into heavy eaves boards. A later development was to set the bottom of the gable end wall planks into grooved sills as well. It now became common to decorate the house with representations of the owner's crest figures. The front (in the center of which was situated the building's main entrance) would bear a huge painted mural, and inside, the framework's heavy uprights would be carved and painted. After the shift of the principal village to Alert Bay in the 1870s, where a sawmill was soon established, the timber-framed house would be permanently clad in sawn lumber, but until then, the shell remained removable and was still transported to the seasonal settlements.

Furnishings within the house included floor-level backrests for the comfort of those who sat near the fire and woven cedar bark mats for the surrounding platform's sleeping areas. Each constituent household's possessions (animal hides, woven blankets, wood or mountain goat horn spoons, wooden dishes, fishing equipment) were stored on the platform between the sleeping areas, often in distinctive decorated wooden chests. Outside each house was usually a fair-weather lounging area—a square patch of level ground or plank platform built out over the bank, surrounded by a low, plank back rest. Sometime during the nineteenth century, free-standing carved crest poles became fashionable and a not-uncommon sight in front of dwellings. In the engraving of Xwulk in 1792, however, there is but one possible example.[13]

Nimpkish fished, hunted sea mammals and birds, and generally traveled about their territory—even up the swiftly running current of the lower Nimpkish River—in dugout canoes. These were of varying size and form, depending on their use. There were small ones, suitable for one or two paddlers and a passenger, that were in frequent use by men or women as they tended the halibut sets, scouted for spawning herring, gathered firewood or shellfish, or undertook a hundred other domestic tasks. Larger versions, with more prominent stem and stern pieces, and often richly ornamented, were used for the main seasonal relocations and as transport for parties of raiders. By the nineteenth century, canoes were often fitted with a mast and sail, but they seem not to have been in earlier times.

Residential and Kin Groupings

The normal large winter dwelling accommodated up to twenty-five or thirty people; an average was perhaps around fifteen. Usually from four to six households, each with its own cooking fire and sleeping and storage platform, comprised the house group. The core would be a group of closely related males—commonly brothers—and their wives and children. But also in the house would be assorted elderly relatives and slaves belonging to the occupants.

Nimpkish house groups were linked as members of one of four major social divisions, each consisting of a cognatic descent group or *numaym*[14] with associated spouses. (A fifth was added during the nineteenth century when the Nenelkenox—the up-river people—joined the Nimpkish.) In a cognatic descent group (sometimes called an ambilineal descent group), the links back to the common ancestor are sometimes through males, and sometimes through females. One had the right to membership in the numaym of either the father or mother; most often the father's group was chosen. The numaym was a generally exogamous unit and a corporate group that was certainly the most important Nimpkish social division. With the numaym were identified village residential areas, resource locations (entire salmon-bearing streams or places to build weirs and traps for salmon on the Nimpkish river or for eulachon on the Kingcome or Klinaklini rivers; halibut fishing areas in Queen Charlotte Strait; clover beds, berry patches, and shellfish beaches; and elk hunting territories along Nimpkish Lake), and a host of incorporeal properties (ranked titles or "seats," crests, songs, performances, myths, and names for people, dogs, houses, feast bowls, and canoes). The most important of these properties, such as the ranked titles, remained always with families in the numaym, usually passed down through the generations in lines formed by a pattern of male primogeniture, but on occasion descending, in trust, to a female for her eldest male child.[15] Properties of another kind or of lesser value might not remain long in the numaym or even within the local group. Their transfer was often negotiated as part of a bride's dowry.

In winter, the four numayms resided together in one or more of the Nimpkish River villages. Only in matters of war or the conduct of the winter season ceremonies did the village act as a unit; even while co-resident, numayms, and individual households retained their essential autonomy.

Rank and Social Stratification

Of paramount import were the ranked positions held by the numaym. These "names," "titles," or "seats" (so called because they gave the holder a place when attending a feast) bore names whose origins and order lay in the distant, mythic past. Titles descending within the numaym were ranked with respect to one another but, as a likely reconstruction of early contact circumstances would have it, when they met at feasts, precedence was based only on the relative position of each numaym's highest ranking title-holder.[16] However, the situation had changed by the latter part of the nineteenth century and, in principle, the almost eight hundred titles that were distributed among the Kwakwaka'wakw could be placed in a single order. In practice, inter-numaym ranking was only of consequence when two or more title-holders were together at a feast or when marriages were being arranged. At feasts, rank was made apparent in a variety of ways to be outlined shortly. For marriage, care was taken to arrange unions that would involve families whose titleholders were of similar status.

Although each numaym harbored several title-holders, the highest-ranking title reflected on the posi-

tion of all. As we have seen, one interpretation suggests that at one time only the principal titles were of significance when numayms met at feasts. But even after development of pan-Kwakwaka'wakw ranking for all titles, the holder of the top rank in each numaym could count on other members for assistance in upholding the worth of the title. Diminishment was of constant concern to all title-holders. If one did not mount feasts and distributions of scale appropriate to rank on those occasions that especially called for such events, the title's mcrit was imperiled.

This particular system of rank seems also to have structured leadership within the local group. The holder of the highest title in each house led the house group, and the highest in the numaym was its leader or "chief," as they are most commonly identified in the literature. With four numayms, the Nimpkish had four such "chiefs" who were graded by rank with respect to one another. The control of day-to-day activities was largely in the hands of the house group leaders as the house groups had a great deal of autonomy of action. Numaym leaders were primarily active in guiding and coordinating the ceremonial activities of their groups. It is said they also decided when villagers should dismantle their houses and move on to the next seasonal settlement, but as these seasonal shifts were so intimately connected to cycles of nature, this responsibility may have been largely a ritual one. Leaders were the nominal owners ("caretakers" might be a better word) of such numaym or house group resource properties as salmon streams or fishing stations, clam beaches, and berry patches.

There were two other formal schemes of rank. Each of the twenty-five Kwakwaka'wakw local groups was ranked with respect to the others. As this grading seems in large measure to have been related to the relative richness of the salmon resources they controlled,[17] with their very productive river, the Nimpkish were high on the list—in sixth place at the end of the nineteenth century and likely about there in earlier times. The other scheme of precedence was most apparent during the winter ceremonies. At these events, the various categories of performers—most of whom were dancers—formed a ranked order.

Occupants of the Northwest Coast were distinctive amongst hunter-gatherers for the presence of two or more social classes. The Nimpkish and other Kwak-waka'wakw had three, cross-cutting or outside the numaym structure. The major distinction was between those free and those enslaved, but even within the free category were distinct strata.

At the top were what we may call the title-holder class. This included all those who currently were possessors of ranked names or "seats," who had occupied such a seat in the past, or who could expect to succeed to a ranked position. Members of the title-holder class married other members of that class. There was no advantage in arranging marriages with any other category as those outside had no titles or other prerogatives to convey to the partner or to the children. Those who did not have and could never reasonably aspire to have ranked positions within their numaym formed a second stratum of free society. These were the commoners—numaym members far removed from the primogenitural line of succession (a fifth child or beyond seems to have been in this category) or persons in lines of descent that simply carried no privileges.[18] As population declined through the nineteenth century, this class essentially disappeared. There were so many titles and so few remaining people that virtually all who wished to remain participating members of Kwakwaka'wakw society could do so as part of the title-holder class.[19]

At the bottom of the status hierarchy were the slaves. They comprised an hereditary class or caste and were, in theory, self-perpetuating in that the children of slaves were raised as slaves, but a more important source was periodic recruitment from captives taken in raids. The fate of captives was to be killed, ransomed, or enslaved. Ransoming was rare, but a possibility if the captive's relatives were able to make contact with the raiders. The outcome of capture for adult males was sometimes death, for females and children more commonly slavery. In the early nineteenth century, slaves would have been readily available to the Nimpkish through the expansionary wars of the Lekwiltok. As a common practice to discourage runaways was for captives to be passed on through the trade network to locales distant from their homeland, many Salish would thereby have found their way into Nimpkish hands.

The lives of slaves were possessed, absolutely, by members of the free classes. Slaves might be traded, given away as feast gifts, or even killed on ceremonial occasions. Owners reaped full benefit of their labor, which was directed to tedious tasks like fetching water and firewood, paddling canoes, and preparing fish for winter storage.

Marriage

One perpetual concern of the title-holder class was to arrange advantageous marriages. Because the numaym was commonly treated as an exogamous group, partners were usually sought amongst the other Nimpkish numayms or, frequently, amongst other local groups. To some extent, such matches served to tie numayms or local groups together, but of even greater importance to the Nimpkish seems to have been the transfer of property that indispensably accompanied a marriage. If we follow through the customary steps of arranging and completing a marriage, the consequences should become clear.[20]

The first initiative was taken by the groom's family or the groom himself if he was a mature adult. A spokesman secretly contacted the father of the desired bride to determine if a proposal would be accepted. If the response was favorable, emissaries of the groom's numaym were sent to the bride's house to announce, loudly and publicly, the intended marriage. Subsequently, a solitary representative of the groom visited the prospective bride's father to work out details of the bride-price and dowry and to agree on when the event was to take place. Once mutually acceptable terms had been negotiated, a token gift of animal pelts or woven blankets was delivered to the bride's father as a down payment on the eventual bride-price.

Up to a year elapsed while the groom's family assembled goods to be given the father of the bride. On the appointed day, the groom's party arrived in canoes at the beach before the bride's house—a custom followed even if the marriage was between residents of the same village. A mock battle might ensue when the party tried to make its way across the beach and into the house. Here, as with other word and action, it is evident much of the marriage symbolism entails analogy with abducting women through warfare—indeed, the Kwakwala words for war and marriage are identical. Once in the house, and after speakers for each side had proclaimed the greatness of the numayms or local groups being linked, the bride-price goods were piled before the bride's father. He, through his speaker, announced what the dowry would be and produced an initial installment composed largely of the boxes, spoons, mats, and blankets necessary to establish the new household. The groom was then led forward and seated beside his bride, concluding the ceremony. Most commonly, the new couple took up residence with the groom's house group.

Later, after the birth of the first child, there was a further ceremony at which more of the dowry was conveyed to the groom. Most valued, perhaps even the objective of arranging a particular match, were rights to winter ceremony performances. Also prized and quite commonly transferred as dowry were "coppers"—large metal shields whose equivalent worth in blankets was established by the scale of the last feast at which they had been delivered to another owner.

Full payment of the dowry brought the protracted marriage observances to a close.

No such formal rites and procedures characterized marriages of those outside the title-holder class[21] and many of the motives for arranging ties would simply not apply to this virtually propertyless group. A variation reported only for very high-ranking title-holders was negotiation of unions within the numaym.[22] The marriage could be between a man and his niece or possibly a step-sister. Here, the attempt would seem to be to avoid loss to the numaym of its highly valued prerogatives.

Feasts and Property Distributions

One important duty of the top-ranking title-holders was to invite other title-holders to elaborate feasts designed to mark significant events in the life of the host or the host group. Accompanying the feast would be a distribution of valuable property—gifts from the host to the assembled guests.[23] Anthropologists have commonly referred to these events as "potlatches," a term adopted by the Nimpkish themselves. What would occasion a feast and distribution could be a memorial for a previous holder of the title or a wish to celebrate such contemporary events as initial assumption of the title, the giving of a name to a child, a marriage, construction of a new house, or the launching of a canoe. The affair might be small, involving only the numayms of a single local group, or of grander scale, with the title-holder and his numaym serving as hosts and title-holders from other local groups attending as guests. The whole local group would commonly cooperate for these larger gatherings, with title-holders from the group's other numayms using the opportunity to host subsidiary distributions.

Years of preparation might be involved in hosting a particularly elaborate feast—one perhaps extending over several days. Gifts had to be manufactured or acquired and in the immediately preceding months, food stockpiled. The usual gift was a hide or woven blanket, but canoes, household utensils, and even slaves might be presented. Suitable items were amassed through the direct labor of the title-holder's house group, by calling in loans previously made at interest to other title-holders, and finally, by borrowing from relatives and friends.

Central elements of these events were the speeches, meals, and property distributions. Orators or "speakers," each acting on behalf of the host title-holder or a guest title-holder, in turn recited the accomplishments of incumbents and their predecessors and in the process listed the important prerogatives and possessions of each numaym present. Throughout the proceedings, the relative status of the guests was made apparent. Rank was evident, for example, in such conventions as the order in which title-holders' presence was acknowledged during speeches. The seating arrangement for title-holders reflected their rank. Generous amounts of food were served to the guests in the order of their rank and when the gifts were distributed, these too were handed out according to standing. The value of the gifts was also graded with respect to rank of the recipient. A high-ranking guest might receive a canoe or slave; one of lower status, some carved spoons. And when blankets were distributed, rank was reflected in the height of the pile before each guest.

Two significant things were happening at these feasts. The host and his numaym were publicly proclaiming their worth and rightful position in the scheme of ranked titles. In addition, guests were having their relative status acknowledged in the elaborate protocol of the event. Perhaps rarely in earlier times, but with increasing frequency during the nineteenth century, the host and his group ventured to promote the title to a higher standing. They would not learn if the attempt was successful until a subsequent feast when the host of that event either did or did not seat the aspirant in the position sought.

Winter Ceremonies

As the Nimpkish settled into their winter quarters, they entered a period in the annual round of activity when subsistence concerns drew into the background. People lived primarily off their stores of dried seafood, dried berries, and eulachon oil and passed much of this rainy time indoors—the women weaving blankets, baskets, and mats, the men carving utensils and preparing fishing and hunting gear for the coming seasons.

Highlights of the period were the winter ceremonies with their colorful dance performances. The ceremonial period was a special time, marked by distinctive observances and behavior, when spirit beings returned after long months spent circling the earth. The insignia of the season was cedar bark dyed a conspicuous shade of red. Cedar bark was charged with supernatural power and figured prominently in the costumes of dance officials and of many performers and their attendants. Additionally, titles and names employed by men and women during the rest of the year were replaced by special ones in use only at this time. Such names might be of ribald nature, reflecting a purposeful relaxation of moral standards—a temporarily free-and-easy approach to matters of sexual conduct.[24]

The dance performances that were the core of each ceremony formed yet another system of rank, as already noted. However, these performances were ordered, not individually, as were titles, but by category so a whole set of dancers would be of higher standing than another set.

Most dance categories were identified exclusively with either males or females, while a few could belong to either. "Belong" is a fitting word to use, because the rights to perform a particular dance and to use the mask and costume associated with it were valuable property passed down through the generations. The right to perform those dances appropriate for males, for example, might be transmitted from father to son, or, more commonly, from father-in-law to son-in-law as part of the bride's dowry.[25] Only one person at a time could hold the individual performance right, but, of course, there would normally be several performers in each ranked category. In addition, there were several officeholders who came by their positions through inheritance. These included a master of ceremonies and his speaker and a host of individuals with special responsibilities in the traditional rituals associated with different stages of the ceremony. They bore designations like "water-carrier," "stone-picker," "cedar-bark worker," and "wedge-splitter."[26]

Winter ceremonies grew in size and complexity throughout the nineteenth century, with the new dance forms apparently coming to the Kwakwaka-'wakw mainly from their northern neighbors, the Heiltsuk and Owikeno. Acquisition in these cases was not through marriage but mainly by seizure. Such property could be obtained by killing the owner and all accounts of how Kwakwaka'wakw gained the *Hamatsa* or Cannibal performances, for example, are of this means.[27] A Nimpkish title-holder killed a Heiltsuk Hamatsa who was passing through the area on the way to his northern home sometime after the Nimpkish had moved to Alert Bay (shortly after 1870) and thereby brought what may have been the first Hamatsa prerogative to that local group.[28] Considerable familiarity with these aggressive, wild-behavior performances and even with "secret" aspects of initiation are implied by resort to this practice.

Notwithstanding the means by which the right to a performance was acquired, before it could be used there was an obligatory stage of initiation. For some categories this might take as long as four months and involve long stays in the woods away from the settle-

ment. For others, initiation required only a short period hidden in a portion of the house. However elaborate, the assumption was the same: A guiding spirit has abducted the novice and carried him or her off for instruction.[29] In time, they reemerge, are captured, and with the help of attendants, dance for the first time at a ceremony in one of the houses.

Those who attended these winter ceremonies were of one of three statuses: the uninitiated (many of whom would never have the right to dance), novices, and active dancers (collectively referred to as "Seals"), and inactive or retired dancers ("Sparrows").[30] Sparrows served as managers and attendants. They were composed of several groups, organized partly to reflect their age, partly the dance category from which they had retired.

It was customary for a dancer to perform for several seasons—four may have been the usual number—sometime after which the right would be transferred to a suitable successor. The formerly active dancer would then join the appropriate division of Sparrows. The eventual possessor of a very high-status prerogative might have first gone through many seasons performing several lower-ranked dances, in effect alternating between Seal and Sparrow. One duty of the Sparrows was to determine when the dancers were ready to join their ranks. This should not be until there were no remaining signs the dancers were under the control of the spirits that had originally captured them. To this end they taunt with words or objects or gestures known to goad the dancer. When there is no longer a response, they are ready.

The presentation of a dance was an elaborate affair, with rich costuming—often including a large wooden head or face mask—designed to depict the essence of the animal spirit that was the performer's inspiration and protector. The dance movements themselves in large measure imitated characteristic actions of the animal. Much use was also made of clever theatrical devices and deceptions. For example, the audience might see a *Tukwid* dancer (usually a female performer) placed in a wooden burial box whose lid is lashed tightly in place. From the box, which was placed on the fire, the Tukwid's singing voice is heard to issue but, in time, it ceases, and attendants pick her charred remains from the fire. These are deposited in a box, out of which, in a short time, she rises, apparently unscathed and whole. The entire performance has been skillfully staged through the use of a tunnel with hidden entryways, a speaking tube made of kelp, and a genuine corpse stolen from its burial location. Similarly miraculous resurrections were staged by

Tukwids who had been beheaded or stabbed. Others caused thunder to sound, or animals, people, or objects to fly through the air.[31]

Before they obtained the Hamatsa dance privileges, the Nimpkish and other Kwakwaka'wakw seem to have had a related but tamer category, the *Hamshamtses*.[32] Many different animals served as spirit protectors for the Hamshamtses with the result their costumes were highly variable. Some masks were of the "transformation" kind, with the face or beak composed of two or more hinged pieces that swung open to reveal an entirely different animal spirit within.

The onset of a typical dance season would see the disappearance of several villagers under circumstances interpreted by the uninitiated as abduction by a spirit being. Many of those who vanished would have danced the previous season, but some would not, and it was on the new initiates, particularly those being inducted to high-ranking categories of performance, that the ceremonies seemed to focus. Each ceremony (there would usually be several in the course of the winter) had a different host wishing to mark the initiation of one or more dancers. As the guests were to witness a display of rights and prerogatives, gift distributions necessarily accompanied each initiation and the hosts' numayms assisted in amassing the requisite quantities of food and goods for what could be an expensive event.

The sponsor of a novice hired songwriters (one for the music, one for the lyrics) to visit the new dancer and assist in developing his or her unique set of songs. The day before the novice was scheduled to reemerge, these writers met secretly with a group of singers to coach them in the new piece.[33] Eventually, one at a time, the dancers appeared at the village, were captured by Sparrows who had once been initiates for the dance category, and were led to chambers at the back of the various houses.

Each host's residence served as a dance house. For this purpose, it was fitted with a secret chamber at the back, behind a painted screen that figured as the backdrop for most performances. On up to four successive evenings, the initiate emerged from in back of the screen, performed, and then withdrew behind the barrier. Each evening, others, those in their subsequent years of dancing, might be moved to perform, usually coming forward from a corner of the house where attendants had been guarding them.

On the fourth evening, the dancers were generally quite subdued—evidence the guiding spirit's control was weakening and that the dancer would soon return to normal behavior. As a final gesture, the host's numaym distributed property and fed those

assembled with what might well be the last of its stored food. Attention then shifted to another host, who for the next several days provided villagers with food and entertainment.

In this manner, the winter season was spent, until the final host numaym had distributed the last of its food, the performers had all been tamed, and the spirits had set off on the return journey to their distant world. With the close of the ceremonies, "summer" names came back into effect and the usual rules of moral conduct were once more in force.

Warfare and Raiding

Kwakwaka'wakw local groups were embroiled in several serious armed conflicts in the nineteenth century and the Nimpkish participated in their share of these. Fighting seems not to have been carried into Nimpkish territory, but there were forays into the lands of distant neighbors. In 1850 they crossed Vancouver Island from the head of Nimpkish Lake in an ill-fated attempt to raid the Nuuchahnulth. Later that decade they were part of a more successful excursion against people far to the north.

This affair[34] is worth examining for it illustrates rather well the major characteristics of Kwakwaka'wakw "warfare." A longstanding conflict between the Nuxalk (Bella Coola) and some Kwakwaka'wakw local groups escalated when a near exterminatory Nuxalk raid on the Kwiksutaineuk resulted also in the deaths of some visiting members of other local groups, including Nimpkish. As among those killed were several title-holders, the losses involved both lives and property—most significantly, valued names with their associated prerogatives. Those groups affected promptly mounted a retaliatory expedition. They would hope to avenge the losses, regain the stolen names, and, as such things were viewed, transfer the burden of grief to the relatives of those they would kill.

However, long before the sixteen canoes of this party reached Nuxalk territory, their scouts fell in with a small group of highranking Oyalidox Heiltsuk on their way to invite neighboring title-holders to a feast. From them they learned the Nuxalk, evidently forewarned, had retired to fortified locations. When the main body of raiders caught up with the scouts, they promptly killed the Oyalidox. The decision was then made to return home. Others would now grieve, and while the lost names and prerogatives had not been recovered, in their place they had gained those of the dead Oyalidox title-holders. Specific revenge against the Nuxalk was less important than attainment of these other objectives.

The main motives for raiding and killing seem to have been of this sort, although territorial expansion was not unknown. Throughout the first half of the nineteenth century, various Lekwiltok local groups, once immediate neighbors of the Nimpkish, were pressing the margins of Kwakwaka'wakw territory southward, wresting lands from Salish control.[35] Nimpkish were amongst the first Kwakwaka'wakw to obtain guns and a reliable source of ammunition, which they did through their overland contacts with the Nuuchahnulth, who were then in regular contact with European and American fur traders. Armed through this channel, the Lekwiltok used their technological advantage to full effect and eventually gained territory to the northern shores of the Strait of Georgia.

The gun, a trade musket throughout the period of concern, was important, but as the principal tactic was surprise of the enemy, other, more silent or less obvious weapons were more often employed. A warrior would be armed with a spear, a dagger, and a short sword-like club of whale bone. Elk hide tunics were used as armor but these were rendered obsolete as guns became more generally available. Trophy heads and scalps were taken from the slain and the heads displayed on the end of upright poles or suspended from a bar back at the home village.[36] As already noted, a not-insignificant outcome of raiding was the acquisition of captives who, if not ransomed by their relatives, could be enslaved.

Religion and Medicine

No clear line can be drawn between the analytical category "religion" and those facets of Nimpkish life that have already been described. Virtually everything had its religious aspect and almost every action had at least potential supernatural consequences. The affairs of humans in the earth world were therefore intimately connected with matters in four other realms.

These additional domains known to the Nimpkish and all other Kwakwaka'wakw were the sky world, where humans had dwelt before they acquired human form and where many important spirits still lived; a world at the bottom of the sea, presided over by a powerful sea spirit; a world beyond the ocean, at the western horizon, where sea and sky met, which was accessible to those who inhabited the world at the bottom of the sea; and beneath the earth, a ghostland, to which humans went after death.[37]

Many inhabitants of these lands, including some in the earth world, were possessed of supernatural power or *nawalak*—the underlying belief of Kwak-waka'wakw religion.[38] Of the earthdwellers, many plants (such as individual cedar and hemlock trees) and animals (wolves and salmon) possessed nawalak but twins were the only humans to have it naturally. However, other humans might acquire it from animals or the supernatural residents of the other worlds. Once gained, it might long remain in human control. Events in the mythical past brought the first humans to earth from the sky world, established the system of ranked titles, and endowed those titles with supernatural power. As the titles have descended through the generations, so also has their associated power. Power long ago obtained was also transmitted with the names and prerogatives that passed, after a marriage, from father-in-law to son-in-law or from maternal grandfather to grandchild. But power was more immediately and directly received by novice performers during their initiation. Although returning to them for several winters, it eventually left, freeing them to join the ranks of the Sparrows.

Some individuals gained shamanic powers, often after being made ill by the being that was to become their supernatural helper—for Nimpkish shamans, commonly the toad.[39] Shamans (or paxala) were of several grades. The highest were associated with the top-ranking title-holders (indeed, some were title-holders themselves) and had the ability to cure or cause illness. Lower down the scale were those who could only cure, and lower yet, ones whose power permitted them only to diagnose.[40] During the winter ceremonies, all who were in the Seal category, were considered and referred to as paxala,[41] and some performances involved seemingly miraculous cures and resurrections that were attributed to shamanic power. However, the paxala status of performers ended with the close of the winter season.

Illnesses were believed to have a variety of causes. If diagnosis indicated intrusion of a foreign object into the body (usually through sorcery), the shaman treated the patient by removing the object. This was accomplished through massage to locate and concentrate the offending material and then sucking to extract it. The object, perhaps a pebble or insect, would be spat out by the shaman, sometimes accompanied by copious amounts of blood.[42] Soul loss was another possibility, which was countered by prolonged and difficult measures to find and restore the soul to its body.[43] Nimpkish shamans sometimes concluded the source of the trouble was an excess of "green matter." Skillful massage would bring about its expulsion.[44] Shamans were also quite familiar with various plant, animal, or mineral materials useful for the treatment of particular ailments.

The Nimpkish Today

The Nimpkish live now at Alert Bay, on Cormorant Island, within sight of their river. Fishing is still a major occupation, but it employs a vastly different technology, involving big seine boats and the smaller gillnetters and trollers, equipped with electronic aids like radiotelephones, radar, long-range navigation, global positioning, and fish-finding sounders. Governed by the complex rules of the commercial fishery, they take many of their salmon now in Broughton Strait as they approach the river, but many Nimpkish vessels range far beyond their traditional territory in pursuit of fish. Canadian legislation for several decades forbade winter ceremonies or the "potlatch" customs. Masks and dance costumes were confiscated and a few leaders jailed. A revision of the Indian Act in 1951 quietly dropped these prohibitions and since then the Nimpkish people have been at the forefront in reaffirming the importance of feasts and ceremonies in their lives. They have also been active in renegotiating their relationship with the governments of Canada and British Columbia. One important outcome is certain to be a return to greater control over the traditional resources of their territory.

Notes

1. Franz Boas, "Geographical Names of the Kwakiutl Indians," *Columbia University Contributions to Anthropology* 20 (1934): Map 22; Edward S. Curtis, *The North American Indian*, vol. 10 (1915; reprint New York: Landmarks in Anthropology, Johnson Reprint Corporation, 1970), p. 22.
2. Franz Boas, "Census and Reservations of the Kwakiutl Nation," *Bulletin of the American Geographical Society* 19 (1887): 231; Donald Mitchell, "A Demographic Profile of Northwest Coast Slavery," in Marc Thompson, Maria Teresa Garcia, and Francois J. Kense, eds., *Status, Structure, and Stratification: Current Archaeological Reconstructions* (Calgary: The Archaeological Association of the University of Calgary, 1985), p. 231; and George Vancouver, *Voyage of Discovery to the North Pacific Ocean and around the World*, vols. I–III (London: Robinson & Edwards, 1798), p. 627.
3. Franz Boas, "The Social Organization and the Secret Societies of the Kwakiutl Indians," *Annual Report of the United States National Museum for 1895* (1897): 331; Boas, "Geographical Names," Map 22; and Curtis, *The North American Indian*, p. 22.
4. Franz Boas, "The Kwakiutl of Vancouver Island," *Memoirs of the American Museum of Natural History* 8 (1909): 471; Curtis, *The North American Indian*, p. 25.
5. Boas, "The Kwakiutl of Vancouver Island," pp. 420, 465–466; Curtis, *The North American Indian*, pp. 23–24.
6. Boas, "Geographical Names," Map 21.
7. Boas, "Kwakiutl of Vancouver Island," pp. 461, 464.
8. Curtis, *The North American Indian*, p. 29.
9. Vancouver, *Voyages*, p. 627.
10. Boas, "Kwakiutl of Vancouver Island," pp. 451–454; Curtis, *The North American Indian*, pp. 4–5.
11. Vancouver, *Voyages*, Plate 28.
12. Helen Codere, "Kwakiutl: Traditional Culture," in Wayne Suttles, ed., *Northwest Coast Handbook of the North American Indians*, vol. 7 (Washington: Smithsonian Institution, 1990), p. 365.
13. Boas, "Kwakiutl of Vancouver Island," pp. 415–416; Curtis, *The North American Indian*, p. 10; and Vancouver, *Voyages*, Plate 28.
14. Franz Boas, *Kwakiutl Ethnography*, Helen Codere, ed. (Chicago: University of Chicago Press, 1966), p. 37.
15. Ibid., pp. 51–52.
16. Philip Drucker and Robert F. Heizer, *To Make My Name Good: A Reexamination of the Southern Kwakiutl Potlatch* (Berkeley: University of California Press, 1967), p. 36.
17. Leland Donald and Donald Mitchell, "Some Correlates of Local Group Rank among the Southern Kwakiutl," *Ethnology* 14 (1975): 340–341.
18. Boas, *Kwakiutl Ethnography*, p. 53.
19. Codere, "Kwakiutl: Traditional Culture," pp. 371–372.
20. Boas, *Kwakiutl Ethnography*, pp. 53–54; Curtis, *The North American Indian*, pp. 124–128.
21. Curtis, *The North American Indian*, p. 124.
22. Boas, *Kwakiutl Ethnography*, p. 50.
23. This section is based on descriptions in Boas, *Secret Societies*, pp. 341–358; and Curtis, *The North American Indian*, pp. 141–143.
24. Boas, *Secret Societies*, p. 418; and Curtis, *The North American Indian*, p. 170.
25. Boas, *Kwakiutl Ethnography*, p. 173.
26. Curtis, *The North American Indian*, p. 185.
27. Boas, *Secret Societies*, pp. 426–427.
28. Ibid., pp. 425–426.
29. Curtis, *The North American Indian*, p. 159.
30. Boas, *Secret Societies*, pp. 419–420; Boas, *Kwakiutl Ethnography*, pp. 174–175. A conflicting interpretation is presented in Curtis, *The North American Indian*, p. 155.
31. Boas, *Secret Societies*, pp. 487–492; Curtis, *The North American Indian*, pp. 209–212.
32. Boas, *Secret Societies*, pp. 463–466.
33. Ibid., pp. 520–521; Curtis, *The North American Indian*, p. 171.
34. Boas, *Kwakiutl Ethnography*, pp. 112–116.
35. Herbert Taylor and Wilson Duff, "A Post-Contact Southward Movement of the Kwakiutl," *Research Studies of the State College of Washington* 24 (1956): 56–66.

36. Boas, *Kwakiutl Ethnography*, p. 105.
37. Franz Boas, "Kwakiutl Culture as Reflected in Mythology," *Memoirs of the American Folklore Society* 28 (1935): 125; Irving Goldman, *The Mouth of Heaven: An Introduction to Kwakiutl Religious Thought* (New York: John Wiley & Sons, 1975), pp. 195–197.
38. Boas, *Kwakiutl Ethnography*, pp. 165–167; Goldman, *Mouth of Heaven*, pp. 179–192.
39. Boas, *Kwakiutl Ethnography*, p. 135.
40. Ibid., p. 120.
41. Boas, *Secret Societies*, p. 505.
42. Boas, *Kwakiutl Ethnography*, p. 127.
43. Ibid., pp. 137–141.
44. Ibid., p. 142.

Suggested Readings

Boas, Franz. "The Kwakiutl of Vancouver Island," *Memoirs of the American Museum of Natural History* 8 (1909): 307–515.

Boas, Franz. *Kwakiutl Ethnography*, Helen Codere, ed. Chicago: University of Chicago Press, 1966.

Codere, Helen. "Kwakiutl: Traditional Culture," in Wayne Suttles, ed., *Northwest Coast Handbook of the North American Indians*, vol. 7. Washington: Smithsonian Institution, 1990, pp. 359–377.

Curtis, Edward S. *The North American Indian*, vol. 10. 1915; reprint New York: Landmarks in Anthropology, Johnson Reprint Corporation, 1970.

North Alaskan Eskimos: A Changing Way of Life

Ernest S. Burch Jr.

"There it is," said the pilot of the small bush plane.

"There is what?" I asked.

"It's the village, Kivalina," said the pilot. "We're practically there."

All I could see was an enormous expanse of empty space as we flew up the coast. The Chukchi Sea was on the left, and a broad, treeless flat area ringed with hills was on the right. The dividing line between land and sea was a beach of dark sand and gravel. It was mid-October. The rivers and lakes were newly frozen and covered with a light dusting of snow, but the sea was still ice free and dark under the overcast sky. I was so overwhelmed by the sensation of openness and space that I could scarcely identify the landscape's components.

Suddenly I saw some irregularities near the beach just ahead. Just as it dawned on me that they were buildings, we zoomed over them. Then we turned, descended, and landed on a small airstrip. The pilot deposited me and a few mailbags on the apron and left. Several villagers had come out to see the plane, and we stood there staring at each other as the plane's roar faded into the distance.

Kivalina in 1960 was a village of about 150 Eskimos, two white teachers and 175 sled dogs. Physically, it consisted of a school, a store, two churches, a National Guard armory, and twenty-four small houses. Of the houses, half were made of sod placed over a wood frame, and half were wooden shacks. There was no electricity or plumbing.

Just out of college, I was in Alaska as a research assistant on an environmental impact study. My job was to learn how dependent the Kivalina people were on local resources for their livelihood. My home was a small house rented from the Episcopal Church.

The day after I arrived I was invited to participate in a caribou hunt with three other men. I accepted, of course. Victor Swan told me to get in his sled. I was young and in reasonably good shape, and I responded that I preferred to trot alongside; I had read many times of how Eskimos travelled slowly across the country with two to three dogs pulling a heavily loaded sled. However, I could not reconcile my book-based vision with the scene in front of me. Victor had fifteen dogs hitched to an empty sled, and they were so enthused at the prospect of going that they were leaping five feet (one and a half meters) into the air and screaming with excitement. So I got in the sled. As soon as I did, Victor raised the hook that had held it and the dogs took off so fast that I fell flat on my back in the sled.

The hunt was unsuccessful because Dennis, who had been my partner during the hunt, had apparently made some tactical errors. Sitting around drinking coffee afterward, Leonard and Victor expressed some negative opinions about his actions. They spoke in Eskimo, but swore in English. Leonard, in particular, uttered amazing strings of profanity. I asked him where he learned to swear, and he responded that he had just retired from the U.S. Army after many years as a master sergeant. It also turned out that, after living for many years in Japan while in the Army, he could speak fluent Japanese, as well as English and Eskimo.

The next day was Sunday, so I decided to see what a service was like in the local Episcopal Church. It was led by an Eskimo from the village who turned out to be a fully ordained deacon (later priest) in the Episcopal hierarchy. The music was led by a pump organ, played by the deacon's brother, and a robed choir; the hymns were sung by the entire congregation in four-part harmony.

What was going on here? Were these people traditional Eskimos or modern Americans? On the one hand, they spoke almost exclusively in Eskimo among themselves. On the other hand, most of them could also speak English. They lived largely from hunting and fishing and ate traditional native foods almost exclusively, but most of the men also worked seasonally as carpenters, miners, longshoremen, or commercial fishermen in other parts of the state. All of the young men were members of the Alaska National Guard, which meant that they had had at least six months of military training at Fort Ord, California. Some of the young men and women had gone to school in southeastern Alaska, Kansas, New Mexico, or California. Every person had an English name, but also one or more Eskimo names.

The answer to the question "Were these people traditional Eskimos or modern Americans?" is that they were both, or, perhaps, neither. I became fascinated by this situation and decided to learn how it came about. That turned out to be more difficult than anticipated, involving hundreds of interviews with native elders and extensive library and archival research. I am still working on it more than thirty years later. What follows is a condensed version of what I have learned so far.

The Iñupiaq Eskimos

The Native residents of Kivalina belong to a larger group of people known as *Iñupiat* (pl.), or "North Alaskan Eskimos." The Iñupiat speak the Inuit Eskimo language, which is spoken across the northern part of North America from Bering Strait, on the west, to the coasts of eastern Greenland and Labrador, on the east. (Several *Yup'ik* Eskimo languages are spoken in south-central and southwestern Alaska and along the coast of easternmost Asia.)

At the beginning of the historic period, in the late eighteenth and early nineteenth centuries, the Iñupiat numbered about eleven thousand people and occupied an area of nearly one hundred thousand square miles (260,000 square kilometers). Their territory extended from the islands in Bering Strait to just east of the mouth of the Colville River, and included most of the drainages of the rivers reaching the sea between those two points (see Figure 1 at the end of this article).

The Setting

Northern Alaska is characterized by a variety of landscapes. At one extreme are the rugged, glaciated peaks of the Brooks Range, which rise to altitudes of nearly

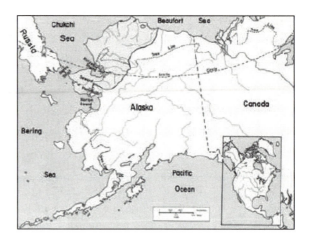

Figure 1

nine thousand feet in their central portion. At the other extreme are extensive lowlands, the largest of which, the Arctic Coastal Plain, covers all of Alaska north of the Brooks Range. Much of the country is comprised of a mosaic of hills, flats, lakes, and streams. The coastline consists of a long sand and gravel beach bordered by lagoons in many areas, and broken here and there by capes and bluffs rising abruptly from the sea. Most of the country is underlain by permafrost (permanently frozen ground).

About seventy-five percent of Iñupiaq country lies north of the Arctic circle. The sun does not rise above the horizon for at least one day a year at the Arctic circle, and is not visible for nearly six weeks at Point Barrow, the northernmost tip of Alaska. On the other hand, it does not get dark at all from mid-May to late July, and there is very little darkness for a month or so before and after that.

Iñupiaq country is also crossed by the treeline, or northern limit of trees, which angles irregularly west, then south across the region. North of the treeline the country is covered with tundra vegetation, which consists of a variety of grasses, sedges, and mosses, but with sizeable shrub growth along waterways and in well-drained or protected areas. South of the treeline the landscape is covered with patches of northern boreal forest (primarily spruce, with some birch and other species) along waterways and in well-drained areas, and by tundra vegetation elsewhere.

Northern Alaska is relatively warm for a region so far north, but it is still very cold compared to most regions of the world. Below zero temperatures Fahrenheit (below -17 degrees Celsius) last for weeks and often months during the winter, occasionally descending into the -40s Fahrenheit (-40s Celsius) along the coast, and much lower inland. Summers are cool along the coast, rarely getting above 60 degrees Fahrenheit (15 degrees Celsius), but it can get fairly warm—in the high 90s Fahrenheit (high 30s Celsius) inland. Rivers and lakes normally freeze in early to mid-October, and thaw in middle to late May. The ocean usually freezes in December. The ice starts to melt in May and breaks up in June. Precipitation is minimal, almost at desert levels. Most of what does fall comes as light rain in mid- to late summer. Snow-fall is light, but because of the cold temperature snow accumulates on the ground for nearly eight months. Wind is an important fact of northern life everywhere, but particularly so beyond the treeline. In general, the southern part of the region is warmer and more moist than the north.

The animal life of northern Alaska is rich and diverse for a region so far north. Of particular importance to the traditional native economy were several kinds of sea mammal, bowhead whales, belukha whales, walrus, and several species of seal. Caribou (wild reindeer) were the most important land animals; others included polar bears, grizzly bears, and a variety of furbearing animals, such as wolves, wolverines, foxes, minks, beavers, otters, marmots, and ground squirrels. The region is favored with sizeable fish populations, including several species of salmon and whitefish, sheefish, char, ling cod, lake trout, grayling, pike, blackfish, and two varieties of small cod. Finally, northern Alaska is visited in summer by birds, such as murres, that nest on bluffs rising from the sea; huge numbers of migratory waterfowl (ducks, geese, swans, cranes); songbirds; and birds of prey. Ravens and two species of ptarmigan stay in the region year-round.

The Traditional Iñupiaq Way of Life

Archaeologists have discovered that people have lived in northern Alaska for at least eleven thousand years. A number of prehistoric cultures have been identified, but for most of the period of human occupation it is difficult to assign ethnic or linguistic labels to them. However, the Iñupiaq Eskimos are clearly the direct biological and cultural descendants of the bearers of the Thule Culture, which emerged along the northwest Alaskan coast toward the end of the first millennium A.D. Over the ensuing centuries they expanded both inland and toward the south.

The first written accounts of the Iñupiat that have come down to us were made by English and Russian

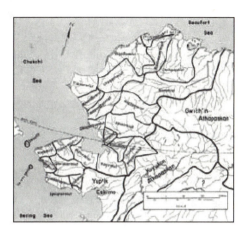

Figure 2

explorers in the late eighteenth and early nineteenth centuries. The latter is also the earliest time for which reliable oral historical accounts have been obtained. For these reasons, it serves as a useful ethnographic "baseline" from which to measure social change in the region, both backward into prehistoric times, and forward into the present. For convenience I refer to this time as the "traditional period," and to the social system that existed then as the "traditional" one.

The traditional Iñupiat were organized into twenty-six socioterritorial units that have been variously referred to in the anthropological literature as "tribes," "regional groups," and "societies." The boundaries of these societies are shown in Figure 2 at the end of this article. Elders from whom I learned about these units characterized them as "nations, just like France, Germany, and England." Although I refer to them here as societies, it is useful to think of them as having been tiny versions of nations or countries as most of us understand those terms. Each society was characterized by a distinctive name, a discrete territory, a clearly identifiable subdialect of the Iñupiaq language, an ideology of distinctiveness, and a number of other distinctive features such as clothing styles, taboos, annual cycles of movement, and burial customs.

The estimated populations of the traditional Iñupiaq societies ranged from about 225 (*Ukiuvangmiut*, on King Island) to 1,340 (*Tikirarmiut*, at Point Hope), with an average of about 425. To modern readers, the idea that such a tiny social system can justifiably be considered the equivalent of a nation is ludicrous, but few modern readers are familiar with societies whose economy is based entirely on foraging (hunting, fishing, and gathering). They were very different from everything most of us have experienced.

The average area of traditional Iñupiaq societal territories was 3,850 square miles (9,970 square kilometers), but there was a considerable range of variation among them. The smallest territory was that of the Ukiuvangmiut, which consisted solely of the four square miles (ten square kilometers) that constitute King Island. The largest was that of the *Nunamiut*, in the northern interior, which encompassed some nineteen thousand square miles (forty-nine thousand square kilometers).

The village of Kivalina, where I first experienced northern Alaska, is located on the territory of a traditional society known as *Kivalliñarmiut*, which encompassed an area of approximately 2,100 square miles (5,400 square kilometers). The Kivalliñarmiut numbered about 320 people, making them one of the smallest Iñupiaq societies.

FAMILIES

The basic social unit in an Iñupiaq society was a large, bilaterally extended family (defined below). This large unit was comprised of several subfamilies.

The core of the system was a conjugal, or nuclear, family composed of husband and wife and their nonadult offspring. A conjugal family was created when a man and woman took up residence together and had sexual relations. That was all there was to it; Eskimos are among the few people in the world who did not recognize a marriage with some kind of ceremony. The Iñupiat had no system of preferential marriage by which certain categories of people were supposed to get married. They also lacked a system of arranged marriage, although in most cases parents seem to have tried to influence their children's choice of spouse. Incest taboos prohibited the marriage of siblings and close cousins, but in these small populations it was often difficult to find someone of the opposite sex and the right age to whom one was not rather closely related. Intersocietal marriage was one way to solve this problem. It did sometimes occur, but it usually led to so many conflicts that it was generally avoided. A few expert hunters had more than one wife (polygyny), the known record being five; having multiple husbands (polyandry) was also possible but extremely rare. Despite these possibilities, monogamy was the norm.

The division of labor along gender lines was sufficiently extreme as to ensure that most people did marry; it was almost impossible for an adult to live successfully without a spouse. Men hunted big game (caribou, mountain sheep, bears, and sea mammals) and most furbearers, and they manufactured tools, weapons, utensils, and most other paraphernalia that did not involve sewing. In some societies they did the fishing, at least at certain times of year, or else shared that activity with women. Except in special cases, women fetched big game animals that had been killed, butchered them, and processed the meat and skins. They also did most of the gathering of vegetable products, hunted small game (such as hares, ptarmigan, and ground squirrels), and in many societies did much of the fishing. Women were in charge of the storage, preparation, and distribution of all edible material from the time it reached the settlement until it was consumed. They also did all work involving sewing, which most notably involved the manufacture and maintenance of skin clothing, and they were the ones to make nets, pottery, and baskets. Child care was also largely the responsibility of women.

Conjugal families rarely lived by themselves. Most of the time they shared their dwelling with other relatives: the parents of one or (rarely) both spouses, married or unmarried siblings or cousins, their own married children if they were old enough to have any, or some combination of any of those possibilities. The families were "bilaterally extended" because they could include relatives from either the wife's or the husband's side, or both.

Extended family households were almost always located next door to other households of relatives of various kinds. Furthermore, the members of this larger unit acted as a single family under most circumstances. The men typically hunted and worked together, and the women spent most of the day together doing their chores. The children moved freely among the houses and felt at home in all of them. To distinguish these neighborhoods of related extended families from extended family households, I refer to the former as "local families" and to the latter as "domestic families." Thus, there were three levels of family in the Iñupiaq system: conjugal, domestic, and local.

Local families that I have been able to document for the late nineteenth and early twentieth centuries ranged in size between seven and nearly seventy members, with the majority involving between ten and twenty. According to elders with whom I discussed the matter, this was a very traditional pattern, except that in a few exceptional cases families had approached one hundred members. For reasons that are not clear, couples seem to have had few children in traditional times, and in most households there were as many adults as children, or more adults than children.

No matter how large or small they were, for all of the people most of the time local families constituted the social universe within which their daily lives were carried out. In one sense it is obvious that this would be so, since most settlements consisted of just one local family, and since settlements were situated several miles apart. But it was also basically true even in the largest settlements, where the houses of several local families were built close together.

Traditional Iñupiaq societies may be usefully conceived as being made up of a network of interrelated local families. Since in most cases the society as a whole involved just a few hundred members, it may be readily understood that most people were related by birth or marriage to practically everyone else. In addition, of course, there were friendships and various other relationships in which nonrelatives could interact, but family ties took precedence over all others to an overwhelming degree.

ECONOMY

The economies of traditional Iñupiaq societies were based primarily on animate resources. The precise details varied from one society to the other according to the specific combination of resources available in their respective territories. At a general level the most critical resources were sea mammals, fish, and caribou.

Sea mammals were hunted with harpoons and spears; the precise techniques and the size of the weapons used varied according to the size of the animals being pursued and the ice conditions existing at the time. In northern Alaska, sea mammals range in size from the bowhead whale, which reaches sixty tons (54,400 kilograms) or more in size, down through walrus, belukha, and bearded seals to the hundred-pound (forty-five kilogram) ringed seal.

Sea mammals differ from land mammals in that their deposits of fat, known as blubber, are concentrated in a distinct layer located between the meat and the skin. Seal blubber renders easily into oil, and was served to the Iñupiat as food, fuel, medicine, and a medium within which dried meat and fish, and also some berries and greens, were safely stored without refrigeration for the better part of a year. Bowhead and belukha whales were a substantial source of meat, and their soft skin, rich in vitamin C, was relished as food. Walrus and bearded seals were also important sources of meat, and their skins were used for boat covers. Walrus tusk ivory was made into components of tools, weapons, utensils, and jewelry. Ringed seals provided meat, and their skins were made into rope, clothing (especially waterproof boots), tarpaulins, and bags. Finally, bowhead whalebones were used as

structural members of the framework of sod houses in coastal regions north of the treeline.

Several varieties of fish are found in northwestern Alaska. They include lake trout, pike, burbot, grayling, and blackfish in freshwater; small species of cod and flounder in saltwater; and Dolly Varden char and several species of salmon and whitefish which move between salt water and freshwater seasonally. Fishing techniques varied according to season and species. In summer, the most productive technique in most areas was seining, whereby a long net made of rolled bark, baleen, or sealskin line was used to herd the fish toward a gravel bar and eventually scoop them up onto the bar. In the fall, when the ice is thin and many species of Alaskan fish move downriver, weirs were used. Otherwise, fish were caught with hook and line and with leisters (specialized fish spears). Although sea mammals and caribou receive most of the attention in the anthropological literature on northwestern Alaska, fish were a very important source of food for the members of practically all Iñupiaq societies, especially those whose territories were located inland.

The final primary animate resource in northern Alaska, and the only important terrestrial mammal, was the caribou. Caribou are a highly migratory species of medium-sized deer. Their meat resembles beef in taste and texture, and their hides can be made into tent covers, storage bags, and exceptionally warm but lightweight clothing and sleeping bags. Their antlers were made into the components of tools, weapons and utensils, and their back sinews (muscles) were made into excellent thread. The most productive way to hunt caribou is to build a circular enclosure, or corral, in an area they commonly cross when migrating and to herd the animals into it. Other techniques were snares set in passageways through forest or brush, pitfalls dug in the snow, bows and arrows, and spears wielded by kayakers chasing animals crossing rivers or lakes.

Vegetable resources ranked far below animate resources in general significance in Iñupiaq economies, although they were important in certain areas. Wood was used in the manufacture of boat and house frames, tools, weapons, utensils, sleds, paddles for umiaks (large open skin boats) and kayaks (small closed skin boats), and as fuel in some districts. Although most of northern Alaska is devoid of trees, driftwood formerly was common along the coast. Willows provided bark for net-twine, and the leaves, bark, and roots of various shrubs were used for medicinal purposes and for staining animal hides and some wooden objects. Finally, several kinds of berries, greens, and some roots were gathered and consumed as food or as medicine.

Minerals were used in a variety of ways. Chert ("flint") was chipped or flaked to make arrow and spear points, scrapers, knives, gravers, and other tools, and used with pyrite to start fires. Slate was made into knife blades, and nephrite (jade) was used to make adz blades, whetstones, jewelry, and occasionally knife blades or spear points. Two or three kinds of rock served as grinding material in the manufacture of slate and jade tools, in the manufacture of pottery, and, in conjunction with scrapers, in the preparation of skins. Clay was made into pottery, and certain kinds were eaten during periods of starvation. Finally, hematite, or red ocher, was made into paint to decorate paddles, the handles of weapons, and some items made from caribou skins.

All of the major animate resources of northern Alaska (including fish) are migratory, and they travel too far and too fast for people to follow. However, the various species take different routes and follow different schedules, so that every Iñupiaq territory had some important resources on hand most of the time except for late February and March. One way the people provided for seasonal variations in food supply was to overharvest in times of plenty and store the surplus for later consumption. They also undertook a series of annual moves themselves so that they could be in the best place to intercept each species of fish or mammal as it went through. As a rule, the members of local families stayed together during these movements, although during the lean season of late winter they often split up into domestic family segments and spread out. This spread the risk on the one hand, and increased the chances of someone finding game on the other.

For most of the year seasonal human movements were within societal territories. In summer, however, many involved trips to other territories as well. The residents of the islands in Bering Strait, for example, had alliances with the members of societies on the Seward Peninsula, which permitted them to hunt caribou on the mainland. In another example, the *Nuataarmiut*, whose territory lies far inland along the Noatak River, traveled to the coast every summer to hunt belukha; while they were away, hunters from the Kobuk River hunted caribou on the upper Noatak. All of the summer encroachments into foreign territory were undertaken at times or in ways that did not infringe upon the activities of the owners. It was a remarkable system of coordinated movements that must have taken centuries to develop.

Extensive movement was made possible by sled in winter and by boat in summer. Most domestic families had three or four large dogs to help haul their goods and possessions. People had to help pull and push when the sleds were fully loaded, but the arrangement still enabled them to transport much more than they could have otherwise. Extensive summer movement along rivers and seacoasts was carried out in umiaks. Umiaks built for travel—as opposed to those built for whale hunting—ranged from about thirty to fifty feet (nine to fifteen meters) in length, and were made of wooden frames covered with seal or walrus skin. A thirty-foot umiak could carry a ton of freight and a dozen people, yet was still light enough when empty for two men to lift out of the water. These large boats were sailed, paddled, or pulled along the beach or riverbank by dogs or people, as conditions permitted or dictated. Birchbark canoes served as the major form of transportation in a few inland districts where sealskins were not easily acquired. In the mountains summer travel was on foot, with the assistance of dogs as pack animals. Kayaks were used primarily for hunting in most areas.

People lived in cone- or dome-shaped tents in summer, during which time they needed no light (because of the midnight sun) and used wood as cooking fuel. In winter they lived in sod houses along the coast, and elsewhere in dome-shaped dwellings made of a wooden framework covered by sod, moss, or caribou-skin tarpaulins. Light and heat were provided by oil lamps. Cooking was done either over the lamps, or with rocks heated in wood fires and then placed in pots containing water and meat. In winter, most meat and fish were eaten raw and frozen except at the evening meal. When travelling, people took their skin-covered dwellings and frames with them, along with most of their other equipment and supplies. When they set up camp for the night they created a brand new settlement.

The overwhelming majority of the goods and services required for survival in traditional northern Alaska were both produced and consumed at the local family level. Most raw materials, especially those used as food, were contributed to the general supply by the individual(s) who originally acquired them. The family stores were under the supervision of the wife (or main wife in the case of polygyny) of the local family head. She redistributed food to the domestic families as needed. However, since the men and older boys all ate together in one building, and the women and children all ate together in another, the redistribution of food was a simple operation.

THE POLITICAL PROCESS

Eskimos have been depicted in some anthropological texts as having lived in a state of anarchy. If, by anarchy, one means the absence of a formal government, that characterization would be correct. If, on the other hand, one means by the term a complete lack of order, an "every man for himself" type of situation, the claim is nonsense.

Local families, which formed the foundation of the Iñupiaq political system, were characterized by a pervasive hierarchical structure based on the factors of generation, relative age, and gender. With regard to generation, parents had authority over children. As long as children continued to live in the same local family as their parents, and as long as the parents were active, vigorous individuals, this authority continued pretty much throughout their lifetimes. With respect to relative age, the hierarchical system was even more pervasive: Older people had authority over younger ones. In most families in our society, children are taught to resist attempts at dominance by older siblings that are not explicitly authorized by a parent (as when baby sitting); youngsters are taught to "stand up" for themselves. Eskimo children were taught just the opposite, to submit. While Eskimos did not record birth dates, they did know people's relative ages. With respect to gender, the picture is more complicated, but, in general, males had authority over females, at least over those of the same or lower generations. However, there were distinct domains, such as control over food supplies, where women's authority was superior to that of men.

Local family leadership was based on individual talent combined with the factors of generation, relative age and gender described above. A local family head was a highly competent hunter between the ages of about forty and sixty who had one or more wives, one or more married younger siblings and/or siblings-in-law and cousins, and one or more nonadult or married offspring living with him in the same local family. His authority over the others flowed almost automatically from his position in the kinship system. The successful head, or *umialik*, of a large local family was a wealthy man. He and at least his primary wife wore the most elegant clothes, ate the choicest food, and generally had the best of whatever they wanted. They bore themselves in a dignified manner, and were treated with deference by others. For these reasons, the first European explorers to visit northern Alaska could tell who the "chiefs" were from a long distance away.

The main check on an umialik's abuse of power was that compliance was voluntary. There was no legitimate source of coercion in the entire system. The various domestic and conjugal family subsystems of a local family could come and go as they pleased, and if an umialik became incompetent or demanding, everyone simply left. Effective umialiks were generous with their wealth and considerate of others in most of their dealings, and they consulted widely before making major decisions.

Disgruntled people had to consider their alternatives. If they left one local family, they had to join another, so they had to decide where they would be better off. Domestic and conjugal families did not realistically have the option of striking off on their own for more than brief periods. They would find it difficult to produce all of the goods and services they needed to survive, and they could not defend themselves against raiders from other societies or even against villains from within their own.

The counterpart of the problem of an ineffective or corrupt leader was a problem individual farther down the hierarchy. Such a person could be a nuisance, or someone who refused to perform his or her share of the work that had to be done in order for them all to survive. Such individuals were cautioned, exhorted, teased, admonished, and otherwise exposed to the sentiments of the other members of the family about their behavior. The ultimate sanction in this direction was to shun the offender. No one would talk to him or her, people would try to avoid him or her as much as possible, and they might even try to move the settlement without warning. In a world where social life and family life coincided, this was devastating treatment, and brought all but the most deviant individuals into line. Truly dangerous individuals were killed, preferably by their closest relatives so as to avoid the possibility of a blood feud.

Religion played a part in the political process in a way that crosscut the kin-based system just described. As discussed in the next section, the Iñupiat believed that the world is governed by a host of spirits. Some of them could control important things, such as the game supply and the weather. If the spirits were alienated by something people did, they sent the game to another country or visited upon the offenders some other kind of disaster. In order that this not happen, people had to obey an enormous set of prohibitions, or taboos, that were communicated to them by spirits via a shaman. This gave shamans considerable influence in daily affairs, since they could tell people what they had to do and when they had to do it in order to prevent hostile spirits from harming them. The authority of the shaman and that of the umialik ordinarily covered different sets of activities, but not always, and conflicts between them could be a source of stress within the local family.

Local families were very self-sufficient politically. Political integration above the local family level was weak, and this fact is what may have led to some of the claims of anarchy noted above. Iñupiaq societies did lack governments or other organizations above the local family level that could have mediated, influenced, or controlled relations between and among families. For most people most of the time, local families were located so far apart that this did not matter. However, in the larger settlements, where the members of two or more local families resided in close proximity to one another, there was often considerable tension, since there was no structured way to resolve interfamily disputes. The political process at this level operated essentially as it did within local and domestic families, through the voluntary cooperation of the people involved. When that did not work, the solution had to be either the departure of one of the contending families to some remote district, or bloodshed.

Religion

Iñupiat religion was based on the animistic belief that every living thing, and many things (e.g., mountains) that we do not conceive of as being alive, were imbued with souls. There were, in addition, a number of spirits who were not normally associated with any particular physical form. All spirits, including those associated with humans, could be temporarily disassociated from their related physical forms, either through their own volition, or through magical practices of some kind.

The Iñupiat believed that the world was basically a munificent place. Fish and game existed in infinite supply, the weather was good, and people were healthy—unless some spirit interfered. If one did, the result was famine, stormy weather, accident, or illness. Spirits were viewed as negative forces that had to be placated in order for people to survive. Unfortunately, spirits were also perverse, because they required people to obey an enormous number of taboos.

No one has ever compiled on paper a complete list of the taboos adhered to by the members of any Eskimo group, and no native elder living today knows more than a fraction of those followed in earlier times. However, some examples from northern Alaska illustrate their general nature:

1. If bear meat had been placed in a dish, the same container could not thereafter be used as a receptacle for belukha flesh;
2. Skins could not be deliberately wet while the salmon were running;
3. A young girl could eat meat only from certain ribs of a mountain sheep; when she was older she could eat only from certain other ribs; and when she was full grown she would have to abstain for a time from eating ribs that she had been allowed to eat up to that point.

If one understands that rules like these numbered in the thousands, one can begin to appreciate the significance of taboos in traditional native life.

The discovery of what activities were tabooed was the prerogative of the shaman. The shaman was a person, male or female, who, through mystical experiences or training, acquired an ability to communicate with spirits. If someone was ill, or the caribou failed to appear at the usual time of year, or the weather had been bad for weeks on end, a shaman was hired to intercede with the spirits to find out what caused the problem. The answer was always that one or more specific taboos had been broken, and the solution was typically the addition of a new one to placate the offended spirit. For the Iñupiat, religion meant avoiding trouble, not seeking a state of grace.

Intersocietal Relations

Hunter-gatherers in general, and Eskimos in particular, are sometimes depicted in anthropological texts as being "free wanderers," as people who could go anywhere they wished. While that may have been true in some areas, it certainly was not in northern Alaska. In northern Alaska, anyone who ventured into foreign territory without permission was killed.

Alliances were arranged between individuals and families rather than between governments. They were of two basic types: trading partnerships and co-marriages. A trading partnership involved an arrangement between two individuals, male or female, to exchange certain basic products, and to provide general support in time of need.

A co-marriage involved the practice misleadingly called "wife trading" in the literature. It did involve two couples—usually from different societies—exchanging sexual partners for a night. But when a man and a woman engaged in sexual intercourse, they were considered married for the rest of their lives, even if they never had sex together again. They were married in a different way than residential spouses, but they were married nevertheless. The two women involved were considered related to one another in the same way that the women were in a polygynous residential marriage, and the relationship of two men was considered analogous to the one existing in a polyandrous marriage. All of the children that any of the four ever had, before or after, were considered siblings, with all of the rights and obligation implied by that status. Whether or not an exchange of sexual partners was undertaken for lustful reasons, the consequences were significant and long-lasting.

Ordinarily partners and co-spouses met at one or another of three large fairs that occurred each summer, and, less frequently, at special feasts that were held during the winter. In time of famine, people could go with their families and live under the protection of their partners or co-spouses in another society until the crisis passed.

Intersocietal warfare was common among the traditional Iñupiat. Usually it was undertaken to settle a grudge rather than to take prisoners or acquire territory. Participation in a raid was strictly voluntary, so resentment had to be widely felt before a fighting force could be mustered. The preferred tactic was a surprise nighttime raid, but the Iñupiat knew how to form and maneuver battle lines, they knew how to construct defensive works, and they wore breast armor made from plates of ivory or bone attached together with thongs. Weapons consisted of bows and arrows, spears, and clubs. Although tiny operations by modern standards, battles often involved a significant proportion of the male populations of the societies concerned. They were also brutal affairs: neither women nor children were spared, and prisoners were tortured and killed. It is not surprising that men kept their weapons in good repair and close at hand at all times.

The Exploration Period

Russian and British explorers began to make their way to northern Alaska in the eighteenth century, but their contacts were brief, and their reports of native life were not particularly informative. Both the number of contacts and the quantity of information increased dramatically in the early nineteenth century.

The natives encountered by the explorers were aggressive people. They were eager to trade, but only on their own terms and only during the traditional summer season of interregional travel. They were obviously experienced traders, for they brought forth their best wares only after the explorers rejected inferior work. When the Europeans tried to buy fresh fish to eat, the natives tried to sell them fish skins inflated with air.

Outside the summer trading season, which lasted from about late June to late August, or whenever the explorers were heavily outnumbered, the Iñupiat were hostile to them. Bloodshed was narrowly avoided on several occasions. For example, when Aleksandr Kashevarov's small party passed along the coast of Kivalina territory in late August 1838, it was frequently threatened by a large number of Iñupiat. Only alert action and a hasty departure by the Russians prevented disaster. The English, under Frederick Beechey, were threatened several times on Chamisso Island in the fall of 1826, and again a year later. Finally, the Iñupiat attacked the explorers with bows and arrows. They produced some casualties but were repulsed, also with casualties, by the English firearms.

After a hiatus of about a decade, exploration resumed in the late 1840s with a number of British expeditions, all of which were involved in a search for the missing explorer Sir John Franklin. For the first time Europeans overwintered in northern Alaska: on the western end of Seward Peninsula, on Kotzebue Sound, and near Point Barrow, the northernmost point of Alaska. Several potentially violent confrontations were defused through wise action on the part of the English captains and, by the time the British left in 1854, peaceful relations between Iñupiat and foreigners had been established.

In 1848, the same year that the Franklin search ships arrived in northern Alaska, an American whaling ship sailed north through Bering Strait for the first time. The venture was so successful that an entire fleet of ships soon began working in the Arctic Ocean off Alaska. During the early years the whalers had little direct contact with Iñupiat, but they had an enormous impact on the bowhead whale population. Within a few decades they reduced it to a shadow of its former self, and turned attention to walrus. It was not long before the walrus population, too, was decimated.

American trading vessels followed the whalers north of Bering Strait. Their initial goal was to supply the whaling fleet, but they soon found a lucrative trade with the natives. They cruised the coastline and, in exchange for furs and various items of native manufacture, they traded whisky, firearms, knives, and various other goods. As the whale and walrus populations declined, some of the whalers also turned to trading as a way to turn a profit.

While these developments were taking place north of Bering Strait, the Russians, who "owned" Alaska, established permanent trading posts just south of Iñupiaq country. Shortly afterward a smallpox epidemic struck the region served by the Russian posts, killing at least half of the native population. For some reason the epidemic did not reach Iñupiaq country, but it almost eliminated the Yup'ik Eskimo population living between it and a Russian post on the south side of Norton Sound. That post lured a number of Iñupiat southward, and the loss of the former native population removed the chief obstacle to expansion. When the United States acquired Alaska in 1867, Americans took over the St. Michael post and began selling firearms and other goods to the Iñupiat.

The cumulative effect of these developments was disaster. The whalers' near extermination of whales and walrus eliminated two major sources of food and other important raw materials. Rifles made caribou hunting much easier than it had been previously. Firm in the belief that caribou existed in infinite supply, with access to them only controlled by the whims of the spirits, the Iñupiat themselves proceeded to wipe out the herds. The US. Revenue Marine (now the Coast Guard), which began regular summer cruises to northern Alaska in the early 1880s, unsuccessfully attempted to prevent this by halting the trade in rifles.

Between 1870 and 1890, famine and newly imported diseases such as influenza and measles combined to reduce the Iñupiaq population by some fifty percent, more in some districts, less in others. Faced with disaster in their homelands, and no longer fearing the few remaining defenders of other territories, people began to move around in search of food, not only within the traditional Iñupiaq area, but beyond it as well. These trends continued into the twentieth century.

Missionaries arrived in the 1890s to attack traditional Iñupiaq beliefs and replace them with new ones. The gold rush of 1898, especially to Nome, but to several other areas as well, temporarily brought in tens of thousands of outsiders, with a number of disruptive effects on native life. The U.S. government imported domesticated reindeer from Eurasia to replace the now nearly extinct caribou, and built schools in most of the places where there still was a resident Iñupiaq population.

By 1910 the demographic basis of the traditional societies was destroyed. The economy had been fundamentally altered by the loss of important game animals (walrus, whales, caribou), the introduction of rifles and the new hunting techniques they required, the importation of reindeer and new types of food, and the introduction of money. Native political independence was lost when the U. S. government imposed its control over the region. And, finally, the traditional cognitive and belief systems were under attack by the teachers and missionaries. The traditional way of life was gone.

The Mission-School Village Period

The years from about 1910 to 1970 were a time in which Iñupiaq life was focused on settlements built around missions and schools. It was a time in which the demands of the new and old ways were in constant conflict. I was fortunate enough to begin my own work in northern Alaska before this period had quite run its course.

Physically, a mission-school village consisted basically of a one-room government school (with dwelling quarters for the teacher and his or her family), a Christian mission of one denomination or another, and a number of native dwellings. Later on, independent traders established stores in many of the villages.

The reason that there was only one mission per village is that representatives of the several denominations had agreed among themselves to divide the Alaskan "field" so that they would not come into conflict with one another. Missionaries met with considerable resistance during the early years, but after a few converts publicly flouted taboos without bringing harm to themselves or their families, conversions came fairly quickly.

Initial composition of the Native populations of these villages varied to some extent from one to another. In Point Hope, for example, most of the people were direct descendants of the traditional Tikirarmiut. In Kivalina, however, the first residents included descendants of traditional Kivalliñirmiut, as well as immigrants from five other societies.

In Point Hope, the mission-school villages were organized along traditional family lines. In the Kivalina-type situation, where there was a mixture of people from different areas, local families initially were few in number and small in size, and many of the domestic units were isolated from other relatives. It was only after several marriages had taken place that local family neighborhoods began to emerge.

Interestingly, about this time couples began having more children than they had had traditionally. Since heating requirements strictly limited house size, this development eventually led to overcrowded houses. Over time, what had been extended family households became conjugal family units. Houses still had five to ten people living in them, but that number now included a married couple and their nonadult children. Married siblings lived next door to one another, not in the same dwelling.

During much of the mission-school village period the natives were faced with a major dilemma. On the one hand, they were legally required—and for the most part genuinely wanted—to keep their children in school during the winter. Most of them also wanted to be near the church and the store. These considerations meant they had to stay in town. However, since they still derived their sustenance almost entirely from hunting and fishing, and since most of their cash income (required to buy rifles, ammunition, and such new staples as flour, coffee, tea, and sugar) was derived from trapping, they also had to be out on the land. Some families were involved in reindeer herding, which required that they, too, live out of the village.

The dilemma was resolved in a number of ways. Several families did spend the winter a long way from the mission-school villages, usually in traditional-style local family settlements. They left their school-age children with relatives in town, and returned periodically to pick up supplies, and during major holidays such as Christmas. The people who stayed in town, on the other hand, started using larger teams of smaller, faster dogs to pull their sleds. Instead of hunting on foot, as they had traditionally, village-based men started going out to hunt with dogs and empty sleds. They could cover much more country in one day this way than they could have on foot. During the early fall and late spring, the major hunting and fishing seasons when the entire village emptied out, teachers accepted the inevitable and closed school.

Mission-school village affairs tended to be dominated by the teachers, or the head teacher where there was more than one. Teachers were the representatives of the federal government in most villages. Much of their influence stemmed from this and from their knowledge of contemporary American affairs and the natives' ignorance thereof. If the teacher told people they should do something, they thought they had to do it. After the government forced the native herders to place their reindeer under government control, for reasons too complicated to discuss here, teachers were placed in charge of herd administration, and also in charge of the cooperative stores formed by the new government reindeer companies to reduce the cost of imported goods.

Disputes in many villages were settled by elected village councils. Most of them were established initially by teachers to show the natives how American democracy worked. The councils generally had no legal authority, but the threat of filing a complaint with a federal marshall (in one of the regional centers) if a troublemaker got out of hand gave their demands some force. Some councils were shamelessly manipulated by teachers, but others—especially those comprised of several local family heads—were effective in managing village affairs.

The situation described above is broadly accurate for the entire 1910–1970 period, but a number of changes also occurred. For example, the Great Depression of the 1930s ruined the fur market, and severely restricted the government's ability to pay the salaries of reindeer herders. In addition to increasing the general poverty level, these developments reduced the need for families to spend winters in small, isolated settlements. They also introduced the Iñupiat to government welfare.

In another, more positive development, the caribou population recovered, beginning in the late 1930s. By the time I arrived on the scene in 1960, caribou were abundant. Moose arrived in the area for the first time in the 1940s, and quickly became an important source of food.

A third important change was the growth of opportunities for men to work at seasonal wage employment. Most of the time this was in places far from the villages, which took them to cities such as Fairbanks and Anchorage for the first time. Other avenues for wage labor came through government programs, such as the Civilian Conservation Corps during the Depression, exploration of the Naval Petroleum Reserve south of Barrow after World War II, and the construction of the Distant Early Warning (DEW line) system of radar sites all along the coast in the 1950s. Other opportunities for Iñupiat to learn about the world at large were provided by the military, by boarding schools and training centers, and by the Bureau of Indian Affairs relocation program.

Disease remained a major problem until the very end of this period. There were two catastrophic flu epidemics early in the century, and tuberculosis became almost universal. At a church conference in Noatak in 1961, all those who had been in a sanatorium were called forward to sing a hymn together. Of the several hundred people present, only about a dozen adults and the children were left in the audience. If, in 1960, one asked a woman just past her childbearing years how many children she had, a typical response was "fourteen, five living."

By 1960 most Iñupiat still preferred village life, their traditional foods, and their native language. However, the formal education provided by the schools, and the informal learning acquired via radio, books, and magazines, and experiences in places outside the villages combined to produce a native population that was reasonably knowledgeable about modern American ways.

During the late 1950s and the 1960s, a number of development schemes were proposed for northern Alaska as well as for other areas of the state. All were conceived without consultation with natives. Nor did they include provisions to compensate natives for losses they might bear because of the plans. That angered not only Iñupiat but natives all over Alaska. Armed with their new knowledge of American society, they formed a number of regional organizations and the statewide Alaska Federation of Natives. Working through the courts, these organizations brought the proposed development of the Prudhoe Bay oil field to a halt. Then, using classic, American-style pressure politics, they effectively pursued their claims with the U.S. Congress. The result was the Alaska Native Claims Settlement Act (ANCSA) of 1971.

The Land Claims Era

ANCSA granted to Alaska natives fee simple title to 40 million acres of land and $962. 5 million in return for their dropping all aboriginal claims. Both the money and the land were to be received and administered by twelve regional corporations and 204 village corporations established under the act. Shortly before ANCSA was passed, hundreds of claims were filed by individuals for allotments, the equivalent for natives of the homesteads by which whites had taken possession of much of the western United States. In 1980 the Alaska National Interest Lands Act (ANILCA) was passed, establishing national parks, monuments, and preserves over huge areas of the state, particularly in northern Alaska. Two boroughs have been created in the region, the North Slope Borough across the northern part of the state, and the Northwest Arctic Borough in the country draining into Kotzebue Sound.

For the first time since the breakdown of the traditional societies, land ownership became a major issue for the Iñupiat. In 1960, one could travel for days in almost any direction without bothering anyone; by 1990, one could hardly go anywhere without trespassing on someone else's property. Even the villages have been surveyed and divided into plots.

ANCSA has had a major impact on life in northern Alaska. The natives had to staff and operate the regional and village corporations despite the fact that a corporation was an alien organizational form to most of them. Although the corporations provided more opportunities for local employment than had ever existed before, more trained people than the native population could supply were required to staff them.

Outsiders had to be hired to fill the gaps, leading a number of nonnatives to immigrate to the region. Similarly, both the new oil field at Prudhoe Bay, near the Beaufort Sea coast, and the Red Dog Mine, about fifty miles (eighty kilometers) inland from Kivalina, employed Iñupiat and brought in lots of outsiders.

Iñupiat are now more in control of their own affairs than they were during the mission-school village period. They run the regional and village corporations, and in most cases the village and local governments. School districts are now under local control, and most church congregations are led by native clergy. Villagers complain that their lives are controlled by the regional corporations and people in the regional centers, but that is very different from having them controlled by an agent of the Bureau of Indian Affairs.

In 1990 there were nearly sixteen thousand people residing permanently in traditional Iñupiaq territory, seventy-four percent of whom were natives.[1] Slightly more than half of the Iñupiat were distributed among 23 predominantly native villages having an average of 290 inhabitants. The rest lived in the regional centers of Barrow, Kotzebue, and Nome, which had average populations of about three thousand.

The physical aspects of community life have been transformed through a process that began shortly before ANCSA. Several projects sponsored by the state, and later by the new local governments and regional corporations, provided much larger houses for almost everyone. They are heated by oil stoves and/or by very efficient factory-made wood-burning stoves. All the villages have electricity, television, and telephone service, and almost all of them have plumbing. In 1960 Kivalina was lucky to get one small bush plane bringing mail and passengers three times a week; thirty years later ten flights a day was not considered unusual. Dog teams are gone, having long since been replaced by snowmobiles and all-terrain vehicles. In 1960 an eighteen-horsepower outboard motor was the biggest thing around; now boats have ten times that. Every village now has a high school, so no one has to attend boarding schools in some other place if they want a high school education. Physically, life in northern Alaska is much more comfortable than it used to be.

Modern life apparently has been acquired at significant psychological cost, however. Alcoholism, drug abuse, suicide, accidental death, and domestic violence occur at unusually high rates in Alaskan villages. The precise causes of these problems remain unknown, and so, unfortunately, do the solutions.

Local families continue to be important in village life, but they are gradually yielding to domestic and conjugal families. People may no longer build a house anywhere they want. With each passing generation, it is becoming more difficult to maintain local family neighborhoods, and closely related conjugal families are increasingly spread all over the village. However, telephones and the ubiquitous citizen's band radios make keeping in touch a simple matter, and snowmobiles in winter and all-terrain vehicles in summer make it easy for relatives to get together no matter how far apart their houses might be.

Traditional food is still preferred by most of the Iñupiat, and people still have to hunt and fish to get it. But many have fulltime jobs, and they must either buy their food or hunt on weekends. Many women hold fulltime jobs, and more than one erstwhile hunter has to spend most of his time babysitting. English is the preferred language in many homes, but Iñupiaq remains the language of choice in others, and is now being taught in the schools.

Anecdotes may capture the flavor of modern village life in Iñupiaq Alaska better than any generalizations can, and I conclude this piece with two of them. Both occurred in June 1983, when I was doing a followup of the 1960–1961 Kivalina study.

The first event occurred one beautiful day when I was standing outside enjoying the view. About ten women were scattered along the shore butchering seals their husbands had taken the night before. Suddenly, as if by some signal, they all stood up, put their things in order, and went inside. Curious, I started visiting around to see what they were doing. Every one of them was watching General Hospital on television. As soon as the show was over, they returned to their work.

The second event occurred a few days later. This time I was visiting a local family at its sealing camp about fifteen miles (twenty-five kilometers) southeast of the village. Its members lived in tents complete with floors, beds, stoves, stereo systems, and lots of tapes. A CB radio was used to maintain contact with the village, and also with hunters boating among the loose pans of sea ice. After a dinner of seal meat, rice,

and seal oil, we listened to world news on the radio. The broadcast concluded with the stock market report, which stimulated among my Iñupiaq friends a discussion of the state of the world economy, particularly on the effect that lower oil prices might have on it. Then they went out and resumed seal hunting. By 1990 the place where their camp was located had become the port site for the Red Dog Mine.

Note

1. These figures do not include the many places to which Iñupiat have spread to the south and east (including northwestern Canada) of traditional Iñupiaq territory.

Suggested Readings

Burch, Ernest S., Jr. *Eskimo Kinsmen: Changing Family Relationships in Northwest Alaska.* St. Paul, MN: West Publishing Company, 1975. A comprehensive study of changing family life from traditional times to the 1970s.

———. "Traditional Eskimo Societies in Northwest Alaska." *Senri Ethnological Studies* 4 (1980): 253–304. The only comprehensive summary of traditional societies in northern Alaska, although somewhat out of date.

Chance, Norman A. *The Iñupiat and Arctic Alaska: An Ethnography of Development.* Fort Worth, TX: Holt, Rinehart & Winston, 1990. A summary of recent changes, especially in the northeastern portion of the Iñupiaq sector of Alaska.

Ray, Dorothy Jean. *The Eskimos of Bering Strait, 1650–1898.* Seattle: University of Washington Press, 1975. A comprehensive account of the traditional and exploration periods in the Bering Strait/Seward Peninsula area.

Spencer, Robert F. *The North Alaskan Eskimo: A Study in Ecology and Society.* Washington, DC: Smithsonian Institution, 1959, republished in 1969 by Random House. A highly regarded general ethnography of the northern portion of the Iñupiaq sector of Alaska during the exploration period.

Van Stone, James W. *Point Hope: An Eskimo Village in Transition.* Seattle: University of Washington Press, 1962. The best description of an Iñupiaq village during the mission-school village period.

A Shaman to Organizations

Andrew W. Miracle

I am a shaman. I am not the kind of shaman you may have studied, such as those in many cultures who foretell the future and heal individuals. Rather, I am a shaman to modern organizations, the kinds of organizations that are the foundation of industrialized nations. To avoid confusion, you need to know from the beginning that while I compare myself to a shaman, more typically I am referred to as an applied anthropologist.

In this chapter I will tell you my story, the story of how I came to be a shaman to organizations. However, before telling you this, it is necessary for you to know a little about traditional shamans, that is, the original shamans. Then you may be able to better understand my views on the work of applied anthropologists.

After comparing my work to that of a traditional shaman, I will tell you specifically how applied anthropologists go about their work—that is, what kinds of research we do and how we use research in our work. Since applied anthropology is so broadly defined, I also will tell you a little about the kinds of work other applied anthropologists do.

Finally, I want you to understand what applied anthropologists do in case you are in the position of needing such services in the future, or in case you want to consider such a career for yourself. Thus I will close my story by telling you about the rewards and the risks of this profession.

The Traditional Shaman

The traditional shaman has served human communities for thousands of years.[1] Men and women who exhibited special skills, shamans were valued as healers in their communities and as forecasters of future events. While in some societies shamans also might engage in other roles (such as dispensing justice and resolving disputes), foreseeing the future and healing are certainly the most common shamanic activities.

In hunting-and-gathering and horticultural societies, traditional shamans predict where hunters might be most successful, whether drought or storm might endanger the group, when to plant and harvest crops, and what the group's enemies might be up to, as well as the best time and manner to attack those enemies.

There are many methods that shamans in various cultures use to foresee the future. These are always seen as involving supernatural forces. One method used in some cultures is scapulimancy—the manipulation of a scapula, or shoulder blade, of an animal and the subsequent reading of the indicated signs.

Moore has assessed the use of scapulimancy to predict the best place to hunt.[2] His conclusion is that by relying on the toss of a bone the decision-making process is randomized. This prevents overhunting in familiar areas, which could lead to repetitive failure to bring game home.

In addition to foretelling the future, shamans, with the aid of natural remedies and supernatural intervention, have been healing the sick for thousands of years. One of the most widespread curing practices used by shaman is the sucking cure. I shall tell you about the sucking cure as an example of shamanic work.

The sucking cure is based on the belief that an individual becomes sick when the balance of the natural is upset. When foreign spirit or matter enters a person's body it violates the harmony of the body and adverse symptoms appear. If the foreign entity can be removed, the natural balance will be restored and the individual will become well. In such situations, the shaman will attempt to remove the foreign entity by sucking it out of the client's body.

There are many cross-cultural variations of the shamanic role. The specific beliefs, symbols, paraphernalia, and practices vary from culture to culture. However, it is possible to summarize a widespread pattern of the traditional shaman and shamanic practices.

Shamans usually believe that they have been called by the supernatural to their shamanic work. Thus by extension they view their shamanic abilities as a gift. However, it is widely recognized by shamans and their clients that these talents require improvement through training and practice.

Shamans often talk about "the path "or "the way." They learn this path through experiences in an ecstatic state. Many describe spirit guides who have taught them their special knowledge.

Shamans also learn many practical skills, usually through an apprenticeship to an older, more experienced shaman. As initiates they have hands-on lessons, learning by watching and assisting a master shaman.

Shamans are usually part-time specialists. That is, they also perform the work that is appropriate for someone of their age and sex. As members of the community, shamans are often marginal; they are marginal because they are different, because they are engaged in work others cannot do. However, their work is central to the well-being of the community.

Shamans mix practical remedies and advice with abstractions, often couched in stories, songs, and dance. Shamans can divert a client's attention from one concern to another focus. Sleight of hand, ventriloquism, and other skills, however, are not thought of as "fooling" clients but as helping them focus on solutions.

Shamans are masters in the use of the symbolic and much of their success derives from the manipulation of "a coherent system of symbolic communication" shared with their clients.[3] They use symbols to help clients connect their individual situations with the universal. In contemporary parlance, it might be said that shamans empower their clients through the power of positive thinking.

Shamans do what works. For them, the outcome or the product, not the means, is of ultimate concern. Shamans also have demonstrated considerable capacity for adaptation. That is, as a culture evolves or encounters forces for change, a shaman may combine the traditional and modern elements into a new system that is fully functional in the contemporary world.[4]

Applied Anthropology in Modern Organizations

Before I explain how I think my work is like that of a shaman, I want to tell you about the importance of organizations in modern societies. Then I will tell you why organizations sometimes need help from someone external to the system and give you some examples of the types of work I have done with organizations.

Organizations are social inventions for accomplishing goals through cooperative effort. Organizations have been important in all agricultural societies. It was the development of industrialization, however, which led to their proliferation. Modern societies as we know them are defined largely by organizations.

Typically organizations come into being for a particular purpose or to meet a specific goal. Organizations usually cease to exist when one or more of three conditions is met: (1) The organization achieves its goal and thus has no reason to continue. Such may be the case with organizations that mobilize resources in times of war or disaster or to fight a specific disease or social condition; (2) There is general recognition of the organization's inability to meet the desired goal. This may be due to internal characteristics of the organization or to conditions in the external environment; (3) Another organization similar in purpose but more effective causes the other one to be unnecessary or redundant. In business this may happen when one company is more successful than a competitor.

Of course, rather than shutting down under such conditions, an organization frequently will adapt or even evolve a new identity. This may mean downsizing, changing the original purpose, or identifying a new goal.

It is when an organization is facing a crisis that threatens its continuation in its current form that directed change is usually perceived as necessary. This is when applied anthropologists are most likely to become involved.

Organizations may need help in such situations for a variety of reasons. We all recognize that sometimes it is easier to identify others' problems than our own. In the same way, the perspective of someone external to an organizational system can be invaluable. In addition, organizations may not have the in-house expertise to direct change. Finally, someone external to the organization, who is not part of its social system, may be necessary to say what others are thinking but no one wants to say. The outside consultant can become a foil for internal politics, a scapegoat for unpopular but necessary adaptive action, a thorn who pricks the complacent, or a comforter to the anxious. The status position of applied anthropologists can be multifaceted indeed.

During my career I have worked with businesses and not-for-profit organizations. Some of these organizations have been quite small, sometimes very large.

In spite of the diversity of the organizations, though, the nature of my work for most of these can be categorized in terms of tasks. These tasks are not exclusive and frequently several will be required by an organization.

1. The collection and analysis of data, often for the purposes of marketing or decisions about service delivery.
2. Strategic planning, that is, looking at the current and likely future characteristics of the environment and the organization's ability to meet its mission.
3. Restructuring of the organization or redefinition of roles and functions in order to meet goals better.
4. Improving relations in a culturally diverse environment, whether multicultural in the traditional (ethnic) sense or in terms of social classes or occupational categories (for example, tensions between management and engineers in high-tech environments).

In almost every case, I find that I have been asked to help only after leadership has perceived it is on the verge of a crisis—things aren't going well, or at least not as well as hoped. From the shamanic view, I am usually called when there are symptoms of an imbalance in the natural order of the organization.

The Shaman and the Applied Anthropologist: A Comparison

The process whereby an individual becomes a shaman typically involves several specific steps. I shall illustrate this with the case of Aymara shamans from the Andean highlands.

First, one recognizes the calling. While this may be a gradual recognition by individuals that they have interests and special abilities well-suited to the work of a shaman, among the Aymara there is often a much more dramatic calling. A potential Aymara shaman reportedly is struck by lightning. There is hardly a more direct way in which the supernatural can imbue an individual with power and publicly validate the calling.

Having been called, one then enters a period of apprenticeship. For many Aymara, this involves a pilgrimage to the sacred Island of the Sun in Lake Titicaca, mythological birthplace of the first Inca ruler and founder of the Inca Empire. It also entails working as an assistant to a master shaman in order to learn necessary skills.

Finally, the shaman enters individual practice, assisting members of the community and the surrounding countryside. Like other professionals, there is a period of professional development until a shaman may be recognized widely as a wise and powerful yatiri, "one who knows."

While I have not yet been struck by lightning, my own career has gone through similar stages. My calling was the gradual sort. My interest in directed change pre-dated my interest in anthropology. After receiving a bachelor's degree I studied development organizations in Mexico and went to Bolivia as a community development specialist. After returning to the United States I enrolled in a graduate program in Latin American studies. It was a couple of more years before I discovered anthropology.

My apprenticeship occurred while I was a graduate student in anthropology at the University of Florida. Even though I was studying the Aymara language and culture, with expectations of focusing my future work on the Andes, I had several opportunities to work with master applied anthropologists. My mentors and role models included Solon T. Kimball, a pioneer in the profession, and Elizabeth M. Eddy, an expert on American schools. I learned a great deal working on projects where I could observe work in progress and then ask questions later in private discussions.

My early professional development occurred almost accidentally. After obtaining a university teaching position, I became involved as a volunteer with local social service agencies. Later the national headquarters of one agency became aware of my efforts and enlisted me to work on a project. This was the beginning of my reputational network.

The diversity of my work with organizations has increased greatly over the years. In addition to numerous social service agencies, I have worked with educational organizations (colleges, museums, professional associations), health care systems (needs assessment and service delivery), and businesses (marketing, public relations, and manufacturing). In most cases, however, my work follows a standard sequence.

1. Work always begins with a diagnosis. Usually I spend time in the organization listening for hiccups and observing blemishes that may indicate an imbalance within the system responsible for the adverse symptoms. I also must come to understand the mission and goals of the organization so that I can develop a vision of the client in the future.

For example, when a large social service agency was unable to make internal changes needed to maintain adequate service delivery to its clients, an accurate diagnosis was needed as quickly as possible. Interviews and focus groups with key staff and board members helped identify the point at which change always became bottlenecked, while also reaffirming a widespread commitment to the agency's traditional mission. Restructuring one department facilitated the much-needed changes.

2. Data collection and analysis is usually of utmost importance. In part, this is because as an outsider I am ignorant of the culture of the organization and this is one way of educating myself. However, the use of data also is important because modern organizations believe in data-based decisions. Even if I could walk into an organization and provide solutions as quickly as a shaman can cast the scapula, few in a modern organization would act upon such recommendations. Today's leaders require strategies supported by data as visible as the regurgitated entity sucked from the client by a shaman.

Strategies for data collection and analysis must be adapted to the needs of each client. For example, a trade association experiencing losses in membership asked for help to revitalize the organization. Data were needed from all the constituencies. I used a Delphi process to elicit opinions from leaders and a mail-in questionnaire was printed in the members' monthly magazine. In addition, there were open discussions at regional and annual meetings. It became clear that there were generational differences between older members who controlled the organization and younger professionals who either were not joining or not renewing their memberships. Once the differences were articulated, solutions could be targeted.

3. Usually the final step in a project is the presentation of a report or recommendations. This step is best viewed as a process, not a product, as a new way of viewing reality rather than as a document to be shelved. This concluding process often involves helping others articulate their inner thoughts and visions in a manner appropriate to share with the organization. In this sense it may be likened to the shaman's efforts to help clients see things as other things—whether this is moving from the abstract to the concrete or vice versa.

The presentation of data is not always routine. For example, I worked with one organization that marketed its services to inner-city neighborhoods; the goal was to increase market share. It became obvious that top leadership in the organization was so removed that they did not know their markets. I plotted maps of the city indicating the presence or absence of demographic traits and I prepared a matrix of market data for decision making. After they had heard the presentation in the boardroom, the key leaders were put on a bus and given a tour of existing and potential markets. The presentation of information in multiple ways resulted in a unanimous decision on the new marketing strategy.

My work is like that of a traditional shaman in many ways. For example, shamans perform sucking cures by bringing together the entire family for the healing and even using family members as drummers or to perform other essential roles. Similarly the organizational anthropologist brings together those who are afflicted so they can facilitate their own healing.

In both cases the individuals must sense that their interests are interdependent, their destinies related, before healing is possible. In both cases the healer creates a shared vision of health, as well as helping individuals to understand the nature of the illness. However, in both cases the cure is provided by the afflicted themselves—it is as if the healer is a midwife to a healthier organism or organization.

This notion that help and healing come from within is important. In his book *Anatomy of an Illness* Norman Cousins quotes the physician Albert Schweitzer's similar observation: "The witch doctor (i.e., shaman) succeeds for the same reason all the rest of us succeed. Each patient carries his own doctor inside him."[5] I always tell clients that they hold the answers to their questions, the solutions to their problems. I am engaged only to help them obtain the vision to see these things within themselves.

To summarize this comparison, my work as an applied anthropologist parallels that of a traditional shaman in several ways, although there are differences in techniques.

1. The submerging of identity and rediscovery of unity. The traditional shaman accomplishes this in a trance state; I usually do this with process groups involving members of the organization. For example, a meeting with the staff of a large museum provided the means for the curators, educators, and sales and marketing staffs to realize that they held different values. They also came to realize that they had to reach a consensus about the future of the organization so they could work more effectively as a team. A sense of unity among those who will implement change is critical.

2. A regression to origins. The traditional shamanic journey is one route. However, I am concerned with the origins of the organization and thus often lead an examination of its primary mission. At a retreat of a college experiencing sharp declines in enrollments and revenues, I asked the faculty and staff to tell me the history of the college. As they recounted the generational history of the institution, I asked them also to describe what society was like at each point in time. This exercise allowed the group to understand what had happened and what to change in order to realign the college with changes in society.

3. Rebirth with restored powers. The traditional shaman's return from the supernatural realm is emblematic of the analogous change desired for the client. I attempt a similar quest by freeing organizational members to create a common vision of the future in which their organization is re-empowered. Such was the case with the college described above.

4. The transference relationship between the shaman and the client. The traditional shaman absorbs the disease by sucking out the intrusive entity, changing places with the client as host for the affliction. While there is no single dramatic moment of transference in my work, inevitably as I work with an organization my language reflects a shift from "I" to "we" as I increasingly identify with the organization. Similarly, organization members often assume my analytical perspective, including the professional jargon of the applied anthropologist.

It should be clear from this comparison that traditional shamans and applied anthropologists are both agents of directed change and utilize some similar approaches. There is, however, at least one important difference—the reliance of the applied anthropologist upon research.

What Is Applied Anthropology?

There is no consensus on the definition of applied anthropology, though most definitions focus on the process or products of directed change. Nor is there a single type of work that is indicative of the profession. Applied anthropologists are individuals trained in the discipline of anthropology who work for clients outside the traditional academic setting. Certainly not all applied anthropologists work with organizations in the ways I have described.

In fact, applied anthropologists may become involved at any of several levels of the change process.

A number of years ago, George Foster identified three basic foci: (1) a target or recipient group; (2) an innovating organization; and (3) the interaction setting where change agents of the innovating organization come into contact with the members of the target group.[6]

Traditionally anthropology has been viewed as consisting of four subfields: archaeology, biological or physical anthropology, linguistics, and socio-cultural anthropology. Usually applied anthropologists are assumed to be socio-cultural experts. However, it should be made clear that there are many applied anthropologists whose primary focus is one of the other subfields.[7]

For example, those from physical anthropology may be forensic experts, epidemiologists, or they may work with industries to ensure that products are fully adapted to the human body. Linguistic anthropology has many applications, most notably in language policy and bilingual education. In addition, a great number of anthropologists are employed today as applied or contract archaeologists.

However, such applications of anthropology constitute different stories. While there may at times be considerable overlap among the subfields of anthropology (e.g., between language and culture), I want to concentrate on those whose work focuses on the socio-cultural dimensions of change.

In such roles, applied anthropologists may work as external change agents, that is, as consultants to innovating organizations, or as internal specialists who are employed full-time. The opportunities and challenges for applied anthropologists today are many, and the possibilities for employment are too numerous to list fully.

In summary, it seems that there are four characteristics that help to define the unique contributions applied anthropologists may bring to their work.

1. Applied anthropologists tap into the universals of human behavior. The discipline of anthropology has accumulated a great deal of information on cultural adaptations to the human condition. Knowledge of such universal principles is a distinct advantage for anyone attempting to direct change in any social system.

2. Applied anthropologists recognize that multiculturalism is the normal human experience.[8] In heterogeneous societies, such as our own, it is obvious. However, even in small homogenous societies continuous change, which is differentially acquired by individuals, creates a variegated cultural environment. Thus all humans live and work in a multicultural

world of different sets of others (managers, physicians, teachers, police, homeless persons, and so on) to whom different cultural attributions are made. Awareness of such microcultures and their differences in beliefs and behaviors allows applied anthropologists to direct change more efficiently and effectively.

3. Applied anthropologists recognize the importance of theory to their work. Theory is necessary because good theory is predictive. It is abstraction from empirical evidence which illuminates regularities and complex patterns, and demonstrates relationships that otherwise might be obscure.[9]

4. Applied anthropologists are committed to the use of empirical data and multiple methodological techniques. Since change in any social system is dynamic and multifaceted, no single prescription can be applied successfully in all cases. Effective applied anthropologists tend to have a broad knowledge of methodological techniques and understand the appropriate use of each one.

The Rewards of a Shamanic Life

The potential rewards for a traditional shaman or applied anthropologist may be similar. For example, one can take personal and professional satisfaction in helping individuals in a community or an organization. Those who are successful also may enjoy considerable prestige and material benefits.

For me there is nothing quite as gratifying as knowing that I have helped an organization. I often can sense a new energy emerge within organizations as I work with them. In addition, there is the possibility that my work may save jobs, increase the dignity of employees in the workplace, or help the organization advance its mission. Of course one does not always succeed, at least not as fully nor as immediately as one might hope. Still, the rewards of the successes are such that I remain motivated to continue. However, it is the process that I perhaps enjoy the most. The excitement of constantly learning, of being put on the spot to find solutions or to provide knowledge—even when none is apparent.

On the other hand, the potential risks to the traditional shaman or applied anthropologist should not be ignored. Both are specialists who work alone. Just as traditional shamans are marginal to their own communities, applied anthropologists are marginal to the organizations or communities in which they work. This marginality can be lonely at times, especially when one wants to share knowledge or the excitement of recent insight. It also can be dangerous.

Just as the disgruntled family of a former client may turn on a traditional shaman, the applied anthropologist may become a scapegoat for an organization's failure or for a community's lack of success. Even though their lives may not be threatened in such instances, their livelihood may be since applied anthropology, like traditional shamanism, is largely a reputationally based profession.

There also is the threat of failure—of misdiagnosis and the application of the wrong treatment or of misreading the indicators when predicting the future. Shamans and applied anthropologists work with statistical probabilities. No matter how much you know or how good your intuition, you must make assumptions based on probabilities (demographic projections, economic indicators, reports on current and future technology). No model of a human system can approximate the complexities of reality. At least occasionally, all shamans and applied anthropologists must suffer from these inadequacies.

So far I have given you my personal perspective on applied anthropology. However, you might consider what it would be like to encounter an applied anthropologist during the course of your own working career. If an applied anthropologist is brought into your office, factory, hospital, or school, the interactions that you will have with that professional will be affected by your knowledge of social science and of your own work environment, as well as by the social system of that environment.

On the other hand, what if you are an organizational executive or community leader? When should you consider using an applied anthropologist? An increasing number of organizations are employing applied anthropologists full-time, usually to deal with issues related to cultural variation or culture change. If your organization does not have a staff anthropologist and you perceive it is stymied because of such issues, then you might consider seeking an anthropologist as a consultant.

If you think you might enjoy the shamanic life, you may want to consider what it takes to become an applied anthropologist.[10] While there are as many routes as there are practicing professionals, a few generalities apply to most situations.

First, you need a graduate degree in anthropology. Many applied anthropologists have a master's degree and an increasing number have a Ph.D. A degree is necessary for obtaining abstract knowledge and for certification (you are not likely to get hired as an applied anthropologist if you don't have a degree saying you are one).

Second, you need an apprenticeship, for practical

knowledge and for the wisdom that comes only from experience. Such an apprenticeship is part of some graduate programs that specialize in applied anthropology. However, it also is possible to acquire such experiences by working with another professional or in a organization specializing in the kind of work you want to do.

Since research capabilities are the mainstay of the applied anthropologist's tool kit, an aspiring professional must learn as much as possible about research. This is necessary because every client situation is unique and calls for specially adapted research methodologies.

As an applied anthropologist you will need a variety of quantitative and qualitative research skills—the more the better. You also must have the ability to synthesize diverse types of information from both large and small data sets. Observational skills and qualitative research techniques have been the trademark of anthropology throughout most of the twentieth century. In addition, today's applied anthropologist also must be comfortable with computer-based techniques for analyzing data statistically.

Presentation skills are important too. Research findings and recommendations must be reported in a clear and cogent fashion. This includes the utilization of visual techniques such as color graphics and maps. You also must be able to judge the research knowledge of the client, and hence the appropriate level for reporting findings. Frequently results are presented as statements for action, while the statistical analyses that support such conclusions are referenced only as footnotes if they are noted at all.

Interpersonal skills akin to the shaman's bedside manner are crucial. These may be the most important factor in the success of an applied anthropologist. Oratorical talent, even a flair for the dramatic and acting skills, may be useful.

Applied anthropologists can benefit greatly from counseling skills, such as the ability to be a good listener while controlling the nature and direction of conversation. You must be able to get clients to provide necessary information. The applied anthropologist also needs the ability to process group discussions and to utilize group dynamics.

In an applied setting, ideas and inspiration come from the totality of life experiences. For an anthropologist this means applying the lessons of pig feasts, potlatches, and the kula ring to businesses, health care systems, and universities. Not only do such cultural phenomena from traditional ethnography provide me with insight, but I often find that explanations

employing such analogies are meaningful for the members of contemporary organizations too. In this fashion, applied anthropologists like traditional shamans are repositories of valued cultural and mythical knowledge.

Notes

1. The term *shaman* is from the Tungus language in Siberia.
2. Omar K. Moore, "Divination: A New Perspective," *American Anthropologist* 59, no. 1 (1957): 69–74.
3. Douglas Sharon, *Wizard of the Four Winds: A Shaman's Story* (New York: Free Press, 1978), p. xii.
4. For an example of this in modern Peru, see Sharon, *Wizard of the Four Winds.*
5. Norman Cousins, *Anatomy of an Illness as Perceived by the Patient* (New York: Norton, 1979), p. 69. I am indebted to Robert Murphy for putting this quote into the context of shamanic healing. See "Review of 'The Way of the Shaman: a Guide to Power and Healing' by Michael Harner," *American Anthropologist* 83, no. 3 (1981): 714–717.
6. George M. Foster, *Applied Anthropology* (Boston: Little, Brown, 1969), p. 71.
7. For examples, see Louise Robbins, "The Nature of 'Applied' Physical Anthropology," pp. 17–22, and Hester Davis, "Applied Archeology: New Approaches, New Directions, New Needs," pp. 72–80, both in Michael V. Angrosino, ed., *Do Applied Anthropologists Apply Anthropology?* Southern Anthropology Society Proceedings, no. 10. (Athens, GA: University of Georgia Press, 1976); Andrew W. Miracle, ed., *Bilingualism: Social Issues and Policy Implications*, Southern Anthropological Society Proceedings, no. 16 (Athens, GA: The University of Georgia Press, 1983).
8. Ward H. Goodenough, "The Elusive Nature of Cooperation and Leadership: Discovering a Primitive Process that Regulates Human Behavior," *Anthropology and Education Quarterly* 7, no. 4 (1976): 4–6.
9. For examples, see Elizabeth M. Eddy and William L. Partridge, eds., *Applied Anthropology in America*, 2nd ed. (New York: Columbia University Press, 1987), p. 53.
10. I have described the similarities in the training of applied anthropologists and shamans in Andrew W. Miracle, "The Making of Shamans and Applied Anthropologists," *Practicing Anthropology* 5, no. 1 (1982): 18–19.

Suggested Readings

Eddy, Elizabeth M., and William L. Partridge, eds. *Applied Anthropology in America*, 2nd ed. New York: Columbia University Press, 1987. The first chapter in this volume is perhaps the best summary of the history of applied anthropology in America. Also included are articles on applied anthropological theory, the practice of applied anthropology and policy issues.

Harner, Michael. *The Way of the Shaman: A Guide to Power and Healing*. New York: Harper & Row, 1980. Written by an anthropologist who is a practicing shaman, this volume presents a unique inside perspective on shamanism.

Human Organization. This journal, published by the Society for Applied Anthropology for over fifty years, is the primary outlet for professional articles. It demonstrates how the interests of applied anthropologists have changed over time.

Stefflre, Volney. *Developing and Implementing Marketing Strategies*. Westport, CT: Greenwood Press, 1985. Based on experience applying his anthropological training to business organizations, Stefflre utilizes case studies to describe systemic organizational obstacles to marketing innovations.

Van Willigen, John. *Applied Anthropology: An Introduction*. South Hadley, MA: Bergin and Garvey, 1986. This textbook is a good introduction to the field of applied anthropology.

Saraguro: Medical Choices, Medical Changes
Ruthbeth Finerman

Health, Illness, and Culture

Health is a mirror to culture. Since it is so basic to survival, the ways that societies conceptualize health and respond to sickness tell us a great deal about the challenges they face in adapting to a setting, and the diverse strategies they employ to cope with these challenges. They also reveal a society's most deeply held values, beliefs, and practices, and lend insight into the process of culture change.

My research into illness and healing in the Andes spans nearly two decades. The long-term focus of my research is the indigenous community of Saraguro, comprising Quichuan descendants of the Inca who today populate the southern highlands of Ecuador. Over the years I have witnessed how Saraguros adopt and modify medical innovations obtained through contact with neighboring groups and with Spanish and mestizo (mixed blooded) colonists. What emerges from this exchange is a rich, contemporary mixture of old and new health customs. Ethnographers often decry contact and change as threats to cultural image. For Saraguros, though, the very ability to incorporate innovation into tradition is a hallmark of the persistence and vitality of their culture and their healing traditions. At the same time, while Saraguros are receptive to many medical innovations, some features of care have resisted pressures for change. For example, families continue to rely on mothers to treat nearly all cases of illness in the household.

Sickness threatens individuals, families, and society as a whole. Consequently, groups make massive efforts to maintain or recover health and constantly search for new ways to resolve health problems. As groups adopt innovative healing concepts and procedures they also spur change in other spheres of culture, introducing new technologies, products, social roles, beliefs, values, and expectations.

The Study of Health

People are concerned about their health and readily discuss issues of sickness and curing. The health issues individuals raise illuminate their ideals and expectations; however, they may not be aware of their most common and serious health threats. For instance, individuals might voice concerns about risk of violence yet they might actually be at much greater risk for accidental injury. Personal concerns reveal cultural perceptions about the nature of violence, while measured risks for injury illustrate how populations might ignore or minimize other health priorities. This makes the topic a popular if challenging one for researchers. Health studies need to strike a balance between popular assumptions and statistical risks.

Health studies also have to distinguish between hypothetical situations and actual behavior. For instance, individuals usually claim that they follow their doctor's orders when, in reality, they regularly disregard diet regimens, medication schedules, and instructions about exercise, smoking, and alcohol consumption.

The best way to distinguish hypothetical cases from real behavior is to combine research strategies, collecting data from a variety of sources. General interviews produce preliminary data on health and treatment ideals. Follow-up interviews help detect subtle variations or changes in attitudes that emerge with time and fresh experiences. Over the years I have repeatedly interviewed more than 350 Saraguro women and numerous traditional and nontraditional health providers on a range of issues, using structured surveys, informal questioning, and group discussions that produced extensive information on health concepts, curing practices, and changes in medical traditions over time.

Participant-observation is an especially valuable

strategy for learning how people actually manage health and healing. This process provides first-hand exposure to illnesses and to the outcome of different treatments. Communities are usually quite receptive to the participatory technique because it frees individuals to demonstrate, rather than merely describe, healing procedures. Personal experience with the participant-observation process is illustrative, if rather humbling. Saraguros tired of simply recounting their healing traditions in interviews showed obvious delight whenever I fell ill, since my suffering offered rare opportunities to demonstrate their skills. On some days Saraguro women lined up outside my door, patiently awaiting their turn to ply me with a battery of remedies for my head colds, tarantula spider bites, and mortifying if brief episodes of diarrhea. While sickness was certainly unpleasant and subjecting myself to the ministrations of numerous healers felt decidedly awkward, these experiences yielded better research results than did an entire year of surveys and interviews.

Many women also took pains to teach me family curing procedures. A few eventually confided that they considered my training essential after reasoning that my pale skin, my labored breathing at high elevations, and my comparatively light build and childless condition demonstrated obvious incompetence in managing my own health. They feared, perhaps quite reasonably, that I would never survive fieldwork without intervention and intensive training. Thus, for my own good I was accorded opportunities to assist with cures in order to learn how to recognize and respond to illness.

The Context of Health in Saraguro

Health and sickness are intimately linked to the physical and historic context of a population. Saraguro's environment poses manifest health risks, but at the same time offers a rich body of therapeutic resources. Historical events, particularly contact with other peoples, exposed Saraguros to innovations that shape current health-related attitudes and behaviors, and provided access to alternative treatment options.

Saraguro is nestled in an inter montane basin in the Andes. This chain of volcanic mountains runs the length of Ecuador, separating the country's hot, humid coastal strip by the Pacific Ocean from the tropical rainforests of the Amazon interior lying to the east. The residential community of Saraguro and its surrounding pasture lands are located at elevations of eight thousand to twelve thousand feet above sea level. The area supports a somewhat moist, cool-to-temperate climate that graduates to a colder, windier, and drier climate at the highest elevations. These extremely high-altitude plateaus, called the *altiplano* or *paramos*, are largely unpopulated and are primarily used to graze cattle.

Saraguros divide their labor between crop cultivation and livestock husbandry. Crops consist largely of corn, beans, potatoes, barley, wheat, and squash. Families often till several fields at different elevations, allowing them to grow a range of crops suited to distinct soils and climates. All family members over the age of five participate in cultivation. Children help to plant, weed, and harvest crops, while adult women also handle heavier digging with mattocks. Plowing, a highly strenuous activity that is regarded as an art, is most often undertaken by adult males, although some Saraguro women have also mastered this skill. Corn is a prized crop and the name Saraguro in the Quichua language means "land of corn." Not surprisingly, the corn harvest each May is the focus for a major celebration in the community.

Many families raise a small number of chickens, pigs, guinea pigs, and goats to supplement their diet or their income, but most pastoral labor is devoted to herding cattle and sheep. Cattle husbandry is usually managed by men, who tend herds that are kept at high elevation pastures and transport the cattle to markets in larger cities. Saraguro women also use milk from these herds to manufacture cheeses that are sold throughout the province. Sheep are raised for their wool, which Saraguros use to fabricate clothing for the household.

Locals maintain a unique dress pattern little changed since the seventeenth century, making Saraguros, like many indigenous communities in the Andes, distinctive and easily identifiable. Both men and women wear their long hair in a single braid that they plait in a complex style from numerous small hair strands. Saraguro males wear short pants, a tunic called a *cushma*, and a blanket-like cloak called a *poncho*, all made from wool. Women wear hand-embroidered blouses, sets of embroidered and pleated wool skirts called *anacos* and *pulleras*, and woolen shawls or *sarapos* held by antique silver shawl pins called *topos*. When they attend church, market, and holiday celebrations, Saraguro women adorn themselves with very large antique silver earrings that hang down to their shoulders, and beaded necklaces woven into fans that drape around their shoulders. Saraguros are never without their hats. Most wear a simple fedora in either a dark wool or a woven straw that is then painted white, but on special occasions many wear a traditional white wool hat with a wide, flat brim. Because Saraguro clothing is made from handspun and hand woven wool, women spend much of their time spinning on hand-held spindles and men pass their evenings weaving on traditional backstrap looms. All Saraguro woolens are dyed a deep blue-black color, which legend claims is in mournful tribute to Atahualpa, the last Inca ruler, who died at the hands of Spanish conquerors.

Social organization preserves a number of traditions. Most Saraguros are bilingual, speaking both Quichua and Spanish. During the 1960s the Quichua language approached extinction but has since been revived through a series of educational programs. Saraguros describe themselves as devout Catholics, although they retain many pre-Christian concepts such as a belief in nature spirits like the sun, the rainbow and winds, and the prevalence of supernatural forces like evil eye, soul loss, and magical fright. The community is organized into a system of work groups known as *mingas*, which cooperate in the management of any community-held lands, maintain roads and irrigation ditches, and supervise the construction of communal buildings. Families also foster powerful alliances through kinship and marriage. Saraguro women retain their family surname and their own lands and property after marriage, which gives these women a degree of financial independence that is rare in the Andes. Children receive both their maternal and paternal surname and inherit through both family lines. Many marry within their own barrio or local neighborhood. This permits offspring to remain close to their parents and allows families to combine their forces for labor and production. In recent decades, though, Saraguro has experienced a population surge that has reduced the availability of land for homes, crop cultivation, and grazing. As a result, the traditional pattern of extended households has begun to erode as young Saraguros migrate to the tropical lowlands in search of grazing lands, or to cities in a quest for wage labor opportunities.

Saraguro's ecology and production systems present a range of health risks. A few common threats include parasitic infection from livestock, unpurified water, and the absence of sewage and waste systems; rabies from dog bites; hypothermia from exposure to the cold climate; respiratory infections aggravated by open hearths with wood fires; and influenza, whooping cough, measles, and tuberculosis promoted by confined sleeping arrangements.

Saraguro's ecosystem and network of social relationships offers health opportunities as well. The environment supports a rich and relatively diverse food supply, making malnutrition relatively uncommon in this population. The diverse ecology of the region also supports a tremendous variety of medicinal plant species that residents exploit for nearly all health conditions. In addition, extended religious, kinship, and community ties offer access to a safety net of labor and financial resources for individuals requiring emotional support and material assistance in times of sickness.

Saraguro's history, like its environment and social organization, has also shaped health. During the Incan Empire (A.D. 1476–1534) Saraguros were conscripted to operate a way station that serviced the Incan highway that ran through the Andean highlands. The Inca also compelled them to supply tribute in the form of labor, crops, and gold excavated from regional mines. After Spanish conquest in the sixteenth century, Saraguro retained the obligation to offer labor, taxes, and supplies to colonial authorities. During this period colonists of Spanish descent appropriated most of the land in Saraguro's administrative center. These colonists, locally known as Whites, or *Blancos*, continue to dominate the town. Still, indigenous Saraguros preserved their ownership of farming and grazing property surrounding the town; most other indigenous peoples in the Andes lost their lands during the colonial period. Historically, Saraguros did not materially benefit from contact with other populations. Instead, the community's energies and resources were exploited, first by Incan and later by European colonial powers. This experience reinforced values of self-reliance and autonomy, and fostered a degree of resentment and suspicion of outsiders that has been extended to all forms of external intervention, including the introduction of innovative health services. As it will become clear, Saraguros resist many new medical programs because they are seen as a threat to their culture and independence.

The Meaning of Health

The more cosmopolitan, biomedical viewpoint on health differs from that of Saraguros in two principal ways. First, the biomedical model draws a distinction between conditions affecting the mind and those affecting the body, while Saraguros see mind and body as integral and mutually interactive in health. Second, biomedicine tends to create the impression that health and disease comprise entirely separate states, so that someone is either problem-free or suffers from some pathological condition, while Saraguros, like many other non-Westernized populations, regard health as a more complex and inconstant ideal.

Mind-body dualism, or separating diseases into physical and mental disorders, is a hallmark of contemporary biomedicine. Physical complaints such as pain or dysfunction are nearly always attributed to organic causes like trauma or infection. Potential psychological triggers like stress or depression tend to be discounted or minimized, as is the impact of physical disease on emotional well-being. Similarly, mental illnesses are infrequently linked to biology, and those cases ascribed to organic origins are usually reclassified and treated as physical dysfunctions.

Saraguros do not distinguish between physical and mental illness. Rather, all conditions are seen as inseparable and interactive. Here, experience and emotion have an equal footing with infection and contagion as risk factors. Sorrow, anger, and fright appear as threatening as bacteria, accidents, and viruses. Moreover, Saraguros contend that harmful emotional states give rise to physical disorders, as when anger produces colic. Similarly, organic dysfunction impairs mental and emotional functioning, as when pain fosters depression. Thus, diagnosis demands evaluation of an individual's emotional life as well as his or her manifest physical condition, and treatment depends on the holistic recovery of both mental and physical faculties.

Physicians and other biomedical practitioners also tend to think of health and disease as contrasting states. Reality, however, is rarely that simple. Individuals can be presumed healthy despite the presence of undetected disease, or ill although lacking any clear signs of disease. Moreover, a healthy or unhealthy status can rapidly change. Anthropologists like to point out that health and illness are filtered through cultural beliefs and expectations, so that the two states can actually coexist. Individuals who appear to be free of diagnosed disease can still feel decidedly ill, as in cases of chronic fatigue syndrome. Others may have a disease but feel perfectly healthy; a frequent occurrence in undetected or asymptomatic disorders like hypertension (high blood pressure), the early stages of cancer, or latent (inactive) phases of some sexually transmitted diseases. Still others learn to manage chronic problems like arthritis, clinical depression, or heart murmurs and consider themselves otherwise healthy. Finally, some disorders such as parasitic infection are so pervasive in some settings that such populations accept the condition as perfectly normal.

Saraguros share this vision of health as a complex and fluid condition. They regard health as an ideal, one that is difficult to achieve and virtually impossible to sustain for very long. They note that people always seem to suffer at least some minor ailment and that everyone eventually experiences serious illness. Several characteristics combine to form the Saraguro definition of health. Some features are fairly predictable, particularly the absence of physical pain and emotional distress. However, Saraguros also describe other less typical qualities as essential components of good health, including an ability to work, harmony within family and community, and freedom from both supernatural and natural illness agents.

Andean populations often equate work and physical activity with health. Most of these groups produce their own food and depend on physical labor for survival. Individuals here cannot turn to social services for assistance if incapacitated. Saraguros often use the refrain that one works or one goes begging and hungry. So it is not surprising that they prize energy and endurance, and view physical activity as a broad health indicator.

Saraguros describe social harmony as another elemental feature of health. Since Saraguros presume that emotional and physical processes interact to shape illness, they reason that anger, sorrow, or suffering brought on by discord could yield both psychological distress and physiological disorders. They report that interpersonal conflicts produce ailments ranging from head and stomach aches to insomnia, fatigue, and susceptibility to infection; symptoms not uncommon to anyone who has experienced a tension headache, upset stomach, or lowered disease resistance following trauma. This link between conflict and illness provides secondary benefits in terms of social control because Saraguro family members and acquaintances feel compelled to conform to social expectations and conventions to avoid the adverse health consequences of disobedience and hostility.

While work and social cohesion are important, Saraguros regard the suppression of harmful forces within the realms of nature and the supernatural as essential to health. Concepts of natural and supernatural blend historic and contemporary influences on beliefs about illness.

Natural illness agents include infection, injury, aging, and dietary deficiency, as well as the belief in humoural forces, a widespread concept in Central and South America. Saraguros assert that two humours, comprising heat and cold, persist in mutual opposition. The qualities pervade the physical environment and the human metabolism. They are not exclusively associated with temperature; rather, they exist in all things, including colors, climates, seasons, plant and animal life, and emotional states. Balancing hot and cold components in personal diet, dress, emotions, and physical activity protects health, while any excess or sudden change in humoural status produces illness.

Heat can be caused by strenuous activity, overexposure to sunlight, excessive consumption of hot foods like red meat, peppers, and oranges, or by hot emotions like anger and passion. Heat imbalances induce disorders such as fever, infection, and colic. Cold may be produced by extreme inactivity or sleep, exposure to cold winds or water, overconsumption of cold foods like sugar, fish, and rice, or by cold emotions such as sorrow and apathy. Cold causes ailments such as chills, bronchitis, sterility, and most cases of diarrhea. Cases of hot or cold humoural imbalance receive allopathic treatment; that is, an excess of a humour like heat is gradually countered by the opposing quality of cold to restore equilibrium. This process is actually quite delicate; sudden exposure of hot ailments to extreme cold can worsen matters and induce a dangerous chilling known as *resfrio*. Rapid warming of a cold disorder produces a risk of excessive heat, called *gangrena*.

Saraguros attribute some illnesses like evil eye (*mal ojo*), soul loss (*espanto*), magical fright (*susto*), and envy sickness (*envidia*) to the deliberate action of supernatural agents, particularly witches and spirits. Cases are actually relatively rare, but children are the most common victims. Infants and children are considered weaker and more vulnerable to supernatural powers, and their very youth is said to make them the targets of envy. Supernatural disorders often produce varied and unpredictable symptoms, and the cause may go unrecognized at first. Cases are usually attributed to supernatural causes only after more conventional diagnoses and treatments fail. This is especially common when a seemingly healthy individual falls ill, when onset is sudden and the condition deteriorates rapidly, when a collection of symptoms lacks conformity with more mundane syndromes, when previously effective treatments are exhausted without success, or when unusual events like a mystical or frightening experience precede or coincide with the onset of a mysterious illness. Such cases are treated by freeing the patient from spirit influences. This is achieved by cleansing, luring or frightening a spirit away from the victim through various treatment combinations, including teas, lotions, baths, steam vapor, purges and emetics, sprays, scents, or powerful prayers and incantations.

Saraguros say one can detect health and sickness from a number of observable signs, including skin tone, energy level, and, most critically, fatness. Ruddy, red skin and active behavior suggest vitality. Weight is a crucial index of health and prosperity. Saraguros

complement each other by noting how fat, or *gordo*, they have grown, and mothers consider it the ultimate compliment to hear their children described as fat. Indeed, Saraguros are puzzled by North America's emphasis on slimness, which most societies equate with emaciation, wasting, and disease. Saraguros do differentiate between a solid build and morbid obesity, which they regard as excessive but not necessarily unhealthy. Still, the relationship of fatness with health among Saraguros is often at odds with the nutritional counseling of biomedical practitioners.

Health Providers and Options in Saraguro

Over the years many traditional and nontraditional medical assistance options have emerged to help Saraguros manage threats of natural and supernatural disorders and their varied physical, emotional, and humoural facets. The notion of a health specialist is a new one for most Saraguros, although an emphasis on medical specialization has accelerated in recent years, accompanied by a marked deterioration of some curing traditions. What has not changed, however, is an almost fierce reliance on mothers to provide most of the health care for family members.

The most traditional practitioners in Saraguro include shamans or *curanderos*, herbalists, and midwives. These healing roles predate the introduction of Westernized biomedicine and hospital care. Traditional curing roles in Saraguro are actually quite informal. The healers rely on their own skills, personal experience, and reputation rather than on formal training, licensing, and titles to attract clients. Nevertheless, changes such as the advent of biomedical care create an uncertain future for some of Saraguro's indigenous healers.

Curanderos usually treat supernatural illnesses, especially cases of soul loss and evil eye. They are occasionally asked to remedy other conditions, such as alcoholism, infertility, and unrequited love. Most Saraguros are unable to specify exactly what treatments curanderos provide, since few have consulted such healers. Most remedies reportedly involve cleansings, sprays, and incantations to drive out evil forces tormenting a patient.

Saraguros agree that magical healers have been known to succeed where other practitioners fail, but most also fear and distrust these curers. This is because curanderos can use powers for either good or evil and seem equally disposed to cure or cause illness. Some clients seek relief from complaints, while others pay curanderos to use their magical skills to inflict illness on enemies. Curanderos do not distinguish between good and bad in their practices; they merely act as their clients bid. Saraguros contend that such healers cannot be trusted and that some curanderos consort with dangerous spirits to achieve their powers. In actuality, virtually all Saraguros refer to the practitioners of magical healing as *brujos*, meaning witches. Few employ the term *curandero*, or *curer*. Public ambivalence and outright antagonism have diminished the status of magical healing in Saraguro and reduced the pool of clients willing to seek such assistance. The emergence of other innovative medical options has further decreased reliance on curanderos. As a result, magical healing seems to be a dying profession in the community. Aged curanderos are disabled and most have died without training apprentices, so that few remain in practice today.

Herbalists treat both natural and supernatural disorders. Treatment, as one could expect, emphasizes the use of medicinal plant preparations such as teas, baths, plasters, and sprays, as well as advice on diet and healing foods. Saraguros rarely consult these specialists because most residents already possess extensive information about medicinal plants. Most consultations occur only after individuals exhaust their own knowledge or when unusual or chronic conditions arise.

Midwives, known as *parteras* in most of Ecuador, assist in reproductive health issues. In Saraguro, the formal title of partera is virtually unrecognized. Instead, residents simply describe these providers as local women who have raised many healthy offspring, or as women with a great deal of experience and skill in matters of childbearing. Such women may be consulted for advice on pregnancy, birth, and child care. Some are called to assist with difficult deliveries or to treat infertility. Most Saraguro women prefer to manage reproductive care themselves, so midwives or women with such knowledge are usually sought by inexperienced first-time mothers, or if complications arise.

Access to biomedical curing options in Saraguros accelerated in the last three decades. Pharmacists, nurse practitioners, and physicians share qualities like formal titles, training, and licensing, which set them apart from the informal roles of curanderos, herbalists, and midwives. They also share a Westernized view of health and illness that differs substantially from the beliefs of most Saraguros. This allows them to offer innovative, if sometimes incompatible, diagnostic and treatment options.

In Saraguro and all of South America, licensed pharmacists and smaller, independent druggists dispense medications without prescription. Pharmacies in Saraguro also stock a range of herbal preparations and exotic imported curatives. By offering this combination of remedies they bridge the worlds of traditional and biomedical healing. Some pharmacists also offer occasional advice on diet and therapy. Pharmacist recommendations and the ability to purchase medication without prescription allows patients to circumvent the intermediate step of seeing a doctor.

Free advice and the availability of both herbal remedies and prescription medications make pharmacists a very popular resource for Saraguros. However, pharmacies have limitations. Druggists are poor at diagnosing conditions, especially if symptoms are unusual or complex. Consequently, most Saraguros visit pharmacies after making their own preliminary diagnosis. Many Saraguros, perhaps justifiably, suspect that druggists might also recommend unnecessary drugs or more expensive brands since they are, after all, motivated by profit. Fewer recognize the additional risk that pharmacists unfamiliar with a patient's history might over prescribe or sell dangerous drug combinations, although several such cases have occurred. Finally, pharmacists do not offer hands-on care; instead, they sell remedies that are usually self-administered. Consequently, Saraguros consider pharmacists to be suppliers rather than health providers.

Nurse practitioners in Saraguro include registered nurses sent to the community to work in the government-run hospital, as well as indigenous Saraguro women trained as nurse practitioners who operate out of smaller neighborhood health posts. Nurses based at the government hospital mainly assist physicians with patient care and administration. Indigenous nurse practitioners at health posts provide assistance with minor health complaints, immunize children against disease, and offer community health and preventive care courses on issues like nutrition, child care, and family planning. In many respects Saraguro nurses are culture brokers. Their shared cultural background helps them communicate biomedical concepts to residents in a culturally appropriate and understandable format. However, neighborhood health posts are poorly stocked and understaffed, so that nurses must refer most cases to the hospital. Limited resources and support reduce their potential impact on public health.

A few physicians in Saraguro operate private practices, but most are medical residents employed in the government-owned hospital. Medical students are required to provide a year of residence service in a rural clinic before pursuing private practice, usually in larger cosmopolitan settings. Saraguros often complain that this residency process continually subjects patients to unfamiliar and inexperienced providers who rotate out of the community every year. A majority also emphasize the fact that most physicians are males, making them appear less nurturant and experienced in healing than are mothers, who spend years tending to the health needs of family members. Historically, doctors have been outsiders to the community. A few were volunteers from the United States who operated a mission clinic, now closed. Currently, most are members of the Spanish-descended middle and upper classes who come from larger, more urbanized cities in Ecuador. None are considered familiar with or sympathetic to Saraguro's culture and people. Recently, one indigenous Saraguro was trained as a physician and operates a private practice. While he is regarded as far more understanding of Saraguro health needs, he remains a secondary option for many residents because females are still widely regarded as more compassionate and experienced healers.

Saraguro's hospital opened in 1978 and provides facilities including laboratory tests and some surgical procedures. However, as already noted, Saraguros can purchase medications without prescription, so most circumvent physician examinations and instructions and obtain the bulk of biomedical advice and pharmaceuticals directly from druggists.

Medical Choice in Saraguro

Saraguros might easily appear overwhelmed by the sheer range and abundance of options for medical assistance. Nevertheless, they are remarkably consistent in their pattern of health-seeking behavior. They select from medical alternatives by weighing treatments likely to help against the sacrifices or costs each alternative might exact.

Most people think of medical costs as financial, such as consultation fees, medication purchases, wages or productivity lost when work is abandoned to obtain treatment, and the cost of transportation to consult a practitioner. However, patients face other less perceptible costs, such as a loss of social status, exposure to frustrating, inappropriate, or unnecessary treatments, or the experience of emotional trauma.

Lost social status is considered a real risk for Saraguros, particularly for women, who attract gossip if they disrobe for private examinations by male physicians. Women also risk lost prestige if they employ midwives or other attendants for births, since women are expected to manage delivery alone or, at most, with the help of spouses. Women lose further

status when they make the decision to surrender control over health care.

The emotional consequences of care can also prove costly, and for many Saraguros such costs take precedence over financial concerns. Patients everywhere are frustrated by long waits for attention and by conflicts with provider views about treatment. Unfamiliar treatment procedures, particularly those provided by outsiders, are also disorienting and stressful for most patients. Few are versed in the technical jargon of physicians or feel comfortable submitting to complex and often mechanized procedures such as physical examination, CAT-scans, and blood tests. The stress, fear, and emotional costs of such care are compounded for indigenous Saraguros, who share neither the health values nor the culture of biomedical providers. However, most Saraguros assert that many traditional practices, particularly magical healing by curanderos, seem equally exotic and produce similar stress, fear, and a reluctance to seek their help.

In an overwhelming majority of cases, Saraguro family members turn to the female head of the household for medical assistance. Reliance on mothers as family health providers is not unique to Saraguro. In fact, it is the most common pattern worldwide. Children in any society are most likely to seek out their mothers when they feel sick. Certainly children are unlikely to schedule medical appointments and consult directly with physicians or other practitioners. Husbands are similarly prone to requesting support from wives when they become ill or incapacitated. A wife or mother is the most reasonable health choice for Saraguros. She is immediately accessible, experienced, compassionate, and intimately familiar with family needs and problems. Moreover, and in contrast to nonfamily practitioners, a wife and mother is more likely to be personally concerned about kin and more willing to do all she can to restore family health.

Family-Based Healing

Mothers, like other traditional practitioners, gain their curing skills through informal training and experience. Women learn about healing by assisting their own mothers with family care and gain extensive curing experience as they manage a broad range of family health complaints on a daily, even continual, basis. In this process they learn to anticipate the unique signs and symptoms of illness in offspring. Saraguro women often claim they can detect illness even before a family member realizes he or she is sick. Women expand their curing knowledge by sharing information with friends and kinswomen and by participating in community health courses. Consequently, many Saraguro women express the opinion that they possess broader knowledge about health than do more specialized practitioners in the community.

Maternal curing beliefs and practices are, in fact, among the most complex healing systems in Saraguro, combining elements of most traditional and biomedical systems. Women possess a broader repertoire of healing knowledge since they interact with many different practitioners, adopting techniques through this contact and through trial and error and experience in treating family members. Women gain initial information on health and healing as young girls, as they assist their own mothers with family care duties. They expand this knowledge base as they marry and tend their own offspring, learning to spot the signs of sickness and discovering effective treatments through testing and eliminating those that fail. Women further enhance their knowledge through information exchanges with neighbors and friends who trade advice and recipes for effective remedies. Women also obtain fresh curing ideas from traditional and biomedical practitioners when they accompany sick family members to consultations. Most women accompany children and spouses to see therapists, and providers usually direct their instructions on treatment to the wife or mother, rather than to a spouse or child who needs care. As a result, women are exposed to new health views, diagnostic procedures, illness categories, and therapies. Such information exchanges rarely occur between other practitioners, who may jealously guard their expertise and scorn other treatment approaches. Thus, curanderos do not tend to consult physicians to learn about biomedicine, nor do they meet with midwives to secure advice on fertility care. Physicians are similarly unlikely to request instruction from magical healers, herbalists, and midwives.

Family-based healing includes traditional and nontraditional approaches to prevention and treatment. It combines natural, supernatural, physical, and emotional elements that women adopt from diverse medical systems and incorporate to produce their own unique healing system.

Saraguro mothers constantly strive to prevent illness among family members. They dress children in layers of clothing to protect them, as doctors and nurses advise, from the chilly climate and, as traditional healers warn, from attack by evil winds and airs. Women also contend that layered clothing prevents humoural imbalance from sudden exposure to the cold. Spouse and offspring are also reminded to wear their hats while outdoors. Saraguro women sug-

gest that this practice protects the head from evil winds and also shows respect for the sun. The sun was an object of worship by the Inca. Its influence continues among contemporary Saraguros, who claim that the sun strikes down the sacrilegious who demonstrate contempt by going out with their heads bared. Infants often go naked at home, but when mothers carry infants outside they are heavily protected from sickness. First, the head is covered with a scarf. The baby is then wrapped with blankets and carried beneath shawls so that he or she remains hidden in public. Saraguro women cover weak, vulnerable infants to protect them from cold and contagious diseases described by doctors, and to shield them from traditional threats posed by the envious gaze of others, which might precipitate evil eye or envy sickness. Finally, mothers tie red cord to the wrist or ankle of each child in the belief that red color wards off witchcraft. They also caution children to burn any hair lost in combing and to bury their waste when they defecate outdoors, since hair and excrement are also used to cast spells.

Women's main contribution to preventive care concerns diet. They supervise all meals and prepare combinations of foods that balance a biomedical emphasis on nutrition with more traditional concerns about humoural equilibrium. They mix individual foods or add herbs and spices to balance the hot and cold qualities of dishes. Women also protect family members from health risks posed by food taboos. For instance, women feed children with hot colics cooling foods to gradually stabilize their condition. Mothers forbid daughters to eat avocado while menstruating, believing the food's cold nature makes it toxic during the particularly cold state of menstruation. I witnessed one mother who snatched her daughter's dish of avocado and flung it down in alarm when the girl remarked that she was menstruating.

Saraguro mothers gain lifelong experience in managing family illness and learn to spot its early signs, such as reduced appetite, changes in sleep patterns, fatigue, or fidgeting. Family members may also approach mothers with symptoms like nausea, injury, or pain. When illness is detected, mothers examine kin for symptoms to establish a diagnosis. They usually check for fever or subnormal temperature and further signs of pain, bleeding, or dysfunction. Most check the eyes, tongue, urine, and spittle for discoloration, and the skin for changes in tone, rashes, or swelling. Mothers question the sick about their behavior preceding illness, inquiring about dress, hygiene, diet, emotional experiences, and (for husbands) drinking and personal comportment, as well as unusual incidents that might suggest supernatural causes. In most cases, mothers can make a diagnosis based on prior experience. In those rare instances when mothers cannot identify a disorder, they may ask a practitioner to determine the problem. Even so, mothers still treat the family member themselves with home-based remedies.

Most home-based healing combines herbal remedies with diet, rest, and limited physical therapy. Saraguro women often pride themselves on their knowledge of medicinal plants. When asked, most can name dozens of varieties at will. Older women with more experience can often recall two to three hundred species. When asked about specific species, women are able to identify still more plants, and describe features like growing habits, seasonal availability, uses for specific parts such as flowers or leaves, preparation methods, and proper applications. Nearly all Saraguro women tend house gardens, or *huertas*, filled with medicinal plants. The gardens are comparable to first aid kits, placing remedies close at hand for emergencies.

Herbal treatments are often quite simple, particularly when family members suffer few symptoms. In such events remedies might contain only one or two ingredients, like a poultice made from potato slices for fever, a steam bath of menthol and eucalyptus to treat coughs, or a tea of lemon grass, chamomile, or peppermint for hot or cold colics. However, syndromes with complex symptoms require greater effort. For instance, treatments for soul loss, nerves, infections, and measles can combine dozens of ingredients and take days to prepare, making family healing an arduous, time-consuming process.

A typical case illustrates the energy and resources Saraguro women expend on home-based curing. "Rosa's" four-year-old son fell ill with a fever, diarrhea, rash, and facial swelling. At first, Rosa treated each complaint individually, making a poultice to reduce the boy's fever, feeding him herbal teas for his diarrhea, and mixing an ointment for the skin rash and swelling. Despite these efforts, the boy's condition did not improve and Rosa grew convinced that her son was suffering from a supernatural ailment. She questioned the boy further and determined that he suffered from *bao de agua*, or soul loss sickness, caused by a snake that had frightened her son and stolen his spirit. Rosa and her two daughters spent days collecting ingredients for her son's cure, including wild and domesticated plants and remedies from neighbors and the local pharmacy. Treatment involved two stages. First, the boy was given a *sahumar* vapor bath, inhaling the steam from a heated basin holding more than twenty aromatic ingredients like menthol, eucalyptus, Spanish broom, tobacco, garlic, roses, and urine. Then the boy was given a *sopla*, or "blow," using an extract boiled from nearly thirty plants such as linseed, elder, garlic, roses, tobacco, fever few, and mallow. Rosa then made the sign of the cross on her son's chest, took the liquid in her mouth, and sprayed it over the boy's skin. Rosa emphasized that the sopla must be performed at high noon and be repeated for four days. After Rosa expended more than thirty hours of care and attention and a month's income to treat this one episode of sickness, her son recovered his soul and his health.

In most cases, Saraguro mothers administer herbal remedies in conjunction with pharmaceuticals. They believe that medications also have hot or cold qualities that can alleviate individual symptoms and correct humoural imbalances. Various brands of analgesic, bicarbonate, and antibiotics are the most popular and heavily used medications, but combinations can be dangerous. Some cases of drug overdose or interaction have been reported as a result of overprescription or the mixing of incompatible medications. It is not uncommon for mothers to administer four or more different brands of aspirin or bicarbonate to a family member at one time. Overmedication is encouraged by the fact that brand names imply that they relieve specific symptoms, not broader ailments. For instance, different aspirin brands imply that they either reduce fever, treat cold, ease pain, relax muscles, or stop infection. Not surprisingly, then, mothers administer a combination of pills to treat each of these distinct symptoms.

Saraguro mothers also feed the sick special foods selected to correct humoural disorders. Less often, they massage and bathe sick kin, and attach red cords or amulets to deflect supernatural agents. Perfumes and plant remedies are sometimes sprayed in the patient's face or on the skin to frighten off spirits.

If herbal remedies and pharmaceuticals fail, Saraguro women may seek assistance from traditional and nontraditional health providers. Rare cases of supernatural illness might be presented to curanderos or herbalists. Midwives may manage cases of infertility, pregnancy, or birth complications. Physicians and nurses attend to most disorders that prove unresponsive to home-based care. However, mothers often combine the advice provided by practitioners with additional home-based remedies, and usually attribute successful recovery to their own efforts, discounting any contributions made by other practitioners.

Saraguro women are often frustrated by specialized care, particularly physician consultations. Much of this frustration stems from a basic conflict between the cultures and medical systems of Saraguro women and that of providers. Mothers often disagree with physicians on diagnostic and treatment approaches. For instance, mothers fear that disrobing for medical examinations exposes sick kin to dangerous cold airs. Doctors may also advise pregnant women to eat citrus fruits and drink milk, foods that Saraguros consider dangerous during pregnancy. Many mothers are also antagonized by doctors, who very often criticize patients for their reliance on home remedies, saying it causes a delay in seeking "proper" biomedical attention. Mothers who take children with diarrhea to a doctor commonly receive stern rebukes and lectures on hygiene and diet instead of the purgatives and warm humoural remedies they expected.

It is important to note that Saraguro's doctors often feel equally frustrated by such exchanges, which most attribute to a mix of stubbornness and superstition on the part of their indigenous patients. Unfortunately, biomedical providers in Saraguro largely resist recommendations that they modify patient treatment to show greater cultural sensitivity, even though culturally appropriate care has been proven effective in encouraging patients to seek medical advice and to obey a doctor's orders.

Innovation in Family-Based Healing

While Saraguro mothers are unwilling to abandon their role as family healers and to place family health care in the hands of traditional or nontraditional providers, they eagerly adopt innovative ideas and resources. Medical innovations are not considered a threat to home-based curing. Rather, fresh concepts and procedures help to expand and revitalize more traditional approaches to family care.

It warrants emphasis that all medical "traditions" receive constant revision, and Saraguro's home-based curing system is no exception. Humoural concepts found throughout Latin America are considered a byproduct of conquest by the Spanish, who themselves adopted the humoural theories of China and Greece. The notion of evil airs could derive, in part, from pre-Inca concepts of winds and from nineteenth-century European medicine, which attributed disease to poisonous "miasmas" or putrid airs.

Saraguro women have also cultivated home-based versions of treatments offered by other traditional practitioners. They incorporated shamanic practices like sprays and cleansings in home care along with

medicinal plant knowledge acquired in part from herbalists. In other words, Saraguro's traditional health system does not reflect a medical process trapped at one point in history; instead, it comprises a successful, complex blend of therapies predating the introduction of more recent, cosmopolitan biomedicine.

Saraguro women adopted biomedical resources as readily as they did other more traditional therapies. They have incorporated pharmaceuticals into their repertoire of home remedies, combining medications with medicinal plants in teas, baths, lotions, and sprays. They allot pharmaceuticals a hot or cold designation on the basis of curative properties and observable features. Women assume that remedies that alleviate hot conditions like fever, colic, and infection are cold, while drugs that relieve colds, coughs, and diarrhea are hot. White, blue, or green coloring suggests a cool medication while red, orange, or yellow indicates the drugs are humourally hot. Humoural classification determines how medicines are used in home remedies. For instance, sodium bicarbonate produces a "cold boil," making medicinal plants bubble and churn in a pot without any heating.

In the last decade Saraguro mothers increased their use of other resources like laboratory testing, vitamin supplements for pregnancy, infant immunizations, and powdered milk and milk substitutes. At the same time, novel medical concepts gained credence as many employed new diagnoses and illness terms. For instance, Saraguro women now identify diseases like parasites, cancer, whooping cough, and tuberculosis and describe the adverse effects of germs and bacteria, concepts discounted a decade ago since microscopic life forms too small to see could hardly be considered real or particularly dangerous. Many Saraguro women also possess newly enhanced, accurate knowledge of human anatomy and organ function as a result of consultations with midwives, lectures by nurses in community health courses, and discussions with children enrolled in biology courses. Women welcome fresh information and new products as opportunities to expand and improve the effectiveness of homebased healing.

Culture Change and Revitalization

Expanded use of biomedical knowledge has not displaced traditional medicine or a tenacious confidence in the value of home remedies. Illnesses like evil air, nerves, and magical fright persist, and Saraguros consider these to be as serious as are biomedical disease categories. Home remedies remain the most common form of treatment, and recovery is invariably attributed to the potency of medicinal plant preparations. Biomedical concepts and practices have not supplanted traditional care; instead, innovations have enhanced and even rejuvenated such care, expanding preventive care, diagnosis, and treatment options. Saraguros can actually increase their reliance on home-based healing because it accommodates new concepts and procedures that improve the quality of care.

Biomedical care has also failed to eliminate the maternal curing role in Saraguro. This might seem surprising, since such services are commonly expected to dominate all other forms of care once they become accessible. After all, biomedicine seems to offer many advantages. Treatment is generally assumed to be more effective, while traditional healing is frequently dismissed as superstition and its practitioners as charlatans. Moreover, the use of hospitals and biomedical services can potentially enhance social status, making clients who abandon tradition in favor of cosmopolitan care seem progressive, modern, and enterprising. In the case of Saraguro, reliance on physicians, nurses, hospital treatment, and similar resources would also relieve mothers of the constant burden of protecting and restoring family health.

Despite these apparent advantages, indigenous Saraguros remain unwilling to abandon home-based healing. Historic events reinforce cultural values stressing autonomy and independence. Families strive to manage health problems within the context of the household and resist external aid, including that offered by traditional curers like curanderos, herbalists, and midwives. Families particularly prefer maternal care because, as discussed earlier, such providers are accessible, familiar with family health needs, and far more nurturant, compassionate, and concerned about their patients than are other practitioners.

Saraguro mothers are equally loathe to surrender their role as family curer since it offers valuable advantages in terms of prestige. Women enjoy enhanced status in the household by virtue of their healing role. Their knowledge accords them power and authority to regulate all health-related behaviors in the family, including diet, dress, work habits, and personal comportment, and they can enforce compliance by cautioning household members about the health risks of disobedience. Mothers derive further kin support, gratitude, and influence with each successful cure. Women also achieve public status and recognition by supervising family well-being. Female friends and neighbors compliment Saraguro mothers who have healthy, vigorous offspring and often seek their advice on curing and child care. By contrast, women with sick children may be targeted for gossip

and ridicule for their perceived inadequacies as family health providers. Thus, any mother who willingly cedes her healing role to traditional or nontraditional providers faces reduced family and social status and scorn for abandoning her duties. Since the self-image of mothers is inherently linked to their role as family healer, growing pressures to shift care to biomedical providers threatens Saraguro women's very identity.

The Future of Health Care

Quality care does not require that populations abandon their health values and popular healing traditions. For instance, traditional and nontraditional medical systems successfully coexist in parts of China, India, Southeast Asia, and the Middle East. Both systems may benefit from this exchange. Traditional options save physicians and hospitals from being overwhelmed by demands to treat minor or chronic complaints that can be managed effectively with home care. More cosmopolitan biomedical services offer an alternative resource for acute and severe conditions.

Cosmopolitan care is also an unrealistic option for the many communities that lack physicians and hospital care. It is unreasonable to expect such populations to depend on biomedical services. Instead, basic care can be funneled through mothers and other traditional providers. Several recent international health programs train women and other local practitioners to supervise prevention and treatment, tracking weight in children to detect and address malnutrition, preparing and administering oral rehydration therapy for infants with diarrhea, distributing vitamin supplements to pregnant women, and directing community sanitation programs.

Mothers can be particularly powerful allies in the quest to promote long-term health improvement, since they train their own daughters in family care and home-based curing. Mothers who are instructed in biomedical therapy can transmit these innovative concepts and procedures to subsequent generations, thereby perpetuating programs for years to come. To succeed, however, projects must be designed to recognize mothers and other traditional curers as opportunities rather than as threats to health promotion.

Suggested Readings

Belote, Linda, and James Belote. "Development in Spite of Itself: The Saraguro Case." In Norman Whitten, ed. Cultural *Transformations and Ethnicity in Modern Ecuador.* Urbana: University of Illinois, 1981, pp. 450–476. Surveys culture change and socioeconomic development in the Saraguro community since the 1960s.

Finerman, Ruthbeth. "'Parental Incompetence' and 'Selective Neglect': Blaming the Victim in Child Survival." *Social Science and Medicine* 40 (1995): 5–13. Describes how medical choices for child health are influenced by economics, physical access, and cultural beliefs and values about appropriate care.

Finerman, Ruthbeth. "The Forgotten Healers: Women as Family Healers in an Andean Indian Community." In Carol McClain, ed. *Women as Healers: Cross-Cultural Perspectives*. New Brunswick: Rutgers, 1989, pp. 24–41. Examines the training of women as family health providers, curing beliefs and practices, and the impact of the health provider role on women's status in the family and community.

Finerman, Ruthbeth. "Tracing Home-Based Health Care Change in an Andean Indian Community." *Medical Anthropology Quarterly* 3 (1989): 162–174. Details the process of blending traditional curing practices with innovative medical practices and materials to create a new system of health care that bridges cultures and value systems.

Finerman, Ruthbeth, and Ross Sackett. "Saraguros." In Johannes Wilbert, ed. *Encyclopedia of World Cultures, vol. 7: South America*. New York: G.K. Hall/Macmillan, 1994, pp. 293–295. Offers a general ethnographic description of the population.

Human Rights Violations

Paul C. Rosenblatt

It would fill thousands of pages to list all human rights violations in recent years with a sentence or two to summarize each separate pattern (not *event*, but *pattern*). It would include each separate pattern of massacre, ethnic cleansing, enslavement, rape, spouse abuse, child abuse, beating, torture, assassination, mass extermination, killing of rights advocates, forced prostitution, press censorship, banning of organizations that advocate specific rights (for example, women's rights, workers' rights), jailing or killing people for expressing ideas, deprivation of the right to vote or of free and honest elections, sexual harassment, deprivation of property, forced relocation, forced religious conversion, terrorizing of those who might become critics, denial of access to birth control, denial of health care, destruction of or denial of access to food sources, destruction of dwellings, and denial of asylum.

Among the many entries in those pages would be the war of the government of El Salvador against its own people in which seventy-five thousand civilians were killed or "disappeared" (kidnapped and presumably killed by government troops or police); the South African system of apartheid that has been responsible for death, forced displacement, terror, family separation, and virtual enslavement of millions of black South Africans; the killings, enslavement, terror, and repression by the Communist governments of China, the Soviet Union, Eastern Europe, and elsewhere; "ethnic cleansing" in what used to be Yugoslavia; Indonesian government massacres and oppression of the Timorese; and Iraqi, Iranian, and Turkish persecution and massacre of Kurds. (Publications by Amnesty International and Human Rights Watch are excellent starting places for finding documentation of these and other patterns of human rights violations.)

The Idea of Human Rights

Human rights became a worldwide issue with the signing in 1948 of the United Nations Declaration of Human Rights (see Appendix). The Declaration has been an inspiration to many, a force for reform, and a charter for governments and nongovernmental agencies that support human rights. An enormous amount has been written about how to understand and apply the statement of rights in the Declaration, and there is also an extensive literature advocating, clarifying, explaining, and extending rights not spelled out in detail, if at all, in the Declaration. Perhaps the most substantial literature in this regard deals with the rights of women. The Declaration set the agenda for much of the debate and much national and international political effort in support of human rights.

Relativist Perspectives

Concern has been raised often about the ways in which pressures to meet the human rights standards set forth by the Declaration are a form of colonialism and ethnocentrism, a way for Western Europeans and North Americans to control other people and to deny the validity of non-Western codes of ethics. Critics say that pressures for individual political and economic rights consistent with the Universal Declaration can be understood as the imposition of outsider standards on societies with their own codes of ethics and understandings of what is moral. What gives the United States, other Western countries, and nongovernmental organizations that are highly visible advocates of human rights (for example, Amnesty International, Human Rights Watch, and Cultural Survival) the right to say how the governments and peoples of other countries should live? What if what human rights advocates want to stop in country X is considered ethical behavior in that country? What if it is seen as necessary to preserve life and order in that country? What if it is consistent with national religious doctrine?

Cultural relativism is an important concept in anthropology and comparative sociology. If we could not think as relativists there would be no hope of understanding cultures other than our own. The concept of cultural relativism takes various forms but basically it is the idea that cultures should be understood in their own terms. If, for example, people in a culture practice plural marriage or cut scar patterns in the skin of adolescents being initiated into adulthood, they should not be judged by the standards of other cultures but understood in terms of their own culture. Do these practices enable people to achieve standards of worth in their own culture? Do these practices have value and meaning in their own culture and receive widespread support? From a cultural relativist perspective, an advocate of human rights would do well to understand the ethical standards of another culture and what Western concepts of human rights and of violations of human rights mean to the people of that culture. From a comparative sociology perspective, it can be risky to compare cultures on dimensions conceptualized and given meaning in only one culture.[1]

A cultural relativist would note that critics of human rights pressures imposed on other countries by the United States government say that the U.S. government is hypocritical. Critics point out that the United States is itself guilty of human rights violations. These violations include the practice of capital punishment, continuing patterns of institutional racism, sexism, and homophobia, economic deprivation of millions of Americans, unwillingness to accept asylum-seekers fleeing for their lives (for example, from Guatemala and Haiti), failure to provide employment or employment at an adequate income to millions, bloody attacks on people of other countries, the denial of adequate health care to millions, failure to redress wrongs committed against Native Americans, the carrying out of government invasion of privacy directed at dissenters (wire-tapping, mail-opening, etc.), and imprisonment for mere advocacy of certain viewpoints (for example, of communism during the McCarthy era or of opposition to World War I).

Given that the United States also violates human rights, we can ask how citizens of the United States would feel about attempts to limit U.S. human rights violations. How would citizens of the United States react if, say, China led the U.N. in condemning human rights violations in the United States? What if economic sanctions were threatened against the United States if these practices did not cease? What if the government of China offered financial support to a U.S. political party that was working to end the rights violations? Just as many Americans would feel upset by such efforts to stop rights violations in the United States and feel that China should address its own human rights problems, so many people around the world react negatively when the U.S. government opposes human rights violations in their own countries.

Another route to understanding the cultural relativist perspective is to recognize that different cultures give different meanings to the individual, the family, the community, the idea of governance, the idea of freedom, the idea of democracy, and, in fact, all concepts used in the Universal Declaration of Human Rights. Consider, for example, Article 17 of the Declaration (see Appendix). There are enormous cultural differences in what ownership means and in what can be owned. Ownership may be a temporary right, it may typically be ownership shared with others in one's family or local community, or it may be open to termination if community members request it. (For example, one might only "own" a piece of cropland while actually farming it and may not own it individually but only in common with one's family or village. One may "own" a piece of jewelry but be required to give it to anyone in one's community who asks for it.) Similarly, cultures differ in whether individual trees can be owned, whether fishing rights in specific locations can be owned, whether the right to hunt specific kinds of animals can be owned, whether children, a spouse, or a worker can be owned, whether names can be owned, and whether certain kinds of knowledge can be owned. Thus, it is not simple to use Article 17 of the Universal Declaration to pass down to people in all cultures a set of instructions on what should be done with regard to property ownership. The concepts in the set of instructions would not be understood in the same way from culture to culture, would not have meaning in some cultures, and would violate fundamental values in still others.

Cultural relativism alerts us to the ways in which cultures may have such different perspectives from our own that we cannot, without a great deal of learning and effort, begin to understand how people in those cultures think. For example, "the person" is understood as more or less free-standing in many cultural groups in the United States, but there are other cultural groups in the United States and throughout the world in which group membership is much more important in defining "the person."[2] In cultures like that, the most fundamental right of the individual may be to continue to belong to groups, and the rights statements that would receive the most detailed attention would be about the rights of groups such as the family, the neighborhood, and the village. Another example of the ways in which cultures might differ markedly from what many Americans consider relevant to life is that there are many cultures in which abstract rights doctrines have never been used and in which government actions have always had another base (for example, community consensus or respect for people who are powerful or religiously learned).

Cultural relativism is more often thought of as a tool for understanding a culture than as a tool for changing it. But to the extent that it is easier to persuade people whose viewpoints and values one understands, relativism can be a tool for change. Instead of pressuring the elite of a society in which violations of human rights occur, a relativist's awareness of the values and understandings of the elite makes it easier to know what arguments would be persuasive. (For example, in a society in which the group rather than the individual has great primacy, it might be persuasive to try to show how respect for individual rights benefits the group.) One can make a relativist case for leaving other cultures alone, but even if one is absolutist about protecting human rights, relativist thinking is valuable.

From the perspective of cultural relativism it is important to understand the ethical doctrines of various cultures in their own terms. We cannot assume that the single set of standards of the Universal Declaration of Human Rights should be employed by all. The Declaration overlooks crucial ethical ideas in some cultures (for example, obligations to God) and asks some people to go against the ethical ideas of their culture (asking them, for example, not to draw distinctions based on religion). So what can we say about cross-cultural differences (and similarities) in ethical standards?

Cross-Cultural Differences in Definitions of Rights

All cultures define ethical obligations, both with regard to insiders and with regard to outsiders.[3] (Of course, who is considered an insider and who is considered an outsider differs from culture to culture.) Cultural injunctions almost always hold people to higher ethical standards with regard to insiders than with regard to outsiders.[4] Thus, the Universal Decla-

ration of Human Rights, by asserting that all people should have the same rights, runs counter to a widespread and deeply held pattern in human societies. It is in the nature of how peoples divide themselves from other peoples, how people learn what is right and wrong, and how individual and group identity is formed that people typically see their own in-group members as superior to outsiders. That way of setting one's own ways and one's own people above the others is often called *ethnocentrism*. The ethnocentric way of seeing the world can be unlearned, but the advocates of universal human rights are asking people to give up ethical standards that are deeply felt and a matter of society-wide consensus when they ask that outsiders be given the same rights as insiders.

The Declaration emphasizes individual political rights and, to a lesser extent, property rights. The emphasis on the political comes out of Western democratic cultural values, and the emphasis on property rights comes out of European and American capitalism. By the ethical standards of other cultural traditions, a statement of rights might emphasize very different things: for example, the rights of kin group authorities over kin group members, rights of men over women, rights of parents over children, rights of elders over younger people, rights to take revenge, the right of governments to do what is necessary to guarantee societal stability and economic growth, the right to share in the food and other possessions of neighbor and relative, or the right to observe one's religion even if such observance violates what some people consider universal human rights.

Political and property rights are not considered primary in all societies. In fact, the vast majority of countries that have come into existence in the latter half of the twentieth century, perhaps reflecting the values emphasized during colonial domination by Britain, France, the United States, the Netherlands, and other colonial powers, have placed economic growth and political order at a higher priority than individual political and property rights.[5] The view of officials from these countries in debates about human rights is often that the demands of the United States and other Western powers to place the rights listed in the Declaration at highest priority denies their countries the right to economic growth. But perhaps the most important point is that international debate goes on in various forums, the most important of which may be the U.N. Commission on Human Rights—most important because most visible.

Precise knowledge about human rights matters is difficult to attain. How can we make moral judgments or carry out comparative sociology when we hardly know what is going on in a country or when sources of information disagree or when people who carry out human rights violations hide their dirty work in order to escape international sanctions, revenge, or legal action? Even when we have information, our source may well be biased. Even such supposedly objective reports as the U.S. State Department *Country Reports on Human Rights Practices*, though often useful and increasingly more objective, will be biased to fit the commitments, ideology, and policy goals of important players in the State Department, the White House, U.S. embassies abroad, and elsewhere in government.[6] There are many challenges in carrying out quantitative, comparative analysis on human rights matters,[7] not the least of which is that we have spotty information.

Effects of Rights Violations

It is easy to assume that one understands the consequences of human rights violations such as killing, torture, or being forced off one's land because someone in power wants to farm it. But the consequences of rights violations are not as obvious as might be assumed.

LIFETIME CONSEQUENCES FOR VICTIMS

Victims who survive human rights violations may never leave their experiences behind. They may carry the health effects of mutilation, rape, starvation, and forced labor throughout life. Their lives may be shortened by physical or psychological damage resulting from the rights violations they experienced or by the economic consequences of their victimization. They may carry their victimization as a stigma. People may shun them. The loss of property, livelihood, or homeland may condemn them to a life of poverty. Moreover, the rape victim, the torture victim, the victim of arbitrary arrest, and other rights victims may forever be haunted by the experience, never to feel safe, never to trust others, never to have what would have been a normal relationship with another person. They also may continue to grieve over what happened, with the grief giving their lives qualities of sadness, searching, emptiness, uncertainty about the meaning of life, feelings of having been abandoned by God or the gods, angry irritability, emotional lassitude, preoccupation with self, and feelings of having no firm ground on which to make life choices.

Grieving seems crucial to getting on with one's life after a loss, but it does not necessarily lead to an end to pain. Perhaps some people are led by horrible experiences to higher levels of wisdom and compassion. But perhaps for many, carrying the burdens of losses due to rights violations may make life always frightening and in some ways bitter and may make it harder for them to connect with others, to find support and to give support. For some, the victimization may have led to the destruction of spirit, to a kind of permanent emptiness. Parents who have been human rights victims may be very wise and good parents or very ordinary parents, but they also may be distant, uninvolved, overinvolved, brutal, or difficult for their children in other ways that mean that their children carry for their own lifetime consequences of their parents' victimization.

Human rights violations make many people move far from where they have been living. People who fear being victims or who have been victims may flee their home and their homeland. Indeed, human rights violations are often calculated to make people who remain alive flee far away. So in a climate of human rights violations people often lose home and the surroundings of people who know their culture and speak their language. Worse yet, forced migration often breaks up families. Parent is separated from child, wife from husband, sister from sister. The loss of home, of familiar cultural situation, and the separation from family members add to the pain, loss of personal grounding, and so on, of victimization. Forced migration often involves starvation and disease and the risk of injury from bullet or bomb, but for many of the people who survive a forced migration the long-run damage is to put them in a situation where they are beginners, outsiders, perhaps temporary residents, and more or less alone in a place where a different language is spoken and different customs are practiced. It puts them in a situation where they will always feel their losses and perhaps always search for those from whom they have been separated and who may still be alive.

There are, here and there, programs of therapy, counseling, and support for victims of human rights violations. In some countries (such as Chile) that have come to better times after a period of extreme human rights abuses, therapists have helped some people to confront their losses, the individual and family costs of silence, and much else. In some of the countries to which human rights victims flee there are therapists available to help with the multiple traumas of victimization in one's country of origin and refugee status in a new land.[8]

CONSEQUENCES FOR FAMILY, FRIENDS, AND COMMUNITY OF VICTIMS

Living in a society where human rights violations occur, many who are not themselves victims of the most direct and obvious violations of human rights will experience heavy consequences of the victimization of others. People will grieve the lost family members and friends, the loss of freedom, the loss of innocence. Grief is not something that goes away, partly because fresh losses occur, partly because there are always new reminders of the loss, and partly because it is in the nature of grief for major losses that the grief will come back again and again, perhaps for the person's lifetime.[9]

People who are grieving are often less available to another's needs. In their grief, they are preoccupied, short of energy, not so good at listening, and focused on their own needs.[10] Thus, even if people do not have direct losses to grieve, they may well lose the emotional support, attention, and good spirits of the people around them who in better times would be fully available to them.

Being connected (by kinship, friendship, organizational membership, ethnicity, or in other ways) with a human rights victim puts people at risk. They may be suspected of being allies of the victim. If people are upset by what has happened to a victim, that makes them suspect as potential new opponents of those in power. (This raises questions about whether governments that use terror are operating in their own best interests, because they constantly create new enemies, but that is beside the point to be made here.) The possibility that they might be the next victims makes people very cautious. Their caution may lead them to hold back support from victims, their families and their friends; make them suspect that anyone could be an informer; and make them unwilling to express feelings or ideas in public, or even in private. (I vividly remember, during a visit to a country where terrible things can happen to dissenters, the terror of a young man who was whispering to me that he had been opposed to the building of an all-weather road into his village.)

A climate of human rights violations may also lead many people to public actions that support the violators of human rights. The only way to feel safe may be to inform on others or to attack those who seem to be enemies of the oppressive government. This can further divide friend from friend and family member from family member, and make many people live with the guilt, brutalization, and self-contempt that can come from violating the rights of others. Of course, when someone's family members or others in the community become agents of the forces in power, they will silence critics to protect them (and themselves). They will teach and reinforce the standards of the victimizers. They will also learn the ways of the victimizers, so if terror is a way of life in the larger society it may well be a way of life at home and in the immediate community.

Human rights violations also occur at the family level in societies where men are granted rights over women. Fathers, brothers, uncles, and husbands may claim the right to control women's labor, sexuality, and so on. As in the case of governmental rights violations, some of the victimizers may be people who are or could be in the victim category, that is, a woman whose labor, sexuality, and so on are controlled by men may find that her immediate victimizer is a woman—perhaps her mother-in-law. Rights violations originating in the family may have similar consequences as those perpetrated by government agents—health problems, destruction of the spirit, reduction of availability to other family members, and so on.

Sociocultural Systems and Rights Violations

Human rights violations are so widespread that it is tempting to say they are matters of human nature, or "That's just the way people are." Nonetheless, there is a pattern to human rights violations that helps us to understand what fuels and sustains rights violations.

Most countries of the world contain a diversity of cultures. By some estimates, among the fewer than 200 member countries of the U.N. there are 5,000 distinct communities, including 575 that are actual or potential nations.[11] A country like India or Indonesia contains hundreds of distinct cultural groups, which differ in language, values, spiritual beliefs, ways of understanding the world, and so on. The United States is certainly not homogeneous. It includes, at the very least, over a hundred different Native American, Eskimo, and Polynesian cultures, African-American groups with ancestors who were brought to the United States as slaves, and a diversity of immigrant and refugee groups that retain substantial cultural distinctiveness.

Human rights violations are most often committed across cultural lines, with the people of one cultural group victimizing people of other cultural groups. This may stem partly from differing cultural standards of what rights should be, but it probably stems much more from a sense that it is acceptable to do to outsiders what one would be less inclined to do to insiders. In fact, along with the ethnic diversity of many countries is a history of conquest and exploitation of one group by another.[12] Often, contemporary rights violations are a continuation of that history.

All countries include patterns of social stratification, differentiating rich and powerful from poor and relatively powerless. Frequently culture and class go together, with the rich and powerful being members of dominant, conquering cultural groups, and the poor and powerless being members of dominated, conquered cultural groups. Human rights violations tend to occur along social class lines. It is the poor and powerless who more often are the human rights victims, and, in fact, that often seems to be part of how they are kept poor and powerless. Although the rich and powerful are often the instigators of rights violations, their agents (their police, torturers, censors, and so on) are often members of oppressed groups. All this is not to say that if the people who are poor and oppressed were to take power, things would be different. It may be in the nature of power that people will tend to use it to protect their advantage and to victimize those with less power.

If we take a cultural relativist perspective, we may find that the people in power in a nation where human rights violations follow lines of culture and class have a very different view of things. They might argue that it is very difficult to hold together a large nation state consisting of a diversity of cultural groups, particularly when most people in the country have had no experience of democracy. They might say that keeping the state together saves lives that would be lost in the chaos of fragmentation, promotes economic development that also saves lives, and leads to the higher quality of life that comes with modernization, participation in the world economy, and technological development. One could argue with such a viewpoint, saying, for example, that economic development is not as important as the development of a tradition of truth-telling about government actions, of free criticism, and of fully informed voters whose votes are honestly counted. But the advocates of state power might reply that individual rights and a democracy that allows multiple parties and a free exchange of ideas can only come when the country is unified and has an adequate economic and educational base. In this view, the country has a separate and preeminent existence in relationship to the individual citizen. In fact, many of the ordinary citizens of

these countries may see things the same way as the ruling elites and be quite concerned when dissent is expressed in public.

It might be noted that many of the countries in which antidemocratic sentiments are expressed were once colonies of countries that are now considered democracies. The colonial powers did not often teach their colonial subjects about human rights or democracy. Even in the post-colonial era, the democracies have not necessarily encouraged democracy. The U.S. government, for example, has exercised enormous influence on who holds the power in other countries, particularly in Latin America and the Caribbean. But the U.S. government has not often acted in a way that fosters and encourages a democracy in which freedom of speech prevails and voters have unrestricted choice about political options. In fact, it could be argued that nationalistic movements and social revolutionary forces have often been reactions to the limitations on rights imposed directly or indirectly by the United States and other Western advocates of human rights.

In trying to understand patterns of human rights violations, it seems clear that external forces typically shape and sustain rights violations. Even though any person or group in power may have the imagination to exploit, torture, murder, and so on, it seems usually to be the case that human rights violations are carried out with the support of powerful governments and businesses outside a nation's boundaries. Paradoxically, the U.S. government and U.S.-based international businesses seem often to be involved as major instigators, supporters, and tolerators of rights violations. Human rights seem, for these governmental and business forces, not an absolute value but a value to be balanced against the economic and political interests of U.S. government agencies and corporations. Thus, the very countries and corporations that at times may speak forcefully for human rights will at other times tolerate or even encourage the imprisonment, torture, or even death of dissenters. To take one of many examples, the leaders of the U.S. government supported the government of Guatemala in the expropriation, displacement, economic enslavement, and murder of thousands of Guatemalan Indians. In fact, many Guatemalan military officers who had leading roles in terrorizing Guatemalan citizens were trained in "counter-insurgency" tactics by the U.S. military.[13] U.S. businesses that advocate freedom in television commercials for U.S. audiences may, at the same time, act to get control of the land of peasants in other countries or support actions in other countries that keep local people working at the lowest of wages in dangerous working environments. The U.S. government may tolerate human rights violations in countries that grant it military bases, favorable economic relations, allies in U.N. voting and in opposing countries currently in disfavor with the United States.

What Is Moral?

Is it moral for the United States and a handful of other powerful nations to impose their will on other nations? By my own standards and those of many in the United States, Canada, and Europe, it would be immoral not to make every effort to stop torture, ethnic cleansing, rape, press censorship, and so on. But it also seems immoral to impose Western standards on countries in which many people have very different understandings of what is moral, countries in which many people see torture as proper, ethnic cleansing as a just righting of past wrongs, press censorship as necessary to prevent a mass chaos in which many would be killed and economic growth would be thwarted. It is even questionable in a moral sense to carry out comparative studies of human rights and human rights violations based on frameworks rooted in a single society. Perhaps what is needed to achieve a culturally sensitive morality, to improve human rights situations around the world, and to carry out insightful comparative studies, is not a simple advocacy based on a universal declaration of human rights but a deeply complicated view of human rights.

We must be aware of the cross-cultural diversity of rights embodied in various cultural systems.[14] We must work with a conception of rights that is sensitive to the irrelevance of property in one culture, the importance of duty to the collective in another, societal differences in the economic resources to support human rights, and so on.

We must also be aware of how saints can be sinners and sinners can be saints. We must acknowledge the ways in which human rights violations are created by the U.S. government. We must also pay attention to the ways sinners may do good things. For example, the revolutionary Chinese government was murderous and oppressive, but it attempted to free women from foot binding, to give young people a say in whom they married, to end prostitution, and to provide work, food, and medical care for the impoverished.

Finally, we must be aware of the cultural and class complexity of other countries. To advocate improved human rights in a country is often to side with one culture and class against others. The route to human rights may not be through advocacy of principles but through work at promoting more respectful, peaceful, and nonexploitive relations among different groups within countries.

Appendix

Excerpts from the Universal Declaration of Human Rights:

ARTICLE 2. Everyone is entitled to all the rights and freedoms set forth in this Declaration, without distinction of any kind, such as race, colour, sex, language, religion, political or other opinion, national or social origin, property, birth or other status.

ARTICLE 4. No one shall be held in slavery or servitude. . . .

ARTICLE 5. No one shall be subjected to torture or to cruel, inhuman or degrading treatment or punishment.

ARTICLE 7. All are equal before the law and are entitled without any discrimination to equal protection of the law. . . .

ARTICLE 9. No one shall be subjected to arbitrary arrest, detention or exile. . . .

ARTICLE 11. Everyone charged with a penal offence has the right to be presumed innocent . . . [and to] a public trial at which he has had all the guarantees necessary for his defence.

ARTICLE 12. No one shall be subjected to arbitrary interference with his privacy, family, home or correspondence. . . .

ARTICLE 13. Everyone has the right to freedom of movement and residence. . . .

ARTICLE 14. Everyone has the right to seek and to enjoy in other countries asylum from persecution.

ARTICLE 15. Everyone has the right to a nationality. . . .

ARTICLE 16. Men and women. . . , without any limitation due to race, nationality or religion, have the right to marry and to found a family. They are entitled to equal rights as to marriage, during marriage and at its dissolution. Marriage shall be entered into only with the free and full consent of the intending spouses. The family is . . . entitled to protection by society and the State.

ARTICLE 17. Everyone has the right to own property alone as well as in association with others. No one shall be arbitrarily deprived of his property.

ARTICLE 18. Everyone has the right to freedom of thought, conscience and religion; this right includes . . . freedom, either alone or in community with others . . . to manifest his religion or belief in teaching, practice, worship and observance.

ARTICLE 19. Everyone has the right to freedom of opinion and expression . . . includ[ing] freedom to . . .

seek, receive and impart information and ideas through any media. . . .

ARTICLE 20. Everyone has the right to freedom of peaceful assembly and association. . . .

ARTICLE 21. Everyone has the right to take part in the government of his country, directly or through freely chosen representatives. Everyone has the right of equal access to public service in his country. The will of the people shall be the basis of the authority of government, . . . expressed in periodic and genuine elections which shall be by universal and equal suffrage and shall be held by secret vote. . . .

ARTICLE 22. Everyone . . . has the right to social security and is entitled to realization . . . of the economic, social and cultural rights indispensable for his dignity and the free development of his personality.

ARTICLE 23. Everyone has the right to work, to free choice of employment, to just and favourable conditions of work and to protection against unemployment. Everyone . . . has the right to equal pay for equal work. Everyone who works has the right to just and favourable remuneration ensuring for himself and his family an existence worthy of human dignity, and supplemented, if necessary, by other means of . . . protection. Everyone has the right to form and to join trade unions. . . .

ARTICLE 24. Everyone has the right to rest and leisure, including reasonable limitation of working hours. . . .

ARTICLE 25. Everyone has the right to a standard of living adequate for the health and well-being of himself and of his family, including food, clothing, housing, and medical care . . . and the right to security in the event of unemployment, sickness, disability, widowhood, old age or other lack of livelihood. . . . Motherhood and childhood are entitled to special care and assistance. All children, whether born in or out of wedlock, shall enjoy the same social protection.

ARTICLE 26. Everyone has the right to education. Education shall be free, at least in the elementary and fundamental ages. Elementary education shall be compulsory. Technical and professional education shall be made generally available and higher education shall be equally accessible to all. . . .

ARTICLE 27. Everyone has the right freely to participate in the cultural life of the community. . . .

Notes

1. Russel Lawrence Barsh, "Measuring Human Rights: Problems of Methodology and Purpose," *Human Rights Quarterly* 15 (1993): 87–121.
2. Rhonda E. Howard, "Dignity, Community, and Human Rights," in Abdullahi Ahmed An-Na'im, ed., *Human Rights in Cross-Cultural Perspectives* (Philadelphia: University of Pennsylvania Press, 1992), pp. 81–102.
3. Theodore E. Downing, "Human Rights Research: The Challenge for Anthropologists," in Theodore E. Downing and Gilbert Kushner, eds., *Human Rights and Anthropology* (Cambridge, MA: Cultural Survival, 1988), pp. 9–19.
4. Paul C. Rosenblatt, "Origins and Effects of Group Ethnocentrism and Nationalism," *Journal of Conflict Resolution* 8 (1964): 131–146.
5. Adamantia Pollis and Peter Schwab, "Human Rights: A Western Construct with Limited Applicability," in Adamantia Pollis and Peter Schwab, eds., *Human Rights: Cultural and Ideological Perspectives* (New York: Praeger, 1979), pp. 1–18.
6. Judith Innes de Neufville, "Human Rights Reporting as a Policy Tool: An Examination of the State Department Country Reports," *Human Rights Quarterly* 8 (1986): 681–699.
7. Robert Justin Goldstein, "The Limitations of Using Quantitative Data in Studying Human Rights Abuses," *Human Rights Quarterly* 8 (1986): 607–627; Andrew D. McNitt, "Measuring Human Rights: Problems and Possibilities," *Policy Studies Journal* 15 (1986): 71–83.
8. Guus van der Veer, *Counseling and Therapy with Refugees: Psychological Problems of Victims of War, Torture, and Repression* (Chichester, England: Wiley, 1992).
9. Paul C. Rosenblatt, *Bitter, Bitter Tears: Nineteenth-Century Diarists and Twentieth-Century Grief Theories* (Minneapolis: University of Minnesota Press, 1983).
10. Paul C. Rosenblatt, "Grief: The Social Context of Private Feelings," in Margaret S. Stroebe, Wolfgang Stroebe, and Robert O. Hansson, eds., *Handbook of Bereavement* (New York: Cambridge University Press, 1993), pp. 102–111.
11. Ted Robert Gurr and James R. Scarritt, "Minorities Rights at Risk: A Global Survey," *Human Rights Quarterly* 11 (1989): 375–405.
12. Ibid.
13. Guillermo Toriello Garrido, "On the Role of the United States and Israel," in Marlene Dixon and Susanne Jonas, eds., *Guatemala: Tyranny on Trial* (San Francisco: Synthesis Publications, 1984), pp. 24–30.
14. Marnia Lazreg, "Human Rights, State and Ideology: An Historical Perspective," in Adamantia Pollis and Peter Schwab, eds., *Human Rights: Cultural and Ideological Perspectives* (New York: Praeger, 1979), pp. 32–43.

Suggested Readings

Donnelly, Jack. *Universal Human Rights in Theory and Practice*. Ithaca, NY: Cornell University Press, 1989. Counters relativist arguments against applying human rights standards to non-Western societies.

Downing, Theodore E., and Gilbert Kushner, eds. *Human Rights and Anthropology*. Cambridge, MA: Cultural Survival, 1988. Explores conceptual and ethical issues in addressing human rights violations; useful bibliography.

Hatch, Elvin. *Culture and Morality: The Relativity of Values in Anthropology*. New York, Columbia University Press, 1983. An important book, dealing with historical and cultural roots of ethical and cultural relativism, philosophical perspectives on them, and recent attitudes in anthropology toward relativism.

Pollis, Adamantia, and Peter Schwab, eds. *Human Rights: Cultural and Ideological Perspectives*. New York: Praeger, 1979. Excellent source on relativist perspectives, with chapters from the perspective of a number of different cultures.

Suggested Viewing

"Rights & Wrongs," a weekly public television program. Powerful visual images; covers human rights issues around the world and the debates and complexities surrounding U.S. government action (and inaction) concerning human rights violations.